CHINA AND RUSSIA
THE "GREAT GAME"

Studies of the East Asian Institute,
Columbia University

O. EDMUND CLUBB *Oliver* *1901 -*

CHINA

&

RUSSIA

THE "GREAT GAME"

COLUMBIA UNIVERSITY PRESS
NEW YORK AND LONDON

O. Edmund Clubb, in the course of twenty years with the U.S. Foreign Service in Asia, occupied such borderlands posts critical to Sino-Russian relations as Consul at Urumchi, Sinkiang, and Consul General at Vladivostok, USSR, and at Mukden and Changchun in Manchuria. He was Director of the Office of Chinese Affairs in the Department of State from 1950 to 1952.

Library of Congress Catalog Card Number: 72-155362
Printed in the United States of America
ISBN 0-231-02740-0 *Cloth*
ISBN 0-231-08305-X *Paperback*
Third cloth and second paperback printing.

To Oliver and Zoë

The East Asian Institute
of Columbia University

The East Asian Institute of Columbia University was established in 1949 to prepare graduate students for careers dealing with East Asia, and to aid research and publication on East Asia during the modern period. The faculty of the Institute are grateful to the Ford Foundation and the Rockefeller Foundation for their financial assistance.

The Studies of the East Asian Institute were inaugurated in 1962 to bring to a wider public the results of significant new research on modern and contemporary East Asia.

PREFACE

FROM THE OUTBREAK of the Pacific War onwards, the United States has played a major role in the affairs of East Asia. Now, three decades after Pearl Harbor, there is still manifest an official intent that, as a Pacific power, we shall continue to exercise a dominant influence in the troubled Asian scene. Many forces will impinge upon the implementation of our design, but it is hardly open to question that one of the most important factors in the whole complex equation will prove to be the course taken in the Sino-Soviet relationship: will the Chinese People's Republic and the Union of Soviet Socialist Republics cooperate for common ends in Asia? Or will their chief efforts be directed in hostility against each other? One way or the other, American power and influence will be affected in important respects. This book is an attempt to depict the nature of the relationship between the two countries, as discovered in historical context, and thus to arrive at a tentative estimate of what the future might hold in that regard.

I would acknowledge my warm appreciation of various assistances I have received in producing this work. I express my thanks to the Rockefeller Foundation and to the Contemporary China Studies Committee of the East Asian Institute, Columbia University, for their financial support of my research travel to the Soviet Union in 1966. I record my deep gratitude to Mrs. Jane Leonard for research assistance and her helpful criticism of the Introduction and first seven chapters of my work; to Mrs. Josephine Burke of *Life* Magazine for valuable aid rendered in connection with my search for illustrations; and to my wife, Mariann, for salutary literary criticism and other aid generously given in connection with preparation of the manuscript. I am especially indebted to Theodore R. Miller, cartographer, who designed the maps.

I express my thanks to the Aldine Publishing Company for their permission to use, as basis for maps depicting China at various stages of its historical development, certain maps from the work by Albert Herrmann, *An Historical Atlas of China* (new edition, 1966), General Editor, Norton Ginsburg; prefatory essay by Paul Wheatley. I thank Yale University Press for their similar authorization to use elements from the maps in the work by Allen F. Chew, *An Atlas of Russian History: Eleven Centuries of Changing Borders* (1967) to the same purpose. I further express my appreciation of the permission granted by Doubleday & Company to quote excerpts from *The Memoirs of Count Witte* by Sergei Witte, translated by Abraham Yarmolinsky, copyright 1920, 1921 by Doubleday & Company, Inc.

O. Edmund Clubb
March, 1971

CONTENTS

MAPS

ILLUSTRATIONS   after page 386

1. Yermak's conquest of Sibir; 2. Manchu conqueror, the emperor K'ang-hsi; 3. Tsar Peter I ("the Great")

4. Manchu siege of Albazin: 5. Mission of E. Izbrandt Ides to Peking; 6. Captain Kruzenstern; 7. State Counselor Rezanov at Nagasaki; 8. Nikolai N. Muraviev; 9. Tso Tsung-t'ang

10. Construction of Trans-Siberian Railway, Nerchinsk, c. 1895; 11. Russian military camel caravan on Amur, c. 1895; 12. Russian soldiers in China during Boxer Rebellion; 13. Goldi tribesmen, Amur region

14. Russian fleet issuing from Port Arthur, February 1, 1904; 15. Retreat of Russian army after Battle of Mukden; 16. Michael Bluecher ("Galen"); 18. Marshal Feng Yü-hsiang

CHINA AND RUSSIA

THE "GREAT GAME"

INTRODUCTION CHINESE, RUSSIANS, AND MONGOLS

THERE IS A NATURAL tendency to view Sino-Russian relations in the perspective of the past twenty years, when Communist regimes have ruled in both countries, or of the past fifty years, when Russia has been cloaked in its Soviet aspect. In historical fact, however, the greatest proportion by far of the Sino-Russian relationship has fallen in the imperial stage of the two countries, during the respective rules of the Manchu (1644–1912) and Romanov (1613–1917) dynasties. During much of those same three centuries, the Mongols, who had earlier conquered both Russia and China, played a highly significant role in the Sino-Russian relationship.

"Ch'ien-ch'e shih chien" say the Chinese: "The cart ahead is a mirror." It is especially true in political developments that what has gone before may show what is to come after, and certain patterns in past Sino-Russian relations are repeated over time. The present work aims to bring out, in brief compass, domestic developments and third-power influences bearing upon relations between the two states, in support of the prime purpose of tracing both continuity and change in that relationship. The basic theme treats the growth of the two empires, and the long struggle for dominance between them, which has continued even after they discarded their "imperial" aspects. Thus

CHINA, RUSSIA, AND CENTRAL ASIA
UNDER THE MONGOLS

1290

if the imperial past is comprehended, the Communist present can be better understood.

The story has its real beginnings before Russia and China were in actual physical contact: it starts when the Mongols ruled both countries, acting as a channel of first communications between them. It was shortly after the expulsion of the Mongol rule from Russia that the Russians began to grope eastward, trying to "discover" China; later, after the Manchus conquered China, the Manchu power thrust westward—at the Mongols. In recounting the history of the Russo-Chinese relationship, one starts naturally with the Mongol imperium.

MONGOL IMPERIUM

In 1223, on the banks of the Kalka (present-day Kalchik), a combined Russian force was shatteringly defeated by Mongol warriors. After their victory, the Mongols disappeared as suddenly and mysteriously as they had come—by orders of their chief, Genghis Khan. Genghis, conqueror of men, had already won important victories in Northeast and Central Asia. The Mongols possessed, in the Great Yasa (decree), a philosophy of universal rule, in which there would be a Pax Mongolica. They would return.

The Mongols of this time numbered perhaps a million people, and they were no more an ethnic amalgam than were the Rus in Eastern Europe, but Genghis Khan's genius for organization, strategy, and command, and his capacity to use other men than those of his own race—Chinese, Uighurs, Arabs, and Persians—gave the Mongols a power surpassing that of other political organizations. Genghis Khan died in 1227 one of the greatest conquerors of all times and transmitted his empire, in four parts, to three sons and a grandson, but with his son Ogodai successor to the position of Great Khan. With the legacy went the task of building world empire upon the foundation Genghis Khan had laid.

At a Mongol *kuriltai* (clan assembly) of 1235, it was decided to wage four campaigns simultaneously: to complete the conquest of Korea and to conquer Sung China, Asia Minor, and Europe beyond the Volga River. The last named was to be the main effort, and in the autumn of 1237 Mongol forces numbering perhaps 50,000, with from 70,000 to 100,000 Turkic auxiliaries, crossed the Volga. The Mongol drive westward was against a Europe riven by feudal and religious quarrels, with each warring faction happy to see the Mongols overcome its particular enemy. When the Saracens of the Near East, under Mongol attack in 1238, appealed to the West for aid, the Bishop of Winchester observed:

> Let us leave these dogs to devour one another, that they may all be consumed, and perish; and we, when we proceed against the enemies of Christ who remain, will slay them, and cleanse the face of the earth, so that all the world will be subject to one Catholic church, and there will be one shepherd and one fold.[1]

The West would persist in its miscalculations of the East for centuries.

The Mongols stormed Kiev in 1240, killing most of the Russian survivors and destroying the town. In April, 1241, one Mongol column defeated a combined force of Teutonic Knights and Poles at the battle of Liegnitz; three other Mongol columns later in the same year surprised and defeated the Hungarian army of King Bela, and occupied Hungary. The Mongol armies were poised for an advance on Western Europe when, in December, 1241, Great Khan Ogodai died in Karakorum. Most of the chief Mongol commanders returned to Karakorum to settle, at a Great Kuriltai, the problem of succession. Western Europe had been saved from Mongol conquest by default, but the Kievan era in Russia ended with the beginning of Mongol rule that same year.

In the period 1246–1251, when Mangu finally became Great Khan in violation of an earlier pledge given the Ogodai house respecting the succession, division developed within the Mongol leadership. Mangu died in 1259 in the siege of a Chinese town, and in 1260 a Great Kuriltai elected his brother Kubilai to succeed him. This act sealed the division between the Juji and Tului clans on the one side and the Ogodai and Jagatai clans on the other. The conquest of China was completed in 1279, but the rule of the Mongol Juchids in Eastern Europe was separated from the Tului dominion in China by the Jagatai power in Central Asia.

The Mongol rule changed the character of Eastern Europe, Persia and the Near East, and India. It also brought the reopening of the great transcontinental trade routes that had been closed since the end of the T'ang dynasty (618–907) in China. For a brief span in history, the Mongols acted to disseminate cultural elements and to draw Asia and Europe closer together. They incidentally conscripted many Russians and others to serve them in Eastern Europe and the Middle East; Russians also served in an imperial guard force in the Great Khan's court at Cambaluc (Khan-balik, "the city of the khan"). It was thus the Mongols who first introduced the Chinese and Russians to each other.[2]

In 1368, with the Great Khan's power weakened through efforts to conquer both Southeast Asia and Japan, the Mongol control over China ended, and the Ming Chinese succeeded to power in the country, but with an evident loss of self-confidence. The psychological trauma suffered by the Chinese under less than a century of Mongol rule led, in seeming compensation, to a substantial increase of their cultural ethnocentrism — and of simple xenophobia.[3] The sense that the Chinese order of things represented orthodoxy and Truth was automatically strengthened.

The Mongol power continued in being, not only in the Khalkha region (eastern Mongolia) and Central Asia, but also in Russia, ruled by the Golden Horde. China was now cut off from Russia by the Mongols in between. In Russia itself, Moscow became semiautonomous, and some Mongols began to enter the service of Russian princes. The Golden Horde began to break up into different rules, and separate khanates were established at Kazan and in the Crimea. In 1480, Grand Duke Ivan III (the Great) of Moscow, with the support of the Crimean khan, refused further payment of tribute and won independence of Mongol rule — a full century after the end of Mongol dominion in China. Moscow had become the new center of Russian power; Ivan III was energetically expanding the frontiers of Muscovy in Eastern Europe. There would be no return to Kievan Russia.

MING CHINA

The great Ming emperor Yung-lo died in 1424 en route back to Peking (which he had built near the site of Cambaluc) after his fifth expedition against the Mongols, and was succeeded on the Dragon Throne by lesser men. The bad features of Confucian society became aggravated, to the detriment of both the government and the people. Bad government and domestic weakness naturally had their influence in the realm of foreign affairs. The Mongols, although ousted from power in China and torn periodically by internecine strife, still exercised dominant power in Inner Asia. The major role in Mongolian political developments between 1423 and 1530 was played by the Oirats (western Mongols). Their able leader Togon (1418–1440) succeeded in extending his rule to most of Mongolia and was laying plans for the conquest of China when he died. He was succeeded by his son Esen, who in the fall of 1449 advanced against the Ming power.

A vast Chinese army took the field against the Oirats in 1450. Esen cut the Chinese force to pieces near the Great Wall and took the emperor captive. The Mongols clearly no longer had anything to fear from the Ming Chinese. They pushed Chinese authority back inside the Wall, and, with the exception of a small holding in the Northeast, it remained there until the end of Ming days. The Mongols thereby established themselves as the dominant political factor in the Inner Asian region. The chief challenge to tenure was their own fratricidal wars. Esen in his turn undertook to unite the Mongols and revive their imperial power, but he died in 1455 with the task still unaccomplished.

The Ming posture, by 1500, had become categorically defensive. Military colonies, a political device used in China as early as the second century B.C., were planted on the borderlands, with the soldiers employed in working state lands. But borderlands defense was not enough; there was decay within. The usual characteristics of the end of the Chinese "dynastic cycle" had made their appearance: the dynasty was weakening.

Early in the sixteenth century, white seafarers from the Occident reached China's shores. The first comers were the Portuguese, who sailed into Canton in 1514. For a time Portuguese ships called and traded without hindrance at ports along the southeastern coast. But the Portuguese by their violent ways quickly alienated the Peking Court, and in succession they were expelled from, and forbidden to trade at, Canton, Ningpo, Chuanchow (a major foreign-trade center in the Sung period), and elsewhere. Only in 1557 were they granted the privilege of residing in isolated quarantine, for trading purposes only, on the minor peninsula of Macao near Canton.

The first British and Dutch visits to China also resulted in armed clashes. Those developments doubtless prejudiced China's later relations with Occidentals. Adding Asian insult to Western injury, Japanese pirates, who had been relatively quiet for nearly a century, returned in force and in 1555 sacked Nanking, which had been the first capital of the Mings. The empire now retired deeper still into the exclusionism implicit in the concept that China, the one supreme culture and the only legitimate civilization, had no need of anything from aliens.

THE BIRTH OF RUSSIA

A contrasting development was taking place far to the west, in Muscovy. In 1483, only three years after the Russians cast off the Mongol yoke, Ivan III sent the *voevoda* (military commander) Prince Fedor Kurbski against the Vogul prince Asyk in the Yugry country on the Ob River. The expedition was successful, in that it caused Asyk to submit and promise to pay *yasak* (tribute in furs). The fur "trade" was a lodestone that would draw the Russians always eastwards. Another, bigger expedition was sent into the Yugry domain in 1499–1500, and completed the conquest of the Yugrians and Voguls. The Russian thrust into Asia had begun.

Consolidating the imperial base in Europe for the time being commanded priority attention. By the middle of the sixteenth century, vast changes had been wrought in Muscovy. The Grand Duke Ivan IV (the Terrible) in 1533 succeeded Vasili III. Ivan III had put forward the claim that Moscow, as successor in religious orthodoxy to Rome and Byzantium, was the Third Rome, and he assumed the title of *tsar* (Caesar). In 1547, Ivan IV became "Tsar of All the Russias." An autocrat now ruled, and no longer in the limited confines of Muscovy, but in that larger political entity, Russia. There had begun to take form a nation which, in its claim to divine legitimacy and orthodoxy, bore a certain resemblance to that Oriental Middle Kingdom which assumed that the occupant of the Dragon Throne at Peking was the legitimate ruler of all mankind.

Tsar Ivan IV launched fundamental reforms in such diverse areas as landholding, state finance, the army, and military obligations of the aristocracy. In the end he succeeded in substantially increasing his autocratic power and in centralizing the authority of the state. Ivan also won victories abroad. He achieved striking successes against the khanates that had continued to threaten Russia from Inner Asia and the direction of the Black Sea and the Caspian. He defeated the Tatars, took Kazan and Astrakhan, and in 1557 brought the Great Nogai Horde, occupying an area east of the lower Volga, into a vassal relationship. The Russian people were thus enabled to populate the lower

Volga region, to the marked benefit of the country's agriculture and trade. But the Crimean khanate, which in 1478 had become a vassal of the Ottoman empire, continued in being, and in 1571 the Crimean khan captured Moscow and destroyed it except for the Kremlin. The Russian struggle with the Ottoman Turks would continue for centuries, with Persia making up the third in a triangle of conflict.

Ivan had little success in extending the imperial sway westwards, but in a long series of wars he first defeated Livonia and finally achieved the elimination of Lithuania (with which Livonia had merged) as a separate political force when, by the 1569 Union of Lublin, Lithuania was joined to Poland. Russia still faced Sweden and a strengthened Poland, but the situation on its western frontier had been sufficiently stabilized to permit more profitable action in the Inner Asian borderlands.

Unremittingly, all this time, the "foreign menace" combined with threats to the internal order to make the Russian rule more despotic.

RUSSIAN THRUST TO THE EAST

In 1558, Tsar Ivan had made a land grant on the upper Kama River, west of the Urals, to the merchant Grigori A. Stroganov. Stroganov and his brothers Yakov and Semyon built up a strong base there and engaged in widespread and lucrative operations. Cossack adventurers and various freebooters swarmed in large numbers to the Stroganov banner, and, with new concessions, the Stroganov power grew. So too did Russian colonization of the region. In 1563, the prince ruling the lands east of the Urals as a nominal subject of Moscow, Ediger Taibugid, was defeated by the Tatar khan Kuchum. Kuchum at first followed the policy of Ediger, continuing to pay tribute to Moscow. When he had consolidated his position over a domain reaching from the Urals to the Ob, however, he stopped his delivery of tribute and gifts and in 1572 began to raid the Permsk *oblast* (district), which was mainly ruled by the Stroganovs.

The Stroganovs in 1574 petitioned the tsar for a grant of land *east* of the Urals as far as the Tura and Tobol Rivers (tributaries of the Ob), where reputedly silver- and iron-ore deposits were to be found. Ivan IV gave them title to those lands and more. The lands in question, however, actually constituted approximately the western half of the domain ruled by Kuchum from his capital at Sibir, on the Irtysh River near its confluence with the Tobol. The Stroganovs, in sum, still had to win the domain they had been granted.

The opening up of the Russian frontier was speeded by a new force in Russian politics—the Cossacks. In Turkic dialects of the fifteenth and sixteenth centuries, *kazak* (as "Cossack" is properly transliterated from the Russian) signified a freebooter, an adventurer. The term came to be applied to Russian frontiersmen as well as to Tatars. With the merging of Poland and Lithuania, Belorussia and the Ukraine (*ukraina*—borderland) came under the Polish system of government, which purposed the transformation of free peasants into serfs. Peasants fled in large numbers to the Ukraine steppe, where the Cossack frontiersmen had already formed military groups to fight the Tatars. They settled *za parogi* (beyond the rapids—of the Dnieper) in military encampments. Dissidents and adventurers were enrolled, and they lived in large measure by plunder. The region became "Zaporozhe," and the Cossacks of South Russia in due course became divided into two main groups, the Zaporozhians and the Ukrainians.

The Poles continued to endeavor to transform the Cossacks from free men into serfs. The Cossacks first resisted and then revolted, thus becoming a separate factor in Eastern European politics. They fought on the side that seemed most profitable to them, whether it was Poland, Sweden, Russia, Turkey, or even the Crimean Tatars. Even as border tribes in the Ming system, these were military colonists charged with maintaining border defense against nomad raids from Inner Asia. The device, however, worked out differently in the two cases. The Ming organization, constructed in a defensive spirit, became an element of weakness. In Russia, on the other hand, the incorporation of adventurous fighters, runaway peasants, and free spirits into Cossack organizations furthered the cause of imperialist expansion: there was always good reason for extending the buffer zone farther in the interest of "state security." For three centuries, adventurous and rebellious Cossacks, often with prices on their heads, were to be found on Russia's expanding frontier. Pushing against the frontier actually became in good part their life's purpose.

Not long after the Stroganovs received the imperial grant of title to lands held by Kuchum Khan, there arrived at their camp one Yermak Timofeevich, a Cossack *ataman* (hetman, chieftain) who, commanding a large band of robbers on the Volga, had been forced to flee with his men by the approach of a government force charged with his destruction. Yermak and his followers reached the upper Kama in their search for refuge. The Stroganovs granted hospitality to the unruly band, but in due course suggested to Yermak that richer fields awaited cultivation farther to the east, and equipped and strengthened his force for an expedition against Kuchum.

The Yermak command of 840 men left on its military campaign in the summer of 1579. The first stage ended when, in October, 1582, it occupied Sibir after a hard-fought battle in which Kuchum's warrior nephew Mahmetkul,[4] who commanded the troops, was wounded, after which Kuchum was forced into flight. The Tatars kept to the field, but in the spring of the following year a Cossack detachment captured Mahmetkul. Various local tribes now submitted to Yermak, who thereupon both reported his successes to the Stroganovs and sent a petition to the tsar requesting a pardon. With his petition, forwarded by his trusted lieutenant Ivan Koltso (who also had a death sentence for robbery hanging over him), he sent a generous portion of the rich loot captured from Kuchum. Yermak took the same occasion to ask for military support.

Ivan IV not only granted the desired pardon but, in his pleasure at Yermak's accomplishments, sent back valuable presents in return, including a richly worked cuirass, and dispatched the voevoda Prince Volkhovski with a detachment of 500 men. But the relief force, including Prince Volkhovski, perished from the weather while en route in the winter of 1583. In August of 1585,[5] Yermak, while out on a foray at the head of a small detachment of his Cossacks, was set upon in a surprise night attack. All but two, Yermak and another Cossack, were killed in the first assault. Yermak, in an effort to escape, plunged into the Irtysh. According to the tradition, he drowned by reason of the weight of the tsar's present, the cuirass, that he wore.

But the foundations for an eastern empire had been laid, by Ivan the Terrible, the merchant Stroganovs, and the freebooter Cossack who would go down in Russian history as Yermak the Conqueror. Kuchum's capital Sibir gave its name to the nucleus of Russia's vast new territory, Siberia. Near Sibir, now once more in Kuchum's hands, the Russians in 1587 constructed a new fortified town, Tobolsk, which long functioned as Siberia's administrative center.

Ivan the Terrible died a year before Yermak. In 1580, in a fit of fury, he had killed his able eldest surviving son Ivan, and succession thus passed to his weak offspring Fedor, who Ivan himself had once said was better fitted to be a bell ringer in a convent than tsar. But there was real power behind the Throne in the person of the tsar's brother-in-law, Boris Godunov, and under his strong influence Moscow went forward with plans for consolidation of its rule in Siberia, and in 1586 Tyumen was founded on the Tura River as a forward base. Kuchum was finally defeated only in 1598, fled to the Nogai Horde, and was there killed. In that same year Tsar Fedor died without legal heir, and the Rurik dynasty ended. Godunov, as Tsar Boris, ruled until his death in 1605, but then there ensued a "Time of Troubles" marked by a confused struggle for the succession, with accompanying revolts of the distressed peasantry.

A *zemski sobor* (territorial assembly) in 1613 elected Mikhail Romanov as tsar, thus ending the Time of Troubles and introducing a new dynasty. The first Romanov tsar was a weak personality and faced massive problems of rehabilitation and reordering of the strife-torn country. Nevertheless, Mikhail succeeded in reconstructing the army and in establishing peaceful relations with Sweden. Under his rule Russia experienced an increase of European cultural and social influences.

At the beginning of the seventeenth century, the Cossacks had waged three campaigns against Khiva, but without success. The Russians found it easier to continue eastward into Siberia, where they faced only minor resistance from such petty forest tribes as the Nentsy, Khanty, and Kets. Along the way, they constructed *ostrog*s (fortified strongpoints) as support positions. The ostrog Mangazeya, on the lower reaches of the Taz River (a tributary of the Ob), functioned as a major base for the new thrust eastward. The ostrog Yeniseisk was constructed on the Yenisei in 1619.

Continuing east from the Yenisei, the Cossacks subdued the Evenki, a Tungusi tribe. There were campaigns against the Buryat Mongols, who offered stronger resistance to the Russian advance, and in 1628 the Cossack *sotnik* (commander of a hundred) Petr Beketov succeeded in getting the Buryats, for the first time, to pay yasak. The Cossacks also ran into the Turkic Yakuts to the east, and Beketov played a further role in empire-building by founding, in 1632, the ostrog Lensk (later renamed Yakutsk) on the middle Lena. In 1636, the Russians discovered the Amur River. Then, in 1639, at the end of their long trek overland, the Cossacks arrived at the Sea of Okhotsk. They had reached the Pacific.

The resistance offered by the Buryat Mongols typified a broader situation: powerful Mongol groups blocked Russian penetration into the vast region south of Siberia.

MONGOLS, MINGS, AND RUSSIANS

The eastern and western Mongols remained disunited. After the death of Altan Khan in 1582, the Khalkha region on the Kerulen split into three main khanates—the Tushet, Tsetsen, and Jasaktu. In western Mongolia, in the meantime, fresh turmoil had wracked the Oirat power. Gushi Khan, who at the beginning of the seventeenth century ruled the Altai region and the rich grazing country north of the T'ien Shan range, came into conflict with Erdeni Batur Khontaiji, was defeated in 1635, and thereupon retreated into the Koko Nor (lake) region of northeastern Tibet. Other Oirat tribes in the turbulent 1630s moved northward into the Black Irtysh valley.

Batur Khontaiji proved himself another Mongolian empire-builder and erected the Dzungarian khanate, which developed such strength that, wielding the balance of power, it would for a full century play a major role in relations between Russia and China. Taking advantage of internal Tibetan strife, Gushi Khan for his part in 1642 consolidated Mongol control over both Tsang (Outer Tibet) and Cham (the eastern Tibetan region).

In China, in the meantime, political decay had accelerated during the emperor Wan-li's long reign (1573–1620). The greedy, luxury-loving, spendthrift emperor developed a nearly total unconcern with governmental processes. In 1592, as the Ming rule continued to deteriorate, the Japanese warrior Hideyoshi Toyotomi invaded Korea preliminary to an attack on China, with the aim of conquering all Asia. The Chinese sent aid to the Koreans, but the Japanese venture failed chiefly because of logistical difficulties and the death of Hideyoshi in 1598. The Tokugawa shogun reached a peace settlement with the Ming Throne in 1607, but there was an increase of Japanese raids along the South China coast.

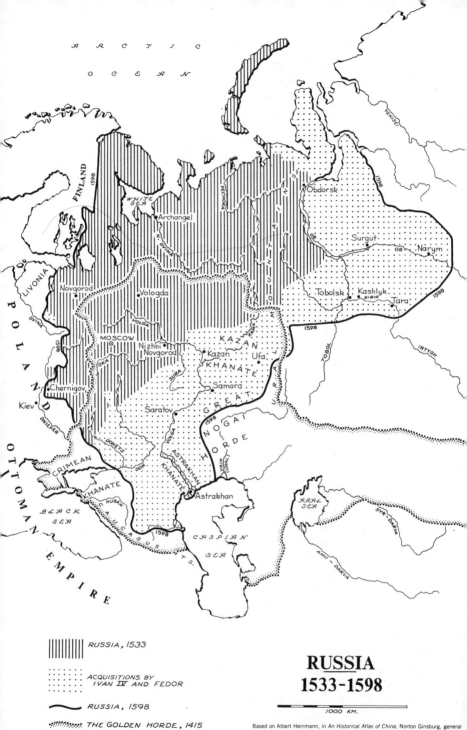

ARCTIC OCEAN

FINLAND

WHITE SEA

Archangel

LIVONIA

Novgorod

Vologda

MOSCOW

Nizhni Novgorod

KAZAN

Kazan

Ufa

KHANATE

Chernigov

Kiev

Samara

GREAT

Saratov

NOGAI

HORDE

ASTRAKHAN KHANATE

CRIMEAN KHANATE

Astrakhan

BLACK SEA

KUBAN

CASPIAN SEA

Obdorsk

Surgut

Narym

Tobolsk

Kashlyk

SIBIR

Tara

1598

ARAL SEA

SYR-DARYA

AMU-DARYA

POLAND

OTTOMAN EMPIRE

CAUCASUS MTS.

URAL MOUNTAINS

PECHORA

YENISEI

OB

IRTYSH

TOBOL

N. DVINA

VOLGA

OKA

SURA

DON

DONETS

DNIEPER

YAIK URAL

||||||||| RUSSIA, 1533

:::::::::: ACQUISITIONS BY
:::::::::: IVAN IV AND FEDOR

——— RUSSIA, 1598

:::::::::: THE GOLDEN HORDE, 1415

**RUSSIA
1533-1598**

1000 KM.

Based on Albert Herrmann, in *An Historical Atlas of China*, Norton Ginsburg, general
ed. (Chicago, Aldine, 1966), and Allen F. Chew, *An Atlas of Russian History* (New
Haven and London, Yale University Press, 1967).

T. R. MILLER

MING CHINA
1415–1580

MING
CHINA,
1415

MING
CHINA,
1580

1000 KM.

Even as pressure by Occidentals and Japanese on China from the sea side was growing, the Russians became increasingly desirous of establishing direct contact with the Chinese empire. In the fifteenth and sixteenth centuries, through their trade in Central Asia, the Russians had acquired a broader acquaintanceship with Chinese goods. When they met up with the Buryat Mongols in the mid-sixteenth century, they found them, too, in possession of Chinese silver and manufactured items. Moscow, which was suffering a shortage of silver, was distinctly interested, and the desire to trade directly with China increased accordingly.

The ostrog Tomsk, founded in 1604, was used as base for the first Russian attempts to make contact with the Middle Kingdom. In 1608, the Tomsk voevoda, V. V. Volynski, charged the Cossack Ivan Belogolov with opening up a route to China via the domain of the Khalkha Mongol *altyn-khan* (literally, "Golden Khan") Sholoi Ubashi (1567–1627), ruling in northwestern Mongolia. But the altyn-khan was then at war with the Oirats, and Belogolov's party had to turn back even before reaching the Mongol lands.

The Russians were not alone among Westerners in the endeavor to reach fabled Cathay and its riches. Boris Godunov had earlier promised to help the English get to China. Now, blocked from trading at Macao by intrigues of the Portuguese, the English ambassador at Moscow, John Mericke, applied increased pressure to obtain facilities for his countrymen to trade with China via Russia.[6] The Russians were deeply interested in the matter in their own behalf, and in May, 1616, the Tobolsk voevoda, Prince Ivan S. Kurakin, sent Vasili Tyumenets and Ivan Petrov as envoys to the altyn-khan. The party reached the nomad camp of Sholoi Ubashi in the vicinity of Ubsa Nur (lake), and Tyumenets was so successful in his diplomatic mission that on the third day of his visit the altyn-khan acknowledged Russian suzerainty.[7] The quick conversion may have been somewhat related to the Russians' exhibition of their skill with the harquebus, which so impressed the altyn-khan that he expressed the hope that they would obtain twenty of the weapons from Moscow for him.

Tyumenets and his companions have come down in history as the first Russians to drink Chinese tea, served to them by Sholoi Ubashi. They incidentally obtained from their host additional information about China and how to get there. They got back to Tomsk in November, 1616. The Russians refrained from communicating to the English the critical elements of the new knowledge obtained about the land route to China, but were themselves led into some error by the report of the existence of a "brick wall" around the country; "and therefore," they concluded, "it can be known that the place is not large." [8]

In May, 1618, Ivan Petlin, supported by the Cossacks Andrei Mundov [9] and Petr Kizylov, left Tomsk with the mission of finding a way to China and obtaining additional information about the country. Accompanied by Mongol envoys, they reached the camp site of Sholoi Ubashi, who not only gave permission for the expedition's passage through his territory, but also assigned two high-ranking Buddhist lamas to accompany them. The lamas' services to the Russians were strikingly effective. The party reached Peking in September.

The Russians had discussions with Chinese officials but, possessing no official character and bearing no gifts (as tribute), did not receive an audience with the emperor Wan-li. The emperor was, however, apprised of the arrival of the Russians, and when they departed in late October they bore with them a message addressed by Wan-li to the tsar granting permission for the Russians to send envoys and to trade with China. Wan-li added, for the edification of Tsar Mikhail, that he himself did not issue from his state, nor did he send out either envoys or traders. [10]

Winter travel through the Mongolian *gobi* (arid steppe) was arduous, and it was May, [11] 1619, when Petlin and his comrades got back to Tomsk. Even so, owing to the inability of the Russians to translate the Chinese-language document Petlin carried, the Russian government remained ignorant of the commercial rights granted therein until the Russian envoy Spathar-Milescu in 1675 found at Tobolsk a man who translated the document into Russian — with many errors. The Petlin mission was the first Russian expedition to reach Peking, [12] and Petlin wrote an account of his trip that was translated into various languages and given wide circulation.

Given the hardships and dangers of the long overland journey between the Russian lands and those ruled by the Chinese emperor, an early attempt was made to discover a water route. Tyumenets and the Cossack Andrei Sharigin in 1620 started out from the ostrog at Kuznetsk with that aim but had to return with a report of failure. In the last decades of the Ming dynasty, the

Russians sent no more missions to China. Russia, however, continued to cultivate relations with the Mongols, sending eleven embassies to the Khalkha altyn-khan between 1616 and 1678. Russian relations were also early established with the western Mongols, with the Bukharans in the beginning acting as both the political and the commercial representatives of the Oirats.

The Mongols continued their own relations with declining Ming China. They also sent missions all the way to Moscow, and the visitors reported on China's riches — gold, silver, and fine satins and damasks. The Russian merchants needed little urging, and early in the seventeenth century began to send trade caravans to the Chinese frontier, while Chinese and Mongol merchants brought goods from China to sell as deep in Russia's interior as Surgut, lying far below Tomsk on the Ob. At that time, a hard economic factor underlay the Russian interest in the China trade: the market for Russian furs had sharply declined in Western Europe. China appeared to offer a promising new market.

1 THE MEETING OF EMPIRES

THERE WAS AS YET no physical contact between the Chinese and Russian empires; other peoples inhabited the borderlands between. An additional factor that may well have discouraged the Russians from undertaking new expeditions for some time after 1620 was the circumstance that Ming China was then entering upon its own Time of Troubles under challenge from a rising borderlands people, the Tungusi Jurchens. The Jurchens, numbering no more than 400,000, occupied a region between the Sungari River and the Chinese-populated area resting on the Chihli Gulf. In 1616, the Jurchen chieftain Nurhachi (or, Nurhachu) declared himself khan (the nomadic equivalent of emperor), thus by unmistakable implication issuing his challenge to the emperor Wan-li in Peking.

Nurhachi did not live to achieve the conquest of China; he died in 1626. The leadership of the Jurchens passed to his eighth son, Abahai (1592–1643), an experienced military and political warrior in the prime of life. From the end of the sixteenth century, one Jurchen objective had been the dividing of the Mongols in order to weaken their power, and thus the eastern Mongols were found involved from the beginning in the contest in Northeast Asia. Abahai in 1632–1634 conquered the Chahar Mongols to the west, and the death in 1634 of the ruling Chahar khan, Ligdan, ended the imperial line of reigning Mongol khans dating back to Genghis. The title "khan" thereafter came to be assumed by numerous Mongol princes, where before it had been limited in use to the rulers of the four major Mongol khanates of Eurasia.

Abahai incorporated the Chahars into his military organization, and they contributed substantially to his growing power. Other Mongol princes, reading the political signs aright, acknowledged Jurchen suzerainty. In 1635, Abahai announced that his people would no longer be called Jurchens or Chienchou Jurchens, as was the Chinese usage, but "Manchus" (for which the rationale is now unknown). And then, in May, 1636, with forty-nine Inner Mongolian princes in attendance, Abahai proclaimed himself emperor of the Ch'ing ("pure") dynasty. In 1638, he added to his governmental apparatus a Li-fan Yuan (Court for the Administration of Borderlands), charged with the handling of Mongolian affairs. The functions of that organ were destined to expand.

Abahai died in 1643 and succession passed to his ninth son, Fu-lin, then only five years of age. The able fourteenth son of Nurhachi, Dorgon, acted as regent and carried on the campaign against Ming China. Dorgon's victory march on Peking was facilitated by the prevalent banditry in China, which had now assumed the proportions that historically had threatened the existence of dynasties. One such bandit, Li Tzu-ch'eng, had taken on the stature of challenger to the dynasty, and in April, 1644, occupied Peking. Dorgon reached an agreement with the disaffected Chinese general Wu San-kuei, and the combined Manchu and Chinese forces in June, 1644, easily ousted Li from his newly won authority in Peking. Abahai's son Fu-lin ascended the Dragon Throne as the emperor Shun-chih.

The Manchus, while maintaining their characteristic social organization, including the clan system and the military "banner" system adapted by Nurhachi from the Ming borderlands defense structure, and their "national identity," nevertheless adopted the Chinese forms of political administration and the Confucian concepts generally. The Chinese scholar-bureaucrats for the most part were content to enter the Manchu service. Wu San-kuei, notably, helped to subdue the rest of the Ming supporters. By 1659, the territory Inside the Wall, as controlled by the Ming Chinese, had all passed into the alien Manchu hands.

Outside that Wall, by subjugation of the Chahars, the Manchus had already begun to move into Mongol domain. Indicative of the importance which the Manchus attributed to the Mongol factor was the circumstance that in the Manchu regime, from the beginning, the Manchu, Mongol, and Chinese languages were all given official status in the Ch'ing Court.

There was one automatic addition to the empire when the Manchus took it over; the Manchus controlled their own homeland, the Northeast (as the Chinese commonly term Manchuria). Abahai had carried on the work begun by Nurhachi of subjugating the tribes to the north of his own clan's holding. Beginning in 1636, he launched several expeditions into the Amur region, and in 1644, the year Dorgon occupied Peking, the Manchu military power was extended to the Amur River.

This had originally been Tungusi land; now Occidentals were also found there. The Russian Cossacks had been extending their conquests at the same time the Manchus were overcoming China. In 1641 a new expedition was sent against the Buryats, who had been harassing the Russian line of communications to Yakutsk. The Russians administered several severe defeats to the Buryats, and finally, in 1652, marked their victory by founding Irkutsk; they thereafter controlled the easier route to the east around the southern tip of long and deep Lake Baikal. This development would have important strategic significance for future developments.

A more direct confrontation with the Manchu empire was impending. In the spring of 1644, Vasili Poyarkov descended the Zeya to the Amur and then proceeded downriver. At the mouth of the Sungari, which he reached in about three weeks, he was met with hostility by the Dyuchers, and a twenty-five-man detachment of the Cossacks was wiped out. But Poyarkov continued on his way. Passing the mouth of the Ussuri, along which, to the south, the Olchei and Goldi lived, after another month he and his sixty companions reached the mouth of the Amur. Wintering there, the company in the spring of 1645 reached the Sea of Okhotsk. They got back to the Yakutsk ostrog in 1646, bearing with them new accounts, obtained from the Tungusi peoples they had encountered, of the richness of China. To the Russian eyes, the Amur River had opened up a new world. In Northeast Asia, the Russian and Manchu empires had met.

The Manchus thus faced a more complex situation with respect to foreign affairs than the defense-minded Mings, for they had to deal politically with both Russians and Mongols, as well as with "barbarian" seafarers. But the unsophisticated Manchus came to power with a confidence born of victory. They already exercised suzerain power over certain Mongol groups, and were allied with others. Here they met direct Russian competition. The Russians had established working relations with the Oirats at the beginning of the century. Contacts with the Khalkhas, located farther to the east, came later. About 1647, a party of Russians reached the camp of the Tsetsen khan, but they refused to bow before his yurt as demanded, and so were not received. In 1648, with the change of authority in Peking, the first Khalkha envoys made the journey to Moscow, with the double aim of working out arrangements for avoiding conflict with the Cossacks—and for trade. Early in their contact with the Khalkhas, the Russians suggested that the Mongols become subjects of Russia.[1] This démarche bore no fruits, but it was one which, under varying circumstances, would often be repeated.

While endeavoring to develop closer relations with the various Mongol groups, Tsar Aleksei, who had succeeded his father Mikhail in 1645, sought to establish ties with the Manchu Court in Peking. There was reason for Moscow to be concerned with Russo-Manchu relations, now that the two expanding empires were in direct contact. The Russians were continuing with their exploration—and colonization. In 1648, the Cossack ataman Semyon Dezhnev headed a party which, starting from the mouth of the Kolyma River, made its way around the Chukotsk Peninsula south through the Bering Strait—eight decades before the arrival of Vitus Bering in the service of another Russian tsar.

On the Amur, Poyarkov's work was continued by Erofei P. Khabarov, who in 1649, by command of the Yakutsk voevoda Frantsbekov, set out on a new expedition down the river. His party ran into some settlements of Daurs, subjects of the Manchu emperor. Khabarov wisely stopped his advance and, leaving a small garrison behind, returned to Yakutsk and reported on the situation. The following summer, reinforced, he made his way down the Amur once more to join his garrison, which was found under siege by the Daurs. Poyarkov had dealt harshly with the initially friendly indigenous tribes; Khabarov resorted to outright barbarous treatment.[2] There was a clash between Khabarov's force and the Daurs. The Daur prince Albaza fled, and Khabarov entered his town, Albazin, at the confluence of the Shilka and Argun, and strengthened it to enable him to pass the winter there. Frantsbekov sent a detachment of 137 men from Yakutsk as reinforcement. On receipt of Khabarov's first report, which had described the riches of the region, he had transmitted the promising intelligence to Moscow, and Moscow, on receipt of the report many months later, dispatched 3,000 troops under the command of Prince Lobanov-Rostovski to the Amur sector.

Khabarov in the meantime was busily engaged in consolidating his position on the Amur. In September, 1651, he occupied a village belonging to the Olchei tribe, constructed an ostrog known as Achansk, and despite Olchei and Dyucher harassment wintered there. The Olchei and Goldi, oppressed and under pressure to pay yasak and supply the Russian detachment, called upon the Manchus for help.

In March, 1652, a Manchu detachment of 2,000 men arrived and attacked the ostrog but was repulsed. Russian losses were small, but Khabarov prudently evacuated the point in April and moved upriver — closer to possible support from Yakutsk. Khabarov actually met up with a relief force, commanded by Dmitri Zinoviev, at the mouth of the Zeya in the autumn of 1653. A dispute developed between the two Russian forces, and Zinoviev returned to Moscow taking Khabarov with him. Command of Khabarov's force fell to Onufri Stepanov.

Stepanov in 1654 made a plundering raid down the Amur and explored the lower Sungari until surprised and defeated by a stronger Manchu force, then went back up the Amur and built an ostrog named Kumarsk. The sotnik Petr Beketov arrived from the trans-Baikal region to support Stepanov, and they beat off a strong Manchu attack on the Kumarsk ostrog in the winter of 1654-1655. The Manchus, however, had in the meantime ordered the Dyuchers and Daurs to remove from the region and resettle on the Nonni River, and Stepanov was forced to forage far afield for supplies. In the summer of 1658, in the course of such a foraging-plundering expedition, he was intercepted by the Manchu general Sarhuda near the confluence of the Sungari and the Amur, and he and most of his detachment were killed or captured. The Russian "presence" on the Amur was thus eliminated for the time being, and Moscow decided that the final conquest of the Amur should be undertaken only after consolidation of the trans-Baikal position. A big step in that direction was taken with the establishment on the Selenga, in 1666, of the ostrog Selenginsk.

It was within this overall context that Moscow had undertaken to establish contact with Peking for the regularization of relations between the two countries. In 1650, Erofei Zabolotski started out on the road to China, but he and his companions were murdered by their Buryat escort south of Lake Baikal. Similarly, a mission headed by the Cossack Tetyak E. Chechigin, dispatched from the Amur region to Peking in the latter part of 1653, was wiped out by Dyucher guides.

A third venture made some advance. In 1653–1655, a Tobolsk merchant who was by birth a Bukharan, Seitkul Ablin, headed a caravan that visited Peking for purposes of trade—and to pave the way for an official Russian mission. Returning by a different route from that by which he had come, he missed the tsar's mission, headed by Fedor I. Baikov. Baikov had departed from Tobolsk, with a suite of some hundred persons, in June, 1654, traveling by boat up the Irtysh and then overland to the point of entry to China at Kalgan. The party was held up at that point, but the Court's permission to proceed finally arrived, and Baikov reached Peking in March, 1656.

Baikov, although illiterate, was an unusually able man. At Peking, however, he faced a hostile bureaucracy, that of the Li-fan Yuan (now charged with handling Russian as well as Mongol affairs), interposed between him and the emperor. He was unsuccessful in presenting either his credentials or the tsar's gifts to Emperor Shun-chih. Months were taken up in an endless wrangle regarding ceremonial, with the Manchu officials insisting that Baikov should kowtow to the emperor's seal and even at the temple before the city gates, surrender the tsar's gifts in advance of any audience with the emperor (the gifts were finally taken from him forcibly), and also deliver his credentials over to them. A genuflection similar to the kowtow was a part of Russian Court ceremonial in the seventeenth century,[3] but there is little doubt that the ritual the Manchus sought to impose upon Baikov was more clearly designed to show subjection, not formal courtesy.

Baikov's refusal to follow the prescribed procedure led to the failure of his mission: in August, the tsar's gifts were returned to his custody, and he was ordered to leave China. He left Peking in September, 1656, and got back to Moscow just under two years later. The arduous round trip had taken four years.

Undaunted, the Russians tried again in that same year. The merchant Seitkul Ablin was in 1658 sent back to China accompanied by Ivan Perfilev, son of a *boyar* (member of the aristocracy). They carried a communication from the tsar to the Manchu emperor, but they themselves bore only the designation of couriers. They naturally received no audience with the emperor, but in any event the Russian gifts were accepted (as tribute), and they were given gifts for the tsar in return. They also took back with them a message from the mandarinate setting forth the reasons why they were not accorded an imperial audience. They reached Moscow in November, 1662, but again there was none there who could translate the Chinese document. They had been despoiled of the bulk of the emperor's presents by Oirats while en route, but one thing they were successful in bringing back was ten poods (360 pounds) of tea, theretofore unknown in Moscow. That commodity would become one of the most highly prized of Russian imports from China.

Ablin had compromised the Russian position in one respect by agreeing that Cossack activities in the Amur region should be halted — a persistent Manchu demand. That concession aimed at furthering Moscow's chief desire, the fostering of trade with China. Ablin would return to Peking once more, in a voyage of 1668–1671, but as the leader of a commercial caravan. His diplomatic days were done.

Political contacts between Russia and the Khalkhas had in the meantime been renewed, with a Russian mission visiting the Jebtsun Damba Khutukhtu (Living Buddha) at the latter's invitation in 1665, and the Khalkhas sending a mission to Moscow in 1667 to protest against the construction of Selenginsk. Perfilev next, in 1668, was dispatched to the Khalkhas to inform them that they were subjects of the Russian tsar, but he gained no acknowledgment from the Mongol princes.

The ostrog built by Khabarov at Albazin (also called Yaksa) had been taken and razed by the Manchus in 1658, the year of Stepanov's disaster. In 1669, Cossacks of Ilimsk under the leadership of Nikofor Chernigovski, after having killed their voevoda, fled to Albazin, reconstructed the ostrog, brought surrounding lands under cultivation for their support, and as usual with the Cossacks extorted tribute from the Daurs and Dyuchers. The Manchu emperor K'ang-hsi had ascended the Throne in 1661, at the age of eight, and when only fourteen took control from the regents who had ruled during his early minority. He faced important power problems in China Proper, however, and for the time being the outlaw Cossacks held sway at Albazin without interference from the Manchu side.

In 1670, there was another Russian mission to China, that of Ignati Milovanov. It resulted from an approach made by the Manchu side, which demanded that the Evenki [4] prince Gantimur (or, Ghantimur) should be handed over to China. Gantimur had originally ruled in Dauria independently of both the Manchus and the Russians, but had sided with the Manchus to oppose the Cossacks, and then, in 1667, went over to the Russian side with his family and his *ulus* (tribe) of some forty persons. The Manchu Court regarded him as a renegade and wanted him back. Further, doubtless with the idea that the Russians would think it an attractive quid pro quo, the Manchus proposed free trade between subjects of the two countries.

The Russian mission proceeded by authority of the voevoda of Nerchinsk, Daniil Arshinski, who probably out of his ignorance proposed in his communication to K'ang-hsi that the latter submit to the tsar.[5] This part of the communication was presumably not conveyed to the emperor, who addressed a letter to the tsar (duly translated to the Nerchinsk voevoda) noting both his complaints and his desire for peace. The Russians made no move to hand over Gantimur, and conditions in the borderland between the two states remained inauspicious for trade. Moscow, when it learned of Arshinski's action, relieved him of his post.

Milovanov, however, five years later made another trip to Peking, this time to inform the Court of the projected visit of a new Russian ambassador, Nikolai G. Spathar-Milescu (Spafari in the Russian). Spathar-Milescu was a Moldavian Greek speaking various foreign languages. Elaborate preparations were made in Moscow for the mission. Upon departure in March, 1675, it included a geographer, a cartographer, and other scientists, and en route in Siberia it was further briefed regarding conditions in China. The mission traveled by land and water to Nerchinsk, then followed the route taken by Milovanov in 1670, proceeding via the Nonni River valley to Peking. After the Spathar-Milescu journey, that route was long favored for Russian diplomatic and trade missions to China.

In May, 1676, after a voyage of over a year, Spathar-Milescu arrived in Peking, bearing the tsar's gifts. It was his function to assure the Manchu government of Russia's friendly intentions and the desire to undertake trade relations, and if possible to get

Peking to send a mission to Moscow. But the usual quarrel over procedure and ceremonial had begun, as in Baikov's case, even while Spathar-Milescu was en route to Peking; it continued after his arrival. The Russian ambassador finally agreed to perform the kowtow. He won the desired audience with the emperor and was later entertained by K'ang-hsi at an official banquet.

But the issue of Gantimur had early been raised, and it was evident that this was a critical matter in the mind of K'ang-hsi. When Spathar-Milescu refused to kowtow in a muddy courtyard in the rain when receiving, from subordinate officials, the emperor's presents for the tsar, the mission came to an inglorious end. There was no reply by K'ang-hsi to the tsar's letter, only an imperial edict read by one of the Grand Secretaries to Spathar-Milescu and his aides, while they were on their knees. The edict made three demands: that Gantimur be surrendered, that the new ambassador (to accompany Gantimur) should be "a most reasonable man who will do all we command him, in accordance with our customs, and oppose us in nothing," and, finally, that the peace be kept unbroken in all frontier places inhabited by Russians.[6]

The last demand clearly had reference to the Cossacks. Spathar-Milescu had earlier been informed by one of the Jesuits that K'ang-hsi proposed to send troops against the Russian positions at Albazin and Nerchinsk and that, if Gantimur were not handed over, China would make war on Russia. On September 1, the Russian ambassador and his mission were ordered to depart Peking that same day. They got back to Moscow in January, 1678.

There had in the meantime been critical developments in the Dzungarian khanate. Batur Khontaiji died in 1653, and power passed to his son Senge (or, Sengge). Another son, Galdan, went to Tibet and entered a lamasery. After Senge was killed by a third brother, however, Galdan renounced the occupation of lama, returned from Tibet in 1671, entered the lists, and killed the murderer-brother in turn. He soon won authority over most of the Oirat chieftains, although at some cost. A number of Khoshote, Derbet, and Torgut princes during this time of turmoil led their people to settle on the Volga.[7] Among them was the Torgut prince Ayuka, who in 1672 united the Volga Mongols under his rule.

By 1673, Galdan had begun to infringe upon Russian authority by collecting yasak from the same peoples on the upper Yenisei who had been paying yasak to the Russians. There were already trade relations and political contacts between Dzungaria and the Russians; in the decade 1671–1680, Galdan sent no less than six missions to various Siberian points and to Moscow. In October, 1673, given Galdan's tax-collecting activities, the Kalmyk (Oirat) representative then in Moscow was informed that Russian subjects might not pay yasak to the Dzungar khanate, and that Galdan himself was a subject of the tsar.[8]

Galdan, given his imperial ambitions, was not prepared to bow to the Russian will. In 1677, he sent a tribute mission to Peking. He was obviously preparing to profit through winning control of the balance of power between China and Russia. Behind Galdan there were others, particularly in the circle of the Dalai Lama at Lhasa, who supported him in the strategic aim of forming a state comprising all Mongols who were followers of the lamaistic Buddhist religion. His aim was the creation once more of a unified Mongolia.[9] By 1679, he had added Kashgaria (the region south of the T'ien Shan range) to the original holding of the Dzungar khanate. He informed Peking that Lhasa had confirmed him in his position of authority, with the title of Boshoktu Khan.

At this time, the Mongols occupied a vast buffer zone between the Manchu and Russian empires. Mongol rule was divided among the Khalkhas of the Kerulen valley, the Buryats in the Selenga valley, the Oirats in the Dzungarian basin and at the sources of the Ob and Yenisei rivers, and the Torguts far to the west with a control extending along the Urals and to the mouth of the Volga – although subject to Moscow. Galdan's purpose in working for Mongolian unity was easy for other imperialists to discern: with such unified power in Inner Asia, he could confront both Manchu and Russian imperialism from a position of strength.

The Russians were awake to the significance of Mongol moves, having by now accumulated over four centuries of experience regarding Inner Asian nomads. Nikita Ya. Bichurin (the monk Iakinf), living a century later (1777–1853), offered a characterization of some Central Asians the Russians had known: "Nomads consider allegiance a bargain with their conscience, in which they expect to win at least four to one," failing which they repaid themselves by pillage, rapine, and murder.[10] The Russians of the seventeenth century had already learned as much and had developed a sense of wariness appropriate for the handling of Inner Asian affairs. When Galdan began to exert pressure on what the Russians regarded as their own preserves, he alienated Moscow, which would thereafter naturally be less inclined to help him against the Manchus.

Galdan's assumption of the title of Boshoktu Khan, reminiscent of Nurhachi's earlier similar action, likewise bore a clear significance for Peking. Where the Throne had been energetically engaged in trying to split the Khalkhas, the better to expand Manchu imperial power, it was now realized that disunity in eastern Mongolia, in circumstances where a threat was looming up from western Mongolia, was disadvantageous for Peking's overall strategic position. Peking therefore reversed itself and began to stress the virtue of Khalkha unity.

And in addition, K'ang-hsi turned his attention to the related Russian question.

2 THE "NORMALIZATION" OF RUSSO-MANCHU RELATIONS

IN 1681, AND AGAIN IN 1682, Peking sent couriers to Nerchinsk to request a conference on outstanding issues, without results. In 1683, K'ang-hsi appointed the Manchu general Sabsu to be military governor of Heilungkiang,* with the particular charge of handling Russian affairs. Sabsu captured a number of Russians at the mouth of the Zeya that same year, and more in the next two years, for a total of about a hundred men. They were formed into a company and put under the command of a Russian who had reached Peking as a refugee in 1648. Some won official ranks in Sabsu's army. Those who resided in Peking were assigned a special quarter in the northeastern part of the town. They intermarried with Chinese and Manchus, but kept to their own religion.

In June, 1685, Sabsu's forces, reinforced by those of the Manchu general Pengcun, appeared in martial array before Albazin. The Russians, now commanded by Aleksei Tolbuzin, retreated after taking heavy losses in the first action. The Manchus destroyed the fortifications, then withdrew. In October, Tolbuzin led a fresh force back, and the ostrog was rebuilt under the direction of the German military engineer Afanase Beiton. The

* So the Amur River is called in China, and the river gave its name to the northernmost region of Manchuria.

next summer Sabsu reappeared on the scene and laid siege to the Russian position. Tolbuzin was killed early in the investment, and Beiton took over command.

Neither side wanted to go to war, however, over the relatively minor issue of Albazin: both had bigger objectives at hand to engage their energies. Two letters, written in Latin, had been received in Moscow in November, 1685. They were dated May, 1683, and were addressed to the tsar by K'ang-hsi, who raised the matter of previous letters, which had gone unanswered, demanding the evacuation of Albazin. The Russian Court promptly dispatched two couriers, Nikifor D. Venyukov and Ivan Favorov, to carry to Peking the news that an envoy would be sent to negotiate the problem. There was to be a political resolution of the dispute.

In 1686, under the patient urging and manipulations of K'ang-hsi, the Khalkhas reached a truce among themselves. Galdan's policy of *divide et impera* had failed, and he was left in that much the more dangerous a position vis-à-vis the Russians, Khalkhas, and Manchus.

Venyukov and Favorov reached Peking in the fall of 1686 and delivered their message. The emperor K'ang-hsi agreed that a diplomatic conference should be held and gave the Russians two letters for the tsar, one in Latin, the other in Mongolian. En route back to Moscow, the couriers met the tsar's envoy, Fedor Alekseevich Golovin, son of the voevoda of Tobolsk, and informed him of their experience. When K'ang-hsi received word that the tsar's envoy was en route, he ordered Sabsu, as promised, to lift the siege of Albazin. The stage was set for negotiations.

Golovin, with a little army of 1,500 men, made his way slowly eastward. When he reached the trans-Baikal region, he was met by envoys from the Khutukhtu and the Tushet khan. After the Buryats, under Russian pressure, abandoned their ancestral lands in the 1650s, the Khalkhas had continued to pursue the issue of Russian penetration of Mongol territory. The chief concern of the Mongol mission appears to have been, as always, that same subject — but Golovin refused to discuss the matter. He went on to the projected conference with the Manchus. His party reached Selenginsk, the agreed meeting place, in November, 1687 — nearly two years after Moscow had dispatched its couriers in response to the emperor's letters.

The Manchu mission was finally constituted, and in May,

1688, left Peking for Selenginsk via Mongolia. But a Mongol struggle intervened. The shaky Khalkha truce had been broken when one of the Khalkha chieftains, the Jasaktu khan, joined Galdan. Galdan moved heavy forces eastward and when the errant Khalkha chieftain was killed by the avenging Tushet khan, invaded the Khalkha domain. The Manchu mission to Selenginsk ran into the side eddies of the Oirat-Khalkha war, halted, and some weeks later was overtaken by an imperial order directing it to return to Peking. The conference was necessarily postponed.

In the meantime, the Khalkhas had brought Golovin and his party under siege, and the Russians were pinned down in Selenginsk until April, 1688, when, disengaging, they flanked and defeated the Mongols. Golovin then forced the Khalkha leaders to sign a treaty of submission. The Oirats were still a factor in the complex equation. In the intra-Mongol struggle of 1688, Galdan defeated the Khalkhas, some of whom, for their salvation, signed a treaty acknowledging Russian suzerainty. Others petitioned the Manchu Court to be accepted as vassals of China. Peking naturally acceded to that Khalkha request, and an ultimate conflict between Galdan and the Manchu power now became inevitable.

Galdan's leadership had unexpectedly been weakened. During his conflict with the Khalkhas, his nephew Tsewang Araptan had mobilized in his rear and appropriated a part of the Dzungar domain. The nephew was the initial victor in the clash that occurred on Galdan's return to Dzungaria in 1689. Galdan that summer sent an envoy to Moscow with an eye to the possible need of an ally. In Russo-Manchu relations there had already been established a pattern: when the Mongols were quiet, Peking tended to be arrogant toward the Russians; when the Mongols threatened China, the Manchu Court assumed a conciliatory stance. That same pattern was mirrored in Moscow's relations with the Dzungar power.

In Russia in 1689, mainly because of Prince Golytsin's disastrous campaigns against the Crimea, the regent Sophia lost power, Ivan V resigned the co-tsarship, and Peter I, at the age of seventeen, came to full de jure power.

That same year, K'ang-hsi again sent out his mission to meet with the Russians. The chief envoys were Songgotu and T'ung Kuo-kang (K'ang-hsi's uncle). They were accompanied by a large military escort comprising both Songgotu's command and some

3,000 men under Sabsu, and by the Jesuit Fathers Jean-François Gerbillon and Thomas Pereira as interpreters. The Russo-Manchu conference, begun in August, was held not at Selenginsk, however, but at Nerchinsk (also, Nipchu), founded by the Russians in 1658. In the negotiations, the potentials for an Inner Asian war, with shifting alliances, was a major factor well known to both sides. Golovin came to the conference table authorized to cede control of Albazin, in return for commercial concessions by Peking.

Given the display of Manchu military force, which Golovin did not come even close to matching with the 1,000 men remaining under his command, the Manchu party was in a good negotiating position. That position was even improved when, during the second session of the conference, the Manchus abruptly departed the meeting place and surrounded the town with their troops; some 2,000 *yurts* (tents — families) of Buryats and Onkotes, responding to Manchu manipulation, renounced their allegiance to Russia and joined the Manchu forces. The Russians, however, had one bargaining lever not visible at Nerchinsk but fully appreciated there: if they chose, they could align themselves with the Oirats and cause considerable embarrassment to Peking. This was a situation in which Manchu compromise was indicated. The Manchus desired to limit Russian holdings to the territory west of Lake Baikal and the Lena River. The Russians, avid as ever for trade with China, were on their part distinctly inclined to be conciliatory. Neither side, at that juncture, had anything to gain from mutual hostility, whereas both might profit from amicable relations.

The Jesuit priests played a pivotal role. The Russians could speak neither Manchu nor Chinese, and the Manchus spoke no Russian. The Mongol tongue common to them both was in the main left unused. The Jesuits, commanding Manchu, Chinese, and Latin, became the essential channel of communications. The bargaining, in the shadow of the opposing military forces, was long and hard. On September 7, 1689, * there was signed the Treaty of Nerchinsk, the first such Western-style agreement between China and an Occidental power. The document was drawn up in five languages: Manchu, Chinese, Mongolian, Russian, and

* August 27, 1689 Old Style. Russian dates, which followed the Julian calendar, will be given in the Gregorian system unless specifically accompanied by the designation "O.S."

Latin. The Latin version was the definitive one, and only it was signed.

The treaty fixed the boundary between the Russian and Manchu powers as following the Argun to the Gorbitsa, proceeding to the watershed between the Amur and the Lena, then continuing on to the Udi and the sea. The geographic description was vague, reflecting the imperfect knowledge of both sides with respect to the geography of the region. There was the interesting proviso that ownership of the country lying between the Udi and the mountain range constituting the watershed should remain undetermined, pending later settlement. Albazin was to be demolished. Golovin refused to negotiate with respect to the Mongolian border, holding that this matter did not fall within the purview of his instructions. In any event, Article III provided, in amicable terms, that "All that has happened up to the present, of whatever nature it might be, shall be buried in eternal oblivion." [1] The Russians thus renounced all territorial claims to the Amur valley proper, and, except for the qualification regarding the country lying between the mountain range and the Udi, limits to the Russian advance had been established.

No hunters from either China or Russia might cross the border, but Russia got the essence of its desire: Article V provided that the subjects of either nation, "being provided with proper passports," might travel across the common frontier for the purpose of commerce. Further, such traders and craftsmen, if committing crimes of violence in the territory of the other signatory power, should be handed over to their own authorities for punishment by the death penalty. The principle of extraterritoriality had thus also been established, a century and a half before it was written into treaties for Occidental sea powers.

The issue of Gantimur was settled by the treaty provision that subjects of China who had gone to Russia, or Russian subjects who had fled to China, before the date of the treaty, might remain in their adopted countries, but fugitives after the signature of the treaty were to be returned to their homeland. Gantimur had been baptized in 1684 and had become a member of the Russian nobility as Prince Petr Gantimurov. He continued to reside in Russia until his death near the end of the century.

The treaty had incidental effects in the two countries' respective Inner Asian relationships. The Russians and Manchus turned with redoubled vigor to deal with the Mongols, who had been a source of embarrassment to both. The Russians fell upon the Onkotes and Buryats and dealt them harsh chastisement. K'ang-hsi, now free to act against the Dzungar khanate, began to prepare for final conflict. Galdan, obviously sensing his disadvantage, in March, 1690, approached Golovin, by then at Irkutsk, with a proposal for an alliance against the Khalkhas. At Nerchinsk, however, Russia had got a deal it valued more highly than a military liaison with the mercurial Oirat. Golovin, while encouraging Galdan to act against the Khalkhas, rejected the proposed alliance.

That same spring, Galdan advanced again into the Kerulen valley and passed the summer in that good Khalkha grazing land without meeting major challenge. However, advancing southward that fall, he suffered a heavy defeat about 350 kilometers from Peking. He was able to extricate his army without disaster, but the political effect of the development was far-reaching: his star seemed to be setting, and other Mongols took due note. In 1691, in an elaborate ceremony at Dolonor in Inner Mongolia, the subjection of the Khalkha Mongols to the Manchu rule was formalized, and eastern Mongolia effectively became a part of the Manchu empire. Conflicting commitments to Russia were conveniently forgotten: in the practice of the day, "solemn" vows of allegiance were ordinarily thought to bow before either superior force or greater political profit.

In their vassal-suzerain relationship with the Manchu Court, the Khalkhas occupied a higher position than did the Chinese, a subjugated people. Manchus might not marry Chinese, for instance, but there was considerable intermarriage between Manchus and Mongols, especially at the higher levels. Nevertheless, both the Chahars and Khalkhas had lost their independence and been gathered into the Manchu fold, and the overall Mongol power was correspondingly weakened. The Oirats remained in being as a major Inner Asian force. Galdan's defeat had not been decisive, and he retired to Kobdo to rehabilitate his military power.

In 1694, Galdan again mobilized for action against the Khalkhas. The Khorchin prince, reputedly by direction of K'ang-hsi, pretended to fall in with Galdan's plans for joint action and proposed a campaign the following spring against the Khalkhas in the Kerulen valley. K'ang-hsi mobilized a force of 80,000 troops, and Galdan arrived at the rendezvous only to be trapped by the

Manchu armies under the personal command of the conqueror-emperor and in June, 1696, suffered a tremendous defeat in the battle of Jao Modo, near Urga. The big Oirat force was almost entirely destroyed. Galdan escaped with about a thousand men, and rather more camp followers, but was denied aid by Tsewang Araptan, and, when a new Manchu army neared his base in early May, 1697, he poisoned himself.

Tsewang Araptan succeeded his uncle to power over the Dzungar khanate as *kontaisha* (prince) and continued to endeavor to implement the imperial Mongol ambition, against both the Manchus and the Russians. He demanded of the Manchu Throne the return of all lands once ruled by the Oirats. But K'ang-hsi's authority over eastern Mongolia had now been consolidated beyond easy challenge, and Tsewang Araptan in eliminating a rival had at the same time substantially reduced the Mongol power available for opposing the Manchus.

While K'ang-hsi was dealing with Galdan, Tsar Peter in 1695 embarked upon war against the Crimean Tatars and their allies, the Turks, and the following year succeeded in taking the Tatar fortress of Azov, at the mouth of the Don. But the war continued. Peter went abroad in 1697 as a member of a "grand embassy" headed by General François LeFort in the capacity of "Petr Mikhailov," a noncommissioned officer, with one of the embassy's objectives being to win support for the war against the Turks. He returned home in 1698 without having obtained allies for his crusade, but convinced of Russia's need for modernization, and he began to reconstruct Russian society and the bureaucracy. Associated with him in the foreign trip and in his new purpose was his negotiator at Nerchinsk, Golovin. Peter I would not forget the East.

Nor would circumstances permit Moscow to forget China. The signature of the Treaty of Nerchinsk had in theory marked the beginning of "normal" political and commercial relations. With the drawing of border lines between the two countries in the area of contact, military action and casual clashes largely ceased for the time being. But that new bilateral, "international" document, so foreign to the Confucian concepts the Manchus had adopted, had not provided an overall, detailed settlement of political and economic relations between the two countries: some outstanding problems had been only half solved, and new ones arose.

There were still disputes, and charges and countercharges of non-compliance with the treaty terms.

Traffic between the two countries was bound up in red tape; by the regulations, each Russian caravan was fully documented, with official passports and a detailed goods manifest. A tithe was collected on all goods, with administration at Verkhotur and Nerchinsk. The Russian Court thus made a substantial profit on the commerce. Beginning in 1694, caravans were dispatched every year, but from 1698, when they took on the character of a Russian state enterprise, they made the trip only every two years.

Commerce between the two countries was early subjected to abuses arising from the cupidity of the voevodas and their friends and agents who operated the caravans into China. The voevodas manifested a tendency, all too natural given the leagues of uninhabited forest that separated them from the Throne in Moscow, to send the best furs to the China market and to deliver only inferior goods to their own Court. There was regular and widespread evasion of payment of the tithe. From the early days of Russo-Chinese contact, Russian traders commonly accompanied diplomatic missions traveling to Peking. As happened with other Inner Asian merchants, Russians avid of the profits to be gained in the China trade frequently passed themselves off as official visitors, and when the Russian envoy Sava Vladislavich, in Peking in 1726, inquired regarding the number of Russian "missions" that had come to China, he was astonished to learn that the Chinese official records accounted for fifty — whereas the Russian government itself had no knowledge of more than a small number.[2] Of those "missions," many were headed by Bukharan merchants — who upon occasion acted as agents of the Oirats, and sometimes of the Russians. The private commerce with China of the voevodas and private entrepreneurs, Russian and Bukharan, made greater profit by far than those which operated strictly within the rules laid down by the tsarist Court.

The Danish merchant Evert Izbrandt Ides, long resident in Russia and known to contemporary Russians as Elizar Izbrant, headed an important mission sent to Peking in 1692 for purposes of both political negotiation and trade. There had been no formal exchange of ratifications of the Treaty of Nerchinsk (a process to which the Manchus were doubtless strangers), and none seems to have been projected. But the Manchu Court had reservations regarding the matter of ceremonial and had not signified its acceptance. Izbrant was charged with clarification of this aspect of the matter, with ascertaining the attitude of the emperor regarding that part of the frontier left undefined, with getting the repatriation of Russian deserters, with obtaining facilities for study of the China market, and with acquiring a site in Peking for erection of an Orthodox church. The church, as the Russians saw it, would assist toward the establishment of a durable peace and, moreover, would promote the political and commercial interests of Russia.

Izbrant reached Peking at the head of his caravan in November, 1693, and, after complying with the Chinese etiquette, had an audience with the emperor, but he achieved no success in his political mission. The emperor refused the tsar's letter Izbrant carried, as being improperly phrased, and Peter's envoy was instructed regarding the appropriate style for addressing the emperor in official communications. The treaty was confirmed by tacit acceptance and observance, rather than through an exchange of ratifications. Izbrant got back to Moscow in February, 1695, bearing a letter (intelligible, because in Latin) generally ignoring the Russian requests.

But Izbrant had been not so much a plenipotentiary envoy as a political and commercial agent charged with learning, on behalf of the Russian Court, more about the Chinese rules of political and commercial intercourse. Moscow doubtless profited to that degree from his mission. For one thing, the Chinese in 1694 fixed at 200 the maximum number of persons, not counting merchants, accompanying an ambassador. This became the effective rule from 1704 onward. (The 1698 mission had 478 persons.) After all, the Chinese as hosts were called upon to provide for both the escorting and the entertainment of the caravans and found as much reason for trying to reduce the costs as did the merchants for expanding their efforts. After 1693, Russians were permitted to trade at Peking itself.

Such was the eagerness of the Russians to trade that, in the seventeen years from 1699 to 1716, prices for Russian goods fell variously 5 percent to 60 percent, whereas the prices for Chinese merchandise remained approximately stationary. That situation reflected the strong competition between sellers of Russian goods in the Chinese market. They were also meeting competition from the sea side, for the British entered the commercial arena in earnest in 1699, and China was being offered more goods than it had any need or desire to absorb. Tea was a highly desirable commodity for the foreign merchants, but the foreigners were increasingly hard put to find goods to offer the Chinese in exchange.

The multilateral power struggle in Inner Asia was continuing on its tortuous course. In 1698, Tsewang Araptan launched an expedition against the Kazakhs, who promptly appealed to Russia for help. The Kazakhs, however, had frequently pillaged the Russians, and their prayers went unanswered. In something like compensation for territories lost by Galdan to the Manchus, Tsewang Araptan defeated both Kazakh and Kirgizi forces and extended his authority to Lake Balkhash on the west. Tsar Peter was in actuality not then well situated to support Inner Asian opposition to the Dzungar power, for he was about to become engaged on another front. When war with Turkey ended in 1700, Russia began a conflict with Sweden that would last two decades and come to be called the Great Northern War. Inevitably, that engagement left its imprint on Peter's Asia policy.

Peking, seeking allies in its conflict with the Dzungar khanate, thought of engaging the Torguts living in refuge on the Volga under the leadership of Ayuka Khan. Ayuka's nephew Arabjur was at this time being detained in China by the emperor. Ayuka, with the approval of Tsar Peter, in 1710 sent a mission to Peking under the escort of the Russian underofficer Surovtsev to request Arabjur's release—fruitlessly, for Arabjur was a valuable pawn. Now the Manchu Court broached to the Siberian governor, Prince Matvyi P. Gagarin, the matter of sending a mission to Ayuka Khan for the nominal purpose of negotiating the matter in point. A mission headed by the Manchu Tulisen duly departed Peking in June, 1712, and got to Selenginsk in August. It waited there five months for the Russian reply.

The real purpose of the Manchu mission was of course known to St. Petersburg (to where the Russian government had removed in 1712). The Russian Senate approved the proposed travel—but took the precaution of advising Ayuka not to go to war on the Manchu behalf against the Kalmyks, with whom the Russians were currently on amicable terms. Russian permission finally in hand, Tulisen resumed his journey in the harsh Siberian winter and reached Saratov, on the Volga, in January, 1714. He waited

long months there for the arrival of Ayuka Khan's envoys to bid
him welcome and reached the khan's camp at Manych — ten days'
travel away on the Volga — only in July, and was received by
Ayuka. The long delay at Saratov had been a sign: Ayuka Khan
had already determined his policy in a sense unfavorable to Tulisen's main mission, and Tulisen for his part could offer Ayuka's
avuncular spirit no more solace than contained in the advice that
Arabjur was best advised to remain in China. Tulisen's visit was
limited to a fortnight mainly filled with courtesies, after which he
began the arduous journey back to Peking, arriving there in
April, 1715. The reason for his failure was perhaps to be found as
much in Ayuka's personal assessment of the military situation in
Inner Asia as in the Torgut chieftain's concern for Russian
advice.

Prince Gagarin, in furtherance of his design to extend
Russian control in Inner Asia, had earlier proposed to Tsar Peter
that a series of strong points be constructed from the Irtysh to
Yarkand (through Dzungar territory), and Peter had approved
the project. In 1715, 3,000 men under Colonel Ivan D. Bukhgolts
made their way from Tobolsk up the Irtysh River with the aim of
constructing a fortification on the Irtysh and searching for gold
deposits on the Amu-Darya. They actually built an ostrog on
Lake Yamyshev, but were brought under siege there the following February by a strong Oirat force led by Chereng Dondub,
cousin of Tsewang Araptan. After a three months' defense, which
was complicated by an epidemic, the position was abandoned, and
at the end of 1716 some 700 survivors got back to Tobolsk. But the
ostrogs Omsk and Semipalatinsk were successfully constructed
in 1716 and 1718, respectively.

In 1717, a Russian force of 3,500 men under the Circassian
prince Bekovich Cherkasski attacked Khiva, but was ambushed
and destroyed. General Likharev in 1720 was dispatched with
440 men to establish a fortress at Zaisan, on the upper Irtysh. He
had reached that point and was ascending the river when he
collided with a large force under Galdan Tseren, the son of Tsewang Araptan. Likharev offered the explanation that his was an
exploratory party, made his escape, and in retreat built an ostrog
at Ust-Kamenogorsk, up the Irtysh from Semipalatinsk. The
Russian advance along the line laid down by Gagarin had been
checked, but the frontier had nevertheless been pushed forward.

The Manchus also advanced. Although Chereng Dondub had

in 1717 seemingly been successful in consolidating Dzungar authority over Tibet, K'ang-hsi's fourteenth son, Yin-t'ai, invaded at the head of a strong force and expelled the Mongols in a campaign of 1718–1720, hunting down and butchering them and their Tibetan supporters with the same ruthlessness the Mongols had displayed toward others. In 1720, K'ang-hsi put his own candidate on the Throne at Lhasa as seventh Dalai Lama, and the Manchu imperium was extended over Tibet. In Dzungaria itself, that year saw the maintenance of an uneasy truce between the Manchus and Oirats.

Given especially the assorted problems posed by the Oirats, political relations between Peking and St. Petersburg took on added importance. Both governments had designs on Inner Asia, and their respective strategies with respect to the Mongol force might well determine the outcome. Besides that important political matter, growing irregularities in connection with commerce between the two countries had given rise to new issues. The Russian Court decided to send a new mission to China for the purpose of achieving an improvement in relations.

In 1719 Lev Vasilevich Izmailov, a military man who, under Peter's orders, had served in the Danish army, was designated envoy extraordinary to the Manchu Court. Peter was still engaged in the war with Sweden and his instructions to Izmailov were drafted with circumspection. Izmailov was to fulfill the Chinese ceremonial if requisite, to endeavor to increase the volume of trade between the two countries, and to secure a tract of land in Peking on which to construct an Orthodox church. The Russians desired to have a permanent church in the Chinese capital to minister to the spiritual needs of the Russian colony and of Russians who might visit Peking as members of trade caravans. With respect to trade, Izmailov was to seek to increase the frequency of caravans to once yearly, with the caravans to meet their own expenses if Peking complained of their cost to the imperial treasury, and with full freedom of trade throughout the empire to be requested—on a reciprocal basis. Further, he was to try to arrange for the stationing of a permanent consular representative at Peking, to render assistance to the Russian commercial efforts in China. The consular officer would exercise jurisdiction over Russian subjects.

En route in the following year, Izmailov met with Tulisen at Selenginsk. Both remained there for some months, and at the beginning of November Tulisen informed Izmailov that the Manchu forces had achieved a major victory over the Oirats and requested that Izmailov inform an Oirat envoy then in Selenginsk that the Russians and Manchus were agreed upon taking joint action against the Dzungar khanate. The Manchus had occupied Hami and Turfan but had not penetrated the Dzungarian basin, and the issue was far from decided. Izmailov refused to take the suggested action (which was of course out of line with his instructions) and shortly afterward left for Peking. He arrived there in November, 1720, nearly a year and a half after his departure from Moscow.

Izmailov at last solved the vexed problem of ceremonial. It was agreed that Russian envoys should perform the kowtow to the Manchu emperor at Peking, and China's envoys when sent to St. Petersburg should repay the compliment in kind. A high Manchu official performed the kowtow before the tsar's letter. Izmailov was received in formal audience by Emperor K'ang-hsi, went through the customary genuflections, and presented his credentials. He was accorded full ceremonial honors in return for his own compliance. He remained in Peking from November to mid-March, 1721, and after his first formal audience was received by the Manchu emperor some dozen times in private audience. The Manchu Court, after all, had good political reason to try to keep the Russians from supporting the Oirats.

Izmailov worked hard to achieve the Russian aims. He already had a strong position from which to argue the case for the construction of an Orthodox church. A priest had been among the Russian prisoners taken at Albazin some thirty-five years earlier. Upon arrival in Peking, the little group had been granted a temple as place of worship, and the temple had been duly dedicated by direction of the metropolitan at Tobolsk.[3] The priest died in 1704, but he had been replaced, and in 1707 a second priest was added. In 1714, accompanying the Tulisen mission on its return, the Russian archimandrite Illarion Lezhaiski arrived in Peking and assumed functions. Two years later the mission was strengthened by a party comprising two priests, a deacon, and seven students. The group got a friendly reception from the Chinese as well as from the Russian colony, and the emperor K'ang-hsi conferred official rank on the clergy and provided subsidies for the support of the students. Lezhaiski died at the end of 1719, but the mission, including students, continued on in Peking, engaged in ecclesiastical work and Oriental studies.

Izmailov was successful in arranging for the construction of a temporary church structure on the premises of the Russian hostel and for the cession of a plot of land as site for the permanent building. In his smooth negotiations with K'ang-hsi's Court, Izmailov also reached an agreement looking toward the establishment of tighter controls over Russian caravans to eliminate private undertakings, and he was able to leave behind him at Peking his aide, Lorentz Lange, a Swedish engineer, who from 1721 acted essentially as a foreign consul in the Manchu capital. Lange had been in Peking in 1715 in the company of an English doctor whom the tsar had sent to learn how to manufacture porcelain stoves. He consequently was already acquainted both with the Jesuit priests, who could be so helpful in relations with the Manchu Court, and with Chinese conditions. The Jesuits, who were being subjected to increasingly severe restrictions by the emperor K'ang-hsi, were inclined to be more helpful than at the time of the negotiations for the Treaty of Nerchinsk.

Lange nevertheless faced considerable difficulties in carrying out his functions. Tsewang Araptan had again made goodwill moves in the direction of Peter I, even making a vague commitment to accept Russian suzerainty, and the Manchu Court complained about St. Petersburg's having political traffic with China's enemies. There was the old topic: Russia's failure to return refugees from the Manchu rule. Lange at Peking contacted an envoy from China's vassal, Korea, and the suspicion and ire of the Court increased. Finally, Lange intervened to get permission for a Russian trade caravan, long held up at the Great Wall, to proceed to Peking. Permission was finally granted, but when the caravan arrived the concerned officials demanded that certain goods be set aside for the emperor — and selected the best sable skins, for which they allowed three ounces of silver each, when they were worth twenty ounces.

A major quarrel ensued. In the end, Lange and the caravan leader were told that, because of various specified shortcomings on the Russian side, the emperor had decided that trade and other relations between China and Russia should be severed. Trade was in fact stopped. Lange left Peking with the caravan in July, 1722. When about thirty-five miles out of town, he was summoned back into audience with K'ang-hsi to receive more complaints—and to be wished a pleasant journey. With the caravan now went Tulisen, who bore a letter to the voevoda at Tobolsk repeating an earlier demand for the return to China of 700 fugitive Mongols. The problem of refugees had taken on increased dimensions in Russo-Manchu relations: eastern Mongolia had become a part of the Manchu empire in circumstances where there had been no border demarcation between Russia and Mongolia. The dangers of dispute and confrontation were thus always present.

This was at a time when Russia was growing in stature. In 1711, by reason of the demands of the Great Northern War, Russia had lost Azov to the Turks; however, Peter's armies had at last succeeded in invading and defeating Sweden, and the 1721 Treaty of Nystad gave Russia possession of ancient Russian lands on the west and broad access to the Baltic. The Russian Senate acclaimed Peter "Father of His Country, Emperor of All the Russias, Peter the Great." What had theretofore been "The Grand States of the Russian Tsardom" became "The Empire of All the Russias." In 1721 also, by order of the tsar, Siberia Governor Prince Matvyi P. Gagarin was hanged in St. Petersburg. One charge against him was that he had schemed to transform Siberia into an independent state; another, dating back to 1714, was that he had been guilty of gross irregularities in the administration of the China trade.

3 THE KIAKHTA AGREEMENT AND MONGOL DISASTER

THE TRIANGLE of jealousy in the relations between the Oirats on the one hand and the Manchus and Russians respectively, on the other, continued in being. Where Tulisen had endeavored to enlist the Russians to fight against the Mongols in 1720, Tsewang Araptan in the summer of 1722 sent an envoy to Tobolsk to say that, if it were true as reported that Russia planned to send troops against the Dzungar power, he would have no other recourse than to submit to Peking. The envoy was assured that Russia harbored no such intention – and it was suggested that those who would circulate such a rumor might well be persons desiring the desperate action conjured up by Tsewang Araptan. A few months afterward, a Russian envoy approached the Dzungar chieftain with a proposal that the Oirats become subjects of Russia, which would then protect them against all threats (including of course the Manchu). Tsewang Araptan refused to renounce independence and imperial ambitions for the Mongols. There had been one recent event that may have given him confidence: the emperor K'ang-hsi had died in December, 1722.

K'ang-hsi was succeeded on the Manchu Throne by the emperor Yung-cheng. Yung-cheng's character is perhaps indicated by the circumstance that five of his brothers, including the one favored by K'ang-hsi for the succession, died in prison. With his advent to power, Yung-cheng continued the current trend toward applying ever tighter restrictions on foreigners and foreign intercourse – including the Russo-Chinese trade. In the course of 1724, nevertheless, Peking several times indicated that it desired direct discussions.

Peter the Great died in February, 1725. He had initiated vast domestic reforms and had also stabilized the western frontiers of the Russian empire. He had been only partially successful in his endeavor to conquer the debilitated Persian empire but had improved the Russian position in the Caspian region. In Inner Asia, thanks in good part to his determination to write *finis* to the "nomadic nuisance," the Russian frontiers had first been strengthened and then advanced. Russia could attribute much of its improved condition to Peter's reign.

Catherine I succeeded Peter to the Throne, and in the first year of her reign sent a mission to Peking under Count Sava Lukich-Vladislavich Raguzinski, charged with achieving delimitation of the common frontiers and reorganization of the commercial relationship, and with reaching an understanding regarding the two countries' respective relations with the Mongols. There had been changes in rule in both China and Russia – and in one Mongol sector. Ayuka Khan, head of the Volga Torguts, had died in 1724. The Dzungar khanate, however, continued under the leadership of Tsewang Araptan who, as had been the case with successive Oirat kontaishas, pursued a strategy of endeavoring to play Russia and China against each other. The Dzungar ruler would also in a sense be present at the forthcoming conference.

Count Sava's embassy, accompanied by a considerable guard force and bearing expensive presents for both the Manchu emperor and his ministers, left St. Petersburg in October, 1725. Lorentz Lange was attached to the party. So too was the Orthodox bishop Innokent Kulchitski, who had been consecrated "Bishop of Periaslav" to head the Peking religious mission, but had been unable to obtain the Manchu Court's permission to take up his assignment. The embassy arrived in Peking a year later and remained for six months, negotiating with three of Yung-cheng's ministers – the president of the Board of Rites, the president of the Li-fan Yuan, and the Manchu Tulisen. Sava made use of the counsels of the French Jesuit priest Dominique Parrenin, who put him in touch with the Manchu Maci, a Grand Secretary. Maci had commanded the Russian company of the Manchu Bordered Yellow Banner after the death of the first Russian captain and had long been concerned with the Russian caravan trade. He thus occupied a position of considerable influence with respect to Russian affairs, and Sava in his pertinent account states that he promised to send Maci from the frontier, in return for the latter's commitment to help with the negotiations, a present of 2,000 rubles.

After over thirty sessions and much hard bargaining the Manchu and Russian sides reached agreement in principle respecting the terms of a new treaty. The Manchu emperor insisted, however, that the actual frontier demarcation take place on the spot and in the presence of the Mongols. The conference site was now moved to the frontier region near Selenginsk, and in early July meetings began there to determine the boundary between the two countries.

The situation had changed to favor the Russians, now free of military engagements in Europe. The first chief Manchu representative, Lungkodo, stubbornly refused concessions and endangered the outcome of the conference, and he was recalled in mid-August and replaced by a Mongol, Prince Tsereng, and Tulisen. On August 30, there was signed the preliminary Treaty of Bura, fixing the border between Russia and China in Mongolia as running west from the Argun River through Kiakhta to Shabin-Dabag. The negotiations reached their culmination in the signature of the Treaty of Kiakhta of October 31, 1727. The assistance of Grand Secretary Maci, who had come to be charged with Russian affairs, seemingly had proved useful in this general connection. Sava, however, finding himself short of money, paid Maci only 1,000 instead of the promised 2,000 rubles and gave 100 rubles to Father Parrenin.

The Treaty of Kiakhta was a much more elaborate document than the Treaty of Nerchinsk. It purported to provide for perpetual peace between the two signatory powers. Moreover, "It is therefore agreed that from this day on each Empire will carefully govern and superintend its own subjects." [1] The extraterritorial principle had now received a further elaboration. The agreement confirmed the new demarcation of the frontier, as set forth in the Treaty of Bura. That border was physically demarcated by the emplacement of monuments. It was agreed that there should be "freedom of trade" between the two countries – but this was interpreted to provide that the number of Russian merchants traveling to Peking once every three years might not exceed two hundred, "as has previously been agreed." Yet, "All sorts of merchandise can be sold, except those which are prohibited by the laws of the two Empires." Trading posts might be established on the common frontiers, at Tsurunkhaita (on the Argun) and at Kiakhta, and then at Peking via the Urga-Kalgan route, duty free. The trading center, however, was now in fact moved from Peking to Kiakhta and trading elsewhere was forbidden. The casual caravans went to Peking no more, and the Manchu Court was relieved of a function that had become an expensive embarrassment to it. And the Russian Court having given up its claim to enjoy sole trading rights with China, trade at Kiakhta now had the character of free enterprise.

Yung-cheng's Court refused to permit Innokent to head the Russian mission in the capital. The treaty instead effectively confirmed the status quo, with Article V providing that Russian travelers would lodge in "the house of the Oros" (Russian hostel) in Peking, and, noting that there had recently been erected a Russian "temple" near that hostel, it provided that "The priest who is in the capital will remain in this habitation with three other priests to assist him."

Further "The Oros are permitted to carry out the duties of their worship with all its ceremonies and to make their prayers." It was, moreover, provided that four young Russians, knowing both Russian and Latin, and two older men whom Count Sava had left at the capital to learn Chinese, Manchu, and Mongol, might also dwell in the same place to pursue their studies; upon completion of those studies, "they will be at liberty to return home as soon as they have been ordered to do so." With establishment of a language school at Peking, the Russians thenceforth would no longer be dependent upon the Jesuits as interpreters in their relations with China. The language students would study China as well as its languages; and the religious mission would regularly thereafter function, in an important degree, as a representative diplomatic mission. As a religious organ, it was subject to the Synod, but it was under the operative control of the Russian Senate of Foreign Affairs.

With the border now further regulated, it was provided (Article VIII) that "The border commanders of the two Empires should decide matters according to the laws of justice and without delay; if they delay because of their own interests each Empire will punish them according to the law." There was further elaboration of the method for dealing out punishment to fugitives, armed persons who might cross the frontier without passports, and military deserters, border raiders, and common people traveling without passports. "Subjects of the two empires who henceforth flee from their government will be punished by death at the spot where they are seized. . . . Soldiers who desert and flee their masters will be beheaded if they are subjects of the Middle Kingdom; if they belong to the Empire of Oros they will be strangled and the things stolen will be restored to the commander or to his government." This time the Russian ambassador, Count Sava, delivered a signed copy of the treaty, in Russian and Latin, to the Manchu side, while the Manchu "Lords of the Middle Kingdom" handed him in return a signed copy of the same document in Russian, Latin, *and Manchu.* There was no provision in the treaty stipulating which text should be accepted as the authoritative version. In June, 1728, there was the exchange of ratifications of the new agreement.

With the Manchu Court's refusal to accept Innokent as bishop at Peking, in 1727 another priest was sent to the Russian mission in his stead. Innokent himself took up permanent residence in Siberia and spent the rest of his energetic life in missionary work there. Back in Peking, the construction of a new Orthodox Russian church began in January, 1728. In June of the following year, the archimandrite Antoine Platkovski and three additional language students arrived in Peking to join the two priests and three students already there. Although the church building would not be completed and consecrated until April, 1732, Russia's religious-cum-diplomatic mission had begun functioning in China's capital.

The Treaty of Kiakhta, added to that of Nerchinsk of some four decades earlier, notably strengthened the political and commercial relationship between Russia and China. This new community of interests would inevitably bring loss to the peoples of Central Asia, who were unable to present to either the Russians or the Manchus attractive alternatives to the Russo-Manchu arrangement. The two empires had reached agreement respecting their common border in Northeast Asia, but not regarding Central Asia — where there were no hard-and-fast borderlines. There was good reason why both Manchus and Russians should interest themselves in the disputed Central Asian zone held by divers Mongol, Kazakh, and Turki chieftains. Given the defeat of first Galdan, and then the Dzungars in Tibet, the Manchus especially were in a good position to extend their conquests.

Time and circumstances were propitious for action against the Dzungar khanate. Tsewang Araptan, ambitious, able, and ruthless, had died in 1727, the year of the signature of the Treaty of Kiakhta, at the hands of lamas bent on avenging the Oirat devastation of Tibet. He was succeeded by his son Galdan Tseren, who promptly put to death four and imprisoned two members of a mission from the Volga Torguts. The emperor Yung-cheng saw an opportunity of exploiting the situation caused by the change in rule and in 1729 charged the Manchu general Furdan with "border pacification," which by the convention meant suppression of restless elements troubling China's Inner Asian frontier.

The military action was as usual accompanied by political maneuvers. In 1729, Peking nominated an embassy to St. Petersburg under the leadership of T'o-shih, vice-president of the Lifan Yuan, accompanied by a weighty entourage. Its nominal purpose was to felicitate Peter II on his accession to the Throne in 1727. The T'o-shih embassy was accompanied by another Manchu mission of nearly equal stature—charged with visiting the Torguts on the lower Volga.

The two embassies comprised a total of six ambassadors and an entourage of a hundred. Traveling via Selenginsk, it was met by Glazounov, who had accompanied both Izmailov and Sava Vladislavich on their respective missions to Peking. The party, duly assembled, departed Selenginsk in June, 1730. At Tobolsk, in October, Glazounov heard the news that Peter II had died in January of that year and been succeeded by Anna Ivanovna. Tactfully, he kept the news of the event from his Manchu guests until the party was well on the way to the Russian capital and return had become manifestly impossible. "Prestige" was protected, and all were satisfied.

The embassy arrived in Moscow in January and was received with elaborate ceremony, including a thirty-one–gun salute at the Red Gate, and had an imperial audience there in early February 1731. The ambassadors delivered their letters of credence from the Li-fan Yuan. The promise made to Izmailov in 1720 was fulfilled: the Manchu envoys not only presented rich presents (valued at 100,000 taels) to the tsarina, but also performed before her the same kind of genuflections required of Izmailov at Peking.[2] Tsarina Anna feasted the envoys (on her birthday) and gave them presents for Emperor Yung-cheng. The mission paid a visit to the Russian Senate and presented that body with a dispatch from the Li-fan Yuan with reference to the observance of the Treaty of Nerchinsk, the proposed mission to the Torguts through Russia, and the purpose of the present mission. The Senate made reply, vowing the observance of treaties between the two countries, expressing the usual hope for freedom of trade, and observing that, since the Torguts were Russian subjects, all matters pertaining to the Torgut prince would necessarily have to be referred to the empress. Anna accorded the Manchu mission another audience on their leave-taking; then, in latter March, the mission departed Moscow for home.

The second embassy, under the Manchu Mandai, charged with visiting the Torguts, left Moscow the same day accompanied by V. Bakunin of the Board of Foreign Affairs and a military escort. The Mandai embassy was in due course received by Tseren Dondok, Ayuka's son and successor. In accord with St. Petersburg's directive, and probably not without reference to the circumstance that the emperor's position respecting the return of Arabjur was equivocal, Tseren Dondok did not enter upon the projected alliance against Galdan Tseren. The Manchu mission departed for home in late June. A month later, Furdan's force of some 10,000 men was ambushed and almost completely destroyed by Galdan Tseren's warriors northwest of Kobdo. The Mandai mission joined the T'o-shih group at Tobolsk, and the combined embassy got back to Peking in the early spring of 1732.[3]

En route home, near Tomsk, the Manchu embassy had passed another party headed for St. Petersburg under the leadership of two ambassadors — Deisin and Bayentai. This second mission, less imposing than the first, arrived at St. Petersburg in May, 1732, and the envoys were received in imperial audience the following day. They fulfilled their mission — to felicitate Anna on *her* accession to the Throne — and two months later, started back over the long, arduous route to Peking. The Manchus had thus sent two diplomatic missions to the Russian Court in the second quarter of the eighteenth century; none would be sent to a Western European court until the reign of T'ung-chih (1861–1874), well over a century later.

The Manchu Court met one setback in connection with the second mission: the Russian Court, knowing the Manchu political aims and doubtless having taken into consideration Galdan Tseren's striking victory over Furdan, refused to permit another embassy to the Torguts to accompany the second diplomatic mission to Moscow, as Peking originally planned. That second mission to the Torguts waited at Kiakhta for three years and then abandoned the project. In the meantime, the Dzungars and Russians sent fresh missions to each other.

In March, 1733, about a hundred yurts of Mongols took refuge in Russian territory in the Selenginsk region. The Manchu Court sent to the Russian Senate a letter demanding that Russian guards aid Manchu forces in rounding up (on Russian territory) the refugees and returning them to China. The Russian government, as in previous similar cases, gave no satisfaction. Russo-Manchu relations again became strained. The period of the two Manchu diplomatic missions to Russia, 1729–1733, may thus be viewed as a brief honeymoon induced by the intense Manchu desire to win Torgut support against the Oirats and to neutralize Russia with respect to that conflict. It was also a period of friendly Russo-Dzungar relations.

Imperial Russia, having reached the Pacific, was still pressing against the borderlands. Vladimir V. Atlasov, at the head of about 120 men, in 1697 discovered and explored the upper part of Kamchatka and in 1700 reached the Kurile island chain. Atlasov was as violent and unprincipled as Khabarov, and in 1711, when furthering the work of consolidation of Russian rule, he was killed in a native uprising; the colonization of Kamchatka nevertheless went on, and was completed. The general Russian thrust eastward also continued. In 1728, the Dane Vitus Bering, in the service of Peter the Great, penetrated the strait between Asia and the American continent that had first been navigated eighty years before by the Cossack Dezhnev—the waterway that came to be called Bering Strait. Bering had gone on in 1741 to discover America from the west by landing on Kayak Island, in sight of Alaska. Wrecked later on "Bering Island," he died in December, 1741. But Alaska had been discovered for Russia, and in the succeeding decades the Cos-

sacks and others went forward with exploration of the region —
and the development of trade with the native Eskimos.

Attention focused intently on Central Asia, where military
actions were still in course. There had been numerous wars
between the Dzungars and the Kazakhs in the first three decades
of the eighteenth century, and civil wars among the Kazakhs,
who were now divided into three *ordas* [*] or, as known in the West,
"hordes." In 1731 (the year the Dzungars defeated Furdan),
the Kazakh Lesser Horde, in their quest for protection, became
subjects of Russia. The Middle Horde in 1740 took the same
course. The Russians in 1735 had constructed a fortress at the
confluence of the Or and Yaik (Ural) rivers. Eight years later that
fortress was reconstructed at Orenburg, which became a major
base for later military expeditions into Central Asia. The Russian
dominion had been advanced nearly to the Aral Sea.

Galdan Tseren died in 1745 and was succeeded by his frivo-
lous youthful second son Tsewang Dorji Namjar. The Dzungar
khanate entered a period of instability and slipped onto the road
to disaster. Dissidents soon overthrew the new ruler and raised
Galdan Tseren's illegitimate son Lama Darja to power. In 1752,
Lama Darja was killed by Davatsi, son of Chereng Dondub,
supported by the Khoit Amursana. Amursana next broke with
Davatsi and, turning over to the Manchu Throne, now occupied
by the emperor Ch'ien-lung, proposed to spearhead a Manchu attack on the divided Dzungar khanate. Ch'ien-lung organized an
expeditionary force, making Amursana second in command in the
northern route army, under the experienced Manchu general
Bandi. The expedition, launched in early 1755, achieved quick
success.

Moved by ambitions of his own, Amursana next turned
against the Manchus and led most of the Dzungars into rebellion.
Bandi's force had its retreat cut off, and was virtually annihi-
lated, with Bandi committing suicide. A new Manchu expeditionary force drove into Dzungaria and recaptured Ili. Amursana
took refuge with the Kazakhs. The main expeditionary force
withdrew, Amursana returned to the field, the Dzungars in late
1756 again rose in rebellion, and once more nearly wiped out the
Manchu force. Earlier, Amursana had laid plans together with
the Khoit leader Chengunjab for a Khalkha uprising against the

---

[*] From the Turkic *ordu:* camp, army; as used with respect to Central Asian nomads such as the Mongols, Kazakhs, and Kirgizi, a tribal grouping.

Manchu authority, and the Khalkha movement of rebellion had in fact begun in the summer of 1756. Other members of the Mongol nobility were favorable to the project, and the Khutukhtu and the Tushet khan approached the voevoda at Selenginsk to ascertain whether arrangements could be made for the transfer of Khalkha allegiance from the Manchu Court to the tsar. In October, 1756, the Russian government authorized Selenginsk to proceed with discussions of the matter.

The conditions for a fruitful collaboration of the Khalkha and Dzungar Mongols against the Manchus seemed present. But Chengunjab showed neither energy nor capacity in organizing the Khalkha opposition, the Khutukhtu played an equivocal role, the rebels failed to go forward with their plan for shifting to Russian suzerainty, and the revolt subsided. In April, 1757, two Manchu armies, led respectively by Chao-hui, second cousin to Ch'ien-lung, and the Mongol Cenggun Jabu, a descendent of Genghis Khan, drove against the rebels in Dzungaria. They won an easy victory, and Amursana fled first to the Kazakhs and then on to Siberia.

Chao-hui had petitioned the Throne to recommend strong action, and his orders now called for the extermination of the Dzungar population. He carried out the letter of the imperial edict with a ruthless efficiency. In some two years of butchery, between 500,000 and 600,000 Dzungars were hunted down and slain. Of the few survivors, some were exiled to Heilungkiang in Manchuria, others were allotted grazing lands in the Ili valley and kept under close supervision there. Use of the name Dzungar was prohibited thereafter, only the name Oirat being allowed. In fact, the Oirats (or Kalmyks) as an organized independent "Dzungar" power had effectively ceased to exist.

A Manchu punitive expedition was sent into Khalkha territory, and harshly suppressed the "rebellion" that had never really crystallized. Chengunjab, the Khutukhtu, and the Tushet khan all met violent deaths. During Chao-hui's engagement with the Dzungar Mongols, the Turki peoples of Eastern Turkestan, the region south of the T'ien Shan range, had seized the occasion to rise. When Chao-hui finished with his killing of the Oirats, he was given the new assignment of extending Manchu control to the south. After some initial difficulties, he completed the conquest of Eastern Turkestan in the summer of 1759. In a four years' campaign, Ch'ien-lung's armies had won for the Manchu empire the whole of the "Western Region," lost to T'ang China nearly exactly a thousand years before.

Amursana had died of smallpox near Tobolsk, at the age of thirty-five, in the fall of 1757. Peking demanded that the rebel's body be handed over, but the Russian government refused, proposing instead that representatives of the Manchu government, if they wished to verify the report of death, could view the body at Kiakhta. That ceremony took place the following March, after which Peking again demanded the body. A new refusal on the part of St. Petersburg resulted in a fresh deterioration of Russo-Manchu relations.[4] It was not until 1765 that Peking finally indicated its readiness to drop the quarrel.

In recognition of the changed political situation in Central Asia, Kazakh and Burut tribes to the west of Dzungaria also acknowledged Manchu suzerainty. The Manchu domain now reached to the Issyk Kul (lake). The Kokand khan voluntarily offered his allegiance to Ch'ien-lung. Earlier, while the Kalmyk threat was still in being, Peking had proposed to St. Petersburg that Russia and China should divide the Dzungar khanate between them (after a joint conquest, still to be achieved), but Tsarina Anna had declined to participate in the enterprise.[5] Now times had changed, and "the appetite comes with eating." Ch'ien-lung not only accepted the Kokand submission but dreamed of greater conquests on the pattern of his illustrious conqueror grandfather, K'ang-hsi. In 1762, he prepared for an expedition against Tashkent and Samarkand.

The Islamic Turks were alarmed, and the *bek*s (princes) of Kokandia and the Kazakh sultans called upon the powerful Kandahar ruler, Akhmed Shah, for help. Akhmed Shah sent a force to the defense of Tashkent, and Ch'ien-lung thereupon stopped the westward movement of his troops. Renewed disorders in Kashgaria then demanded his attention and diverted his ambitions from Western Turkestan. An Uch-Turfan revolt of 1765 marked the final effort of the Turki rebels against the Manchu rule. After a three months' siege, the Manchu armies reduced the walled town and slaughtered its entire population. Ten years after Amursana's betrayal of his fellow Mongols, the Manchu rule had been fully consolidated over both Dzungaria and the Tarim Basin.

There was a bizarre sequel to the Manchu conquest. Tulisen had presumably made attractive offers to Ayuka Khan when he

EASTERN AND CENTRAL ASIA
1760

1000 KM.

RUSSIAN EASTWARD EXPANSION 1598-1762

ed on Albert Herrmann, in *An Historical Atlas of China*, Norton Ginsburg, general
(Chicago, Aldine, 1966), and Allen F. Chew, *An Atlas of Russian History* (New
en and London, Yale University Press, 1967).

visited the chief of the émigré Torguts at his encampment at Manych on the lower Volga in 1714; it can further safely be assumed that the 1731 mission built on the foundation Tulisen had laid. In any event, having "pacified" Dzungaria by annihilating the existing Mongol population, the Manchus in 1771 invited the Volga Torguts to return to Dzungaria. The Torguts, seemingly with scant regard for the fate of the Dzungars but presumably not unmindful of the fact that the rich grazing lands of sometime Dzungaria were now practically empty, accepted the invitation. In the dead of winter, without having previously made arrangements with their Russian hosts and suzerain authority, 160,000 of them set out for their homeland. Their march was beset by the winter, with which they were of course familiar, but also by Russian troops and by the wild Kirgizi who harassed their flanks. Only 70,000 of the original number survived to return to the Manchu empire.

It was not only the Islamic Turkic rulers who had been alarmed by the Manchu advance; St. Petersburg, too, had taken due note of the development. In Russia a new period of expansionism had been introduced when the princess Sophia of Anhalt-Zerbst, by virtue of a military coup, in 1762 replaced her husband Peter III on the Throne and permitted him soon afterward to be murdered. She became Catherine II ("the Great"); she, even as Peter I, was an empire-builder.

Catherine's chief enterprises lay in the west and the south, not the east. She evolved plans to recover the lost Russian territories from Poland and (as Peter I had planned) to expel the Turks from Europe. With the cause discovered in Russian intervention in Polish affairs, in 1768 Turkey was led to declare war on Russia—only to be badly defeated. By the 1774 Treaty of Kuchuk-Kainardji, Turkey acknowledged the independence of the Crimean khanate, and the Sublime Porte granted Russia what was interpreted as being the right to protect Turkish Christians. The "Eastern Question," revolving around the issue of Russia's newly established position as a Black Sea power and its claim to the right of intervention in the domestic affairs of the decaying Ottoman empire, had been born, and would long dominate Russo-British relations.

In 1783, Russia annexed the Crimea. The Turks, with British support, four years later again went to war with Russia, only to be defeated once more. The 1791 Treaty of Jassy gave Russia additional Black Sea littoral. That development, coupled with Turkey's concession of the right of free navigation of merchant vessels through the Dardanelles in times of peace, gave Russia new importance – in its role of a Black Sea power. Besides, in a series of actions between 1772 and 1795, in collaboration with Prussia and Austria, Catherine partitioned Poland.

Not all the Russian populace benefited from the glories and material gains of empire, and there had already been popular movements of revolt of major dimensions. In 1773, Emilyan Pugachev, a Cossack pretending to be Peter III, mounted a revolt of some 25,000 Cossacks, Tatars, Bashkirs, Old Believers, and others, in the Urals. Kazakhs of the Lesser and Middle Hordes also joined that peasant rebellion and gave it added danger. The government armies after suppressing the revolt in 1774 advanced southward into Kazakh territory, further expanding the empire and strengthening its eastern defenses against the Central Asian horsemen and against the Manchu thrust now confronting Russian power in that vast region where no border lines had yet been drawn between the two empires – Central Asia.

Even after the signature of the Treaty of Kiakhta, Russo-Manchu relations, whether with regard to politics or trade, had not proceeded smoothly. It would appear that the Peking government in the beginning had meticulously observed the treaty provisions requiring the handing over to the Russians, or the punishment by itself, of offenders falling within the purview of the treaty. The Russians of Siberia, farther from their central government, were notably much more careless in this regard. That initial difference of implementation of the political provisions may well have influenced observance of the treaty stipulations governing trade between the two countries, and the theft of livestock along the frontier was clearly an important element making for friction between the two sides.

In any event, trade experienced frequent interruptions, usually caused by the Manchu side breaking off relations on a variety of pretexts, ranging from the way a communication might be addressed to a quarrel regarding apprehension and punishment of drunken soldiers charged with killing a Chinese merchant. The disputes centered on Kiakhta and the Chinese trading center nearby, Maimaicheng. Intermittent disputes and dislocations of trade continued until the 1760s, when Tsarina Catherine sent Captain of the Guards Ivan I. Kropotov to Kiakhta with the mission of effecting a resolution of outstanding differences. Kropotov reached a supplementary agreement of October 28, 1768 by virtue of which Article X of the Treaty of Kiakhta was revised. His efforts to get Chinese agreement to freedom of trade between the border and Peking, however, were unavailing.

So "incidents" on the common border went on. A break that occurred in 1778 after Mongols who were Russian subjects had robbed some Russian merchants and taken refuge in Chinese territory continued until a settlement was effected by a special commission two years later.[6] A new break came in 1785, and this time accord was even slower in coming. It was not until February, 1792, that an agreement of five articles for further regulation of the Kiakhta commerce was finally reached. Trade began again some three months later, and the Kiakhta-Maimai-cheng market once more functioned reasonably smoothly.

4 TRIANGLE IN
EAST ASIA

TRADE RELATIONS between the Manchu empire and the sea powers had not followed quite the same course as Russo-Chinese relations, but there were parallels to be discovered. The Manchus upon consolidation of their rule relaxed the strict controls over visitors by the sea route, in 1685 abrogating the existing restrictions on trade. But the experiment had undesirable results, and in the late K'ang-hsi period tight controls were progressively reimposed. From 1757, foreign seaborne trade was once more confined to Canton and Macao. Even that traffic was stringently circumscribed, and the Canton trade, as that with the Russians at Kiakhta, was subject to arbitrary interruptions by the Manchu side and was attended by corruption and a variety of abuses.

Industrialization had begun in Europe, and there was felt a need to expand markets — everywhere. Alone among the Occidentals, the Russians had sailed the North Pacific from 1643 to 1778, and during that period were practically the sole foreign suppliers (via the land route) of furs to China. In 1778, however, the Englishman James Cook penetrated the North Pacific and passed through the Bering Strait. The first American ship, the *Empress of China*, called at Canton in 1784, and furs became a prime American export to China. The British for their part had a surplus of cotton and woolen textiles demanding a market.

Private British manufacturing and commercial interests in

particular, as distinguished from the monopolistic British East India Company, were dissatisfied with the existing state of trade relations with China and began to exercise pressure for amelioration of the situation in that regard. So when Canton officials put forward the suggestion that England might well send a representative to convey felicitations to the emperor Ch'ien-lung on the occasion of his eightieth birthday, London thought the opportunity an auspicious one. In 1793, Earl George Macartney Macartney, who thirty years earlier had served as envoy to Russia, headed a mission to the Court of Ch'ien-lung. The underlying purpose of the mission was to obtain a liberalization of China's trade regulations and the right of permanent British representation at Peking — a privilege not yet enjoyed by the seafarers.

The instructions given Macartney evinced optimism with respect to his mission. As regards the "common opinion" that the Chinese studiously avoided any intimate intercourse with the Occident, it was stated that

> If political jealousy were the chief principle to excite such alarm in the Chinese as should lead them to discourage the entrance of foreigners, it is probable that it would apply with singular force against the Russians, who, from the propinquity of their Dominions, the reputed greatness of their power, and the danger of their leaguing with the Princes of those Tartar countries which have sent forth the former conquerors of China, would be most likely in imagination at least to cause distrust in the reigning Government, and might possibly affect its security.

The home secretary, Henry Dundas, referring to the successful dispatch of a Russian embassy to Peking under Peter I, the residence of a Russian agent at Peking, the commercial intercourse "frequently" allowed since, and "the reputed wisdom of the Chinese Administration," thought that indeed the contrary inference might be drawn.[1]

Macartney and his suite (including military escort) of upwards of a hundred persons duly disembarked at Taku in August, 1793. The English envoy succeeded in obtaining an audience with the emperor and presented his sovereign's requests, but the mission was fruitless. The Russians retained their advantage in the overall relationship of the Occident with Imperial China.

Russia, numbering some 35 million people, was, however, at this time heavily engaged in the west, with focus of attention on the Balkans and Persia. The European situation had now been complicated by the French Revolution, and the Napoleonic wars would follow. The Russian empire in the Pacific area, thanks to European distractions, and to neglect and maladministration besides, had not prospered. In 1784, a Russian group led by Grigori I. Shelikhov reached Kodiak Island with the aim of settling Russia's new territory, Alaska (called by the Russians "Russian America"). But Shelikhov worked against heavy odds, and without much support, and there was little development until after the formation in July, 1799, of the Russian American Company (patterned after the British East India Company and Hudson Bay Company) and the appointment of a new head for the Russian colony, the energetic Aleksandr A. Baranov. That same year, Baranov constructed an ostrog as headquarters for the colony at New Archangel (near present-day Sitka). In 1801, however, the venture received a severe setback when most of the inhabitants of the fortress were wiped out by the Tlingit Indians.

The Russian empire-builders pushed on. In August, 1803, the Russian vessels *Neva* and *Nadezhda* (British-built, of 370 and 450 tons, respectively) set sail from Kronstadt with the aim of circumnavigating the globe, from east to west, to show the flag. The two ships were under the overall command of Captain Adam Y. Kruzenstern (Ivan Fedorovich Kruzenshtern), who had served six years with the British navy. The expedition was accompanied by Nikolai Petrovich de Rezanov, the Russian counselor of state and grand chamberlain — and a strong proponent of the Russian American Company. Rezanov bore a major mission — to open relations with Japan.[2]

The Japanese, after their first experience with the West, had established a policy of exclusionism by edicts of 1636 and 1638, leaving the door to the outside world open only a crack at Deshima, where once a year a Dutch ship might call. This situation held disadvantages for Russia, whose seamen were now plying Pacific waters and whose merchants sought ever broader avenues of trade. As early as the end of the seventeenth century, Russian seamen had been blown onto the Japanese shores. A Russian mission had endeavored to establish relations with the island empire during Catherine's reign, but without success.

The two ships sailed west around Cape Horn, touched the Marquesas, and reached the Sandwich Islands (Hawaii) in June, 1804. There they parted. The *Neva,* under command of Yu. F. Lisyanski, proceeded to Russian America to aid Baranov in recovering New Archangel. Kruzenstern and Rezanov, aboard the *Nadezhda,* first went to Petropavlovsk-on-Kamchatka, where they remained about seven weeks, then proceeded to Japan, arriving at Nagasaki about the end of September, 1804.

Rezanov's mission was to deliver the tsar's presents to the emperor of Japan and to strive for an opening of commerce between Japan and Russia. He and his crew were kept in virtual imprisonment, if with elaborate ceremony, for several months. Then, instead of Rezanov's being taken to the hoped-for audience with the emperor (who they thought, even as did the Western Europeans and Americans, resided in Yedo—whereas he lived in seclusion at Kyoto), "a very Great Man of the Court" came to Nagasaki and gave three audiences to Rezanov. In the first, there was a "rather impertinent and ungracious interrogatory" by the Great Man. In the second, the shogun's envoy (for that was doubtless the official's identity) handed Rezanov a communication incorporating "a peremptory injunction that no Russian should ever again show himself in Japan." [3] The tsar's gifts were rejected. The final meeting was only for ceremonial leave-taking. In early June, 1805, the *Nadezhda* got back to Kamchatka.

Kruzenstern in his account reconciled himself to the failure of his mission by the observation that "the Russian trade will not suffer much in consequence of it." [4] But there were still no arrangements for political intercourse between Russia and Japan —and Russian ships and men would continue to fall upon occasion into Japanese hands. Vice Admiral Vasili M. Golovnin was one such: in 1811, while exploring the Kuriles aboard the *Diana,* he and his crew were seized by the Japanese and imprisoned for two years. Finally released, Golovnin wrote a book on his experiences in which he said that Japan's neighbors should properly thank Providence that Japan had forbidden its people to adopt foreign ideas and concepts. He gave a prophetic warning:

> Let them beware how they give occasion to the Japanese
> to abandon this policy and in its place to imitate European
> methods! . . . if the Japanese were to take it into their
> heads to introduce our civilization and imitate our methods

the Chinese would soon feel obliged to do the same. In that case those two great powers might give quite a new turn to European affairs. . . . I do not say that the Japanese and Chinese could in a very short time become European powers, and so be a danger to Europeans of the present day. But the thing is possible, and sooner or later the danger will make itself felt.[5]

Back again in Petropavlovsk, Rezanov received instructions to put Russian America and the company on a firm footing, and he went on to Alaska. The *Nadezhda* continued a survey of Sakhalin begun in the course of the voyage out of Nagasaki. The captain was eager to determine, by a survey of the western coast, whether Sakhalin was a part of "the Tartar mainland" or an island, but was restrained by orders received in Kamchatka to avoid that enterprise as being likely to excite the hostile suspicion of the Manchu government. He did, however, discover the approximate location of the mouth of the Amur River.

The *Nadezhda* duly returned once more to Petropavlovsk, then made a good run to the Chinese trading port of Macao, arriving there at the beginning of December, 1805. By the arrangement, the *Neva* should already have preceded its companion ship there, but was discovered not yet to have arrived. (It had first run onto a coral reef and, after getting off with difficulty, had then been battered off Saipan by a heavy storm.) The Chinese at once wanted to know whether the *Nadezhda* was a naval or merchant vessel, to enable them to determine whether it would be permitted to remain at its present anchorage. Kruzenstern replied that his craft was a naval vessel, but he had orders to load Chinese goods in a part of it on the account of the Russian American Company; however, he had to wait for the *Neva*, and would in the meantime load water and provisions for the return trip to Europe, without proceeding to Whampoa. He remained at anchorage.

A week later, the *Neva* arrived with a rich cargo of furs. A Chinese source makes it 100,000 bales, but the limited burden of the ship makes the figure suspect. According to that same source, the furs were under commission from a British firm (the Hudson Bay Company?) for sale,[6] but the ships were undeniably Russian. Lisyanski informed Kruzenstern that in his opinion the *Neva*'s cargo had sufficient value to permit them to fill

both ships with Chinese cargo for the return voyage, and Kruzenstern now informed the local officials that his ship as well as the
Neva would proceed to Whampoa.

After a delay, the ships were permitted to proceed, but the
Russians immediately found themselves in difficulty because
they were without a factory, and thus without access to the
cohong (official trading combine), at Canton. But one of the
younger cohong members finally agreed to undertake the matter,
the ships' furs were unloaded (the *Nadezhda* carried a small
cargo of sea-otter and fur-seal skins from Kamchatka), and the
loading of tea began. Just as the loading was about to be completed, however, a Chinese guard was placed on the ships and all
activity stopped.

This was at the time when there was a change of viceroys at
Canton, and with the arrival of the successor official, Wu Hsiung-
kuang, Kruzenstern demanded through the cohong that permission be granted for loading the remaining cargo. The request
was refused, and the indications were that Canton officialdom
was waiting for instructions from Peking, which had been
informed of the arrival of the Russian vessels. Kruzenstern had
spent some six months at Canton and Macao in 1798, at which
time he became acquainted with James A. Drummond, the
head of the British factory. Drummond by 1805 had occupied that
position for nineteen years. He was wise to the Chinese and their
ways and commanded great esteem. Kruzenstern now enlisted
the aid of his old acquaintance. Drummond intervened energetically and adeptly, finally demanding either action or an
audience with the viceroy.

This stirred the *hoppo* (superintendent of trade) to action,
and he promptly (almost certainly by the authority of the viceroy)
issued orders for the loading of the last goods and gave assurance
that permission for the ships to depart would be promptly forthcoming. He was as good as his promise, and the ships sailed
from Whampoa in February, 1806. Not long after getting back to
St. Petersburg, Kruzenstern received a letter from Canton
informing him that, twenty-four hours after they had sailed,
orders had come from Peking strictly commanding that the Russian ships should be detained; if those orders had caught them
in port, "then, probably, our ships would never have returned to
Russia."[7] As it was, they got back to Kronstadt at the end of
August, 1806, having been away from home port on their world

voyage for just over three years. Behind them, at Peking, the ruling had been laid down that, since the Russians already enjoyed trade with China via the land route, they might not in addition trade by sea. Russian ships, therefore, should not return. The unfortunate Wu Hsiung-kuang was dismissed from his new post.

It was Kruzenstern's opinion, expressed in his report on his voyage, that the Russian American Company could not flourish without being enabled to trade at Canton, and he urged that there be an effort to get the Manchu agreement as soon as possible. The arrangements at Kiakhta were still, as before, subject to capricious and periodical interruption. At the very time that Kruzenstern was in Canton, in fact, he had confidently assumed that Count Gavril Golovkin was at Peking on a mission for St. Petersburg. That assumption was, however, incorrect.

Golovkin had been charged with obtaining the Manchu Court's agreement to trading not only at Kiakhta but all along the land border between the two countries; with arranging for regular navigation of the Amur, in order to facilitate the transport of supplies to Alaska; and, finally, with obtaining rights of sea trade from Kamchatka and Alaska to Canton—and, if possible, Nanking. He was also confidentially instructed to ascertain the state of China's relations with neighboring countries and to find out whether Peking was prepared to enter upon an agreement for the waging of a joint struggle against the aggressive nomad peoples of Central Asia. He was, moreover, to offer Russia's services as mediator in case of conflict between England, the expansive conqueror of India, and China.[8]

Golovkin's route had him proceeding via Kiakhta and Urga to Peking, but he was stopped at Urga and prevented from continuing his journey when he refused to perform the ceremonial demanded of him at a feast given in his honor by the Manchu *amban* (high commissioner) and other representatives of Peking's authority in Mongolia. Golovkin consequently returned to Russia, his mission unaccomplished, and the Russian Senate sent a strongly worded protest to Peking regarding the treatment accorded him. The Russians thus missed the occasion for trying to negotiate, at Peking, the navigation and trading privileges desired for Russian ships. China, however, for its part, stood alone when a British naval squadron commanded by Rear Admiral William O'Brien Drury in September, 1808, occupied Macao and defeated Chinese troops sent against them. Peking stopped the British trade at Canton, and after three months, during which he had been unable to command cooperation from the British merchantmen at Canton, Drury withdrew his forces in the face of imperial orders from Peking.

The Court cashiered both the viceroy and the Kwangtung governor for their failure to prevent the British military intrusion and then, in 1809, probably having become aware of the political error committed in the Golovkin affair, took steps to repair relations with Russia. The amban at Urga communicated to the Russian governor at Irkutsk, one Treskin, his desire for a personal meeting. The meeting actually took place during February and March, 1810. The Manchu side invited the dispatch of a new Russian mission. Treskin, in accordance with instructions received from St. Petersburg, proposed in substance that the Golovkin rebuff be considered to have been caused by a misunderstanding and be buried in oblivion, and that the Russian mission indeed be renewed—but on the basis of equality and reciprocity, with China to send a mission to Russia. As for ceremonial, he proposed that envoys should be required to observe state ceremonial only before state representatives, and that they should enjoy freedom of movement and of communication with their respective governments.

The Chinese side rejected the proposal envisaging equality and reciprocity, so the negotiations ended without agreement—but the ending was amicable. Moreover, the channel of communication that had been established between Urga and Irkutsk was thereafter maintained. With the changes introduced by the impact on China of the seafarers, St. Petersburg was acting with care and adjusting to the new situation. The Russian mission at Peking was given altered functions, with inspiration for the change probably coming naturally from the work of the learned monk Iakinf, who took up the post as head of the mission at Peking in 1807 and immersed himself in Chinese studies. Iakinf remained at that post for fourteen years and earned the title "the father of Russian Sinology"; he was indeed the outstanding Sinologue of the time.

The value of Iakinf's contributions received implicit recognition in instructions issued to the mission in 1818 to the effect that thereafter its chief function was not to be work in the field of religion, but the general study of the economy and culture of

China—the mission being charged also with informing the Senate of important political events. As of the end of the eighteenth century, the caliber of men assigned to the mission had been declining, but now selection was made from university or seminary graduates, and the nominees were given advance training in the Chinese and Manchu languages. In China, enrolled as member-correspondents of the Russian Academy of Sciences and other Russian academic organs, they studied all aspects of the country and its society, from geography, agriculture, and jurisprudence to the arts. In Russia, the Kazan and St. Petersburg universities introduced the study of Chinese, and the Board of Foreign Affairs organized a section for the study of Eastern languages (including Chinese); at Kiakhta, there was established a school for the study of Chinese and Mongolian, and the teaching of Mongolian and Manchu was begun at Irkutsk. The Russians sought a fundamental understanding of the Orient.

In general, as pressure on China from the sea side built up, Russia adopted an increasingly flexible position, which would enable it to take advantage of possible developments. The Russian policy was not exigent. The director of the Asiatic Department of the Board of Foreign Affairs at St. Petersburg, Rodofinkin, in a letter of April, 1833, stated the policy:

> The chief and constant aim of the Russian Ministry in relation to China is political and commercial. The first consists of the preservation and acceleration of friendly ties with China, as with a state with which we border over so significant an expanse. The second consists of the expansion and development of our trade relations with the Chinese for the benefit of Russian native industry and mutual profit.[9]

In that same letter, the mission was warned to exercise great care in the work of evangelism, so as not to arouse the suspicions of the Chinese government. At that time, the sea powers were pressing to obtain privileges in China for their evangelists. Peking began to manifest, at least occasionally, a greater disposition to maintain a workable relationship with the Russians.

The developing situation in China had to be viewed against the background of changing relations between Russia and Britain. The 1814 victory over Napoleon, and the Congress of Vienna of 1815, effectively marked the emergence of Russia as a first-class European power with stable western frontiers. Poland and Sweden had both been effectively eliminated as major threats to Russian security. But there was a new factor of great complexity, and potential for trouble, in the international sphere: the Ottoman empire was now manifesting serious debility. The Congress of Vienna had left unsettled the issue of Turkey's security, and at such time as the crumbling of empire might evoke the question of how the spoils should be divided, the threat of war between jealous powers was likely to arise. With the expanding Russian and British empires now in contact at various points, the rivalry of the two would in due course extend from the Middle East to various critical sectors of south, central, and even northeast Asia. There had begun the "Great Game" of the nineteenth century — the power struggle between England and Russia in Asia. Their rivalry would exercise an important influence in the area of China's foreign relations.

After the Congress of Vienna, the Russians failed to make any substantial advances in East Asia. In 1815, 1816, and 1817, they tried again to start negotiations with the Japanese, but with no more success than before. Their territorial expansion on the American continent ended: by 1819, they possessed nineteen settlements on the American Pacific coast, but in 1821 their activities became limited on the south by the Fifty-first Parallel. They now contented themselves with consolidation of their holdings on Kamchatka, the Kuriles, the Aleutians, and Alaska.

The imperial scepter came into new hands at St. Petersburg. Alexander I died in 1825 and was succeeded by Nicholas I, narrow-minded and rigid, who ruled in accord with his concept that divine right gave him unquestioned and autocratic authority. Tsar Alexander, together with King Frederick Wilhelm III of Prussia and Francis I of Austria, had in 1815 formed a Holy Alliance to hold revolution in check. Nicholas I, who had come to power to the accompaniment of the Dekabrist (Decembrist) revolt, was counterrevolutionary by deepest inclination and well fitted in that regard for the role he assumed of "Gendarme of Europe." In that capacity, his attention was focused in the main on Europe and the Middle East.

In the Far East, however, the nearly total exclusionism adopted by the Manchus as grand strategy against the seafarers at last came under the sea powers' direct challenge. The cohong system did not meet the needs of the times, as those needs were seen by the foreign traders at Canton. The opium trade in the end provided a critical issue. Britain fought the "Opium War" of 1839–1842 and breached the Manchu barriers; the United States and France followed to reap a share of the benefits and incidentally widened the breach in the Wall of Exclusionism. By the Treaties of Nanking (1842), Bogue (1843), Wangsia (1844), and Whampoa (1844), the three sea powers laid the foundation of what China came in due course to term the "unequal-treaty system," which imposed an inferior legal status on China. The signatories of those treaties thereafter enjoyed new trading privileges in specified ports (the "treaty ports"), certain rights of evangelism, and extraterritorial jurisdiction over their own citizens. Not least, the seafaring states now had the benefit of the most-favored-nation clause in their treaties: the gain of one was the prize of all.

During a state visit by Nicholas I to Queen Victoria in 1844, there was reached what the Russians believed to be the understanding that there should be Anglo-Russian cooperation for the protection of Turkish political integrity, that is, for maintenance of the status quo with regard to the Ottoman empire. The easily inferred corollary was that neither should endeavor to beat the other's game with respect to the decadent empire. If the situation in the Middle East appeared in the 1840s to have been put into a nice balance for Russia, it was quite different in the Far East. During the period when Russia enjoyed a preferential position with respect to relations with China, its trade had grown despite the difficulties. Russian exports to China in the first half of the eighteenth century averaged 38,000 to 42,000 rubles a year by the public caravans, with private trade through Kiakhta perhaps two or three times as much; by 1740 Russian goods shipped through Kiakhta to Peking were valued at 400,000 to 600,000 rubles. Even assuming Russian private trade through Kiakhta to be no more than the public trade, Russian exports of goods (excepting silver bullion) to China were twice those of Britain during the period in question.[10] British imports from China, on the other hand, were notably higher than Russian purchases.

After 1792 and up to the signature of the Treaty of Nanking, the Russian trade through Kiakhta had shown further promise. In the period from 1830 to 1839, the trade turnover increased from 12.8 million to 17.3 million rubles, reflecting a substantial growth of exports of Russian cotton and wool textiles and an increase from 2.3 million to 8.3 million rubles in the value of Chinese tea imported into Russia. The character of the trade was changing rapidly. Where, at the beginning of the century, furs constituted over one half of all Russian exports through Kiakhta, by the end of the 1830s they accounted for only 28 percent; textiles moved into first position, accounting for over 50 percent of Russian exports at the end of the 1830s where they made up only 29 percent at the beginning of the decade. Further, whereas theretofore Prussian, Austrian, and even English textiles in transit by the land route had been important in the commerce through Kiakhta, by the beginning of the 1840s those foreign goods had been almost entirely displaced by Russian manufactures. Russian imports from China had grown correspondingly. Here tea was dominant. Russia had begun to import that product in substantial quantities only in the second half of the eighteenth century, but by the beginning of the 1840s it made up 97 percent of the total Russian import. At last, Sino-Russian trade seemed to be bearing out some of the promise Russian merchants had always seen in the situation.[11]

The Opium War of 1839–1842, however, proved to be an important turning point in China's trade. In May, 1840, even as the war was in course, the Russian Board of Foreign Affairs informed the Li-fan Yuan that Russian subjects would be strictly prohibited from engaging in the smuggling of opium, and the orders were in fact issued and enforced. This action nevertheless won no advantage for Russia. The 1842–1844 treaties between China and the sea powers, opening up China to cheap imports transported over the relatively easy and economical water route, instead introduced a radical change, to the detriment of Russia.

As early as 1845, after signature of the treaties with England, the United States, and France that opened five ports to their trade with a fixed low import tariff, China granted Belgium and Denmark the same trade privileges — without any new treaty arrangements. In 1847, Sweden and Norway were also brought into the "unequal treaty system" governing sea trade. By the Manchu interpretation, however, Russia fell outside the provisions of the new treaty dispensation: it was governed separately by the agreements already existing between Peking and St. Petersburg and, not having a most-favored-nation clause in its treaties, it could not claim more rights still.

Russia thus suddenly found itself in an inferior position relative to all other trading countries, and the Kiakhta trade suffered a severe slump. Not unnaturally, Russia sought new commercial facilities on the land side. When Russia in July, 1847, requested trading facilities at Tarbagatai, Ili, and Kashgar in the Western Region, however, the Li-fan Yuan rejected the petition. In September, 1848, another Russian ship tried approaching China from the sea side and called at Shanghai for purposes of trade. On the basis of the principle laid down at Canton thirty-two years earlier, the vessel was turned away, and the Court instructed Chekiang and Fukien officials to prevent it from returning. Russia thus, at mid-century, found itself losing ground through trade by the restricted and costly land routes governed by the old treaties, and it was denied the possibility of change, or even modest adjustment, in circumstances where its Far Eastern position was coming under increasing challenge from Britain.

Russia did not at the time have its hands entirely free to act in East Asia. The upsurge of revolutionary fervor in Europe in 1848 shattered the 1815 concept that a Holy Alliance of conservative powers would suffice to hold down the forces of revolt. Russia was thus confronted with revolutionary change in the very nations it had counted on as being allies in the work of suppressing revolution. In mid-1849, Nicholas responded to a request for help from Prince Felix Schwartzenberg, representing the Austrian dynasty, and intervened with an army of 90,000 men to restore the Hapsburgs, now in the person of Ferdinand's nephew Franz Joseph, to power in Hungary as well as Austria. Louis Kossuth and other revolutionaries fled to the refuge of Turkey. Then, in 1850, Russia intervened in a dispute between Austria and Prussia, first against Prussia and next to block the fulfillment of Schwartzenberg's purpose of joining the Austrian empire to the Germanic Confederation to create a unified Central Europe. The Russian western flank was again stabilized.

The same could not be said for Russia's relations in the Middle East. Regardless of the Anglo-Russian "understanding" of 1844, England supported Turkey's refusal to extradite Kossuth and other Hungarian and Polish refugees from the counterrevolutionary reaction of 1848–1849. British naval actions in the Dardanelles in 1849 and against Greece (which had won its independence from the Ottoman empire two decades earlier) in

1850 were settled without seeming to do permanent harm to Anglo-Russian relations, but Russian suspicions were doubtless increased. Then, also in 1850, a dispute between Orthodox and Roman Catholic monks regarding their respective rights in the holy places of Constantinople brought about a clash between France and Russia: France, basing its position on the capitulations granted in 1740 by Mahmud I to the benefit of the Roman Catholics, supported the church that was its protégé; Russia, taking its stand on the position granted it by the Treaty of Kuchuk Kainardji, stood by the side of the Orthodox Christians. By 1850, the potential of the Eastern Question for danger had clearly increased.

By that time, the emphasis in Sino-Russian relations had already begun to shift from the economic to the political aspect. Reference by Peking to the time-honored Chinese device of endeavoring to maneuver one barbarian force against another would logically have dictated the grant of concessions to Russia equivalent to those forced from China by the sea powers, with the aim of maintaining Sino-Russian relations on a basis which, if still mutually profitable in the commercial aspect, would have had a different political base and content—of the greater advantage to China. The Manchu Court had not chosen that approach to the policy problem, and St. Petersburg, under pressure of its own commercial interests, and having due regard for the worsening of the political situation in the Near East, was in effect caused to meet the competition of the sea powers by resort to their own strategy with respect to China.

Russia possessed sufficient resources to be able to maneuver politically on all fronts. There had earlier been a sign that Russia proposed, in the face of a changing situation, to adopt a new line of action in the Far East: in September, 1847, Tsar Nicholas had appointed Nikolai Nikolaievich Muraviev to be governor general of Eastern Siberia, with authority to further Russian interests in the Amur sector in particular.

The political situation in China was changing, and the occasion for action would soon arise. In 1850, when the emperor Tao-kuang died and was succeeded by the emperor Hsien-feng, China, as the Ottoman empire, was entering upon a period of grave weakness and disorder. The seafarers, with the victories of the early 1840s in hand, could see further opportunities for political expansion at the cost of the declining Manchu empire—

even in the region of the Amur and Ussuri. The Russians, for their part, having been the first to win a foothold in Northeast Asia, were naturally alert to both the opportunity for consolidation of their gains, and the danger that threatened. By the beginning of the 1850s, the Amur region had taken on a major importance in the eyes of St. Petersburg. There was also that other borderland between China and Russia which held the potential for trouble or gain — Central Asia.

5 CONFRONTATION IN THE WEST PACIFIC, MID-NINETEENTH CENTURY

AT THE BEGINNING of the Hsien-feng reign, China was plagued by both foreign and domestic troubles. At Canton, now legally an open port, local opposition fed by ire at deteriorated economic conditions prevented the British from entering the walled town in implementation of their new treaty rights. In April, 1847, British troops occupied the Boca Tigris fortress and attacked Canton. The American envoy, A. H. Everett, reported adversely on the British action and proposed that the United States, France, and Russia should join together in opposition to Britain and in support of China's independence.[1]

The frustrations experienced by the victorious sea powers with respect to access to the "vast market" of China that seemed always, like a will-o'-the-wisp, to move toward the horizon before them, combined with the common urge to gain the right of diplomatic residence in Peking, would work changes, however, in the relationships between China and the Occident and among the foreign land and sea powers themselves. The T'aip'ing Rebellion, which took form in South China in 1850 and, inspired by a sinicized Christianity and fed by social discontent, in 1853 swept into Nanking and then drove north nearly to within sight of Peking, was an important factor in the equation. That revolutionary movement would constitute the backdrop for China's foreign affairs until it was crushed in 1864.

The Opium War, in which a small force of Englishmen fighting from their ships half a world away from their homeland vanquished the Manchu power, had demolished for St. Petersburg as well as other Occidental capitals the idea theretofore current that China was a mighty power and probably invincible. Russia now saw no great risk in making new political moves. The Russians had not relaxed their interest in arranging for trade facilities across the Central Asian frontier, and St. Petersburg in 1849 commissioned Major E. P. Kovalevski to accompany an ecclesiastical mission to China in anticipation of negotiating further for the privileges denied by Peking. There were personnel changes on the Manchu side. Prince I-shan, member of the Imperial Clan, had fallen temporarily into disgrace because of the part he played in the negotiation of the Treaty of Nanking, and in 1850 he was appointed military governor of Ili.

I-shan thereafter played a significant role in Sino-Russian relations. The archimandrite Palladius, head of the Russian mission at Peking, reported that the Li-fan Yuan was considering the matter of trade facilities. Kovalevski, then at Peking, was appropriately instructed by St. Petersburg, with the aim of making arrangements similar to those reached *locally* between the governor general of Eastern Siberia and the Urga amban, and he departed for Kiakhta. The record is not clear as to the factors that caused the Court to shift its position, but Peking now accepted all but one of the Russian proposals. On July 25, 1851, acting on instructions from Peking, I-shan and Buyentai, the deputy military governor, signed an agreement with Kovalevski by virtue of which trade was permitted at Tarbagatai and Ili, although still denied at Kashgar. The agreement comprised seventeen articles, of which the four most important provided that:

1. Kuldja and Tarbagatai were opened for trade, with designation of Russian consuls to supervise the affairs of Russian subjects, while the affairs of Chinese merchants would be governed by a functionary of the higher administration of Ili. Further, "in case of conflict between the subjects of the one and

the other Power, each of these agents will decide the affairs of his nationals according to all justice."
2. Chinese authorities would not interfere with the trade of private Russian merchants.
3. Russian imports might be made from March 25 to December 10, by caravan, but Russian merchants might remain after the latter date to dispose of imported goods.
4. There was to be the extradition of criminals.[2]

The agreement was duly ratified by the Manchu Court January 1, 1852. The foundation for regular commercial relations between Russia and China via Central Asia had now been laid.

In the meantime, in 1848, Muraviev had assumed his post as governor general of Eastern Siberia, making Irkutsk his headquarters. His appointment bore an important collateral aspect: Muraviev was hostile to the Russian American Company's concern with Alaska. He set about the task of expanding the Russian empire—in Asia. Using New Archangel as base, the Russians undertook to explore the lower Amur, using the camouflaged brig *Constantine*. They discovered the estuary of the Amur, found the natives friendly—and saw no sign of Manchu authority. With the admonition that due care should be taken to the end that Russian activities in that region should not come to the attention of the Manchu headquarters at Aigun, the government now authorized the Russian American Company to begin occupation of the lower Amur.[3] The project was put in the charge of a naval officer then serving with the Russian American Company, Vasili S. Zavoiko, who began the transfer of Russians from New Archangel—to settle on the Amur. In June, 1853, Russia proposed to Peking that the northeastern frontier be demarcated, but the Manchu Court made only limited response, granting permission for the erection of border markers on the Gorbitsa River. Patently, Peking was not at the moment in a frame of mind to take up border matters left unsettled by the Treaty of Kiakhta.

It was at this very juncture that Russia became involved in an international affair that exerted an important influence on developments in Northeast Asia, and on the lower Amur in particular, during the 1850s. Nicholas I had abandoned the policy of trying to provide for the "neutralization" of the Ottoman empire, and the issue that arose in 1850 between Russia and France with respect to the exercise of religious rights by the two Catholic sects in Constantinople once more inflamed the Eastern Question. At the beginning of 1853, the tsar proposed to the British ambassador at St. Petersburg that Turkey be divided. Whatever chances there had been of Anglo-Russian collaboration to effect a settlement were wrecked, however, by the presence in Constantinople of a British envoy who was personally hostile toward the tsar; by the tsar's dispatch of the inept Prince Aleksandr S. Menshikov to Constantinople to deliver an ultimatum to the Turkish government demanding respect for the Russian position in the dispute; and by the devious diplomacy followed by the Ottoman government. When Russian forces crossed the Pruth River in June, 1853, and occupied the Danubian principalities, war became practically inevitable.

The Crimean War began with the destruction of a Turkish naval squadron by the Russian Black Sea fleet at Sinope on November 30, 1853. A combined Anglo-French squadron passed through the Dardanelles to enter the Black Sea a month later. On March 27, 1854, England and France declared war on Russia; the Crimean War, which was to prove so disastrous for Russian policy and military prestige, took on its full dimensions. For the time being, the Eastern Question commanded precedence over China affairs in Russian strategic considerations. China, getting an unearned respite from British and French pressures, felt even less need than usual to be conciliatory toward the Russians.

In July, 1853, Russia had requested that Efim V. Putyatin, charged with a mission to Japan, be permitted to put in at Shanghai with his naval squadron for rest, and also that Russian merchants should be permitted to trade at the open ports, specifically Shanghai. The Li-fan Yuan, as was its custom, rejected the request. Putyatin's squadron called at the port of Nagasaki, reaching there a short time after Commodore Matthew Perry had dropped anchor at Yedo Bay to the north. Putyatin's visit was related to the standing Russian desire to open diplomatic and trade contacts with Japan, and he had the further mission of fixing the boundary between Russia and Japan. Unsuccessful on the occasion of his first visit, he called again in January, 1854, but still made no progress and departed upon the outbreak of the Crimean War to escape possible hostile action by the allied forces.

In the light of the conflict with Britain and France, Russian military men once more, as on other historical occasions, presented plans to their tsar for an invasion of India. The factor of chronology is unclear from the official Chinese history, but it is logical to assume that it was after the Anglo-French intervention in the Black Sea that Russia approached Peking with the proposition that China dispatch 20,000 troops via Burma and Tibet for a flank attack on India.[4] That proposal possibly reflected the Russian military plan. The diversionary move was, however, not undertaken by China. Nor did Russia send an expeditionary force of its own: it already had its hands full of military matters.

The Russians had in the meantime been strengthening their position in the Amur region. Muraviev had proceeded to Petropavlovsk-on-Kamchatka shortly after assuming his post in 1848, found it an excellent naval anchorage, and in 1850 shifted the Russian Far Eastern naval base from Okhotsk to the new site. He entrusted the task of exploration of the Amur and the Pacific coast to a young naval officer, Gennadi I. Nevelskoi, who discovered, among other things, that Sakhalin was an island. In August, 1850, Nevelskoi raised the Russian flag over a position on the Amur that he named Nikolaevsk. The storm his action caused in St. Petersburg was ended when Nicholas I made his sensational statement: "Where the Russian flag has once been hoisted it must not be lowered."[5]

With the development of tense Russian relations with Britain and France after the outbreak of the war with Turkey, Muraviev in January, 1854, was given increased powers in the field of foreign affairs. In May, embarking at Nerchinsk, he sailed down the Amur with 800 troops in a motley fleet as if the river belonged to Russia, to establish a line of communications with Kamchatka. En route, at the junction of the Ussuri and the Amur, he named the site of Khabarov's ostrog "Khabarovsk," in honor of the early explorer, and that is the name by which the town is known today.

An allied Anglo-French squadron in due course sought to sail up the Amur and destroy the Russian power in that vicinity, but it was unable to discover the river's mouth. It sailed then for Petropavlovsk and in August, 1854, attacked the Russian naval units there and put a landing party of upwards of 1,000 men ashore. The defender of the position was Muraviev's man Zavoiko, who in 1850 had been appointed military governor of Kamchatka and commandant of the port of Petropavlovsk. Zavoiko had a total garrison force (including volunteers) of only 930 men, but he had prepared his defenses well. The landing party, after suffering some 450 casualties (compared to about 100 on the Russian side), was forced to retreat to its boats, and the Anglo-French squadron withdrew. Russian prestige rose accordingly—especially in China. In February, 1855, Peking instructed the Heilungkiang military governor I-ko to permit the Russians to travel via the Amur for return (via the Gorbitsa) to their homeland, but not to permit them to navigate the river thereafter.

The matter was not to be settled so simply. In that same year, Zavoiko evacuated the population and garrison of Petropavlovsk to the mouth of the Amur and undertook the construction of a fortified port at Nikolaevsk. Muraviev, just returned from Moscow, launched a new expedition down the Amur, this time carrying prospective settlers and their cattle. At Kuotuntun on the Sungari, he met with the Manchu representative Funiyanga and put forward the proposition that the entire left bank of the Amur belonged to Russia, and that the river mouth should be Russia's as well, but Funiyanga made no concessions.

Russia, however, made significant progress at this same time in its relations with Japan, which by the treaty of March, 1854, negotiated by Commodore Perry finally abandoned its policy of exclusionism. Britain pressed forward to enter the door that had been opened, signing an agreement with Japan on its own behalf in October of that year. Putyatin ran the risk of being caught by a British naval force by returning to Shimoda shortly afterward in a single vessel, the *Diana,* presumably successor to Vice Admiral Vasili M. Golovnin's ship of the same name. The *Diana* sank as the result of a battering it received in harbor during an earthquake, and the Russians had to have a new ship built for their outward voyage. Admiral Putyatin nevertheless crowned his mission this time with the Treaty of Shimoda, signed in February, 1855. The Russian treaty provided for the opening of the port of Nagasaki, in addition to Hakodate and Shimoda (both opened by the American treaty). It provided, further, for Russian extraterritorial jurisdiction. The American and British treaties lacked such a clause. Since both, however, had with foresight included a most-favored-nation clause, the United States and Britain automatically enjoyed the privilege conceded to the Russians. There was another provision which would have historical significance: Urup and the islands north of it in the Kurile chain were acknowledged as belonging to Russia, while Kunashir and the Shikotan-Habomai island group were recognized as the possessions of Japan.

With the entry of Japan into contact with the outside world, the seeds of great change had been planted in East Asia, as Vasili Golovnin earlier in the century had suggested might happen. In 1855, Putyatin was rewarded for his services by being made a count; three years later, he was given the naval rank of admiral. He would return to the Asian scene, for he had proved his diplomatic worth to the empire.

In February, 1856, the Crimean War ended with the signature of the Treaty of Paris. France and Britain were now free to press their cause against China, and Russia was in a better position than ever before to exploit the situation to its own benefit. One British point of view of the period was set forth by Thomas Taylor Meadows, an interpreter in the British consulate at Shanghai, who wrote in 1856 that, although the Russians were not to be held "more hateful, as aggressors and conquerors, than other peoples," nevertheless:

> . . . this does not make it the less our duty to oppose Russia in China, with all our intelligence, our wealth, and military force. The cause of civilization alone would justify it; for the Chinese are freer and happier, even under the Manchoo government, than they would eventually find themselves under that of Russia.
> . . . The important fact is, that not only England and France but America too, will, if they are wise, wage, severally or collectively, a war of exhaustion with Russia, rather than allow her to conquer China: for when she has done that she will truly be the Mistress of the World.[6]

The Russians undertook to exploit their improved maneuverability by new moves on China's northern frontier. The chief Manchu official on the spot was a man the Russians had met before, I-shan; early in 1856, he was appointed military governor of Heilungkiang. In June, he informed Peking that the Russians had again entered the Amur and said that the only way to handle the matter was to be outwardly conciliatory and covertly to take defense measures, but he proposed to discuss the matter with Muraviev when the latter arrived. In September, I-shan reported again on the Russians' navigation of the Amur: he was in the course of taking control measures, but his purpose was to employ magnanimity. The Manchu Court, its attention fixed on the developing situation at Canton, where the British, French, and American envoys were being held at arm's length by Governor General Yeh Ming-ch'en, obviously did not feel in a position to advise any other line of action.

The Russians pressed their suit. In March, 1857, the Li-fan Yuan received a communication from Russia requesting that Count Putyatin be received as official envoy, for confidential negotiations. The Li-fan Yuan rejected the request, and Chinese officials at Urga and in Heilungkiang and Kirin were instructed to prevent such travel to the Chinese capital. I-shan and the Kirin military governor, Ching-shun, were instructed specifically to reject any Russian requests regarding trade or residence. Muraviev had meetings with both men and discussed territorial and other issues with them but made no progress.

St. Petersburg shifted tactics for the mission to Peking. Putyatin left Kiakhta in May, traveled down the Amur, and in August proceeded by sea in his ship the *Amerika* to the mouth of the Peiho, off Tientsin. He then sent a message to the Chihli provincial treasurer, Ch'ien Hsin-ho, requesting demarcation of the northeastern boundary. In mid-September Ch'ien delivered the Li-fan Yuan's reply: a high official had been dispatched to the Amur to handle the matter there. Appropriate instructions went out to I-shan.

Putyatin, however, had no thought of returning to the Amur. After making two trips each to Japan and Shanghai, in mid-November he arrived at Hong Kong and there met with the British and French envoys, Lord Elgin and Baron Jean Baptiste Louis Gros. He also met with American Minister William B. Reed, and over the months that followed he and Reed established a close working relationship. Rebuffed by China in its unilateral approach, Russia was associating itself with the sea powers, including its recent enemies England and France. Peking showed no signs of appreciating the significance of the move.

In December, 1857, British and French forces occupied Canton and took over its rule. That local victory of course did not settle the issues of new trading privileges and diplomatic residence at Peking, and in early February, 1858, the British and French invited the American and Russian envoys to join them in a démarche vis-à-vis the Manchu Court. At the end of the month all four sent communications to Grand Secretary Yü-ch'eng requesting that a plenipotentiary be dispatched to Shanghai for negotiations.

Putyatin's note remarked that Peking's refusal to receive him was warrant for his joining with the other envoys for the purpose of obtaining the right, theretofore denied, of direct communication with the superior authorities at Peking. He proceeded to send the Grand Council a supplementary statement proposing that the Amur and Ussuri rivers should constitute the boundary between Russia and China. This was an advance beyond anything the Russians had suggested before.

The Manchu Court stubbornly rejected the exigent requests of the "barbarian" envoys. In its replies, delivered at Shanghai, it directed that the British, French, and American representatives should undertake any negotiations with the Canton viceroy, while Russia should deal with the Amur commissioner. The Court also instructed I-shan to refuse Russia's request that the boundary be fixed on the Amur and Ussuri rivers.

Putyatin acted as vanguard and sailed north aboard the *Amerika*. He reached the Peiho on April 12, and was soon joined there by the other envoys — and a joint Anglo-French naval force. At Taku, on April 24, the representatives of the four powers in a message to Yü-ch'eng fixed a time limit of six days for the dispatch of a high official to Taku for negotiations, failing which they would take appropriate action. Putyatin, acting on behalf of Russia, met with Ch'ung-lun and Wu-erh-kun-t'ai at Taku on the following day and demanded that he be permitted to proceed to Peking for the purpose of clarifying boundary matters and to obtain permission for trade at the open ports.

The Court, perceiving differences between Russia and the United States on the one hand and England and France on the other, undertook to try to divide the four powers. The new Chihli viceroy, T'an T'ing-hsiang, together with Ch'ung-lun and Wu-erh-kun-t'ai, in late April met with Putyatin at Taku, only to find that he still wanted to discuss the matters of boundaries and entry into Peking. The Court directed T'an to refuse the Russian demand for border demarcation and to tell Putyatin, once more, to return to the Amur and negotiate there with I-shan. A few days later Peking summarily rejected the British and French requests. In actuality, however, Putyatin was already effectively negotiating the boundary question; he also had begun to take on a media-tory role between the Manchu Court and the seafarers.[7]

On the Amur, in the absence of Putyatin, I-shan in May sent the assistant military governor, Chi-la-ming-a, to see Mura-viev and *urge* him to discuss border matters. On May 23 and 24, Muraviev met with I-shan at Aigun. Muraviev proposed the signature of a new treaty fixing the Amur and Ussuri rivers as the common boundary between the two states. I-shan rejected the proposal, whereupon Muraviev withdrew from the conference in feigned anger, and Russian gunboats on the Amur cannonaded during the night. The following day I-shan sent a representative to mollify Muraviev to the end that he would resume negotiations. Muraviev graciously consented to return to the conference table, and on May 28, 1858, the two sides signed the Treaty of Aigun, by virtue of which the Amur River from the Argun to its mouth was accepted as the boundary between the two countries. Only vessels of the two countries might ply the Amur, Ussuri, *and Sungari*. The agreement provided further that, "for the mutual friendship of the subjects of the two states," mutual trade of the subjects of both states was permitted along the three rivers. This gave the Russians the right of trade (and navigation) on the Sun-gari—a Chinese inland river. As for the region east of the Ussuri, it would remain under joint dominion of the two countries pending future determination of the common frontier in that region.

In the meantime, the negotiations of the four envoys lying off Taku had proved fruitless. On May 20, the British and French forces attacked and occupied the Taku fortress. The envoys en-tered Tientsin at the end of the month and informed Yü-ch'eng that a representative with plenipotentiary credentials must be sent, otherwise there would be a military advance on the capital. Peking at long last sent plenipotentiaries, and between June 13 and June 27 signed treaties with all four powers. The spirit in which the Manchu Court signed the documents, however, was indicated by a memorial submitted by Kuei-liang before signa-ture, stating that the treaties of peace should not be conscien-tiously observed, that in future they could be regarded as so much wastepaper.[8]

The first of the several treaties was that of June 13 between China and Russia, with Grand Secretary Kuei-liang and Hua-sha-na signing on behalf of the Manchu Court and Putyatin for

St. Petersburg. The document comprised twelve articles. Russia wrote into its new treaty the most-favored-nation clause of American invention, and thus became automatically entitled to enjoy all the privileges, whether with respect to trade, evangelism, or politics, that accrued to other treaty powers. Article 3, however, took the precaution of stipulating that Russia thereafter might trade not only by the land route, but at certain specific ports that had been opened in the past, "and in other places open for foreign trade." [9] It was provided further that relations between the Russian and Chinese governments should not as before be carried on through the Russian Senate and the Li-fan Yuan, but by the Russian minister for foreign affairs and a senior member of the Grand Council, or the prime minister, on the basis of complete equality. Former limitations on the dimensions, frequency, and participants in trade were removed: the idea of one caravan every two or three years was cast into the discard. It was provided that Russia might send its *military* courts into the open ports for supervision of the activities of Russian subjects and maintenance of the authority of Russian consular officers. Article 9 stipulated that undefined sections of the boundary between China and Russia would be investigated "without delay" by authorized representatives of the two governments, and conditions fixed by them for the marking of the frontier would be made a supplement of the existing treaty.

On June 18, June 26, and June 27, respectively, the American, English, and French envoys signed treaties on behalf of their respective countries. It was stipulated that ratification of the several instruments should take place in Peking. After having striven with some success to act as a shield for the Manchu Throne against the importunities of the British and French, and having in the end signed a treaty very favorable to Russia's interests, Putyatin departed and, on August 19, 1858, signed the Treaty of Yedo with Japan.

A Foreign Ministry official who had acted as Muraviev's Manchu interpreter at Aigun, Petr Perovski, was assigned the task of exchanging ratifications of the Russo-Manchu treaty, and arrived at Peking in October. Delay was incurred because of differences discovered between the Russian, Manchu, and Chinese texts, but the exchange of ratifications of the Treaty of Tientsin finally took place on April 24, 1859. In the meantime, Perovski had been instructed to negotiate a new treaty providing, inter alia, for outright Russian title to the region east of the Ussuri. Perovski, who lacked ambassadorial status, made no progress toward either the exchange of ratifications of the Treaty of Aigun or the reaching of a new agreement. On June 27, a more prestigious envoy, Count Nikolai P. Ignatiev, reached the Chinese capital to assume the negotiating task. Perovski departed a few days afterward.

In the meantime, true to the spirit of Kuei-liang's memorial, the Manchu Court had endeavored to transform the British and French treaties in particular into wastepaper. After the Anglo-French naval force had withdrawn to the south, the Taku defense position was restored, and Peking sent Kuei-liang and Hua-sha-na to Shanghai to negotiate major changes in the agreements just reached with England and France. That Manchu mission was fruitless, but when the British, French, and American envoys arrived, with naval escort, at Taku in late June, 1859, for the exchange of ratifications, they found the route to Tientsin blocked, and on June 25 a new military clash occurred at Taku. The British lost heavily, and the joint force, in view of the unexpected resistance, pulled back to Shanghai to await reinforcements.

The Taku battle, taking place just before Ignatiev's arrival, left the Russian envoy in a weak negotiating position: the Manchu Court had become convinced anew of China's prowess. Ignatiev was unable to get the exchange of ratifications of the Treaty of Aigun. The dispute over the validity of the document actually led Prince Shun to threaten another stoppage of Sino-Russian trade. The gambit was an old one and had lost much of its effectiveness. The Court nevertheless manifested its temper when, in August, it recalled I-shan and stripped him of his posts for negotiating the Aigun treaty.

Russia again exploited the conflict between the seafarers and the Manchu Court. American Minister John Ward exchanged ratifications of the Sino-American Treaty of Tientsin at Peitang, on the coast, in August, 1859. The British and French, unappeased, insisted on fulfillment of the agreements that treaty ratifications should be exchanged at Peking, and that foreign envoys should have the right of permanent residence in the capital. The emperor Hsien-feng, xenophobic, narrow-minded, and poorly served by his advisers, refused to yield. Nor would Peking concede anything to the Russian demands. At the end of May, 1860, Ignatiev left Peking for Shanghai and began to play an intricate game of manipulating the British and French against the Manchu power, while posing to Peking as ready to help the Court against the Anglo-French combination — for a price.[10]

In August, 1860, after having concentrated some 17,000 men, the Anglo-French allies landed their force in North China and occupied Taku and Tientsin. Then they advanced on Peking. Hsien-feng in late September fled to the Manchu hunting area in Jehol, outside the Great Wall, leaving China's critical foreign relations in the hands of Prince Kung, then twenty-eight years of age. The Anglo-French forces entered Peking in mid-October, and the British and French envoys duly exchanged ratifications of the 1858 treaties there as originally planned. They moreover signed new treaties increasing the concessions and indemnities to be made by the Manchu government. Ignatiev, entering the capital on the heels of the Anglo-French troops, on November 14, 1860, signed with Prince Kung a new agreement of fifteen articles.

That document confirmed the provisions of the Aigun treaty, making final and definitive the demarcation of the Sino-Russian border along the Amur and Ussuri rivers. Further, the boundary on the west was now demarcated. It ran from Shabin-dabag to Lake Zaisan, from there to Mount Tengri south of Issyk Kul, and along the mountain range to the Kokand domain. All boundary questions were thereafter to be settled on the basis of those first two articles of the treaty. In the Western Region trade was to be permitted at Kashgar as well as at Ili and Tarbagatai. Chinese merchants were likewise given freedom of trade at Russian sites open to commerce. China might, if it chose, appoint its consuls, enjoying position and powers like those of Russian consuls in China, in the "capital and other cities of the Russian empire." A protocol signed in June, 1861, provided for an exchange of maps fixing the Ussuri boundary, and one of October, 1864, provided in detail for the delimitation of the Russo-Chinese boundary in the west. A further protocol of March, 1862, set forth in detail (twenty-two articles) new regulations to govern trade by land between Russia and China.

On November 22, 1860, Count Ignatiev left Peking en route home to Russia. His was a truly triumphal journey.

The old order of international relations in East Asia was dead; Russia was now one of the powers of the "unequal treaty system." Nikolai N. Muraviev, for his negotiation of the Treaty of Aigun, was made a count, with the appended title "Amurski."

He had earned no less. In all this, China was the big loser. Had the Manchu Court in the first six decades of the nineteenth century used more expertly the tactic of playing one "barbarian" against another, in particular making some calculated concessions to the Russians during the critical period of the first half-century, it might well have been found in a more favorable position by the end of the T'aip'ing Rebellion.

In 1858–1860 that rebellion was still in course, but its strength was on the wane. And after 1860, with a satisfactory settlement at last reached at Peking, Americans, British, and French contributed to the defense of the Manchu authority in the Shanghai-Ningpo sector in particular. The forces in the field were now too much for the dispirited and badly led rebels. In July, 1864, Nanking was taken by the imperial forces, and the great peasant revolt against the Manchu Throne was ended. It is noteworthy in this connection that, although the three sea powers were all involved in some way or another with the final suppression of the T'aip'ing revolutionaries in behalf of the Manchu rule, the land power Russia was not.

Muraviev's rule of Eastern Siberia had thus brought valuable increment to the Russian empire in Northeast Asia. It also brought major changes affecting the future of Russian America, with the United States the reluctant beneficiary. Muraviev in 1853 had set forth the thesis that "the United States are bound to spread over the whole of North America. . . . Sooner or later we shall have to surrender our North American possessions." [11] The Crimean War began that year, and the war evoked strong American sympathy for Russia. In 1858–1860, when Russia was making substantial territorial gains at the expense of China, Russian Minister to the United States Eduoard de Stoecki and Alexander II's brother Grand Duke Konstantin (a champion of Muraviev, and also an enemy of the Russian American Company) began to push the idea of selling Alaska to the United States.

The campaign was waged in desultory fashion over years but reached a culminating point in December, 1866, when, in a meeting at which Alexander II himself presided, it was decided to ask Stoecki (who had just been appointed to The Hague) to go to Washington to sell Russian America. The Russian idea was that this move would be a favor to the United States. U.S. Secretary of State William H. Seward presented the matter to the Senate as being a way to show amity to Russia (which had manifested a friendly attitude toward the North during the American Civil War), and Russian America was sold to the United States for the nominal sum of $7.5 million — with payment made only grudgingly. As observed by one who recorded the process: "A nation having small desire to sell did so to a nation that was not eager to buy, their motives the belief that they would please each other. History does not invariably make sense." [12] As a result, however, the Russian empire now found its easternmost limit in Northeast Asia, not in the Western Hemisphere.

In the meantime, in the 1860s, when the treaties of Tientsin, Aigun, and Peking had given new forms to the Russo-Manchu relationship in East and Northeast Asia, and Russia was disengaging from the American continent, there were critical developments in Central Asia that engaged the political energies of China and Russia.

6 THE "GREAT GAME" IN CENTRAL ASIA

BY THE BEGINNING of the nineteenth century the Russians had completed a continuous line of fortifications along their Central Asian frontier, running from Guriev (at the mouth of the Ural) to Semipalatinsk and Bukhtarminsk on the frontier with China. They thus possessed a strong barrier against the forays of the nomadic peoples of Central Asia. The defense system could also serve, if the occasion arose, to support offensive action against unruly neighbors. In addition, it constituted a base for operations against the British and Manchu empires.

Russian strategy in Central Asia reflected in no small measure the course of relations between the Russian and British empires elsewhere. Strategic planning in that regard began to take serious form about the time of the Napoleonic wars. There had been the ill-conceived scheme of Tsar Paul and Napoleon envisaging the conquest of India and Napoleon's revival of the project when he met at Tilsit with Alexander I in 1807. Various Russian projects for the invasion of India as a means of thwarting British imperial power would make their reappearance over the decades, but after Paul's reckless venture none was ever finally adopted by the Russian Court. The British public, however, and sometimes the British government, watching developments in Central Asia in the course of the nineteenth century, upon occasion developed the fear that the real Russian strategic objective was indeed India.

At this time the three khanates of Kokand, Bukhara, and Khiva ruled in Western Turkestan. The frontiers of those khanates were undetermined and fluid, shifting according to the fortunes of the incessant wars. In both Bukhara and Kokandia, Uzbek elements were potentially dissident. In the steppe to the north, the Lesser, Middle, and Greater Hordes [1] of the Kazakhs were dominant. The Lesser and Middle Hordes had acknowledged the suzerainty of St. Petersburg, but their oaths were lightly sworn and lightly broken. A similar situation prevailed with respect to the nomadic Turkomans (descendents of the Seljuk Turks), located west of the Bukhara khanate: they had nominally given their allegiance to Russia in 1791, but this action had not truly brought them under Russian rule.

The peoples under those dominions naturally preferred independence, but their concept of "independence" was primitive, and they took it as a fact of Central Asian life that they might be caused, by force or for reasons of expediency, to renounce that independence temporarily. And when they found themselves in that position, they seemingly had no especial preference between the Russian empire and their fellow Asians as masters. They felt no Asian "nationalism."

The Russians were concerned with the safety and extension of land trade routes in Asia in circumstances where they were unable to compete in the markets of Europe and were losing out in China to the seafarers with their cheaper transport; they were concerned likewise with extending their authority over Central Asians who acknowledged no rule. The Russian position on the fringe of Central Asia was strengthened when, in the treaty signed October 12, 1813, ending the Russo-Persian War, the Persian shah acknowledged Russian sovereignty over Georgia and the Caucasus—"the whole country between the boundary as at present established and the line of the Caucasus, and all the territory between the Caucasus and the Caspian Sea." Further, "no other nation whatever shall be allowed ships of war on the Caspian." The Caspian Sea had become a Russian lake. A year later, Persia came into play in the Great Game between the Russian and British empires by signing a treaty with Britain pledging itself not to permit any European army to enter Persia for the purpose of invading India. For the Russia of that period, however, the Great Game was directed more immediately toward Central Asia than South Asia.

In Bukhara, under Nasrullah (1827–1860), the emirate

gained fresh power. Nasrullah even developed ambitions to restore the Timurid empire, which would have required the subjugation of Kokand. In Kokand, Alim in 1800 [2] assumed the title of khan, and that state too entered upon an expansionist cycle. In the course of four decades, under Alim Khan and his successors Omar Khan and Muhammed Ali (Madali Khan), the Kokandian rule was extended over Tashkent, Khojent, and other towns. A line of fortifications was constructed along the frontier facing the Kazakh power. Prominent among the strongpoints were Ak-Mechet (present-day Kzyl-Orda), Aulie-Ata (Dzhambul), and Pishpek (Frunze). In Khiva a series of rulers held the khanate on the traditional Central Asian track in the first half of the century.

Bukhara, Kokand, and Khiva alike harassed Russian merchant caravans, looting the merchants' goods and carrying Russian subjects away to slavery. The three principalities also purchased Russians who had been taken captive by Kazakh raiders, for the same purpose of enslavement. The death rate under harsh treatment and heavy labor was high, but the raiding of Russian caravans provided an easy way of replenishing the labor supply. The condition of the unfortunate slaves was long a matter of concern for St. Petersburg.

In 1819–1820, the military officer Nikolai N. Muraviev was sent on a diplomatic mission to Khiva and Bukhara. Regarding Khiva, he reported that as a Russian possession it "would have become a point of assembly for all the commerce of Asia, and would have shaken to the centre of India the enormous superiority enjoyed by the rulers of the sea, the British." [3] Such a consideration would have acted as an additional impulse for Russian action against the obstreperous Central Asian polities. In 1820, the Russians launched an expedition from Orenburg against Bukhara, occupying the town in December and releasing many Russian and a number of English captives.

A new Russo-Persian conflict occurred when Persia tried, in the 1820s, to reconquer Georgia. The war ended in another Russian victory, embodied in the 1828 Treaty of Turkmanchai, by virtue of which the Persian boundary was fixed at the Aras River. Persia now threatened Herat in an apparent move to compensate for its losses to Russia. Britain saw Russian influence in the move and feared that success on the Afghan front would advance Russian power that much the closer to the Punjab. .

The Persian military campaign against Herat was launched

in 1837, with Russia supplying both money and officers for the enterprise, but the assault on the town failed and the shah, upon receipt of a warning from the British government that it would view the occupation of Herat as a hostile act, lifted the siege and retreated. The Russians, by this time, had turned their attention to Khiva.

Seeing the movement of Russian military units into the steppe, the Khivan khanate seemingly felt that a conciliatory gesture was in order, and in 1837, for the first time, released twenty-five Russian subjects, who arrived at Orenburg in November of that year. The military governor of Orenburg, V. A. Perovski, in a letter to Count Nesselrode, the minister for foreign affairs, in August, 1839, reported the arrival of two Khivan ambassadors with eighty more Russian prisoners for return. Perovski termed the number "notable enough" but remarked that it was still insignificant compared to the number remaining in captivity; as regards the letter for the tsar carried by the ambassadors, this, said the governor, consisted "simply of bombastic drivel." [4]

Russia was at this time experiencing renewed trouble with the Kazakhs. The nomads' unrest and forays against Russian positions were viewed by St. Petersburg as having been instigated by Khiva — which in any event seemed to constitute a barrier to commerce with Bukhara and India. The tsar had approved military action against Khiva in the spring of 1839, and General Perovski's preparations were already well advanced. Late in the year (to avoid the torrid summer heat) the main expeditionary force of 5,325 men began their march into the Ust-Urt plateau. The column experienced great hardships, however, because of the rigors of the winter in that desolate steppe, and reached Ak-Bulak two and a half months later, in February, 1840, with only 1,856 effectives left. Perovski ordered retreat. The British came forward as mediators and got Khiva to release 416 Russian prisoners. The Russians were thus deprived, for the time being, of due cause for subjugation of the troublesome khanate.

Madali Khan of Kokand had in 1826 engaged in the imperialist venture of endeavoring to help Jehangir Khoja oust Chinese rule from Kashgar. The undertaking was unsuccessful — and Madali Khan fell from power when Nasrullah captured and sacked Kokand in 1842. Shir Ali Khudayar Khan succeeded Madali Khan to power with Kipchak support, recovered Kokand from the invaders, and went on to harass the Kazakh lands that were under Russian protectorate.

The Russians established three advance posts southeast of Orenburg and north of the Aral Sea, in 1845 and 1846. They strengthened their flank against Khiva by construction of the fortress Raimsk at the mouth of the Syr-Darya (Jaxartes) in 1847 and then, in the same year, began a series of campaigns to destroy the Kokand line of fortifications. The action against Kokand was facilitated by the internecine warfare between sedentary Sarts and semi-nomadic Kipchaks that had afflicted the country after the death of Omar Khan in 1822.

It was near the end of 1847 that the Tadjik Yakub Beg, who had been chamberlain to Khan Khudayar, was promoted to the position of *kush-begi* ("lord of the family" – commander) and posted to Ak-Mechet ("White Mosque") on the lower Syr-Darya. Yakub Beg carried on a series of raids against the Russian position at Fort Raimsk and neighboring Russian settlements, and in the summer of 1852 a Russian detachment of 468 men and officers advanced against the Kokand fortress. They succeeded in occupying the outer defenses of Ak-Mechet, but were unable to take the inner citadel, and retreated. A year later, however, in August, 1853, a new expeditionary force under Perovski took Ak-Mechet, killing 230 of the 300 defenders of the citadel, including the then commander, Wali Mohamed. Yakub Beg had in the meantime departed.

A Kokand force of some 7,000 men counterattacked against Ak-Mechet, but was defeated in September. Yakub Beg in November issued from Tashkent at the head of an even larger Kokand force of about 13,000 men and 17 guns and moved against the Russian positions on the Syr-Darya, but the Kokandians were again defeated, losing some 2,000 dead – as against 18 dead and 49 wounded on the Russian side. Yakub Beg, having provoked the Russian attack on Ak-Mechet by his attempts to expand Kokand's rule into the Kazakh steppe, was reduced in rank to *mir* (chief) and in the years immediately ahead was found involved in the plots and counterplots of Kokand's domestic politics.

The Kazakh Greater Horde had not followed the Lesser and Middle Hordes in extending allegiance to Russia in the eighteenth century. The Russian expansion took on new form after the construction of the fortress Akmolinsk: now Russian and Ukrainian colonists began to settle on Kazakh lands. Pressed by Kokand in the south and the Russians to the north, elements of the Lesser Horde rose up against the Russians, and then Sultan Kenesary Kasymov led the Middle Horde into the battle. The campaign was long and bitter, and rendered the more complex by the divided loyalties of the Lesser Horde and the casual intrusions of Kokandians and Kirgizi into the turmoil. In 1846 Sultan Kenesary Kasymov was forced south, and took refuge with the Greater Horde. He was killed in the following year, fighting the Kirgizi near Issyk Kul. The Russians extended their fortified line farther by constructing the fortress Kazaly in 1848.

In 1853, with the capture of Ak-Mechet, the Russians crossed the Ili River and began operations against the Greater Horde — nominally for the Horde's "protection." But the Crimean War began, and Russia was for the time being forced to halt military action in Central Asia. It limited itself to an advance, in 1855, to the northern slope of the Khungai Ala-tau (mountains) and the establishment there of a fortified position named Verny — present-day Alma-Ata, capital of Kazakhstan.

After peace with England had been restored, however, Russia again turned its attention to Central Asia. Following up the visit to St. Petersburg of envoys from Khiva and Bukhara to congratulate Alexander II on his accession to the throne, the Russian government in 1858 sent Nikolai P. Ignatiev, of later China fame, on a return mission to the two principalities. Ignatiev failed to negotiate an agreement with the Khivan khan, Said Mohammed, but achieved a measure of success at Bukhara by negotiating a treaty of friendship with the emir.

With its politico-military position in Central Asia strengthened, Russia was in a position to take advantage of the chronic weakness of Kokand, where the Sarts and Kipchaks were still at each other's throats. The Kokand resistance was now led by the Sart Alim Kuli, who in 1860 proclaimed a holy war against the Russians. The Russians that year took the Kokand fortresses of Pishpek and Tokmak, but were forced to retreat before the advance of Khanayat Shah at the head of 30,000 troops, and abandoned the region south of the Ili.

In the summer of 1864 the Russians launched a major campaign with the strategic objective of linking up the Orenburg and Siberian defense lines. Colonel Mikhail G. Chernyaev at the head of 2,500 men drove from the Siberian front and in June attacked Aulie-Ata on the Talas River and promptly secured the town. It was nearly exactly eleven centuries since the defeat of Kao Hsien-chih in the battle of Talas had brought an end to the T'ang effort to dominate Central Asia; 1864 marked an ebb tide of Manchu power in the same region. Colonel Verevkin led a second column of 1,200 into battle and captured Hazret-i-Turkestan. With the gap between the Orenburg and Siberian lines thus effectively closed, Chernyaev led the combined force of some 5,000 men in an attack on 10,000 Kokandians, supported by artillery, at Chimkent. On October 3, 1864, the Russians took the fortified position from the demoralized defenders, with the loss of only five men.

This was clearly military conquest, and Chancellor A. M. Gorchakov, in a circular communication sent shortly afterward to Russian foreign missions, expounded his country's Asia policy. He began by saying that "The position of Russia in Central Asia is that of all civilised States which are brought into contact with half-savage, nomad populations, possessing no fixed social organizations." For the security of its frontier and its commercial relations, Russia was caused to establish a certain ascendancy over its turbulent neighbors, and in this connection the following principles had been determined:

1. "It has been judged indispensable that our fortified frontier lines . . . should be united by fortified points, so that all our posts should be in a position of mutual support. . . ."
2. The line of advanced fortifications should be located in a country fertile enough not only to insure supply but also to permit regular colonization, "which alone can prepare a future of stability and prosperity for the occupied country. . . ."
3. The line should be definitely fixed, "so as to escape the danger of being carried away, as is almost inevitable, by a series of repressive measures and reprisals, into an unlimited extension of territory." [5]

Gorchakov, in short, designed to indicate to other countries, and particularly to Britain, that Russia's ambition was strictly limited.

In 1861, the governor general of Orenburg, General A. P. Bezak, had made an inspection trip to the Syr-Darya line and reached the conclusion that, in order to fix a viable frontier with the Kokand khanate and incidentally to promote Russian trade, Tashkent, nominally subject to Kokand suzerainty but not viewed as an integral part of the khanate, should be occupied as soon as feasible; "with Tashkent in our hands we shall not only dominate completely the Kokand khanate but we shall strengthen our influence on Bukhara which will greatly increase our trade with those countries and particularly with the populous Chinese towns of Kashgar and Yarkand." [6]

In early October, after the capture of Chimkent, Chernyaev attacked in the direction of Tashkent. He was met by the joint forces of Alim Kuli and Yakub Beg, and defeated them. The Kokand forces, however, retired inside the town and Chernyaev, seemingly feeling the inadequacy of the force at his command, withdrew to Chimkent. Relations between Alim Kuli and Yakub Beg deteriorated after the defeat outside Tashkent, and at this juncture the Kirgiz leader Sadic Beg sent word to Alim Kuli that he had captured Kashgar and desired to have an heir of the *khojas* * for the throne. Buzurg Khan, the sole surviving son of Jehangir, expressed his willingness to accept the honor. Alim Kuli, probably with alacrity, gave Yakub to Buzurg Khan as his *baturbashi* (commander in chief). The ambitious politicians, commanding a force of native Kokandi, left for Kashgar in late 1864, just in time to miss a new Russian move on Tashkent.

Mozaffar ed-Din, who had succeeded Nasrullah as emir of Bukhara, mobilized his forces at Ura-Tyube. For a while, there were divided counsels in the Russian Court over the Tashkent question; however, it appeared that Britain had not taken undue alarm at the Russian moves.[7] In the spring of 1865, anticipating the enemy attacks, Chernyaev threw his forces into action again, won a preliminary battle in which the doughty Alim Kuli was killed, and then, in June, occupied Tashkent. With both Yakub Beg and Alim Kuli out of the picture, Mozaffar ed-Din, in traditional Central Asian manner, took the opportunity to seize control of Kokand and Khojent from Sultan Seyyid and to restore Khudayar Khan to power in Kokand—but with Kokand now a vassal of Bukhara, and Khudayar Khan ruling only as Mozaffar ed-Din's viceroy.

Unable to make headway against Bukhara by political negotiation, Chernyaev in January, 1866, marched against the Bukharan fortress Jizakh (Dzhizak), commanding the Zerafshan valley in which Samarkand was situated. He reached his

* Members of a religio-political clan having its origins in the sixteenth century.

objective in February with his forces weakened by the rigors of winter, and was caused to retreat. Even before his retreat, orders had been issued relieving him of his command. He was succeeded by Major General Dimitri Ilyitch Romanovski, who took up the task of invading Bukhara and met the army of Mozaffar ed-Din at Irdzhar. He inflicted a heavy defeat upon the vastly greater forces of the Bukharan emir, captured the strongpoint of Ura-Tyube, and went on to occupy Jizakh in October, 1866. The following spring, Russian forces reduced the fortress Yani-Kurgan, and Mozaffar ed-Din sued for peace. St. Petersburg removed the newly conquered territories and that part of Semipalatinsk south of the Tarbagatai range from the jurisdiction of the Orenburg command, and by an *ukaz* (decree) of July, 1867, proclaimed the creation of a new district, Turkestan, to be under the rule of a governor general directly responsible to the War Office with headquarters in newly captured Tashkent.

The first governor general of Russia's new territory, General Konstantin P. Kaufmann, in January, 1868, negotiated with Mozaffar ed-Din a commercial treaty bringing Kokand into close economic relationship with the Russian empire. Kokandia had lost a major portion of its independence. The Bukharans played into St. Petersburg's hands with the proclamation, in April, 1868, of a holy war against Russia. Kaufmann promptly took the field and defeated the main Bukharan force in a battle fought at Zara-bulak. He went on to occupy Samarkand in May, and on June 30 there was signed a treaty of peace by which Bukhara ceded to Russia the Zerafshan valley and the fortress Katti-Kurgan. The document also granted to Russian subjects the long-sought freedom of trade, and Bukhara was caused to pay an indemnity. Bukhara clearly retained a nominal independence only by Russian sufferance. In 1882, St. Petersburg appointed an official resident to Bukhara, and the emirate was thus brought even more closely under the political supervision of Russian-controlled Turkestan.

By this time, Khiva had also become a target for new Russian moves. The khanate was flanked by the founding of Krasnovodsk on the Caspian shore in 1869. Prince Gorchakov informed the British envoy at Moscow that the projected base was to be only a factory, not properly to be termed a fort, although necessarily protected by a small military force. It had the commercial aim of providing a shorter caravan route to Central Asia, with increased protection against the predatory actions of the Turkomans.[8]

In 1873, however, after careful preparation, General Kaufmann launched an offensive against Khiva from three different bases—Tashkent, Chkalov, and Krasnovodsk. Khiva fell almost without resistance, and the Khivan khan, Seid Mohammed Rakhim Kuli, on August 24, 1873, acknowledged Russian suzerainty. He was forced at the same time to cede title to all territory on the right bank of the Amu-Darya. That territory was annexed to Turkestan, under the Russian governor general. Khiva was also forced to engage itself to pay, over nineteen years, an indemnity of 2.2 million rubles to defray the cost of the Russian expedition.

Russia's striking advances since 1860, viewed against the background of previous gestures in the direction of India, had inevitably heightened the suspicions and increased the alarm of the British. In 1869, Lord Clarendon, the British foreign secretary, initiated negotiations designed to achieve an understanding regarding Russian intentions and proposed that some territory located between the Russian and British spheres should be viewed as neutral ground. It was Prince Gorchakov's suggestion that Afghanistan should constitute that neutral buffer, but Lord Clarendon's counterproposal would have drawn the line at the Amu-Darya (Oxus). This exchange resulted in no agreement,[9] and the matter rested with Gorchakov's assurance that Russia had no designs on Afghanistan.

In the light of the Russian conquest of Khiva, the new British foreign secretary, Earl Granville, in January, 1874, again moved to avoid a clash of Russian and British interests in Southwest Asia. He instructed the British ambassador at St. Petersburg, Lord Loftus, to bring to the attention of the Russian government the concern of the emir of Afghanistan over the report that Russia was planning to send an expedition against Merv and the Turkoman tribes of that region. Lord Loftus was to inform Gorchakov that the British government "think it right to state candidly and at once that the independence of Afghanistan is regarded by them as a matter of great importance to the welfare and security of British India." Furthermore, dangers might arise if Turkoman tribes were to be driven into the neighborhood of Herat, "now or hereafter," by Russian military operations.[10]

Gorchakov in reply said that he believed the understanding between Russia and Britain with regard to the matter in point was complete and observed that he had reiterated to Loftus "the positive assurance that the Imperial Cabinet persists in considering Afghanistan as entirely outside its sphere of activity."[11] Gorchakov referred to "l'oeuvre civilisatrice" of the British and Russian empires and said, with respect to Kabul's apprehensions, that Russia had no intention of undertaking an expedition against the Turkomans, but if those turbulent tribes committed acts of aggression or brigandage against Russia, "force was at hand for their chastisement."

Khudayar Khan was as usual the target of domestic intrigues and in 1875 was forced from power in favor of his son, Nasridden Bek. Kokand now in turn declared a holy war against the Russians. Kaufmann again took up arms against the dissidents, and the Russian forces reduced the fortress of Makhram and occupied Kokand at the end of August. An agreement in September provided for peace at the cost of Kokand's independence, but Kokandian dissidents renewed the struggle early the following year. Their campaign was a vain effort. Russian forces again occupied Kokand and Andijan, and the victors abolished the Kokand khanate, which on March 3, 1876, was transformed into Fergana province and annexed to Russia as a part of the Turkestan governor-generalship. Mikhail D. Skobelev, who had won promotion to the rank of major general by distinguished performance in the campaigns against Khiva and Kokand, became Fergana's first military governor. China, Kokand's nominal suzerain, seems not to have protested the Russian move. At that moment of history, it had effectively lost control of the Western Region.

Soon after taking up his new post, Skobelev proposed to Kaufmann a project for the invasion of India through the combined use of military and political measures. Afghanistan would constitute a critical arena. In April, 1877, however, Russia became involved in a new war with Turkey, and Skobelev was called into service in that field instead. Britain was again backing Turkey, and after the Russian armies had captured Kars and stood outside the gates of Constantinople, peaceful relations between Russia and Britain hung by a thread. The British fleet intervened by entering the Dardanelles in February, 1878. Never since the Crimean War had the Eastern Question taken on so menacing an aspect, but on March 3 the Russo-Turkish War ended with the signature of the Treaty of San Stefano, highly favorable to Russia, and the main danger had passed.

On June 13, the Congress of Berlin convened under Prince Bismarck to revise the March treaty. On the same day a Russian mission under Stoliev set out from Samarkand for Kabul. Emir Sher Ali Khan entertained the Russians in friendly fashion, and refused to receive a British mission. In November, after delivering an ultimatum, British forces invaded, and on December 13 Sher Ali Khan fled from Kabul together with the Russian mission. The Russian military force, which according to the Skobelev plan should have taken the field, was mobilized but did not march. The value of the repeated Russian assurances of disinterest in Afghanistan had been called into question.

The Turkomans were actually next on the Russian list for subjugation. They were natural warriors, were protected by the inhospitable Kara Kum (Black Desert), and proved a tough foe. The war with Turkey being over, however, Skobelev returned to Turkestan to take charge of the campaign against the obdurate Turkomans. He reduced the Geok Tepe fortifications in January, 1881, and put all the occupants of the place, some 8,000 men, women, and children, to the sword. He was relieved of his command and recalled. The Russian forces under Aleksei N. Kuropatkin, who had won high repute as Skobelev's chief of staff in the war against Turkey, went on to capture Ashkhabad.

After the battle of Geok Tepe, the Turkoman chieftains came to the conclusion that further resistance to Russia would be fruitless, and in March 1881 they declared their submission. Three years later to the month, Russian forces occupied Merv without a fight, and St. Petersburg proclaimed annexation of the oasis to the empire. The Turkoman lands, now designated as the Trans-Caspian oblast, became a part of Russian Turkestan. British alarm regarding the Russian imperial expansion now reached its peak, and again there was talk of war. The situation was further aggravated when, in 1885, the Russians took vigorous action to counter Afghan aggressiveness and occupied an Afghan border town. There had, however, already been agreement in 1884 to have an Anglo-Russian commission demarcate the northern Afghan border, and diplomacy won the day. The commission's work was completed in 1886, and a final agreement on the matter was reached between Britain and Russia at St. Petersburg the following year. This sufficed to calm British fears of further Russian advances against ill-defined frontiers and amorphous Central Asian principalities, and quiet reigned.

By the efforts of men like Kaufmann, Skobelev, and Kuropatkin, Russia had gained, in Central Asia, a vast territory, occupied by a population of some 7 million. Its Central Asian frontiers had at last been secured against the unruly nomads who had long harassed Russian merchant caravans. According to a Russian historian, Russia had lost only some 400 dead and 1,600 wounded in the campaigns of 1847–1873 that had won so great a territorial prize.[12] The figures seem possibly suspect. The casualties suffered by the Central Asian armies were in any event doubtless much greater than the Russian, and the Asian peoples involved had moreover lost their independence. The Great Game between Britain and Russia had been won, so far as Central Asia was concerned, by Russia; now, the Russian empire abutted directly upon the Manchu empire — already sinking in decline. In Dzungaria and Eastern Turkestan, even as in western Central Asia, there had been critical developments over the decades.

7 CONFRONTATION IN CENTRAL ASIA, MID-NINETEENTH CENTURY

WITH CH'IEN-LUNG'S suppression of the revolt at Uch-Turfan in 1765 and the return of the Torguts to Dzungaria in 1771, the Manchu rule over the Western Region had been further consolidated. The Manchu domain now included all of Central Asia as far as the Pamirs on the south and Issyk-Kul on the west. It reached into Bukhtarma on the north, but only in a kind of condominium with the border oblasts of Russian Siberia. Ch'ien-lung's ambitions with regard to Western Turkestan seem never to have revived after he was turned back from his attempted conquest of that region in 1763.

Repercussions of Muslim unrest both to the east and the west, however, were to upset the fragile stability and bring new changes in the balance of power between the Manchus, Russians, and British in the mid-nineteenth century. There were Turki revolts against the Manchu authority, notably the "Uprising of the Seven Khojas" in 1847. For a time, the incompetence and petty political jealousies of the rebels served the Manchu cause, but a fresh occasion for revolt against oppressive rule occurred. The T'aip'ing Rebellion in 1855 sparked an insurgency of Muslims in Yunnan Province. In 1861, Muslim Dungans in Kansu also rose, and the movement then spread to Shensi. Rebel emissaries plotted with their coreligionists in Urumchi, and in the summer of 1863 the Urumchi Dungans staged a surprise uprising in which they gave quarter only to those who accepted Islam. They captured the citadel with little resistance from the Manchu garrison and in one day's action killed thousands.[1] A Dungan sultanate was then set up in Urumchi.

The revolt spread farther west still. In the summer of 1864 a combined Dungan-Taranchi force took the Kuldja citadel, burned most of the town, and killed all the Manchus. The last Manchu stronghold in Ili fell to the Dungans in 1866. By a Chinese account, only 10 to 20 percent of the local Manchu and Chinese populations survived the rebel victory.

The political situation had in the meantime become more complicated for the Dungans by the arrival of Yakub Beg and Buzurg Khan in Kashgaria in January, 1865, and their entry into the conflict at the head of a force of native Kokandi. Buzurg Khan took over the reins of power. Yakub Beg won initial successes in the field *against the Kirgizi* and captured Kashgar and Maralbashi. Timeserving leaders joined his colors, more Kokandi arrived to enter the camp of the man on whom fortune seemed to be smiling, and for the first time Buzurg Khan's new government commanded a truly respectable military force.

Buzurg Khan, not content to witness the growth of Yakub Beg's power, had begun to maneuver to rid himself of that potential rival. Baturbashi Yakub before long put Buzurg in a state of honorable surveillance at Kashgar. In 1868, however, Yakub discovered that Buzurg was plotting his death, whereupon he suggested that the sometime ruler would be well-advised to make a pilgrimage to Mecca. The more or less devout Buzurg Khan wisely made the trip and was finally able to return to Kokand. He had played his part in history by acting as the instrument for Yakub Beg's appearance on the political stage of Eastern Turkestan. There Yakub now stood preeminent. In the meantime dissensions had arisen between the Dungans and their Taranchi allies in the Ili region, and as early as the spring of 1867 Yakub Beg launched a campaign against his fellow religionists and took the Dungan strongpoints of Aksu and Kucha.

Yakub continued his drive against the declining Dungan power, and in 1872 the campaign was brought to an end with the shattering of the Dungan military strength at Urumchi and annihilation of the sultanate which had functioned as the center of Dungan political authority. Yakub Beg had achieved his ambition. The cost, however, had to be counted in the fundamental weakening of potential support for his rule.

While wrestling with problems of domestic politics and organization, Yakub also found himself involved with foreign powers. The conflict between the Dungans and the Taranchis in the Ili valley had given rise to problems between Russia and China—and between Russia and Yakub. Russian expansion eastward into Western Turkestan, facilitated by the progressive weakening of the Kokand khanate, had been temporarily halted to permit consolidation of the territorial gains. Both Russia and Britain, however, were concerned with the situation in Eastern Turkestan and Dzungaria, for the area seemed to both powers to constitute a buffer region between the growing Russian power in Central Asia and the recently strengthened British authority in India.

The Russians appreciated that Muslim successes in Eastern Turkestan were stimulating a feeling of rebellion among the followers of Islam over whom Russia had recently established control, with the turbulent Kirgizi already manifesting signs of restlessness. The British felt that the situation offered opportunity for an ambitious Russia to resume its eastward advance and to pose a potential threat to the British rule in India. Both governments, therefore, fearful of each other, at first acted to support the Manchu authority in Central Asia, even as foreign governments in China Proper had helped the shaky dynasty in its struggle with the T'aip'ing rebels a short time before. Yakub by this time judged that his domestic authority was sufficiently well established to warrant bargaining with his neighbors for official recognition of his position. In the natural course of events, such recognition would bring him needed additional support.

Yakub chose his nephew, Seyyid Yakub Khan, better known as Hadji Torah, to make the projected diplomatic effort. The scope of Hadji Torah's activities was commensurate with the breadth of Yakub's ambitions. He visited St. Petersburg, Constantinople, Calcutta, and London in service of Yakub's plan to join the international community of independent nations. The success of his missions was varied and came slowly, but the gain in the end was inconsiderable only by reason of the general debacle which finally overtook the government he represented.

The Russian government had in 1858 found it requisite, in view of the unfavorable effects of the uninterrupted disorders in Eastern Turkestan upon the subjects of the tsar, to send an envoy to Kashgar to obtain firsthand information of conditions. The governor general of Western Siberia selected for the mission the aristocratic Kazakh officer Chokan Chingisovich Valikhanov and charged him with the additional task of carrying out a survey for a commercial route to that part of Central Asia. Valikhanov left Semipalatinsk in June and reached Kashgar only in October. He remained there for several months, arriving at Verny on his return journey in April, 1859. (Valikhanov went on to win fame as Central Asian scholar – and liberal.) In the next nine years two other envoys made similar journeys designed to keep St. Petersburg informed of the course of events, but evidently without undertaking formal negotiations whether with Yakub or his predecessors.

The British were naturally interested in ascertaining the lay of the land and first sent T. Douglas Forsyth to see Yakub Beg – but Yakub refused to receive him. In 1869, however, Robert Shaw visited the haughty Central Asian potentate. The attitude of Yakub Beg with respect to Britain has been described as follows: "All that the sovereign of the Six Cities [Alty-shar – Eastern Turkestan] understood by diplomatic relations with England was, in the first place, money and arms; in the second place, money and arms; and in the third place, money and arms. Beyond these his mind never reached."[2] Excepting, that Yakub doubtless considered playing Britain and Russia against each other for his own advantage. But Shaw was in any event favorably impressed and after his trip wrote to Forsyth to report that Yakub Beg had erected "almost an empire" and commanded wide popularity in Kashgaria, while Qomul (Hami), Urumchi, and Ili were tributary to his rule.[3]

The care with which Russia approached the matter was indicated in exchanges between Russian and British diplomats. In November, 1869, the British ambassador to Russia, Sir A. Buchanan, informed his government that Gorchakov had told him that Forsyth, in conversation a few days earlier, had suggested that it seemed expedient to establish relations with Yakub Beg's government at Kashgar. Gorchakov's position was, however, that although Yakub Beg might have established a de facto government, Russia was not in a position, given its treaty relations with China, to enter upon diplomatic relations with an insurgent regime. Forsyth, in a letter to Buchanan, reported with respect to the same conversation that "Eastern Turkestan the Prince Gorchakov considered to belong to China, and could only be dealt with by Russia through the Chinese." [4]

St. Petersburg, however, did not remain indifferent to the de facto situation. In 1870, the Russians sought by word conveyed indirectly through Khudayar Khan of Kokand to get Yakub Beg to take the initiative for conclusion of a commercial treaty. They were somewhat nonplussed by receiving from Yakub the bold reply that it was useless for them to use Khudayar as an intermediary; if they wished an alliance with him, Yakub, they might send emissaries to negotiate with him directly for commercial and other treaties.

St. Petersburg did not immediately respond to the invitation. In the first several years of turmoil in Eastern Turkestan, Russia had generally maintained a hands-off attitude. That position had been made requisite by the circumstance that, from 1866 to 1871 in particular, Russia had been struggling to consolidate its own control over Bukhara, Kokand, and Khiva. Yakub, just as he had blinded himself to the basic fact that the Dungans were fellow Muslims with a common enemy in China, similarly took no overt notice of the subjugation of the Turki Muslims of Western Turkestan by Russia and remained neutral with respect to the conflict. His attitude of benevolent neutrality won for him no active support from the side of Russia, which (regardless of British suspicions) for the time being had no special interest in Kashgaria. The interest of the Russians was limited mainly to Dzungaria, "with which they were intimately connected by trade and political association, stretching back for almost a century." [5]

It was only when events affected their interests in Ili and also threatened indirectly to introduce an element of instability into their newly established authority in bordering areas by fomenting unrest among the Kirgizi that the Russians intervened. Admittedly they acted with an eye on their competitor in Asia, Great Britain. The Russian point of view of that time has been reflected even in later accounts: "Behind the back of Yakub Beg stood England, directing him against Russia." [6] When the Kirgizi, evidently stirred into movement by the machinations of emissaries of Yakub Beg and Akhmet-Jan Khoja, began to create disorders of dangerous dimensions, St. Petersburg considered that the time for action had come.

The Russian government first offered to aid the Manchus in bringing order once more into the affairs of Dzungaria and Eastern Turkestan. The Manchu Court rejected the proposal on the grounds that it did not feel itself in a sufficiently strong position to undertake the pacification of the pre-T'ien Shan region. To guard against the possible uprising of the Muslim population in the Russian borderlands, therefore, the Russian Throne charged Major General Kolpakovski with occupation of the Ili region. Kolpakovski's forces entered Kuldja in July, 1871. There is one report indicating that the Russians sent troops into Alty-shar as well,[7] but no confirmation of this appears in other sources. Upon occupation of Ili, Russia promised that the territory would be returned to the Manchu government as soon as the latter was able to restore peace and order in Dzungaria.

The Russians were thus in Ili when St. Petersburg dispatched Baron Aleksandr V. Kaulbars as envoy to Yakub Beg, then at the height of his power. Kaulbars left Kuldja for Kashgar in May, 1872, to negotiate a commercial treaty with Yakub—if such an agreement seemed desirable in the light of existing conditions. The Kaulbars mission was undoubtedly motivated by the Russian desire to forestall anticipated British moves in the same direction.

Baron Kaulbars' secondary mission was to obtain reliable information on the extent and stability of Yakub Beg's power and its significance for the Russian position in Central Asia. It was clearly to the benefit of Yakub that he should sign an agreement with St. Petersburg if at all possible, and the Russians had themselves provided the opportunity. Kaulbars succeeded in signing a commercial treaty on June 8, 1872. Subsequent events proved, however, that Yakub had been successful in deceiving the Russian representative, and perhaps even himself, regarding his real strength. Kaulbars' error of judgment rendered sterile his accomplishment of obtaining a treaty with an autocrat soon to pass from the stage of history.

Yakub achieved another tour de force in the same year. After signing with Kaulbars a treaty which, by the Russian concept, might well have been expected to bring Yakub closer to the Russian authority in Western Turkestan, Yakub concluded negotiations that he had been carrying on secretly with Constantinople through the medium of Hadji Torah. By this new agreement, Yakub acknowledged the suzerainty of the Porte, which in return designated Yakub emir of Kashgaria. Kaufmann, then in Tashkent, wished to take armed action against Yakub after this development, but was refused permission by St. Petersburg.

It was in 1873, when Hadji Torah made a visit to St. Petersburg, that the Russians undertook their great expedition of conquest against Khiva. Yakub again remained a passive spectator of the defeat of his fellow religionists. In the following year, the victorious Russians entered upon fresh negotiations with Yakub with the aim of effecting the removal of restrictions on Russian trade with Eastern Turkestan. The discussions bore no fruit, and in the autumn of 1874 the Russians massed 20,000 troops on the border of Eastern Turkestan. Yakub Beg was probably saved from chastisement, and Eastern Turkestan possibly kept from going the way of Western Turkestan, only by virtue of the fortuitous circumstance that rebellion in Kokand caused General Kaufmann to divert his military strength to another endeavor.

Yakub Beg had in the meantime been negotiating with the British. The Englishmen Robert Shaw and Hayward arrived in Eastern Turkestan about the same time, in December, 1868. They were not, however, on the same mission, Hayward going to Yarkand and Shaw proceeding to Kashgar. Shaw met with Yakub Beg for his first official interview on January 12, 1869, and expressed the British pleasure at the establishment of Yakub's rule in Turkestan in place of the Chinese (Manchu) rule. In another interview in April, Yakub asked whether he should send an envoy to India, and Shaw replied that it was most desirable that he do so. Yakub proposed at that time to send his envoy in the company of Shaw, with a letter to be delivered to the viceroy of India for forwarding to Queen Victoria. In any event, when Shaw left shortly afterward, the Kashgarian envoy did not accompany him. Hayward, however, finally released from the close confines of Central Asian hospitality, was able to return to India together with Shaw.

During the first part of his trip to Kashgar, Shaw had been informed by the *mahrambashi* (chamberlain) that in the Kokandi books it was prophesied that Russia would conquer all Turkestan and then perish. The British in India were not desirous that the first part of the prophecy, at least, should come true, and in 1870

Shaw, Hayward, and T. Douglas Forsyth made a second trip to Kashgar. Forsyth, commissioner of the Trans-Sutlej States, was a strong advocate of the development of British intercourse with Central Asia.

When they arrived in Kashgar, Yakub was personally engaged in pursuit of his campaigns against the Dungans in the north. In September Forsyth left Yarkand en route back to India, Shaw followed him shortly afterward, but Hayward was assassinated. Yakub's representative, Ihrar Khan, in turn made the trip to India in 1871, but failed in his mission of establishing something in the nature of diplomatic relations. The Baron Kaulbars treaty of 1872 led to a revival of the British desire to gain a position that would enable them to exert an influence on the destinies of the new Central Asian state, and in the following year Forsyth therefore made another trip to Kashgaria, as representative of the Indian government.

On February 2, 1874, at Kashgar, Forsyth signed on behalf of the government of India a treaty with Yakub Beg to govern trade, travel, residence, and legal jurisdiction over British subjects in "the dominions of His Highness the Ameer." The Forsyth mission then returned home, and the agreement was duly ratified by the Indian government. Yakub evidently considered that he had formed a new friendship on which he could rely for support against Russia. As events were to demonstrate, he was mistaken: the British, having been misled as were the Russians in their estimate of the probable durability of Yakub's regime, quickly saw their mistake and refused to come forward in support of a lost cause. Yakub Beg, who had often changed sides in a battle when he thought it to his advantage, was hardly in a position to complain of bad faith.

Nemesis was now stalking Yakub Beg. In 1868, after a long series of victories over first the T'aip'ing and then the Nienfei rebels, the able Chinese general Tso Tsung-t'ang was charged with suppression of the Muslim rebellion in China's Northwest. Proceeding as carefully as he had campaigned against the T'aip'ings, Tso in 1873 brought the long Dungan revolt in China Proper to a bloody end. In October of the following year, he was put in charge of the provisioning and transport of forces involved in the expedition for the reconquest of the Western Region. He met opposition, but in April, 1875, was found stoutly arguing that failure to recover that territory would jeopardize the hold on Outer Mongolia, which was vital for Peking's own safety. Tso was soon afterward put in charge of the entire military campaign.

In June, 1875, an official Russian five-man mission, traveling via Peking, reached Lanchow and met with Tso Tsung-t'ang. The Russians assured Tso that Ili would be handed back to China once the Manchu authority had recovered Urumchi and Manas. They also contracted for the delivery of a large quantity of Siberian grain at Kuchengtzu, on the T'ien Shan North Road, for use of the expedition. Tso continued his preparations and, against the opposition of the influential Li Hung-chang, persuaded the Throne to borrow 10 million taels from foreign banks in Shanghai for the financing of the undertaking. The loan was floated early in 1876, and Tso was ready.

True to the contract, Russia by April, 1876, delivered 40,000 piculs (something over 1,000 metric tons) of grain for Tso's expeditionary force. In August, the Manchu forces reached Urumchi, breached the walls, and massacred the garrison. They repeated the same process the following month at Manas. By the end of the year, most of the armed rebel strength in Dzungaria had either fallen on the field of battle or, subsequent to the Manchu victory, had succumbed to the sword of the executioner.

Yakub at that time had an army of 15,000 to 17,000 men, widely scattered throughout Kashgaria, and in addition commanded the halfhearted allegiance of about 10,000 Dungans. Most of his troops still carried bows and arrows, or at best matchlock or flintlock rifles, with only a small percentage equipped with modern weapons. He concentrated such forces as he could muster in the vicinity of Turfan. The Manchus had about 50,000 men at their headquarters at Kuchengtzu and 10,000 at Hami. In March, 1877, they advanced on Turfan and inflicted a severe defeat on Yakub's army. The retreating Muslims were closely pursued and were defeated again at Toksun and Karashar. Yakub probably lost 20,000 men in those three battles, and was left with his power broken. He appealed to Russia for aid, but Captain A. N. Kuropatkin (of later Manchurian fame) had made an unfavorable report on his prospects, and the requested assistance was refused. Yakub Beg died at Korla in May, 1877, and the rebel regime he had erected crumbled soon after.

Again internal conflicts, resulting from that parochial political naïveté which led to the neglect of mutual nationalistic interests, had brought the peoples of Eastern Turkestan under the control of an alien power. The struggle that ensued had been only the latest in a series of myopic political errors by the Muslim Turki. Those errors, resulting in the division instead of unification of Turanian strength against the common foe, had given the Manchus an easy victory.[8] There remained the task of restoring Manchu rule over the entire Western Region. By Kolpakovski's pertinent proclamation, the Ili valley (designated as "Dzungaria" in the original) would have been annexed by Russia in perpetuity. By the promise made by St. Petersburg to the Manchus, on the other hand, the territory was to be restored to the Chinese empire at such time as peace and order should again prevail. That condition had at last been fulfilled.

The Manchu Throne, for the first time since the eighteenth century, now sent an envoy to St. Petersburg. The emissary was the Manchu Ch'ung-hou, who from 1861 to 1870 had been superintendent of trade for North China and after the 1870 "Tientsin Massacre" had carried China's official apologies to France. Ch'ung-hou arrived in St. Petersburg at the end of December, 1878, and after long negotiations there was finally signed on October 2, 1879, at Livadia (the royal family's Black Sea resort) a treaty designed to effect an appropriate readjustment of the situation with respect to the Western Region. The Treaty of Livadia provided for the cession to Russia of the western (and richer) part of Chinese Ili and of the Muzart Pass, for payment to Russia of an indemnity for the costs of its military occupation, and (in a separate set of trade regulations comprising seventeen articles) for important trade concessions.

Ch'ung-hou had proved an inept diplomat. Upon his return home, he met strong opposition both in the Court and in the bureaucracy for having signed a treaty which gave up valuable territory and made broad trade concessions. He was removed from his post, imprisoned, and later condemned to decapitation. Tso Tsung-t'ang was among the stalwarts who opposed the treaty. He proposed that he march on St. Petersburg with 2,000 troops and dictate a treaty which would omit Ch'ung-hou's humiliating concessions. Soberer counsels prevailed. Tseng Chi-tse, China's minister to England, was named minister to Russia for the purpose of reopening the matter. Queen Victoria intervened in behalf of Ch'ung-hou, and Tseng recommended that the unfortunate envoy's life be spared. The death sentence was commuted to life imprisonment. (After Ch'ung-hou in 1884 contributed 300,000 taels to the Throne's military budget, he was released, and lived in retirement until his death nine years later.)

Tseng Chi-tse arrived in St. Petersburg at the end of July, 1880, to the accompaniment of suggestions that China was prepared to go to war with Russia. St. Petersburg made warlike moves of its own; but the Congress of Berlin had deprived Russia of much of the gains won from the Turks by the Treaty of San Stefano, and with the Middle Eastern question still far from being settled to the Russian satisfaction, there was little support for the idea of a war with China over territory which, by St. Petersburg's commitment of 1871, should in any event have been returned to China.

After extended negotiations, the Treaty of Livadia was superseded by the Treaty of St. Petersburg, signed on February 24, 1881. By this new agreement, China recovered most of the lost Ili territory, including the Tekkes valley, with the Khorgos River to constitute the common boundary. Control of strategic passes between Kashgaria and Kokandia went to China, excepting that the border post of Irkeshtam was assigned to Russia. The opening of additional Russian consulates in China was authorized, and the indemnity due Russia for expenses of the occupation was increased from 5 million to 9 million rubles. Nevertheless, there was a net territorial gain to Russia in the western sector of the Ili region, the "indemnity" (in circumstances where there had been no war) was substantial, and the Russians had won additional trade facilities. In the end, the Russian empire was still the winner.

Tso Tsung-t'ang remained discontented with the settlement. He believed that China, with its millions, was omnipotent in the international sphere, and he recommended to the Throne to "make an end, once and for all, of all the obnoxious foreigners, whose presence creates grave difficulties and dangers for the Empire." [9] But the Manchu Court generally viewed the partial restitution of territory as a victory won by Peking's intimidation of St. Petersburg. Indeed Tseng Chi-tse's achievement was no mean diplomatic feat, as most European capitals agreed.

There was an epilogue to the Manchu reconquest of the Western Region. Tso Tsung-t'ang's victory had been followed by the customary measures of "pacification." Death, accompanied often enough by tortures considered befitting the crime, was the usual fate of those deemed to have been guilty of rebellion. The Manchus energetically pursued the Eastern Asian tactics of fomenting tribal antagonisms, the easier to rule the various mutually jealous tribes, and "tens of thousands" of Dungans and Uighurs were killed. Evacuation of Russian troops did not begin until the spring of 1882, and was completed only in 1883. A Russian report gave a crystal-clear indication of the forebodings of the local population regarding the turn of events: "In order to understand fully the alarm and trepidation which seized the population of the whole borderland, it is enough to say that, simultaneously with the withdrawal of the Russian troops from Kuldja, completely, almost to a man, the population of the Kuldja region emigrated past Khorgos." [10]

This was the culmination of a movement that had been in course for some time. During the rebellion itself, according to a contemporary note in a Russian periodical, Tungusi, Sibos, and Solons had been the first to flee across the border for refuge; in 1863, over 10,000 Torguts arrived in Russia; in the one month of August, 1866, 13,861 Torguts, Sibos, and Solons reached Russian territory from the troubled land across the frontier. [11] Then came Tso Tsung-t'ang, who, as Chao-hui before him, followed the tactic of extermination of those categorized as "rebels" and converted to wasteland settlements through which he passed. Thousands of Dungans then fled into Russia, and Governor General Kaufmann, apprehensive that such a massacre would adversely affect Russian trade with Western China, protested Tso's actions. [12] Now, with yet another turn of fortune's wheel, there was a still greater influx of refugees from the Manchu empire. The 1881 agreement permitted most of the Uighur and Dungan refugees to remain in Russia. They were given land and took up residence in Semireche.

In November, 1884, the Manchu Throne welded Eastern Turkestan and the Dzungarian Basin into a single administrative unit, Sinkiang (New Borderland) Province. The Ili, Tarbagatai, and Altai regions were not included. The political status of the territory which had been brought under challenge by Yakub Beg was thus defined for some time to come. The bloodletting to which it had been subjected kept it quiet for many years.

There was one faint revival of the Anglo-Russian contest in Central Asia in the early 1890s. The 1887 agreement had fixed the Afghan border only as far east as Zor Kul, with the Pamir sector, bordering on China, left undefined. Ch'ien-lung's forces had penetrated the Pamirs in the eighteenth century, but then withdrew, and did not put in another appearance in that region until the latter part of the nineteenth century. Nominally, the eastern Pamirs were under the rule of Kokand, but when Russia conquered the khanate in 1876 it failed, through apparent oversight, to extend its sovereignty effectively into the Pamirs, which continued torn by the feuds of the warlike Tadjiks. The demarcation of the frontier between Fergana oblast (ex-Kokandia) and Sinkiang, as effected by the Sino-Russian protocol of 1884, extended south only as far as Uz-bel Pass, the Pamirs thus by inference not being included in the Russian domain. However, with fresh ventures of Manchu troops into the Pamirs in the 1880s, and Britain's occupation of Hunza in 1891, the Russians took alarm and acted to give effect to their dormant claim. Afghan forces drove out both Manchu and Russian military expeditions in 1892, but a fresh Russian expedition achieved partial success, with the establishment of Russian control to the Sarykol range.[13]

China in 1894 became concerned primarily with Korea and the menacing conflict with Japan, and Li Hung-chang looked to the possibility of employing Russia in support of the Manchu cause. In those circumstances, Peking agreed provisionally to accept the Sarykol range as the de facto boundary, pending final border demarcation. A further agreement in that region followed. Russia the land power and Britain the sea power had seemingly become better acquainted with each other's aims and operating procedures over the years and, when Japan manifested its growing might by going to war with China, St. Petersburg and London reacted to the new challenge by improving upon their understanding in Central Asia. A new border commission was set up, and a settlement of 1895 awarded most of Wakhan, in the southwestern corner of Eastern Turkestan, to the emir of Afghanistan, while Bukhara, Russia's protectorate, received the rest of the disputed territory. The Manchu Throne, with its attention currently concentrated on the disaster of the war with Japan, was not a party to the determination of that one last bit of disputed terrain on its Inner Asian borders.

The last of the Central Asian border issues outstanding between Britain and Russia had been settled. A pair of contemporary English observers of the Asian scene reflected the new British mood. The Crimean campaign of forty-five years earlier, shattering the long-standing Anglo-Russian friendship, had been the "blunder of the century." The Russian advance had been interpreted as a menace to the British position in Asia, with "public opinion goaded to frenzy by such baseless fears." That India should be absorbed by Russia was a dream too wild for even the most aggressive of the tsar's advisers: "Such is the geographical position of the peninsula, that it can be held by no European Power which is not Mistress of the Seas." And finally, what would be the profit to Russia of assuming the responsibility for governing 300 million Asians "whose ignorance of Malthusian doctrines renders them a prey to perennial pestilence and famine?" [14]

The economic factor was at long last also served. There had been a rapid rise in trade between the Western Region and Semireche after signature of the Kuldja treaty in 1851, but with the Dungan uprising commerce had inevitably fallen off. The Russian occupation of the Ili region and overthrow of the Kokand khanate had brought a measure of economic recovery. Now there had been the final restoration of peaceful relations with all Sinkiang and the establishment of Russian consulates in important towns of the new province. Trade in the 1880s surpassed previous records, with manufactured goods occupying an increasingly important place in Russian exports. A firm foundation for regular economic commerce between Sinkiang and Russia's new dominion to the west had been laid, and would be assiduously built upon.

8 FIN DE SIÈCLE IN EAST ASIA

CHASTENED by the events of 1858–1860, China had entered the 1860s with the idea that a "restoration" of the true Confucian order would lead to regeneration of state power. But any urge in the direction of increased political virtue was checked by the advent to power of the narrow-minded, reactionary Empress Dowager Tz'u-hsi, who acted as regent during the minority of her son, the emperor T'ung-chih. Tz'u-hsi proposed neither to undertake domestic change nor to have more dealings with the Occident than necessary. In 1861, a Tsungli Yamen (Office for General Management) was established to replace the Board of Rites and the Li-fan Yuan in the handling of foreign affairs, but a decade later the initial limited willingness to try to adjust to the ways of the world had faded, and there was a regression to old attitudes.

Across the East China Sea, with the Meiji Restoration of 1868, Japan undertook the modernization of its own state system, and with the signature in 1871 of its first treaty with China, a new day began in East Asia. An Asian power had entered the imperial lists. In the 1870s, Japan demonstrated its newborn strength by winning the Ryukyu Islands from China and gaining a Manchu indemnity because of an "incident" on Formosa. The Sino-French war of 1884–1885 confirmed the growing impression that China was inherently weak, and even as the war was being waged Japan launched an initial challenge to Manchu control over Korea, the vassal "Hermit Kingdom."

In Russia, after the abolition of serfdom in 1861, there began a substantial flow of settlers into Siberia. Their movement into the Far East was politically quite as easy as the parallel settlement of the American Far West, for the scattered tribes of Samoyeds, Buryat Mongols, Yakuts, and Tungusi now offered no more impediment to the Russian advance than did the Sioux, Blackfoot, and Navaho to the American. The population of Siberia, estimated at 2,681,000 in 1851, by 1897 grew to 7,788,000. This was little strength with which to oppose China's hundreds of millions – or even Japan's 41.5 million.

Russia was bent, however, on the further development of its Far Eastern empire. In 1891, Tsar Alexander III authorized the construction of a Trans-Siberian Railway, and on May 31 his son Nicholas, who had been wounded shortly before by a would-be assassin in Japan, went through the ceremony of beginning the construction work – at Vladivostok. En route to Japan, the tsarevich had visited China, but was not honored by an invitation to proceed to Peking, and received discourteous treatment at the hands of Governor General Chang Chih-tung in Wuchang. It seems probable that his Far Eastern reception would have left a lasting impression on the young man destined to become tsar.

Following in the footsteps of the United States, Britain, and Germany, Russia in 1886 entered upon treaty relations with Korea. By a decision of an Extraordinary Council of 1888, Russian policy with respect to Korea was fixed in support of the status quo – in the face of what was patently a threat to the existing order. In June, 1894, as tensions built up between China and Japan over developments in Korea, Chihli governor general Li Hung-chang, who wielded major influence in foreign affairs, informed Count Cassini, the Russian minister, that China had categorically rejected a Japanese proposal for the establishment of joint Sino-Japanese control over Korea and would appreciate Russian mediation.

This was only the beginning of the Manchu Court's attempt to mobilize international support against Japan. While Li Hung-chang put his main reliance on the possibility of Russian intervention, the Tsungli Yamen wooed the British. In the end, the British inclined in favor of Tokyo, and the Russians, while presenting so sympathetic a mien to Li that he was convinced as late as July 22 that they would send troops against the Japanese,[1] had definitely decided against becoming involved militarily on

China's behalf. On July 23, Japanese forces occupied Seoul; on August 1, 1894, the Sino-Japanese War formally began. China remained without a champion.

At the beginning of November, as the Japanese advanced against Talien and Lushun on the Liaotung Peninsula, the representatives of Britain, Russia, the United States, Germany, and France were invited to the Tsungli Yamen to receive a formal request for mediation. (A similar request was wired to the Italian representative, then absent from Peking.) Talien fell two days later, and the Lushun fortress surrendered on November 21 without offering serious resistance. Britain had fixed its policy in favor of Japan. The United States refused to participate in joint efforts with respect to the war and inclined more toward Japan than to China. Germany refused support to the Manchu Court. This left Russia and France, who had become allies in March, 1894, to try to stem, or limit, the Japanese advance.

Liu K'un-yi, the powerful governor general at Nanking, memorialized the Throne to propose the strengthening of China's international position by the negotiation of an alliance with Russia, suggesting that certain concessions be made to achieve that end. The Manchu regime was not currently in a position, however, to offer major benefits to Russia in return for its intervention, and the politico-military situation was not in any event conducive to third-power action. An Extraordinary Council of February 1, 1895, at St. Petersburg decided that Russia's strategic aim should be to support the independence of Korea. This shift from the policy position adopted seven years before reflected the changing circumstances. There was reason for Russia to be concerned with Japan's evident aim of obtaining a foothold on the Asian mainland, but there was no prime reason for Russia to go to war for China in circumstances where the Manchu arms were giving a miserable performance on the battlefield.

Manchu military actions were hopelessly ineffective: by land and on the sea, the Japanese smashed the antiquated formations that opposed their advance. In overwhelming China, a nation which then numbered some 400 million, little Japan suffered some 60,000 casualties. Nor was Peking any more successful in enlisting enough foreign support to stave off defeat in the peace negotiations. By the Treaty of Shimonoseki of April, 1895, Peking recognized Korea's independence, ceded Formosa, the Pescadores, and the Liaotung Peninsula to Japan, granted new commercial concessions, accorded Japan the most-favored-nation clause (which Japan had not possessed before), and promised to pay an indemnity of 200 million taels. Among the casualties of the Sino-Japanese War was Li Hung-chang, who lost his high position as governor general of Chihli and was transferred to a sinecure post in the Tsungli Yamen at Peking.

Russia was interested in preventing the dismemberment of China at that juncture and was naturally concerned with any Japanese advance that might seem to offer a potential threat to its own position in Northeast Asia. The powerful minister of finance, Count Sergei Yu. Witte, recorded developments on the Russian scene at this time:

> Emperor Nicholas . . . was anxious to spread Russian influence in the Far East. Not that he had a definite program of conquest. He was merely possessed by an unreasoned desire to seize Far Eastern lands. As for myself, I clearly saw that it was to Russia's best interests to have as its neighbor a strong but passive China, and that therein lay the assurance of Russia's safety in the East. Therefore, it appeared obvious to me that it was imperative not to allow Japan to penetrate into the very heart of China and secure a footing in the Liao-tung peninsula, which to a certain extent occupies a dominating position. Accordingly, I insisted on the necessity of thwarting the execution of the peace treaty between Japan and China. To discuss this matter a conference was called. . . . At this conference I advocated the principle of the integrity of the Chinese Empire. Russia's best interests demanded, I pointed out, that China remain unchanged and that no power be allowed to increase its territorial possessions at China's expense.[2]

The tsar accepted Witte's suggestions, and on April 7 Prince Aleksei Lobanov-Rostovski, newly appointed minister for foreign affairs, instructed the Russian ambassadors in London, Paris, and Berlin to invite the attention of the governments to which they were accredited to the circumstance that Japan's acquisition of Lushun would militate against good relations with China and create a threat to the peace of the Far East. Britain refused to associate itself in an international move of opposition to the treaty, but it was entirely within the imperial reason of things that, six days after signature of the Treaty of Shimonoseki, Russia joined with Germany and France to force Japan to drop the spoils of war, the Liaotung Peninsula. The Russian government advised pointedly in its formal note to Tokyo that "the possession of the Peninsula of Liaotung, claimed by Japan, would be a menace to the Capital of China, would at the same time render illusory the independence of Korea and would henceforth be a perpetual obstacle to the peace of the Far East." [3] Japan loosed its hold, but to compensate for the retrocession of Liaotung, the indemnity China had to pay was correspondingly increased.

With the war over, and China's weakness fully unveiled before the interested world, there soon ensued the struggle for territorial concessions, leaseholds, and "spheres of influence," which came to be called "the Battle for Concessions." St. Petersburg was now committed to playing a major role in that vast competition. Kaiser Wilhelm II favored deeper Russian involvement in Asia, assuming that this would diminish the power that Russia could pose against the German border, would lead Russia into inevitable conflict with Japan, and would, moreover, possibly lead to serious conflict between Russia and Britain.[4] Any or all of those developments would favor the German cause.

Russia's advance was facilitated by Peking's urge to obtain international support — with none but the Russian in sight. The emperor Kuang-hsu in June, 1895, receiving the Russian envoy Count Cassini in audience, pointedly remarked: "We deeply hope that henceforth the relations between the two neighboring empires will take on a most friendly character." [5] Russia in fact early rendered substantial aid to the harassed Manchu regime, confronted with the need to pay a big indemnity to Japan. Working through a Franco-Russian syndicate in which the French financial interest was predominant, in July 1895 it floated on China's behalf and guaranteed a 400 million gold-franc loan, secured on the Chinese Maritime Customs. In December, 1895, there was founded the Russo-Chinese Bank, with capital subscribed by the Russian treasury and (to the extent of 6 million Kuping taels) by China, but with the major share contributed by Russia's ally, France. That bank was authorized to perform various customary banking functions, but its chief missions were to constitute a bank of deposit for payments made against Russian loans to

China and to acquire concessions for the construction of railways and telegraph lines in China.

Given Japan's striking rise to political prominence, the Russians had already begun to formulate new objectives. At the time of the joint Russo-Franco-German démarche against Japan in April, 1895, there had been evolved the entirely logical idea of extending the Trans-Siberian Railway eastward by the short route from Chita across Manchuria to Vladivostok, instead of following the arc of the Amur. Then, in December, 1895, an Extraordinary Council evolved the idea of seeking a warm-water port in either Chinese or Japanese waters – with action however to wait upon favorable circumstances.

Cassini transmitted to the Tsungli Yamen the Russian request for a concession for the projected railway across Manchuria. At this time, however, Peking was following the principle that China should rely on its own resources for the construction of railways, and the response to Cassini was framed accordingly – the while it was indicated that China hoped to obtain the services of engineers, and get rails and other construction materials, from Russia.

Peking was, however, in a poor bargaining position. If the Manchu Court desired to negotiate the projected Sino-Russian alliance, it would be called upon to offer a quid pro quo – since the alliance demonstrably would contribute little to Russia's military strength. Li Hung-chang went to St. Petersburg at the end of April, ostensibly to attend the coronation of Nicholas II, but actually bearing the mission of bringing the desired alliance into being. In the secret negotiations that followed his arrival, there were thus two major issues: first, the mooted alliance, but second, the railway concession desired by the Russians. There was, further, a pecuniary consideration – a promise conveyed by Witte that Li Hung-chang would receive three million rubles for expediting the matter of the railway concession.

On June 3, 1896, at St. Petersburg, Li Hung-chang and Foreign Minister Lobanov-Rostovski signed a secret treaty of alliance, comprising six articles, by which China and Russia bound themselves to support each other militarily in opposition to any aggression by Japan against Russian East Asia, China, or Korea. It was moreover agreed that, in time of war, Russia would enjoy the right to use Chinese ports. Further, it was provided that

Russia might construct a railway across Manchuria. On September 8, at St. Petersburg, Minister Hsu Ching-ch'eng on behalf of Peking signed a contract with Prince Ukhtomski and one Rotshtein, acting in the name of the Russo-Chinese Bank,* for construction of the Chinese Eastern Railway (CER) across Manchuria.⁶ The Russo-Chinese Bank in December set up a joint-stock company to construct and operate the projected railway. By virtue of the contract, that company enjoyed "absolute and exclusive right of administration of its lands." The contract also provided that China might purchase the railway after thirty-six years; if not so redeemed, the railway would revert to China at the end of eighty years without cost.

Li Hung-chang returned home in October, 1896, with, presumably, a sense of mission well accomplished. The June treaty had been ratified a few days before his arrival. He nevertheless received less than a conquering hero's welcome in Peking, and was protected from devastating attack only by the intervention of the empress dowager—who, reputedly, herself acted only for a substantial consideration.

On November 1, 1897, two German missionaries were murdered in Shantung. Kaiser Wilhelm promptly ordered a German squadron to proceed to Kiaochow Bay, which possessed the excellent harbors Kiaochow and Tsingtao. He informed Tsar Nicholas by telegram of November 7 that he proposed to "punish those Chinese."⁷ Nicholas replied immediately, suggesting that the contemplated punitive action might well evoke broader disorders and even increase the gulf between missionaries and the Chinese, but the German squadron was not long in arriving at its destination, and on November 14 German forces occupied the Tsingtao fortress. Li Hung-chang at once went to Russian Minister Pavlov and requested Russia's assistance. It was not forthcoming.

Two years before, Peking had granted permission to Russia to use Kiaochow Bay as a winter station for its Pacific Ocean squadron. The privilege had been little used, and Kaiser Wilhelm in the course of a visit to Nicholas in August, 1897, was assured by the latter that Russia had no interest in acquiring the position, while the new Russian foreign minister, Mikhail N. Muraviev, had gone on to inform the German ambassador that Russia was

---

* Subsequently renamed "Russo-Asiatic Bank."

prepared to have Germany take Kiaochow to avoid its acquisition by Britain.[8] Muraviev now suggested that Russia should in turn occupy the Liaotung Peninsula. Witte protested that such action would violate the principle of China's territorial integrity that had provided the excuse for forcing Japan to withdraw from its claim over the same piece of territory, but War Minister Petr S. Vannovski supported Muraviev. So too did Tsar Nicholas II, and in December, Admiral Fedor V. Dubasov led his squadron into Lushun and announced his intent of wintering there. Witte anticipated that "disastrous consequences" would follow the act,[9] but General A. N. Kuropatkin, who succeeded Vannovski the following month, next submitted the proposition that Russia should demand cession of the entire Liaotung Peninsula.

Kuropatkin at this time nevertheless placed limits on Russian imperial ambitions with respect to China. He was later to cite a report made after becoming minister of war in 1898, in which he considered the position of Manchuria in the context of Northeast Asian affairs:

> What shall we do with it [Manchuria] in the future? To annex it would be very unprofitable, not to mention the fact that seizure of this — one of the most important provinces of China — would forever destroy the ancient peaceful relationship between China and ourselves. It would result in many Manchurians settling in our territory, in the Amur and Ussuri districts, which now are only thinly populated by Russians, and our weak colonies would be swamped by the flowing tide of yellow. Eastern Siberia would become quite un-Russian, and it must be remembered that it is the Russians alone who form, and will form in the future, the reliable element of the population. . . . It would, therefore, be preferable if Manchuria remained an integral part of China. But if we decide against this annexation, we ought undoubtedly to take every means to obtain absolute commercial control, consolidating our position by constructing lines through it, such as the Trans-Baikal–Vladivostok and Port Arthur railways.[10]

Events took on a threatening aspect. In 1897, the Russian Court had sent to Peking a mission headed by Prince Ukhtomski, charged with delivering to Li Hung-chang the first installment of a million rubles – but also with obtaining for Russia the right of constructing a railway from the CER into South Manchuria. The prince was unable to achieve any success whatsoever with respect to the second part of his mission. In March, 1898, however, Germany obtained a ninety-nine-year lease of Kiaochow Bay, mining rights in Shantung, and the usual indemnity. Just three weeks later, Russia forced Peking to grant it a twenty-five-year lease to the Liaotung Peninsula, knocked from the hands of Japan only three years before, with the right of constructing a railway from Harbin to Talien. The following day the Russian representative Pokotilov handed over 500,000 taels to Li Hung-chang as a sign of "gratitude" for the successful outcome of the negotiations and described Li as being very satisfied.[11] But Li's tribulations were not yet ended: later that year, he was first relieved of his post in the Tsungli Yamen, and then sent to supervise conservancy work on the Yellow River. It was only in late 1899 that he was partially rehabilitated by being appointed Liang-Kwang governor general at Canton.

Talien (the Japanese Dairen) now became "Dalny"; Lushun was renamed "Port Arthur." Those were signs of the times.

The Russian actions tended naturally to push Britain and Japan closer together. St. Petersburg realized this and took steps to reach an understanding with Tokyo. A Russo-Japanese treaty (the "Rosen-Nishi agreement") of April 13, 1898, stipulated joint respect for the independence of Korea, with noninterference by either signatory. This went a long way toward delineating Russian and Japanese spheres of influence respectively, given Russia's lease of the Liaotung Peninsula the month before and Japan's concern with Korea. Witte said, in retrospect, that:

> If we had faithfully adhered to the spirit of this agreement, there is no doubt but that more or less permanent peaceful relations would have been established between Japan and Russia. We would have quietly kept the Kwantung [Liaotung] Peninsula while Japan would have completely dominated Korea, and this situation could have lasted indefinitely, without giving occasion to a clash.[12]

The actions of Germany and Russia had, however, inevitably set other forces in motion. Britain demanded, and received, rights of occupation of Weihaiwei for as long as Russia might occupy Port Arthur. France received a ninety-nine-year lease over

Kwangchowwan on the southeast China coast. There was introduced into the picture a new device — "nonalienation" promises by Peking, leading to the delineation of spheres of influence. By the end of the century the southern provinces were regarded as falling within France's sphere of influence, the Yangtze valley and Shansi Province were counted as in Britain's, and Germany claimed dominance in Shantung and the Yellow River valley.

In a communication to Germany, Russia demarcated its sphere of influence as enveloping Manchuria, Chihli Province, and Sinkiang. By an Anglo-Russian agreement of April 28, 1899, however, Russia abandoned its claim to priority of interest in Chihli, while reiterating its claim to a sphere of influence embracing Manchuria, Mongolia, and Sinkiang. It was mutually agreed further that Russia would refrain from seeking railway concessions in the Yangtze valley, and that Britain, for its part, would not lend support to private British railway undertakings north of the Wall.

But not all was at harmony inside China. An attempt in 1898 by Kuang-hsu to effect sweeping reforms for the modernization of China met a calamitous end when Tz'u-hsi by a coup removed the emperor from power and imprisoned him. A year later, reflecting popular distress mixed with antidynastic sentiment, the Boxer movement began. It was soon diverted to antiforeign channels, and from North China spread to Manchuria.

Muraviev at this time worked to bring Russia closer to the Manchu government, but he died suddenly on June 21, 1900. On June 20,[13] the Manchu Court joined cause with the Boxers, declared war on the powers, and ordered the extermination of all foreigners in China.

Russia became engaged against the Boxers on two fronts. In North China it participated in an eight-power expedition of some 20,000 troops who, after some delay incurred by international rivalries but with relatively little difficulty, drove inland from Tientsin to occupy Peking and lift the siege of the beleaguered legations on August 14. Then, in contrast to the actions of Britain, Germany, and France in particular, Russia withdrew its troops and diplomatic personnel to Tientsin in line with Witte's purpose of manifesting friendliness for China. The German soldier who had been named commander in chief of the international force, Marshal Alfred von Waldersee, arrived in North China only in mid-October. In late 1900, when the international force had been built up to some 45,000 men, von Waldersee carried out punitive expeditions against various North China towns. The Russians, however, did not participate, and likewise withheld support from the demand of the other powers for severe punishment of Court officials deemed to bear major responsibility for the direction events had taken in 1899–1900. The empress dowager had fled to Sian, deep in the interior, taking the luckless emperor Kuang-hsu with her. Li Hung-chang, summoned back from his exile in Canton in late August to make peace with the victorious powers, turned toward Russia for support in his arduous task.

Russian Minister Mikhail de Giers in fact acted as a moderating influence at various stages in the negotiations, but there was another struggle in course that had an important bearing on the Russian position: in Manchuria the fighting between the Manchu/Boxer forces and Russian units had taken on aspects not discovered inside the Wall. After the Court's declaration of war in June, Boxers and regular forces alike went into action against Russian railway-construction workers on the Harbin-Dairen railway section. Protected only by weak guard forces, the Russians, after sustaining losses, retreated to the northern part of the Liaotung Peninsula. Behind them, the opposing forces destroyed bridges and tore up the tracks of the newly constructed line.

But the antiforeign forces met a foe possessing a special determination of his own. With the upsurge of the Boxer Rebellion in 1900, Kuropatkin called on Witte, who made note of his colleague's feelings:

> He [Kuropatkin] was beaming with joy. I called his attention to the fact that the insurrection was the result of our seizure of the Kwantung Peninsula. "On my part," he replied, "I am very glad. This will give us an excuse for seizing Manchuria." I was curious to know what my visitor intended to do with Manchuria, once it was occupied. "We will turn Manchuria," he informed me, "into a second Bokhara." [14]

With the attack on the Russian positions, the cautious counsels of Witte no longer governed in the Russian Court. On July 11, he informed the Chinese minister at St. Petersburg, Yang Ju, that it was found necessary to send Russian troops into Manchuria, but that they would be withdrawn when the disturbances ended. The pattern was that of Ili three decades before.

On July 15, regular Manchu forces on the south bank of the Amur suddenly opened fire on the town of Blagoveshchensk, on the Russian side of the river, and the bombardment was stepped up on the following day. With many Chinese and Manchus resident in the town, and lacking a military garrison adequate to meet any sustained enemy attack, the authorities of Blagoveshchensk panicked and caused Chinese and Manchu residents to be rounded up and driven into the Amur — en route back to China. Most of the persons thus harshly "repatriated" naturally drowned. For nineteen days Blagoveshchensk was held under ragged bombardment from the Amur's south bank, but the feared attack never materialized. And at the end of that time the Russians had so reinforced their position that they were prepared to carry the fighting into Manchuria.[15]

The Russians now undertook to establish firm control of the 1,300-mile-long CER. Advancing from the south, a Cossack force had on July 18 reached Harbin to reinforce the small garrison there. Attacking from the west, a Russian detachment took Hailar. On the night of August 1, Russian forces crossed the Amur from the north. They occupied and razed Saghalien and took Aigun. General Pavel K. Rennenkampf at the head of somewhat over 500 men pushed on to occupy Tsitsihar on August 29. The Heilungkiang military governor, Shou Shan, committed suicide, and Lieutenant General K. N. Gribski assumed his functions. In the meantime, there had been trouble with the Boxers at the treaty port of Yingkow, and on August 5 Vice Admiral Evgeni I. Alekseev occupied the town and set up a provisional Russian administration.

By the end of August, the Manchu regime was seeking peace, and most of the fight had gone out of both the Boxers and the Manchurian regulars. Kirin on September 21 surrendered to Rennenkampf without resistance. There were battles at Anshan and Liaoyang at the end of the month, but the Russians, although many times outnumbered, won the victory. On October 1, a small vanguard of Russians by a surprise move took Mukden, Nurhachi's capital. By armed force, Russia had displaced the Manchu governmental structure in Manchuria.

Given what the Russians considered the treachery of the original attacks on their railway-construction men, the destruction of railway installations, and barbarous treatment customarily meted out by the Manchu forces to Russian prisoners, the

military occupation was harsh in its impact on the local population. The Russian army, recorded Witte, "behaved in Manchuria
as in a conquered country, thus preparing the ground for a catastrophe." [16] The Russian action attracted widespread foreign
criticism, inspired in part no doubt by the assumption that St.
Petersburg fully intended to make the occupation lasting.

Against the background of the battle of Manila Bay and the
acquisition of the Philippines, by virtue of which twin facts the
United States became a West Pacific power, Secretary of State
John Hay during the Boxer troubles circulated two notes embody-
ing what came to be known as the Hay Doctrine. By the first, sent
in September, 1899, he proposed that the various powers should
agree to maintain equality of opportunity for the merchants of
all nations within their respective spheres of influence in China;
by the second, sent in early July, 1900, after the Manchu declaration of war, he argued, mildly, for respect for the territorial and
political integrity of China.

Russia, as most of the other recipients, replied in noncommittal fashion: major power plays were already in course. Even
as the international expedition was advancing on Peking, a Japanese suggestion was conveyed informally to the Chinese minister at Tokyo that, if China were to fight Russia to prevent
seizure of the Northeast, Japan would assist with munitions
and military advisers. Li Hung-chang, at Canton, advised against
pursuing such a course. On instructions from Peking, however,
in August, 1900, he twice communicated, through the Chinese
minister at St. Petersburg, a request that Russian forces be withdrawn from Manchuria. The Russian government replied that
first there must be restoration of order and assurance that there
would not be a recurrence of trouble.

On November 9, 1900, [17] a representative of Tseng-ch'i, the
military governor of Fengtien, signed an agreement with Alekseev
that conceded to the Russians broad authority, including the
right to station troops, in the Fengtien military area. When the
contents of the document became known to the foreign powers—
and to the Peking Court—at the beginning of 1901, alarm increased with respect to Russia's intentions. Peking was now
strengthened by the knowledge that Britain and Japan were
intensely interested in the arrangements which might be made
respecting the future of Manchuria. Tokyo in mid-January made
independent representations at St. Petersburg regarding the

Manchurian situation, linking the matter with the question of Korea. In the first part of February various powers, led by Japan, in one manner or another advised China against entering upon new treaty arrangements with an individual power before reaching a general settlement of the Boxer affair with all the powers.

The situation was now roughly similar to that prevailing after Ch'ung-hou's signature of the Treaty of Livadia: discretion dictated that Russia should renounce some of the gains obtained from an inept Manchu representative. A month after receipt of the Japanese representations, Count Vladimir N. Lamsdorff, who had become foreign minister in 1900, presented Yang Ju with a proposed agreement, in twelve articles, to take the place of the Tseng-ch'i–Alekseev treaty. It provided for the eventual restitution of Manchuria to China, with the withdrawal of Russian forces after order might have been restored. There was to be effective demilitarization of the area, however, and China was not to employ the nationals of another power for the training of its military forces in North China and was to arrange with the CER Company for indemnification of losses caused by destruction of the rail lines.

Li Hung-chang was in favor of reaching a settlement with Russia, but strong opposition had now developed in China against the Russian proposals, with the powerful Yangtze valley governors general Liu K'un-yi and Chang Chih-tung playing a leading role. Japan and Britain were kept informed of the course of the negotiations, with the obvious purpose of enlisting their support. Peking refused to agree even to modified, milder proposals. By March, Japan had begun to explore the attitudes which would be assumed by other powers, particularly Britain and Germany, in the event of a war between Japan and Russia. On July 1, Count Lamsdorff in a communication to the Ministry of War set forth the now-cogent reasons for giving up the project for negotiating a separate arrangement prior to a general settlement between China and the powers, and the matter was shelved for the time being.

With the distraction eliminated, the powers went forward to reach a final settlement of the Boxer affair. The Boxer Rebellion was brought to a formal close with the signature on September 7, 1901, of a protocol levying suitable punishments, indemnities, and restrictions on China. The international expeditionary force was to evacuate Peking on September 17, and Chihli Province, with the exception of specified points that the powers might occupy for maintenance of communications between Peking and the sea, by September 22, 1901. There was, naturally, no parallel provision with reference to Russian troops in Manchuria. One month after signature of the protocol, the Imperial Court began its journey from Sian back to the capital. On November 7, long before Tz'u-hsi and Kuang-hsu reached Peking, Li Hung-chang died. His final major service to the Manchu Throne had been the signature, on China's behalf, of the Boxer Protocol.

9 WAR, REVOLUTION, AND IMPERIALISM

WITH THE "CHINA PROBLEM" once more temporarily "settled," the powers were again in a position to devote their prime attention to particular imperial enterprises. The political stage appeared to have been set for a further substantial Russian advance in the Far East, and the imperialist urge was stimulated, at least locally, by fears that the new territories would be engulfed by a Chinese flood. By the end of the nineteenth century Chinese had come to occupy a predominant position in Eastern Siberian trade, and more Chinese were pouring in. At a conference held at Khabarovsk in 1903, a stark picture was painted with reference to the mass immigration:

> Every speech exhibited utter helplessness in resisting the impending storm. Some of the members presented in the darkest colours the future Calamity and insisted on drastic measures. The Chinese should not be allowed to enter the frontiers of Russia, those who had settled down there should be expelled — such was the keynote of the oratory. Those who opposed these opinions produced an even more distressing impression, for they frankly stated that the Chinaman and his cheap labour were indispensable to us, and that without it our Far East would probably die a natural death.[1]

With the ending of the Boxer Rebellion, the most venturesome of Russia's empire-builders pressed to the fore in the Court at St. Petersburg. Some of the more influential figures in that group had become interested in the exploitation of the natural resources of Korea and Manchuria. Involved were the Grand Duke Aleksandr Mikhailovich, Count Illarion I. Vorontsov-Dashkov (who had been an intimate of Alexander III), Captain Aleksandr M. Bezobrazov, Vice Admiral A. M. Abaza, and powerful merchants. They had easy access to the Throne and in due course established a strong influence over Tsar Nicholas. In 1901, having obtained a timber concession from the Korean government, they formed a "Russian Timber-Industry Association" for the exploitation of forest reserves in the Yalu valley. The plan had strong political undertones.

There was, however, a major obstacle to the attainment of Russian ambitions of dominion in that region—the newly fledged Asian power, Japan. Given especially the Russian occupation of Manchuria, Tokyo obviously would not be content to rely upon the toothless Hay Doctrine for the protection of its interests on the continent. Tokyo was confronted with the necessity of choosing strong allies in a situation where political tensions were increasing. Japanese statesmen weighed for some time the relative merits of joining forces with either Russia or Great Britain and actually made a démarche toward Russia. Russia, however, was not inclined toward such an alliance, whereas Britain was. The British in 1898 and 1901 had made proposals to Berlin for an Anglo-German alliance, but Chancellor Prince von Bülow and Foreign Minister Baron von Holstein of Germany had opposed the liaison in the belief that England desired to involve their country in a war with Russia. Germany opted instead for a strong navy and what von Bülow termed "the free hand." For Britain, heavily engaged after May, 1899, in the Boer War, the German position was full of menace.

In the British foreign office's view as set forth in a memorandum of March, 1901,[2] a defeat of Japan by the Franco-Russian combination might bring about such renewal of the understanding between those two powers and Germany as would push Britain to the wall in China, whereas Japan's defeat of Russia would not seriously endanger European interests in the Far East—and would in any event probably not be permanent. The post-Boxer dispute within the Japanese government as to whether it should strive for liaison with Britain or Russia was finally resolved by the intervention of the emperor,[3] in favor of seeking ties with Britain. On January 30, 1902, Japan and Britain entered upon an alliance.

One factor influencing the British decision to enter upon an agreement clearly directed against Russia was the old fear for the security of India; this time, the British perceived a Russian thrust into Tibet, that tremendous massif on India's northern frontier. In the 1890s, British intelligence was aroused by rumors of the presence of Russian travelers in Ladakh. In early October, 1900, the *Journal de St. Petersburg* reported that the tsar had on September 30 received at Livadia an official of the Dalai Lama's government, one "Dorjieff" – a Buryat Mongol named Dorje who had actually been in Tibet since about 1886.

In the summer of 1901, Dorjieff was back in Russia on a second trip. He brought letters from the Dalai Lama, and was again received by Tsar Nicholas. St. Petersburg let it be known that he was only discussing religious matters; Foreign Minister Lamsdorff said that his mission had no political significance whatsoever. Lord Curzon, who had become viceroy of India in 1899, was nevertheless convinced that Russia aimed at establishing its influence over Tibet and designed to make that country into a protectorate within a decade.

In 1902–1903 there were rumors suggesting that Russia and China had reached certain agreements regarding Tibet. In 1903, Curzon sent Francis Younghusband at the head of a small armed force to Kampa Dzong, fifteen miles north of the presumed Tibetan border, for the nominal purpose of discussing boundary and trade problems with the Tibetans – and the representatives of the Manchu government. The end result was an armed invasion, the flight of the Dalai Lama to Urga, and the signature at Lhasa on September 7, 1904, of a British-Tibetan treaty that stipulated, inter alia, that there should be no alienation of Tibetan territory to any foreign power. Britain had thus taken the first steps toward inclusion of Tibet within its own sphere of influence.

In the meantime much bigger developments had occurred in China's Northeast. In a secret communication of March 16, 1901, to the minister of war, Vice Admiral Alekseev had recommended the indefinite occupation of Manchuria, until pacification was fully accomplished. International protests could be generally disregarded. But there was an exception:

The only serious objections against our military occupation can be presented by Japan, who has large commercial interests in Manchuria and, perhaps, will take advantage of this convenient pretext to attain her objectives in regards to Korea. In view of this, we ought to forestall the possibility of active measures on the part of Japan, enter into an agreement with her on the basis of the Korean question, and obtain for ourselves full freedom of action in Manchuria, even [if this has to be done] by means of concessions and temporary compromises.[4]

The Anglo-Japanese alliance confronted Russia with a new and more threatening situation. Responding to political exigencies, St. Petersburg by a new agreement of April 8, 1902, undertook a commitment to Peking to remove Russian troops from Manchuria, by stages, within eighteen months.

Bezobrazov in May, 1903, became state secretary to Tsar Nicholas II. In July, the tsar established the position of "His Majesty's Viceroy for the Far East" and appointed the adventurous but incompetent Vice Admiral Evgeni I. Alekseev, who was Alexander II's natural son, to the post. Significantly, in August Count Witte was removed from his influential position as minister of finance and given the high-sounding but powerless post of president of the council of ministers. Thus his steadying hand was removed from Russia's foreign policy. The "Bezobrazov Clique," as it had come to be called, now played the dominant role in the formulation of Russia's Far Eastern policy. Alekseev sided with Bezobrazov, and Russian plans were pushed forward with rash disregard for either Chinese sovereignty or the implicit warning of the Anglo-Japanese alliance. Russia completed the first stage of troop withdrawal from Manchuria but then delayed the further withdrawals to which it was committed. Beginning in April, 1903, it even sought to wring new concessions from China.

Russia also continued to exert pressure on Korea in contravention of the Rosen-Nishi agreement. In extended negotiations from July, 1903, onward between Tokyo and St. Petersburg regarding such matters of common concern, the Russian side took an aggressive stand. In latter September Baron Roman R. Rosen, the Russian minister to Tokyo, left his post to consult with Admiral Alekseev. He and Alekseev drafted a set of counterproposals, which were duly sanctioned by the tsar, and on October 3 he returned to Tokyo and presented them to Foreign Minister Komura. While outwardly in line with the earlier Rosen-Nishi agreement, there were two striking features: (1) while various limitations were to be imposed on Japan's freedom of action in Korea, Manchuria and its littoral were to be recognized as "in all respects outside her sphere of interest," and (2) that part of Korea lying north of the thirty-ninth Parallel was to be regarded as a neutral zone "into which neither of the Contracting Parties shall introduce troops." [5]

"A well-known Russian officer" having close relations with Alekseev and "in a position to know the real views of the higher Russian authorities with regard to Manchuria, Korea, and Japan" was quoted at the beginning of 1904 to the effect that Russia had no intention of evacuating Manchuria. He elaborated:

> We made certain conditional agreements, it is true, but they were only diplomatic promises, and never really amounted to anything. Our interests in the Far East are too important to be sacrificed at this stage of the proceedings, and we shall stay there, even at the risk of war with Japan. [6]

The Russian Timber-Industry Association had already begun lumbering operations on the Korean side of the Yalu, and in January, 1904, Russian troops arrived on the scene to act as a guard force. The Russo-Japanese negotiations were still in course at this time, and Japan finally proposed on January 13 that it acknowledge that Manchuria was outside its sphere of interest, while Russia should agree to respect China's territorial integrity in Manchuria, and should recognize that Korea and its littoral were outside the Russian sphere of interest—with suppression of the proposal for the establishment of a neutral zone in North Korea. [7] The Russians, torn by divided counsels, showed themselves insensitive to the dangers of their situation: they had not made adequate military dispositions in anticipation of the critical eventuality of war; for another thing, a hundred miles of track of the Trans-Siberian Railway around the tip of Lake Baikal were still uncompleted. Despite Japanese pressure for an early reply, the Russian Court delayed, and Count Lamsdorff as late as January 31 was unable to inform Japanese Minister Kurino when a response might be forthcoming. In a meeting of February 4 at St.

Petersburg, Lamsdorff touched upon the crux of the matter when he volunteered to Kurino the personal opinion that Russia required free passage of the Korea Straits (en route to Port Arthur), and, as Kurino reported the conversation to Komura, "Though Russia is willing to make every possible concession, she does not desire to see Korea utilized for strategic purposes against Russia. . . ." [8] Lamsdorff informed Kurino that the substance of the Russian reply had just been sent to Alekseev for transmittal to Rosen. The Court's communication reached Rosen on February 6, but it was too late: on the same day, Japan broke off diplomatic relations.

St. Petersburg now fully expected that the Japanese would both invade Korea and undertake naval action within twenty-four hours. Late on February 8, in fact, the Russian gunboat *Koreets* issued from Chemulpo harbor to confront a Japanese squadron of six cruisers and eight torpedo-boats,[9] commanded by Admiral Uriu, convoying a troop transport. The *Koreets* fired the first shot of the Russo-Japanese War at the torpedo-boat screen, then retired to the harbor and the protection of the (American-built) cruiser *Varyag*. During the night of February 8, Vice Admiral Togo Heihachiro's main fleet attacked the Russian fleet drawn up in battle array in the roadstead at Port Arthur. On February 9, Uriu summoned the two Russian warships out of Chemulpo harbor (now Inchon). They issued, with bands playing, to meet hopeless odds. The *Varyag* was badly damaged, made it back to harbor, and was there scuttled by its crew; the *Koreets*, with one 6-inch and two 8-inch guns, had escaped shelling by reason of the Japanese concentration on the *Varyag*. It too made it back to harbor, and there the crew blew it up. That same day, Japanese troops from Uriu's convoy occupied Seoul. The talking stage in Russo-Japanese relations was over.

Kuropatkin, now Russian minister of war, proceeded to the field to take command of the Russian armies. But he, who had unsuccessfully opposed the forward policy of the Bezobrazov group in Northeast Asia, now had his cautious strategy undercut by Admiral Alekseev and his powerful friends in Court. The Russian military machine thus operated under various serious handicaps from the beginning.

By a strict interpretation of the provisions of the Li-Lobanov treaty, China was not required to come to the aid of Russia, since there had been no attack on Russian territory, but had Peking desired to join with its ally in overcoming a troublesome potential enemy, an occasion had arisen. Peking did not choose to seize the opportunity. Secretary of State Hay on February 10 instructed the American envoys to Russia and Japan to inform the respective ministers for foreign affairs that the United States earnestly desired that Russia and Japan respect the neutrality of China and that the area of hostilities be localized. This intelligence was communicated to the Peking government, which on February 12 declared its neutrality. Prince Ch'ing noted that it might be difficult to maintain neutrality in the Northeast, but remarked that, regardless of which belligerent won, "The sovereignty of the frontier territory of Manchuria will still revert to China as an independent Government." [10] By somewhat laborious construction on the part of Russia and Japan, it was agreed that the neutrality of China did not preclude the waging of war in Manchuria.[11]

This was not the line of thought followed by Admiral Alekseev. He issued a proclamation ordering Chinese in Manchuria to render all possible aid to the Russian forces; furthermore:

> on this occasion the interests of Russia and China apart
> from Manchuria are indissolubly allied, and . . . the duty
> of China should be to join in attacking the destroyers
> and invaders. But China has announced to me her
> resolve to be neutral and to look on with her hands in
> her sleeves.[12]

It appears that Alekseev went further than expressing his irritation: he was reported to have threatened to exterminate the Chinese population of Manchuria if it were to become hostile.[13] Since various groups of overseas Chinese had earlier begun to agitate in favor of China's joining with Japan in the war on Russia, and Yuan Shih-k'ai, who had succeeded Li Hung-chang as governor general of Chihli and as North China superintendent of trade, was reported about this time to have recommended that China declare war on Russia,[14] Alekseev's action had greater motivation than simple nervousness. Indeed, one of the features of the fighting in Manchuria turned out to be Japan's enlistment of Chinese bandits for irregular warfare against the Russian forces.

As was the intent of the Anglo-Japanese alliance, the support of Russia by potential allies was blocked. President Theodore Roosevelt in a letter of July, 1904, to British secretary of embassy Cecil Spring-Rice at St. Petersburg had stated (for the information of the Russians) that if Germany and France aided Russia, the United States would at once go to the assistance of Japan. Britain gave a similar warning directly to the German government in August.

The Russo-Japanese War was thus pregnant with potential disaster for Russia. Despite competent leadership by individual commanders and heroic fighting by Russian units, the Port Arthur fleet was practically destroyed in August when it left harbor in an attempt to reach Vladivostok; General A. M. Stessel (Stoessel) after a prolonged siege, but while he still commanded strong effectives, munitions, and food supplies, surrendered Port Arthur to the Japanese on January 2, 1905; the Russian armies suffered heavily, although they were not decisively defeated, in the battle of Mukden in March; and then, in the battle of Tsushima on May 27–28, the Russian Second Pacific Ocean Squadron under the command of Admiral Zinovi P. Rozhdestvenski was nearly totally destroyed.

Japan's victories were striking in outward aspect, but they were not decisive, and Japan faced shortages of both finances and manpower. In full appreciation of the possibilities inherent in American sympathy for the Japanese cause, Tokyo in April had approached Roosevelt with a request for good offices. Under American auspices the two countries advanced toward peace in a conference begun at Portsmouth, New Hampshire, in August. Witte negotiated for the Russians, and Baron Komura Jutaro represented Japan. By the Treaty of Portsmouth signed a month later, Russia transferred to Japan its lease over the Liaotung Peninsula and its property rights in the rail line between Changchun and Dairen (thereafter called the South Manchurian Railway), ceded South Sakhalin to Japan, and granted Japan fishing rights along Russian coasts in the Japan, Okhotsk, and Bering seas. It was, moreover, agreed that both Russian and Japanese troops, excepting railway guards, should be evacuated from Manchuria. Not least, Russia acknowledged Japan's paramount interest in Korea. One item required no formal treaty recognition but flowed naturally from Admiral Togo's victories at Port Arthur and in the Tsushima Strait: Russia for the time being no longer counted as a naval power.

There had been a major domestic factor bending the Russian Court toward acceptance of a compromise peace with Japan: labor agitation, peasant riots, and student disorders beginning at the end of the century had combined with popular dissatisfaction regarding the course of the Russo-Japanese War to culminate, almost accidentally, in an outbreak at St. Petersburg in January, 1905, in which the troops, firing upon demonstrators, killed about a thousand people. The 1905 Revolution had started, and it continued to take on added dimensions after the peace talks began and even after they were concluded. A general strike in October affected all Russia, and Nicholas II considered abdication, but was saved once more by Witte, who drafted a manifesto of October 30 promising liberal reforms. Leon Trotsky, vice chairman of a *soviet* (council) of workers' delegates formed in St. Petersburg in October, proclaimed the doctrine of permanent revolution. Vladimir I. Ulyanov (N. Lenin), in exile abroad, evolved his doctrine for the seizure of power but arrived in Russia only in November. In December, Trotsky's soviet of rebels was arrested, an uprising in Moscow was put down by troops, and punitive expeditions in the countryside suppressed any remnant signs of rebellion. The October Manifesto had saved the dynasty, but the reactionaries, strongly supported by the tsarina, gave credit to the application of plain military force.

The 1905 Revolution seemed superficially to have failed. But there was initiated from the top, just as in contemporary China, a program of moderate social reforms, implemented between 1906 and 1911 by the president of the Council of Ministers, Petr A. Stolypin. The seeds of both revolution and reform were thus planted deep in the Russian soil, and some would in time bear fruit. Further, the 1905 Revolution had a major impact abroad and left a lasting imprint in Asia especially. Prior to this event, Russia had been viewed simply as an imperialist power; now it was seen as a nation composed in no small measure of working people and intellectuals opposed to autocracy. The Revolution itself was seen as a new popular challenge to the established order, and those who lived under autocratic rule in the Orient were inspired by the example thus given them. Where the Russian influence in Asia had been mainly military and political, now it began to take on a cultural aspect.

In China, revolutionary thinking now advanced from the embryonic nationalism manifested in the Boxer Rebellion. Some Chinese looked to developments in Russia for lessons that might prove useful in changing China. In Tokyo, in July, 1905, exiled Chinese revolutionaries led by Sun Yat-sen, Huang Hsing, and

THE MANCHU

RUSSIAN AMERICA
1741–1867

Based on Albert Herrmann, in *An Historical Atlas of China*, Norton Ginsburg, general ed. (Chicago, Aldine, 1966), and Allen F. Chew, *An Atlas of Russian History* (New Haven and London, Yale University Press, 1967).

T.R. MILLER

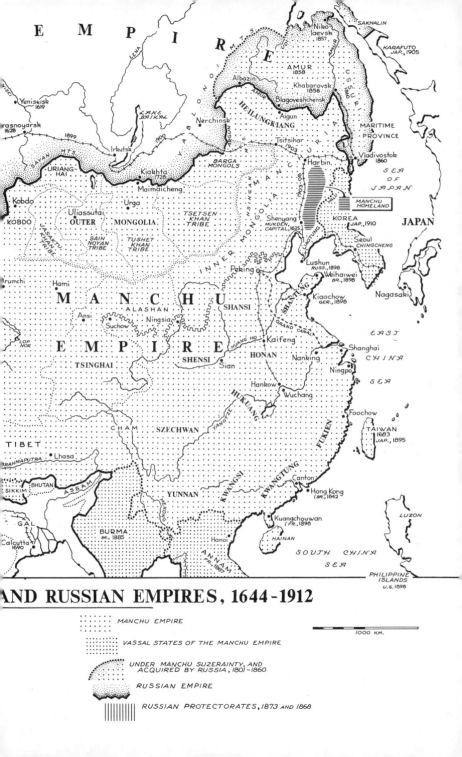

E M P I R E

Yeniseisk
1619

rasnoyarsk
1628

LENA

1899

Irkutsk

Kobdo

KOBDO

LAKE
BAIKAL

Kiakhta
1728

Maimaicheng

Urga

Uliassutai

OUTER   MONGOLIA

SAIN
NOYAN
TRIBE

TUSHET
KHAN
TRIBE

rumchi

Hami

M A N C H U

ALASHAN

Ansi

Suchow

Ningsia

SHANSI

LOP
NOR

E M P I R E

TSINGHAI

SHENSI

Sian

TIBET

Lhasa

BRAHMAPUTRA

SIKKIM   BHUTAN

ASSAM

GAL

Calcutta
1690

BURMA
BR., 1885

SAYAN MTS.

URIANG-
HAI

SASAKTU
KHAN TRIBE

Kobdo

BARGA
MONGOLS

TSETSEN
KHAN
TRIBE

YABLONOI MTS.

Nerchinsk

Albazin

ARGUN

HEILUNGKIANG

Tsitsihar

1903

1901

URIANG

1900

INNER   MONGOLIA

GREAT   KHINGAN MTS.

Peking

Kaifeng

HUANG HO

HONAN

Hankow

Wuchang

HUKUANG

Nanking

Ningpo

YANGTZE

SZECHWAN

CHAM

MEKONG

YUNNAN

KWANGSI

KWANGTUNG

Canton

Hanoi

ANNAM
FR., 1887

Niko
laevsk
1857

SAKHALIN

KARAFUTO
JAP., 1905

AMUR
1858

Khabarovsk
1858

Blagoveshchensk

AMUR

USSURI

MARITIME
PROVINCE

Vladivostok
1860

SEA
OF
JAPAN

Harbin

1900

1905

MANCHU
HOMELAND

Shenyang
MUKDEN,
CAPITAL, 1625

LIAOTUNG

KOREA
JAP., 1910

Seoul   CHINGCHENG

JAPAN

Lushun
RUSS., 1898

Weihaiwei
BR., 1898

SHANTUNG

Kiaochow
GER., 1898

Nagasaki

GRAND CANAL

Shanghai

EAST

CHINA

SEA

Foochow

FUKIEN

TAIWAN
1683
JAP., 1895

Hong Kong
(BR., 1842)

Kuangchowan
(FR., 1898)

HAINAN

LUZON

SOUTH   CHINA

SEA

PHILIPPINE
ISLANDS
U.S. 1898

AND RUSSIAN EMPIRES, 1644-1912

· · · · · · ·   MANCHU EMPIRE

VASSAL STATES OF THE MANCHU EMPIRE

UNDER MANCHU SUZERAINTY, AND
ACQUIRED BY RUSSIA, 1801-1860

RUSSIAN EMPIRE

RUSSIAN PROTECTORATES, 1873 AND 1868

1000 KM.

Ts'ai Yuan-p'ei combined forces to organize the T'ung-meng Hui (Alliance Society), dedicated to overthrow of the Manchu dynasty and formation of a republican government.

The period saw major shifts in the structure of alliances in the international sphere. Britain, in view of Germany's attitude, had reached an understanding with France in the spring of 1904 regarding their respective spheres of influence in Africa. When Germany in the following spring threatened Morocco, in the French sphere of influence, it unwittingly — or as carelessly as Russia had acted with respect to Korea — fostered a new combination of powers against it.

The first Moroccan crisis contributed substantially to the enhancement of Japan's power position in East Asia. Not only was the Anglo-Japanese alliance renewed in 1905, but Britain withdrew warships from the Far East in order to strengthen its position against Germany in European waters. Germany became Britain's prime enemy in Europe and proceeded to confirm itself in that position by ventures into the Middle East (particularly Turkey and Persia). In East Asia the United States, after having sided with Japan against Russia, soon came to be regarded by Japan as its chief competitor for commercial privilege and political power. In practical political fact, Japan's victory in the Russo-Japanese War, and the Treaty of Portsmouth that formalized the victory, had launched the long Japanese struggle with the United States that reached a climax in the Pacific War of 1941–1945.

Change in relations with the United States was not limited to Japan. During the nineteenth century, the friendliness of Russo-American relations had been manifested by the Russian naval demonstration in behalf of the North at the time of the American Civil War, the transfer of title to Alaska, and occasional collaboration with respect to China and Japan. American business interests had not only sold much machinery and railway equipment and other materials for use in Manchuria, but were deeply involved in Siberian enterprises. An American testified at the beginning of the century:

> Commercially we are the dominant power in Asiatic
> Russia today. The Pacific ports, and every river of Siberia
> has been thrown open, duty free, to our imports. . . . All
> through Siberia, Americans have millions of dollars
> invested in iron mills and other industries, from flour

mills to liquor stills, while a Russo-American party of prospectors has recently secured a concession for an immense area of gold-bearing country which they are now exploring. Everywhere in the country, Yankee prospectors are spying out the land in the interest of capitalists at home.[15]

But American support of Japan in the Russo-Japanese War naturally brought a metamorphosis of Russian official and private sentiment. A situation had in fact been created in which Russian and Japanese interests in Northeast Asia were closer to each other, despite recent enmity, than the interests of either Asian power to those of the United States.

Political conditions thus facilitated realignments. France worked to bring Russia and Britain together. Russia, however, in view of its long conflict with Britain, felt it necessary first to reach an understanding with England's ally, Japan, to gain protection for the Russian position in Northeast Asia. Given the new Japanese expansionism, Russo-Japanese conflict was otherwise easily possible. The task St. Petersburg set itself was not very difficult. Many Japanese believed (wrongly, but with fervor) that at Portsmouth they had been robbed of the full fruits of their military victory. In 1906, American–Japanese relations were exacerbated by California's promulgation of regulations discriminating against Japanese school children. Russia, for its part, was ready to abandon old antagonisms and seek new friendships.

In June, 1907, a meeting of King Edward VII and Tsar Nicholas II at Reval was viewed by the world as the manifestation of a new Anglo-Russian entente. Other agreements swiftly followed. By a secret Russo-Japanese convention signed July 30, 1907, by Foreign Minister Aleksandr P. Izvolski and Ambassador Motono Ichiro, North Manchuria was recognized as constituting Russia's sphere of influence and South Manchuria as being Japan's. Further, Russia, "recognizing the joint political relations between Japan and Korea," undertook not to interfere with or obstruct the further development of those relations. Japan for its part recognized the "special interests" of Russia in Outer Mongolia and agreed to refrain from action prejudicial to those interests.[16] The United States and other nations were thus excluded from equal participation in those areas.

King Edward's visit to Reval and the Russo-Japanese agreement, taken together, paved the way for a broad agreement between the traditional imperial antagonists, Britain and Russia. On August 31, 1907, Sir Edward Grey and Izvolski signed a convention defining British and Russian spheres of interest with respect to the old arenas, Persia and Afganistan, and also regarding Tibet. In defining the respective spheres of interest in Persia, Russia obtained the better deal. In return for what was effectively a British guarantee that Afghanistan would not be used as a base for hostile actions against Russia, however, Russia agreed to keep entirely out of that country.

The way to agreement on the Tibetan problem had already been paved by events. The Dalai Lama, upon his arrival in Urga in 1904, had seemingly endeavored to enlist the support of Russia against Britain. Russia, however, at that moment engaged in a difficult war with Britain's ally Japan, was in no position to intervene in Tibet against Britain. St. Petersburg's choice was "that the Dalai Lama should return to Lhasa and restore the status quo ante, but Britain being opposed to this, the matter was quietly dropped." [17] China, too weak a suzerain to protect its vassal from the British forces, maneuvered politically to maintain its legal position intact. On April 27, 1906, there was signed an Anglo-Chinese treaty by virtue of which China adhered to the Lhasa convention (and paid the indemnity assessed against Tibet), while Britain recognized China's sovereignty over Tibet and pledged itself not to interfere in Tibetan affairs.

Now, by the August, 1907, agreement, Britain and Russia bound themselves not to negotiate with Tibet except through the Manchu government, and agreed that neither should station representatives in Lhasa. That arrangement was designed to keep Tibet neutral territory where neither power should transgress. In the face of the German advance into the Middle East, Russia and Britain had come to see eye-to-eye on their interests in Persia and Afghanistan, and Tibet was no longer to play a part in Anglo-Russian relations — or in Sino-Russian relations. After a full century, the "Great Game" of Anglo-Russian competition in Asia had been brought completely to a close; and the Triple Entente came into being to confront the Triple Alliance — in Europe.

Japan naturally pressed forward with the development of its new empire in South Manchuria. Russia, in the north, consolidated its position in the Chinese Eastern Railway zone, with Harbin the administrative center for an imperium in imperio com-

plete with civil government, a military establishment in the form
of railway guards, a growing Russian population (but no peasant
colonists), and of course a bustling trade. The next strengthening
of the Russian and Japanese relationship in Manchuria derived
directly from moves by the United States to expand American
railway holdings in Manchuria.

The American railway magnate Edward H. Harriman, even
prior to the Russo-Japanese War, had conceived of the idea of
financing and constructing a round-the-world rail system, and
at the time of the Portsmouth peace conference obtained the
agreement of Prince Ito Hirobumi, then acting as special adviser
to the emperor, to the leasing of the South Manchuria line. The
project was canceled when Baron Komura, on his return from
Portsmouth, raised strong objections. Harriman continued with
his efforts to acquire both the South Manchurian and Chinese
Eastern railways. In the summer of 1909, Russian Minister
of Finance Vladimir N. Kokovtsov promised Harriman that,
after he had returned from a trip to the Far East, he would
recommend that the CER be sold to American interests.[18] Harriman's round-the-world railway scheme came alive again. On
October 4, 1909, in violation of secret commitments it had
made to both the Japanese and Russian governments, Peking
granted to American interests a concession for the construction of
a railway from Chinchow to Aigun, that is, through the Japanese
and Russian spheres of interest. In December Secretary of State
Philander C. Knox (the proponent of "dollar diplomacy"), acting
in behalf of the Harriman interests, proposed the internation-
alization of the (Japanese and Russian) Manchurian railways.

Harriman had died in September, and the American financial community lacked others of his capacities to push forward
with so vast an undertaking. Britain refused to support the American secretary of state's incursion into the spheres of influence of
its two allies. The Chinchow-Aigun concession and the Knox
proposal alike died natural deaths. St. Petersburg and Tokyo
moved still closer together before what they regarded as a common menace, and a new secret Russo-Japanese treaty was signed
on July 4, 1910, providing, as a counter to the American démarche,
that the two signatories should consult regarding common action
to be taken in case of any threat to their special interests in Manchuria. In July, 1910, also, Russia signed an agreement with the
moribund Manchu Court that had the effect of legitimizing the

Russian navigation of the Sungari River that had begun in 1898. For good measure, Japan in August annexed Korea.

Thus, five years after the end of the Russo-Japanese War, the sometime enemies were discovered collaborating with each other. China, on the other hand, was found without major international support. The Li-Lobanov convention had become a dead letter when China chose neutrality in 1904. Japan, with imperial ambitions, saw less reason for joining forces with the Manchu dynasty than in collaborating with Russia. The tsarist regime consequently had been able to restore, in some measure, its damaged position in Northeast Asia. Russia had threatened China's sovereignty in Manchuria before, but now both Russia and Japan were solidly entrenched there.

At this juncture, China and the powers were severally confronted by two major developments — the Chinese Revolution and a world war.

10 REVOLUTION AND THE MANCHU BORDERLANDS

THE FORCES OF CHANGE that had been operative in China since the time of the T'aip'ing Rebellion were having a cumulative effect. Reforms undertaken by the Manchu government after the disaster of the Boxer Rebellion had come too late to bring the massive adjustment to the modern world demanded by the times. New ideas imported from abroad, pressures exerted by foreign governments on the Manchu Throne over the preceding half century, new railway loans being foisted upon the Chinese nation by foreign banks in bland disregard of attendant corruption and popular attitudes, and the convocation in October, 1910 of a national assembly that offered a platform for the presentation of criticism of the existing order, all went to swell the revolutionary tide. Widespread disorders in Szechwan due to dissatisfaction with Peking's railway policy were followed by a military revolt at Wuchang on October 10, 1911. The Chinese Revolution had officially begun, and it was entirely apparent that the dynasty faced its doom.

Those developments were a matter of concern to China's immediate neighbors. The American chargé d'affaires at Tokyo in a telegram of October 15 informed the secretary of state that Japan would not intervene in China to put down the disorders unless Japanese interests were seriously threatened or unless the powers urged Japan to act. Inferentially in the latter event, "Japanese Government will be ready to take speedy and efficient action, which Russia will not oppose. . . . If the rebellion becomes serious in Manchuria, Japan and Russia will send troops at once without consulting the powers." [1]

There was the slaughter of Manchu garrisons at various points, but the Chinese Revolution did not lead to a national upheaval. The Manchu rule was brought to an end largely through the political maneuvers of the man charged with saving the dynasty, Yuan Shih-k'ai, in circumstances where the Manchus had forgotten how to rule. The Revolution ended officially with the abdication on February 12, 1912, of the Manchu imperial house in favor of Yuan. Yuan had thoughtfully arranged that the articles of abdication transfer to the new Chinese Republic title to all the territories of the Manchu empire. "China," in short, should include Manchuria, Mongolia, the sometime "Western Region," and Tibet, as well as the lands of the Han Chinese as taken over from the Mings.

The advent of the Republic was received without visible enthusiasm by the autocratic Russian government. American Ambassador Curtis Guild reported from St. Petersburg that "The Minister for Foreign Affairs frankly states that Russia does not wish to see a strong military power in China." [2] The foreign minister (Sazonov), according to Guild, doubted that a republican China could maintain law and order; Russia, however, was prepared to join interested powers in emergency loans to China, with the proviso that its interests in Manchuria, Mongolia, and "Western China" (Sinkiang) would be maintained and with the further stipulation that such Russian participation did not imply recognition of the Chinese Republic. In the event, however, Russia, France, Japan, and other powers (excepting the United States, which had acted independently several months earlier), recognized the new Republican government on October 10, 1913, when Yuan Shih-k'ai was formally installed as president.

The situation in China in 1912 was thus in the usual disordered end-of-dynasty pattern. Semi-independent military men held important segments of political power in the field, and political unification had not yet been effected. With lack of unity, there was the usual tendency for the non-Chinese periphery of the Chinese empire to crumble and fall off. Witte had foreseen this development, and Russia had already staked out claims to a part of Manchuria and to Outer Mongolia and Sinkiang, as falling properly within the Russian sphere of influence.

By the Anglo-Russian agreement of 1907, Russia was debarred from action with respect to Tibet. If there were to be any change in that situation it would more probably be to the benefit of Britain. In fact, after the Dalai Lama in 1913 made an amateurish move designed to assert his country's independence, Britain, Tibet, and China in 1914 entered upon the Simla Convention, which acknowledged a large measure of autonomy for Outer Tibet. Peking, however, refused to ratify its plenipotentiary's action, leaving Lhasa and London in the closer agreement. In Manchuria, there was the division of authority agreed upon earlier between St. Petersburg and Tokyo—with some strengthening of the Japanese position by virtue of a 1915 Sino-Japanese agreement. The situation there was thus held in a somewhat uneasy balance.

The Chinese Revolution had, however, sparked developments which seemed to promise countervailing benefits to Russia in Outer Mongolia. Here was a region of prime strategic importance to the Russian empire, flanking as it did Central Siberia and offering a potential threat to Russia's thin line of communications running south of Lake Baikal, and of major interest to Japan because of its similar relationship to southern Manchuria. Mongolia had from the beginning been of considerable importance in Russo-Manchu relations, and Siberian Governor General Muraviev in a memorandum of 1854 had written that, in the event the Manchu dynasty were overturned, "it ought not to be permitted that a new Chinese government should extend its authority over Mongolia, which in such circumstances must be under our protection." [3] And if Mongolia's aspiration to be subject to Russia were clearly indicated, Muraviev suggested, there would be no reason to obstruct its desire.

The problem had to be viewed against the background of Manchu-Mongol relationships. Beginning in 1910, Peking had begun to make strong moves to bring Outer Mongolia more directly under the Throne, with severe constriction of Mongolian autonomy. When the Mongols resisted, the Manchu authority threatened to launch a punitive expedition. A colonization bureau was opened in 1911 with the aim of increasing the flow of land-hungry Chinese peasantry into the Mongol grazing lands, and there was projected an increase of the Manchu garrison stationed at Urga.

By the Peking convention of 1860, Russia had obtained the right to maintain consular representation in Outer Mongolia and had established consular offices at Urga (1861) and Uliassutai (1905). St. Petersburg in the year 1911 could normally be expected to concern itself with actions that might threaten Russian political and commercial rights. The international situation had changed substantially, however, from that existing when Muraviev wrote, a half century earlier. Russia had reached an understanding with both Britain and Japan regarding the balance of power in Asia, and tensions were rising in Europe, where Russia, as a member of the Triple Entente, had major obligations. There were compelling reasons why Russia should not now embark upon a Mongol policy apt to awaken the suspicions of newfound allies.

In July, 1911, acting on the suggestion of Sain Noyan Khan, the leader of one of the Khalkha *aimaks* (tribes), the Jebtsun Damba Khutukhtu convened a conference of Mongol princes and lamas. It was decided that help should be requested of Russia, and in August a mission headed by Sain Noyan Khan arrived in St. Petersburg, bearing a letter requesting that Outer Mongolia be made a Russian protectorate.[4] Muraviev would have leaped at the opportunity thus presented. In the new circumstances, however, the Russians acted with marked restraint. The delegation was received and was promised Russian help to maintain its autonomy in the face of the new aggressive Manchu policy; further, representations were duly made at Peking in protest against the administrative and military reforms being undertaken with respect to Outer Mongolia. St. Petersburg, nevertheless, offered no support for the Mongols' proposition that they should sever Outer Mongolia from China — doubting the Mongol ability, for one thing, to move effectively in that direction,[5] and apprehensive of opposition from the powers, for another.

St. Petersburg did express to Peking Russia's concern regarding the Manchu policies, but Peking replied in effect that the reforms were for the good of the Mongols. That response promised no satisfaction for Mongol aspirations, whether for maintenance of the status quo of autonomy or for the achievement of full independence of China. The October, 1911, Revolution came soon after, and the Mongols took the occasion to announce their divorcement from an oppressive rule: on November 3, they formally declared their independence. Referring to the civil war that threatened to overturn the Manchu dynasty, they declared that:

> Our Mongolia was in times past an independent State, therefore, standing on the ancient right, Mongolia proclaims itself an independent State, with a new government, with an authority independent of others in the administration of its affairs. In consideration of this, it is announced that we, the Mongols, submit ourselves no longer to Manchu and Chinese functionaries.[6]

The Mongol view was that allegiance had been to the Manchu Throne, not to the political entity "China."

There occurred in this connection a minor incident, of significance because of the personality involved. The Russian consular Cossack guard at Urga was at the time commanded by Grigori M. Semenov, half Buryat by blood. With the Mongolian declaration of independence Semenov disarmed the forces of the Chinese Amban. For that political faux pas, he was reprimanded and removed from his command. But the Cossack firebrand would be heard from again.

Coincident with the move for independence, the Khutukhtu demanded arms from the Russians, and the Irkutsk military district delivered 15,000 rifles, 15,000 sabers, and 7 million cartridges to the rebel Mongol regime. On December 28, 1911, there was formally established the "Empire of Mongolia," with the Jebtsun Damba Khutukhtu assuming the additional title of "Great Khan." The Mongols, remembering the days of Genghis Khan, and imbued as always with the dream of pan-Mongolism (although as usual divided on means to achieve their ends), desired that Russia support their aim of incorporating Inner Mongolia in the new empire. In January, 1912, the Barga region of Manchuria, ethnically Mongolian, actually declared its adherence to Outer Mongolia. Tokyo, however, its suspicions aroused by the developments, in the same month of January demanded that Russia concede that Japan possessed special interests in Inner Mongolia and proposed that the line dividing the Russian and Japanese spheres of influence should be drawn from Urga to Kalgan.

This would have meant a notable advance of the Japanese

sphere of influence and a corresponding retreat for the Russians. On July 8, 1912, after extended discussions, there was concluded another secret Russo-Japanese convention in which it was provided that the line of demarcation should pass on a north-south axis through the Peking meridian (116°27'E). By that division, Eastern Inner Mongolia appertained to the Japanese sphere of influence, and Russia had another reason not to support the desire of the Outer Mongols to extend their rule over Inner Mongolia. Nor did St. Petersburg support the desire of the Barga region to become a part of the new Mongolian empire; after all, if Barga's program had been supported, why should Buryat Mongolia not also have been enabled to join that new Mongol state?

The Mongols at Urga nevertheless felt sure enough of their new position to abolish the system whereby the *hoshun* (clan) guaranteed individual Mongol debts to Chinese merchants, and there was a prompt decline in Chinese trade – to the benefit of the Russians. President Yuan refused to acknowledge as valid the withdrawal of Mongol allegiance and endeavored to win the Mongols back,[7] but failed. In the Barga region the separatist movement continued.

On November 3, 1912, Russia and Outer Mongolia, without reference to Peking, signed a bilateral agreement by virtue of which Russia committed itself to help Mongolia "to maintain the autonomous regime which she has established, and therein to exercise her right to have her national army, and to admit neither the presence of Chinese troops on her territory nor the colonization of her land by the Chinese." The agreement further provided that, as in the past, Mongolia would permit Russian subjects and trade "to enjoy the rights and privileges" set forth in an attached protocol, and no rights *not* enjoyed by Russia would be granted to the subjects of any third power. Finally, it was stipulated that the Mongolian government might not make a treaty with China or another power infringing the provisions of the present agreement, or modify provisions of that agreement without Russian consent.

In an attempt to protect what it viewed as China's paramount interest in Outer as well as Inner Mongolia, the Peking Foreign Office undertook negotiations with Russia to get cancellation of the autonomy provided by the 1912 agreement. It was unsuccessful in this, but achieved a half-measure. In a joint Sino-Russian declaration of November 5, 1913, Russia recognized China's suzerainty over Outer Mongolia, China accorded recognition to Outer Mongolia's autonomous status, and the signatory parties jointly pledged themselves to abstain from intervention in the internal affairs of Outer Mongolia, the dispatch of troops to that country, and colonization — a direct reference to the earlier Manchu plan to flood the region with Chinese bodies. China expressed its readiness to accept Russia's good offices for a settlement of relations with Outer Mongolia. Finally, the two parties agreed to settle questions appertaining to their respective interests in Outer Mongolia in subsequent conferences.

In sum total, Outer Mongolia was put in the position of a joint protectorate, with reduction of China's authority indeed, but also with specific reference to its suzerain authority — which made that country a vassal once more. Urga protested, stating that it would not recognize any condition of dependency determined without its consent. It was essential, for stability's sake, to achieve a trilateral agreement. The necessity became more exigent for Russia in particular, after the outbreak of the European War in July, 1914: the Triple Alliance had engaged the Triple Entente.

From September, 1914, to June, 1915, in something of a historical parallel to the negotiations at that point in the eighteenth century, a conference of representatives of Russia, Mongolia, and China sat in Kiakhta. The negotiations were long-drawn-out, given especially the Chinese aim of expanding rather than contracting its authority over Outer Mongolia, but in due time developments at Kiakhta reflected the course of events elsewhere, and the matter was brought to a close. Russia, during this period, was subject to the exigencies of the European War, but its position had not as yet been seriously weakened. China, however, in early 1915 was presented with Japan's onerous "Twenty-one Demands" proposing the creation of a special privileged position for the Japanese with reference to Manchuria, Inner Mongolia, and China as well. The Chinese were forced to accept the major part of those demands in May, 1915.

Peking then bowed to another necessity and signed an agreement with the Russians and the Outer Mongols. In that treaty of June 7, 1915, Outer Mongolia gave its recognition to the Russo-Chinese declaration and notes of November, 1913, that is, acknowledged Chinese suzerainty. China and Russia were found in agreement, as in 1913, that Outer Mongolia was a part of China, with the Outer Mongol ruler to be invested by the president of the Chinese Republic, but it was further stipulated, as before, that Outer Mongolia should enjoy autonomy in the administration of its internal affairs without interference from the other contracting parties, and, except for a limited number of consular and military guards, no Russian or Chinese troops were to be stationed there. Outer Mongolia had no right to conclude treaties with foreign powers regarding territorial or political matters, but it might conclude agreements of a commercial or industrial nature. Finally, it was provided that the Russo-Mongol protocol of 1912 remained in force. In sum total, Russian commercial prerogatives remained unimpaired, and Outer Mongolia was to rule itself free from Chinese authority, protected by Russia. Obviously, the Russians and Mongols obtained greater satisfaction from the arrangement than had the Chinese. The arrangement would last until Russia got into trouble.

There remained the final segment of the China borderlands, that vast area that had once been termed only the Western Region and had in 1884 become Sinkiang. The situation there had been quiet since the putting down of Yakub Beg's rebellion in 1877. The 1911 Revolution saw the Manchu power still dominant over the Turki peoples of Chinese Turkestan. With the abdication of the Manchus, the then *tutuh* (military governor) of Sinkiang, Yuan Hung-wu, issued a proclamation accepting the Republic and setting forth the new credo. Turki unrest welled up in the province, and Yuan abandoned his post — which, however, was then occupied in turn by another Chinese, the Yunnanese Yang Tseng-hsin. By able political maneuvering and the judicious use of military force, Yang succeeded in consolidating his rule throughout the province. That rule, if quasi-independent in the circumstances prevailing in China at the time, was still Chinese, not Turki. Sinkiang, different from both Tibet and Outer Mongolia, showed no signs of detaching itself from the shattered empire.

Under Yang's administration, there were certain exchanges with neighboring Russia that might have been viewed as pointing up potentials for the future. In the early days of the Chinese political upheaval, the Russians sent military detachments to both Ili and Kashgar, but this was probably for the protection of their nationals and consular establishments, and the action led to nothing in the order of permanent occupation. The outbreak of the European War diverted both British and Russian attention from Central Asia for the time being, but it at the same time gave rise to fresh developments in that region.

One problem centered on the movements of the nomadic Kazakhs. From 1910 onward, with Russian settlers flowing onto their grazing lands in Russia, many Kazakhs had moved to new pastures in Sinkiang. In the period from 1912 to 1914, Yang on various occasions requested the Russian consul at Ili to take back those migrant Kazakhs, and on two occasions Chinese troops were dispatched to herd the nomads back to the Russian frontier. But the Russian consul refused to commit his government regarding the matter, and border officials expressed an unwillingness to receive the voluntary expatriates.

In 1914, several thousand more yurts (equivalent to the same number of families) arrived in the Ili region. The Kazakhs technically remained Russian subjects, and the question of jurisdiction was becoming increasingly complicated. A local agreement was reached between the Russian consul, presumably acting with the approval of his government, and Sinkiang Foreign Affairs Officer Feng T'e-min, that Kazakh subjects of Russia who had come to Sinkiang and had not returned to their homeland as of July 20, 1911, were to be considered to have lost their Russian citizenship and to have gained Chinese citizenship, with exactly the same status as other Chinese, but that Kazakhs who had arrived after the indicated date were to be received back by Russia.

There were over 2,000 families, or approximately 6,000 persons, involved in that transfer of citizenship. The Chinese Foreign Office and the Russian minister stationed at Peking approved the agreement, with the stipulation that the number 6,000 was not to be exceeded. In a telegram of February 18, 1915, to the Foreign Office, Yang pointed out the essence of the problem. If China were to refuse to grant grazing lands to the Kazakhs, he said, and the nomads were driven to rent land from the Mongols, the Russians would be able to entice the Kazakhs away from the Chinese fold and there might come a day when the Kazakhs would orient themselves in another direction. Then, as had been shown in the case of Mongolia, neither the lands nor the people would belong to China.

Yang went on to point out that there was no reason why the Russians (presumably including the Kazakhs who migrated between summer and winter grazing grounds each year across the international frontier) should enjoy the rights currently exercised in the Altai region of freely residing, cultivating the soil, hunting, and fishing, all without payment of rental. He recommended that the Russian minister at Peking be informed that such activities would thereafter be prohibited, and that movement across the Sinkiang-Russian frontier must cease. Yang would have known that the Kazakhs and Kirgizi had freely roamed the borderlands for centuries without regard to political frontiers, and that it was hardly probable that they would now be content to observe fixed boundaries.

A bigger issue still grew out of the production of opium. The Manchu Throne had finally issued proscriptive measures, aimed at eventually extinguishing traffic in the drug, in Sinkiang as well as elsewhere. Yang Tseng-hsin, upon his accession to power, succeeded in implementing the prohibition, at least to a degree. With opium production barred in Sinkiang, however, large numbers of Chinese began regularly to cross the frontier into the Issyk Kul region of Russia, where they would grow the opium poppy in the summer, reap the harvest, and return home—with the opium. This activity led to conflict with the Kazakhs, on whose lands the Chinese presumably infringed, and one summer a large number of Chinese opium cultivators were killed. Yang Tseng-hsin, under orders from Peking, undertook to collaborate with the Russian authorities in an effort to halt that seasonal opium production—but when the Russians applied repressive measures and moved to expel the Chinese immigrants by force, without their opium, Yang stood behind his compatriots in their demand for compensation. The whole matter was brought to an end only by the Russian Revolution, which in due course caught up Russian Turkestan in a turmoil which made poppy cultivation—and indeed most agricultural activity—out of the question.

In the meantime, foreign and domestic factors were combining to cause major changes in China Proper. It was in the summer of 1915 that Yuan Shih-k'ai launched his campaign to become emperor. Japan and its ally Britain reached agreement that the attempt to restore the monarchy would probably bring disorders in China in its wake, and then, at the end of October, the Japanese embassy at Petrograd (St. Petersburg) proposed to the Russian Foreign Office that Russia should join the two allies in a démarche at Peking recommending that the project be set aside for the time being. Russia agreed, and Sazonov instructed Minister Vasili N. Krupenski at Peking to act in consultation with his colleagues. The three ministers at Peking made their joint representations on October 28. The United States refused to associate itself with the action, on the ground that this would constitute interference in China's internal affairs, but Italy and France a few days later supported the démarche by representations of their own.

Yuan nevertheless, in response to a "popular demand" created by his agents, in December announced his acceptance of the invitation. On December 15, the Japanese minister on behalf of his and the other four governments informed the Peking Foreign Office that the five powers proposed to maintain an attitude of watchfulness regarding future developments in China.

Yuan Shih-k'ai failed to realize his dream of becoming emperor, not by reason of the opposition of the powers, but because of a spreading national revolt against his scheme. He died in June, 1916, and with his passing the "warlord era" of national division began, with individual militarists ruling severally at Peking and in various provinces. The powers were thus given increased opportunity to play politics in China for their own benefit. Germany was out of the running, given its defeat in the Far East; Britain and France were too heavily engaged in the war in Europe to pay much attention to Asia. Of the belligerents, Russia and Japan, both Asian powers, were primarily concerned with developments in China, and the United States, still "neutral," also endeavored to play a role there.

By the time Yuan died, Russia was beginning to suffer deeply from disastrous defeats on the European battlefield. Negotiations begun six months before brought the signature, on July 3, 1916, of a new secret Russo-Japanese convention. The agreement provided that the signatory powers, "recognizing that their vital interests demand that China shall not fall under the political domination of any third Power whatsoever, which may be hostile to Russia or Japan," would "whenever circumstances demand" confer on measures to be taken to prevent such a development; and in the event war were to be declared between one of the signatories and a third power by reason of the implementation of those measures which had been mutually agreed upon, "the other Contracting Power, at the demand of its Ally, shall come to its aid. . . ." [8] Japan in January and February, 1917, went on to obtain Russia's commitment, together with similar agreements by

Britain and France, to support at the peace conference the Japanese position with respect to Germany's rights and interests in China and the German islands in the Pacific. It also obtained something in the nature of a blanket American acknowledgment of its "special interests" in the "contiguous" part of China by the Lansing-Ishii agreement of November, 1917.

Japan's actions in the period 1915–1917 in particular were designed to bring about a reduction in the stature of the Western sea powers in the West Pacific, and for this purpose it showed itself the readier to cooperate with the Occidental land power in Asia, Russia. It was nevertheless evident that the Japanese political strategists kept in mind the further possibility that a Russian defeat in the European War would create even greater possibilities for the expansion of Japan's position in East Asia.

In the meantime, a fundamental reorientation, favorable to Japan, had occurred in China. In November, 1915, when Britain, France, and Russia sounded out Tokyo on the desirability of endeavoring to bring China into the war against Germany, Foreign Minister Ishii Kikujiro had opposed the proposal, on the grounds (according to his later explanation) that China was then in a critical political condition because of the impact of Yuan Shih-k'ai's monarchical movement, and that the military value of China's participation on the side of the Entente would have been almost nil.[9] Japan had subsequently established ties with Premier Tuan Ch'i-jui which seemingly gave Tokyo confidence that it would be able to guide developments in China to its benefit. When the Peking government was approached by the United States in February, 1917, with the suggestion that China, as the United States, break off diplomatic relations with Germany, it consulted Tokyo and received its approval. Tuan Ch'i-jui thereupon undertook to bring China into the war.

On August 14, 1917, after a domestic struggle in the course of which the parliament was dissolved and President Li Yuan-hung ousted from power, Peking declared war on Germany. Tuan Ch'i-jui had fulfilled his commitment to Japan. In September, at Canton, an opposition government was set up under the leadership of Sun Yat-sen as "generalissimo," and it likewise "declared war" on Germany. It was entirely evident that, with China so divided, Japan for the time being was confronted with no military threat from the Asian mainland.

11 THE RUSSIAN REVOLUTION AND CHINA

AT THIS SAME TIME, Russia was undergoing violent transformation. The Russian Revolution of March, 1917, was the natural consequence of the same kind of insensate autocratic rule that had brought ruin to the Manchu dynasty, and of the military disasters and popular suffering brought upon the nation by the war. The Provisional Government had not attended to the second factor, but when the Bolsheviki succeeded the Kerensky regime in November, they called for an immediate end to hostilities — for a general peace, without annexations and without indemnities.

Soon after coming to power, the new regime endeavored to regularize relations with China. In November, the People's Commissariat for Foreign Affairs (Narkomindel) under Leon Trotsky undertook discussions with Minister Liu Ching-jen with the aim of reaching agreement on procedures for liquidating the old "unequal treaty" arrangements and the provisions directed against China in Russo-Japanese agreements of the 1907–1916 period. The Narkomindel in December dismissed Minister N. A. Kudashev and other tsarist diplomats from their posts in China and named as new minister A. N. Voznesenski. The Bolshevik authority attempted at the same time to send consular representatives into Sinkiang. The Peking government, however, refused to accept the new appointments, instead maintaining relations with Kudashev at Peking and tsarist consular officials elsewhere.

Manchuria early entered the equation. The CER was a property having considerable value from both a pecuniary and political point of view. Dmitri L. Horvath (Khorvat), a Russian nobleman who had been the line's general manager since 1902, was a royalist to the core. With the overthrow of the monarchy in March, Horvath seized control of the CER, and set up an opposition "All-Russian Provisional Government," with himself at its head, in Harbin.

But a soviet of workers' deputies had been created at Harbin after the March Revolution, and on December 12, after the Bolshevik Revolution, the soviet announced its seizure of power and formed a revolutionary-military committee that ordered Horvath and his associates relieved of their posts. The foreign powers, which had viewed with equanimity Horvath's autocratic administration of the CER railway zone, now reacted in alarm, and asked Peking to support Horvath with troops. Peking was only too willing to oblige, and on December 25 Chinese forces entered Harbin, dispersed the soviet, and forced the surrender of the Bolshevik railway guards. The following day, the railway guards, with their leaders, were expelled from Chinese territory. The new Sino-Russian relationship was off to a bad start.

The Bolsheviki won a measure of relief in Europe. In December, they reached an armistice agreement with the Germans, and on March 3, 1918, they signed the onerous Treaty of Brest-Litovsk. Russia had left the war.

This was in line with Lenin's thesis that, instead of an "imperialist war," there should be both peace—and world revolution. From Brest-Litovsk, the Bolsheviki proclaimed that "The reign of capitalist pillage and violence is crumbling. . . ." They called upon the workers of the world to "struggle against all the imperialists." That stance was naturally viewed with distaste by the Allied powers, who desired above all to maintain intact the eastern front against the Central Powers; they feared that Bolshevik Russia might actually join imperial Germany or be forced to act as its cat's-paw. There were Russians, supporters of the monarchy, who might indeed lend themselves to such endeavors. The seizure of power by a radical regime promising social revolution had given rise to internal division in Russia, and where the foreign war ended the civil war began. The Allied powers in March,

1918, landed troops at Murmansk, and "White" leaders who professed to fight for the true faith of the monarchical principle saw a potential source of aid for their cause.

The Bolsheviki moved their government from Petrograd to Moscow. As the internecine struggle progressed, the periphery of the Russian empire loosened and threatened to fall off, in a Chinese-type syndrome. In January, 1918, with Germany acting as midwife, the Ukraine had become independent. Finland, the Baltic states, Armenia, Azerbaijan, and Georgia all severed themselves from the Russian rule. In Kazakhstan, Cossack forces remained in power, but in Turkestan, Muslim sentiment welled up in favor of autonomy within a Russian federation, as demanded by an Extraordinary All-Muslim Congress meeting in Tashkent. Poland, by virtue of the Treaty of Brest-Litovsk, was now again free to play an independent power role — and threaten its ancient enemy, Russia. Russia had returned to a "Time of Troubles."

In Asia, if the Bolshevik disaster were to prove complete, the Russians stood to lose all the fruits of conquest since the time of Yermak. Hideyoshi had nurtured the idea of a Japanese world empire, and the Russo-Japanese War had started Japan on the way. Korea, Mongolia, and Siberia were stepping-stones to the achievement of domination of a continent. If the Russian empire in Asia were really to be dissolved, Japan would obviously be a competitor for the legacy.

The rulers of what remained of the shattered Russian empire thus appeared to be in a desperate position. It was nevertheless to be remarked that the anti-Bolshevik forces were agreed upon no common philosophy or strategy. In 1918, there were some thirty different "governments" ruling in different parts of the country; in the period 1917–1920, Kiev changed political hands a dozen times. In Asia the revolutionary power achieved an early advance: at the beginning of 1918, the Provisional Siberian Government, which had been established at Tomsk under the leadership of the Social Revolutionary Derber, fled before the Bolsheviki to Harbin.

But in January, 1918, China closed the Russo-Manchurian border, thus anticipating the Allied powers' imposition of an economic blockade of Soviet Russia the following autumn. In Manchuria, with Japanese funds, there was undertaken the organization of counterrevolutionary forces under the leadership of the Cossack ataman Grigori M. Semenov (the sometime Urga consular-guard commander), assisted by his friend and lieutenant, the half-Magyar, half-German "Baron" Roman Nikolaus von Ungern-Sternberg. Farther east, in the Ussuri region, the Japanese groomed another Cossack, Ivan Kalmykov, as ataman of the Ussuri Cossacks.

China had a place in Tokyo's plans. In line with its design to utilize Tuan Ch'i-jui's faction as an instrument of its Asia policy, Japan in early 1917 had thought of bringing China into a military arrangement, and Deputy Chief of Staff Lieutenant General Tanaka Giichi presented the idea to Generals Chin Yun-p'eng and Chu T'ung-feng on the occasion of their official visit to Japan the following November. In February, 1918, General Tanaka became head of the general staff's Siberian War Planning Commission, which in due course proposed the dispatch of five Japanese divisions into the Primorye and Trans-Baikal region, the employment of Russian anti-Bolshevik forces, and the negotiation of a military agreement with China, to destroy the Bolshevik power. On March 25, 1918, three weeks after signature of the Brest-Litovsk treaty, Japan and China in an exchange of notes agreed that, "Having regard to the steady penetration of hostile [nominally, German] influence into Russian territory, threatening the general peace and security of the Far East," the two governments should promptly consider "the measures to be taken in order to meet the exigencies of the situation." [1]

This agreement did not reflect any Japanese disposition to share spoils of conquest with a weak China: Tokyo simply desired to legitimize its position, to keep the Peking government trailing steadily in the wake of Japanese policy, and to obtain a secure base in China for its operations against Asiatic Russia. The Japanese "Nishihara loans" to the Peking government, negotiations for which began in March parallel to talks on the first military agreement, gave Tokyo reasonable assurance that Tuan Ch'i-jui's Anfu clique would persist in its pro-Japanese orientation.

The day after Japan had reached its agreement with Peking, Foreign Minister Viscount Motono in an address to the Japanese Diet stated that, if the situation in Siberia so developed as to threaten Japan's security or vital Japanese interests, the government was determined "to take prompt and adequate measures of self-defense." [2] He denied that Japan had proposed intervention *to the powers* (which would seem to exclude China), or that any *formal* proposal to the same end had been received from the Allied and Associated powers (which would include the United States). On April 5, however, after the killing of three Japanese nationals, Japanese marines were landed at Vladivostok.

In May a leading White Guard personality, Admiral Aleksandr V. Kolchak, visited Horvath in Harbin. Kolchak had fought at Port Arthur during the Russo-Japanese War, and in the European War had commanded the Black Sea fleet. His present aim was to obtain the use of Manchuria as a base for White Russian operations against the Bolsheviki. Parallel action by China and Japan facilitated the Kolchak purpose. On May 16, the two countries signed a secret treaty by which, in view of "the gradual extension of enemy influence towards the East," they agreed "to take concerted action against the common enemy." [3] On the basis of this agreement, the Japanese would eventually move 60,000 troops into northern Manchuria, the Russian sphere of influence. In June, the Peking government ordered the dispatch of Chinese troops to Vladivostok, and the Fifth Mixed Brigade was transformed into the Ninth Division and assigned to the task.

By this time, Horvath's "government" had found sources of financial support. The Russo-Asiatic Bank had been nationalized by the Bolsheviki after the November Revolution, but the board of directors, meeting in Peking in April, 1918, under French auspices, in effect declared the bank's independence of Soviet Russia — and General Horvath was made its acting general director. The Peking government had continued regularly to pay the Russian share of Boxer indemnity funds over to Minister Kudashev, but with the bank's reorganization the Entente declared that those funds should be paid into the Russo-Asiatic Bank. From there, they flowed to the support of the White Guard forces. Horvath also received direct financial support from Japan. In July, he appointed Semenov field commander for the All-Russian Provisional Government, with the mission of waging war against the Bolsheviki in Siberia. In the beginning, Semenov's "army" had comprised some 550 Cossacks and Mongols (mostly Buryats); now, augmented by Chinese and Koreans, it numbered about 12,000 troops.

The Bolshevik power at the time faced a critical situation in Asiatic Russia. Earlier, in European Russia, some 40,000 to 50,000 Czechoslovak prisoners of war had been released to fight against Austria-Hungary, their imperial fatherland. In February, 1918, the Bolsheviki agreed that the Czech Legion might proceed to the Western front, via Siberia. Transport delays put the Czechs into a rebellious mood, and at the end of May, when they were extended along the Trans-Siberian Railway all the way from Kazan to Vladivostok, one detachment suddenly seized Chelyabinsk. Other groups also rose up, and the Legion turned against the Bolshevik authority. Trotsky as commissar for war issued orders for their suppression, but in the course of June the Czechs overcame the Bolshevik power all along the Trans-Siberian line and established a heterogeny of new administrative authorities. At the end of the month, the Czechs disarmed the Bolshevik troops at Vladivostok and overturned the Soviet authority there.

The Bolshevik regime's international position had also deteriorated. At the Inter-Allied Conference of November 29 to December 3, 1917, Field Marshal Ferdinand Foch had proposed that a combined Japanese-American force should "take possession of the Trans-Siberian Railroad at Vladivostok first, then at Harbin, and from there to Moscow, by means of detachments which would extend their action progressively along the line." [4] With the rail line secured, the military operations could then be further extended to the southwestern sector of Russia.

For the moment, particularly given American opposition, the plan did not go forward. In mid-January, 1918, however, British and Japanese warships dropped anchor at Vladivostok. The U.S.S. *Brooklyn* joined them on March 1. In the following months, under the pressure of both its own representatives in the field and recommendations from other governments, Washington's opposition weakened. On June 29, the day that the Czechs overthrew the Bolshevik authority in Vladivostok, the British and Japanese landed additional troops there. The Bolsheviki lost Irkutsk a fortnight later. With the action probably related to the general pattern of events, the tsar and his family were executed at Ekaterinburg on July 16 and 17.

On the day after the executions, Washington extended implicit recognition to the faits accomplis in Northeast Asia by proposing a joint expedition of Japanese, British, and French forces, each contingent to comprise 7,000 men. The express purposes of the undertaking were to aid the eastward movement of the Czech troops to Vladivostok and to keep Allied military stores from falling into revolutionary hands. American-Japanese agreement to that end was made public on August 2, and Allied expeditionary forces disembarked at Vladivostok within a fortnight. The Siberian Intervention had begun. Also in August, the British expanded the Murmansk operation, similarly justified in the first instance by the need to safeguard war supplies, by landing several thousand troops at Archangel. Semenov was at this time active in the Trans-Baikal sector at the head of his strengthened force and assisted by Japanese military advisers. The Red forces lost Verkhneudinsk and Chita. At a conference in the railway town Urulga at the end of August, the Bolshevik leaders decided to wage partisan warfare against their enemies.

Moscow also undertook political maneuvers, aimed at splitting China off from the enterprise of encirclement. In a report of July 4, 1918, to the Congress of Soviets, Georgi V. Chicherin, who had recently succeeded Leon Trotsky in the position of commissar for foreign affairs, stated that Soviet Russia was renouncing special rights and interests acquired by the tsarist regime in China. With the Tuan Ch'i-jui regime committed to collaboration with Japan, there was naturally no response from Peking. The Bolsheviki probably had cherished no great hopes in that regard. But Sun Yat-sen had sent a telegram of greetings to Lenin shortly after the establishment of the Soviet regime in Russia, and now, on August 1, 1918, Chicherin sent a letter to Sun setting forth the proposition that Russia and China held common aims in the struggle against imperialism and calling upon the Chinese people to join with the Bolsheviki in that common cause: "For our success is your success, our destruction is your destruction."

Peking had no impelling concern with the balance of power in Europe — were they not all Occidental "imperialists" fighting each other? — and no discernible interest in the fate of the Czech Legion. China nevertheless desired to have an acknowledged role in the Siberian venture, both for reasons of domestic and international prestige and to win support from Britain, France, and the United States against its "ally," Japan, with respect to the future of the strategic CER system in particular and postwar power dispositions generally. The Chinese needed support: where the May 16 convention between Peking and Tokyo had provided that "both parties shall be considered to be on an equal footing," a supplementary military agreement of September 6 stipulated that the operations of Chinese forces in Siberia should be under Japanese command.

In the light of China's obligation under the 1915 Treaty of Kiakhta to respect the autonomy of Outer Mongolia, Article 1 of the new agreement held especial interest:

> With the purpose of obtaining the giving of mutual assistance by the forces operating from Manchuli and from Trans-Baikalia each to the other, the Chinese forces shall operate from Urga toward Trans-Baikalia. If China desires the assistance of Japanese forces in this locality, Japanese forces may be sent to work in cooperation with the Chinese forces and be under Chinese commanders. China shall herself see to the protection of her borders to the west of Central Mongolia.[5]

The record shows no reference to the wishes of the Mongols in this connection.

Alien power naturally shaped events in Russia. A moderate "All-Siberian" government had been set up at Omsk in June, 1918. With the adherence of other groups, this body was in October transformed into an "All-Russian" government headed by a five-man directorate. Kolchak became minister of the army and navy in that regime, but in a coup of November 18 he overthrew the directorate and declared himself "supreme ruler of all Russia." Horvath promptly abolished his own "government" and threw in his lot with Kolchak. The British, French, and Americans likewise directed their support to the new autocrat. The Japanese, on the other hand, closely associated with both Chang Tso-lin in Manchuria and the Anfu government at Peking, employed Semenov and Kalmykov as their chief instrumentalities in the Siberian intervention. Nor did Semenov acknowledge the authority of the Kolchak regime.

In December, Allied intervention was undertaken in yet another sector, in Odessa – occupied until the November armistice by the Germans. Kolchak, after his November coup against the Russian moderates, made what seemed on the surface to be notable progress.[6] The British, French, and Americans gave him important aid in arms and supplies. He consequently was able to create an army of 300,000 men and extended his rule from

Vladivostok to the Urals. He looked strong to the Allies, and they put their cards on him and other White Guard generals in Russia Proper, Anton I. Denikin in the Caucasus and Nikolai N. Yudenich in the North. Support to the three was extended from the three sectors of intervention based respectively on Vladivostok, Odessa, and Murmansk. The triangle of containment seemed strong.

In the end, China committed no more than one division of troops to the intervention (as compared with Japan's approximately 72,000 men). The Chinese were assigned guard duties over 1,225 miles of railway, including much of the CER. The Czech Legion was charged with guarding the Trans-Siberian railway section west of Lake Baikal. The strategic aim of the Allied force was now openly discovered to be not the prompt evacuation of the Czechs, but the overturning of Bolshevik power. The future of the intervention would be determined mainly, however, by the character of the "loyalists" whom the powers had chosen as their instruments—and who maneuvered to exploit great-power support for their own narrow, selfish political ends.

Kolchak, as his nominal authority increased, became the more arrogant and disdainful of Allied advice. Semenov was at loggerheads with Kolchak. Kalmykov was sadistically cruel and relied chiefly upon violence and terror for "the restoration of peace and order." None seemed ideally constituted to help make the world "safe for democracy." The intervening powers, even as the Whites, were of different minds. The French general Janin was commander in chief of the expeditionary forces and General Knox, British, the deputy commander. But the command structure was hardly to be viewed as unified—particularly as regards the Japanese.

In March, 1919, Kolchak launched an offensive westward, broke through the Red defenses, advanced on the Volga, and threatened Kazan and Samara. This success was offset, to a degree, when the Bolsheviki in April succeeded in establishing themselves in Odessa. The French troops, having become semi-mutinous, were withdrawn, and the foreign intervention in that sector ended. The Bolshevik high command had by now come to regard the Kolchak offensive as decisive for the civil war, and in May and June the Red Army counterattacked in force. In July, it thrust Kolchak from the Urals.

Even as the Red Army was swinging into its counteroffensive, the Chinese nation had been thrown into a paroxysm of nationalistic fury. The Paris Peace Conference had finally decided, in the face of Chinese aspirations, to award German rights and interests in Shantung Province to victor Japan. As a consequence, a wave of popular protest which came to be called the May Fourth Movement swept the nation, and China refused to sign the Versailles Treaty on June 28, 1919. The pro-Japanese Anfu government was seriously discredited and weakened. The situation on the battlefield and in the Chinese political arena alike clearly was favorable for a new Soviet move, and on July 25 Deputy Commissar for Foreign Affairs Lev M. Karakhan addressed a new declaration to both the Tuan regime at Peking and the opposition military government at Canton — and to the Chinese people as a whole. The Bolshevik proposition had undergone amplification and clarification since Chicherin's statement of one year before: it was no longer either as general or as generous.[7]

Referring to the struggle against Kolchak, the statement declared that the Red Army had crossed the Urals not for conquest but to liberate peoples from the yoke of foreign bayonet and foreign gold, "which repress the enslaved peoples of the East, among whom are, in the first place, the Chinese people." Remarking that the Workers' and Peasants' Government's peace proposals of 1917 had probably been hidden from the Chinese people by "the mercenary American-European-Japanese press," Karakhan reviewed those proposals, and also those for abrogation of all secret tsarist treaties and for negotiations for the nullification of the Treaty of 1896, the 1901 Peking protocol, and all Russo-Japanese treaties from 1906 to 1916. Renouncing (once more) the Russian share of the Boxer indemnity, and indicating that the Soviet government was abandoning all special (extraterritorial) privileges on Chinese soil, Karakhan voiced the Soviet government's readiness to negotiate with the authorized representatives of the Chinese people on "all other questions." Karakhan included a word of advice that could not but leave an impression on Chinese whose nationalism had been stirred so recently by developments at the Paris Peace Conference:

> If the Chinese people desires to be free, like the Russian people, and to escape that fate prepared for them by the Allies at Versailles with the aim of turning them into a second Korea or a second India, let them understand that

their sole ally and brother in the struggle for freedom is
the Russian worker and peasant and their Red Army.

At the time of Karakhan's declaration, Kolchak was in retreat, but not finally defeated; and Denikin's armies were still
advancing. The grand strategy was still in being. Sun Yat-sen
as early as December, 1912, had proposed to the Japanese people
that the yellow races should follow a common policy. Japan had
been rebuffed in its effort, at the Paris Peace Conference, to win
acceptance of the principle of the equality of races. Now some
Japanese conceived of developing a Pan-Asian movement which
would bring into being an "Asiatic League," under Japanese
leadership, for furtherance of the Asian cause. In 1919, at Mukden, a new Japanese journal entitled *Great Asia* made its appearance. An editorial in the first issue proclaimed as the journal's
purpose "the endeavor to raise up the hundreds of millions of inhabitants of Asia, inspiring them with the thought of the insults
and injustices which they bear as a consequence of the oppression
of the white race of Europe and America"; further, "the freedom
of Asians must be achieved through the unification of the strength
of the yellow races." [8] The war cry was "Asia for the Asians."

The Anfu government, allied to Japan militarily and ideologically, clearly saw no reason to reply to the proposals set forth
in a public declaration by Karakhan. It clung to hopes for greater
gains. Even when Narkomindel representative Ya. D. Yanson
at the beginning of March, 1920, delivered the text of the declaration to the Chinese consul at Irkutsk for transmittal to the
Peking Foreign Ministry, there was still no reply. In strict law,
the offer might in due course have been considered forfeited by
want of takers.

The Peking government turned its attention to an area
where it hoped to make a coup against beleaguered Soviet Russia,
Outer Mongolia — which had entered into Sino-Japanese military
planning the year before. At Urga, Resident High Commissioner
Ch'en Yi had been cautiously negotiating to bring the Mongols
back into the Chinese fold. The Chinese suit was favored by the
circumstance that Russia, Mongolia's protector, was in a weakened condition: Mongols despairing of outside aid might well
shift back voluntarily to their ancient suzerain.

Peking was not content, however, with a slow evolutionary

process, and in June, 1919, Tuan Ch'i-jui's chief lieutenant, Hsu Shu-cheng, was charged with the task of bringing Outer Mongolia back into the Chinese fold in short order. Ch'en Yi was instructed that he would remain in charge of negotiations with the Mongols and that Hsu Shu-cheng would act only in a military capacity. But Hsu, upon his arrival at Urga in the wake of his armed forces in October, disregarded the position and accomplishments of his colleague and by threat of the use of his military contingent forced the Mongol princes and ministers to petition Peking on November 16 that Mongolian autonomy should be canceled. President Hsu Shih-ch'ang graciously obliged on November 22 by declaring such autonomy at an end.

The tsarist Russian legation at Peking protested the violation by China of the Russian agreements of 1912, 1913, and 1915 with China and Mongolia, and voiced a reservation of Russian rights under those agreements. The tsarist chargé d'affaires at Washington, in a memorandum of December 4, endeavored to enlist the aid of the United States to get respect for the 1915 treaty and the guarantee of "the freedom and self-determination of the Mongolian people." The Russian embassy at Paris on December 15 sent a note of protest to the representatives of the Allied and Associated powers.

All was in vain.[9] It appeared on the surface as if the Chinese had won a major victory against the Mongols — and against the Russians. In that same November, however, the Red Army captured Omsk, and Kolchak's regime collapsed. The Mongolian situation had finally to be viewed in the context of the Siberian intervention and the condition of Bolshevik power. Kolchak had withdrawn to Irkutsk, and at the end of December came under the protection of the Czechs. On January 5, 1920, at Nizhneudinsk, he resigned his position as "supreme ruler" of Russia in favor of Denikin, but entrusted to Semenov military and civil authority over "the whole territory of the Russian Eastern borderland."[10] On the same day, a Social Revolutionary "political center" was set up at Irkutsk.

Seemingly shortly afterward, the Czech unit guarding Kolchak in the course of military operations was cut off by the Fifth Red Army, and it asked permission of the Red commander to withdraw to Vladivostok. Permission was granted — on condition that Kolchak be surrendered. The Czechs, acting by authority of General Janin, handed Kolchak over to the "political center" on

January 15. He was tried by a revolutionary military tribunal and shot on February 7, 1920, together with two of his chief lieutenants—Viktor Pepelyaev (chairman of his Council of Ministers) and the "hangman" Ch'eng T'ing-fan, who had been responsible for many atrocious crimes. Kalmykov had fled from the scene of the Kolchak disaster only to be captured and shot (by the Chinese) in China. Semenov, with the Japanese at his side, for the time being held out in Chita.

The intervention against the Bolshevik power was effectively over. The Allies had implicitly acknowledged this by lifting the economic blockade against Soviet Russia on January 16. In February, the intervention in the Murmansk-Archangel sector was terminated. The last of the French, British, and American forces, as well as the Czech legion that the whole Siberian Intervention was supposed to be about, were withdrawn from Siberia by early April. There remained behind only the considerable Japanese forces, now based on Primorye (excepting the contingent supporting Semenov at Chita), and their allies the Chinese.

The failure of the Siberian Intervention patently created a new situation with respect to both Manchuria and Outer Mongolia. On January 24, 1920, Horvath endeavored again to extend political authority over the Russian residents in the CER zone. The Kirin governor and concurrently CER president, General Pao Kuei-ch'ing, protested Horvath's action—for the time being ineffectively. The Bolshevik supporters organized a United Conference at Harbin, and on March 12 they issued an ultimatum to Horvath calling upon him to give up the authority he had seized—and on the following day the Russian employees of the CER began a general strike. On March 15, General Pao announced that Horvath had been stripped of political authority in the CER zone. Under pressure from the Ministry of Communications, Horvath was forced to resign his CER post, and in April he was made an adviser of that ministry. In due course he took up his sinecure in Peking. His long reign as tsar of the CER zone was over, but the CER question remained unsettled.

China's power relationship to the Bolshevik authority in Siberia had now been substantially altered from what it was in the spring of 1918. The Bolsheviki, by defeating their hydra-headed antagonist in Siberia, had won the strategic initiative. On April 6, 1920, shortly after the withdrawal of the main foreign expeditionary forces from Vladivostok, there was established at Verkhneudinsk (present Ulan-Ude) the government of a new political entity, the Far Eastern Republic (FER). That nominally independent state was in reality under the control of Moscow, but had taken its particular form the better to be a buffer against the Japanese in the Maritime Province [11] and to act as well as a political front for operations vis-à-vis a China under Japanese influence.

As Bolshevik control in Russia was being consolidated, the division of China, now deep in its warlord era, had increased; the central authority was weaker. The Peking government dominated by Tuan Ch'i-jui was nearing the end of its term. Not only did its Japanese liaison bring disrepute upon it in the eyes of all patriotic Chinese, but Hsu Shu-cheng's penetration into Outer Mongolia had seemed to threaten the rule of powerful Chang Tso-lin in Manchuria, and Hsu's Frontier Defense Army was developing a strength that menaced other important *tuchüns* [*] on the Chinese political state as well. In July, 1920, a combination of eight tuchüns headed by the Chihli militarist Ts'ao K'un, with Chang Tso-lin playing a prominent role, overthrew the Anfu regime. Tuan Ch'i-jui fell from power, and Hsu Shu-cheng, who had so recently dominated the scene with his unbridled arrogance, was forced to flee for his life – not unfittingly, to the refuge of the Japanese legation in Peking. The Peking government now came under the sway of Ts'ao K'un and his lieutenant Wu P'ei-fu. Japan's influence in the Chinese capital went into a sharp decline. The situation in Northeast Asia, which upon the advent of the 1917 Russian Revolution had seemed to offer so many glittering political opportunities to empire-builders, had patently undergone a fundamental change.

---

[*] The term "tuchün" in 1916 officially replaced "tutuh" as the designation for a military governor; in the usage of the era, it came to mean, more generally, "warlord."

12 CHINA, OUTER MONGOLIA, AND THE FAR EASTERN REPUBLIC

THE OVERTHROW of the Anfu regime at Peking had indirectly reflected the retreat of Japan before revolutionary forces on the Asian mainland. It naturally introduced new elements into the situation in Outer Mongolia, dominated so short a time before by the ominous personality of Hsu Shu-cheng.

Grigori M. Semenov and Ungern-Sternberg, fighters for Japan's cause in Siberia, were both pan-Mongolists. The half-Buryat Semenov had a deep interest in Mongolian affairs; Ungern-Sternberg in due course became convinced that, to turn back the tide of Communism, it was essential to mobilize the Mongolian people. The Japanese were desirous of stimulating movements in Outer Mongolia, as in Sinkiang, which might further their campaign against Soviet Russia. The Buryat Mongols of Russia were found variously on the side of the Bolsheviki, Semenov and Ungern-Sternberg, and the Japanese; sometimes, particularly in the period before the Siberian Intervention, they had endeavored to lay the base for Buryat-Mongol autonomy. Those various factors combined to give a special contemporary importance to the "Mongol Question."

The Siberian Intervention had introduced into Buryat Mongolia forces too great for the Buryat nationalists to handle. They were compelled willy-nilly to fit into the Japanese mold, which was designed to sever Buryat Mongolia from Russia and bring a "unified" Mongolia into the Japanese mainland orbit. At a conference held at Dauriya in February, 1919, with Semenov and a Japanese military officer in attendance, there had been launched a movement for creation of a "Great Mongolian State" that would include Inner Mongolia (right up to Tibet) and the Barga district of Manchuria, Outer Mongolia (including both the Khalkha and Kobdo districts), Urianghai, and Buryat Mongolia. Its nominal "leader" was the venerable Inner Mongolian khutukhtu, Neisse Gegen.

In August, 1919, Moscow addressed a declaration to the people and government of Outer Mongolia renouncing all unequal treaties between tsarist Russia and Mongolia, acknowledging the Mongol right of independence, and proposing the establishment of diplomatic relations. Doubtless having in view the presence of Japanese and other foreign forces on the Mongol flank in the Trans-Baikal region, the Jebtsun Damba Khutukhtu at Urga sagely made no response. In September, a delegation from Neisse Gegen Khutukhtu's Dauriya government visited Urga with the aim of getting the Outer Mongolian khutukhtu's concurrence in the scheme for creation of a Great Mongolian State under the Japanese aegis, but for equally good political reasons it also failed.

As a consequence of Kolchak's collapse and the inevitable adjustment of Japanese plans, the Dauriya government broke up and disappeared; Neisse Gegen fell into the hands of the Chinese troops stationed in Outer Mongolia, and was shot for his ultra-nationalism. In January, 1920, taking the place of the Mongols who had pinned their hopes on Japanese assistance, a "Mongolian People's Party" appeared on the scene. It had been formed by the amalgamation of two revolutionary groups led respectively by Sukhe Bator and Choibalsan.

In June, 1920, as the political crisis was building up around the Anfu clique at Peking, the Mongolian People's Party met in conference at Urga and adopted a nationalistic program. It was decided to send a delegation to Moscow under the leadership of Sukhe Bator and Choibalsan, and the Urga khutukhtu duly approved their mission. The delegation proceeded to Irkutsk, and was then invited to go on to Moscow. In the meantime, however, the Anfu regime had fallen from power in Peking, and when the delegation resumed its travel Sukhe Bator and Choibalsan remained behind in Irkutsk, to watch the developing situation.

Sukhe Bator, on August 28, addressed a letter to Boris Z. Shumyatski, premier of the Far Eastern Republic. In the name of the Mongolian party, he requested Russian aid in restoring Mongol autonomy. This move supplemented the démarche being made directly to Moscow. There, the Mongolian delegation was in September received by Lenin, and obtained a promise that Soviet aid would be given to the Mongol people. Sukhe Bator and Choibalsan had in the meantime been studying revolutionary organization and military doctrine under Russian tutelage; now, upon receipt of the news from Moscow, they returned to Outer Mongolia.

Ch'en Yi, who had been restored to authority as Peking's representative in Urga in mid-August, proceeded to relax the oppressive rule that had been imposed on the Mongols by Hsu Shu-cheng. A new directive from Peking ordered the reorganization of the administrative system of all Outer Mongolia. The liberalization of the system was patently designed to mollify the outraged Mongols. Circumstances did not permit the undisturbed working out of the experiment. At the beginning of October Ungern-Sternberg suddenly invaded Outer Mongolia with a force of some 2,000 troops and attacked in the direction of Urga, in service still of the "Greater Mongolia" strategy.

The Chinese garrison force repulsed the attack and then proceeded to loot the Russian residents in Urga, with much killing. They made the khutukhtu a virtual prisoner in his palace, thus further alienating the Mongols. One result was an accession of Mongol strength to the ranks of Ungern-Sternberg. He returned to the attack and captured Urga early in February. The Chinese garrison suffered heavy losses, with the survivors fleeing to Maimaicheng – accompanied by Ch'en Yi. In a communication of February 19, Ch'en in his turn called upon the Russians for aid; his assistant Li Yuan renewed the plea on March 3.[1]

But on March 1, 1921, the Mongolian People's Party was transformed into the Mongolian People's Revolutionary Party (MPRP), and convened its first congress – not in Outer Mongolia, but at Kiakhta, on Russian soil. Sukhe Bator and Choibalsan, who had in the meantime established close ties with the Far Eastern Secretariat of the Comintern at Irkutsk, were among the twenty-six delegates present. So was a representative of the Comintern. The conference bore fruit: on March 13, at Kiakhta, a Provisional People's Revolutionary Government of Mongolia was formed. It was supported by a Mongolian People's Revolutionary Army (MPRA) of 700 men, commanded by Sukhe Bator. Choibalsan was his political deputy. A week later, the MPRA captured Maimaicheng and set up a branch of the new revolutionary regime there. It appeared evident that the Russians, long plagued by the troublesome Mongol Question, had decided on a new approach to the problem.

The Mongolian revolutionaries next proposed to Urga that joint action be undertaken against the forces of "foreign imperialists" — which of course meant Ungern-Sternberg, supported by Japanese funds and aided by Japanese military advisers. The Jebtsun Damba Khutukhtu rejected the proposal, and on April 10 the Revolutionary Government asked Moscow for military aid in fighting the White Guard bands in Mongolian territory. Moscow had agreed earlier to assist the Mongolian people in its struggle for independence; now the Soviet government issued orders for the deployment of Red Army units against the common foe, the Russian White Guards in Outer Mongolia.

Peking remained concerned with developments. Warlords Ts'ao K'un, Chang Tso-lin, and Wang Chan-yuan conferred at Tientsin in April, and it was decided that Marshal Chang should restore order in Outer Mongolia. On May 30, he was appointed high commissioner for the Mongolian borderlands, and funds were allocated to finance a military expedition. Here there was a conflict of interest. At an earlier meeting between Chang, Semenov, and the Japanese at Mukden, there had by report been a division of spheres of influence, with Semenov to control Outer Mongolia and Chang to have southern Manchuria and Inner Mongolia; in April, Semenov, Ungern-Sternberg, and one Kaigorodov had met in Peking with the apparent purpose of determining future campaign plans.[2]

Ungern-Sternberg had of course made no secret of his ambition to overthrow Soviet power in the Trans-Baikal and create a Greater Mongolia. He appears in fact to have become by that time something of a megalomaniac, and is reported to have thought himself a reincarnation of Genghis Khan. In May, commanding 11,000 troops and possessing a well-staffed officer corps, he drove northward, captured Maimaicheng, crossed the frontier, and attacked Troitskosavsk, the fortified strongpoint immediately north of Kiakhta. His evident objective was Verkhneudinsk, for the severing of the Far Eastern Republic's communications with Soviet Russia. Marshal Chang Tso-lin sat by in evident unconcern.

On May 26, at Vladivostok, a counterrevolutionary coup brought the brothers Merkulov, supported by the Japanese, into power. The relationship of that move to the military actions of Ungern-Sternberg appeared clear. The Soviet power, however, had anticipated the threat and had made appropriate dispositions to meet it. The Far Eastern Republic was the political entity technically concerned with the Ungern-Sternberg attack, and Vasili K. Bluecher (Blyukher) now was appointed FER minister of war and put in command of the Republic's armed forces. Bluecher, son of a peasant family, was a revolutionary of outstanding military capabilities. He had just been awarded his third Order of the Red Banner for his performance in the 1920 Perekop campaign against General Petr N. Wrangel, successor to Denikin.

White Russian leaders, including Kaigorodov, had advanced into western Mongolia and Urianghai. The joint FER-Soviet-Mongol command (for it amounted to that) dispatched a part of the MPRA into the same region, and, under Bluecher's direction, it also addressed itself to the threat posed by Ungern-Sternberg in the Troitskosavsk sector. At the beginning of June, Ungern-Sternberg's attack was repulsed, and the Red Army pursued him into Outer Mongolia. On June 15, Chicherin informed the Peking government that this incursion had been necessitated by Ungern-Sternberg's military operations in FER territory. A proclamation addressed by Moscow to the Mongolian people shortly afterward gave assurances that "The armies of Workers' and Peasants' Russia and the Far Eastern Republic will not remain any longer in Mongolia than will be necessary to defeat the common enemy: the Tsarist General, the bloody Ungern." [3]

The combined Red force drove southward and on July 6 occupied Urga. On July 10,[4] the Mongol insurgents transferred their People's Revolutionary Government to Urga and dropped the "Provisional" from its title. The Jebtsun Damba Khutukhtu was still head of the state, as theocrat. The premier was the lama Bodo, but Sukhe Bator became minister of war and concurrently commander in chief of the Mongol forces.

Ungern-Sternberg had not yet been decisively defeated, and the Urga government promptly requested Moscow to keep Red

Army forces in Outer Mongolia to help rid the country of the White Guards. Ungern-Sternberg actually invaded the Trans-Baikal region again shortly afterward, but in early August he was decisively defeated in the vicinity of Lake Gusinoe. A fortnight later, he was captured south of Urga while trying to escape. He was duly tried and executed at Novonikolaevsk (present-day Novosibirsk) on September 22, 1921.

The White Russian force under Kaigorodov's command was driven from western Mongolia into the Russian Altai and there wiped out. But the Kalmyk Mongol Ja Lama, who claimed to be the reincarnation of Amursana, remained in western Mongolia as an opposition force. A strong supporter of Mongolian independence, he had wrested control of Kobdo from the Chinese in 1912 and joined with Urga, but in 1919 he had returned to Kobdo to re-establish himself in a position of independence from the troubled capital. As strongly anti-Russian as anti-Chinese, he still maintained his independent role.

Outer Mongolia, ruled by a theocrat (who now enjoyed only limited powers) was not yet a republic. It was, however, a sign of the times when, in August, Urianghai proclaimed itself an independent Tuvan People's Republic; given the Russian interest in the area, and the landlocked location of that region, it was entirely evident that this new political entity would tend naturally to gravitate toward its strong neighbor, Soviet Russia. Moscow was not unwilling that Outer Mongolia should go in the same direction. In a communication of September 10, Urga requested Moscow's intervention to aid in putting Mongolian relations with China on a new basis. Chicherin accepted the mediatory function. Another Mongol delegation headed by Sukhe Bator made the pilgrimage to Moscow, and on November 5 there was signed a secret Russo-Mongol treaty of friendship.

That treaty made no reference to China's sovereignty or suzerainty over Outer Mongolia, nor did it any longer pay lip service to the simple "autonomy" of the country. It provided for mutual recognition, as between two independent states, and thus laid the cornerstone of a new foundation for Outer Mongolia in the field of international relations. It was the evident intent of both Mongols and Russians that Outer Mongolia should be independent of China, under the Russian aegis. The Chinese were categorically out of the Mongolian picture, and Russia was in. The southern flank of Siberia was now protected by a massive buffer zone. The

Chinese Republic had in the end reaped bitter fruit from Hsu Shu-cheng's violent destruction of the status quo.

The People's Revolutionary Government and the Jebtsun Damba Khutukhtu in that same November entered upon a "sworn agreement" providing a new procedure for the validation of legislation. Thereafter, the theocrat enjoyed only a pro forma position as head of the state; "The Bogdo Gegen * reigned, but he did not govern." [5] There had been a complete bouleversement of the situation in Outer Mongolia, and the Mongolian events would strongly influence the development of Sino-Russian relations.

While revolutionary change was in course in Mongolia, the Chinese and Soviet sides respectively had made tentative moves toward establishing political contact. In March, 1920, after the execution of Kolchak had signaled the effective end of the Siberian intervention, Peking directed a military man, Lieutenant General Chang Shih-lin, to proceed to Irkutsk "for discussions with the Soviet government." [6] Chang got only as far as Harbin, where he met with the chairman of the Soviet-controlled United Conference, N. E. Gorchakovski. The first contact had been made. In April, shortly after the formation of the Far Eastern Republic, a Chinese "military-diplomatic" mission which included General Staff officers from both Harbin and Peking arrived at Verkhneudinsk and held discussions with representatives of the new regime on matters of common interest – including the Chinese Eastern Railway. The mission departed on April 27 and, according to a Soviet source, upon its return recommended that there be convened a conference of representatives of China, the Far Eastern Republic, and Soviet Russia, and that Peking receive an FER diplomatic mission. [7]

In June, the FER government appointed a mission to Peking under the leadership of Ignatius L. Yurin, and the group duly started out with the aim of traveling via Outer Mongolia (Chita still being in the hands of Semenov). In view of French and Japanese protests at reception of the envoy, however, Peking refused visas, and the party was halted at Kiakhta. Instead, Peking in June sent three foreigners, the American Sinologue John C. Ferguson, the British journalist Lennox Simpson ("Putnam Weale"),

---

* "Bogdo"–heavenly; "Gegen"–holy man, a title conferred by the Chinese government on various khutukhtus. "Bogdo Gegen": the title of the Jebtsun Damba Khutukhtu, which can be liberally rendered as "Living Buddha of Urga."

and the Frenchman Georges Padoux, to the FER for the purpose of making a survey of conditions. The foreign mission got to Vladivostok and there had talks with Vladimir Vilenski, representative of the Narkomindel.

In mid-June likewise, General Chang Shih-lin, without advance notification to the FER government, crossed the lines between the Semenov forces and the FER People's Revolutionary Army, and asked permission to proceed to Verkhneudinsk. After arriving there, at the end of June he sent a message to Lenin and Chicherin requesting that his mission be permitted to go on to Moscow. Chicherin in a telegram of July 8 asked Peking to confirm that Chang was appropriately accredited and possessed plenipotentiary powers. There was no reply from Peking, not unnaturally, given the political crisis in which it found itself at the time — but perhaps Peking would have preferred in any event not to be specific with respect to the issue. Moscow finally, without waiting for Peking's reply, gave permission for the Chang party to proceed, but Chang then delayed (to await the outcome of the Anhwei-Chihli war in course). In late August he resumed his journey and arrived in Moscow on September 5. He promptly made a handsome gift of furs for the children of Moscow and Petrograd. General Chang and an American named Vanderlip were guests of honor at a dinner given by Lenin, who gave a speech of welcome "in which he stated that the purpose of the occasion was to bring together these representatives of the people of the three nations, the United States, China and Russia, with a view to drawing them closer together." [8]

The Chang Shih-lin mission proved of short duration. The Moscow government on September 27 delivered to him a "Declaration of the Government of RSFSR to the Government of the Chinese Republic" in which there were set forth what Moscow considered the essential elements for agreement.[9] The next step was taken by Chang, who informed the Narkomindel in mid-October that Peking had named consuls general for assignment to Moscow, Omsk, and Irkutsk. The Narkomindel welcomed the action and in its reply informed Chang that the Soviet government had decided to send diplomatic representatives to Peking and to appoint consuls to Tientsin, Shanghai, and Canton. On October 18, the Chinese minister at London informed the local Soviet trade representative there, Leonid B. Krasin, that General Chang lacked full powers and was being recalled. Chang was given a ceremonial farewell by Chicherin and other Narkomindel personnel on October 31, was received by Lenin in audience two days later, and returned home in December. Not long after Chang's departure, the Soviet authorities accepted a Chinese consul general for Moscow and consuls for Irkutsk and Omsk. For the time being, however, Soviet consular officers were unable to take up their duties in China.

It is worth noting that the then American minister to China, Charles R. Crane, met with Chang and Chu Shao-yang, the Chinese consul at Irkutsk, at Peking in the following January for a discussion of Chang's "visit of investigation," and it was recorded by the American side that:

> For the sake of appearances they [Chang, Chu] informed Mr. Crane that their mission to Russia had been for the purpose of investigating conditions so that China might be in a position to take adequate measures of defense against the incursions of Bolshevism, but when they were questioned as to the dangers against which China would have to defend herself, they stated with a smile that the dangers were those that were apprehended by western nations and that China desired to conform her policy to that of the Allied countries, but evidently they themselves felt that right-minded people could not but admire the doctrines of the Soviet Government, their only doubt being as to its too great idealism.[10]

In the meantime, with the overthrow of the Anfu regime and the consequent reduction of Japanese influence in Peking, the new Chinese government had begun to readjust its position. In August, Peking withdrew from its agreement with Japan for "joint defense" against Soviet Russia; for China, too, the Siberian Intervention now ended. Then the Chinese government prepared to entertain Bolshevik representatives. Assuring the French and Japanese ministers that there would be no discussion of political questions with the FER representatives, it now permitted the Yurin mission to proceed to Peking. The FER delegation arrived in the Chinese capital in August. There promptly arose the issue of Yurin's full powers: he came by the authority of the Verkhneudinsk government, but the Chinese demanded that he show that he was authorized to speak for the Amur and Vladivostok governments as well — whereas, by virtue of the Japanese coup of May at Vladivostok, they knew that he could not produce such evidence.

Thus, in line with Peking's assurances to the foreign envoys, there was in the beginning no more than informal discussion with the Russian delegation regarding the restoration of trade relations. Even those contacts were suspended when, not long afterward, Wrangel won some successes in the Crimea. The Peking government took a step of considerable legal significance, however, when it informed Kudashev on September 8 that it considered the Russian legation at Peking and the tsarist Russian consuls in China to have lost their status and that it expected him to close the Russian organs forthwith. Minister Crane promptly reported this development to the Department of State, remarking that it constituted the first tangible victory for the Yurin mission. The State Department, which had viewed without perturbation Hsu Shu-cheng's overturning of Russian treaty rights in Outer Mongolia a year earlier, now undertook to intervene in support of the tsarist treaty position in China. Crane was instructed to invite the Chinese government's attention to the necessity of acting so as to avoid the charge "of having connived with the Bolsheviks to violate or ignore the treaty rights of the Russian people." [11]

To what must have been the surprise of Washington, Peking stood firm. A presidential order of September 21 set forth the current Chinese policy with respect to Soviet Russia and at the same time announced the withdrawal of recognition from former tsarist officials in China. In a response to Washington, the Peking Foreign Office asserted that there was no relationship between the arrival of the Yurin mission and the withdrawal of official recognition from the tsarist Russian diplomatic and consular officials, and announced that China itself proposed to "protect and administer" Russian settlements and property in China until such time as a proper Russian government might be established and recognized. With regard to the suggestion of connivance, Peking offered some salve that seemed to have an admixture of acid: "As to the internal affairs of Russia, the Government still follows a policy of non-interference in conjunction with the allied and associated powers." [12]

The diplomatic corps, including Minister Crane, sent a joint note protesting the Chinese actions. So did the Wrangel "government," in the capacity of lineal successor to the Russian provisional government and the Kolchak and Denikin regimes. In its discussions with Yurin, the Peking government quite possibly held back because of the foreign pressure — more than might otherwise have been the case. Nevertheless, the signing of the Russo-Polish armistice, the ousting of Semenov from Chita in October, and the decisive defeat of Wrangel in November, could only have convinced Peking that its move to establish contact with the Bolshevik power was in the Chinese national interest. In January, 1921, tsarist Prince Kudashev left China.

The interest of Moscow in relations with China was sharpened and defined as a result of considerations set forth in the Second Comintern Congress and the First Congress of the Peoples of the East, both of which were held in the summer of 1920. At this time, with their power consolidated after so bitter a struggle, the Bolshevik theoreticians viewed the Russian Revolution as the forerunner for new revolutions to come. It was nevertheless recognized that Asian revolutions would necessarily follow a course somewhat different from revolutions in the industrialized societies of the West, and it was proposed in this connection that revolutionaries in those essentially peasant societies of the Orient should follow united-front tactics, joining forces with the revolutionary bourgeoisie. The countries of the Orient, after all, were for the most part colonies or (as China was called) "semicolonies," and the enlightened bourgeoisie could be expected to experience such nationalistic fervor as that manifested in China's May Fourth Movement and to constitute useful allies of the weak working class in the revolutionary struggle. M. N. Roy, the Indian Communist, agreed with Lenin at the Comintern congress that the peasantry of Asia, where the industrial proletariat was so weak a force, had a major role to play in revolution; however, he argued further, against Lenin, that (1) the ultimate success of the European revolution depended entirely upon victory for the Asian revolution, and (2) consequently, the Asian revolution should be given priority over the European revolution.

The Moscow government was thus well adjusted to political opportunities that might issue in the China arena. A contemporary Chinese development presented an attractive potential. In late 1920, another in a long series of political upsets occurred in Canton, and Sun Yat-sen and his supporters were enabled to return there from their refuge in Shanghai. In December, they restored the Canton military government of 1917 to its functioning in opposition to the Peking warlord regime. This was a "bourgeois democratic" force of the type the Russian theorists had in mind.

For the moment, the Yurin mission was heavily engaged in negotiations with the Ts'ao-Wu regime at Peking. Wu P'ei-fu, at this juncture, was regarded by Moscow as an outstanding candidate for the role of "the best of the militarists." [13] The bilateral talks appeared at first to offer substantial promise. At the end of November, Foreign Minister Yen Hui-ch'ing (W. W. Yen) had a meeting with Yurin in which it was agreed to start official negotiations. Yurin on November 30 presented Yen with an exposition of the FER government's point of view respecting outstanding problems — and this could be taken as representing Moscow's position. But that position was already known, by virtue of the "declaration" earlier delivered to Chang Shih-lin at Moscow. The Peking Foreign Office in its reply proposed only a limited field of discussion: (1) the mission's abstention from propaganda in China, (2) indemnification for losses and damages sustained by Chinese merchants in Siberia, (3) guarantees for the protection of Chinese residents in Siberia, and (4) measures for the prevention of recurrence of incidents. [14]

The FER mission accepted those proposals — on the basis of mutuality. It then proposed, in mid-December, that there be considered the working out of a trade agreement, which was of course the nominal objective of the mission. Since the final article of the draft treaty proposed to Chang Shih-lin at Moscow in September had included provisions for settlement of the CER question, it is to be presumed that Yurin would have included a similar proposal in his present proposition — for he was effectively acting both as Moscow's representative and as the delegate from Verkhneudinsk. Yurin seemingly in due course received counterproposals from the Foreign Ministry, [15] and in May, 1921, now designated FER minister for foreign affairs, he went to Chita for consultations.

Yurin returned to Peking on July 25. The Yurin mission had earlier found no Chinese agreement for the proposition that there should be joint Sino-Russian administration of the Chinese Eastern Railway; now, another major issue besides that of the CER had obtruded into Sino-Russian relations. With Ungern-Sternberg out of the Outer Mongolian picture, the Chinese were desirous of reestablishing in that wayward vassal region the authority Hsu Shu-cheng had endeavored to impose upon the Jebtsun

Damba Khutukhtu—but the Red Army stood in the way. The CER and Outer Mongolian issues not only were deemed by Peking to be of first priority in any discussions with the Russians: by their nature, they automatically evoked the doubt that a representative of the patently temporary regime having its seat at Verkhneudinsk was qualified to negotiate a definitive settlement. On August 1, Yurin left Peking, without having achieved any settlement of major problems outstanding between China and Soviet Russia. He left behind him, to maintain the existing contact, his deputy A. F. Agarev.

Yurin's mission was not to be viewed as a total failure. He had during his residence at Peking established contacts in the academic community that would later prove fruitful for the Soviet effort. At least, coincident with his mission, Peking had withdrawn recognition from the tsarist diplomatic and consular representatives in China. Yurin had laid the foundation for later exchanges.

13 TURMOIL IN CENTRAL ASIA

THE RUSSIAN REVOLUTION and the ensuing civil war inevitably had an impact on Sino-Russian relations in Central Asia as well as in the Northeast Asian sector. In theory, the Bolsheviki acknowledged the right of the minority peoples of tsarist Russia to exercise self-determination, even if this meant secession; in practice, they had to take into sober account the probability that, if weak elements of the empire's periphery were to be detached, those territories were more apt to fall into hostile hands than to become "neutral" independent political entities. Finally, the Russian borderlands contained valuable resources. Bolshevik political theory therefore early came to be tempered by considerations of the strategic and economic value of the borderlands to Soviet Russia – in the role of a political power.

The Bolsheviki came into control in Tashkent soon after the October Revolution, and on May 1, 1918, Turkestan became an Autonomous Soviet Socialist Republic. The base for future action in opposition to Turki nationalism had been established. The situation in the Steppe Region developed very differently. There, the Bolsheviki organized a soviet at Orenburg, but the ataman of the Orenburg Cossacks, Aleksandr I. Dutov, in a coup of November 27 destroyed the Bolshevik apparatus and proceeded to mobilize the Cossacks, who soon controlled the southern Ural, Orenburg, and Semireche regions. Dutov aimed at formation of a Cossack state which would embrace those three regions and Russian Central Asia as well.

Organization of the Red Army was begun, in Petrograd, in January, 1918, and Turkestan followed that lead by forming its own Red Army units. Here, an important role was played by Vasili K. Bluecher. He organized workers and peasants and campaigned for some months against Dutov's Cossacks before leading 10,000 men over a 1,500-kilometer fighting march to join the Red force engaged against Kolchak on the eastern front.

After Kolchak's November coup at Omsk, the Dutov force, based at Orenburg, technically became a part of the Kolchak command. The military situation in Turkestan became more complex with the appearance of an anti-Bolshevik "Peasant Army" and the development of guerrilla warfare against the Bolshevik power by the Basmachi (from the Turki *basmak,* "to raid"). Circumstances dictated an adjustment of Moscow's Bolshevik Central Asian policy.

A new approach was foreshadowed in an article by Stalin, head of the Commissariat of Nationalities, published in *Izvestiya* on March 2, 1919: the Bolsheviki faced the task, he said, of winning over the approximately 30 million inhabitants of the region, thus to build a bridge to the proletarian movement of the East, "to construct a citadel of Soviet power in the East, to establish a socialist beacon in Kazan and Ufa, Samarkand and Tashkent, lighting the way to the freeing of the tortured people of the East." The task, then, was more political than military.

Tashkent's policies were subsequently moderated, to give a larger measure of recognition to the political aspirations of the Turkic minorities. Nevertheless, the fate of the overall Bolshevik program would patently depend in the first instance on the outcome of the fighting against the White forces commanded respectively by Kolchak, Denikin, and Yudenich. In August, 1919, the Bolshevik authority created the Turkestan front, under command of Mikhail V. Frunze. By mid-September, the Red forces had defeated Kolchak's Western Army and destroyed the Southern Army. The chief White forces remaining in that sector were Dutov's Cossacks, a Steppe Cavalry Corps led by the Cossack ataman Boris V. Annenkov, and elements of the Fourth Armenian Corps under Admiral Bakich, one of Kolchak's former naval associates.

With the collapse of the Kolchak power, Frunze at the beginning of March, 1920, addressed a proclamation to "the Kazakh and Taranchi people of Semireche" in which he called upon them to discard ties with the Whites and side with the Red Army. A few days later, he issued orders for an attack on Kopal, a Cossack stronghold. Bakich and his forces, numbering several thousand, accompanied by families and some merchants, crossed the Sinkiang border and reached Chuguchak, and the White leader Boiko surrendered Kopal to the Reds. Frunze ordered a general advance, and with the support of the Fifth Red Army from the Siberian front the Semireche forces went into action against Annenkov. Annenkov's main force was defeated at the beginning of April, and he retreated to a point near the Chinese Ili border and stubbornly hung on there for some time still.

War between Poland and Soviet Russia had begun in March, and a May drive by the northern Red Army was beaten back. Those developments raised the esprit of counterrevolutionary elements in Turkestan and Semireche. But a revolt that began with an uprising of the garrison at Verny was quickly suppressed. In late August, Bukhara proclaimed the establishment of a People's Republic. An armistice in October, 1920, brought an end to hostilities in the Russo-Polish war. And developments in Russian Central Asia entered upon a new stage.

The scene shifted to Sinkiang. Where a measure of quiet had succeeded the turbulence caused by the influx of Turki and Kazakh refugees from tsarist conscription in 1916, the upsurge of civil strife in neighboring Russia in 1918 had brought a new overflow of trouble into that Chinese Central Asian province. Tuchün Yang Tseng-hsin found himself increasingly engaged in diplomatic and other exchanges with the Russians, both Red and White. In May, 1918, he received a message from one Golikho, who stated that he had been appointed by the people's congress (at Tashkent) to be consul at Chuguchak and was planning to proceed, with an escort of twenty-five cavalry, to take up his post. Yang informed the aspirant consul that the matter of exchange of consular officers after the overturn of one government and the setting up of another depended upon the establishment of regular relations between the new regime and other governments, and he was without instructions from Peking regarding the matter; in the circumstances, it was necessary to request that Golikho delay his coming.

About a month later, the imperial Russian consul at Urumchi, one Dyakov, transmitted to Yang Tseng-hsin a message received from his colleague at Kuldja, Consul Lyuba, citing the report of Kazakh and Muslim arrivals from Semireche that it was feared the "old party" in their home oblast would be unable to resist the wiles and depredations of the "party of disorder," and requesting the intervention of the Chinese government. In a telegram of June 21 to the Peking government, Yang reported his "polite refusal" of that request that he send troops to aid the tsarist forces.[1]

The first defeated Cossacks to retreat into Ili came about this time. There were some 275 troops, accompanied by refugee women and children. The Chinese disarmed them. Dyakov asked that the unit be given back its arms and be permitted to return to Russia. Yang requested instructions from Peking, and was informed by the Ministry for Foreign Affairs that defeated Russian troops crossing the Manchurian border at Blagoveshchensk and Manchouli had been disarmed and brought under control of the Chinese authorities, and that Yang should be guided accordingly. The policy regarding refugee Russian troops entering Sinkiang had thus been fixed, and would govern thereafter — at least nominally.

Matters were further complicated for Tuchün Yang by the arrival of Japanese on the scene. Tokyo was deeply concerned with developments in Soviet Asia at that juncture, and it would have been unlike the Japanese strategists to neglect the Bolshevik flank. A successor ruler of Sinkiang, Sheng Shih-ts'ai, would in due course report that in 1918 there arrived in the province from China Proper an official Sino-Japanese "joint investigation group" of twenty persons, comprising ten Chinese and ten Japanese. The group had the nominal function of investigating political and military conditions and "regulating" the Sino-Russian frontier. According to Sheng, the Japanese were actually engaged in planning "aggression" against Sinkiang, with one of their main functions being the establishment of contacts with White Russian officers and the organization, with those officers' help, of espionage work. The Sino-Japanese group appears to have made Ili the base of their activities, and they remained there for two years. Then, with the collapse of the Siberian Intervention and the changed situation, that "joint investigation group" departed.

Yang Tseng-hsin's records give a measure of support to Sheng's allegations. In a telegraphic report of November 29, 1918, to the Peking government, Tuchün Yang remarked in passing that the Russian consul in Ili and a Japanese "investigator" had been jointly obtaining information regarding conditions prevailing among refugee Russian troops. In a telegram sent two days later to his Ili defense commissioner, Yang remarked that people of "a certain country" (Japan?) had on various occasions proposed at Urumchi that (Japanese?) troops be stationed at Ili and Chuguchak to assist in the border defense, but that luckily the Peking government had taken the position that the national defense of Sinkiang was China's own responsibility. Those same quarters had urged him, Yang, to dispatch troops to attack the Reds, arguing that certain future benefits would derive from such action.

Yang admonished his defense commissioner that to send troops across the border for that purpose would be "most disadvantageous." Twice more before the end of the year the shrewd old tuchün castigated the White Russian proposal to move troops through Sinkiang as deriving from the machinations of "a certain country" that wished to stir up trouble between Sinkiang and the Bolsheviki so that it would have an excuse to intervene with military force in Sinkiang. Given the experience of Manchuria, Yang's suspicions may well have been correct. In any event, the proposal was eventually dropped.

With the first Red victories over Kolchak's forces in Semireche, and the crumbling of Cossack power in Sinkiang's close neighbor region, Yang Tseng-hsin became increasingly harassed about what to do with Consul Lyuba at Kuldja. Lyuba was apparently both a loyal tsarist and an energetic and hardfisted man besides, and he had undertaken the organization on Chinese soil of a White Guard junta to overthrow the Red power in Semireche. The matter took a critical turn when the Peking Foreign Ministry in May, 1919, instructed Yang to escort Lyuba from the country with troops. Yang replied — and there was no reason to doubt the sincerity of his words — that he would very much like to take the suggested action, but that at the moment over 10,000 White troops were attacking the Reds in Semireche, and if Lyuba were expelled from China at that juncture the Whites might seize the opportunity to quarrel with Ili. On July 10, Yang instructed the Ili defense commissioner and the *taoyin* (circuit intendant) that the Whites should be forbidden to recruit troops in Ili. It was not until September, 1919, however, that he was at last able to report to Peking that Consul Lyuba had consented to stop his recruiting activities.

The Bolsheviki pressed their case. In September, they requested via the Ili officialdom: (1) the opening of the border to the Bolshevik authorities, (2) the release of Reds held by Lyuba, and (3) the exchange of consular officers. Yang instructed his Ili officials that the first and third requests pertained to international relations and would have to be taken up with the central government, but that the illegal actions of Lyuba would be given consideration upon receipt from the Bolsheviki of a listing by name of the detained persons.

With the collapse of the Kolchak government, the question of Sinkiang's harboring Russian refugees became a major issue with the victorious Reds. In January, 1920, a Bolshevik delegation to Kuldja presented four demands, the nature of which was indicated by Yang's subsequent instructions to his Ili subordinates. Yang directed that: (1) it was difficult to extradite White officers and consular officials, and the Bolsheviki could not make threats in contravention of international law; (2) the matter of designation of a Soviet commercial agent in Sinkiang should be taken up with the Chinese central government; (3) it was difficult to agree to the establishment of a Russian telegraph service to Ining (Kuldja),* but if it were desired to connect the Russian line to the Chinese service at Khorgos (on the Sinkiang-Russian frontier) the matter might be taken up with the central government; and (4) the extradition to Russia of Russian refugees was permissible, with delay in the case of those hampered by poverty or illness, but to obviate difficulties there should be a clear statement by the Bolsheviki that they would follow international law in this regard and would not, because of the personal ideas of one or two persons, take independent action (that is, would not arbitrarily execute the refugees).

As the White breakup progressed, the position of the tsarist representation in Sinkiang also deteriorated. On March 20, 1920, Yang directed the Ili defense commissioner to place Lyuba and the rest of the tsarist consular staff at Kuldja under surveillance and escort them to Urumchi. When the defense commissioner re-

* "Ining" is the Chinese name that was given Old ("Tatar") Kuldja, the administrative center of Ili Special District, which was incorporated into Sinkiang Province only under the Republic.

plied that Lyuba was still unwilling to depart, Yang directed that Lyuba be "urged" to begin his journey quickly. The obstreperous consul left within ten days.

In 1919, the first few refugees into Sinkiang had been followed by a small military group led by General Shcherbakov, the earliest of the high Cossack leaders to seek asylum in China. Now Ataman Dutov and over 1,000 troops crossed the frontier into Sinkiang. They were disarmed and temporarily lodged in barracks. Bakich led his remnant force over the international frontier in March, 1920.

In May, Annenkov's troops, assailed by hunger and disease as well as by the Reds, began to abandon their hopeless position and make their way into the Sinkiang haven. An interesting aspect of the retreat was that the troops carried little in the way of munitions; the third group of Annenkov's men, comprising 587 troops, turned over to the Chinese only 127 rifles and 4,000 rounds of ammunition. Yang, however, held that it was of no concern to China whether or not it was true, as reported, that Annenkov had buried his good rifles in Russia. Annenkov and his rear guard, numbering only 1,400 men including sick and wounded, crossed the Sinkiang frontier in mid-May. Of his original force of about 20,000 men, somewhat over 80 percent had been killed or had shifted to the side of the Reds; only 2,000 to 3,000 reached Sinkiang. Ataman Annenkov and his men took up a position near Borotala, in Chingho Hsien.

Soon afterward, the Ili defense commissioner informed Yang that Chinese troops had apprehended some twenty Cossacks sent to Russia to bring back arms that had been buried there. From Chuguchak, Yang received the further intelligence that the White forces there had dug up some buried weapons with the purpose of killing Admiral Bakich. The situation was taking on more ominous aspects, and Yang instructed Kuldja that Annenkov and his men should not be permitted to proceed to Urumchi. He further ordered that the Chinese forces surrounding the White troops at Chuguchak should be replaced by Mongol and Manchu troops. Yang knew fighting men, and he seems to have had a healthy respect for the military capacities of the tsarist Cossacks who had come to Sinkiang with nearly a decade of war experience behind them.

Yang was also appreciative of the fact that the Bolsheviki had won the civil war in Russia. In May, 1920, when a congress, attended by Lenin himself, convened at Tashkent, Yang dispatched a delegation to that Turkestan town. There, on May 27, the Sinkiang envoys and Soviet commercial representatives signed the so-called Ili Trade Agreement.[2] It comprised three parts, the first governing trade relations and providing for the mutual establishment of commercial and foreign affairs bureaus; the second, laying down provisions for the repatriation from Sinkiang of Russian troops and civilian refugees; and the third, providing the first measures for consideration of Chinese losses sustained in Russia as a consequence of the Revolution.

Both the Annenkov and Bakich forces were involved in the June uprising at Verny. It was only at the end of June, all too late, that Yang Tseng-hsin directed that strong measures should be taken to prevent the White forces at Chuguchak from joining Annenkov. Evidently disturbed at the possible results of Chinese negligence in this connection, Yang directed his Chuguchak taoyin to reply to the pertinent inquiries of the Red commander, Klotov, with a confidential proposal that, in future instances where China might have informed the Bolsheviki in advance of impending "special actions" on the part of the tsarist forces in Sinkiang, China should be absolved of blame.

The Chinese efforts to moderate the irritation of the Bolsheviki came after Sinkiang had for some time demonstrated ineffectiveness with respect to the disarming and administration of the White forces. Sinkiang's shortcomings in that regard derived at least partly from the province's own political and military weakness, but the Bolshevik authorities had passed the point where they were inclined to be indulgent. Frunze on July 27, 1920, reported by telegram to the revolutionary military council (at Moscow) that the troops of Dutov, Annenkov, Bakich, and other White Guard leaders had not been disarmed upon entering Chinese territory and had in fact retained in part their military organization. He charged that the great mass of the Whites' equipment had been buried and remained at the disposition of the enemy forces; further, according to latest information, the White generals were recruiting local Russians and Muslims and organizing new detachments. The activities of the Whites in Sinkiang, he said, included the establishment of ties with the Basmachi of Fergana and secret agitation in Semireche itself. By his estimate, Kuldja was the center for the anti-Soviet movement in all Turkestan: it harbored a Muslim organization that planned the waging of a holy war for the liberation of the peoples of Afghanistan, Persia, India – and first of all Western Turkestan.

Frunze said that the (Turkestan) revolutionary military council considered that, for the establishment of complete peace in Turkestan, it was essential that the White Guard center in Sinkiang be liquidated. He proposed that the Chinese authorities should be categorically required to disarm all White bands and transport them into deep China and that, in case of refusal, the Soviets should temporarily occupy Kuldja and Chuguchak. "The [Turkestan] Revvoensovet [revolutionary military council] awaits the appropriate orders of the center."

The deliberations of "the center" in this regard are not a matter of public record. It was clear, however, that the day of final reckoning was approaching for the White forces, of which the strongest group was that commanded by Bakich, who had reputedly received a million rubles in gold from the director of the Russo-Asiatic Bank at Chuguchak for the support of "troops for the salvation of Russia." [3] Commanding over 12,000 men, he was in camp with his main force on the Emil River, near Chuguchak.

The White forces had become a thorn in the flesh of Yang Tseng-hsin, and he proved cooperative. To achieve the objective of Frunze's demand that the White forces in Sinkiang be disarmed, the Chinese and Soviet sides reached an agreement for joint military operations, and in the spring of 1921 the Soviet Seventeenth Rifle Regiment and a Chinese mixed brigade collaborated (at least nominally) to surround the White headquarters unit at Chuguchak. The Red unit took 500 prisoners, including 100 officers, who were sent back to the homeland from which they had come. By May, the Thirteenth Division from the Siberian front as well as troops from Semireche were cooperating with several Chinese regiments in the field against Bakich's forces.

Operations were at last undertaken against the main unit under the personal command of Bakich. He made a fighting retreat, but battle between the two armies was finally joined at Sharasume. There, in August, 1921, the White force was defeated.

Bakich led his remaining troops into Urianghai; from there, he was driven into Outer Mongolia. The Red Army caught up with the hard-fighting Cossack force at Ulankom, and the Cossacks met their end there in October. Bakich was captured by a Mongol unit in mid-December and handed over to the Bolsheviki for trial and execution. The turbulent influence of the White Cossacks in Sinkiang had been eliminated as a political factor in Central Asia.

The Russian struggle for "pacification" of the Turki peoples themselves had not yet been completely won: the Basmachi were still active. Bukhara had become a rallying point for Muslim rebels against Russian authority. Among the arrivals in 1921 was Zeki Validov Togan, who set about the organization of a secret Turkestan National Union, with the long-term objective of ousting Russian authority and setting up a Turki government for Turkestan. The Basmachi movement entered a new stage.

The situation was complicated by the entry into the political arena of Enver Pasha, Turkey's sometime minister of war, in October of that year. Enver, who had been prominent in the Young Turk movement in his native land, came in the first instance as an agent for the Soviet government, but then he shifted to the side of the Muslim revolutionaries and went to eastern Bukhara. Early in 1922, he began to enlist support for a Turki movement having as its objective the creation of a great Central Asian Muslim state. Togan argued against Enver's ambitious plan, which he considered impracticable in the face of Russian military superiority — and doubtless he also had in mind the lack of cohesion among different Turki groups. Enver Pasha nevertheless went ahead, and soon had recruited some 7,000 troops for his cause. He also established liaison with the Basmachi of Fergana. In April, he was visited by a ten-man Soviet delegation with the offer of peace negotiations. Disregarding the advice of Togan, Enver rejected the offer of a political settlement,[4] and on May 19 issued an ultimatum demanding the removal of all Russian forces from Khiva, Bukhara, and Turkestan within fifteen days.

With his alliances, Enver Pasha at that juncture commanded (nominally) an army of some 16,000 men. He had extended his control over much of Bukhara as well as Fergana. The Soviet government, however, sent against him General Sergei S. Kamenev, who had taken part in the fighting against Kolchak and was now commander in chief of the Russian Soviet Federated Socialist Republic (RSFSR) armed forces, and Grigori K. Ordzhonikidze, a member of the party central committee. The Red Army in mid-June administered a severe defeat upon Enver's army near Kofryun. He sustained another defeat at Dushanbe. Then, in early August, a Soviet detachment of 300 troops came upon Enver

Pasha's remnant force, and Enver, attacking recklessly at the head of some twenty men, was killed.

The backbone of the Basmachi movement had now been broken. By 1926, except for occasional guerrilla raids from bases in Afghan territory, the movement was ended. The conservative Basmachi leaders had made much more trouble for the revolutionary Russian power than had the Turki liberals. All alike had been weakened politically by their internecine jealousies and dissensions, and this proved a major factor in the failure of their struggle for national independence and pan-Islam.[5]

Thus it was that Russian Turkestan was pacified. In October, 1924, Russian Central Asia experienced a change in political boundaries. The Turkestan Autonomous Soviet Socialist Republic and the Bukharan and Khorezmian People's Republics all went out of existence, and were replaced by the Soviet Socialist Republics (SSR) of Uzbekistan and Turkmenistan, the Autonomous Soviet Socialist Republic (ASSR) of Tadjikstan, and the Kara-Kirgiz and Kara-Kalpak Autonomous Oblasts. The Kirgiz ASSR (the former Steppe Region), with more accurate nomenclature, became the Kazakh ASSR. From this development, with a number of subsequent adjustments of boundaries or status, what had once been Russian Turkestan and the Steppe Region was duly incorporated into the Union of Soviet Socialist Republics (USSR) that had come into being at the end of 1922.

On the other side of the Central Asian international frontier Yang Tseng-hsin, long experienced in adjusting to political change, continued to maintain good relations on the basis of the 1920 Ili Trade Agreement. In September, 1923, he and the Soviet side drew up a new agreement to replace the 1920 treaty, but Peking, when asked to approve the document, would authorize signature only "with slight modifications." The Soviet side found Peking's recommended changes unacceptable and refused to sign. It was only after Peking itself in May, 1924, signed a treaty with Moscow reestablishing normal relations between the two states that Yang Tseng-hsin, by an exchange of notes of October 6, 1924, with a Soviet representative from Omsk, achieved what he had long desired—the establishment of five Chinese consular offices in neighboring Russian areas in exchange for the reestablishment of Russian consulates in Sinkiang. The Chinese offices were to be set up at Semipalatinsk, Alma-Ata, Zaisan, Andijan, and

Tashkent; the Soviet organs at Urumchi, Chuguchak, Kuldja, Sharasume, and Kashgar.

Yang's "foreign affairs" were on a sound basis. The Cossack elements remaining in Sinkiang were seemingly now under firm control. Annenkov was imprisoned for a time by Yang Tseng-hsin but was released, and then made his way to Kalgan — the gate to Inner Mongolia. There he was arrested by Feng Yü-hsiang and turned over to the Soviets in Outer Mongolia, whence he was returned to Semipalatinsk, tried by a Soviet court, and shot. Dutov was killed at Kuldja by Soviet agents in 1921 or 1922, whereupon his military organization fell to the control of his lieutenants, chief among whom were Colonel Papingut and Colonel Eric (Aleksandr I.) Franck, a Volga German who had been under Admiral Kolchak at the time of the Russian Revolution. Papingut and Franck would still, in due course, play minor roles in Sinkiang political disorders. Many White officers and Russians of the aristocratic class made their way as best they could to China port cities. Even more rank-and-file soldiers and peasant émigrés, seeking to build a new foundation for their existence, settled in Sinkiang. They were deprived of their own military organization, but Yang Tseng-hsin did not force them to enter the Chinese military service. Some simply returned to Soviet Russia, to adapt themselves to a way of life which, if radically different from what they had known in the past, was still Russian.

Russia's international position had by this time improved still further. Bluecher, as FER minister of war, had in January, 1922, assumed personal direction of the Red forces operating against the Whites in Primorye and, beginning with a critical victory at Volochaev, his troops on February 14 captured Khabarovsk. With the withdrawal of Japanese forces from Vladivostok October 24 and 25, 1922,[6] the FER People's Revolutionary Army occupied the port. The Soviet Far East, excepting northern Sakhalin, had been cleared of foreign interventionists.

14 REESTABLISHMENT
OF STATE RELATIONS

ONE OF MOSCOW'S prime purposes was the reestablishment of regular relations with the warlord government at Peking: China on the side of Japan was a potential enemy; in friendly relationship with Moscow and neutralized, it would constitute a buffer zone protecting Soviet Russia's eastern flank. The Russians thus did not long delay in making new moves after the return of the Yurin mission to the Far Eastern Republic in 1921. On December 12 of that same year, another Russian delegation, led by Aleksandr K. Paikes, arrived in Peking. That delegation came from Moscow.

The appointment of the Paikes mission had in a sense derived from the Chang Shih-lin visit. The Chinese consular officers whose appointment had been announced by Chang duly arrived in Russia, and were tentatively acknowledged by the Moscow government. But when Moscow endeavored to get its own representatives into China, Peking finally announced that Moscow's consular officials could not be accepted prior to China's recognition of the Soviet government. The Soviets thereupon informed the Chinese consul general at Moscow that recognition of him in that capacity could only be on the basis of mutuality.

There were many Chinese resident in Russia, and Peking desired protection for their interests. In March, 1921, the Chinese government finally acknowledged receipt of the communication handed Chang Shih-lin in the previous September, and stated that it was prepared to engage in direct discussions. Moscow welcomed the interest of the Peking government, not omitting to remark the usefulness that the exchange of consular personnel would have with respect to the matter of Peking's concern for Chinese citizens living in Soviet Russia. After a lengthy exchange of correspondence, Peking in April gave its agreement, hedged by conditions, to receive an "unofficial" delegation from Moscow. The Paikes mission was the result of that agreement.

Upon its arrival in Peking, the Moscow mission was joined by Agarev, as representative of the FER. The Mongolian question was clearly up for discussion. At this time, White Guard forces commanded by Bakich, Kaigorodov, and Kazantsev were still active in the Kobdo region, and Moscow had no intention of removing its Red Army units from Outer Mongolia — particularly given past Chinese delinquencies with respect to the activities of Semenov, Ungern-Sternberg, and others. Further, the November, 1921, treaty with Urga had changed the situation to Moscow's considerable benefit.

In the end, it was the Soviet-Mongol treaty that tripped up Paikes's mission. At Harbin en route to Peking, he had given an interview in which he denied that Soviet Russia harbored any agressive intent with respect to Outer Mongolia and asserted that the Soviet forces there would be withdrawn as soon as the danger to Soviet Russia offered by hostile organizations in Outer Mongolia had been removed. Rumors of the signature of a Soviet-Mongol pact reached Peking about the same time as Paikes himself, however, and soon after his arrival the Foreign Ministry questioned him regarding the reported agreement. Paikes denied the existence of any such treaty.

Another factor was operative at that time. In November, the Washington Conference convened for the settlement of outstanding issues in the Pacific, and with regard to China — and Russian Asia as well. Russia, for all of its protests, had not been invited to attend, and was only able to look on, at a distance, through the medium of an unofficial FER delegation present in Washington. China, on the other hand, was a participant and a primary object of American concern. Rather naturally, Peking chose for the moment to give greater emphasis to prospective gains from the Washington meeting than to the potential of Sino-Soviet negotiations which had already been frowned upon by the great powers represented at Washington.

On January 8, 1922, Peking proclaimed the abrogation, as of April 1, of the Sino-Russian treaty of 1881. In the preface of the declaration it was stated, doubtless with reference to Moscow's expressed readiness to review with Peking various Sino-Russian agreements that had been signed between China and the tsarist regime, that there existed at the time no formally recognized government in Russia to which the Chinese government might propose a review of the treaty. The formal discussions between the Paikes mission and the Foreign Ministry, which were to have begun a few days after the mission's arrival, failed to start.

The Washington Conference took up the question of the disposition of the Chinese Eastern Railway. In the end, however, in circumstances where China was still in effective control, and the powers—particularly Japan and the United States—were suspicious of each other's "imperialist" ambitions in that regard, the result was a mild resolution recommending more economical and careful administration of the railway, for preservation of the interests of its owners. Even though not present at the conference, Soviet Russia benefited further from the deliberations of the conferees by Japan's being caused to agree to withdraw from the Primorye.

China was disappointed in its larger ambitions with respect to the conference. While offering promises for the future, the great powers abandoned none of the substance of their privileged position under the "unequal treaties." There was indeed signed a "Nine-Power Treaty Relating to Principles and Policies to Be Followed in Matters Concerning China," in service of the American desire to have a codification of the Hay Doctrine. Soviet Russia, not being a party to the conference or its instruments, was naturally not bound by the treaty's provisions. The conference adjourned in February, 1922. The fundamental error of the Washington Conference powers in assuming that it would be possible to keep Soviet Russia isolated was demonstrated when Moscow, to the surprise and consternation of the Allies, in April signed the Rapallo Pact with defeated Germany—bearing the implicit threat of overturning the Versailles Treaty provisions. Conditions were no longer what they had been in 1918–1920.

China was nevertheless still under pressure from its putative benefactors not to enter upon any agreement with Soviet Russia. It was also, as usual, under internal strains. In April, 1922, Chang Tso-lin's forces entered the Great Wall from Manchuria in a move that could easily be interpreted as having the support of Japan. On May 1, under this threat, the Peking government sent Paikes a note that seized upon the issue of the Soviet-Mongol pact, the existence of which had by now been confirmed, and asserted that: "Mongolia is a part of Chinese territory and as such has long been recognized by all countries. In secretly concluding a treaty with Mongolia, the Soviet Government has not only broken faith with its previous declarations but also violates all principles of justice." [1]

With Paikes unable even to get formal negotiations started, Moscow in June named Adolph A. Joffe as plenipotentiary for the Peking mission, charging him to undertake discussions in Japan as well. Joffe arrived in the Chinese capital in mid-August, and Paikes returned to Moscow in defeat. In his first contacts with the Chinese Foreign Ministry, Joffe indicated the readiness of the Soviet side to enter upon negotiations for new agreements based upon the principles of the two Karakhan declarations of 1919 and 1920. In a note of September 7, Peking agreed to negotiate — but stipulated, as a precondition for talks, that Soviet military forces should be withdrawn from Outer Mongolia.

In the exchanges that followed, it became evident that the main issues between the two sides would indeed be, as before, the Chinese Eastern Railway, Outer Mongolia, and, besides, Russia's share of the Boxer indemnity. The first issue was related in the Chinese mind to the faulty text of the 1919 Karakhan Declaration as received from Irkutsk. Peking desired simply that the CER be turned over to China, gratis; Moscow proposed joint operation, with recognition of China's sovereignty over the railway zone. With regard to the second issue, the Soviets were quite evidently unwilling to cede more than had been provided in the tripartite agreement of 1915, but Peking, for its part, was desirous of reasserting the status imposed upon Urga by Hsu Shu-cheng. As for the third matter, Moscow had long before renounced the Russian share of the Boxer indemnity — but not unnaturally objected to those funds being used against it.

Joffe in September broke his residence in Peking to attend a fruitless conference with the Japanese at Changchun respecting the rendition of Primorye. After his return, in a memorandum of October 13, he dealt with the Chinese demands. He contended that the immediate withdrawal of Russian troops from Outer Mongolia, in the face of another possible attack by White Guard forces, would be in the interest of neither Soviet Russia nor China. He complained again that Russian White Guards enjoyed the use of China as a base for attacks on Soviet territory. Peking in late October ordered local Chinese authorities to disband White Russian groups seeking shelter in Chinese territory. But this order naturally did not affect the status of White Russian units fighting for Chang Tso-lin.

When Peking continued to dwell on the allegedly binding effect of the 1919 and 1920 declarations, Joffe on November 5 finally warned that those declarations could not be regarded as valid forever and that, unless the Chinese government ceased ignoring Russian interests, "Russia will perhaps, after all, be obliged to consider herself free from those promises which she voluntarily gave."[2] For all of the haggling, it was the general belief in Peking that the projected Sino-Soviet conference would open early in 1923. But a new, and doubtless more attractive, possibility opened up before the Soviet diplomat: he was invited by Viscount Goto Shimpei, mayor of Tokyo and one of the leading proponents of a Russo-Japanese rapprochement, to visit Tokyo — not officially as Moscow's envoy, but for treatment of an illness incurred during the trip to Changchun. Joffe accepted without any notification to his Chinese hosts, and to the surprise of Peking departed for Japan in early January, traveling via Shanghai. The Soviet mission as such remained behind in Peking in the charge of Davtian.

Joffe never returned to Peking; he departed Tokyo en route home the following summer. He was succeeded in China in early September by Lev M. Karakhan, sometime acting commissar for foreign affairs and since 1921 Soviet ambassador to Poland. Karakhan was much feted in Peking, and, like Joffe, he talked over the heads of the Peking government to reach the Chinese people. In line with the Comintern policy of the time, he advocated an alliance between China and Soviet Russia. The imperialist powers, he warned, desired to keep China divided and weak: "Only the Soviet Republics, only the Russian people, desire to see China strong, powerful, possessing a strong Army, and capable of defending the interests and the sovereignty of its people." Further, "The friendship of Russia and China is a pledge of the peace of the Far East."[3]

Karakhan in the beginning assumed an advanced bargaining position: he demanded, as a condition precedent to negotiations on outstanding problems, the formal recognition of the Moscow regime. But he was quick to settle for China's counterproposal that, even without Peking's recognition, a bilateral conference be held for consideration of the issues in dispute. Again the representatives of the foreign sea powers evinced concern, and the American, British, French, and Japanese ministers sent the Foreign Office a note stating that their governments were interested in having China adhere to the Washington Conference resolution with respect to the disposition of the Chinese Eastern Railway. American Minister Jacob Gould Schurman went further by holding that China had no right to settle the CER question without the sanction of the great powers, under whose guardianship the railway would have to remain.[4]

Peking made bargaining moves designed to manifest its indifference to the working out of an agreement with Moscow. Its negotiator, Wang Cheng-t'ing (C. T. Wang), as Joffe before him, made a trip to Tokyo. Karakhan, however, manifested no signs of distress or urgency; in an interview given at the time, he evinced confidence that, once the CER issue was settled, there would be little difficulty in disposing of other issues.[5]

The bargaining position of Moscow was becoming stronger, while that of the tuchün regime at Peking did not change. The Far Eastern Republic, having served its purpose, had ceased its "independent" existence in November, 1922, and Siberia was once more an integral part of a united Russia. Karakhan's actions reflected a growing Soviet confidence. He sent a telegram of warm congratulations to the rebel Chinese at Canton on the occasion of the convening of the First Kuomintang National Congress in January, 1924, and received a friendly acknowledgment from Sun Yat-sen in return. The new Soviet minister to Outer Mongolia and the Mongolian minister to Moscow both presented their credentials in that same January, without either paying even lip service to Mongolia's traditional ties to China. On February 1, 1924, Britain extended diplomatic recognition to the Soviet government, and Italy, Norway, and Austria followed suit later in the month. Between February and October a total of eleven countries would recognize the new Soviet state. All the time, Karakhan continued to protest to the Foreign Office regarding alleged violations of Russian rights and interests in China. Chinese public opinion, particularly as voiced by the articulate academic community at Peking and by the press, became increasingly insistent upon the unconditional restoration of normal diplomatic relations between the two countries.

Those were developments which even Chinese warlords could not afford to ignore indefinitely. Peking got down to business. On February 25, a few days after Austria's recognition of the Moscow regime, Karakhan and Wang reached agreement on negotiation procedures. Then, on March 1, they settled upon a draft treaty.[6] Wang delivered the draft to President Ts'ao K'un on March 3,[7] and on the following day it was forwarded to the Cabinet for consideration. The Cabinet duly approved the draft agreement, and on March 14, after the exchange of full powers, it was duly signed and sealed by the two plenipotentiaries. It was scheduled for formal signature in clean draft that same day, but instead the Peking government suddenly disavowed Wang's full powers, citing, in a circular telegram of March 23 to top military and civil officials in the provinces, three chief changes it professedly desired: (1) treaties between Soviet Russia and Outer Mongolia should "immediately" be canceled; (2) Soviet troops should "immediately" be withdrawn from Outer Mongolia; and (3) former Russian property in China such as churches and immovable property should not be handed over to the Soviet government.

One cannot believe that Wang had negotiated the instrument without the full knowledge of Foreign Minister V. K. Wellington Koo in particular and the Cabinet in general. Peking's circular telegram had probably not set forth the true explanation for the government's bizarre action. French minister A. J. de Fleurian on March 12 had warned the Foreign Ministry that "serious consequences" might follow the signature of an agreement by China and Russia regarding the Chinese Eastern Railway without consultation with the Russo-Asiatic Bank. Peking had actually been warned for months not to act on the CER matter without regard for the interests (and opinions) of the great powers. The Peking Foreign Ministry offered the facile argument that Wang had exceeded his authority, but the probability was that, at this time, "American, French, and Japanese representatives were applying heavy pressure against conclusion of so far-reaching a pact with Soviet Russia,"[8] and that in an eleventh-hour panic the Peking government decided to withhold action, making Wang the scapegoat, in the hope of at least getting some further concession from the Soviet side.

Wang was in fact at first instructed to continue negotiations, in order to obtain the desired revision.[9] But on March 20 he was removed from his artificial position as chief negotiator, and the negotiations were transferred back to the Foreign Ministry, that is, to Wellington Koo. On April 1, the Ministry proposed to Karakhan that the March 1 draft should be the basis for agreement, with the addition, as desirable changes, of three points—those set forth in Peking's telegram to the provinces. It was, moreover, proposed that, contrary to a provision in the Wang-Karakhan draft, regular diplomatic relations should after all *not* be established between the two countries coincident with signature of the treaty.

The French and American legations put new pressure on the Foreign Ministry to the end that there should be no agreement, and beginning May 20 the intensive negotiations between Koo and Karakhan were carried on secretly, where they had been semipublic before. Neither Karakhan in Peking nor Chicherin in Moscow bowed to the arguments marshaled by Koo in support of a better bargain for China. There were, moreover, rumors that circulated to the effect that the USSR and Japan were preparing to enter upon a deal, and that Moscow was in negotiation with both Canton and the Mukden government. On May 31, 1924, without having won any concession of substance, Peking surprised the international community by signing a treaty with the Soviet Union.

The document as signed by Wellington Koo was essentially that negotiated originally by C. T. Wang. It provided for the resumption of normal diplomatic and consular relations "immediately" upon signature of the treaty. All treaties and agreements that had been concluded between the Chinese government and the tsarist government would be annulled at a conference to be held within a month of signature and would be replaced with new treaties and agreements based upon the principle of equality and reciprocity, "as well as the spirit of the Declarations of the Soviet Government of 1919 and 1920." The Soviet government "recognizes that Outer Mongolia is an integral part of the Republic of China, and respects China's sovereignty therein," and would withdraw its troops therefrom as soon as the envisaged conference had brought agreement on "the measures to be adopted in the interests of the safety of the frontiers" and the matter of the time limit for such troop withdrawal.

Article VI provided that "The Governments of the two Con-

"SOVIET RUSSIA" TO
UNION OF SOVIET SOCIALIST REPUBLICS

1000 KM.

SPITZBERGEN (NOR.)

ARCTIC

BR., & FR., 1918-1920

BR., FR., & U.S., 1918-1920

GREAT BRITAIN

London

NORTH SEA

NORWAY

SWEDEN

Murmansk

NOVAYA ZEMLYA

Paris

BELG.

NETH.

DEN.

FRANCE

GERMANY

Berlin

FINLAND

Petrograd

Archangel

YUDENICH

BALTIC SEA

R

U

S

URAL MOUNTAINS

S

ITALY

Vienna

Rome

AUSTRIA-
HUNGARY

Budapest

POLAND

LITH.

Brest-Li.

WHITE RUSSIA

Smolensk

MOSCOW

Vologda

Kirov

Kazan

Perm

Ekaterinburg

Tobolsk

Ob

ALBANIA

SERBIA

GREECE

RUMANIA

BULGARIA

Kiev

Odessa

FR., 1918-1920

DENIKIN

Rostov

BLACK SEA

VOLGA

Ufa

Orenburg

URAL

KOLCHAK

Omsk

KOLCHAK'S
HEADQUARTERS
TO NOV., 1919

MEDITERRANEAN

OTTOMAN

EMPIRE

BR., 1918-1920

Batum

TRANS-
CAUCASIA

Astrakhan

CASPIAN SEA

ARAL SEA

LAKE BALKHASH

EGYPT

RED SEA

Mosul

Tabriz

Baku

Alma Ata

Tashkent

Kashgar

ARABIA

PERSIAN GULF

Teheran

BR., 1918-1920

PERSIA

AFGHANISTAN

INDIA

T. R. MILLER

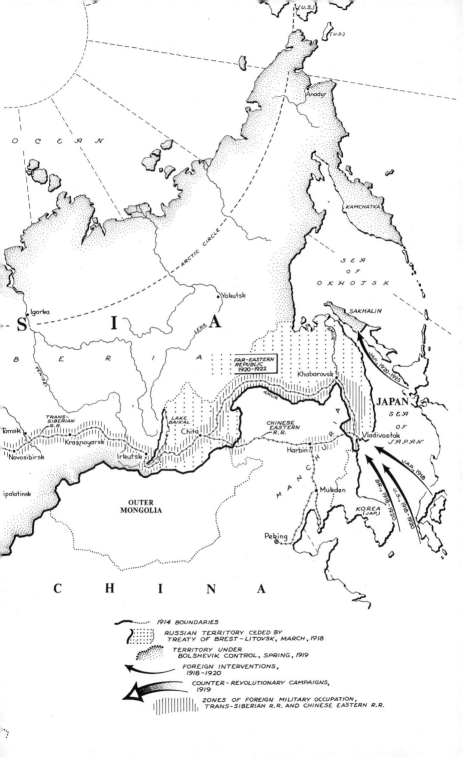

O   C   E   A   N

(U.S.)

(U.S.)

Anadyr

ARCTIC CIRCLE

KAMCHATKA

SEA
OF
OKHOTSK

Yakutsk

S   I   A

SAKHALIN

B   E   R   I   A

LENA

FAR-EASTERN
REPUBLIC
1920-1922

Igarka

Khabarovsk

JAP. 1920-1925

YENISEI

AMUR

JAPAN

SEA
OF
JAPAN

TRANS-
SIBERIAN
R.R.

LAKE
BAIKAL

AMUR

Tomsk

Chita

CHINESE
EASTERN
R.R.

Vladivostok

Krasnoyarsk

Harbin

JAP. 1918

Novosibirsk

Irkutsk

M
A
N
C
H
U
R
I
A

ipalatinsk

Mukden

KOREA
(JAP.)

Br. 1918-1920

U.S. 1918-1920

OUTER
MONGOLIA

Peking

C   H   I   N   A

1914 BOUNDARIES

RUSSIAN TERRITORY CEDED BY
TREATY OF BREST-LITOVSK, MARCH, 1918

TERRITORY UNDER
BOLSHEVIK CONTROL, SPRING, 1919

FOREIGN INTERVENTIONS,
1918-1920

COUNTER-REVOLUTIONARY CAMPAIGNS,
1919

ZONES OF FOREIGN MILITARY OCCUPATION,
TRANS-SIBERIAN R.R. AND CHINESE EASTERN R.R.

tracting Parties mutually pledge themselves not to permit, within their respective territories, the existence and/or activities of any organizations or groups whose aim is to struggle by acts of violence against the Governments of either Contracting Party." This provision clearly debarred Japanese as well as White Guard use of Chinese territory as a base of operations against the USSR. Another long article set forth the principles on the basis of which the CER question would be settled at the contemplated conference, the essence of the matter being that the administration of political, military, and police matters over the CER zone now pertained to China, that the railway remained the property of the USSR but might be redeemed by the Chinese government "with Chinese capital," and that "The Governments of the two Contracting Parties mutually agree that the future of the Chinese Eastern Railway shall be determined by the Republic of China and the Union of Soviet Socialist Republics, to the exclusion of any third party or parties." The Soviet government for its part unilaterally renounced the special rights and privileges relating to concessions obtained in China under the provisions of tsarist treaties (such concessions existed in Hankow, Tientsin, and Harbin), the rights of extraterritorial and consular jurisdiction, and, finally, the Russian portion of the Boxer indemnity.[10] Certain accompanying declarations and notes dealt with individual problems, including the provisional management of the Chinese Eastern Railway.

Russia had been one of the last of the Western powers to obtain for itself "unequal treaty" status in China; after the defeated powers Germany and Austria, it was the first to abandon that status. Chicherin hailed the agreement as "an historical event in the emancipation of the Eastern peoples," and went on:

> The appearance of the Soviet Union on the coast of the Pacific Ocean as a power friendly to China immediately raises the question of the world importance of the basin of the Pacific Ocean. Formerly the cultured world was concentrated around the Mediterranean. Now the political and economic interests of the world reach out more toward the Pacific. It is the ocean of the future.[11]

The reaching of this agreement with the Peking government, in the face of the opposition of the powers, was a clear victory for Soviet diplomacy. The victory was still incomplete, for Chang Tso-lin in Mukden considered his government a law unto itself, not bound by the actions of the enemy central government at Peking. He therefore refused to accept as applicable to Manchuria — where the CER was located — the provisions of the May 31 treaty. Peking sent Pao Kuei-ch'ing to Mukden to get Chang's acquiescence in the state treaty just signed, but the mission was unsuccessful. Chang demanded that, as far as Manchuria might be concerned, a new agreement be signed with his regime. Now, his hands freed by Peking's admitted inability to cause the Manchurian warlord to abide by the provisions of the treaty, Karakhan sent his aide, Nikolai S. Kuznetsov, to Mukden for "unofficial talks." Chang, who at this time still retained his close Japanese connections, proved himself an obstreperous negotiator, repeatedly breaking off the talks.

> Finally, the Soviet representatives let it be known that, inasmuch as the question of the CER had been regulated with the Chinese government, and Chang Tso-lin hindered the implementation of the Peking agreement, the government of the USSR would be compelled to have recourse to such measures as might cause the Shenyang militarist to respect the agreement.[12]

Chang Tso-lin was not desirous of constituting himself the main target of hostile Soviet efforts: he still retained those ambitions with respect to North China that had twice before been frustrated. At this juncture he was in contact with Feng Yü-hsiang of the Wu P'ei-fu camp and proposed, with the help of Feng, to oust President Ts'ao K'un and his military supporter Wu P'ei-fu from power in Peking. On September 20, at Mukden, Kuznetsov signed with three representatives of "The Government of the Autonomous Three Eastern Provinces of the Republic of China" a new agreement effectively confirming the provisions of the May 31 treaty insofar as the latter document affected the Chinese Eastern Railway in particular, except that it was now provided that the Chinese government would obtain gratis possession of the railway and appurtenant properties sixty, instead of eighty, years after construction as provided by the original contract of 1896.

The Treaty of Rapallo had breached the quarantine barriers erected in the West to "contain" the Bolshevik regime; the 1924 treaties with the Peking and Mukden governments were comparable in their effect: the Soviet Union had thereby forced open the door to the East. On October 24, after negotiation of the agreement with Chang Tso-lin, Karakhan made a significant statement:

> The restoration of the Soviet Union's title to the Chinese Eastern Railway opens up broad vistas for economic and political collaboration with China. At present the Soviet Union is gaining a firm foothold in the Far East by occupying one of the most important positions of which its enemies were trying to deprive it.[13]

Chang Tso-lin and Feng Yü-hsiang duly achieved their coup at Peking, ousting the Ts'ao-Wu regime. Feng promptly transformed his armed forces into the Kuominchün (People's Army). On November 24, Tuan Ch'i-jui returned to power in Peking, under the aegis of Chang and Feng, as provisional chief executive. The new Peking government organized in March, 1925, could without qualms approve Chang Tso-lin's treaty of the previous September, and did so.

Events in China Proper during 1924 were accompanied by important changes in Outer Mongolia. Major developments had been in course there ever since the signature of the Soviet-Mongolian agreement of November, 1921. In January, 1922, while Paikes was still in Peking, Bodo lost his positions as premier and foreign minister of the Mongolian People's Revolutionary Government at Urga. In August, he and fourteen other alleged conspirators were executed, among the charges being that they "aspired to overthrow the people's government, to set up the old autonomous government dependent on and subject to China," and that Bodo and the Jebtsun Damba Khutukhtu in particular had sent representatives to Chang Tso-lin to discuss with him "whether to govern the Mongolian nation as a part of the Chinese Three Eastern Provinces."[14]

On February 22, 1923, Sukhe Bator died, at the age of thirty, poisoned (according to the version that has been written into the official history) by the Bogdo Khan, Jebtsun Damba.[15] The Urga regime in 1923, however, staged a coup that resulted in the final consolidation of its authority over western Mongolia. Ja Lama had defied a move of February, 1922, by Urga to extend its rule over Kobdo by fiat, and some time later, presumably after the purge of August, 1922, he moved his small military force (and his larger popular following of some 500 yurts) to the border region between Outer Mongolia and Sinkiang and there established a fortified position. In 1923, a Mongol detachment ran him down *in Sinkiang,* killed him, and sent the longtime rebel's head and heart to Urga. This marked the end of resistance by Kobdo to the new revolutionary rule: the district now was brought directly under Urga's control.

Soviet Russia had in various times and circumstances asserted that it had no imperialistic designs on Outer Mongolia and no intention of causing that territory to break off from China. Moscow was confronted, however, by a double threat from the side of Outer Mongolia: there might emerge from the increasingly sophisticated Mongolian nationalism an urge to pan-Mongolism which would, at the least, threaten to engulf both Buryat Mongolia and Tannu Tuva and, at the most, might stimulate a growth of nationalism among the Turkic elements in Russian Turkestan; or, as experience had demonstrated, Mongolia might be used by either China or Japan as a sharp-edged instrument against Soviet Siberia.

The enhancement of the Soviet Union's international position in the 1922–1924 period gave it further freedom of action vis-à-vis both Japan and China. It was therefore not surprising that, after the death of the (eighth) Jebtsun Damba Khutukhtu on May 20, 1924, it proved impossible to find his reincarnation. In June, it was announced that Outer Mongolia was to be transformed into a republic. The Mongolian People's Revolutionary Congress sat from August 4 to September 1, 1924, and consolidated the foundations of the new state. The nationalist Danzan, who had contributed largely to the creation of an independent Mongolia in the first instance and had come to occupy the positions of chairman of the Mongolian People's Revolutionary Party central committee and commander in chief of the army, was arrested by order of the congress, tried by a special commission on charges of corruption and collusion with the Chinese, and shot. He appears to have stood for an anti-Soviet policy line and had clashed, in the congress, with the Comintern agent, the Buryat Mongol Rinchino, over the issue.[16]

The first Great People's Huruldan (*khural* – council) met in November, 1924, and adopted the national constitution. By the first article, Mongolia was proclaimed "an independent People's Republic in which all power belongs to the labouring people."[17] All international agreements antedating the 1921 Revolution were declared null and void. Foreign trade (in which both Chinese and Russians had long been so interested) was thereafter to be a state monopoly. The name of the capital was changed from Urga to Ulan Bator (Red Warrior); the ancient Russo-Chinese trading point Maimaicheng became "Altan Bulag."

Theocracy had reached its term in the land of the Mongols; so had Chinese rule. In March, 1925, the Soviet Union informed the Chinese government that Soviet forces had been withdrawn from the Mongolian People's Republic (MPR) and pointedly advised the Peking government to deal peaceably with the Mongols thereafter. Chicherin about the same time made a significant statement to the Congress of Soviets:

> We recognize this republic of Outer Mongolia as part of the Chinese Republic, but we also recognize its autonomy as sufficiently wide to preclude any interference in the internal affairs of Mongolia on the part of China, and to permit independence in its foreign policy. . . . In Mongolia we have a government completely directing its policy along the lines of close rapprochement with the USSR.[18]

Russia had effectively won the centuries-long struggle with China for preeminent influence in Mongolia. The Mongols of the Mongolian People's Republic, for their part, had obtained a shield against two dominations, either of which threatened to be more onerous than the Russian—the Chinese and the Japanese. In August, 1926, as a separate act of insurance, Moscow by a treaty with Tannu Tuva acknowledged it to constitute a separate political entity, independent of the Mongolian People's Republic.

Bemused by the advice of its great-power "friends," the Chinese government had waited several years too long to get a good bargain with the new Russian government at Moscow.

15 PEKING-MOSCOW RELATIONS IN CRISIS

THE OLD, IMPERIAL relationship between Japan and Russia had ended in 1917; what form the new relationship would take was then still to be determined. Certain trends, however, could be foreseen. The war of 1904–1905 had given good reason to anticipate that Manchuria would be a future arena of contest between Russia, Japan, and China, and the Siberian Intervention had offered substantiating evidence. Japan was bound to note the possible significance of the Sino-Soviet rapprochement of 1924 for the balance of power in Northeast Asia. Analyzing the causes of conflict in Manchuria, the Lytton Commission at a later date would remark the effect of the procession of events:

> The Russian Revolution of 1917, followed by the
> declarations of the Soviet Government of July 25, 1919,
> and of October 27, 1920, regarding its policy towards the
> Chinese people and, later, by the Sino-Soviet agreements
> of May 31, 1924 and September 20, 1924, shattered the
> basis of Russo-Japanese understanding and cooperation
> in Manchuria.[1]

The advent of Shidehara Kijuro to the Foreign Ministry of the Kato Cabinet in June, 1924, brought important shifts in Tokyo's strategy: Shidehara undertook to carry out a conciliatory policy toward both China and the Soviet Union. At a time when Moscow was still endeavoring to develop good relations with

Peking and its ties with Canton had not yet borne substantial fruits, Soviet relations with Japan experienced a remarkable advance. In September, 1923, shortly after his arrival in Peking, Karakhan had called on Japanese Minister Yoshizawa to inquire whether Japan desired to resume the talks discontinued upon Joffe's departure from Tokyo. Japan was not, at the moment, interested. With the initiation of the Shidehara policy, however, Yoshizawa resumed negotiations with Karakhan, and on January 20, 1925, there was signed, at Peking, a basic treaty, with accompanying agreements, incorporating a settlement of outstanding issues and Tokyo's recognition of the Soviet regime. Notably, it was provided that Japanese forces should evacuate Northern Sakhalin by May 19, 1925. That evacuation was duly accomplished, and the Siberian Intervention was finally ended, for all concerned.

Peking, after winning in 1924 an initial advantage in relations with the USSR, was by 1925 again lagging behind. The Sino-Soviet conference that was to convene within a month after signature of the May 31 treaty was blocked in the first instance by Mukden's unwillingness to be bound by the agreement's provisions. Then, the Second Fengtien-Chihli War that began in October had brought about yet another exchange of tuchüns at Peking and the installation of a new government under the uneasy front man, Tuan Ch'i-jui. It was only in March, 1925, that Peking designated C. T. Wang to be director general, and Mukden's man Cheng Ch'ien vice director, of the projected conference.

The meeting nevertheless still did not take place. Conflict between Chang Tso-lin and Feng Yü-hsiang naturally complicated matters. Further, there developed a wrangle over operation of the CER under the provisional procedures established by the May agreements. Five Chinese and five Russian directors had been appointed to administer the railway, with Soviet citizen A. N. Ivanov holding the positions of director and general manager, and General Pao Kuei-ch'ing functioning as vice director and chairman of the board of directors. When Ivanov moved to dismiss employees possessing other than Chinese or Soviet citizenship (that is, White Russians), a dispute occurred between the Chinese and Soviet directors. It was settled in June on the basis of Ivanov's interpretation, and more than two hundred employees in the proscribed category were discharged from their posts.

The Sino-Soviet conference was at last formally convened on August 26, 1925. The following day, Karakhan left on a trip to Moscow, and the full-dress sessions necessarily adjourned. Various subcommittees went to work, however, on outstanding tasks, such as the negotiation of a consular convention, the drawing up of a trade agreement, and the verification of frontiers. Clearly, the settlement of CER matters had a primary importance, but by the time Karakhan returned Feng Yü-hsiang and Kuo Sung-ling were engaged in a war against Chang Tso-lin, and for the time being little progress was to be expected regarding issues centered on Manchuria.

The formal conference resumed on December 1, and work on a draft consular convention and the projected trade agreement made fair progress until, in March, 1926, the Chinese negotiator was taken ill. The claims subcommittee began with reasonable chances of success, with the Chinese side asking 40 million gold rubles in compensation (mainly for losses allegedly sustained by Chinese merchants in Russia during the Revolution). The subcommittee on verification of existing frontiers, on the other hand, held only three sessions.

The Kuo Sung-ling rebellion had a long-term effect on the negotiations. On November 10, after the revolt had begun, CER General Manager Ivanov directed that Chinese troops would be transported only upon payment in cash. This action was viewed by Chang Tso-lin, who was the antagonist desirous of transporting troops by rail, as a manifestation of Soviet sympathy for his enemies Feng and Kuo; the circumstance that the Japanese intervened in the dispute in *his* behalf evidently did little to salve his sense of injury.

Manchuria's endemic banditry provided the occasion for a direct confrontation on the troop-transport issue. The railway guards by virtue of the 1924 agreement between Chang Tso-lin and Moscow were no longer under CER administration. In mid-January, 1926, the commander of the guards, General Chang Huan-hsiang, decided to send a force of sixty men from Kuanchengtzu to deal with a bandit menace in the vicinity of Yaomen, and his troops undertook to commandeer a mail train for their travel. Again by authority of Ivanov and in accord with the

November precedent, free transportation was refused, whereupon the troops prevented the train from leaving and seized other trains as well. Ivanov thereupon suspended rail traffic between Harbin and Changchun, an action that automatically brought losses to the connecting Japanese South Manchurian Railway (SMR) trunk line between Changchun and Dairen. General Chang Huan-hsiang ordered resumption of traffic, but his order was disregarded by the Russian railway management.

General Chang Huan-hsiang had acted by authority of Chang Tso-lin, who was quite beyond the control of the Tuan Ch'i-jui government in a Peking occupied by the troops of Feng Yü-hsiang. Moscow knew this, and it was therefore quick to act when, on January 21, General Chang Huan-hsiang effected the arrest of Ivanov, the three Soviet CER directors, and numerous Soviet employees of the railway. On the following day, Moscow addressed a telegraphed ultimatum to the Peking government demanding the release of Ivanov and the others arrested, and restoration of "order" on the railway, within three days. The message went on to say that, in the event that the Peking government for any reason found itself not in a position to achieve the desired results within the indicated time period, the Soviet government was ready, with permission of the Chinese government, to assure with its own strength the protection of the joint interests of China and the USSR in the Chinese Eastern Railway.[2]

Tokyo dealt a blow to Chang Tso-lin's presumed hopes of outside support when the Foreign Office announced that the Japanese government had no intention of mediating the CER matter, that is, would not support Chang's arbitrary action to possess himself of foreign railway property in Manchuria. After all, why should Japan condone a move that might establish a precedent prejudicial to its own holdings in China? Without foreign support, Chang was in no position to continue with his challenge to the Soviet Union, and an agreement for the settlement of the dispute was signed at Mukden between the Soviet consul general and a representative of Chang Tso-lin a full day before expiry of the time limit.

The agreement made little provision for saving the political face of the Manchurian dictator. It was stipulated that there should be release of the arrested Soviet citizens, that railway traffic should be resumed, and that transportation of troops should be in accordance with railway regulations, with the cost of transportation of Chinese troops to be charged against China's share in railway profits; other issues would be settled by later negotiation. Ivanov was released the next day, and rail traffic resumed. But, as demanded by Karakhan, Chang Tso-lin on January 30 dismissed railway guards commander Chang Huan-hsiang, replacing him by Ting Ch'ao. Later, in April, there was something in the nature of a quid pro quo: Ivanov was removed as CER director and general manager by action of the board of directors, and replaced by A. I. Emshanov.

Turbulent change in Manchuria was paralleled by deadlock in Peking. When the claims subcommittee of the Sino-Soviet conference met in March, the Soviets were confronted with a new Chinese demand, purportedly based upon the Soviet declarations and the enabling May, 1924, agreement, for compensation in damages now computed at 3.4 billion rubles. The Soviets rejected the demand outright. The work of the other subcommittees stalled about the same time. Chinese politics had taken their toll. The circumstance that Chang Tso-lin and Wu P'ei-fu were heavily engaged against the forces of Feng Yü-hsiang until mid-April, while the First Kuominchün controlled Peking, had an obvious influence on negotiations; after mid-April, with the collapse of the Tuan government, Chang Tso-lin permitted Wu P'ei-fu for the time being to run Peking as he chose.

Chang had other work at hand. He had developed a strong animus toward Karakhan by reason of the defeats suffered at the Soviet diplomat's hands and in March launched a campaign against him. Chang's representative, Chang Kuo-ch'en, negotiated with the Soviet consul general at Mukden with the aim of obtaining Karakhan's recall, on the grounds that Karakhan was inciting Chinese students to bolshevize China and had also helped Feng Yü-hsiang to prolong civil disturbances in China.[3] In a reply of April 6, the consul general remarked that the demand had considerable international importance and requested that the marshal consider the matter carefully. Chang Tso-lin blandly hoped in turn that Karakhan's departure from Peking would not affect diplomatic relations between the two countries.

Chang's demand for Karakhan's recall, it was reported, was made with the support of Wu P'ei-fu.[4] Karakhan, however, did not yet take his leave. On April 20, there arrived in Mukden the Soviet vice commissar of communications, L. P. Serebriakov, who had previously served on the Chinese Eastern Railway. He was charged with discussing matters pertaining to the administration of the CER – and also Chang's demand for the recall of Karakhan.

Serebriakov on May 21 formally got down to the work of negotiation with Chang's representative in an effort to resolve the outstanding issues. The prospects were not good. The Soviet side offered an eight-point program for a broad settlement. The Chinese presented Chang's charges that Karakhan was involved in Communist propaganda and political movements in China and had generally interfered in China's internal affairs. The charges were basically true. But an even greater difficulty in reaching agreement was found in the circumstance that Chang had no intention of accepting any settlement of CER issues that might confirm the Soviet position. On June 7, Chang's chief of staff, Yang Yü-t'ing, announced that the conference was terminated. Serebriakov started for home, whereupon the Fengtien authorities reconvened the meeting. Serebriakov returned – only to be met with the old Fengtien proposals regarding Karakhan. He then departed for good.

On July 31, the Peking Foreign Office, dutifully voicing the sentiments of Chang Tso-lin, instructed the Chinese chargé d'affaires at Moscow, Cheng Yen-hsi, to demand Karakhan's recall. With Moscow denying that the move was in response to the Chinese demand, Karakhan on September 10, 1926, finally left Peking. The Soviet embassy was left in the hands of Chernykh, as chargé d'affaires. Karakhan would not return to China – he died in the Soviet purge of 1937.

The Sino-Soviet conference having been effectively aborted, the Chinese abolished the committee headed by C. T. Wang and unilaterally organized, under the overall chairmanship of Wang Yin-t'ai, six new committees, three to sit in Peking and three in Mukden, to deal with outstanding Sino-Soviet issues. They then invited Moscow to send representatives to take part in the work. Moscow seems not even to have replied.

A military drive launched from the South in July by the revolutionary Nationalists had now reached the Yangtze, and posed a new threat to warlord power. There was still trouble ahead for the USSR, however, in the territory controlled by Chang Tso-lin. It had been reported in Harbin in late August that the Fengtien government had issued orders to the naval authorities to seize the shipping department of the CER. Chicherin, in a note of August

31 delivered to the Chinese chargé in Moscow, demanded immediate cancellation of the order, saying that the Soviet Union would not tolerate further violations by Chang Tso-lin of existing Sino-Soviet agreements.

Two days later, General Shen Cheng-chang, commander of the Sungari defense forces, by authority of Chang Tso-lin seized eleven river steamers and thirty barges of the CER Sungari River fleet. Then, on September 4, he occupied and sealed the educational department of the Chinese Eastern Railway. As justification for their action, the Chinese argued that the new agreements of 1924 gave the Soviets no rights of navigation on the Sungari — and besides, the Soviets had confiscated certain Chinese ships at Vladivostok in 1922. The activities of the CER's educational department, it was charged, infringed upon Chinese sovereignty. That the action was perhaps not based on principle alone was indicated by General Shen's report that he had turned over to the Chinese authorities (Chang Tso-lin) the sum of Y$1.6 million discovered in the educational department's treasury. The personnel of the department were summarily dismissed. The Soviet government in a note to the Peking government expressed the hope that "illegal" actions would be promptly countermanded, and on October 9 it expressed its willingness to review all disputed issues pertaining to the CER.

This time, in the face of Chang Tso-lin's growing authority, the Soviet protests proved ineffectual. In December, 1926, after disaster had overtaken his occasional comrade-in-arms Wu P'ei-fu on the Yangtze front, Chang moved personally into North China, created the Ankuochün (National Pacification Army), and took direct charge of the Peking government. In February, 1927, his campaign against the Soviet Union was advanced yet another stage. His old-time associate, Shantung military governor Chang Tsung-ch'ang, occupying a prominent position in the Ankuochün hierarchy, had moved troops to the south in support of General Sun Ch'uan-fang and with Sun established a joint headquarters at Nanking to confront the Nationalist military threat. On February 28, his troops (which included a contingent of 4,000 White Russians) seized at Nanking the Soviet ship *Pamyati Lenina,* which was en route to Hankow to load tea, and arrested the ship's crew, several diplomatic couriers, and the wife of Soviet adviser Mikhail M. Borodin. All were sent to Chang Tsung-ch'ang's provincial capital, Tsinan, and were there imprisoned. Incidental to the arrest, propaganda literature and presumably Soviet documents were obtained — and doubtless conveyed to Chang Tso-lin in Peking.

The Soviet embassy at Peking was not in a good position to protest the arrest of the couriers, since their visas, as issued by the Chinese mission in Moscow, were valid only for travel via Manchuria, inferentially to the Soviet embassy at the capital, and therefore could not except by some stretch of the imagination be deemed to cover travel by Soviet ship proceeding via the open sea and the Yangtze River to a Soviet consular office in "enemy" territory, Hankow. The Soviet government nevertheless on March 10 made its protest, demanding the release of the arrested Soviet citizens and return of the ship and diplomatic mail.

Chang Tso-lin was not moved by the Soviet demand, nor was he inclined to make a chivalrous exception even in the case of Mme Borodin. Borodin's wife, née Fannie Orluk, was an American citizen. In an interview granted American Senator Hiram Bingham in late April, Chang informed his distinguished visitor that he planned to execute Mme Borodin the following day. He was quite evidently disagreeably surprised to be told by the American that the world would judge him a beast and a barbarian if he were to shoot Mme Borodin without a trial, that the Western world didn't treat women in that manner, but after a tense moment the marshal said, "Well if the Westerners are so foolish about their women as that, I will not execute Mrs. Borodin." [5]

Still, it was not Moscow's protests, but luck, that finally brought about the release of Fannie Borodin. She and the diplomatic couriers were actually given their freedom by a Chinese court at Peking in July — and they immediately disappeared from the scene and the court judge just as promptly went into hiding. Orders were issued for the rearrest of the Russians, and for the arrest of the judge besides; the judge's wife, two children, and a brother were thrown into prison, while wrathful pressure exercised by Chang Tso-lin on the minister of justice resulted in the resignation of the chief justice of the high court. It was perhaps to compensate in part for this judicial mishap that the ship's complement of forty-seven officers and men were held in prison at Tsinan, without trial or charges laid against them, until January, 1928 — by which time Chang Tso-lin's position faced a renewed threat from the Nationalist side. Then they were released.

The Nanking warlords had originally intended to use the

Pamyati Lenina in the fight against the Nationalists, but the Chang-Sun forces were defeated at both Shanghai and Nanking in March, and as they retreated they blew up and sank the ship. The setbacks at Shanghai and Nanking however probably only stimulated Chang Tso-lin's hostility to Moscow: he was a man who held to plans to destroy an enemy. On March 20 and 29 his police descended upon Peking colleges and arrested a number of students. Lists of alleged Kuomintang and Communist student leaders were also handed to the college authorities with a demand that the suspects be delivered over. A number of the "wanted" students and intellectuals fled, some taking refuge in the Soviet embassy. Among other refugees found already in residence there was the revolutionary leader Li Ta-chao, who had in 1926 written a denunciation of Chang Tso-lin that was published in a local newspaper. After the fearsome warlord moved to Peking in December of that year, Li had fled for his life to the presumed sanctuary of the Soviet embassy.

The main fear of Chang Tso-lin, and of the foreign powers, at that time was not of the Chinese Communists but of the Nationalist revolutionary movement, generally considered to have been "bolshevized," and the Moscow influence that was assumed to be advancing pari passu with the Nationalists toward the capital. Chang clearly appreciated that Soviet aid to the Nationalists was substantially aiding the revolutionaries to build up a real threat to the Peking government. He now discussed with various Peking missions a project for raiding the Soviet establishment in the legation quarter. It was agreed by the British and French that permission for such breach of the Boxer Protocol would be forthcoming, but express arrangements should be made by direct negotiations between the Fengtien authorities and the doyen of the diplomatic corps, Netherlands Minister H. E. W. J. Oudendijk. On the morning of April 6, Chang's representative formally requested Oudendijk's authority to raid the premises of the Dalbank (Far Eastern Bank) and of the Chinese Eastern Railway, adjoining the western portion of the Soviet embassy in the legation quarter, on the grounds that those places were known to be the headquarters for subversive "agitation."[6] Oudendijk had seemingly already been in contact with his American and British colleagues (at least) regarding the matter.[7] In any event, he gave prompt approval "in behalf of the diplomatic quarter" (in the words of American Minister John Van A. MacMurray's pertinent report), and a party made up of nearly 500 Peking police and Fengtien gendarmerie was admitted to the legation quarter shortly after 11 A.M. of the same day and began the raid.

When a black cloud of smoke from burning documents began to rise from the chimney of the Soviet military attaché's office, the raiding party soon "went beyond their authorization," and extended its action to the quarters of the military attaché, which were located *inside* the Soviet mission compound with its presumed diplomatic immunity. The American and British legation guards had been alerted (as they had to be in order to grant admission of the Chinese forces into the sacrosanct legation quarter), but they made no effort to intervene against this expansion of Oudendijk's authorization. The Chinese were thus able to cart away masses of propaganda material and confidential documents. They also arrested and took off to jail eighteen or nineteen Russians and over sixty Chinese.

Just after 5:00 P.M., Chargé Chernykh went to the Foreign Office to protest the violation of embassy territory. The Foreign Ministry was closed for the day: it was a Chinese holiday. Chernykh was thus unable to deliver his note of protest. Before the day was out, however, he *received* a note from that same Ministry protesting with respect to the documents and inflammatory materials seized, and the Communist agitators arrested, in the course of the raid. The Foreign Ministry received a second note of protest that same day: Oudendijk now protested to the Foreign Ministry regarding the intrusion into the office of the Soviet military attaché. Yet, the time limit of the original authorization was extended to permit continuation of the work at hand. The deed had been done, and an eyewitness to the affair reported that there was evident general approval of the action on the part of members of the diplomatic corps.[8] Dr. Charles Fox, editor of the *China Star,* went further. He offered the opinion that the British minister, Sir Miles Lampson, was the prime mover in getting the Chinese to stage the raid, with Minister MacMurray, however, playing the more active role while Lampson remained behind the scenes.[9] The Japanese, oddly enough at first glance, had been reputedly lukewarm with regard to the project.[10] But perhaps they had again thought of the danger of establishing certain precedents.

Soviet Commissar for Foreign Affairs Maxim Litvinov promptly demanded the withdrawal of Chinese police and gendarmerie from the Soviet embassy premises, return of the seized documents, and release of all arrested persons. But where Moscow had been able effectively to resist encroachments on its position by threat of the use of pressure vis-à-vis Chang Tso-lin in Manchuria in 1924 and 1926, now, with Chang at the head of the central government in Peking, the Soviets found themselves without the means to obtain retribution. The Peking government rejected the Litvinov demands on April 16, and Moscow was forced to limit itself to withdrawing all diplomatic personnel from Peking. Chargé Chernykh and his party of some twenty persons promptly departed the Chinese capital, leaving behind only consular personnel. Chinese Chargé Cheng Yen-hsi remained at his post in Moscow. It had been a little under three years since the establishment of official relations.

In a first message of April 6 to Ankuochün leaders, Chang Tso-lin explained that he had effected the raid because the Soviet embassy constituted the headquarters for *Kuomintang* propaganda in North China.[11] Far from returning the seized material, he in due course published some of the documents, *and* documents seized from the *Pamyati Lenina* couriers, in Chinese translation, in the meantime making them available to the American, British, and French military attachés. There was indeed evidence obtained of Soviet ties with Kuomintang revolutionaries,[12] but this was hardly to be considered new intelligence. Documents established the fact that Feng Yü-hsiang had developed tenuous ties with both the Kuomintang and the Soviet embassy and that, in the six months from October, 1925, through March, 1926, Moscow had made payments to the First, Second, and Third Kuominchün totaling US$383,933. In a sense, Chang had obtained some evidence supporting his suspicion that the Soviets had had a hand in the Feng-Kuo rebellion against his power.

There were also, as further concrete corroborative evidence of "subversive activities," the prisoners. Foreign legations in Peking, as the foreign concessions in Shanghai and other treaty ports, had in the past often played host to Chinese politicians suddenly feeling the compulsion to seek safety from their domestic enemies. Tuan Ch'i-jui, Ts'ao K'un, and Premier Chia Teh-yao had all taken refuge in the legation quarter upon the fall of Tuan's regime in April, 1926. But the Soviet embassy proved an insecure haven. Chia Teh-yao was among the refugees seized in Chang Tso-lin's raid. Further, besides reputedly discovering a list of 40,000 Kuomintang members, Chang had netted a number of Kuomintang activists, his critic Li Ta-chao, and a half dozen members of the Peking branch of the Chinese Communist Party. On April 28, after a drumhead court martial, twenty-four of the arrested Chinese were put to death, most of them by strangulation. Among those executed was Li Ta-chao, who had contributed so largely to the founding of the Chinese Communist Party and the introduction of contemporary Russian radicalism into China. His death would prove a sign of things to come.

The arrested Soviet citizens were held in prison until the overthrow of Chang Tso-lin's regime a year later automatically closed the case of the Soviet embassy raid. They were evidently spared the fate accorded to Li Ta-chao and his comrades by Oudendijk's advice that, for the Russians, "A proper and public trial would be necessary, in accordance with China's new laws, in the presence of the foreign Press and with proper defence for the accused." [13]

The April 6 events in Peking seemingly had a shock effect well outside the perimeter of the capital – and even of Chang's authority. In the international settlement at Shanghai on the evening of the same day, by authority of the Shanghai Municipal Council (comprising six British, one Japanese, and two American nationals), armed pickets were thrown around the Soviet consular office and Chinese entering the building were stopped and searched. On the following day the picketing force, made up of White Russian volunteers in the employ of the council and a sprinkling of British police officers, was further strengthened. The foreign Municipal Council had thus taken sides in the tuchün regime's dispute with the Soviet Union. On April 7, in the French concession at Tientsin, the Soviet consulate together with offices of the CER and other Soviet enterprises were also raided and documents seized.

Major forces were coming into play. This was confirmed when, in May, the British in London raided Soviet House, location of Arcos, the Soviet trade agency, in disregard of the Soviet claim to diplomatic immunity by virtue of the 1921 agreement. The British based their action on the grounds that a document involving military secrets had been stolen. The lost document was not discovered on the Soviet premises; the British found other documents they deemed to show Soviet involvement in subversive Communist activities, however, and on May 27, 1927, London broke off diplomatic relations with Moscow.

Chang Tso-lin's actions would thus appear to have been justified by similar action on the highest "imperialist" level. But his motives in moving against the Soviet Union were not to be considered simply in the light of his own preferred explanations, or yet against the background of his earlier feud with Karakhan. Marshal Chang was in deep trouble and was looking about for aid. He had been endeavoring for some time to win foreign financial support against the advancing Nationalists, whom he labeled "the forces of Bolshevism." The propaganda approach had, however, proved insufficiently attractive — against the background of his record.

16 MOSCOW AND CHINESE REVOLUTIONARIES, 1923–1926

AS THE SOVIET UNION'S diplomatic relationship with the Chinese central government waxed and waned, Moscow worked hard at building up a parallel relationship with the forces of revolutionary Chinese nationalism. Beginning in 1920, various Comintern representatives visited China. They both established contacts with Sun Yat-sen and helped to organize, in July, 1921, the Chinese Communist Party (CCP).

Sun Yat-sen, a man of many political devices, during the winter of 1921 and spring of 1922 was engaged in a search for foreign aid, his governing concept envisaging a Chinese-German-Russian alliance. Sun's scheme naturally had his Canton regime, not the Peking government, in the role of representative government of China. There was some basis in logic for Sun's idea: defeated Germany and pariah Soviet Russia, alike "oppressed" by the seafaring nations and bereft of their former positions of privilege in China, seemed superficially qualified to be allies of a "semicolonial" China opposed to those same sea powers. It was to be noted, nevertheless, that the plan was conceived entirely on the basis of China's self-interest. The proposition in that form carried little attraction for the sober politicians of Berlin and Moscow. In any event, Sun was again thrust from power in Canton by his military supporter Ch'en Chiung-ming's coup of June, 1922. It had been demonstrated anew that Sun could not speak for China.

Supported in the early days of the T'ung-meng Hui by individual Japanese, Sun did not at this time omit consideration of Japan as a possible source of aid. Back in Shanghai, he gave an interview to a Japanese newsman in which he said that, "In joining in the World War on the side of the Allied Powers, Japan failed to utilize the golden opportunity of making Asia exclusive for the Asiatics. Such an Asia would have opposed the Whites, especially the Anglo-Saxons." [1] He was prepared to offer obiter dicta. "As Japan has shown herself incapable of seizing this opportunity, it will be China that will be called upon to make Asia a place for Asiatics in the future." But he assured his Japanese audience that it was not too late for Japan to correct its error.

> If Japan really wishes to see Asia controlled by the
> Asiatics, she must promote relations with the Russians.
> Russians are Asiatics. . . . Japan must make common
> cause with the Russians in opposing the aggression of
> the Anglo-Saxon. In shaking hands with Russia in the
> work of asserting the rights of the Asiatic alone lies
> hope of salvation from the catastrophe to which Japan
> and the other Oriental countries are being forced by
> the unsatiable ambition of Anglo-Saxons.

The editor of the *Japan Advertiser,* which had printed the interview in English translation from the Japanese original, remarked that on several occasions in the past decade Sun had raised his voice in the wilderness "to cry the coming of a Messiah who will preach the gospel of freedom for the colored peoples of Asia from the hated domination of the whites." [2]

As things actually turned out, there was after all a temporary joining together of Soviet Russia and the Chinese revolutionaries, instead of the projected alliance of the yellow races. Sun Yat-sen at the head of the Canton military government had given only restrained response to the first Russian overtures; in defeat, and back in his Shanghai refuge, he was in a more receptive frame of mind. An exchange of communications between him and

Joffe built upon the correspondence begun with Chicherin. Sun helped to create a propitious atmosphere by proclaiming, on New Year's Day, 1923, a new Kuomintang (KMT) political platform in which his vaguely conceived Three People's Principles were imbued with a somewhat more revolutionary spirit – derived from the Russian Revolution.

With the ground thus prepared, Joffe, when passing through Shanghai, met with Sun for a series of discussions which quickly bore fruit. On January 26, 1923, the two revolutionaries issued a joint communiqué, comprising four main points:

1. Sun and Joffe were in agreement that "the Communistic order, or even the Soviet system, cannot actually be introduced into China."
2. Joffe reaffirmed the principles set forth in the Soviet government's note of September 27, 1920, and declared that "the Russian Government is ready and willing to enter into negotiations with China on the basis of the renunciation by Russia of all the treaties and exactions which the Tsardom imposed on China, including the treaty or treaties relating to the Chinese Eastern Railway."
3. Sun expressed the opinion that "the realities of the situation point to the desirability of a *modus vivendi* in the matter of the present management of the railway."
4. Finally, "Mr. Joffe has categorically declared to Dr. Sun Yat-sen (who has fully satisfied himself as to this) that it is not and has never been the intention of the present Russian Government to pursue an imperialistic policy in Outer Mongolia or to cause it to secede from China. Dr. Sun Yat-sen, therefore, does not view an immediate evacuation of Russian troops from Outer Mongolia as either imperative or in the real interest of China." [3]

It is not to be concluded that, in January, 1923, the Soviet leaders harbored any considerable hopes that they would be able, by collaborating with Sun's Kuomintang, to convert China within the foreseeable future into a "Bolshevik" state. They had, after all, a considerable knowledge of Asian history – and some relatively recent experience in unsuccessful revolutions. The China of that period, however, fell under various separate rules, and Moscow had as yet been unable to establish relations with the "legitimate" government controlled by the tuchüns at Peking. In the circumstances, it was good Asian politics, and the politics of pragmatism, to deal with any local authorities who might offer promise of serving Russian interests. One of Moscow's prime concerns was the combating of the hostile sea powers in East Asia. The deep-rooted and frustrated Chinese nationalism bore a potential favorable to the Soviet purpose. By Joffe's design, the Kuomintang was to become the vehicle for a vigorous Chinese "anti-imperialism." One of his several China tasks accomplished, Joffe proceeded to Japan for the avowed purpose of attending to his health.

A possibility for putting the Joffe-Sun agreement to practical use soon arose. Sun's military supporter Hsu Ch'ung-chih recovered control of Canton at the end of January. Sun returned to the South, and in early March resumed the leadership of his rebel regime at Canton. The revolutionaries invited Moscow to provide technical assistance, and the first group of Soviet advisers arrived in Peking on June 21, 1923.[4] For the time being, however, they remained in the tuchün capital, and thus were on hand to welcome Karakhan when he arrived at Peking in early September.

Accompanying Karakhan was Mikhail M. Borodin, who had become a member of the Russian Social Democratic Revolutionary Party in 1903 at the age of twenty-one. He had resided in the United States from 1907 until July, 1918, when he returned to Soviet Russia to assume duties as a Comintern agent which took him first to England and then, in the capacity of Soviet ambassador, to Mexico. In the United States, Borodin had become acquainted with Dr. Sun Yat-sen, and his present trip to China was at Sun's invitation. He went not as Comintern agent but simply as a member of the Russian Communist Party and representative of the Moscow government, to be Sun's adviser. As of September 8, while still in Peking, he was appointed political adviser to the KMT Central Executive Committee.[5] He and another Soviet adviser, Volodya Polyak, arrived in Canton at the beginning of October.

At this juncture, there was a Nationalist politico-military mission in Moscow. Sun had sent to the Soviet capital a delegation headed by his young military adjutant, Chiang Kai-shek. Included in the party was the Communist Chang T'ai-lei. The group met with both party and governmental leaders, including Trotsky, Chicherin, and Grigori E. Zinoviev, but omitting Lenin (who was in his final illness), and studied party as well as military organization. By the evidence of later developments, the delegation also accomplished its other, major mission – that of obtaining Soviet military aid for the Chinese insurgency.[6] The Soviet commitment for extension of such aid was presumably qualified by a proviso that the Nationalist movement should meet certain political requirements.

With Borodin on the ground in Canton, the work of rebuilding the Kuomintang went rapidly forward. A declaration regarding the proposed party reorganization and the draft for a new party program were published on November 25.[7] In sum, the Kuomintang was to be transformed into an effective revolutionary political machine, on the pattern of the Russian Communist Party. The First Kuomintang National Congress convened at Canton on January 20, 1924, and Sun addressed the gathering in support of his proposal for a pro-Soviet orientation. He pointed to the successes achieved by Soviet Russia in the face of great difficulties, and proposed that that revolutionary state be used as a model. "We live in a dangerous time, we must learn the lessons of history, the results of the Russian revolution are visible to all, and we must take it as an example, if we desire to construct a strong, organized and disciplined party."[8]

In line with Sun's proposal, the congress resolved that, in foreign affairs, the party should act in alliance with the Soviet Union. The new Kuomintang-Soviet collaboration took on concrete form in the Whampoa Military Academy. This was a revolutionary politico-military school, designed to turn out indoctrinated military men to lead a new National Revolutionary Army. With Chiang Kai-shek as commandant, the academy was formally inaugurated on June 15.

This was at a time of political strain in the Soviet Union. Lenin had died on January 21, on the morrow of the opening of the KMT congress. Ever since his first stroke of 1922, with his growing incapacity, disputes at the top of the Soviet hierarchy over domestic and foreign policies had become increasingly exacerbated. The chief figures in the controversy were Joseph Stalin, Comintern chief Zinoviev, Lev B. Kamenev, and Trotsky. Trotsky in particular stood for "permanent revolution," holding that it was impossible to "build socialism in one country" (the Soviet Union) unless imperialism were distracted by world revolution from its self-imposed task of destroying Russian socialism. After Lenin's death, the dispute over policy became transformed into a struggle for the succession that took on aggravated form during 1924, just as the Kuomintang-Communist relationship in China was being evolved with Soviet military and financial aid.

The Trotskyite approach to the issue of world revolution was rejected. At the Fifth Comintern Congress, held in June and July, 1924, M. N. Roy, the Indian Communist who had contended ideologically against Lenin at the second congress, still inclined toward his own more radical approach. It was Roy's argument that the thesis that Communists should form a united front with oppressed national groups did not signify collaboration with bourgeois nationalist elements. But a pertinent congress resolution directed the Comintern to "give support to the movements of all oppressed nationalities directed against imperialism . . . bearing in mind that these movements represent one of the most important phases of that great movement of liberation which alone can lead to the victory of the revolution, not only on a European but on a world scale." [9] This remained the policy line of Moscow, and it would govern the CCP in its relationship to the Kuomintang, but both Soviet Russia and the revolutionary camp in China still confronted the problem of reconciling differences between Right and Left, standing respectively for the broad, gradualist and narrow, "radical" approaches.

In service, then, of the concept of giving support to a bourgeois nationalist revolution "directed against imperialism," Moscow's aid to the Chinese revolutionaries went forward. A large number of Russian military men joined the Whampoa Military Academy as advisers. When the Russian training ship *Vorovskii* cast anchor at Whampoa in early October, 1924, with a cargo of military supplies for the Nationalist revolutionaries, it found cadres ready and waiting. In the same month, presumably also aboard the *Vorovskii*, there arrived at Canton a man possessing experience that could be of great value to the Nationalists in their projected campaign against the warlords — General Vasili K. Bluecher, known in his China career as "Galen." [10] He now succeeded Polyak as senior military adviser at Whampoa.

Borodin early became concerned about the political unsteadiness of Sun Yat-sen, who was renowned for a proclivity for making temporary alliances — with anyone. Sun's was not a firm revolutionary character. Two days after Chang Tso-lin had begun the second Fengtien-Chihli war in mid-September, Sun formally launched a "Northern Expedition." That move from the South had no significant effect on the outcome in the North, but when Chang Tso-lin and Feng Yü-hsiang by concerted military action toppled the Ts'ao-Wu regime and brought Tuan Ch'i-jui back to power, Sun doubtless felt the victory to be one in which he had a part. Consequently, when the victors invited him to proceed north to discuss the national future, he was quick to accept.

This was bad enough, from the standpoint of the Russians, but the situation was worsened by Sun's announced intention of traveling via Japan. Right-wing Kuomintang elements in the Nationalist military establishment were known to be eager to exchange their Russian advisers for Japanese, with whom they would have felt much more at ease. Bluecher endeavored to point up the untimeliness and danger of the projected visit to Japan, but the Chinese offered an argument that was doubtless Sun's own: the journey would strengthen Sun's position in the struggle with the Northern militarists, and thus redound to both the Chinese Nationalist and the Russian benefit. On November 13, at a time when the Nationalist camp was wracked by internal dissensions and the Kwangtung militarist Ch'en Chiung-ming was preparing an offensive against Canton, Sun left for Japan, in his final attempt to stage a political tour de force in the traditional Chinese pattern.

It was Bluecher's strong conviction that the Nationalist base should be consolidated and the rear made safe before the revolutionary armies should venture upon a military campaign against the powerful forces of Wu P'ei-fu and Sun Ch'uan-fang in the Yangtze region. He was fearful that Sun would insist upon the launching of his oft-projected Northern Expedition at this time, to join forces with his "allies" in Peking. But on March 12, Sun died of cancer in the enemy capital. He had failed, as was logically to have been expected, to maneuver Tuan and Chang Tso-lin into sharing an authority they had won by their own efforts. Instead, he had contributed to the unsteadiness of the "revolutionary" regime in Canton.

Sun bequeathed an ideological legacy to the Kuomintang. In a letter addressed shortly before his death to the Central Executive Committee of the Soviet government, he stated:

> I leave behind me a party which . . . will be allied with you in its historical task of liberating China and other suppressed peoples from the yoke of imperialism. . . . I

. . . charge my party to maintain permanent contact with you. I cherish the firm belief that your support of my country will remain unaltered. In taking my leave of you, dear comrades, I express the hope that the day is approaching when the Soviet Union will greet in a free and strong China its friend and ally, and that the two states will proceed hand in hand as allies in the great fight for the emancipation of the whole world.[11]

Upon the death of Sun Yat-sen, an expression of condolences came from the Soviet side, while the KMT Central Executive Committee, in a telegram addressed to Stalin and Zinoviev, affirmed a determination to carry on Sun's work. In a resolution of May 23, 1925, the committee affirmed that it could cooperate only with the government of the USSR, and that the party should strive to obtain the cooperation of the Soviet Union, for the emancipation of the Chinese people and the reform of the Chinese Republic.[12]

One of the problems before the Soviet political and military advisers, from the beginning, had been to achieve a closer integration of the clashing, self-serving, disparate elements in the Nationalist combination. Some advance was made with the organization, in mid-April, of a party army. A "Nationalist Government" was formally inaugurated at Canton on July 1, 1925, with Wang Ching-wei as chairman, but it was far from united in its outlook. For one thing, opposition to the pro-Soviet orientation was strong in the Nationalist camp, dividing it automatically into Right and Left factions. The political assassination on August 20 of Liao Chung-k'ai, close associate of Sun Yat-sen and strong supporter of the Kuomintang's pro-Soviet orientation, was a manifestation of the antagonism between the two factions. The KMT Right would not readily cede power.

Military affairs continued to exert their predominating influence. In late August, the heterogeneous units that had made up the Nationalist fighting force were reorganized into five armies comprising the National Revolutionary Army. A first Eastern Expedition against Ch'en Chiung-ming had achieved a limited success in the spring, and in October a second Eastern Expedition was launched against his main strength. By the end of 1925, eastern Kwangtung had been brought firmly under Nationalist control.

Bluecher had played a critical role as strategic adviser in the first Eastern Expedition. He had returned to the Soviet Union in the summer for reasons of health, and Chief of Staff Viktor P. Rogachev functioned as top military adviser until General N. V. "Kisanka" [13] (Kuibyshev) arrived on November 1 to act as chief of the Soviet military mission in Bluecher's absence. Kisanka would play his part in future developments. But Soviet advisers played a lesser role in the second expedition than in the first: the Whampoa cadets demonstrated the worth of the training received at the hands of the Russians.

The Kuomintang at this time betrayed new schisms within its ranks. Rightist elements fled from Canton and, in November, met outside Peking in what came to be called the Western Hills Conference and strongly condemned the pro-Communist and pro-Soviet policies of the Canton regime. They called for the expulsion of Communist members from the KMT Central Executive Committee and the dismissal of Borodin as KMT adviser. The riposte of the Canton regime, effected at the Second KMT Congress of January, 1926, was to expel the ringleaders of the schismatic movement from the party. The Canton group had just won the adherence of the Kwangsi military men to the Nationalist cause, and the Kuomintang now spoke out more bravely. Addressing the oppressed peoples of the world, the congress asserted that the party's mission was to advance along the lines laid down by Sun Yat-sen together with all oppressed peoples and classes to accomplish the national revolution, help hasten the World Revolution, and realize true peace for mankind; in yet another message, it called upon the Soviet government to cooperate even more closely with the Kuomintang in the fight against imperialism.

There was additional reason for the Kuomintang's bravura. During 1925, a realignment of forces in North China changed the balance of power between South and North. Feng Yü-hsiang had been alienated from his colleagues even before the arrival of Sun Yat-sen in December, and had set up headquarters at Kalgan, on the eastern edge of Inner Mongolia. From that position, however, he could only look for support inland, toward Soviet Russia, and southward, where the Nationalist revolution threatened.

At that time, there was in Peking a Soviet mission headed by A. S. Bubnov, then chief of the Political Administration of the

Workers and Peasants Red Army and member of the central Revolutionary Military Council. Some time between late February and April, the mission and Soviet military attaché A. I. Egorov (subsequently Marshal of the Soviet Union) visited Feng in the vicinity of Paotow and got his agreement to accept Kuomintang political workers for his First Kuominchün and to "oppose imperialism," in exchange for Russian munitions and military instructors. The first tie between the Northern militarist and the Canton-based Kuomintang was thus established — through the intermediary of the Soviet missions.[14]

The Russians now had on their hands another difficult personality to work with. They fully realized this, but Feng possessed an earthiness, and a feeling for the common people, that others did not, and Moscow decided to make a modest gamble on the man. The fact that Moscow viewed both Tuan Ch'i-jui and Chang Tso-lin as being strongly pro-Japanese and anti-Soviet doubtless was a basic factor in its risk-taking.

In the beginning, Feng gave little reward to either the Kuomintang or the Soviet endeavor. He applied close controls over the KMT activists attached to his army and channeled the Soviet advisers' skills chiefly into the organization of various military training schools. His native peasant suspicion caused him to hold back from full collaboration. In that early period, Karakhan received a report that Feng, in the propaganda material circulated among his troops, employed a "national humiliation map" marked to show territories to be recovered by China. Those territories included the Trans-Baikal and Amur provinces and Vladivostok. Further, "Feng refused to recognize the independence of Outer Mongolia."[15] Giving little, he received only some 15,000 rifles and 30,000 hand grenades from Moscow in 1925.

The defeat of Feng and Kuo Sung-ling in their revolt of October, 1925, against Chang Tso-lin changed the situation and made Feng more susceptible to the "united front" approach used by Borodin and the Kuomintang. Feng now found himself temporarily without allies and isolated in defeat; his needs were greater than before. And the circumstance that he had struck at the anti-Soviet Chang Tso-lin, and that the equally inimical Japanese had seen fit to save Chang by intervening against Kuo Sung-ling, cloaked him with a certain desirability in Soviet eyes.

At the beginning of February, 1926, Borodin left Canton for

the North, to see Feng Yü-hsiang. Feng, then in a busy "retirement," maintained a headquarters at Pingtichuan, Suiyuan Province. It seems probable that Borodin first communicated indirectly with him through the Russian advisory group attached to the First Kuominchün. In any event, in mid-March Feng left Pingtichuan for Ulan Bator, where a party of some thirty persons from the revolutionary South arrived on April 3 with Borodin at their head. The group included such Left KMT luminaries as Hsu Ch'ien, Ku Meng-yü, and Eugene Ch'en. On April 5, there was an important meeting, at which it may safely be assumed that there was intensive review of revolutionary — and also strictly military — considerations. Two days later, his purposes presumably accomplished, Borodin departed on the return journey via Vladivostok to Canton.

Feng Yü-hsiang's Kuominchün had come under the combined attack of Chang Tso-lin and Wu P'ei-fu, now allied to each other. His First Kuominchün forces, after toppling the government of Tuan Ch'i-jui in mid-April, abandoned Peking in favor of making a defense at Nankow, gateway to Inner Mongolia, to permit the construction of a new base in China's Northwest. For the implementation of that purpose, Feng needed help. He delayed no longer. Accompanied by his chief Russian adviser Henry A. Lin and Hsu Ch'ien, he left Ulan Bator en route to Moscow, for the striking of such bargains with Stalin as might prove possible. He arrived at the Soviet capital in early May. Behind him, Russian advisers helped the Feng generals defend the Kuominchün position at Nankow.

Borodin got back to Canton at the end of April to face the arduous task of bringing order into a situation rendered unstable once more by an anti-Leftist coup of March 20, subsequently known as the "Chung Shan Incident," staged by Chiang Kai-shek. In that action, taken by the authority of Chiang alone without reference to Government Chairman Wang Ching-wei, Chiang had declared martial law in Canton, arrested various Communist personalities, and disarmed the guards stationed at the Russian advisers' quarters, on the basis of an assumption that the gunboat Chung Shan, commanded by the Communist Li Chihlung, planned a move against him. At the time, Chiang made no specific accusation.[16]

The Russian advisory group was shaken by the action and the threat it bore for the whole Nationalist enterprise they were supporting. When the coup occurred, Bubnov's mission was in Canton. As senior Soviet official present — if only as visitor — he seemingly took charge of the situation,[17] and in a conciliatory move reflecting his judgment that some Soviet advisers and the Chinese Communists had perhaps endeavored to go too far and too fast, Moscow relieved of duties and ordered home Chief of Staff Rogachev, Acting Chief of Mission Kisanka, and eight other Russians. The chief Soviet aim was patently to hold the fragile KMT-CCP coalition together. The dismissed Russians departed, almost precipitately, on March 25. The Chinese Communists likewise adopted a conciliatory line, and various Communists were removed from commanding positions in the KMT central party headquarters. At the beginning of May, after Borodin's return to the scene, Wang Ching-wei left China for a trip abroad. The whole episode had been a clear-cut victory for Chiang Kai-shek, who incidentally took over the post of Military Council chairman vacated by Wang Ching-wei.

In the spring of 1926, the Nationalists were confronted by the old strategic question: should the Northern Expedition against Peking now be launched? Certain Nationalist leaders and the Soviet advisers were divided on the issue. When Chiang Kai-shek proposed at the Second Kuomintang Congress in January that the campaign should be undertaken, Borodin had offered no objection. Kisanka had been actively hostile to the idea, but Kisanka had since departed, and Bluecher had returned to the China scene. One of the major concessions that Borodin made to Chiang Kai-shek in order to achieve the final liquidation of the Chung Shan Incident was to give definitive agreement to the enterprise.[18] Chiang Kai-shek was made commander in chief of the National Revolutionary Army, and at a ceremony of July 9, 1926, the Northern Expedition of which Sun Yat-sen had dreamed so long was formally launched. By the end of the month, the Nationalist forces were at the borders of Hupeh, Wu P'ei-fu's stronghold. In September, they advanced against Sun Ch'uan-fang's position in Kiangsi.

Those developments were the object of close attention in Moscow, where Feng Yü-hsiang as well as Stalin had a deep interest in the course of the Nationalist Revolution. Feng, as Chiang Kai-shek, had met there with persons critical for his enterprise: Chicherin, Zinoviev, Karl Radek, Commissar of Defense Kliment E. Voroshilov, and even Trotsky — who then occupied the minor post of head of the Central Committee for Concessions. Usmanov, who had previously been Bluecher's chief of staff, replaced Henry Lin as Feng's adviser. Feng's revolutionary protestations, or perhaps his conveying to Stalin (through an intermediary) the impression that he desired to thrust the Japanese from Manchuria, had evidently carried a measure of conviction, and on August 15 he signed obligations to pay over 6 million rubles for military supplies delivered up to June 1, and 4.5 million rubles for munitions for future delivery. On the previous day the Kuominchün, having fulfilled its military and political functions, had begun a strategic withdrawal from the Nankow front into Northwest China.

Feng left Moscow immediately after reaching the agreement for Soviet support of his projected contribution to the revolutionary cause, and upon his arrival back in China swore his Kuominchün into the service of the revolution at a ceremony staged at Wuyuan, in western Suiyuan. He could congratulate himself on having made a good deal.

After a long siege, Wuchang was occupied by the Nationalist forces on the anniversary of the 1911 Revolution, October 10. By a decision reached in December, the Nationalist government removed from Canton to Wuhan, and began functioning in the new locale on January 1, 1927. It was to prove significant for China's political future that the rebel government in its new phase was under the domination of the Left Kuomintang, supported by prominent Communists.

17 END OF THE REVOLUTIONARY ALLIANCE

IN ACCORDANCE with the "Theses on the Chinese Question" adopted by the Executive Committee of the Comintern (ECCI) in November, the Communists at this time were following a policy of endeavoring to convert the Kuomintang into a true people's party by practicing moderation, and struggling against Rightist tendencies while supporting the KMT Left — without endeavoring to seize leadership from the Left. It had chosen to cause the Kuomintang to become radical of its own volition.

The Joint Council that functioned as the governing body in Wuhan at that period was composed entirely of members of the Kuomintang Left and Communists, with Borodin in close liaison. The Right Kuomintang was effectively not represented, and that circumstance bore a threat to the future of Chiang Kai-shek. Chiang, after the Chung Shan Incident of March, 1926, was no longer to be counted even nominally in the Kuomintang Left. He had made various "revolutionary" and pro-Soviet statements at Canton, but many politicians have upon occasion voiced phrases appropriate to their desired aims without necessarily feeling personally involved in the content of their statements. Chiang's personality had also become a factor. He was a hard man to deal with, even for Chinese. Entries appearing in Chiang's diary beginning in early 1926 give evidence of policy clashes with Rogachev, and in one entry he asserted that he had been ridiculed by Kisanka. His staff adviser V. A. Stepanov, in a contemporary report, characterized him as "a peculiar person with peculiar characteristics, most prominent of these being his lust for glory and power and craving to be the hero of China." [1]

It seems probable that personality clashes made Chiang distinctly more anti-Russian in attitude than he had been originally, and that, when it became evident that the few Communist members of the Kuomintang were exercising an influence along certain lines quite out of proportion to their numbers, he turned increasingly anti-Communist besides. His personal ambitions, doubtless fortified by the elimination of major competitors, eventually completed the transformation. Chiang's action in the Chung Shan Incident had marked his first overt commitment to counterrevolution. The Russians had not been oblivious to the possible significance of the affair. But they had weighed the pros and cons of the matter, and their general conclusion was embodied in Stepanov's observation: "No one can guarantee at present that Chiang will always be one of us, but we must utilize him for the cause of the National Revolution." [2] They went ahead, acting with greater circumspection in the hope that they could avoid the worst. After all, they had few alternatives.

The estrangement of Right and Left begun in China's revolutionary camp with the assassination of Liao Chung-k'ai in 1925 now built rapidly up to a climax. Trotsky and his followers had urged the "revolutionary" line of heading straight for a proletarian dictatorship in China through the organization of popular soviets. But Trotsky's faction had declined in power, and the sixth plenum of the ECCI, meeting from February to March, 1926, had called upon the CCP to continue with the united-front tactic.

At the seventh ECCI plenum in November, Stalin made obeisance to Trotskyism by supporting the idea that the revolution should be spurred in the countryside, while holding that it was still premature to embark upon the organization of peasant soviets. The plenum's final theses found that "The development of the national-revolutionary movement in China at the present time depends upon the agrarian revolution," with the capitalist bourgeoisie destined gradually to abandon the revolution, the leadership of which would fall increasingly into the hands of the proletariat (i.e., the Communists). [3] The program proposed a radical approach for winning the peasantry over to the revolution.

That program was designed, however, for joint implementation by the CCP and KMT, for the CCP was to remain aligned with the senior bourgeois party in order to "strive to develop the Kuomintang into a real people's party – a solid revolutionary bloc of the proletariat, the peasantry, the urban petty bourgeoisie, and the other oppressed and exploited strata – a party dedicated to a decisive struggle against imperialism and its agents."

Doubtless in the light of the latest ECCI directive, a CCP Central Committee plenum held at Hankow in mid-December decided on a policy of restraint with respect to the peasant movement, in service of the concept that unity of the overall revolutionary movement should be preserved for achievement of the Northern Expedition's prime purpose of destroying the tuchün regime in Peking. Mao Tse-tung was present at that meeting in his capacity of chairman of the Hunan party committee. On this same occasion, Mao was directed to make an inspection of the Hunan peasant movement.

The evidence indicates that, far from feeling under compulsion to hold the peasant movement back, Mao actively whipped up peasant radicalism. His report of February, 1927, on the potential of the peasant revolution in his home province manifested a highly optimistic faith in the successful outcome of a course of violence. In practice, the Communists pressed forward with the organization of peasant associations, which they spurred on to deal summarily with "local bullies" and landlords and to proceed with the confiscation and division of land in Hunan. Quite naturally Nationalist military officers, many of whom came from landed families, were increasingly alienated.

It was thus in tense circumstances that Chiang Kai-shek's representative, Ch'en Kuo-fu, visited Leftist Wuhan in March, 1927, in an effort to retrieve Rightist fortunes by political maneuver. Ch'en was unsuccessful. He returned to Shanghai and met there with other KMT conservatives to formulate strategy for a counteroffensive against the KMT Left. At the beginning of April, Wang Ching-wei returned from the European exile to which he had consigned himself the year before. His return clearly threatened further incursions into Chiang's political power. The stage for a power struggle was set.

As late as April 8, Chiang was outwardly sufficiently radical to send a note to Soviet chargé Chernykh denouncing Chang Tso-lin's raid on the Soviet embassy as an outrage engineered by imperialists with the aim of wrecking the national revolution and fomenting international conflict. The first documents seized in the raid were not made public until April 19, but in the interim, as if Chiang had obtained prior knowledge of some of their contents, a strange thing happened: on April 12, he launched a sudden attack on the Communist and workers' organizations that had helped him capture Shanghai a month before. A large number of Leftists were slaughtered, and labor unions and radical organizations were smashed. The threat implicit in the Chung Shan Incident of March, 1926, was being borne out. Chiang had launched a "party purification" movement, and was now preparing to strike out on his own.

In an editorial of April 15, Moscow's *Pravda* condemned Chiang's action, asserting that "he and his supporters have become the center, the focal point of the national counter-revolution. . . . In the eyes of the millions of Chinese people, Chiang Kai-shek has now become a renegade and is on the side of imperialism." [4] The Wuhan government promptly broke with Chiang Kai-shek, expelled him from army and military posts, and ordered his arrest. Chiang's response was to organize his own "Nationalist government" at Nanking. The revolutionary issue was being presented to Chinese leaders in more categorical terms. Was the Nationalist revolution to be heavily social, or the old admixture of politics and military force?

The CCP now stood alone with the KMT Left. Here the personality of a newly arrived Comintern agent, the Indian M. N. Roy, played a critical role. It was Roy who had contended with Lenin at the Second Comintern Congress in favor of an enhanced role for the peasantry in Asian revolutions. His counsels now proved to be in line more with Trotsky's views than with Stalin's. He was opposed by Borodin, who by this time had three and a half years of experience in China behind him. Roy, however, could count on his side Ch'ü Ch'iu-pai, central committee member and prolific pamphleteer.

The Fifth CCP Congress convened in Hankow on April 24, confronted by the easily perceived warning conveyed by Chiang Kai-shek's coup: if Chiang could shift sides, so might other Kuomintang generals. The CCP had grown to new strength. Where it had a membership of 950 at the time of its fourth congress in January, 1925, now it numbered nearly 58,000, of whom 53.8 percent were "workers" (a category patently including mostly peasants), 19.1 percent intelligentsia, 10.0 percent women, but only 3.1 percent military personnel. The party had just suffered heavy losses in Peking and Shanghai, and it could not well accept without struggle further disaster at the hands of the Right, whether outside or within the Kuomintang.

The congress was attended by KMT leaders Wang Ching-wei and Hsu Ch'ien as guests, as well as by representatives of both the Comintern and the Profintern (Trade Unions International). But attendance was no sign of a stable relationship. Owing in large measure to the split between Right and Left Kuomintang, serious strains had developed between the Left KMT and their yet more radical Communist collaborators at Wuhan. Differences of opinion regarding tactics had also arisen within the Communist ranks.

Wang Ching-wei, addressing the gathering, spoke once more in favor of the CCP-KMT collaboration. Ch'ü Ch'iu-pai contrariwise proposed that the CCP break with the Kuomintang. He was opposed by Ch'en Tu-hsiu, who had joined with Wang Ching-wei at the beginning of April in a joint declaration (on the existing Moscow political line) reaffirming collaboration between the two parties. Mao Tse-tung, although present, came under strong criticism from the assembled delegates by reason of his report on the peasant situation in Hunan and was deprived of his right to vote. Ch'en Tu-hsiu, given his position of preeminence in the party hierarchy, was able to carry the day with respect to policy, and was moreover reelected to the position of general secretary.

The Fifth CCP Congress thus ended its deliberations on May 6 with the party on the old line. But the peasant excesses in Hunan, T'ang Sheng-chih's home province, were continuing unabated under the ardent leadership of Mao Tse-tung. On May 21, in what came to be known as the Ma Jih [Horse Day] Incident, Nationalist troops went into action at Changsha to wreck, bloodily, labor unions and peasant associations alike. It is logical to assume that the Ma Jih Incident was a factor that entered into Moscow's calculations. On June 1, Borodin and Roy received a telegram from Stalin worded close to Roy's own wishes. The directive found the KMT leadership wanting in revolutionary spirit, and proposed rejuvenation:

A large number of new peasant and working class
leaders must be drawn into the Central Committee of the

Kuomintang from below. . . . The present structure of
the Kuomintang must be changed. . . . It is necessary
to liquidate the dependence upon unreliable generals
immediately. Mobilize about 20,000 Communists and
about 50,000 revolutionary workers and peasants from
Hunan and Hupeh, form several new army corps, utilize
the students of the Party school for military commanders
and organize your own reliable army before it is too late.[5]

It would appear as if Mao Tse-tung's enthusiastic report of
February that 2 million Hunanese workers and peasants had ris-
en in revolt had perhaps deceived people in Moscow as well as
Mao's own followers in the CCP. But it was in fact already "too
late" for the CCP to undertake any such action as that proposed:
at this juncture, the Wuhan government commanded a military
force of 140,000 to 180,000 men. If Feng Yü-hsiang had 100,000 to
120,000 more, they were hardly to be counted on the Communist
side—and the Communists possessed no military units of their
own. To enlist 20,000 Communists into military formations would
have meant incorporating one-third of the entire Communist
membership, including women, into the armed forces—with an
officer corps composed of cadets. Where would such an army, even
if raised, have obtained its arms? And, if armed, what would it
have been able to accomplish against forces ten times its strength?

The author of that amateurish approach to the problem of
continuing revolution in circumstances where the Right wing of
the Kuomintang had already split off and the Left wing, with no
place else to go, had promptly recommitted itself to the alliance
with the Communist radicals, was patently more Trotsky than
Stalin—but Stalin, for reasons of Soviet domestic politics, had
chosen to adopt his opponent's idea as his own and had given it
his imprimatur. And then, the concept probably in some measure
reflected the heady estimates and braggadocio of a CCP faction.

The scheme was put to the test in unexpected ways. The message was constructively a secret instruction to the Chinese Communist Party. In a move hard to surpass for naïveté, Roy showed
the telegram to Wang Ching-wei, presumably believing that
Wang would be frightened into accepting, and following, the new
Communist line. Instead, as was entirely logical, Wang first confronted "Kuomintang adviser" Borodin with the telegram and
then consulted with his KMT colleagues. Next, he headed a

weighty KMT delegation, which, arriving in Chengchow on June 6, met with "revolutionary" Feng Yü-hsiang for the purpose of reaching a supporting agreement. Borodin accompanied the delegation. Significantly, the only Chinese Communist present on the delegation was the relatively unimportant Yü Shu-teh, who had performed political work in the Kuominchün.

Wang Ching-wei's mission made a great effort to win Feng over to the Left KMT camp and policies. There is every reason to believe that Wang also communicated to Feng the contents of the Comintern telegram shown him by Roy. He moreover indicated his readiness to turn against the Communists.[6] Feng gave nothing in return but an equivocal statement.

At this juncture Chang Tso-lin, in a countermove aimed at the insurgents in the South, organized a new government. On June 18 he issued a circular telegram proclaiming a policy designed to appeal as much to foreign powers as to conservative domestic elements, stating, inter alia:

> The Chinese Communists have surrendered to Soviet Russia and are preaching Communism among the Chinese. . . . The goal of the Communists is to bring about a world revolution. It therefore follows that to exterminate Communism should be the common enterprise of mankind. . . . But there can be no compromise with Communism.[7]

Chang Tso-lin's bid for a united anti-Communist front was too late. After the departure of the Wuhan delegation, Feng Yü-hsiang traveled to Hsuchow, at the junction of the Lunghai and Tsin-Pu rail lines, and there conferred from June 19 to 21 with an imposing group of military and political figures headed by Chiang Kai-shek. At the end of the meeting, "revolutionary" Feng joined with conservative Chiang in a statement in which the two military chieftains paid due lip service to Sun Yat-sen's revolution and vowed to destroy the warlords in power. In a message to Wang Ching-wei and T'an Yen-k'ai of the Wuhan group that was, in effect, his leave-taking of them, Feng referred with disapproval to the (Communist-inspired) class struggles in course within Wuhan's jurisdiction and to the terror planned by those who had borrowed the name of the national revolution (this being a clear reference to the content of the Comintern telegram) and, adopting the position of the Western Hills group and (now)

Chiang Kai-shek, proposed that Borodin should be dismissed and return to the Soviet Union.

At Hankow, shown a copy of the Feng telegram by Dr. Krarup Nielsen, correspondent of the Copenhagen *Politiken*, Borodin said that "If my Chinese friends think they can consummate the revolution without me, let them do so and I will withdraw." He went on, however, to express the belief that the militarists would soon wipe out the results of the preceding four years of revolutionary work, and that (in the words of the recorder of the conversation) "China would return to her old time chaos of perpetual internal warfare." [8]

Presumably written about the same time, although published only about a month later in China, an analysis of developments in China by a Russian Communist held that there was no inconsistency between the earlier Communist support of Chiang Kai-shek and the current condemnation of the same man, for the progress of revolution was to be thought of as uneven.

> Both the Third International and the Communist Party of China realized from the first that with the progress of revolution, and the increasing prominence of the working classes and the peasantry in it, a time would come when the bourgeoisie would desert the cause and would go over to the reactionaries. [9]

By previous party resolution, the commentator continued, it had been anticipated that arrival at that critical point of the revolution would result in the transfer of the entire burden of continuance of the revolutionary struggle onto the shoulders of the workers and peasants. The current massive shift of the bourgeoisie to the side of reaction made it requisite for the Chinese Communist Party to change tactics, and fight against the bourgeoisie instead of fighting by its side while aiming still at the primary strategic objective of carrying the national revolution to an end and creating a socialist state. "So now we witness the opening of the class struggle proper."

There was no long wait for a testing of those Communist theses. Feng's message was followed in quick order, on June 25, by an anti-Communist proclamation by General Ho Chien, commander of the Thirty-fifth Army stationed at Hankow. The KMT Leftists were thus confronted with the choice of bending to the will of the military men who were their source of real power, or joining the Communists, in line with Roy's presumed expectations, in the hopeless adventure of striving to overwhelm the huge armies of the "enemy" faction and mobilize the revolutionary spirit of the amorphous "masses."

On the revolutionary anniversary July 14, the ECCI at Moscow passed a resolution condemning the KMT Left for having sanctioned the disarming of labor organizations, punitive action against the peasantry, and repressive military actions. It called upon the Chinese Communists to "unmask" the "cowardly position" of the Wuhan government and the KMT Central Executive Committee and push both the government and the Kuomintang toward "the true revolutionary road." [10] The CCP was also enjoined to press forward with construction of a militant organization and to purge opportunism from the party's leadership.

The Wuhan regime, isolated in its adherence to Sun Yat-sen's grand strategy of alliance with the USSR and the Chinese Communists, now far weaker militarily than either the Northern grouping or the Feng-Chiang combination as supported by the Kwangsi forces, disillusioned regarding the bona fides of Borodin, whom they had stood beside against the importunities of the Right, and now clearly facing even a Communist challenge to their retention of power, chose the road to political salvation. At a meeting held July 13 in the residence of Wang Ching-wei, it was decided to outlaw both the Communist Party and Communism; at a meeting the following day in the premises of the Central Bank at Hankow, it was further decided that Borodin should be sent back to the Soviet Union.

In mid-July, consequently, shortly after the ECCI had again called upon the Chinese party to arm the workers and peasants and take "decisive action," Wuhan military men undertook the destruction of Communist organizations and the radical labor unions, in the Shanghai pattern. On July 26, the KMT Central Executive Committee made the action official by proclaiming its break with the Chinese Communist Party. Wuhan's military action against "radicals" now was given full rein, and from April through July, by Communist count, 337,000 revolutionaries lost their lives in the Right and Left Kuomintang purge.

Borodin and other Soviet advisers on July 27 took their departure. They were accorded safe conduct, and even a measure of hospitality, in passage through Feng's territory in the Northwest, and returned by way of Mongolia to Soviet Russia. Bluecher left later, traveling via Shanghai and Japan. KMT personalities who continued to adhere to the pro-Soviet line of Sun Yat-sen — such as Mme Sun Yat-sen and Eugene Ch'en — also made their way abroad, for the suggested "rest."

By the urgent recommendation of Borodin, Roy had been ordered to leave China and was replaced by Besso Lominadze, who was still in his twenties. Lominadze probably arrived in the country about mid-July, with the essential mission of keeping the Chinese Revolution alive. With the alliance wrecked, however, he had perforce to adopt the Trotskyite tactics of direct revolutionary action. He also bore Moscow's instructions to stage a military uprising against the Wuhan regime. At the very juncture when Chang Fa-k'uei, Chu P'ei-teh, and Ch'eng Ch'ien were undertaking preparations in the Kiukiang area for a drive on Nanking, two Communist Chang Fa-k'uei officers, Yeh T'ing commanding the Twenty-fourth Division and Ho Lung at the head of the Twentieth Army, supported by a training regiment of the Ninth Army commanded by Chu Teh, on August 1 staged a revolt at Nanchang, in Kiangsi.

The insurrectionists succeeded initially in capturing the town, and August 1 came in time to be celebrated as the birthday of the Chinese Red Army. Chang Fa-k'uei and his colleagues now abandoned their plans for an attack on Nanking, however, with Chang instead throwing units against Nanchang and on August 5 expelling the rebels from the town. The Communists' adventurist coup within Chang Fa-k'uei's military organization had destroyed the possibility of collaboration with him against the common foe, Nanking. The defeated putschists retreated southward in the general direction of Canton.

There had been Moscow's directive to purge the CCP leadership. With the help of Lominadze, Ch'ü Ch'iu-pai and his faction convened an extraordinary session of the CCP Central Committee, with Lominadze present, at Kiukiang on August 7. The session was hardly to be termed plenary and legal, since it was attended by only twelve regular and three alternate members, with Ch'en Tu-hsiu himself absent. The session nevertheless condemned Ch'en in absentia for right opportunism, removed him as general secretary, and elected Ch'ü to the post instead. Somewhat belatedly, the new leadership decided to break with the Kuomintang and devote itself to the peasant revolution. The next day, Roy left Wuhan for Moscow. Ch'en Tu-hsiu took up residence in the Shanghai International Settlement, and in 1929 turned to Trotskyism.[11]

The Communist force retreating from Nanchang was joined while en route south by Chang T'ai-lei, who had participated in the August 7 meeting at Kiukiang and been elected to the posts of head of the South China bureau and chairman of the Kwangtung provincial committee of the CCP. The Communists captured the Kwangtung port city of Swatow on September 24, but were forced to abandon their prize a week later. Ahead of them lay Canton, the cradle of the Nationalist Revolution. Chang Fa-k'uei by a coup in November had seized the city for Wang Ching-wei from the forces of Li Chi-shen (who was currently on a trip to Shanghai). But he was soon forced to deploy his troops east and west of the town in order to meet the threat of strong units thrown against him by the irate Li, with Communist Yeh Chien-ying left behind in Canton in command of two regiments to perform garrison duties. Again the Comintern became involved. Lominadze had been replaced in November by Hans Neumann, and at this juncture Ch'ü Ch'iu-pai, with Neumann evidently playing to the hilt his role as adviser, directed Chang T'ai-lei to stage an uprising in Canton, with P'eng P'ai's peasant militia to participate. The Kwangtung party committee passed the appropriate resolution on November 26. On December 7, a government was secretly formed.

In the early morning of December 11, the uprising began under the leadership of Chang T'ai-lei and Yeh T'ing; Yeh Chien-ying of course joined them. In the circumstances, the insurrectionists achieved a quick initial success, and by the end of a bloody day the town was in their hands. On December 12, approved by a mass meeting held at noon, the Canton soviet government was formally established and the previously selected personnel confirmed in their posts. But Chang Fa-k'uei, upon receipt of news of the developments, had rushed troops back to town, and his counterattack was already beginning. Chang T'ai-lei was killed by KMT agents as he left the popular meeting that had been organized to confirm the Communist victory. Yeh T'ing assumed Chang's functions as commissar of war, but titles were no substitute for organization and firepower. With the support of British, American, and Japanese gunboats in the East River,[12] Chang Fa-k'uei's forces on December 12 began their assault on Canton. On the following day, they penetrated into the town, and by December 14 had consolidated their control. Chang's troops gave the City of Rams a second bloodbath that more than matched that of Communist origin. In three days' time, some 6,000 to 7,000 insurrectionists were killed in the fighting or executed. Thus the Canton Commune ended.

In the course of the uprising, Chang's troops took into custody and executed five Soviet consular officials, including the vice consul, Abram I. Khassis. On December 14, the day the Canton Commune died, Nanking ordered the closure of all Soviet consular and commercial offices and other Soviet state agencies within its jurisdiction, and the Soviet officials from the Canton, Hankow, and Shanghai establishments now followed Borodin in returning to their homeland. But Soviet consular offices in Manchuria (Chang Tso-lin's domain) and Sinkiang remained open and continued functioning.

In February, 1928, the ECCI met again in Moscow and assessed the reasons for the failures in China. Now it was held that the Chinese Communist Party, and also Neumann, had erred by embarking upon adventurism: "To play with insurrections instead of organizing a mass uprising of workers and peasants is a sure way of losing the revolution." [13] Ch'ü Ch'iu-pai, although elected to the ECCI, was removed from his newly won position as CCP general secretary on the charge of *Left* opportunism. He took up his residence in Moscow.

The consensus of Trotskyite and other opposition opinion was that Stalin's policy had "failed" in China—with the way left open for the easy inference that Trotsky's policy, or some other tactic than that adopted by the Comintern in the 1924–1927 period, might well have "won," and the social revolution have been consummated at that time. From any objective point of view, the inference is not to be accepted without challenge. In the period under reference, the Chinese Communists were weak in numbers and in political—and especially military—power, and there had not been time for a true social revolutionary tide to rise massively—Mao Tse-tung to the contrary notwithstanding. The forces of conservative militarism were too strong, in the China of 1924–1927, for revolutionaries to have stood a chance of seizing power. The chief charge of tactical error to be made against the Communists in that period was not that they had proceeded too slowly, but that they had pushed forward too aggressively, and thus alienated elements of the Kuomintang Left and Center who might otherwise have stood with them against the KMT Right. Roy's move vis-à-vis Wang Ching-wei, and Mao's actions in Hunan Province, were pure examples of Left adventurism.

And, despite the debacle, there was to be no return to the status quo ante with respect to the national sentiment regarding social change. The effects of the efforts of Borodin and Bluecher and Li Ta-chao and Ch'en Tu-hsiu in that early period of China's social revolution would remain to influence events. A contemporary observer remarked that "there is no disputing the fact that this man Borodin, a Russian Jewish emigrant to the United States, has placed his stamp on the Chinese revolution and the stamp, whether for good or evil, will remain for many months and years after he has passed from the scene." [11] The judgment would be borne out by subsequent events.

18 CONFLICT IN MANCHURIA

WITH THE MOMENTUM of the initial thrust from Canton, the Nationalists continued with the Northern Expedition and in June, 1928, overthrew the tuchün rule at Peking. Because of the events of 1927, however, when the new National government was formally established at Nanking in October, 1928, it had relations with the United States and other sea powers, but none with Moscow. This seemed on the surface to be essentially a return to the situation existing from 1917 to 1924, but there were new factors in the equation: in particular, the situation in China's borderlands had changed radically. Outer Mongolia had achieved de facto independence. New disorders threatened in Sinkiang. And the Chinese Eastern Railway had been returned to Russian hands by the two treaties signed in 1924. With none of those situations would the highly nationalistic regime at Nanking rest content.

Chiang Kai-shek had early paved the way for new undertakings with respect to Manchuria. In the summer of 1927, forced out of power at Nanking, he had visited Japan. He met there with Tanaka Giichi, the sometime deputy chief of staff now become baron and premier, and with Tanaka's vice minister for foreign affairs, Mori Kaku, and reached an understanding touching on Manchuria predicated upon a Nationalist victory: Chiang extended recognition to Japanese rights and interests in Manchuria, while Tanaka agreed to recognize the united China that would emerge from a successful Nationalist Revolution—with the proviso that the Kuomintang should dissociate itself from Communist elements (as it had already undertaken to do).

The Japanese were thus assured that, whether Chang Tso-lin won or lost, their position in Manchuria would receive protection. Chang lost, and as the train carrying him in retreat from Peking to Mukden approached its destination in early June, 1928, it was blown up as the result of a plot by activist members of the Kwantung Army general staff. Marshal Chang was killed. His son Chang Hsueh-liang succeeded him to power, and in December the "Young Marshal" divorced Manchuria from the ties with Japan long maintained by his father and brought the rich region into the Nationalist camp.

The Nationalists still harbored the "anti-imperialist" spirit that had helped bring them initially to the Yangtze. Following the strategy of attacking the seemingly weakest and most vulnerable adversary, the National government and Chang Hsueh-liang began to formulate a coordinated campaign against the Soviet position in Manchuria. At the end of 1928, the American consul at Harbin remarked a significant straw in the wind: Chang Hsueh-liang's secretary in an interview with representatives of the local Russian press had stated that, unless Soviet citizens in Manchuria showed themselves loyal to China and obeyed its laws and regulations, and unless the Soviet CER administration introduced full parity in employment and otherwise adhered to existing agreements, the local (Manchurian) authorities would be compelled to take action against them along lines adopted earlier by the Southern (Nanking) government. The consul continued his report: "There is much talk regarding the taking over of the entire railway by the Chinese authorities." [1]

The first overt move came in early January, when the Chinese authorities at Harbin on instructions from Mukden confiscated, without provision for compensation, the telephone system that had been installed in the town by the Chinese Eastern Railway. The U.S. consul at Harbin reported that "The Soviet officials fear that this drastic move will be followed by the taking over of the whole railway." [2] The American consul at Mukden reported more positively that "there seems to be little doubt" that the Chinese were considering means for implementing their "set scheme" of taking over the Chinese Eastern Railway. [3] In fact, Chang Hsueh-liang, in a conversation with Soviet Consul General Melnikov near the end of February, threatened that he might be forced to take further measures for the protection of Chinese rights.

On May 27, the Chinese suddenly swooped down upon the Soviet consulate at Harbin, arrested all persons present (including both Harbin consul N. K. Kuznetsov and Consul General Melnikov of Mukden), and in the pattern of Chang Tso-lin's raid on the Peking embassy made off with large quantities of documents. The Chinese officially announced, as justification for the raid, that "the Russians were conferring on an urgent problem for the Third International having special reference to the future of Russia in North China, that is, the creating of great disturbances in North China in cooperation with General Feng Yü-hsiang." [4] Since Feng, after receipt of substantial Soviet aid, had by joining forces with Chiang Kai-shek in June, 1927, undercut the overall Wuhan position and was only now entering openly upon his contest with Chiang, a less likely plot would be hard to imagine. Nor was the allegation actually substantiated.

Karakhan, as acting commissar for foreign affairs, promptly sent a message of protest to the Nanking government, demanding the return of confiscated items and release of the arrested persons. His protest was in the main fruitless. The Chinese released Melnikov and his Harbin colleague, but held thirty-eight other Soviet citizens under arrest.

As late as June 10, it was officially denied at Nanking that there was any intention, as rumored, to seize the Chinese Eastern Railway. Just one month later, however, the Chinese suddenly seized the CER telegraph system and then, on the following day, took over the railway, dismissing all Soviet heads of railway departments and divisions. CER General Manager A. I. Emshanov was replaced by the Chinese Fan Chi-kuan, and Emshanov and Soviet Assistant Manager Eismont were expelled from Chinese territory. Lü Jung-huan, president of the CER board of directors, assumed "emergency" powers and effectively took over control. There were wholesale dismissals of Soviet citizens, with about sixty shipped off to the Soviet Union and some 200 others held under arrest. The Chinese in addition closed the offices of the Soviet Merchant Marine, the Far Eastern Trading Organization, the Naphta Syndicate, and the Textile Syndicate, and dissolved the existing Soviet trade unions and cooperatives. Chang Hsueh-liang deployed some 60,000 troops, including White Russian detachments, facing the Soviet frontier.

On July 13, the Narkomindel (People's Commissariat for Foreign Affairs) at Moscow handed to Chinese chargé d'affaires Hsia Wei-sung, for delivery to Mukden and Nanking, a note lodging a strong protest and laying down three propositions:

1. There should promptly be convened a conference for the resolution of all questions pertaining to the Chinese Eastern Railway.
2. There should be promptly countermanded all illegal actions by the Chinese authorities regarding the railway.
3. There should be the prompt release of all arrested Soviet citizens, and cessation of oppressive actions against Soviet citizens and organizations.

In that note, Karakhan termed the Chinese actions "a gross violation of the existing agreements between the U.S.S.R. and China," entered "the most emphatic protest against these actions," and invited the attention of the Mukden and Nanking governments to "the extreme seriousness of the situation created by these actions."[5] Finally, he demanded a satisfactory response within three days. This, then, was an ultimatum.

The seizure of the railway, according to reliable information later obtained by American officials, had been the result of a final decision reached between Chiang Kai-shek, Chang Hsueh-liang, and Foreign Minister C. T. Wang in a meeting at Peking on July 10.[6] On July 15, Chiang Kai-shek officially announced the National government's intention to possess itself of the railway. In a reply of July 16 to the Soviet note, transmitted through Chargé Hsia at Moscow, the National government began by saying, surely with tongue in cheek, that "Since the signing of the Sino-Russian Provisional [sic] Agreement in 1924, diplomatic relations between the two countries have been firmly established." It went on to complain of "organized propaganda" conducted by Soviet Russia against the interests of the Chinese government and society, observed that it had received reports from Manchuria that the Soviet railway administration had failed to observe the terms of the 1924 agreement "from the very beginnings," and that consequently "the authorities of the Three Eastern Provinces" had been forced to take action. Taking note of reports that Moscow had arrested over a thousand Chinese merchants in the Soviet Union, Nanking proposed that, if those merchants were released and guaranteed "adequate protection and facilities," then the National government would be prepared to act similarly with respect to arrested "Soviet agents" and the closed office buildings, "at the appropriate time." The message ended on an admonitory note: ". . . we hope the Soviet Government will respect China's law and sovereignty and refrain from submitting proposals contradictory to the actual facts of the case." [7]

There was no suggestion of returning the Chinese Eastern Railway to the status provided by the 1924 agreements. On July 18, the Soviet government rejected the Chinese reply as "unsatisfactory in content and hypocritical in tone." And it informed the Chinese that it was breaking off all relations and withdrawing diplomatic, consular, trade, and CER personnel from China. It declared at the same time that it reserved to itself all rights accorded it by the May, 1924, agreement, and agreements reached with local authorities (meaning those of September, 1924). Moscow incidentally turned over to Germany the protection, pro tem, of Soviet interests in China.

The Soviet moves shook Mukden and Nanking. Nanking sought now to enlist third-power sympathy for its position by issuing, on July 19, a public statement on the matter, incorporating alleged evidence of secret Soviet activities as reputedly discovered in the search of the Harbin consular office two months earlier. China had undoubtedly expected to be able to enlist substantial foreign support for its action. It had reckoned without the highly probable adverse reaction that treaty-power governments would naturally have toward a move by Nanking to alter arbitrarily a situation governed by international treaties, even where the treaty partner might be the Soviet Union. Chinese Minister C. C. Wu, meeting on July 18 with Secretary of State Henry L. Stimson, must therefore have been unpleasantly surprised to have Stimson observe that China's actions appeared to violate the Sino-Russian agreement of 1924 and could be interpreted as an attack on the Soviet Union — and that he thought China had acted hastily.[8] Nor was American opinion unique in this regard. Minister MacMurray reported about the same time that foreign press comment in China condemned the Chinese position "and apparently regards the present issue as a test whether China may or may not be held to any of her contractual obligations." [9]

On July 20, just two days after Wu's meeting with Stimson, in a move patently designed to justify its action, Nanking issued a public statement in which it invoked the specter of Communism and charged that the documents seized in the May 27 raid on the Harbin consulate indicated the fostering of conspiracies "involving the shattering of the national unification of China, the organization of an assassination corps to operate in Nanking, Liaoning [sic — Mukden?] and other important cities of China, the destruction of the Chinese Eastern Railway, the dissemination of communist propaganda, the perpetuation of internal unrest in China, etc." [10]

If in any quarter, Nanking might have expected to find support in Japan for its attack on the Soviet position in North Manchuria. But these were not the bygone halcyon days of Japanese collaboration with either Old Marshal Chang Tso-lin or the Anfu Clique. Chang Hsueh-liang had roughly rejected the Japanese advice to maintain Manchuria separate from the Nanking regime, and Nanking even earlier had indicated its intention to apply Chinese laws and regulations to Japanese subjects in China — only to be pulled up short by Tokyo. Moreover, the South Manchurian Railway occupied a legal position not quite the same as, but distinctly similar to, that of the Chinese Eastern Railway. The Japanese vice minister for foreign affairs on July 19 informed the American chargé d'affaires at Tokyo that the Japanese government had no intention of commenting upon, or interfering in, the CER dispute. The Japanese had decided to remain "neutral."

Given the minatory Soviet attitude, and the state of international isolation in which it unexpectedly found itself, Nanking sought to extricate itself by enlisting third-power mediation. In the July 18 meeting with Stimson, Minister Wu had asked whether the United States could offer its good offices, only to be informed that the United States would never do so excepting at the request of both parties — and a Soviet request was hardly to be expected. (The United States had not yet recognized the Moscow regime.) Two days later, Wu called upon the French ambassador to argue that China had not seized the Chinese Eastern Railway, but had only replaced Russian with Chinese employees. He evidently made little impression on the Frenchman's logical mind. The French ambassador had just received a telegram from his government setting forth the belief of the French foreign minister that the issue of Communist propaganda was only a pretext and that the Chinese intent was to seize both the receipts (assets?) and administration of the railway.

All these developments were on the eve of the formal ceremony, scheduled for July 24, of deposit of ratifications of the Kellogg-Briand "Pact of Paris" for the Renunciation of War. With martial action threatening, France (acting on the suggestion of Washington) on July 19 made representations to the Soviet Union, through both Ambassador Valerian S. Dovgalevsky at Paris and Ambassador Jean Herbette at Moscow, with the aim of furthering a pacific settlement of the dispute. The Narkomindel on July 23 issued a statement acknowledging the démarche but noting that "The proposal becomes without point in view of the refusal of the Chinese authorities to restore the legal basis . . . , which is the necessary prerequisite for an agreement, pursuant to the note of the Soviet government of July 13." [11]

By initiative of the Chinese, on July 22 there was a meeting at Harbin between Foreign Affairs Commissioner Ts'ai Yunsheng and Consul General Melnikov at which Ts'ai, acting in behalf of Chang Hsueh-liang, transmitted proposals to the Soviet side that seemed to offer a way out of the deadlock. On July 31, however, Minister of Railways Sun Fo, in a press interview at Peiping, set forth what had presumably become the guiding concept of the Nanking government: he said that the Soviet Union, given its international isolation and internal difficulties, would not risk a war with China. On August 1, in the border town of Manchouli, Ts'ai handed Melnikov a series of proposals that differed substantially from those made earlier in Harbin.

At this time, according to Soviet charges, Chinese and White Russian forces had begun to make attacks into Soviet territory. Significantly, by decision of August 6, the Soviet Union created a Special Far Eastern Army under command of Vasili K. Bluecher, with headquarters at Khabarovsk. On the following day, August 7, the Narkomindel issued a public statement: the Soviet government was in receipt on August 1 of a communication from Chang Hsueh-liang respecting the CER issue, but the difference between the August 1 proposals and those of July 22 "frustrates the possibility of settling the conflict by an agreement." [12]

By mid-August, minor border clashes involving Soviet troops were being reported from various points, including Manchouli. Nanking had thus far failed to muster any international support.

On August 19, Minister Wu handed the American secretary of state a communication addressed to the signatories of the Kellogg-Briand Pact of Paris. Trouble was patently brewing for the Nanking regime, and even earlier, on August 12, the Chinese minister at Berlin had approached the officer in charge of Far Eastern affairs in the German Foreign Office in the search for a "face-saving formula" for solution of the CER conflict, "saying he was acting under his Government's instructions." [13] The German government refused to intervene in China's behalf but, acting through Ambassador Herbert von Dirksen at Moscow, endeavored to mediate. The Soviet government did not reject the mediation attempt out of hand, and on August 28 [14] Dirksen communicated to the Narkomindel the draft of a manifesto, which Nanking proposed be issued jointly, setting forth the conditions for a settlement of the CER question.

The Chinese project did indeed propose agreement that: "Both sides declare that they will settle all disputed questions between them in accordance with the 1924 agreement, and in particular will determine the conditions for redemption of the Chinese Eastern Railway in accordance with Article 9 of the Peking agreement." [15] A conference was to be promptly convened to this end. However, Nanking's draft also manifested a clear intent to reduce the Soviet control in administration of the railway by proposing that the new CER general manager and assistant manager, to be nominated by Moscow, should be appointed only upon conclusion of the projected conference. Further, in providing for the release of each other's citizens, Nanking proposed the release only of those arrested in connection with the CER affair. Soviet citizens seized at the time of the raid on the Harbin consular office, in short, were to remain under detention.

On the following day, Litvinov conveyed to Dirksen the Soviet government's readiness to subscribe to such a joint declaration—with modifications. Moscow proposed the *immediate* appointment of a general manager and assistant manager of the CER as nominated by the Soviet government, without committing itself to nominate new officials to those posts, and it proposed the release by both parties of all of each other's citizens arrested *after May 1, 1927*. Nanking evidently hoped for a bigger profit from its adventure. No agreement ensued. As regards the Soviet citizens arrested at Harbin, in fact, on October 15, after five months' imprisonment under extremely harsh conditions, they were brought to trial and given prison sentences of from two to nine years at hard labor.

Border incidents continued, and in what was obviously a warning gesture the Soviets on September 7 bombed the Chinese frontier railway town of Suifenho. The Soviets charged specifically, among other things, that there was harassment of their shipping on the Amur, especially from October 1 onward, and that during the same period White Guard forces upon occasion penetrated into Soviet territory with Chinese military support. (Minister Wu, in a conversation of August 20 with the American secretary of state, had admitted that White Guard troops were present in the Northeastern forces.) On October 10, Chinese mines loosed at the mouth of the Sungari appeared in the Amur, and on the following day the Chinese fired all day long from their entrenchments at Lahasusu, at the confluence of the Sungari and Amur, against Soviet military emplacements and guard vessels. The Soviet forces went into action two days later and attacked the Chinese concentration at Lahasusu, routed the Chinese garrison, and then retired back into Soviet territory. The broken Chinese force retreated to Fuchin, thirty miles up the Sungari.[16]

On October 25, the Chinese government addressed a manifesto to all signatories of the Kellogg-Briand Pact that, beginning with the statement "The authorities of the Three Eastern Provinces (Manchuria) unearthed on May 27, 1929, a dastardly plot within the Soviet Consulate General at Harbin to overthrow the National Government and destroy the Chinese Eastern Railway," invited the attention of the world to the aggressive acts committed against Chinese territory.[17] And Minister Wu at Washington on October 30 renewed the official appeal to Kellogg-Briand Pact signatories.

The following day (it would have been October 30 in Washington), the Soviet Amur Flotilla and a landing party attacked and destroyed the already once-defeated Chinese troops at Fuchin — and again pulled back to Soviet territory. In other military actions, Soviet troops inflicted defeats on Chinese forces concentrated at Mishan, deep inside eastern Manchuria, and at Suifenho, the railway border point opposite Pogranichnaya. Then, on November 17, the Soviets attacked in the west, striking hard at the Chinese concentrations at Manchouli and Chalainor, and routing them — with destruction of the nominally crack Seventeenth Heilungkiang Brigade and the taking of some 8,000 prisoners.

With morale shattered by Soviet air attacks, the Chinese forces fled in wild disorder. In close pursuit, the Soviets occupied Hailar on November 27.[18] With the 40,000 Chinese troops originally located between the Hsingan range and Manchouli smashed and converted into a burning, looting mob, the Chinese command seemingly had moved its headquarters to Pokotu, and planned to make a new stand only at the mountain range.[19] On November 21, however, a Russian named Kokorin, who had been assigned to the German consulate in Harbin to assist in rendering aid to Soviet citizens, had arrived at Suifenho with a message from Ts'ai Yun-sheng to the effect that he, Ts'ai, was fully empowered to negotiate a settlement of the dispute. A reply of November 22 from Litvinov was returned through the same channels, and on November 26, the day before Hailar fell, Chang Hsueh-liang gave his full acceptance of Litvinov's conditions. The Soviet terms were essentially the same as those which had been set forth by Karakhan on July 13.

On December 1, the United States, Britain, and France, as signatories of the Kellogg-Briand Pact, reminded Nanking and Moscow that "the respect with which China and Russia will hereafter be held in the good opinion of the world will necessarily in great measure depend upon the way in which they carry out these most sacred promises [as set forth in the pact]." Nanking on December 3 piously protested its scrupulous adherence to the pact and, with reference to the Soviet military actions of November 17, petitioned the pact signatories "that such measures be adopted as may be necessary and appropriate in view of Article 2 of this treaty." [20]

But the gambit was in vain. On that same December 3, Ts'ai Yun-sheng in plenipotentiary capacity signed at Nikolsk-Ussurisk, with Simonovski of the Narkomindel acting for Moscow, a preliminary protocol by virtue of which the Chinese side acknowledged that the 1924 agreements should strictly govern with respect to the Chinese Eastern Railway. Ts'ai reported that Lü Jung-huan had been dismissed from his position as president of the CER board of directors; Simonovski declared that the Moscow government was prepared to replace Emshanov and Eismont in the posts of general manager and assistant manager, but reserved the right to appoint them to other positions in the railway administration. In those circumstances, Moscow charged tartly that the démarche of the three Kellogg-Briand Pact powers at that juncture represented an attempt to exert pressure on direct Sino-Soviet negotiations already in course for a settlement of the dispute, and could "in no way be considered as a friendly act."[21]

There was no saving the situation for the Chinese. On December 22, Ts'ai, with written full powers authorizing him to act in behalf of both the Nanking and Mukden governments, signed with Simonovski at Khabarovsk a definitive agreement which became known as the Khabarovsk Protocol. This document incorporated the preliminary conditions set forth in the Litvinov telegram of November 27 and the Nikolsk-Ussurisk protocol of December 3.[22] It provided generally for the settlement of outstanding issues at a future conference, but specifically for certain "immediate" measures:

1. the restoration of railway administration based upon the old agreements, with restitution of Soviet employees to their duties, and with orders issued from July 10 onward to be invalid unless confirmed;

2. all Soviet citizens arrested by the Chinese authorities after May 1, including both those arrested during the May 27 raid on the Harbin consulate and those arrested in connection with the CER conflict, to be released "without exception," while the Soviet government was charged with releasing without exception all Chinese arrested "in connection with the conflict" and interned *Chinese* soldiers and officers;

3. all Soviet citizens discharged or resigned from July 10 onward to have the right to recover their previous positions, with payment of money due them, or, failing exercise of that right, to be paid wages and pensions due them;

4. "Chinese authorities immediately to disarm the Russian White Guard detachments and deport from the Three Eastern Provinces their organizers and inspirers";

5. there to be restoration of the functioning of Soviet consular offices in Manchuria, and Chinese consulates in the Soviet Far East, with the Mukden government undertaking to assure to the Soviet offices "full inviolability and all privileges to which international law and custom entitle them";

6. Soviet and Chinese commercial organs to resume functioning;

7. guarantees for observance of the agreements to be fixed at the forthcoming conference;
8. the conference for resolution of outstanding issues would be convened in Moscow on January 25, 1930;
9. there should be the immediate restoration of peaceful conditions on the common frontier, with the subsequent withdrawal of troops by both sides; and
10. the protocol would be effective "from the moment of its signature."

In short, there was to be effectively the restoration of the status quo ante May 27, 1929.

Chiang Kai-shek, one of the prime movers in the 1929 adventure, looking back with the perspective of nearly thirty years, viewed the matter in his work *Soviet Russia in China* rather narrowly. His account, in full, of the 1929 events that began with the May 27 raid on the Soviet consulate in Harbin is as follows:

> On October 12, 1929, there occurred the Chinese Eastern Railway Incident. Russian troops invaded Manchuli and Hailar in Manchuria, and forced our local authorities to sign the Khabarovsk Protocol on December 22, another proof that Soviet Russia was continuing Czarist Russia's aggressive policy toward China.[23]

19 CHINA, JAPAN, AND THE USSR, 1931-1935

THE SINO-RUSSIAN conference did not begin in Moscow on January 25 as scheduled. The Chinese had good reason to drag their feet, for they could not possibly win at the conference table what they had been unable to obtain by a tour de force. They started perforce from where they had been in 1924. Mo Teh-hui, of Manchurian origin, was made Chinese president of the CER upon the enforced retirement of Lü Jung-huan in accordance with the Khabarovsk Protocol; he was duly designated China's delegate to the impending conference, but arrived in Moscow only in May, 1930. The belated conference at once struck a serious obstacle. In a unilateral statement of February 8, Nanking had purported to restrict the impending conference to the CER question and, in defiance of the provisions of the Khabarovsk Protocol, Mo carried authority to deal only with questions related to the Chinese Eastern Railway. Karakhan insisted that, as provided by the protocol, the issues of trade and Sino-Soviet state relations should be discussed as well. Furthermore, Nanking soon became engaged in the great civil war of 1930 against the Northern Coalition and therefore marked time in its foreign relations—while Moscow, with a natural interest in the conflict's outcome, did not press Mo Teh-hui toward an agreement that might not be worth the paper it was written on.

The long-scheduled conference finally opened on October 11, but stalled immediately on the matter of the agenda. The impasse was followed by exchanges of notes through November, with Karakhan insisting on full compliance with the terms of the Khabarovsk Protocol. At the end of November, Mo set forth the unoriginal idea that, after all, the continuance of the conference was the essential thing. Karakhan agreed, and on December 4 the delegations took up their work — on the basis of the Soviet agenda. But then, on December 12, Mo Teh-hui reported that he had been ordered to Nanking for consultation. The conference again adjourned.

The situation was clear enough: regardless of the provisions of the Khabarovsk Protocol, Nanking did not desire to negotiate a new agreement that would inevitably grant important benefits, in one form or another, to the Soviet Union. Mo Teh-hui returned to Moscow in late March of the following year, whereupon, on April 11, 1931, the conference held its third formal session. The Soviet side presented a project for the establishment of a commission to determine the value of the Chinese Eastern Railway and procedure for its purchase by China in accordance with the Sino-Soviet agreement of 1924. The Chinese presented their own project to the same end. The two plans were far apart. Major differences developed regarding the issue of whether, as Moscow insisted, China would be permitted to purchase the strategic rail line only by the use of its own resources, and whether the line also should in other respects be kept out of the sphere of possible international intrigue. Nanking and Mukden had, moreover, failed thus far to give effect to the commitment made in the Khabarovsk Protocol (and earlier in the 1924 agreements) to disarm and disperse White Guard detachments in Manchuria, and Moscow evidently felt that it had reason to fear that the Chinese Eastern Railway might once again be used as an instrument in some anti-Soviet campaign in Northeast Asia. Then, long before Moscow and Nanking had come even close to bridging the gap between their bargaining positions, there began a development that would render the whole conference meaningless.

The Russian revolutionary strategists had early focused their attention on another Asian country than China. Zinoviev, speaking at the First Congress of the Toilers of the Far East in 1922, had proclaimed that "The key to the solution of the Far Eastern question is in the hands of Japan." [1] By his judgment, other Far

Eastern revolutions would merely be relatively unimportant local events—until a Japanese revolution had occurred. The task facing the congress, then, was "to co-ordinate the activities of the oppressed, the nonproletarian masses of the entire Far East with those of the industrial village proletariat of Japan." [2]

The Japan of 1931 was, however, not revolutionary in a Marxist-Leninist sense, but imperial; its strategy would be framed accordingly. By this time, post-World War I problems had badly dissipated Allied strength and jarred wartime friendships as well. The economic woes of Germany and Central Europe had been dramatized by the Credit Anstalt crash, and an exhausting debility had assailed even the victor nations. The League of Nations, deprived of the membership of both the United States and the Soviet Union, was in poor condition to function as the guardian of international peace and order. The concept of collective security had gradually faded into the pious and pallid expression of the Kellogg-Briand Pact, which in its first major test, that of the 1929 affair, had proven totally ineffective. There were, moreover, unmistakable indications that the Washington Nine-Power Treaty of 1922 did not guarantee such stability within China, in particular, as would leave foreign rights and interests inviolate.

The world at that juncture was at a critical turning point between two world wars. Under the impact of the world economic depression, the upsurge of nationalism in China, and the advent of fascism in Europe, absolutist concepts had made substantial headway in the Japanese body politic. Extremist societies such as the old-fashioned Black Dragon Society and the new fascist-type parties were in agreement on one point: the Japanese empire should extend its frontiers. One of the aims of the Sakurai Kai (Cherry Blossom Society) in particular was to reach a "solution" of the "Manchurian Problem." A number of Japanese military men, returning in some respects to the thinking of 1917–1920, saw the conquest of Manchuria as the first stepping-stone to a war with Soviet Russia that would give Japan the Siberian region east of Lake Baikal.

It was quite apparent that the Japanese army had ideological support in influential quarters for countermeasures that it might undertake against Chinese threats to the imperial interests of Japan. And Nanking and Mukden, in the same blind disregard of potential danger that had led them earlier to become embroiled with the Soviet Union, in 1931 staged such threats. On the night of September 18, the Kwantung Army struck, and in the "Mukden Incident" began the drive to wrest Manchuria from Chinese control—and the remnant Russian influence.

In Moscow, Karakhan approached Mo Teh-hui with the proposition that events demanded the restoration of regular diplomatic relations between their two countries. Mo, in the absence of instructions from Nanking, refused to discuss the proposal. For the moment, significant movement was discovered in the Soviet-Japanese rather than the Sino-Soviet relationship. In a note of November 19, Ambassador Hirota Koki invited the attention of the Soviet government to the circumstance that Tokyo had followed a policy of nonintervention in the Sino-Soviet dispute of 1929 and requested that the Soviet Union likewise observe a policy of neutrality with respect to the present developments in Manchuria. Hirota went on to assure the Moscow government that Soviet interests in Manchuria would be protected and that the Kwantung Army would not interfere with the Chinese Eastern Railway in particular. Litvinov expressed his government's satisfaction at receiving those assurances and stated that the Soviet government would observe a policy of strict noninterference in the Manchurian crisis.

However, the movement toward an understanding between Moscow and Tokyo advanced no further. In December, the Soviet government proposed to Tokyo that the two countries enter upon a nonaggression pact. For a full year, Japan did not even make formal reply.[3] The United States, with regard to the critical developments in the Far East, contented itself with a reiteration of the Bryan nonrecognition doctrine, and the League of Nations, which on December 10 created the "Lytton Commission" to investigate the Manchurian affair, could hardly do more. In the face of Chinese passivity and nonintervention by the great powers the Japanese occupation of Manchuria proceeded apace. On March 1, 1932, there was born a new state of Manchoukuo in the place of Manchuria, and a few days later the sometime emperor Hsuant'ung of China, P'u-yi, assumed the post of chief executive of that new state, his homeland.

In due course, the Foreign Office at Tokyo adduced a simple argument in justification of the Japanese action in Manchuria: Japan combated Communism:

Japan is exercising very strict control over Communist movements at home, but in view of the international connections adroitly maintained by those who take part in them and on account of other circumstances, she cannot regard with equanimity the "bolshevization" of China, because her policy against communism must necessarily be shaped in accordance with the situation existing in that country.

In particular, the statement went on, Japan was deeply concerned with the possibility that Manchuria and Eastern Inner Mongolia (western Manchuria) might "turn communistic," thus affecting the peace and order of Korea and thereby Japan's own national security.[4]

The Lytton Commission's report, published in October, came up for debate in the League in early December, 1932. The reactions of Tokyo and Nanking, neither of which was prepared to compromise its political position, were predictable: they both rejected the commission's proposed solution. And neither the Soviet Union (which doubtless bitterly remembered the Siberian intervention of 1918-1920) nor the United States was prepared to participate in the construction of a united front against the aggressor nation. The outcome of the League's efforts, in those circumstances, could be foreseen in advance. The League failed and entered upon the decline that led to its death.

The Kwantung Army remained dominant in Manchoukuo. The Japanese had now taken a second great step, after the incorporation of Korea into the empire, toward the establishment of a continental base from which they could proceed with the plan for the creation of a Greater East Asia under their hegemony, waging war if necessary. Nor were Western powers basically inclined toward the use of force to check the Japanese mainland advance: it was regarded by some as being in essence designed to thwart the Soviet Union, and therefore not the greatest of visible evils.

The significance of the Japanese moves was clear to the strategists at Moscow. They could see the near certainty that the Japanese action would give rise to a new wave of Chinese nationalism and that other nations, especially in Asia, might eventually also become involved. For the moment, their moves were defensive. They performed a minor function for the Chinese nation by giving asylum, at the end of 1932, to "volunteers" under Li Tu and Su

Ping-wen, who had resisted the Japanese in Manchuria and lost. Moscow rejected Tokyo's demand that Su Ping-wen and his men be returned to Japanese hands with the observation that the Soviet Union was neutral to the Sino-Japanese conflict and that the disposition of the troops in question was a Soviet domestic affair not subject to negotiation with any other government. Moscow disarmed those Chinese forces but, instead of interning, "repatriated" them – to Sinkiang Province, where it seemed that they might perform a function useful to Soviet policy.

Even before this, the National government had come around to the idea that China's interests might be served by a restoration of regular diplomatic relations with the Soviet Union. True, pro-Japanese elements such as Wang Ching-wei and Chang Ch'ün had stood out in opposition, basing their case on the anticipation that such a move would irritate the Japanese government; but pro-Westerners like T. V. Soong, H. H. K'ung, and V. K. Wellington Koo believed that the restoration of Sino-Soviet relations would more likely check Japanese expansive actions vis-à-vis China – and at the same time offer the possibility of bringing about a conflict between the Soviet Union and Japan.

Chiang Kai-shek agreed with the latter position. So, on June 6, 1932, the Kuomintang Central Executive Committee passed a resolution enjoining the restoration of diplomatic relations with Moscow. China's delegate to the League Assembly, W. W. Yen, at the end of June communicated to Commissar for Foreign Affairs Litvinov in Geneva the proposition that the two countries enter upon a nonaggression pact. Foreign Minister Lo Wen-kan informed the press that a nonaggression pact (viewed naturally as strengthening China's position vis-à-vis Japan) was a prerequisite for the resumption of Sino-Soviet relations. Lo, however, found Moscow in disagreement regarding priorities: Litvinov in his reply proposed the *simultaneous* resumption of diplomatic relations and signature of the projected nonaggression pact.

Nanking at this juncture, in one of its characteristically indirect moves, with the approval of Foreign Minister Lo Wen-kan had a note from V. K. Wellington Koo delivered to Karakhan at Moscow through the medium of an Englishman, Harry Khassi (Hussey?), proposing exchange of ideas regarding the resumption of diplomatic relations on the basis of mutual understanding and goodwill. Karakhan in a letter of reply to Koo remarked that inasmuch as negotiations regarding diplomatic ties were then in course at Geneva, a personal exchange of ideas was not convenient. In early September, Yen announced that his government was ready to exchange notes for the resumption of relations conditional upon the maintenance of former treaties (that is, inferentially, to be in full effect with respect to Manchuria) and the dispatch of a Soviet delegation to Peking for the resolution (under the noses of the Japanese) of outstanding questions. Litvinov replied that the Soviet government was prepared to exchange notes for resumption of relations—without any conditions. Nanking, in its anxiety to strengthen its position vis-à-vis Japan, perforce acceded to the Soviet position.

On December 12, 1932, almost exactly five years to the day after the Nationalist regime at Nanking had ordered the withdrawal of all Soviet consular and commercial representatives from territory under its control, Yen and Litvinov exchanged notes providing for the resumption, as of that date, of formal relations between China and the Soviet Union. Dr. Yen's note observed that publication of the Lytton Report with its suggestion that the United States and the Soviet Union be invited to participate in the deliberations on the Mukden Incident made obvious the desirability of reestablishing normal relations. He added: "The Chinese Government and the Chinese people are very sincere in their desire to cultivate friendly relations with their great neighbour, and they are convinced these feelings are reciprocated."[5]

Litvinov's statement reflected some of Moscow's exultation as victor in the episode, but it contained a significant passage: "the improvement of relations with one country is not a means of rendering worse relations with another." Moscow knew full well why Nanking had come around to the idea of resuming relations, and was letting it be known in both Nanking and Tokyo that it did not propose to be used as a Chinese cat's-paw in the Sino-Japanese imbroglio.

The mission of Mo Teh-hui had come to a fruitless end: there was no point in negotiating further regarding the Chinese Eastern Railway, over which Nanking now obviously had no authority whatsoever, and normal diplomatic relations had been restored between the two countries without Mo Teh-hui's even having participated in the pertinent negotiations. W. W. Yen was appointed Chinese ambassador to Moscow, and Dmitri Bogomolov became Soviet ambassador to China. Yen took up his post in March, 1933; Bogomolov reached Shanghai in late April and presented his credentials on May 2.

Diplomatic relations with Moscow gained no early help for Nanking. When the League of Nations, by resolution of February 24, 1933, established a consultative committee to consider the matter and invited the Soviet Union to participate, Moscow refused. Nor did the committee prove its worth in action. In March, Japan withdrew from League membership and, in the absence of even token Chinese resistance, proceeded to round off its occupation of Manchuria by the conquest of Jehol Province, immediately north of the Great Wall. Chahar, to the west, was brought under threat.

The crisis caused in North China by the Japanese movement was temporarily ended with the signature on May 31 of the Tangku Truce—highly favorable to Japan. With the new agreement in hand and the conquest of Jehol consolidated, the Japanese temporarily halted their military advance and turned to political measures to achieve their ends. It was still requisite that Japan impose its will upon China, or at least neutralize China's strength, for the attainment of its overall objectives.

Nanking, for its part, from the beginning of the conflict had hoped to be able to make a deal with its imperial Asian neighbor —or else to maneuver a third power into fighting China's war. Moscow was naturally aware of the Chinese design. However, the Japanese thrust into Jehol, threatening to flank the Mongolian People's Republic, and the Tangku Truce, evoked a political countermove by Moscow: in August, Nanking was informed that the USSR was prepared to enter upon a nonaggression pact.

A Soviet draft treaty was in fact delivered to the Chinese Foreign Ministry on October 13. But the draft proposed that, in the event of a military attack on one of the two powers, the other would observe neutrality. Nanking desired Soviet support, not neutrality, in the event of Sino-Japanese hostilities. Bogomolov consequently had to report that the Chinese government was apparently little interested in the projected pact.[6] Moscow had indicated a readiness to collaborate, in a qualified and limited manner, with a China prepared to take a stand against a threat that loomed up for both countries in Northeast Asia; but it patently was not at all inclined to rush in gallantly to save a nonresisting Nationalist regime.

For the Japanese, the determination of tactics regarding

China would be influenced in some degree by their decision regarding their ultimate target: should it be the eastward advancing Soviet Union, or the Anglo-American naval power ranged between Japan and the oil, rubber, and rice of Southeast Asia?

In deciding the strategic orientation of Japan's "continental war base," three major factors had to be taken into consideration: (1) it was difficult to reach vital parts of the sprawling body of the Soviet Union by blows launched from the East; (2) the spirit of modern nationalism, with its strong antiforeign overtones, remained alive in China despite repressive measures taken against it by the Nationalists from 1931 onward in service of their conciliatory Japan policy; and (3) it was apparent that social revolution, in the form of Chinese Communism, was reviving from the blow it had received in 1927. There were sound reasons to scotch the Chinese dragon, at least, before proceeding with other mainland — or maritime — ventures.

This was not to mean that the short-range secondary problems with the USSR would be neglected. The immediate strategic issue confronting Japan was seen in the continued presence of Soviet interest and influence in northern Manchuria, now viewed by Japan as part of its domain. With the consolidation of Japanese control confirmed with the erection of Manchoukuo, Tokyo turned, with a neat disregard of Ambassador Hirota's assurances of a short few months earlier, to maneuver the Soviet Union out of control of the Chinese Eastern Railway. Mo Teh-hui, Nanking's appointee, had been replaced as CER president by a Manchoukuo man, Li Shao-keng.

Harassment of the Soviet administration began in 1933 with a demand for the return of CER rolling stock being held in Siberia. Moscow refused satisfaction, arguing that the locomotives in question at least were the property of the Soviet Union, not of the railway. Manchoukuo blocked passage of trains at the two exit points on its borders, Manchouli and Suifenho. On May 2, 1933, doubtless having in view the dubious future of the Russian position in a northern Manchuria dominated by Japan, Litvinov made an offer on behalf of the USSR through the new Japanese ambassador to Moscow, Ota Tamekichi, to sell its interest in the Chinese Eastern Railway to Manchoukuo. Litvinov, in an interview published by Tass on May 11, set forth the essence of the Soviet rationale for treating with Manchoukuo regarding the matter:

The Chinese Government or the powers under its control have ceased to be actual partners with the U.S.S.R. in the Chinese Eastern Railway over eighteen months ago. They have been deprived of this possibility by causes not dependent upon the U.S.S.R., and are unable to exercise their rights or discharge their undertakings in terms of the Peking and Mukden Agreements.[7]

Litvinov was on unassailable ground when he argued that Nanking and Chang Hsueh-liang had lost their de facto authority in Manchuria. But the proclaimed independence of Manchoukuo from China per se, and the clear derivation of P'u-yi's power from Japanese armed strength, did give Nanking occasion to protest where Peking had remained silent when Chang Tso-lin had played an independent role. On instructions of his government, Ambassador Yen lodged strong objection to the proposed transaction, only to meet the suggestion of Litvinov that the deal really favored China, inasmuch as it would eventually obtain possession of the Chinese Eastern Railway without having to pay for it — since China reputedly expected to recover Manchuria. Moscow's reply of June 19 and a further Chinese note of June 25 were not published, and there the correspondence between Nanking and Moscow regarding the projected sale of the railway ended. The Chinese side, in truth, had little more that it could say about the matter.

Formal negotiations of the three parties regarding the projected transaction began in Tokyo at the end of June, with the Soviets asking 250 million gold rubles — a price that did not include the detained rolling stock, still held to belong to the Soviet Union. Manchoukuo offered 50 million yen (40 million gold rubles) as a counterproposal. There were, naturally, other points at issue, such as the matter of providing for the retirement of Soviet citizens employed by the railway, and the question of responsibility for the satisfaction of shareholders and other creditors, but the price factor was obviously the chief consideration. And the contention of Manchoukuo that, as successor to China's position in Manchuria, it already possessed a share in the railway for which it was not required to pay, had a major relevance to the matter of price. On those major obstacles, the negotiations ground to a halt within a fortnight.

The railway became the object of "bandit" attacks, sabotage, and theft – obviously a part of the Manchoukuoan-Japanese bargaining process. In February, 1934, the Soviet Union dropped its price to 200 million yen, at the same time expressing a willingness to take one-half the purchase price in Japanese goods. There followed a series of bargaining exchanges, with the gap between asking and offered prices becoming ever smaller until, in mid-September, the Soviet side reduced its price to 145 million yen (not including payments for Soviet citizens leaving CER employment), and Japanese Foreign Minister Hirota increased the other side's offer to 140 million yen. Soviet Ambassador Yurenev on September 19 accepted that last "final offer" on behalf of the Soviet government.

Only details remained to be ironed out, and the subsequent negotiations proceeded without major hitch. On March 23, 1935, fittingly in Hirota's Tokyo residence, there was signed the agreement for the sale of the Chinese Eastern Railway (including "all the rights, enterprises and properties appurtenant thereto") to Manchoukuo, with Japan guaranteeing payment by Manchoukuo. One-third of the purchase price was to be paid in cash, in part on signature of the agreement and the remainder in installments over three years. Two-thirds of the due amount would be paid in kind, in either Japanese or Manchoukuoan goods, as determined between the Soviet trade representation in Japan and subjects or juridical persons of Japan or Manchoukuo, also over a period of three years. The Soviet Union kept possession of the detained locomotives and freight cars, but renounced claim to other property (excepting specified consular premises) in Manchuria, and was left responsible for claims of CER shareholders and creditors – for the period prior to 1917. With this exception, Manchoukuo succeeded to the assets and liabilities of the Chinese Eastern Railway. The purchaser was called upon to provide 30 million yen for the payment of salaries and allowances for discharged Soviet railway employees.[8]

If the purchase price was far less than the real value of the railway, Russia had probably long before obtained full return on its original capital investment; and, it had besides obtained an intangible present benefit of great value in the existing circumstances, namely a strategic disengagement permitting withdrawal to a less dangerous political position in Northeast Asia. With Moscow's sale of the Chinese Eastern Railway, a whole era of imperialistic endeavor in East Asia did indeed come to a close;

a new era, which Japan proposed to dominate, was palpably beginning. That P'u-yi had on March 1, 1934, been enthroned Emperor of Manchoukuo was a datum of only secondary significance.

Japan had continued to argue that it acted to combat Communism. Foreign Minister Hirota Koki, in his maiden speech of January 23, 1934, to the Japanese Diet, said that "we are watching not without grave misgivings the activities of the Communist Party and increasing rampancy of 'red armies' in China." [9] But, as the pattern of events clearly showed, the Japanese long-range strategy was designed quite as much for Soviet Russia as for disordered China. On April 17, a spokesman of the Japanese Foreign Office, Amau Eiji, issued a statement to the press contending that Japan had "special responsibilities in East Asia" and in particular had a special concern in developments bearing on China; and he warned other powers against launching political, commercial, or financial undertakings in China that might be prejudicial to Japan's interests. Amau said that, "to keep peace and order in East Asia, we must even act alone on our own responsibility and it is our duty to perform it. . . . We oppose any attempt on the part of China to avail herself of the influence of any other country in order to resist Japan; we also oppose any action taken by China, designed to play one Power against another." [10] In this "hands-off-China" statement, the Japanese government thus arrogated to itself the responsibility for acting as the policeman and for becoming the arbiter of destiny for East Asia.

Where the United States and Britain had been indulgent to the Japanese idea of "containing Bolshevism," the Amau statement aroused considerable concern. If elements of the doctrine were clearly aimed at the Soviet Union, the statement as a whole applied as well to the Western sea powers. This estimate was categorically confirmed when, in late 1935, Chinese Minister Chiang Tso-pin conveyed to Foreign Minister Hirota certain proposals for improvement of Sino-Japanese relations, and in response Hirota set forth three "principles" on which any improvement would have to be based, as follows:

1. China should cease trying to maneuver European countries and the United States against Japan, and reach a full alignment with Japan.

2. China should extend de facto recognition to Manchoukuo and recognize also Japan's special interests in North China.
3. China must agree on joint action together with Japan against the anti-Japanese Communist movement.[11]

Japan naturally had no intention of entering upon a relationship of equality with weak and divided China. At this particular juncture, it had embarked upon a course destined to bring it into close relationship with another major power, Nazi Germany. It must by now have become clear to Chiang Kai-shek that there was slight possibility of an accommodation with Japan that would leave China with its sovereignty, and him with his power. It was presumably after the rebuff of Chiang Tso-pin's overture that Chiang Kai-shek's close lieutenant, Ch'en Li-fu, head of the KMT organization bureau, sounded out Bogomolov on the possibility of negotiation of a secret Sino-Soviet alliance. Bogomolov suggested that Ch'en visit Moscow and take up the matter with Stalin, and in late December Ch'en sailed from Shanghai under an assumed name. He arrived in Berlin and then, instead of proceeding to Moscow to present his full powers and the Chinese proposals, waited for word from Stalin agreeing to the negotiations. The cagey Stalin sent no word, and Ch'en returned home in April. A Chinese diplomat who reported on the matter observed that "The only explanation for Stalin's attitude seems to be that he was willing to help China fight an all-out war against Japan on the condition that the Soviet Union would not be directly involved in it." [12] That Stalin did not propose to become directly involved in a war with Japan on China's behalf is plausible. But that Stalin was not prepared to talk to Ch'en Li-fu is not, in the light of Bogomolov's recommendation. The more likely explanation appears to be that, as had been the frequent practice of Chinese rulers in the past, Chiang Kai-shek had given Ch'en authority to explore the possibilities of a deal advantageous to China but had not given him full powers to negotiate.

The Amau declaration of April, 1934, and Japan's denunciation, at the end of the same year, of the five-power naval pact of 1922, marked the beginning of a major exacerbation of Japanese relations with the sea powers Britain and the United States. The potential for improvement of Japan's relations with the Soviet Union increased correspondingly, and this circumstance had doubtless contributed to the successful denouement in 1935 of the protracted negotiations for sale of the Chinese Eastern Railway. Coincident with that transaction, Sino-Japanese relations were building up to a climax because of Japanese pressure on North China and Inner Mongolia. The Sino-Soviet relationship was consequently brought to the threshold of a new stage: as in the case of the Sino-Japanese crisis of four decades earlier, China looked to Russia as a possible source of help against imperial Japan.

It was noteworthy in this connection that, as the result of the fifth "bandit-suppression campaign" waged by Chiang Kai-shek, the Chinese Communists, driven from their base area in Kiangsi Province, had in October, 1935, reached a weak haven in Northwest China.

20 SINO-SOVIET RELATIONS IN SINKIANG, 1934-1937

THE JAPANESE CONQUEST of Manchuria was followed by the establishment, in March, 1933, of the "autonomous" Mongolian province of Hsingan in Eastern Inner Mongolia (western Manchuria). With the nearly simultaneous advance into Jehol, the Japanese came into a position to exploit the nationalism of the Mongols of Western Inner Mongolia, who like their brothers to the east had by 1930 been despoiled of much of their lands by Chinese colonists. By late 1935, the Japanese had made good headway toward winning over to their side the Mongol nationalist leader Demchukdonggrub, better known by his Chinese appellation of Teh Wang ("Prince Teh"), chief of the West Sunid Banner of the Silingol League. The Japanese were flanking the Mongolian People's Republic.

But Tokyo aimed at an even more distant target – Sinkiang. There the old warlord, Yang Tseng-hsin, had been assassinated in July, 1928, and the misrule of the successor governor, Chin Shu-jen, brought the Turki peoples of the province once more to a state of incipient rebellion. A revolt that began at Hami in 1930 under the leadership of Yollbars Khan and Khoja Niaz was put down by the use of refugee Cossacks mobilized by Chin, but the situation deteriorated with the intervention of a hard-fighting Dungan warrior from Kansu, Ma Chung-ying. Ma was initially repulsed, and retired back to Kansu. Chin, given his continued malfeasance, was in April, 1933, cast out of Urumchi by a coup staged by the White Russians, with tsarist Colonel Papingut playing a leading role, and Sheng Shih-ts'ai came to power in northern Sinkiang.

Sheng was a Manchurian military man, a sometime subordinate of Kuo Sung-ling. He had served on the Nationalist general staff after the Northern Expedition, and thus had Nanking connections, especially with the powerful political operator P'eng Chao-hsien, but his ambitions were his own. It was only natural that he should reject the request of Khoja Niaz, as Turki representative, that the Uighurs (the majority people of Sinkiang) be granted one of the two highest posts in the government. Khoja Niaz thereupon transmitted to Ma Chung-ying, through Yollbars Khan, the message that Sinkiang was ripe for conquest, and he appealed to Ma to aid the Muslim cause.

Ma, who had in the meantime become commander of the Nationalist Thirty-sixth Division, reacted promptly. By mid-May, his force was attacking at Chitai, east of Urumchi. Complicated military and political actions ensued, with Nanking endeavoring through emissaries to impose its own control over the province.[1] The emissaries failed either to effect a reconciliation of Sheng and Ma, or to bring Sheng to renounce his ambition to rule undisturbed by Nanking. Nanking found it advisable to confirm Sheng in the post of defense commissioner of Sinkiang, confronting the challenger Ma Chung-ying.

The conflict between the two ambitious men was direct and irreconcilable. Where there had before been political negotiations looking toward a compromise settlement, Sheng would obviously no longer be ready to agree, even in temporization, to any division of territory and power with Ma Chung-ying. And the arrogant Dungan leader, insufficiently aware of the state of the world to recognize natural political limitations, proposed to establish a Central Asian Turki-Muslim state that would have included not only Sinkiang but also an important slice of Western (Russian) Turkestan.[2] Ma was believed to have Japanese backing. He had as advisers the Turk adventurer Kemal Effendi Pasha, a Korean Tatar named Jakar, and the Japanese agent Onishi Tadashi.

In January, 1934, Ma Chung-ying once more attacked Urumchi, and Ili garrison commander Chang P'ei-yuan advanced from the West, at the head of 3,000 troops, to his assistance. In the vicinity of Chuguchak another Dungan, Ma Ho-ying, likewise moved his forces against Sheng. The situation at Urumchi quickly became critical. Ma Chung-ying boasted in propaganda addressed to the town that he was going to transform Sinkiang into an independent "Eastern Turkestan," and it appeared that he would be able to make a significant start by capturing the provincial capital.

But when Ma seemed on the point of grasping victory, there occurred a strange reversal. Earlier, in October, 1933, Sheng Shih-ts'ai had sent to Moscow a delegation made up of Special Foreign Affairs Commissioner Ch'en Teh-li and air force commander Yao Hsiung to request a loan and the delivery of arms as provided earlier in a deal negotiated by Chin Shu-jen. Moscow, evidently without committing itself, had designated Garegin A. Apresoff, diplomatic agent at Tashkent, to be consul general at Urumchi, and Apresoff had gone to Sinkiang with Ch'en and Yao on their return in December. P'eng Chao-hsien was at the time in Urumchi. He had been a student together with Apresoff in Moscow. Now, with Ma Chung-ying's troops threatening to capture the town, P'eng took the occasion of a visit by Apresoff to Sheng's *yamen* (administrative office) one day to feel out the visitor on the matter of emergency aid.[3]

P'eng reminded Apresoff of Russia's supply of grain to Tso Tsung-t'ang in the latter part of the nineteenth century, at a time when Tso was engaged in suppression of the Muslim rebellion led by Yakub Beg, and went on to observe that Ma Chung-ying was endeavoring to subjugate Sinkiang with the aid of a foreign country (Japan), and that Ma's success in establishing an Eastern Turkestan Republic would be inimical to the interests of the Soviet Union; the maintenance of political authority over Sinkiang in the hands of China, contrariwise, would redound to Soviet benefit in three ways: (1) Sinkiang in those circumstances would not aggress against the Soviet Union; (2) communications with China Proper being difficult, and with the USSR easy, the latter country could readily derive economic benefit from the resources of Sinkiang; and (3) Sinkiang, being a nonindustrialized area, offered a natural market for Soviet manufactured products.

The Soviet representative manifested his sympathy with that point of view, and Sheng thereupon requested Nanking to authorize Ch'en Teh-li to discuss the matter of aid with the Soviet side. The result of those complicated negotiations was a Soviet military intervention in Sinkiang in support of the Chinese warlord Sheng Shih-ts'ai against his enemies, the Dungans. Two brigades of G.P.U. (state police) troops, who came not as Soviet military units but in the guise of unidentified "men from the Altai," equipped with cavalry, artillery, armored cars, and planes, advanced swiftly by two routes, through Khorgos and via Chuguchak. One Soviet force attacked Ma Chung-ying's concentrations on January 24, and Ma, without trying to make a stand against the superior force, withdrew in the direction of Toksun, pursued by avenging planes. Chang P'ei-yuan's men were ambushed and killed almost to a man in the vicinity of Manas. Chang, in defeat and with capture and death his manifest future lot, committed suicide. Ma Ho-ying, driving down from the direction of Chuguchak, was caught in a pincers movement and hard hit. The defeat of the Ma Chung-ying coalition in northern Sinkiang was complete, and the beaten Dungan began his retreat into the south that had at one time seemed too small for him. The Soviet forces left the major part of the work of mopping up to the provincial forces, and withdrew back to their homeland in about forty-five days. With the shattering of Ma Chung-ying's power, P'eng Chao-hsien after a ten months' stay in Sinkiang returned to Nanking.

In interpreting the Soviet intervention, it is helpful to remark the circumstance that the time, 1934, was midway between the Mukden Incident of September, 1931, and the Lukouchiao Incident of July, 1937, that began the Sino-Japanese War. The period, that is, was one of further Japanese expansion. It was still unclear which direction the main thrust would take; nevertheless, as early as 1919 one Japanese concept had envisaged the separation of eastern Asia from the Soviet Union by the creation of a buffer belt comprising Mongolia and Sinkiang. For attainment of that objective, it was thought desirable to develop a strategy of Pan-Turanianism, for an ultimate unification of Muslim peoples with the Japanese, in order to link Japan with Turkey in Europe and with Arabia. The strategic value of success along those lines, as regards Japan's expansionist aims in Asia generally, and the objective of containing Soviet revolutionaries, would naturally have been great.

Sheng Shih-ts'ai has charged that Ma Chung-ying received Japanese arms and munitions via Tientsin. It is evident that the

Soviets also believed that there were Japanese influences behind the Sinkiang disorders. By report, Tashkent newspapers of the period charged that Ma had Japanese advisers, and pointed out that, if Japan got control of Sinkiang, the Baku oil fields would be within range of Japanese bombers. In a lecture at the Hong Kong University in October, 1941, Dr. Sun Fo revealed that, on the occasion of a meeting with Stalin at Moscow in April, 1939, Stalin had told him that the conquest of Sinkiang by Ma Chung-ying with Japanese backing would have meant the creation of a Japanese threat to the Soviet position in Western Turkestan, and that it had been for this reason that Moscow had dispatched two brigades of disguised Soviet troops to defeat Ma's army at the gates of Urumchi.[4]

Ma had thus apparently been employed as the instrument of a Japanese-inspired Pan-Turanianism, but had come into collision with Soviet power. The Soviet position in Central Asia at the beginning of the 1930s was stronger by far than it had been in Kolchak's time, or when the Basmachi movement had proved so troublesome for the young Soviet power. The Turkestan-Siberian (Turk-Sib) Railway had been completed in 1930, and paralleled the Sinkiang frontier from south to north. This had notably strengthened the Soviet Union in Central Asia, in economic, political, and military terms. In sum, circumstances in 1934 were favorable for bold Soviet action in the Central Asian sector against Japanese "imperialism," with Sheng Shih-ts'ai playing a willing role.

The Soviet military intervention had been the critical factor in January, 1934. Despite the divisions within the Muslim camp, Ma Chung-ying would have won Sinkiang, had not his (real or suspected) Japanese connections caused the Soviet Union to intervene against him. A British observer later offered a summary comment: "First among the factors which have contributed to the restoration of Chinese rule in Sinkiang must be placed the assistance afforded by the Russians to the Chinese authorities at Urumchi in their struggle with Ma Chung-ying."[5]

In November, 1933, there had been established at Kashgar the government of an "Eastern Turkestan Republic," with Khoja Niaz (by now at odds with Ma Chung-ying) as president and the Khotan *ahung* (religious teacher) Sabit Mullah as premier. A proclamation issued at the time declared both the Chinese and Dungans to be the republic's enemies — with the Dungans the worse of the two. The new regime's founders had reverted to the intolerant political position of Yakub Beg. In their retreat from the north in early 1934, Ma's Dungans destroyed that separatist Muslim government.

Ma Chung-ying himself arrived at Kashgar in March, and was reputedly urged by his brother-in-law and supporter, Ma Hu-shan, to continue the fight for the Dungan cause. But, given the essentially anti-Dungan attitude of the Sarts of southern Sinkiang, Ma Chung-ying rather naturally did not receive that popular support for his cause which he deemed requisite. Reputedly persuaded by a Soviet consular officer at Kashgar that his position was hopeless, Ma handed command of his faithful Dungan warriors over to Ma Hu-shan and on July 7, 1934, accompanied by his higher officers and one Konstantinov of the Soviet consulate general, passed through the border town of Irkeshtam into the Soviet Union. Ma Chung-ying thus accepted the hospitality of the country that had brought his troops to defeat and his dreams of empire down into the dust. Ma Hu-shan and the remnants of Ma Chung-ying's forces withdrew first to Yarkand and then to Khotan.

For the time being, Sheng Shih-ts'ai did not undertake to extend his authority over southern Sinkiang by military means, but resorted to political measures instead. He maneuvered the chief remaining opponents of his rule either into his government or else off the political stage. In that way, he established himself, at least nominally, as the ruler of all Sinkiang. But Sheng knew that latent opposition to his rule still existed, and by long training in intrigue he "saw a soldier in every bush." His capacity for suspicion was boundless, and his rule of Sinkiang was marked by the discovery of a series of "plots" — some doubtless real, others his own concoction.

Among those who early came to grief was Papingut. His offense appears to have been that, becoming apprehensive of what might happen to the Whites in Sinkiang given Sheng's new alignment with Moscow, he requested Sheng's permission for the White Russian troops under his command to leave the province. Sheng rejected the request, and Papingut and his followers secretly made preparations to leave anyway — but when they had collected their horses and carts and were ready to depart with their families and belongings, Sheng discovered their plans. For that "crime," Papingut and a large number of his officers were in

1934 thrown into prison.[6] It is doubtful whether any ever got out alive.[7]

So Sheng put his own peculiar stamp on the new rule in Sinkiang. He had consolidated his power, however, only with the aid of the Soviet Union, and, since he consequently had a continuing debt to pay, Sheng's policies reflected not only his own personality, but his ties with Moscow as well. The Soviet aid had been extended in the first instance on the secret understanding that Sheng should adopt an anti-Japanese stance, eliminate certain anti-Soviet elements from the province, and effect various changes in the provincial administration. Sheng actually assumed an "anti-imperialist" position as categorical as that of Moscow. An Anti-Imperialist Society (the only political "party" permitted to function in the province) was organized, and promptly directed its propaganda against both Japan and Britain. And Sheng adopted, as Sinkiang's emblem, a suggestive six-pointed red star.

Sinkiang's foreign-affairs stance was for the most part strongly suggestive of that of the Soviet Union. By Sheng's interpretation, the imperialists, and especially Japan, Britain, and Germany, objected strongly to Sinkiang's pro-Soviet orientation and proposed to conquer the province and occupy it, with two aims: (1) to convert that vast territory into a colony in order to relieve the imperialist home country from strains suffered as a result of the world economic depression, and (2) to make Sinkiang into the base for an attack on the Soviet Union.

Japan early manifested a lively interest in the new course of events in Sinkiang. Japanese Counselor of Embassy Wakasugi Kaname in November, 1934, asked Chiang Kai-shek for a clarification with respect to Sinkiang developments, only to get the unsatisfactory reply that Nanking was too concerned with Japanese relations to be able to act effectively with respect to Soviet influence in that distant province.[8] The Japanese government had resort to its embassy at Kabul, Afghanistan, headed by Kitada Masamoto, as a source of information and contact with anti-Sheng or anti-Soviet elements. In June, 1935, a personage identified in Japanese correspondence as the emir of Khotan, presumably Sabit Mullah, visited Kitada and submitted a proposal for the establishment of a new "Eastern Turkestan Republic" to be supported with Japanese money and arms. Preparatory moves, according to the plan, would comprise "(1) anti-Communist propaganda, (2) unifying the Moslems, (3) enlightenment of the people, (4) working jointly with other races, and (5) establishing Mahmud Sidjan as our leader." Then, with Japanese military action, there would be staged an armed revolt, to "disturb the rear, assisting the advance of Japanese troops." [9] By this concept, Japan would enjoy special political and economic privileges in the envisaged "independent" Eastern Turkestan Republic.

Kitada himself patently favored a forward policy in Central Asia, feeling that "Sinkiang will furnish a point of advantage to Japan against Britain and the Soviet Union if coalition with the Moslems is secured." [10] But Japanese strategists favoring a "positive" policy, if naturally interested in possibilities for action to checkmate any prospective antagonist in Asia, in 1935 still had not achieved dominance in the Tokyo government. Moreover, Japan was at the time heavily engaged in endeavoring to achieve the creation of an autonomous North China by political measures. Finally, the Japanese as well as the Russians were quite aware of the political frailties of Central Asian leaders, customarily more given to internecine feuding than to unified movements of conquest (or revolt) under an acknowledged common leader. They showed no strong urge to gamble heavily on the Sart Sabit Mullah, who had performed so ingloriously once before as leader of an "Eastern Turkestan Republic."

It is logical to assume that, just as the Japanese and (later) Chiang Kai-shek played upon the taut apprehension of certain Western countries with respect to the "Communist menace," so did the wily Sheng upon occasion paint the "imperialist" wolf at the doors of Sinkiang bigger than he was, the better to extract sympathy, and material aid, from the Soviet Union. In any event, Sheng manifested a firm conviction that Japan had a definite plan for the conquest of Sinkiang. He held that the plan envisaged a three-pronged thrust by: (1) Inner Mongolian forces from the command of Teh Wang; (2) Dungans from Kansu, Ningsia, and Tsinghai; and (3) Japanese forces advancing from Suiyuan, with a vanguard under the leadership of Yollbars Khan. According to Sheng, two Japanese visited Yollbars Khan in May, 1935, with the object of obtaining the latter's collaboration in exchange for a commitment that, with the occupation of Sinkiang, the province would be converted into an independent state after the pattern of Manchoukuo, and Yollbars Khan, Mahmud (a sometime Uighur supporter of Ma Chung-ying), and Khoja Niaz would occupy the chief ruling positions (no doubt with Japanese advisers at their elbows).

Sheng held that the basic Japanese project was to have Ataman Semenov thereafter use the Sinkiang base as a springboard for an attack, supported of course by the Japanese, against the Soviet Union. It was his contention that Yollbars Khan welcomed the Japanese proposal for the conquest of Sinkiang, but he refrained from stating categorically that the Japanese had succeeded in transforming Yollbars Khan quite into an instrumentality for the service of Japanese imperial purposes. Yollbars Khan probably aimed at serving his own nationalism first, and Japanese aims only second — if at all.

The Soviet designs in Sinkiang had a clear and direct reference to the Mukden Incident and subsequent developments in Manchuria and Eastern Inner Mongolia. By 1934, the year of P'u-yi's accession to the throne of Manchoukuo, Moscow probably had a fairly acute appreciation of the potential dangers which the Japanese program of imperialistic expansion in Asia held for both the Soviet Far East and Russian Turkestan. In Sinkiang, given Sheng Shih-ts'ai's political ambitions, the cost of establishing a barricade to the Japanese advance was relatively modest. But it did include the buttressing of newly won political influence by economic measures. In view of that problem, Stalin sent a commission headed by his brother-in-law, Svanidze, to Sinkiang, to help with economic planning for the province.

In July, 1934, at which time the Soviet commission was presumably at work on its survey, Sheng requested Nanking's approval for a Soviet loan of 4 million gold rubles, to be repaid in kind over a period of five years. Nanking instructed Sheng to forward the text of the proposed agreement, and in addition informed Ambassador Bogomolov at Nanking and the Narkomindel at Moscow that the National government's approval was a prerequisite for signature of any such agreement between the Soviet government and local Chinese authorities. Nanking received no satisfaction from either Sheng or the Soviets. Ambassador Bogomolov contended that the matter in point was not one involving an international loan but a commercial transaction, and refused to entertain the issue. Sheng responded to Nanking's stern injunction with the pro forma assurance that, when an agreement might be negotiated, he would report it to the central government for consideration and approval.

Actually, Sheng went on to reach a secret agreement by virtue of which the Soviet Union promised to supply him with munitions and, in case of need, Red Army forces to put down any disorders in Sinkiang. He committed his provincial government to the employment of Soviet advisers and technicians in important governmental organs and construction enterprises. And there was provision for a Soviet loan of 5 million gold rubles, repayable in kind, at 4 percent interest, in five years. The agreement was formally signed on May 16, 1935, between Sovsintorg (Soviet-Sinkiang Trading Company) and the Yü-Hsin Native Products Company. Sheng wired the Executive Yuan * at Nanking in July to report the signature of agreement by the two trading companies, remarking the loan factor, and said that a copy of the document was being forwarded by mail. It did not arrive, and during Sheng's tenure of office in Sinkiang, Nanking never learned of the other provisions of the May, 1935, agreement.[11]

In 1936, the economic relationship had been sufficiently developed for Urumchi to launch the province on its first three-year economic plan. Soviet advisers and technical experts served in provincial economic enterprises, including agriculture, animal husbandry, and mining. They were also employed in fiscal and economic departments of the provincial government. The Soviet Union provided medical workers and hospital supplies for the improvement of hygiene and public health. In return, through the agency Sovsintorg, Sinkiang exported to the Soviet Union wool, hides, and other animal products, and livestock on the hoof. Soviet geologists began the survey of Sinkiang's mineral resources.

The Soviet aid program was early made manifest as well in the political realm. Secret-police work was not the least of Sheng's enterprises, given his unending concern with plots against his power, and in July, 1934, to meet his needs, Moscow sent to Sinkiang a Brigadier General Pogodin. It also supplied the services of one Tseng Hsiu-fu — the alias of the Communist Wang Li-hsiang, who had long served in Outer Mongolia. Thanks to the organizational skills of those two men, there was set up a provincial public-safety bureau headed by one Chang I-wu, with an able deputy in the person of Chang Hsien-ch'eng, who had been

---

* "Yuan" — literally, hall or court. The Kuomintang central government was organized on the basis of Sun Yat-sen's five-yuan system, embracing the executive, legislative, judicial, civil service, and censorial branches. The Executive Yuan comprised the various ministries.

Borodin's interpreter at the time of the Northern Expedition. In 1936, the secret-police network was further expanded and strengthened by creation of a border affairs office, with Sheng himself assuming the position of chief. From this time onward there was a tight control over all entry into and exit from the province—and over travel within the province.

For the time being, Japanese influence did not make itself outwardly manifest in Sinkiang. But the Kazakh and Turki nationalists remained discontented, and in 1936 there occurred a revolt that was in any event in the pattern of the Japanese plot alleged by Sheng. Ma Shao-wu spearheaded a movement through which the Muslims designed to escape from the Chinese warlord's authority. With the support of other Dungan groups, Ili Sarts, certain White Russian officers, and Yollbars Khan, Khoja Niaz, and Mahmud, Ma came out with the war cry "Oppose the Chinese and save Sinkiang" (fan-Han chiu-Hsin).

After the rebellion had been launched, it was joined by the Kazakhs of the Altai. The coalition against Sheng looked formidable, but it failed. The Soviets had made an investment in Sheng, and it promised to pay dividends. The Soviet Union once more intervened to save Sheng Shih-ts'ai from the consequences of mistaken Chinese policies in Sinkiang. The intervention was swift, and effective. Soviet warplanes strafed the Kazakh horsemen, who were armed only with rifles, and under the withering fire the Kazakhs broke and dispersed. The other rebels, reading correctly the lesson of that defeat, called off their offensive.

In April, 1935, under the inspiration of his new relationship, Sheng had advanced his philosophy of rule by enunciating Three Great Principles—anti-imperialism, peace, and construction. With the suppression of the 1936 rebellion, these were elaborated upon, and became the Six Great Principles. The first two principles now comprised anti-imperialism and friendship for the Soviet Union. As given fuller definition by the provincial government's official journal, the "imperialist countries" included all strong powers having relations with China—with the exception of the Soviet Union—and the blackest of them all was Japan.

Sheng's political philosophy was now essentially complete. His domestic rule had been upheld by force of alien arms, and was evidently judged to be further guaranteed by the grant of some cultural autonomy to the Turki peoples and an increased concern for their economic well-being. The Chinese militarist was, nevertheless, to face yet another Muslim revolt. The action began in an indirect fashion when, in May, a Mahmud supporter made an aggressive move in the Kashgar region – and the Dungan Ma Hu-shan, reacting to the Sart move, attacked Kashgar. From victory in that sector, he advanced in the direction of Aksu.

Sheng Shih-ts'ai, not without some grounds, viewed developments as constituting more of a threat against himself than against any residual Mahmud force, and sent some 4,500 troops of all arms to Aksu to check the march of Ma Hu-shan's men. Soviet military advisers accompanied the contingent. The two forces clashed in the Aksu sector in early June, and after an initial success the provincial troops were driven back on the town. With the accession of discontented Turki elements to his ranks, Ma Hu-shan's strength grew during the fighting of the summer. In late August, Sheng, driven to admit his inability to put down the southern Sinkiang disorder by his own efforts, once more called upon the Soviet Union for help.

Moscow again responded, this time sending in a regiment of fierce Kirgizi cavalry to collaborate with the Soviet tanks, armored cars, and planes. In a lightning strike, the Soviet forces caught the main insurgent elements on the flank and with hard blows drove them into retreat. The Soviet air force continued to pursue and harass the retreating men, inflicting heavy casualties. Ma Hu-shan's army was shattered. The surviving Dungan forces retired to Khotan, with Ma Hu-shan going on to take temporary refuge in India. The troops in Khotan came under the command of Ma Fu-yuan, but in October this force was attacked by the Kirgiz regiment and heavily bombed by Soviet planes. Only remnants finally reached a refuge in Tunhuang, in the Kansu panhandle. And in October also those officers and men of Ma Chung-ying's Thirty-sixth Division whom Sheng Shih-ts'ai had earlier captured were put to death.[12] Nothing remained of Ma Chung-ying's power.

Now Sheng purported to discover 435 persons involved in a "Trotskyite conspiracy." The plot, he contended, had been masterminded by the "Trotskyite" Soviet consul general, Apresoff (who had presumably been caught up in the Soviet purge of the same period). The grand design, he said, had been to achieve the murder of himself and other provincial military and political leaders, so that the "loyal Trotskyites" could effect the takeover of power and the conversion of the province, with the help of German and

Japanese advisers, into "a base in the vulnerable rear of both Russia and China." [13] Among those charged with participation in this nefarious plot were, naturally, Ma Hu-shan and Mahmud, and also sometime Special Foreign Affairs Commissioner Ch'en Teh-li, Burhan Shahidi (the Tatar general manager of the Sinkiang Native Products Company), and Sinkiang Vice Chairman Khoja Niaz. There were many other prominent officials listed—so many, in fact, that one is hard put to discover who remained who might have been of sufficient importance for those "Trotskyites" to kill.

Moscow, after being duly apprised of developments, sent one Yekulov to Urumchi to handle the trials of the accused, and Sheng remarked in his report the circumstance that he shifted all of the work of the trials onto the shoulders of that Soviet official. But in due course Yekulov seemingly discovered that most of the confessions had been obtained from the prisoners by means of torture, and he reported accordingly to Stalin. Sheng thereupon accused Yekulov of himself being a Trotskyite, and Yekulov was recalled, nominally for investigation, and replaced by another Soviet official. Of the 435 men arrested in connection with the 1937 affair, most were executed,[14] including Khoja Niaz. Mahmud and Ma Hu-shan, having been farther from Sheng's vengeful arm, escaped with their lives. So did Yollbars Khan, who fled to China Proper, to become a counselor on the National government's military affairs commission. In China, an entirely new situation had arisen.

21 YEAR OF
DECISION: 1936

IN EUROPE, in 1935, Hitler pushed forward with the re-
armament of Germany; in the same year, fascist Italy invaded
Abyssinia, and undertook a deliberate campaign of conquest in
the face of world horror at the aggressor's bombing of defenseless
mountain villages. War in Europe came perceptibly closer. The
year 1936 saw a drawing of lines, marshaling of forces, and the
fighting of initial engagements looking toward larger conflict, in
various parts of the uneasy world. Japan early took significant action by withdrawing from the London naval conference, where
the Japanese demand for naval parity had collided with an un-
compromising American stand. The naval competition in the Pacific between Japan and the United States, predestined by Japan's victory over Russia in 1905 and clearly visible after World
War I, had now been resumed after a truce of fourteen years.

Japan shortly afterward provided another critical indication
that the status quo was under challenge. On February 26, ultra-
nationalistic young officers of the Imperial Way faction led by
General Araki Sadao (lately relieved as minister of war) staged a
coup in Tokyo aimed at the creation of a predominantly military
government devoted to national strengthening and the implementation of a program of imperialistic aggrandizement.

The putsch was put down by loyal forces. In defeat, however,
the radical elements of the army nevertheless won the essence of
their objective; for Hirota, who became the new premier, was

forced to accept army views and frame a new foreign-affairs strategy which he himself described, in something of an understatement, as "positive diplomacy." It proposed the extension of Japanese domination over Asia. Hirota, questioned by American Ambassador Joseph C. Grew regarding the objectives of that new diplomacy, assured his interlocutor that it was directed only at China and the Soviet Union.[1] But all logic suggested that, if Japan had its way in overcoming the opposition of one or the other of those Asian antagonists, the position of the United States as a major naval power in the West Pacific would come under challenge.

The threat those developments in West and East bore for the Soviet Union's national security was clear. At the Seventh Comintern Congress, sitting in Moscow from July to August, 1935, there was formulated the united-front strategy with which Moscow proposed to confront its powerful potential enemies: Communist parties would join in common cause with social democrats and bourgeois nationalists alike for the struggle against fascism and imperialism. The Chinese Communist representative Wang Ming (Ch'en Shao-yü) on August 7 gave a lengthy address on revolutionary movements in colonial and semicolonial countries. He, too, opted for the strategy of the united front. Among the forty-seven persons elected to the Comintern's new executive committee were four Chinese: Wang Ming, Mao Tse-tung, Chou En-lai, and Chang Kuo-tao.

On August 1, through Moscow, the Chinese Communist Party had issued a call for the formation of a united national front of all concerned Chinese groups, against Japanese aggression. The manifesto expressed a willingness, once KMT forces ceased their advances against Communist territory, to let bygones be bygones and join hands with them in the common task of national salvation.[2] The Kuomintang per se was excluded. On November 28, after they had reached a haven of safety at the end of their Long March from Kiangsi, and after also receiving the decisions of the Seventh Comintern Congress, there issued over the signatures of Mao Tse-tung and Chu Teh a new manifesto to the nation now phrased to welcome "any political grouping." This patently included the Kuomintang. And the remnant Communist force at this juncture took on a new and more appealing title – the "Chinese Anti-Japanese Red Army."

The Chinese nationalistic temper was rising. An Anti-Imperialist League had been formed at Shanghai in 1933. In 1935, the anti-Japanese "December 9th Movement," having its beginnings at Peiping, gathered converts throughout the country and added strength to Chinese nationalism. A National Salvation Association was organized in May, 1936, and demanded an end to the civil war in favor of a united front against Japan. In the Northwest, the Communists helped the movement along.

In May also, CCP leader Chou En-lai, and P'an Han-nien representing the Comintern, met in Shanghai with a representative of the Kuomintang, Chang Ch'ung. From Shanghai, P'an Han-nien went on to Nanking and conferred with Ch'en Li-fu. In the May meetings, the KMT representatives set forth conditions for a political settlement that would have meant virtual surrender for the Communists, with literally nothing in return, and there was for the time being no deal. But by now the Communists had aligned themselves with the major trend in national political sentiment, and their position had become correspondingly stronger.

The confrontation of Japan and Soviet Russia in China's borderlands had in the meantime been building up. The sale of the Chinese Eastern Railway had led to relaxation in only one sector. The Japanese occupation of Jehol in 1933, and Japanese-inspired actions in Chahar in 1934, were taken by Soviets and Mongols alike to be the development of a threat against the Soviet Union's protectorate, the Mongolian People's Republic. An early substantiation of that assumption came in the form of a demand by Manchoukuo, based nominally upon ancient Chinese maps, for revision of the common boundary in the vicinity of Buir Nor (lake) to the benefit of Manchoukuo, which laid claim to Mongol territory south of the lake.

There was a predictable political reaction to that thrust. In November, 1934, Moscow and Ulan Bator entered upon a new agreement for joint defense. In late January, 1935, coincident with Japanese action against Dolonor in eastern Chahar, there was a serious clash between Manchoukuo and Mongolian forces along the Khalkhin River, near Buir Nor, and other "border incidents" followed. The issue focused on the exact location of the boundary, and the two countries held a conference at Manchouli for the purpose of resolving border problems. On July 4, the Mongolian delegation was confronted with a Japanese demand that Japanese "military observers" be admitted to the Mongolian People's Republic, and further that Japan be accorded the right of establishing a military telegraph on the Republic's territory for "better communications with Japan and Manchoukuo." [3]

The Mongolian government rejected the demand, and the Manchouli conference ended after five months of discussion without accomplishing the tasks it had set itself. It was thereupon announced, through the medium of the Manchoukuo press, that:

> Manchoukuo does not consider Mongolia an ordinary normal state, and therefore Manchoukuo now claims [*sic:* proclaims?] that, viewing Outer Mongolia as an incomprehensible and dangerous country, it intends to regulate all issues and settle all disputes by force of arms as it sees fit. [4]

Relations between Manchoukuo (Japan) and the Mongolian People's Republic (Soviet Russia) continued to worsen.

There was another armed clash at Bulum Dersu, in the Buir Nor sector, in mid-December, 1935. Soviet Foreign Affairs Commissar Litvinov now proposed that there be established a mixed commission to investigate such border incidents, but the proposal never bore fruit. It was evident that the Japanese preferred to have the situation remain fluid. A more important military clash occurred in the same general vicinity between the proxy forces of the two powers as a result of a Japanese-Manchoukuo assault of February 12, 1936. The attack was beaten off, with heavy losses sustained on both sides. It was only a few days afterward that the Young Officers group attempted their big putsch in Tokyo.

Moscow seemingly promptly grasped the significance of events. Evidently relating recent developments on the MPR frontier to the bouleversement in Tokyo, Stalin in a press interview of March 6 declared that, in the event of a Japanese attack on the Mongolian People's Republic, the Soviet Union would go to the Mongols' aid. On March 12, one month to the day after the big border clash, the Soviet Union and the MPR signed a protocol of mutual assistance. Article 1 provided for joint consultation in cases where there might be the threat of an attack on the territory of either by a third country, and Article 2 incorporated the operative provision: "The Governments of the U.S.S.R. and the M.P.R. pledge themselves in case of a military attack on one of the Contracting Parties, to render mutually any assistance including military assistance." [5]

It would seem only logical to assume that, just as the Japanese were endeavoring to subvert both Inner and Outer Mongols to their purposes, so too were the Soviets actively working against Japanese interests in the newly autonomous Hsingan Province of western Manchuria. There would have been fertile ground for such Soviet enterprises. The governing regime was indeed Mongolian in name, and was headed by a Mongol prince, but the decisive power resided in the hands of a Japanese general, and Japanese "advisers" were attached to the Hsingan administrative organs. The nationalistic Mongols, excited by the nominal grant of autonomy, must inevitably have chafed under the Japanese restraints, and some perhaps sought the possibility of greater freedom of action by using methods of intrigue. In any event, in April, 1936, the Japanese purported to have discovered a pro-Soviet plot at the very top of the Hsingan government. And as leaders in Outer Mongolia had in the past been executed for having intrigued with the Chinese, now the top leadership of Hsingan Province, including the governor, General Ling-sheng, the military commander, General Fu-ling, and the chief of the political bureau, Chun-teh,[6] were put to death for alleged pro-Soviet activities. It was charged that the accused persons had transmitted secret Japanese military information to the Outer Mongols on the occasion of the 1935 Manchouli conference and had, moreover, plotted with Soviet and Mongol agents to effect the secession of the Barga region from Manchoukuo.

Japanese pressure on China had been increasing ever since the enunciation by Hirota of his three-point policy. When Hirota became premier after the events of February, 1936, he named a new ambassador to China, Kawagoe Shigeru. Kawagoe took with him to Nanking a restatement of Hirota's concept, now in the form of Three Principles: (1) joint defense against Communism, (2) economic collaboration, and (3) "friendly good neighborliness." Implicitly, those three principles still envisaged Nanking's recognition of Manchoukuo, and the "autonomy" of the five northern provinces of China.

Confronted with this threatening situation, Chang Ch'ün approached Bogomolov with proposals for joint action for the maintenance of peace in Asia, only to see the Soviet Union enter upon a treaty for mutual defense with the Mongolian People's Republic. The dispute that ensued over the propriety of Moscow's entering upon a military alliance with a country China claimed as its own naturally inhibited the fruition of Chinese efforts to get the Soviet Union to assume the role of China's military bulwark against Japan, and closer Sino-Soviet collaboration was put off for the time being. In fact, the disclosure by Bogomolov, after a stormy session at the Foreign Ministry, of the substance of the recent talks between himself and the ministry, effectively discouraged further Chinese advances along those lines.

The Japanese pressed forward with their plans for severing North China from the Nationalist holding. At Tientsin, from August 17 to 28, 1936, there was held a series of conferences between various high Japanese officials, including Lieutenant General Tashiro Kanichiro, commander in chief of the Japanese forces in North China, Major General Itagaki of the Kwantung Army, and Ambassador Kawagoe, to deliberate upon North China and its economic development, and the situation in Inner Mongolia. By report, Kawagoe argued the necessity of blocking Soviet penetration into Inner Mongolia in order to keep the Soviet Union from thereby exerting a flanking pressure on Manchoukuo and Japan. Kawagoe and Itagaki were found in agreement on the strategic importance of Suiyuan.

In due course, it became evident that the Tientsin conference had resulted in a plan for the invasion of Suiyuan by Mongol and Manchoukuo forces acting in Japan's behalf. Teh Wang in February, 1936, had convened a conference at Pailingmiao, Suiyuan Province, for the purpose of engineering a Mongol declaration of independence from Nanking. However, the conference actually ended in a split, with the majority of the Mongol princes breaking away from Teh Wang's movement and setting up a new Mongolian political council at Kweisui, under the aegis of Suiyuan chairman Fu Tso-yi. Teh Wang, faced with that menacing combination, removed his headquarters from Pailingmiao eastward to Tehhua (Coptchil), near the protective strength of Manchoukuoan Li Shou-hsin — and the Japanese. There, on June 28, he set up an "Inner Mongolian government." In September, discussions were held at Tehhua on measures for implementation of the general decision reached in the August conference at Tientsin.

In early November, some 25,000 to 30,000 Manchoukuo and Mongol forces drove on Suiyuan, with one column advancing from Pailingmiao. Fu Tso-yi gave every evidence of having been forewarned (and truly he could hardly have missed being alerted), and his tough fighting force had been strengthened by the central government's Thirteenth Army, under the command of T'ang En-po. Teh Wang's campaign went badly from the start. The government forces promptly occupied Pailingmiao, and Fu and T'ang exploited the initial military success fully, thrusting the Manchoukuo-Mongol invaders out of Suiyuan and into eastern Chahar. In late December, 1936, Teh Wang announced the termination of hostilities.

In the capture of Pailingmiao, Fu's men seized both important quantities of supplies and, by report, secret documents divulging a Japanese plan to establish an east-west buffer zone comprising Chahar, Suiyuan, Ningsia, Kansu, and Sinkiang, in the form of a "Great Yuan empire" (Ta-Yuan ti-kuo), "to prevent China and Russia from coming into contact with each other." [7] A sum of $400 million had been allocated for the project and, by the first part of 1936, $60 million had been expended. The results of the Japanese investment had fallen far below normal expectations.

Developments in Europe during this period were making the situation ever more critical for Moscow. Nazi Germany had taken the exchange of ratifications of the Franco-Soviet mutual-assistance pact in February, 1936, as sufficient reason to denounce the Locarno Pact and reoccupy the Rhineland in March. In early May, the Italians had taken Addis Ababa, thus completing their conquest of Abyssinia. The democracies had not moved. In mid-July, the Spanish civil war began with General Franco's insurgency, and by the initiative of France (the Soviet Union's political mainstay in Western Europe) and the strong support of Britain, the European countries adopted a "nonintervention policy" by virtue of which they embargoed the shipment of arms to Spain. The United States aligned itself with the same policy by invoking the provisions of its Neutrality Act. The embargo worked the greater hardship on the republicans, for fascist Italy and Nazi Germany promptly began to supply the rebels, first with arms and then with fighting men. The Soviet Union, distant as it was from Spain, undertook at the end of October to support the republicans. But it operated at a logistical and tactical disadvantage.

The Soviet Union was at this time caught up in the beginnings of a vast Stalinist purge. In August, a military tribunal had begun proceedings against Grigori E. Zinoviev and Lev B. Kamenev and fourteen others. They were now charged with having formed a Trotskyist-Zinovievist cabal and with plotting the murder of party and government leaders and overthrow of the Soviet government with the aid of foreign states. In the course of the trial, they pleaded guilty to the charges, and by their testimony implicated others, including Nikolai I. Bukharin, Karl Radek, Mikhail P. Tomsky, Alexei I. Rykov, and other outstanding leaders of the anti-Stalin opposition. The defendants were all executed. Nikolai I. Yezhov replaced Genrikh G. Yagoda at the head of the Commissariat of the Interior (governing internal security), and Stalin marked down his next intended victims. The Great Purge fed upon developments on the country's borders.

About the time that Teh Wang was driven into retreat, Japan took a major step in the field of international relations: on November 25, 1936, Tokyo and Berlin entered upon an Anti-Comintern Pact. Two of the three main provisions were of prime interest to Moscow: the signatories mutually agreed to consult regarding necessary measures for "defense" against the Comintern and to collaborate in carrying out those measures, and to seek the participation of third governments. Nominally, the new alliance was directed against the international Communist organization and not the Soviet state, but the subterfuge deceived no one. It was entirely evident that the German-Japanese pact had been negotiated with a view to joint action against the Soviet Union, which thus faced the threat of a war on two fronts, in Europe and in Asia. In Europe, Moscow had in 1935 signed mutual-assistance pacts with France and Czechoslovakia, but in Asia the Soviet Union's only supporting alliance was with the weak Mongolian People's Republic. In the East, the Axis partners patently proposed to enlist the collaboration of China in their political enterprise. Moscow's strategic task was to keep China out of the Anti-Comintern Pact and if possible to maneuver it into opposition against Japan.

Hirota's Three Principles took on a new significance in the light of international developments: acceptance would effectively mean China's alignment with the "anti-Communism" of the Axis. But it was entirely obvious that, despite any superficial attractions the proposition might hold for Nanking, there would be serious disadvantages to China in any such move. The Japanese proposals, as developed in detail, envisaged an economic "collaboration" that would have been notably more profitable for Japan than for China, with dominance of the Chinese economy by the Japanese; the introduction of Japanese advisers into both military and civilian branches of the Chinese government; and the actual incorporation of Japanese into Chinese military units for action against major Communist forces – and in the borderlands facing the Mongolian People's Republic. For the anti-Communist provision, according to testimony elicited at the Tokyo War Crimes trial in 1946, required China's cooperation with Japan to eliminate the threat of external Communist influence from Outer Mongolia as well as other areas.[8]

China, in that unequal "partnership," would become the economic vassal and military auxiliary of its more powerful neighbor. In such a relationship, especially if it were to become a member of the Anti-Comintern Pact, as proposed by Tokyo, China might soon be found involved in a war with the Soviet Union from which it could only emerge the loser – regardless of the outcome for Japan and Germany.

Foreign Minister Chang Ch'ün had endeavored to effect a détente in Sino-Japanese relations by conceding the existence of a special Japanese position in North China in exchange for the relatively minor concession that the area remain within Nanking's overall jurisdiction. But the Japanese were not content with simple maintenance of the status quo. On Ambassador Kawagoe's insistence, new bilateral talks began in mid-September of 1936. In general, Chang Ch'ün followed delaying tactics, going through the motions of consideration of the Japanese proposals, but in the end giving no satisfaction. In their third meeting, Chang unexpectedly assumed a stiff bargaining position, and the talks ended on December 3 with Chang's rejection of an aide-mémoire presented by Kawagoe, on the grounds that it pictured him as having made greater concession to the Japanese point of view than was in fact the case.

Three days before, the foremost Communist chieftains, headed by Mao Tse-tung, Chu Teh, Chang Kuo-tao, and Chou En-lai, in the capacity of the leaders of "the 200,000-man Red Army," had sent a message to Chiang Kai-shek to propose the cessation of civil war and the creation of a united front against Japan.[9] There was a special reason for the Communists to make such a move at that particular time: Chiang Kai-shek had moved into headquarters at Loyang, Honan, with the purpose of launching a new anti-Communist drive. On December 4, the day after the frosty Chang-Kawagoe meeting at Nanking, Chiang proceeded to Sian to launch the sixth "bandit-suppression campaign" against the badly weakened Communist forces. (The real Communist strength was only a fraction of what they had claimed for political purposes.)

Chinese bargaining tactics were familiar to the Japanese from of old, and they could quite appreciate the significance of Chang Ch'ün's approach to the matter of "negotiations." It seems logical to assume that the next move to bring China closer to the Axis might have come from Berlin, but a startling event now intervened. On December 12, the day the orders for the projected general offensive against the Communists were to have been issued, Chiang Kai-shek was taken captive by his deputy commander, Chang Hsueh-liang, acting in collaboration with Shensi Pacification Commissioner Yang Hu-ch'eng. On the same day, the rebels broadcast to the nation their "eight demands" for a settlement. Three significant points comprised the reorganization of the Nanking government with inclusion of representatives of other parties and national groups, the complete cessation of civil war, and the prompt convening of a conference for national salvation.

The detention of Chiang Kai-shek came as a stunning surprise to the Nationalist camp; likewise, the Chinese Communists were seemingly caught unawares by the development. But they had months before established liaison with Chang Hsueh-liang, and they were quick to react: on December 15, Chou En-lai, CCP Central Committee member Ch'in Pang-hsien, and Yeh Chien-ying (chief of staff of the First Front Army), arrived in Sian.

The first Communist thought respecting disposition of the matter envisaged, all too simplistically, that Chiang Kai-shek should be sent to the Communist camp for trial by a people's court. But a sager head than Mao's bent to the problem: Stalin wired the Chinese Communists that the safety of Chiang should be assured for the purpose of presenting a united front against Japan. At Sian, the Communist delegation now acted as a moderating force. And the CCP Central Committee addressed a telegram to Nanking expressing the hope that the National government would adopt the proposals of the Northeastern forces.[10]

The Soviet thinking seemed logical enough: if Chiang Kai-shek could be committed to the idea of heading a united front against Japan, in circumstances where an aroused Chinese nationalism was coming to constitute a major political force, the Japanese energies would be engaged on the China front for some time to come; if the Nationalist faction were contrariwise led by the killing of Chiang Kai-shek (as some of the more ardent rebels proposed) to adopt an antirebel posture, the nation would in the first instance be split, and the government in the second instance might well fall into pro-Japanese hands. Acting Premier H. H. K'ung in fact was quick to announce that he would not deal with the insurgents; and Minister of War Ho Ying-ch'in was inclined from the first to take strong action against Sian. Ho, moreover, communicated with ex-Premier Wang Ching-wei, recuperating in Germany from wounds received in an assassination attempt the year before, and summoned him home. Wang conferred with Hitler, then started back to China with the obvious purpose of getting into a position to succeed Chiang Kai-shek in power should the opportunity arise. Moscow clearly regarded Wang as being pro-Japanese, and assumed that he would serve Japan's purposes. *Pravda,* in an editorial at the time, actually charged Wang with having instigated the plot to seize Chiang on behalf of the Japanese militarists.[11] There were grounds for Soviet alarm: would not a National government headed by Wang Ching-wei, with Ho Ying-ch'in in command of the Chinese armed forces, be inclined to take China into the Anti-Comintern Pact? The danger was real.

The Japanese charged that the Soviet Union was behind the whole affair. That allegation, in the circumstances, probably only made Moscow the readier to demonstrate by deed that Chiang Kai-shek in the role of national leader (particularly against Japan) was entirely acceptable to it. Seemingly anticipating the adverse Chinese national reaction to the coup by Chang Hsueh-liang and Yang Hu-ch'eng, and almost certainly not unmindful of Chang's role in the attempted seizure of the Chinese Eastern Railway in 1929, Moscow in the beginning charged Chang of complicity with Wang Ching-wei. Japan made its contribution to the complexity of the Nationalists' problem, with Foreign Minister Arita Hachiro informing the Chinese ambassador at Tokyo that, if Nanking made a deal with Chang Hsueh-liang (on the basis of the eight demands), the Japanese government could not maintain the position of an unconcerned onlooker.

There was no compelling reason for the Soviets to endeavor to save Chang Hsueh-liang from the consequences of his coup. It was certain that Chang's action, even if attended by success, would in no way endear him to Chiang Kai-shek; if he failed, it would be better for the Soviet Union, with regard to its relations with Japan, to have disavowed any connection with the matter. Moscow and Nanking had been cagily moving toward a rapprochement ever since Ch'en Li-fu's démarche vis-à-vis Bogomolov a year earlier. Since that time, despite the failure of Ch'en's visit to Europe, there had been meetings at Shanghai and Nanking between Chou En-lai and P'an Han-nien and KMT representatives — including Ch'en himself. Chang Hsueh-liang was not essential to the larger scheme of things.

With Chinese Communist support for a solution that would bring about the release of Chiang Kai-shek on condition that he quit civil war and turn to the formation of a united front of resistance to Japan, the "Sian Incident" was brought to a close. Chiang Kai-shek signed no document, but quite evidently accepted the essence of the "eight demands" presented to him by Chang Hsueh-liang and Yang Hu-ch'eng, although the points of agreement had now been reduced to six. In particular, he agreed to reorganize the Nanking government by replacing pro-Japanese elements with personalities in favor of resistance to Japan, to stop the bandit-suppression campaigns and join with the Communist forces to organize joint resistance to the Japanese aggressors, and to call a national conference of representatives of all parties and groups to work out a general program for national salvation. There was one point that was new: Chiang agreed to improve collaboration with states sympathetic to the struggle against Japan.[12] This could hardly mean any other country than the Soviet Union.

After he had capitulated, Chiang Kai-shek was released on December 25. Upon return to his seat of power in Nanking, he proclaimed that any Sian agreements were null and void. But that announcement probably was primarily for the Japanese benefit; it appears logical to assume that, in some form or other, sanctions had been provided to guarantee Chiang's fulfillment of his part of the bargain.

For the immediate present, there was no outward sign of positive collaboration between the Nationalist and Communist forces — although the sixth "bandit-suppression campaign" that Chiang Kai-shek had gone to Sian to launch never started. The Chiang machine actually removed Yang Hu-ch'eng from office, incarcerated Chang Hsueh-liang, and dispersed Chang's Manchurian armies, thus incidentally leaving the Communist forces largely without counterweight in Shensi Province and relatively free to develop their power there. The civil war ended, and the Kuomintang turned to the formulation of a strategy of resistance against Japan. Nanking, which had hoped to enlist the Soviet Union to fight its war against Japan, was about to begin to fight that war itself. It would thus be serving Moscow's aims, by becoming a military buffer between Japan and the Soviet Union. The design to make the Anti-Comintern Pact into a tripartite alliance, in which China would have played an important if subordinate role, against the Soviet Union, had failed of realization.[13] Instead, the first difficult steps had been taken toward the formation in China, in line with the Comintern "united front" concept, of an anti-Japanese combine. The intricate power struggle that had been waged in Sinkiang took on clearer meaning.

22 THE USSR AND THE
SINO-JAPANESE WAR,
1937–1941

IN THE SOVIET UNION, the purge begun in August, 1936, was carried forward with vigor. In January, 1937, seventeen persons, including Karl Radek (sometime director of the Sun Yat-sen University in Moscow) and others of similar stature, were put on trial, accused of constituting a "Trotskyite anti-Soviet center." At the end of the month, thirteen of the accused received death sentences; the remaining four, including Radek, were given prison terms. The execution of the thirteen was followed by the arrest of the remaining members of Stalin's "opposition," including such prominent Old Bolsheviks as Bukharin and People's Commissar for Communications Rykov, successor to Lenin in 1924 as president of the Soviet of People's Commissars.

A number of high military men headed by Marshal Mikhail N. Tukhachevski, who had played so important a part in the creation of the Red Army that vanquished Denikin, Dutov, and Kolchak, were now charged with treasonable contacts with Nazi Germany and swept up in the purge. The accused were tried by a military tribunal on which sat, among others, General Bluecher. Tukhachevski, Leningrad garrison commander I. E. Yakir, commander of the Moscow Military Academy General A. I. Kork, commander of the western military district General Jeronim Uborevich, and four other generals, were all found guilty of treason and executed in June, 1937.[1] The Red Army's political commissar, General I. B. Gamarnik, had beaten the executioner by committing suicide as he was about to be arrested. The purge of the Red Army spread, to take on vast proportions.

In China, negotiations between the Communists and the National government, brought to a new stage by virtue of the Sian Incident, were continuing. But they had not yet borne fruit.

In March, 1937, there were new contacts at Shanghai between Legislative Yuan president Sun Fo and Ambassador Bogomolov; then Bogomolov made a trip to Moscow. Upon his return in April, he proposed that China should take the initiative in calling for a conference of Pacific Ocean powers, specifically Britain, the USSR, the United States, France, and Japan, with the aim of getting agreement for a regional mutual assistance pact (which would of course have been in effect a nonaggression pact with built-in guarantees for mutual aid against any aggressor). Failing such an agreement, the Soviet Union was prepared to consider the conclusion of a mutual-assistance pact with China.[2]

Another political figure arrived in China in April – Chiang Kai-shek's first son, Chiang Ching-kuo. The younger Chiang had in 1925 gone to Moscow to study and, after breaking with his father's anti-Communist line in 1927, had remained in the Soviet Union for a decade more. On February 11, 1936, the *Leningradskaya Pravda* published a letter attributed to Chiang Ching-kuo and addressed to his mother in which, after proclaiming himself a Communist, the younger Chiang condemned his father as "the enemy of the whole people" and rejected his father's putative invitation to return home in service of filial affection.[3]

But after the Sian Incident, Chiang Ching-kuo had requested permission (inferentially of the Chinese delegation to the Comintern) to return home, and after addressing a second request to Stalin himself, he was invited to Moscow by the Ministry of Foreign Affairs and told that his request was granted. He was visited in his hotel by an intimate friend of Stalin, and then saw Bogomolov, who said that he was glad Ching-kuo was returning home. He also had an interview with the vice minister for foreign affairs, and then, on the day of his departure from Moscow, Comintern chairman Georgi M. Dimitrov invited Ching-kuo to his home and asked him to convey his warm regards to Chiang Kai-shek.[4]

Now, in circumstances leading one to suspect that Stalin might have thought that Chiang Ching-kuo could possibly perform a useful function in the task of bringing China and the Soviet Union closer together, the prodigal son returned home. He met with his father at Hangchow, and, persons close to the generalissimo were quoted as saying that the long-standing reports of estrangement between the two were no more than Russian inventions.[5] There was as yet no agreement between Nanking and Moscow.

On July 7, there occurred an armed clash between Japanese and Chinese forces at Wanping, near Lukouchiao (Marco Polo Bridge), just outside Peiping. The affair was at first approached by the Chinese side as if it were just another "incident," which might lend itself to settlement by political negotiations of the order that led to the Tangku Truce of 1933 and the Ho-Umetsu agreement of 1935. The Tientsin mayor, General Chang Tzu-chung, undertook negotiations with the Japanese military, and on July 11 a preliminary local agreement for disposition of the matter was actually worked out at Tientsin — on the basis of a new Chinese surrender. There were four stipulations, one of which envisaged joint action against Communism.[6]

Already bound, at least to a degree, to the united-front concept, Chiang Kai-shek issued a statement on July 19 proclaiming an intention to resist further Japanese pressure, and laying down the dictum that any local agreement had to be sanctioned by the central government. The provisions of the Chang Tzu-chung agreement, in short, were not to prevail. Japanese troops had early begun to pour into North China. This was an earnest of Tokyo's determination not to let matters rest, this time, with a compromise that would leave North China under the control of Nanking.

The German and British governments energetically undertook to mediate the conflict — for different reasons. The United States, asked (together with the British) to take action to bring about a peaceful settlement, refused to become involved. But Germany had an important military mission working in China to achieve political as well as military ends, and some Germans hoped at least to keep China from being pushed into closer relations with the Soviet Union. Approached by Chinese Ambassador Cheng Tien-fong a week after the "Lukouchiao Incident" with a report on developments and a request for an opinion, German Foreign Minister Constantin von Neurath voiced his government's hope that the matter could be peacefully resolved, and commented: "If the conflict extends in scope China and Japan will both be playing into the Soviet hands."[7]

Various strong pressures were now making for war. The Chinese garrison on August 8 abandoned Peiping to the enemy, but there had been no surrender. On August 13, the Japanese attacked at Shanghai, only to meet strong resistance from the Nationalist Ninth Group Army, headed by one of Chiang Kai-shek's right-hand men—Chang Chih-chung. The Nanking regime had evidently at last resolved to fight, and the Shanghai battle marked the real beginning of the second Sino-Japanese War. The foundation for Nanking's decision was discovered in the signature, on August 21, of the long-contemplated nonaggression pact between China and the Soviet Union. Innocuous in its published provisions, it was important in the implied agreement: China had committed itself to presenting real military resistance to any further Japanese advance; the Soviet Union had agreed to support such resistance. Clearly also, the Soviet Union had not agreed to do China's fighting for it. It was not an alliance: correct in form, it did not require either of the signatory parties to aid the other in case of aggression.[8]

It looked as if the von Neurath estimate stood a good chance of being proved correct. But this possibility did not cause the Atlantic powers to go to the rescue of China. In the League of Nations' debate, the USSR called for joint sanctions against aggressor Japan. Britain and France failed to respond. Tokyo and Berlin exchanged views regarding the developments, and on November 5 German Ambassador Oscar Trautmann submitted to Chiang Kai-shek the Japanese terms for a settlement.

Although the China question was at that moment before the Brussels conference of nineteen nations (including the USSR), and the Chinese had their new agreement with the Soviet Union, Chiang Kai-shek nevertheless informed Trautmann that he would negotiate with the Japanese on the basis of conditions the latter had set forth earlier.[9] The Brussels conference ended on November 24 after rejecting the Chinese proposal (supported by the Soviet delegation) that economic sanctions be imposed upon Japan. The assembled powers contented themselves with a declaration addressed to both Japan and China expressing the hope that the two countries would cease hostile actions and have resort to peaceful methods for settling their dispute.

Japan was thus assured of freedom of action. In the meantime, the Japanese had overcome the stubborn Chinese resistance in the Shanghai-Woosung sector, and were advancing on Nanking. So when the German ambassador to Tokyo, Herbert von Dirksen, on December 7 informed Hirota that the Chinese were prepared to talk peace, Hirota expressed doubts that negotiations could be on the basis proposed a month earlier. Nanking fell to the Japanese on December 13. When Hirota finally, on December 23, informed Dirksen of Japan's willingness to enter upon peace negotiations, it was conditional upon the National government's prior agreement to (1) the establishment of demilitarized zones and special regimes where "necessary"; (2) abandonment of Nanking's pro-Communist and anti-Japanese policies; (3) close economic cooperation between China, Japan, and Manchoukuo; and (4) China's payment of an indemnity to Japan.[10] A reply was required before the end of December. This was an ultimatum. But the price for peace was too high for the Chinese. On January 14, 1938, in the absence of agreement on the part of Nanking, the Japanese ruling group reached a decision to proceed with the conquest of China. The die was cast.

The Soviet Union had early, inferentially in 1937, given the National government a loan of Y$100 million.[11] But this sum was soon exhausted, and in March, 1938, Sun Fo arrived in Moscow with a request for another loan. Ambassador Yang Chieh in May signed, at Moscow, an agreement for a new Soviet credit of U.S.$100 million, for the purchase of military supplies. Some 200 Soviet "volunteers" flew Soviet planes in defense of such Chinese towns as Wuhan, Chungking, Lanchow, and Sian, strafed Japanese shipping on the Yangtze, and bombed Taipei on Formosa. More than a hundred Soviet airmen were lost in the Sino-Japanese war. Soviet engineers assisted in the construction of motor highways and air bases. At a time when Britain and the United States were continuing their profitable trade with the Japanese, the Soviet aid to China was substantial and critical.[12]

The German military advisory group headed by General Alexander von Falkenhausen had begun to thin out in late 1937, but was not withdrawn from China as a body until about March, 1938 – and then only under pressure exercised by Tokyo on Berlin. Shortly after signature of the Sino-Soviet nonaggression pact, however, Moscow dispatched a new military mission to China. It was headed by A. I. Cherepanov, who had been Bluecher's second in command at Canton. Figures of the stature of Generals Grigori K. Zhukov and Vasili I. Chuikov also early appeared on the Chinese scene. The Soviet mission was in due course built up to a strength of 500 officers, who acted in the capacity of technical consultants in China's tank and artillery training centers, but it never took on the importance of the advisory mission to Canton in the old revolutionary days. For one thing, it was given no role in the formulation of strategy. Discovering that there were definite limits to the military effort that Nationalist China was prepared to make, and that there was only a limited use to which Chiang Kai-shek would put the Soviet general officers, Moscow recalled Zhukov and Chuikov to the Soviet Union. There, they found plenty of work to do.

At this time, there existed in the Japanese high command two opposing factions, one favoring the subjugation of China as a matter of first priority, the other bent on confrontation of the greater enemy, the Soviet Union. To meet the anticipated threat, Moscow had already effected a reorganization of its military forces garrisoned along the frontier facing Manchoukuo. The region had been divided into two separate military districts—the Trans-Baikal and the Far Eastern—and put under separate commands. In February, 1937, Bluecher's Far Eastern command of some 240,000 men was reorganized as the Special Red Banner Far Eastern Army.

The purges that rocked the Soviet army in 1937 and 1938 had their effect on the thinking of the Japanese strategists. After the execution of Tukhachevski and his comrades in June, 1937, Major General Homma Masaharu, who had just traveled through the Soviet Union on the way back from London, wrote in the *Osaka Mainichi* that, as a result of the executions, the Red Army no longer constituted a threat to Japan. A few days later, there was an armed clash between Soviet and Japanese-Manchoukuo forces arising out of the Soviet occupation, a short time before, of two small islands in the Amur. On the Japanese demand, the Soviet forces withdrew. When the Japanese occupied Bolshoi Island contrary to prior assurances, the Soviets protested—but did no more. The Japanese were able to draw an easy inference: General Homma was right. In November, 1937, Italy joined the German-Japanese Anti-Comintern Pact; the Japanese strategic position was thus further buttressed.

The Japanese judgment would naturally have been consolidated by the departure from the China scene of not only Zhukov and Chuikov, but Ambassador Bogomolov as well: the envoy was recalled from his China post in late 1937, and in due course assumed the more important position of ambassador to France. The purge of the Red Army that had begun in European Russia reached Bluecher's Special Red Banner Far Eastern Army in May, 1938, with devastating effect. It seemed that the army had been seriously weakened. And when a small Soviet force in early July moved onto a minor height immediately west of Lake Khasan known as Zaozërnaya (called by the Chinese Changkufeng) on the common frontier of the Soviet Union and Manchoukuo, the Japanese demanded withdrawal, claiming that the hill was Manchurian territory. Moscow rejected the demand, claiming the hill for its own. On July 29, the Japanese attacked, and dislodged the Soviet force.

The Japanese were at this time engaged in the difficult campaign directed at the capture of Wuhan, in the Yangtze valley. Ambassador Grew reported from Tokyo on July 25 that, according to a memorandum submitted by the U.S. military attaché, one school of Japanese thought was then contending for the suspension of military actions beyond Hankow, in favor of taking strong action respecting the (Soviet) border situation, while undertaking to overthrow Chiang Kai-shek by political means; whereas a second proposed that border actions be avoided "in order to operate more vigorously toward a complete destruction of the Chiang government, and with it the likelihood of future Russian operations in support of that government." [13]

On the Manchoukuo-USSR border, Bluecher reinforced, and so did the Japanese. Shortly afterward, Bluecher was removed from his command and put under arrest. As the battle developed, the new commander of the Special Red Banner Far Eastern Army, General Grigori Shtern, built up the Soviet force on the Zaozërnaya front to a total of about twenty-seven infantry battalions, several artillery regiments, and tank units. It was presumably about this time that Foreign Minister Joachim von Ribbentrop, approached by the Japanese ambassador, informed him that Germany would not render assistance to Japan in connection with the incident, and counseled moderation.[14] Politically and militarily, the Soviets occupied the more favorable position. They had in their possession a map appended to the Sino-Russian Hunchun Protocol of 1886 evidencing Russian possession, and, with plenty of troops in the Far East and unengaged in fighting elsewhere, they commanded an important military advantage.

On August 2, the Japanese Cabinet reached a decision to undertake a negotiated settlement of the conflict. Two days later, Ambassador Shigemitsu Mamoru at Moscow communicated to Foreign Affairs Commissar Litvinov the Japanese government's proposal that the Lake Khasan fighting be regarded as a local incident, and be settled peaceably. Moscow was willing. On August 11, the two sides signed a truce that provided face-saving formalities for the Japanese but left the Soviets in possession of the disputed height. The Japanese test of the resolve of the Soviet high command, rocked though the Red Army was by the purge, had failed. The Japanese lost over 500 killed, as compared to an admitted 236 dead on the Soviet side. On November 9, Vasili K. Bluecher, who had played so important a part in Sino-Soviet relations, was executed – a victim of the purge he had furthered by sitting in judgment on Tukhachevski.

After the Zaozërnaya affair, the Soviet Far Eastern forces underwent still another reorganization. They were now divided into four separate commands, of which one, comprising the Fifty-seventh Rifle Corps, was garrisoned in the Mongolian People's Republic. The total strength of the Soviet Far Eastern military establishment was estimated by the Japanese general staff to number twenty-four divisions, with 1,900 tanks and 2,000 planes.[15]

The Munich agreement of September, 1938, in Europe convinced the Soviets that Britain desired to appease Nazi Germany and guide it into a collision with the Soviet Union. In China, the Japanese occupied Wuhan in October and then called a halt to their campaigning against the Nationalist Chinese. The Nationalists, who had removed their capital to Chungking in west China, were content not to arouse the ire of the enemy by harassing him, and the Sino-Japanese War went into the doldrums.

Events in 1939 proceeded at a more feverish pace. The Spanish civil war ended in March of that year, after nearly three years of fighting that had cost about a million lives, with the defeat of the republican forces. Since liberals and Communists (including Soviet "volunteers") had been engaged on the republican side, while Nazi Germany and fascist Italy had aided General Franco against them, the denouement was regarded as a setback for the Soviet Union. On April 16, Moscow formally proposed the formation of a Soviet-British-French united front of mutual assistance, with Poland to be added if possible. The following day, the Russian ambassador made a cautious démarche to the German Foreign Office looking toward a détente in the relations between the two countries.

In the face of the Soviet offer, Prime Minister Neville Chamberlain hesitated, indecisive. On May 3, Moscow announced that Maksim M. Litvinov, the advocate of better relations with the Western European powers, had relinquished the post of commissar for foreign affairs, and was being replaced by Vyacheslav M. Molotov. The British finally, on May 8, made a preliminary reply to the Soviet proposal of the month before, but the Soviet government, suspicious of Anglo-French bona fides, had by now begun to stress the negotiations at Berlin. When even the signature on May 22 of the "pact of steel" between Germany and Italy failed to spur the British and French to manifest an active interest in the Soviet proposal, the Soviet commitment to attempting the other alternative was consolidated. Writing long afterward, Winston Churchill recorded his estimate:

> There can . . . be no doubt, even in the after light, that
> Britain and France should have accepted the Russian
> offer, proclaimed the Triple Alliance, and left the method
> by which it could be made effective in case of war to be
> adjusted between allies engaged against a common foe.[16]

Because the overcautious allies hesitated, however, history took a radically different course from what it might have.

The Soviet Union continued to buttress its eastern front by cementing relations with the Chinese National government. Sun Fo in 1939 made another trip to Moscow for the purpose of obtaining additional Soviet aid. He succeeded in signing, on June 16, a new Sino-Soviet commercial treaty of fifteen articles, significant chiefly for the further definition of trade arrangements — and assurances given respecting the treatment of Soviet trade representatives located at various places in China. The signature of the treaty, however, had an important incidental result: it facilitated China's negotiation of a new Soviet credit of U.S.-$150 million, bringing the total to U.S.$250 million.

In the meantime, tensions had been building up on the Manchoukuo-Mongolian frontier. From the time of the establishment of Manchoukuo in 1932, Moscow had labored to transform the Mongolian People's Republic into a stout bulwark for protection of the Trans-Baikal region against advance from either the east (Manchoukuo) or the south (Western Inner Mongolia). The Japanese grant of (nominal) autonomy to Eastern Inner Mongolia, as Hsingan Province of Manchoukuo, with the implicit promise of resurrection of the Mongolian empire, had aroused Mongol sentiments of nationalism and irredentism and created difficulties for the Soviet program. Soviet troops had intervened in 1932 and 1934, as in Sinkiang, to help the Ulan Bator government suppress movements of rebellion having anti-Soviet aspects. In January, 1935, the Soviet forces already in the Mongolian People's Republic were reinforced by the arrival of an additional 2,000 Red Army troops, ten artillery pieces, and 300 armored cars. Soviet troops had again taken up garrison functions in the Mongolian People's Republic.

This was the background for the Japanese purge of the Hsingan Province leadership in April, 1936, and the signature of the Soviet-Mongol mutual-assistance pact the month before. In the same year, Choibalsan, who together with Sukhe Bator had created the Mongolian People's Army, became first deputy premier and minister of internal affairs (charged with internal security). In extensive purges from 1937 to 1939, Choibalsan eliminated from power those who might have wavered—and perhaps joined Teh Wang and the Japanese. Premier and Foreign Minister Gendun, who had negotiated both the 1934 "gentlemen's agreement" and the 1936 pact of mutual assistance between Ulan Bator and Moscow, was shot in August, 1937, for alleged "counterrevolutionary activities and Japanese espionage." [17] His successor in both posts, Amor, was likewise purged in the spring of 1939—again on the grounds of counterrevolutionary activity. Choibalsan assumed the premiership. The Republic by then was solidly in the Soviet camp.

Writing in Tokyo in 1939, two Japanese observers estimated that the Soviet Union needed a sovietized (Outer) Mongolia to protect its flank and had actually transformed the region into a "closed country," where military preparations were in course. They offered a prognostication for the future: "In the opinion of many Japanese specialists as well as the authors of this book, Outer Mongolia will be the scene of the coming Japanese war with the Soviet Union." [18]

The character of the Soviet-Mongolian relationship, and the suitability of Outer Mongolia as an arena for a war with the USSR, were soon to be tested. About mid-March, 1939, General Shtern, in a speech duly published in Moscow, charged that the Japanese were preparing to make an attack on the Mongolian People's Republic. On May 11, in fact, Japanese troops suddenly attacked Mongol border guards in the vicinity of Nomonhan, a small hillock east of Buir Nor and near the Khalkhin Gol (river) in a section of the Mongol-Manchoukuo border that had since 1935 been the scene of strife. According to a Soviet source, the Japanese command planned to thrust through the Mongolian People's Republic to cut the Trans-Siberian Railway and thus make it impossible for the Soviet government to transfer armed forces from European Russia to the defense of the Soviet Far East.[19]

Moscow had doubtless visualized that possibility long before. Stalin, in an interview of March 1, 1936, with American newspaperman Roy Howard, had stated that: "If Japan should venture to attack the Mongolian People's Republic and encroach upon its independence, we will have to help. . . . We will help the MPR just as we helped it in 1921." [20] Now Molotov, speaking on May 31, 1939, made reference to the mutual-assistance pact of 1936 between the two countries and announced that the Soviet Union would defend the borders of the Mongolian People's Republic with the same resolution that it would defend its own. That announcement was made against the background of fighting between Soviet-Mongol forces and Japanese-Manchoukuoan troops along the Khalkhin Gol on May 28 and 29.

Tokyo pressed the issue, and moved up reinforcements. With the significance of developments now quite clear, Moscow about mid-June assigned General Zhukov to command the Soviet forces stationed in the MPR, and he took charge of the joint Soviet-Mongol operations. His first move was to ask for reinforcements, which were promptly forthcoming. Sporadic fighting characterized by some fierce air battles continued for weeks — while Zhukov prepared. Undetected by the Japanese, he concentrated a powerful striking force designated the "First Army Group," made up of strong infantry and cavalry contingents supported by nearly 500 tanks, about the same number of planes, and large numbers of armored cars. When the movement was completed, he commanded thirty-five Soviet rifle battalions and twenty cavalry squadrons as compared with a concentration of twenty-five Japanese infantry battalions and seventeen cavalry squadrons. But it was on the tanks that Zhukov depended in good measure to make the battle one in which he would annihilate the enemy.

The Japanese had organized their main strength into a special Sixth Army. They opened their attack on August 17, with the main thrust scheduled for August 24. On August 20, however, Zhukov launched a well-prepared counteroffensive. He had the superior firepower, and, as anticipated, his tank force proved decisive: the Soviet-Mongol forces succeeded in encircling the main Japanese force and on August 30 effectively destroyed it. In the battle of Nomonhan, Japan probably sustained as many as 55,000 casualties; the combined Soviet and Mongol losses were put at about 10,000.[21]

The military defeat, which could not be easily repaired in the best of circumstances, was attended by a political move that threw the Japanese badly off balance in the international sphere. Ambassador Oshima Hiroshi had earlier been negotiating with von Ribbentrop for a triple alliance of Germany, Italy, and Japan that would have been directed against the Soviet Union, but Germany had kept its Oriental anti-Comintern ally in the dark regarding the German-Soviet negotiations. And on August 23, as the Nomonhan battle was building up to its peak, Germany and the Soviet Union signed a nonaggression pact. Japan was patently caught by surprise. The American chargé d'affaires at Tokyo on August 25 reported to Washington that he had been reliably informed the day before that the Soviet government had proposed to the Japanese ambassador at Moscow that there also be concluded a Soviet-Japanese nonaggression pact. He reported further, however, that "The terms of the German-Soviet treaty have so infuriated the Japanese that I cannot conceive of any reply which the Japanese Government will make other than a flat and categorical refusal." [22]

Thus, when the European war began with the German invasion of Poland on September 1, Tokyo was caused to reassess its grand strategy. It was obviously impolitic for Japan to press issues with the Soviet Union under circumstances where the war with China, if stalemated, was not ended, and Berlin had committed itself not to attack the Soviet Union in Europe (at least, for the time being). On September 16, Foreign Affairs Commissar Molotov and Japanese Ambassador Togo Shigenori reached an agreement to terminate hostilities on the Mongol-Manchoukuo frontier as of that date, with each side to remain in occupation of positions occupied at 1:00 P.M. Moscow time the day before. This of course gave the victory to those who had won it in the field — the Soviet and Mongol forces. This Soviet-Mongol achievement was effectively confirmed by a border agreement announced simultaneously at Moscow and Tokyo on June 9, 1940. Zhukov was duly honored by being named a "Hero of the Soviet Union." Before long, in World War II, he would again, as at Nomonhan, make strikingly effective use of the tank arm. In a long-delayed denouement, a Soviet military court in February, 1946, sentenced a sometime follower of Semenov to twenty-five years in prison for having forged a map of the disputed frontier to help Japan provoke the Nomonhan incident.[23]

The big war between the Soviet Union and Japan did not, as envisaged by some Japanese, begin in the Mongolian People's Republic. The battle of Nomonhan proved to be one of those critical turning points in history. Coupled with the coincident signature of the German-Soviet nonaggression pact, it led directly to the defeat of the Japanese faction that gave priority to a war with the Soviet Union, and the consequent rise to predominance in the Japanese government of those who favored a grand strategy built around a plan for collision with the sea powers. As the events of September 1, 1939, clearly demonstrated, the Munich policy of appeasement had not paid off; the Soviet strategy of stubborn resistance at Zaozërnaya and Nomonhan did. On April 13, 1941, Moscow and Tokyo themselves entered upon a nonaggression pact. When Germany launched its blitzkrieg against the Soviet Union two months later, it attacked alone: its anti-Comintern ally, Japan, was by this time committed to the strategy of attacking the Pacific sea powers — Britain and the United States.

23 THE USSR AND
SINKIANG, 1937-1943

CHINA, SOON CUT OFF from access to the sea, and without support from the sea powers in any event, was dependent
upon the overland route through Central Asia for receipt of military supplies from the Soviet Union for waging the war against
Japan. Sinkiang thus took on a new significance. At the end of
1937, the Chinese set about feverishly constructing a motor highway between Khorgos, on the Soviet frontier, across Sinkiang,
through Hsinghsinghsia (Ape Pass), to Lanchow in Kansu Province, whence the line of communications reached southward to
Chungking. This was a distance of over 5,200 kilometers. Under
the supervision of military contingents, a vast corvée of laborers
completed the highway by the end of 1938, thus bringing Sinkiang
more intimately than ever before into contact with the outside
world.

This was the communications system over which essential
war supplies were transported to China and Chinese tungsten,
tea, and wool were shipped to the Soviet Union in return. The old
route from Urumchi to Chuguchak was now largely abandoned,
but a new highway from Urumchi southward to Kashgar was built.
That southern branch had little significance for the direct military traffic, but it strengthened the regional economy and played
a role in the developing trade relations between Sinkiang and
the Soviet Union. The Soviets used their own trucks for transport
of products purchased in Sinkiang. In addition, the Soviet Union

supplied to the provincial government, in a credit sale, something over a thousand trucks, thus substantially increasing the meager transport facilities of the region.

In that era of collaboration, the Sheng Shih-ts'ai regime and Soviet interests embarked upon various joint undertakings. There was organized a Sino-Soviet airline, with termini at Alma-Ata in Kazakhstan and Hami in eastern Sinkiang. A so-called "agricultural implements factory" was constructed at Toutungho, lying at the foot of a mountain about twenty-five kilometers northwest of Urumchi. The designation was a misnomer, probably to mislead the Japanese: this was actually an airplane assembly plant, with a modest airfield that was easily constructed on the flat countryside. However, it would appear that the plant had been constructed more with a mind to possible future eventualities than to present needs, for its actual production seems to have been small.

A third, and the most important, of the joint economic enterprises was an oil field located at Tushihshan (also, "Tushantzu"), in the vicinity of Wusu. Soviet geologists had discovered the petroleum deposit, and the USSR supplied the engineers, technicians, and equipment for development of the field. Profits of the enterprise were shared by the two countries. Finally, in the mountains near Borotala, in the northwestern part of Sinkiang, there was a joint mining enterprise engaged, it was widely believed, in the exploitation of a deposit of uranium ore.

There was in addition an aviation training center at Kuldja, with separate military airport, supported by the Soviet Union. The airplanes and instructors at the institute were alike Soviet, and the trainees included not only fliers for Sinkiang's very modest air force, but also for the National government's central air establishment.

Some 5,000 Soviet troops, accompanied by planes, had entered Sinkiang in May, 1937, to help put down the rebel challenge of Ma Hu-shan and Ma Shao-wu. With the occurrence of the Lukouchiao Incident on July 7, and the rapid transformation of that "incident" into the second Sino-Japanese War, some of those Soviet troops returned home, but a reinforced mechanized brigade remained behind. Now designated as the "Eighth Regiment," the unit took up station at Hami, at the eastern gateway to the province. The troops wore Chinese uniforms, and it was not publicly acknowledged by either Moscow or Urumchi that a Soviet force occupied a semipermanent garrison position in the province. Regardless of the uniforms, however, the troops were officered by Soviet military men, and took orders from no one else. It is logical to assume that the National government at Chungking was apprised of the presence in eastern Sinkiang of the Soviet force, and had agreed to the arrangement. The military position at Hami was an initial block to any possible Japanese thrust in the direction of Central Asia.

Sheng obtained another loan from Moscow, this time for 15 million gold rubles. The program of construction prospered. The three-year plan was concluded in early 1939, and its reported accomplishments, if small in the absolute, did indeed bear promise for a brighter future for the long-suffering people of Sinkiang. The Soviet aid program was bearing economic fruits long desired by the province.

Sheng was in the meantime acting to further his political relations with the side that seemed to offer promise of advancing his power interests. When the Chinese Communist leaders Wang Ming and K'ang Sheng in 1937 passed through Sinkiang en route home from the Soviet Union, Sheng proposed to them that he join the CCP. The Chinese party, by Sheng's version, in due course responded that, because of the special relationship between Sinkiang and the USSR, they thought it desirable to consult with Moscow. Word finally came through that it was felt that Sheng should temporarily shelve his plan.

But Sheng had attracted the interest of the Communists at Yenan, and in 1937 they sent their special-service head, Teng Fa, to Urumchi with the mission of further developing the triangular relationship between Sheng and the Chinese and Soviet Communist parties. Sheng asked that Yenan send Communist representatives to help him with the task of construction of the projected "New Sinkiang," and got quick fulfillment of his request. In early 1938, Ch'en T'an-ch'iu, who had been one of the founders of the CCP, led a group of Communists to Sinkiang to take up service under Sheng Shih-ts'ai. Ch'en, a member of the CCP Central Committee, seemingly went on to Moscow, but returned in 1939 and took the place of Teng Fa as head of the CCP mission. Various important figures, including Mao Tse-tung's younger brother Mao Tse-min and Ch'ü Ch'iu-pai's wife Yang Chih-hua, were in the group. Under assumed names, they occupied various important posts in Sheng's establishment. Ch'en himself, under the name Hsu Chieh, functioned as the representative of the CCP and of the (Communist) Eighth Route Army. Mao Tse-min had in the past demonstrated ability in the fields of economics and finance, and Mao Tse-tung had leaned upon him heavily. Now, under the alias Chou Pin, he became Sheng's provincial commissioner of finance.

In 1938, Sheng Shih-ts'ai made a trip to Moscow, to see Stalin. He asked the Soviet dictator to expedite shipments of industrial equipment to Sinkiang and also brought up the question of his application for membership in the Chinese Communist Party. Stalin, according to Sheng, ordered Molotov to speed deliveries to Sinkiang and directed that Sheng be granted membership—but in the Communist Party of the Soviet Union (CPSU). Sheng agreed, and was duly enrolled as a member of the Soviet party.[1]

Another political development followed upon Sheng's meeting with Stalin. On July 15, 1934, after Ma Chung-ying had gone into exile in the Soviet Union, the Urumchi government had demanded his extradition, but Moscow had rejected the demand. Now, with more intimate relations existing between Sheng Shih-ts'ai's government and Moscow, Ma was reportedly executed, in the Soviet Union, in the spring of 1939.[2]

It was against the background of apparently increasing radicalization of the Sinkiang administration that, in September, 1939, the European war began. It did not at once affect the Sinkiang-Soviet relationship. On November 26, 1949, Sheng Shihts'ai and two Soviet representatives signed an agreement by virtue of which Sinkiang granted to the Soviet Union, for a period of fifty years, "exclusive rights to prospect for, investigate and exploit tin mines and its ancillary minerals." [3] That agreement gave the Soviet Union extensive rights with respect to the construction and maintenance of secondary enterprises, including power stations and transmission lines, communications facilities, and adjunct offices, hospitals and schools. It offered substantial promise of greatly increased Soviet political and economic influence in Sinkiang. The second three-year plan was scheduled for launching in 1941.

The year 1941, however, saw two striking developments, both of which introduced changes into the position of Sheng's ally and mainstay, the Soviet Union. In April, Moscow and Tokyo entered upon their nonaggression pact; in June, Nazi Germany launched its blitzkrieg against the Soviet Union. The first action might have led Sheng, who had been linking numerous "plots" he discovered in Sinkiang to Japanese machinations, to suspect the bona fides of the chief "anti-imperialist," the USSR. But the second development was far more important: it quickly brought into question the very capacity of the Soviet Union to survive. By November, the German armies had brought Leningrad under siege, were within some thirty miles of Moscow, and had thrust deeply into the Ukraine.

On December 7, 1941, the Japanese attacked at Pearl Harbor, and the Chinese Nationalists won a new ally—and a promising new source of money and military supplies—in the United States. The Soviet Union, on the other hand, now hard put to withstand the German onslaught, was caused to divert its major efforts, and all available military strength, to the European front, and was no longer able to play an important role in Asian developments—not to mention the matter of assisting with Sheng's new three-year economic plan. Matters were not long in taking a critical turn. Early in 1942, Ch'en T'an-ch'iu as head of the Communist mission requested that they be allowed to return to Yenan. Sheng refused permission, whereupon Ch'en proposed that they be allowed to go to Moscow. Sheng again withheld approval, and put the whole group under surveillance in Ch'en's headquarters. Sheng Shih-ts'ai was said now to have had a serious falling out with his brother Shih-ch'i, reputedly strongly pro-Soviet, regarding the question of Sinkiang's policy with respect to the Soviet Union. In mid-March, Sheng Shih-ch'i was murdered. His wife Ch'en Hsiu-ying was promptly arrested, tried in camera, reputedly confessed to the crime as part of a larger plot for the staging of an anti-Sheng uprising on April 12, and, still incommunicado, was executed by order of Sheng Shih-ts'ai.[4]

This development occurred immediately before, or shortly after, an event that seems to have been related: Sheng Shih-ts'ai was visited by a powerful emissary from the Chungking government, General Chu Shao-liang, commander of the Eighth War Area, with headquarters at Lanchow. Chu bore the major proposal from Chiang Kai-shek that Sheng should change sides, particularly in view of the apparently shifting balance of power with respect to the Soviet Union. The quid pro quo would presumably have been Chungking's agreement to Sheng's continuation in power—with a share in the American support already pledged to the Nationalists, who since 1938 had done little fighting. Sheng now informed Moscow that he had found the Soviet advisers in

Sinkiang to be untrustworthy and that it was no longer possible for Sinkiang to cooperate with the Soviet Union.

Whether by design or accident, the death of Sheng Shih-ch'i acted as an earnest of Sheng's intent to dissolve his close relationship with the embattled Soviet Union.[5] In April, Sheng had Ch'en T'an-ch'iu, Mao Tse-min, and another prominent Communist official, Lin Chi-lu, imprisoned on charges formulated, or at least announced, only months afterward, that they had participated in an international Communist conspiracy to overthrow the Sinkiang regime, that is, Sheng Shih-ts'ai. Included also in the plot, according to Sheng, were Consul General Bakulin (who had signed the 1940 "Tin Mines Agreement") and Soviet military adviser Latov. Hundreds of other arrests were made; Sheng Shih-ts'ai counted 656 persons involved in the conspiracy. Significantly, the periodical of Sheng's Anti-Imperialist Society, the *Fan-ti chan-hsien*, ceased publication.

Moscow endeavored to adjust matters with Sheng, but the Soviet winter counteroffensive had failed to break the front in western Russia, and the Germans in the spring of 1942 were preparing a new big drive. Sheng consequently had the less reason to listen to the arguments of Moscow and became more receptive still to blandishments from Chungking. In May, when the Soviets launched an ill-fated offensive against Kharkov, Chu Shao-liang and Minister of Economics Wong Wen-hao met with Sheng in Urumchi, and it would appear that Sheng now entered upon a definitive agreement to abandon his pro-Soviet orientation in favor of alignment with Chungking. In a "confession" of June 20, 1942, attributed to Chancellor of the Sinkiang Academy Tu Chung-yuan, classmate and longtime supporter of Sheng Shih-ts'ai, Tu (not, so far as is known, a member of the Chinese Communist Party) was made to say that he had gone to Sinkiang at the behest of Chou En-lai with the final mission of causing a Communist regime to be set up in Sinkiang. Mao Tse-min, in *his* "confession" of a few days later (June 25), not unnaturally corroborated Tu's reputed testimony, adding somewhat unconvincingly that, "On the surface, Chou's purpose of undermining Sinkiang was to control the land route to Russia. As a matter of fact, his real motive in seizing Sinkiang was to expand his own influence."[6]

The Germans crossed the Donetz in early June and launched their main offensive eastward, toward the Caucasus, at the end of the month. On July 3, after a siege of one month, Sevastopol and the rest of the Crimea fell to the German arms. On that same day, Sheng received the Soviet vice commissar for foreign affairs, V. G. Dekanozov, dispatched by Stalin in an effort to shore up the crumbling Soviet political position in Sinkiang. Moscow's emissary spoke at a considerable disadvantage in power terms, and Sheng informed him that, inasmuch as Consuls General Ouyanjak and Bakulin, Communists Ch'en T'an-ch'iu and Mao Tse-min, and Tu Chung-yuan, had conspired against his life, he had renounced his belief in Marxism and was turning to the study of the Kuomintang's San Min Chu Yi.* The message was clear, and, with the arrival on the following day of an imposing delegation from Chungking, Sheng's agreement with Chu Shao-liang and Wong Wen-hao was formalized. According to Sheng's account, there were subsequent meetings with Dekanozov; but Sheng by now had crossed the Rubicon. On August 29, a formal delegation from Chungking arrived in Urumchi, to celebrate the return of the prodigal Sheng Shih-ts'ai to the Nationalist fold. Chu Shao-liang was once more among those present. One member of the mission was to remain behind in Urumchi — Special Commissioner for Foreign Affairs Chaucer H. Wu (Wu Tse-hsiang).

The Communists and other suspects in the "plot" against Sheng Shih-ts'ai had been held in prison in the essential capacity of pawns in Sheng's power game. The game had now been played out, with Sheng having shifted from what seemed the losing side to join a camp whose fortunes appeared on the upturn. Between June of 1942 and the spring of 1943, many of the arrested persons were progressively liquidated, so secretly that the Communists at Yenan for three years did not know whether their comrades were alive or had died. Ch'en T'an-ch'iu, Mao Tse-min, and Lin Chi-lu, and a large number of other Communists, were executed; others remained incarcerated, to be released — under a new administration — in 1945. In December, 1942, some nine months after the event, Urumchi's official newspaper, the *Sinkiang Jih Pao,* announced that investigation had discovered that Sheng Shih-ch'i had been done to death by (unnamed) "enemies of the country." The report added that, for his meritorious services to the country, Sheng Shih-ch'i had posthumously been awarded the rank of lieutenant general and would be given a public funeral.

* Sun Yat-sen's "Three People's Principles."

In the meantime, the German advance in southern Russia had continued, and in September General Friedrich von Paulus' Sixth Army penetrated the outskirts of Stalingrad. It was thought in Chungking as in various other capitals that, even if the Soviet armies held out during the winter, they would very probably be beaten to their knees by fresh German blows in the course of 1943. The time seemed propitious to press the issue with the Soviets. On October 5, 1942, Sheng Shih-ts'ai communicated to the new Soviet consul general at Urumchi, Georgi M. Pushkin, a demand that Soviet military and technical personnel be withdrawn from Sinkiang. This meant that, among other elements, the "Eighth Regiment" stationed at Hami should depart. Sheng fixed a time limit of three months for compliance.

It had been just five years since the Soviet Union came to the aid of China against the Japanese invaders. It seems highly improbable that without that aid the Nationalists could have held out, under the Japanese blows, and remained in power. But it was of course entirely evident that Moscow was not motivated by a pure altruism in rendering such aid: Japan was viewed as the USSR's potential enemy, too. In any event, Chiang Kai-shek must have viewed the triangular Sino-Soviet-Japanese relationship from 1932 onward as being one in which his proper strategic approach was to endeavor to manipulate one barbarian force against the other—the Soviet against the Japanese. Now the situation had notably improved in that respect for the Nationalists. There had been injected into the politico-military arena yet another barbarian to be played off against the other two—the United States. From the conflicts of those three powers, Chiang Kai-shek anticipated obtaining major benefits for China.

The Soviet Union enjoyed one advantage which, in the dangerous situation existing in late 1942, seemed perhaps indecisive, and of only small comfort: when the Japanese strategists launched their attack on the positions of the Americans, British, and Dutch in December, 1941, they relieved Moscow of the immediate danger of having to fight a two-front war. This circumstance incidentally reduced China's value, for the time being, as a buffer between the Japanese and Soviet arms, particularly with regard to Central Asia. And it was certain that Stalin, who was no man to forget injuries, would link Chiang Kai-shek to the apostasy of CPSU member Sheng Shih-ts'ai and make due note of the bouleversement in Sinkiang, for some possible later accounting.

At the end of 1942, the military situation shifted notably in favor of the Soviet Union. Three brilliant Soviet strategists had devised the defense of Stalingrad. One of them was Chuikov, who might have helped Chungking evolve a more effective military strategy against the Japanese. Another was Zhukov, the victor of Nomonhan. In November, the Soviet forces achieved the encirclement of the besieging German army of over 200,000 men. On January 31, 1943, von Paulus surrendered at the head of his command. Field Marshal Paul Ludwig von Kleist's First Panzer Army retreated back across the Don River. Soviet armies had already begun a drive that was to result in the reconquest of the Ukraine. The expectation on which Sheng Shih-ts'ai had based his policy shift in 1942 had proved in error: the USSR was not, after all, to be conquered by Hitler's Wehrmacht.

Sheng now had to confront the political manipulations of Chiang Kai-shek at Chungking. In November, 1942, Sheng had accepted an agreement for the linking of Sinkiang's currency to that of the National government at an exchange rate that substantially overvalued the inflated Nationalist currency. Immediately, near worthless Nationalist dollars began to flood into Sheng's domain, and valuable products flowed out in exchange. Sinkiang had both a political and economic price to pay.

In the same month of January that marked the Soviet victory at Stalingrad, the new Chinese ambassador to the USSR, Foo Ping-hsiung, went to Moscow to take up his post. He was accompanied by Sinkiang's new special commissioner for foreign affairs, Chaucer H. Wu. Details of the conversations are not known, but logic suggests that the Chinese side, in the light of changing international conditions, proposed that the Soviet Union while withdrawing its political and military "influence" from Sinkiang should continue with economic and technical activities beneficial to the province.

Judging by subsequent events, such a one-sided agreement to permit China to eat its cake and have it too was not reached. Wu returned to Chungking. On April 5, Consul General Pushkin informed Sheng's government that (1) the Soviet government was withdrawing the "Eighth Regiment" from Hami; (2) the Soviet air unit stationed at Hami was also being withdrawn; (3) the "agricultural implements factory" (airplane assembly plant) would be liquidated; and (4) all Soviet technical and administrative personnel, and all Soviet materials and machinery, were also being removed from Sinkiang.

It had been anticipated in Washington and Chungking that

it would prove possible to arrange for the shipment of American war supplies to China via the Soviet Union and Sinkiang. Such was not to prove the case. The Sino-Soviet negotiations to that end struck a snag in that same spring of 1943. The nominal reason for the difficulty was Moscow's reputed concern for the attitude the Japanese (with whom the Soviets were still at peace) might adopt regarding the matter. The Soviet leaders had not been so solicitous of Japanese feelings when they sent Soviet planes piloted by Soviet airmen to knock Japanese planes out of the Chinese skies earlier in the war. But if the Nationalists had chosen to take advantage of the Soviet difficulties in the war against Germany to lever Soviet influence out of Sinkiang, Moscow could now afford to play a similar game. After all, if Chiang Kai-shek could depend upon the Americans and British to keep the Japanese engaged in the South Pacific, so could Stalin.

Chaucer Wu hurried back to Urumchi, but it was already too late. The Soviet Union not only pulled out its military and police advisers, but also ordered doctors, agronomists, mine workers, and other technicians to return home. When the Soviet personnel left, they took with them the machinery, medical equipment, and everything else to which they held title. The USSR also withdrew from joint enterprises such as the Tushantzu oil field, the "agricultural implements factory," and the Borotala mining project, removing most of the plant equipment (which was the property of the Soviet Union) on the ground that the equipment was needed in the home country. The "Eighth Regiment" was kept at Hami until the Soviets got Chinese agreement with respect to the take-over of the military installations, and until the Chinese had further agreed to procedure for the liquidation of other Soviet interests in the province. Then, when all was settled and signed, the last Soviets, comprising the "Eighth Regiment" and remaining technicians, left Sinkiang, taking with them what remained of the Soviet machinery and equipment, and the visible assets of the Soviet trade agency, Sovsintorg.

Nationalist officials loyal to Chungking rather than to Sheng had early moved into key provincial posts. Sheng Shih-ts'ai had only about 20,000 troops — and they had never proved effective against dissident local forces without direct Soviet support. He now stood alone before both the local non-Chinese population and the Nationalists. Chu Shao-liang began to move troops into Sinkiang from Kansu in June, 1943, but their advance was stalled at Hami by the necessity of negotiating the Soviet "Eighth Regiment" out of the way. It was only when the Soviet unit was finally withdrawn in October, 1943, that the way was cleared for the advance of Chu's troops – into Sheng's "own" territory.

By this time, at the end of a summer's seesaw campaigning, the Soviets were developing a strong offensive against the Germans along the Dnieper. In late December, General Nikolai F. Vatutin's armies thrust out from the Kiev sector to recapture Zhitomir and Korosten; at the beginning of January, 1944, they drove across the prewar frontier into Poland. The war in Eastern Europe was definitely going in favor of the USSR. In Sinkiang, Sheng was experiencing the eroding of his autocratic power before the advance of Nationalist authority. In power terms, he had patently blundered and stood in danger of being eliminated from the scene. He began to absent himself from official meetings at the provincial capital.

In April, the Japanese launched their first major drive of six years in China, thrusting swiftly southward from a position on the Lunghai rail line in Honan to roll up Nationalist positions before them, until they reached South China. Sheng now had recourse to the hoary device of discovering a new "plot," and on April 17 arrested a number of Nationalist officials. In June, when the Nationalist debacle was becoming daily more grave, he caused the arrest of large numbers of students and teachers allegedly connected with the April "plot." On August 11, after the Japanese capture of the stubbornly defended position of Hengyang in southern Hunan, Sheng called an emergency meeting of officials in the provincial capital – and detained various Nationalist officials who were so unwise as to attend. Over 300 KMT officials and cadres who had entered the province during 1943 were next arrested, and Sheng declared martial law.

There were Nationalist troops stationed nearby at that time, and Sheng moved fast. He sent word to Lo Chia-lun, the Nationalist supervisory commissioner, that he had uncovered a big plot for the overthrow of the existing governmental authority and the establishment of a Communist regime in its place. He alerted his military forces for action against the Nationalist garrison. And finally, by one report, he sent his chief of staff, Wang Hung-tsao, to the Soviet consulate general with the request that the Soviets intervene militarily to "settle" the National government's influence in Sinkiang – offering as a consideration the Altai gold mines and the petroleum fields as concessions, and 450,000 sheep.[7]

Stalin, who doubtless had had enough of the vagaries of the petty Central Asian autocrat, did not reply to Sheng's final call for help. Sheng was thus left essentially defenseless before Chungking's superior power. The National government on August 29 officially transferred him to the position of minister of agriculture and forestry at Chungking, and made Chu Shao-liang acting chairman of Sinkiang pending the arrival of the new permanent chairman, Wu Chung-hsin. Command of all troops in Sinkiang was transferred to the Military Affairs Commission (headed by Chiang Kai-shek), with frontline forces to be under the command of Chu Shao-liang.

General Chu, acting in a triple capacity in which the military element was plainly visible, now made another trip to Urumchi. On September 11, in Chu's company, Sheng Shih-ts'ai left Sinkiang—forever. Behind him, the people of Eastern Turkestan compiled a two-volume work entitled *Record of the Calamity of Sinkiang,* in which, after charging the departed despot with an assortment of violent and perfidious actions, it was stated in summary: "from the distant past up to the present time the great traitors and biggest knaves didn't dare this, but Sheng Shih-ts'ai ruthlessly did. . . ."[8] During his decade of power in Sinkiang, an estimated 100,000 persons had been imprisoned by his orders, and thousands had been tortured and died. Sheng Shih-ts'ai left behind him a legacy of Turki hatred for his rule. Then, there was Moscow's deep resentment at the Chinese actions with respect to Sinkiang in particular and the Sino-Soviet relationship in general. The Soviet experience would have a natural influence on the subsequent development of the Sino-Soviet relationship.

24 TWILIGHT IN THE SINO-JAPANESE WAR

IN ONE RESPECT, the developments in Sinkiang were expressive of Chungking's as well as Sheng Shih-ts'ai's policy toward the Soviet Union. The Chungking KMT regime, to outward appearances, decided promptly after Pearl Harbor that its greater profit now lay in reliance upon the United States, and that the situation would permit it to attack the weakening Soviet position. From the Nationalist viewpoint, the Soviet factor had depreciated in value with the USSR's involvement in the European War, while the American factor had taken on a new importance with injection of the United States into the Pacific War.

The new relationship, even so, did not work out to the full satisfaction of Chungking. The establishment by the allies of a China-Burma-India (CBI) Theater of War in January, 1942, led to no quick victories; the allies, in fact, were badly beaten in the Burma campaign of early 1942. The campaign projected by Lieutenant General Joseph W. Stilwell, American commander of the CBI Theater, for the recovery of Burma in 1943 was postponed. During this critical period, the Chungking regime maneuvered to advance its political fortunes in the domestic field and vis-à-vis the Soviet Union, always to the neglect of the war against Japan, and sought as well to lever greater amounts of aid from the United States. On May 17, 1943, Minister of Foreign Affairs T. V. Soong (Soong Tzu-wen) appeared before the Combined Chiefs of Staff in Washington and informed them that China would make a

separate peace with Japan unless there were wholehearted operations for its relief and for fulfillment of the Casablanca "commitments" (for the recovery of Burma through joint operations).[1]

It was thus against a background of deteriorated relations
with the Soviet Union and of Chinese harassment of Washington
that, on October 30, 1943, the United States, the Soviet Union,
Britain, and China signed, at Moscow, a Four Nations Declaration on General Security wherein the signatory powers pledged
themselves, inter alia, to carry on a united military effort against
the Axis powers with whom they were at war, to make no separate peace, and to collaborate for the creation of an international
organization for maintenance of the peace in the postwar period.
Despite the lukewarm attitude of Britain and the opposition of
the Soviet Union, Secretary of State Cordell Hull had succeeded
in having China included among the signatories. This was in line
with the basic Rooseveltian concept that China should have the
status of a great power.

In November, Chiang Kai-shek met with Prime Minister
Churchill and President Roosevelt at Cairo. The original project
had envisaged a meeting of Roosevelt, Churchill, and Stalin for
a discussion of the projected landing of American and British
forces in Europe, and Stalin had opted for Tehran, while Roosevelt
leaned toward Cairo. But Roosevelt invited Chiang Kai-shek to
attend, whereupon Stalin chose to absent himself and other Soviet representatives from the meeting. The American, British,
and Chinese chiefs of state thus met first in Egypt. At the Cairo
conference, it was agreed that China should recover certain territories lost previously to Japan. President Roosevelt in the face
of objections from Prime Minister Churchill[2] also promised
Chiang Kai-shek that, within a few months, there would be
undertaken a British amphibious operation in the Bay of Bengal,
Operation Buccaneer, in support of Chinese ground action in
Burma.

Stalin met with Roosevelt and Churchill at Tehran, with the
Chinese out of the picture. There, the three statesmen entered
upon an understanding that effectively wrecked the Buccaneer
project. It was a matter of primary agreement among the three
powers concerned that the military operation of first priority was
the cross-Channel invasion of Nazi-occupied Western Europe,
Operation Overlord. But in October, the month in which the
Soviet "Eighth Regiment" withdrew from Hami, Stalin had

"astonished and delighted" Secretary of State Hull at the Moscow conference by stating categorically that, after the defeat of Germany, the Soviet Union would help to defeat Japan. At Tehran, Stalin unequivocally reiterated that promise.

Any need for Chinese bases or the laborious reconstruction of the Chinese army so that it could participate in the final struggle against Japan vanished completely. Back once more in Cairo at the beginning of December, Roosevelt and Churchill threshed out the matter of the projected amphibious operation in the Bay of Bengal. Roosevelt "was dubious about staking everything on Russian good will, for he feared that the Allies might sacrifice the esteem of the Chinese without later securing the aid of the Russians," [3] and argued for implementation of the plan to which he had agreed. "The British were adamant in opposing Buccaneer as a diversion from Overlord, and Churchill made it clear that he felt no obligations to the Chinese." [4] On December 6, President Roosevelt acceded to abandonment of Operation Buccaneer. Russia's standing in the Allied combine had been enhanced, while that of China was notably depreciated.

The Chungking government thus approached the end of World War II, from which it had hoped (and had initially stood) to gain so much, in a weakened political position vis-à-vis both the United States and the Soviet Union. In June, 1944, the Allies landed in France to implement Operation Overlord; at the same time, the Soviets launched a tremendous offensive on the eastern front that soon brought them to the Baltic. China, on the other hand, was then being buffeted, and its armies scattered to the winds, by Japanese Operation Ichi-go. Burma was recovered in the Chinese-Anglo-American campaign of 1944, but this hardly balanced the collapse of the entire East China front.

Major General Patrick J. Hurley, as President Roosevelt's special envoy, stopped off in Moscow in August, 1944, while en route to China to deal with serious problems that had arisen in Sino-American relations because of clashes over strategy and the Allied war effort centered in the China-Burma-India Theater. In the Soviet capital, he discussed the China situation with Foreign Minister Molotov. The latter emphasized the significance of Soviet intervention to the benefit of Chiang Kai-shek in the Sian Incident of December, 1936, saying that Moscow had hoped that this action would bring a change for the better in Sino-Soviet relations; however (in the words of Hurley's report), "the Chinese had shown little interest in strengthening relations which had on the contrary deteriorated in recent years."[5] Hurley went on to report that the Soviet foreign minister

> confirmed statements made previously that his government would be glad to see the United States taking the lead economically, politically, and militarily in Chinese affairs. Molotov made it clear also that until Chiang Kai-shek tried by changes in his policies to improve Sino-Soviet relations, the Soviet government did not intend to take any interest in Chinese governmental affairs.

Molotov also in effect disavowed Soviet interest in the Chinese Communists, and the American envoy seemingly accepted his comments without any misgivings. In December, within three months after arrival in China, Hurley made a progress report to the State Department:

> At the time I came here Chiang Kai-shek believed that the Communist Party in China was an instrument of the Soviet Government in Russia. He is now convinced that the Russian Government does not recognize the Chinese Communist Party as Communist at all and that (1) Russia is not supporting the Communist Party in China, (2) Russia does not want dissensions or civil war in China, and (3) Russia desires more harmonious relations with China.[6]

This was at a time when the Soviet press had shifted to a position strongly critical of the reactionary character of the Chungking regime — without, however, directly attacking Chiang Kai-shek himself. Hurley's credulity appears in this instance to have been compounded: he inferentially assumed that Chiang Kai-shek, too, was setting forth his inner conviction, whereas Chiang quite obviously was merely embarking upon a new political maneuver.

Moscow had major national enterprises afoot: it was vitally concerned with the impending victory over Germany, and with being able to influence the shaping of postwar Europe; it was, moreover, planning (unknown to Chungking) that the Soviet Union should next enter the war against Japan for the achievement of important political gains. Those enterprises would naturally take precedence over any moves, certain to be of little profit in the unfavorable environment of wartime China, that conceivably might be made in the direction of Chungking. Chiang Kai-shek had in 1927 betrayed the working arrangement that he had helped set up between the Kuomintang and Moscow; he had gone on fifteen years later to bring about the ouster of the Soviet influence from Sinkiang. Molotov's words, so soothing to American ears, were not to be taken at face value.

The Soviet interest in wartime, just as the American interest, was to see the Chinese government broaden its base and take on a different character. But the American and Soviet concepts of the broadening of the base of the Chinese government were formulated differently. The U.S. government had been laggard in the first instance with respect to obtaining an objective appreciation of the significance of the revolutionary movement in China,[7] and it was only in mid-1944, when Chungking felt itself under heavy pressure on all fronts, that the Nationalists permitted Washington to assign "observers" to the Communist headquarters at Yenan. In early 1945, on Hurley's insistence, the experienced Foreign Service officers assigned to that mission were withdrawn.

Moscow, on the other hand, had maintained representatives in the guise of war correspondents at Yenan from 1942,[8] and in addition Chinese emissaries traveled between Yenan and Moscow during the war years. The Soviets, much better informed than the Americans regarding the Communist movement in China, would not have failed to remark the massive development of the Communist organization in both its political and military aspects during the years since the Sian Incident, and logically could only have anticipated that the Communists would play a major role in postwar China, Hurley to the contrary notwithstanding. After all, it was a basic Communist thesis that modern wars foster social revolutions.

Social revolution in fact had a low priority with the Chinese Communists during wartime, when the revolutionaries' primary concern was the broadening of their political base and the development of their armed forces. Naturally, social revolution in China also ranked very low on Moscow's table of priorities: winning the war against the USSR's external enemies came first. And the war against Germany was now patently nearing its end.

At the beginning of February, 1945, the Soviet armies under Zhukov and Konstantin Rokossovski were proceeding with the occupation of Pomerania, and Marshal Ivan S. Konev was driving into lower Silesia. A spearhead of one of Zhukov's columns had reached a point on the lower Oder forty miles from Berlin. Early in that month, Churchill, Roosevelt, and Stalin met in conference at Yalta, to discuss not only the course of operations in Europe, but also the war in Asia—and the shape of the future.

The U.S. Joint Chiefs of Staff, and the American leadership, harbored no doubts in February, 1945, respecting the desirability of bringing the Soviet Union into the Pacific War. This attitude was founded upon the anticipation that the war against Japan, even with Soviet aid, would continue for another eighteen months after the surrender of Germany. There was also a realization that the Soviet Union, if left out of the enterprise, would still be free to act in accordance with the dictates of Soviet national interests —which might prove, unless limited by an agreement with its allies in the war against Germany, to embrace elements distinctly detrimental to the American position, in particular, in the post-war Far East. For one thing, the Soviet Union was still in a state of peace with Japan and could, if left uncommitted, reach a separate arrangement with that country that would undercut American and British aims. The United States and Britain were interested as well in obtaining some fundamental concessions from Stalin with respect to European questions and the shape of the postwar Atlantic world.

In approaching the diplomatic situation at Yalta, Stalin and his advisers would have had prominent in their minds the long-standing strategic issues of Northeast Asia: how to reduce the menace of Japanese power, how to confront the insistent thrust of the United States in the direction of East Asia and (coinciden-tally) the Soviet Far East, and how to provide for buffer protection on the south against American sea and air power as well as against an unreliable and traditionally imperial-minded China. The Soviet tactics early evidenced a clear intent to define the issues: Moscow's prime concern was determination of the political terms to govern Soviet entry into the war. Stalin stipulated a high price. He desired the recovery by the USSR of the Kuriles and South Sakhalin (Karafuto), leases on Dairen (as a commer-cial port) and Port Arthur (as a naval base), long-term leases on both the CER and the South Manchurian Railway systems, and acknowledgment by China of the status quo (effectively, inde-pendence from China) for Outer Mongolia.

China would obviously be concerned, directly or indirectly, with all elements of the Soviet proposals excepting those having reference to South Sakhalin and the Kuriles. But China was not represented at Yalta, or informed respecting the matters concerning it, for the very same reason that kept it out of high military councils at Washington and London: the Chinese, whether at Chungking or in Washington, were notoriously poor at maintaining security. The British were prepared to permit the main bargaining respecting the Far East to be the responsibility of the Americans; it was as if they already had a foreboding of the end of empire. And the Americans, strongly desirous as they were of getting Soviet concessions with respect to Germany and Poland, concerned with getting the Soviet entry into the war against Japan so as to reduce the probability of substantial American casualties, and hopeful of obtaining permission to use bases and establish weather stations in Kamchatka and the Primorye in order to further the American war effort against Japan, did little bargaining with respect to the issues in question.

The secret Yalta agreement respecting the Far East was signed on February 11, 1945, and provided as follows:

The leaders of the three Great Powers — the Soviet Union, the United States of America and Great Britain — have agreed that in two or three months after Germany has surrendered and the war in Europe has terminated the Soviet Union shall enter into the war against Japan on the side of the Allies on condition that:

1) The status quo in Outer-Mongolia (The Mongolian People's Republic) shall be preserved;

2) The former rights of Russia violated by the treacherous attack of Japan in 1904 shall be restored, viz.:

a) the southern part of Sakhalin as well as all the islands adjacent to it shall be returned to the Soviet Union,

b) the commercial port of Dairen shall be internationalized, the preeminent interests of the Soviet Union in this port being safeguarded and the lease of Port Arthur as a naval base of the USSR restored,

c) the Chinese-Eastern Railroad and the South

Manchurian Railroad which provides an outlet to
Dairen shall be jointly operated by the establishment
of a joint Soviet-Chinese Company it being
understood that the preeminent interests of the
Soviet Union shall be safeguarded and that China
shall retain full sovereignty in Manchuria;
3) The Kuril Islands shall be handed over to the Soviet
Union. It is understood, that the agreements concerning
Outer-Mongolia and the ports and railroads referred
to above will require concurrence of Generalissimo
Chiang Kai-shek. The President will take measures in
order to obtain this concurrence on advice from
Marshal Stalin.
The Heads of the three Great Powers have agreed that
these claims of the Soviet Union shall be unquestionably
fulfilled after Japan has been defeated.
For its part the Soviet Union expresses its readiness
to conclude with the National Government of China a
pact of friendship and alliance between the USSR and
China in order to render assistance to China with its
armed forces for the purpose of liberating China from the
Japanese yoke.[9]

The Yalta agreement had provided for a new distribution of
power in the Far East. It was proposed in essence that Japan
should be forced, as Germany, to surrender unconditionally, and
then should be stripped of the empire it had accumulated since
the time when Russia and the United States together had pried
it out of its self-imposed isolation a century before. The Soviet
Union would have its territory and power in Northeast Asia
correspondingly enhanced, at the expense of Japan — and of China.
As for China, not represented at Yalta, it would indeed recover
from Japan what it had lost in the past fifty years, but its power
gains were not commensurate with those won by the Soviet
Union.

One reason for the apparent inequity in rewards was obviously the circumstance that the final contribution of the USSR to
the war effort against Japan, as contemplated at Yalta, would
patently be more decisive in character than that made by the
Chungking regime. But another reason was very probably
Chiang Kai-shek's earlier alienation of both Stalin and Roosevelt

by his manner of approach to the respective problems of Sino-Soviet and Sino-American relations. Chiang paid something at Yalta for the excess of machiavellianism with which he had in the past tried to manipulate one "barbarian" against another.

On April 5, when Moscow announced that it would not renew the Soviet-Japanese neutrality pact of April 23, 1941, the Japanese saw a straw in an ill-omened wind. The treaty had a year more to run, and Japan was naturally not informed respecting the secret Yalta agreement providing for the Soviet Union's entry into the war. In theory, Tokyo still had room for political maneuver.

The bitter-enders were predominant in Tokyo's war counsels, and it was not until after the unconditional German surrender on May 8 that some Japanese leaders began to consider enlisting the good offices of the USSR to obtain a compromise peace. The Supreme Council for the Direction of the War, meeting from May 11 to 14, reached a basic decision aiming at three objectives:

1. Prevention of entry of the USSR into the Pacific War.
2. Evocation from the Kremlin of an attitude of friendliness toward Japan.
3. Mediation of the war, on terms favorable to Japan, through Soviet good offices.[10]

Foreign Minister Togo Shigenori, one of the Big Six who made up the Supreme Council, accordingly asked Hirota Koki, sometime prime minister and earlier (1930–1932) ambassador to Moscow, to approach Soviet Ambassador Yakob A. Malik with the aim of improving the deteriorated Soviet-Japanese relations and performing the spadework for an arrangement that would keep the Soviet Union out of the war against Japan. With the delay reflecting the military clique's reluctance to accept defeat, Hirota met with Malik only on June 4. He failed to arouse the Soviet diplomat's interest with proposals that patently served the Japanese purpose first and foremost.

When Hirota visited Malik again on June 24 (Okinawa had just fallen to the Americans), he proposed the negotiation of a stronger agreement to take the place of the Soviet-Japanese neutrality pact and suggested that Japan trade products from the conquered southern regions (with Japan, be it noted, no longer possessed of shipping to perform the task of transportation) for Soviet petroleum, sorely needed by both Japanese army and navy.

Hirota offered a prospect that would have had greater attraction if presented four years earlier: "If the Soviet army and the Japanese navy were to join forces, Japan and the Soviet Union together would become the strongest powers in the world!" [11]

On June 29, Hirota at last made concrete proposals to Malik, in writing, for a new nonaggression treaty. If Moscow agreed to such a pact, Japan would then commit itself to give independence to Manchuria, withdrawing its troops after the war was over and entering upon an undertaking with the Soviet Union to guarantee Manchuria's sovereignty and territorial integrity. Such an arrangement would have given Japan the essence of what it had in Manchoukuo — that region's independence from China. Hirota also proposed that Japan abandon its fishing concessions in the Soviet Far East in return for Soviet petroleum. Tokyo would be willing as well to consider any other matters of interest to the Soviet government. Malik at last promised to transmit the proposals to his government. But the time for Japan to woo Moscow was long past. This was acknowledged after the war by Hirota, who, asked about the talks with Malik, said: "We acted too late. We should have begun negotiating earlier; only the Government dillydallied so much." [12]

It was not until July 12 that Foreign Minister Togo directed Ambassador Sato Naotake at Moscow to inform Foreign Affairs Commissar Molotov that Emperor Hirohito desired the war terminated at once and proposed to dispatch Prince Konoye Fumimaro to Moscow in the capacity of special envoy. Konoye would carry a personal letter from the emperor and would also bear full powers to discuss all issues in Soviet-Japanese relations. The meeting between Konoye and his hosts, it was suggested, might take place upon the return of Stalin and Molotov from Potsdam.

For the Soviets were about to participate in the Potsdam Conference respecting the disposition of Germany — and the matter of the Pacific War. Sato was not even able to meet with Molotov, who was just about to depart for Berlin, but saw Vice Commissar Aleksandr Lozovski instead. In telegrams of July 21, Togo explained that Prince Konoye would set forth Japanese intentions and, after Soviet demands in East Asia had been given consideration, Japan would then request the USSR to undertake mediation with the United States and Britain for the purpose of achieving a negotiated peace settlement. On July 17 and 18,

Stalin at Potsdam had already told Truman of the Japanese peace feelers — and had reported that the Soviet armies would be ready for action against Japan in early August. The United States had the A-bomb, tested and in hand; by the Yalta Pact, the USSR had already obtained commitments for gains far greater than anything Tokyo could even promise. The Sino-American-British Potsdam Declaration of July 26 called for Japan's unconditional surrender, the A-bomb hit Hiroshima, and on August 8 the Soviet Union declared war on Japan. Prince Konoye never had the opportunity of trying to fulfill his mission.

As far as the Chinese Nationalists were concerned, it was apparent from early 1944 onward that they stood to suffer losses by reason of their deteriorated relations with Moscow. Chiang Kai-shek was too acute a politician not to appreciate the disadvantage of China's position, and the question of Sino-Soviet relations had arisen when Vice President Henry A. Wallace visited Chungking in June, 1944. On that occasion, the generalissimo gave Wallace a message to convey to President Roosevelt: "If the United States can bring about better relations between the USSR and China, and can bring about a meeting between Chinese and Soviet representatives, President Chiang would very much welcome such friendly assistance." [13]

Wallace informed Chiang that the United States would not act as "middleman" in the negotiations. But Hurley tried a mediatory role. As noted above, when in Moscow in August en route to Chungking, he discussed with Molotov the Soviet attitude with respect to the Chinese Communists. He did so, he reported to Washington, "believing that understanding of this was essential to settlement of the Chinese Communist and National Government controversy." [14] The soothing assurances Molotov gave in that regard were perhaps accepted the more readily by Hurley in that they fitted in generally with his own estimate, voiced the following spring, that "the [Chinese] Communists are not in fact Communists, they are striving for democratic principles." [15] Given that sad misjudgment, it is not surprising that, as shown by the record, Hurley also failed lamentably to appreciate the significance of the KMT–CCP dispute for the future of Sino–Soviet relations.

In a telegram of February 4, 1945, Hurley informed Washington that Chungking contemplated sending T. V. Soong to Moscow, as Generalissimo Chiang Kai-shek's personal representative, for a conference, and he transmitted Chungking's tentative agenda for that conference, with the National government's request for any suggested changes. The State Department refused to shoulder that responsibility, instructing Hurley that "while we are at all times anxious to be helpful to the Chinese government we should not permit the Chinese government to gain the impression that we are prepared to assume responsibility as 'advisor' to it in its relations with the USSR." [16] Soong did not make his proposed trip in February, that being the month that the American, British, and Soviet heads of state were sitting in session at Yalta. But the United States was patently involved in the matter, and it committed itself further under the provisions of the Yalta Pact, and by Roosevelt's engaging himself to get Chiang Kai-shek's agreement to the Pact's provisions affecting China.

Hurley was in Moscow again in April of 1945, once more en route back to China after a visit to Washington for consultation. That time he met with both Stalin and Molotov. Again China figured largely in the discussion, with Hurley describing the American policy as being designed to achieve the creation of a democratic government in China under the leadership of Chiang Kai-shek. The incongruity of proposing that the dictator Chiang should have prime responsibility for the nurturing and protection of a budding democratic system appears never to have caught Hurley's attention, but there is little doubt that it was prominent in the minds of the Russians. Nevertheless, Stalin expressed an outward agreement with the reported aims of American policy. Moscow incurred neither obligation nor disadvantage by doing so; the burden of solving China's domestic quarrel had been assumed by the United States. And the Yalta Pact, with the considerable benefits it held for the Soviet Union, was in any event still to be implemented. Hurley interpreted the statements of Stalin as an expression of Soviet willingness that the United States should play the primary role in China after the war with Japan was over. He patently did not know his Far Eastern history.

When Harry Hopkins in the capacity of President Roosevelt's special envoy met with Stalin in Moscow on May 28, 1945, Stalin voiced the desire to meet with T. V. Soong in Moscow not later than July 1, for the purpose of discussing the Yalta agreements. This information was duly conveyed to Soong at the San Francisco Conference at the beginning of June. A few days later, President Truman at Washington informed Soong, in general terms, of the Yalta agreement. Then Hurley at Chungking conveyed the same information to Chiang Kai-shek. Chiang promptly proposed that the United States and Britain be parties to any Sino-Soviet treaty that might be signed in implementation of the Yalta Pact. His proposal evoked no enthusiasm in Washington. China faced the negotiations alone.

Soong thus headed the considerable delegation that arrived in Moscow on June 30 from Chungking for the purpose of negotiating a new agreement for friendly relations — and for satisfaction of the Yalta Pact provisions concerning China — after years when those relations had been exacerbated by Chungking's excessive profit-taking in time of Soviet military distress. His entourage included, among others, Vice Minister for Foreign Affairs Victor Hoo, Sinkiang Special Commissioner for Foreign Affairs Liu Tse-yung, and the minister-counselor of the Chinese embassy in Washington, Liu Chieh.

A new personality in China's foreign affairs also accompanied T. V. Soong on the mission to Moscow — Chiang Ching-kuo, Chiang Kai-shek's son. Chiang Ching-kuo's return to China in April, 1937, had presumably been with the charge, whether avowed or not, of helping Moscow to mend Sino-Soviet relations under circumstances in which the USSR, as well as China, was threatened by Japan. Now, as the war neared its end, he returned to Moscow with a somewhat similar assignment, but on behalf of China. Times had changed: the Soviet Union in June, 1945, was readying itself to attack its ancient enemy, Japan, while China was experiencing domestic strains markedly more severe than those of 1937. Nominally, Ching-kuo was an aide to T. V. Soong; actually, he functioned as his father's personal representative. Soviet Ambassador Appolon A. Petrov had accompanied the party from Chungking, and Chinese Ambassador Foo was present in Moscow as well. The stage was set for the negotiation of a new Sino-Soviet relationship.

25 THE CRITICAL YEAR

WHEN THE NEGOTIATIONS got under way in Moscow, T. V. Soong found that the Soviets were starting with a high asking price.[1] Stalin wanted full Soviet ownership of the Manchurian trunk rail lines and associated coal mines and enterprises, the restoration of the original (1898) Russian lease to the Liaotung Peninsula in its full territorial extent, and Chinese recognition of the independence of the Mongolian People's Republic. Such sweeping concessions went beyond Soong's authority to grant. Furthermore, the Chinese wanted *Soviet* recognition of China's sovereignty over Outer Mongolia – in effect, the withdrawal of the Soviet protectorate, thus to permit China to restore its authority over the region, by force if need be.

Chiang Ching-kuo by instructions of his father met with Stalin in private capacity. He found that Stalin, who had shown himself prepared to make some concessions respecting Manchuria, would make none with regard to the Mongolian People's Republic.[2] Ching-kuo explained that Nanking could not grant independence to Outer Mongolia, since it would then be condemned for alienating national territory and thus betraying the purpose of the war against Japan. Stalin indicated that he understood the Chinese position well enough, but it was necessary that Outer Mongolia be independent because of its strategic position, highly important for the Soviet Union: if a military power were to attack through Mongolia and cut the Trans-Siberian Railway, the USSR would be finished.

Chiang Ching-kuo urged that the Soviet Union need have no fear: with Japan defeated, only China would be left as a power in the Far East — and China would be willing to sign a thirty-year treaty with the Soviet Union. Stalin's response was the soul of hard practicality: Chiang was wrong in his argument about Japan and bilateral treaties, for though defeated, the Japanese people would rise again. Moreover, he said, treaties were unreliable, and a unified China would progress more rapidly than any other country. A strong China, he must have implied, would be inclined to disregard any treaties that might impede its progress toward a position of power in Asia.

Stalin and Molotov departed to attend the Potsdam Conference, and on July 14 Soong returned to Chungking for consultation. On his departure, Soong expressed the belief that the impending Sino-Soviet agreement would constitute the cornerstone for permanent peace in the Far East.[3] The Nationalists wished for something else besides to emerge from the new treaty arrangement: it was hoped that Stalin, in exchange for the National government's agreement to the benefits guaranteed him by the Yalta Pact, would commit Moscow to neutrality vis-à-vis the Chinese internal struggle, thus enabling the Nationalists (so Chiang Kai-shek thought) to handle the Chinese Communists with the greater facility.[4]

At Potsdam, President Truman expressed to Stalin his concern with respect to the dimensions of the concessions being demanded of China by the Russians. Stalin assured Truman that Soviet control of the Manchurian railways would not be exercised to block American trade in the region. The assurances did not suffice to reduce T. V. Soong's apprehensions, and he resigned his concurrent post as foreign minister. He returned to Moscow on August 7 accompanied by the new foreign minister, Wang Shih-chieh, who was now to act as chief negotiator. But the day before, a week after termination of the Potsdam Conference, the United States had dropped the world's first A-bomb on Hiroshima. Moscow's August 8 declaration of war on Japan was effective August 9, and Soviet troops attacked on the Manchurian front at 12:10 A.M. August 9.

On that same day, the second American A-bomb shattered Nagasaki. On August 10, Tokyo announced that Japan was ready to surrender, and on August 14 the de facto surrender took place — except in Manchuria, where the Soviet forces still drove forward.[5] The issue could not be in doubt, and the significance of the replacement of Japanese by Soviet power in Manchuria was clear in the light of history. Stalin, when he suggested to Soong on August 10 that China had better reach an agreement quickly, or the Chinese Communists would enter Manchuria,[6] was only stating the half of it, and Soong knew it.

Soong made the best bargain he could, but the provisions of the agreements signed on August 14 encompassed larger grants on the part of China than originally contemplated by the Yalta agreement. By the Treaty of Friendship and Alliance of that date, "The High Contracting Parties undertake in association with the other United Nations to wage war against Japan until final victory is won."[7] In actuality, general hostilities ceased as of the date of the treaty. China and the Soviet Union by this same instrument agreed "to take jointly all measures in their power to render impossible a repetition of aggression and violation of the peace by Japan," and in the event of Japanese attack upon either of the signatories, the other party to the treaty was bound "at once" to extend to the party thus involved in hostilities "all the military and other support and assistance with the means in its power" (Art. 3). Each signatory undertook not to conclude any alliance or participate in any coalition directed against the other (Art. 4), and the two agreed to respect mutually their sovereignty and territorial integrity, and to refrain from interference in each other's internal affairs (Art. 5). China and Soviet Russia agreed further "to render each other every possible economic assistance in the postwar period with a view to facilitating and accelerating reconstruction in both countries and to contributing to the cause of world prosperity" (Art. 6). As earlier suggested by Chiang Ching-kuo in another connection, the treaty was to remain in force for thirty years. T. V. Soong, by resigning the post of foreign minister, was relieved of the duty of signing the agreement on behalf of Chungking; that chore fell to Wang Shih-chieh.

A number of notes and secondary agreements accompanied the treaty. By one note, the Soviet government committed itself to render to the National government alone "its moral support as well as aid in military supplies and other material resources." Moscow reaffirmed its respect for China's sovereignty over Manchuria, and "As for the recent developments in Sinkiang the Soviet government confirms that . . . it has no intention of interfering in the internal affairs of China." In a separate instrument,

Moscow and Chungking agreed that the main trunk lines of the Chinese Eastern and South Manchurian railways should be combined into one system to be known as the Chinese Changchun Railway, owned and operated by them jointly. Subsidiary enterprises constructed at the time of Russian and joint Sino-Soviet administration of the CER, and during Russian administration of what had become (in 1905) the South Manchurian Railway, and directly serving the railways in point, should also be under joint ownership and administration. The president of the board of directors was to be Chinese, but the manager of the railway should be Soviet. China would possess sovereignty over the railway, and be responsible for its protection. This agreement, too, was to run for thirty years, at the end of which time the Chinese Changchun Railway, with all its properties, was to be transferred without compensation to China.

By two other accords, Chungking agreed to the joint use by China and the USSR of Port Arthur as a naval base and to the designation of Dairen as "a free port open to the commerce and shipping of all nations." The Soviet government was charged by the first agreement with the defense of Port Arthur and was authorized to erect, at its own expense, such installations as might be necessary for that defense. The Soviet government was accorded the right to maintain its army, navy, and air forces within the military area as defined (with Dairen excluded from the military area), and that area was thus in effective military charge of the Soviets, who appointed the chairman of the five-man Sino-Soviet Military Commission charged with handling matters pertaining to joint use of the base. The Chinese, however, were charged with civil administration of the area.

Finally, there was the matter of Outer Mongolia. Ulan Bator, in nominal satisfaction of the provisions of the Soviet-Mongol mutual-assistance agreement of 1936, had on August 10 also declared war on Japan and participated in the military action against the Japanese in Manchuria and Inner Mongolia. The Yalta Pact had provided simply for preservation of the status quo in Outer Mongolia. In the August 14 agreements, however, Chungking committed itself to the position that, if a plebiscite held after the defeat of Japan were to confirm the repeatedly expressed desire of the Outer Mongolian people for independence, "the Chinese Government will recognize the independence of Outer Mongolia with the existing boundary as its boundary."

The Soviet-Japanese hostilities continued. Whereas Japan's unconditional surrender of August 14 was taken by the United States, Britain, and China as effectively marking the end of the war, Moscow held that Tokyo had not yet ordered its forces in the field to cease fire; and, since the Japanese were still offering resistance in Manchuria, the Soviet army continued its advance. The fighting in Northeast Asia terminated officially, from the Soviet government's standpoint, at 10:00 P.M. Moscow time on August 23 (August 24 in the Far East). The Soviets put their own dead at 8,200, Japanese dead at 83,700, and Japanese prisoners at 594,000. The Soviet Union's actual engagement in the fighting in the Pacific War had been limited to exactly two weeks.

In the global fight against the Axis powers, the Soviet Union had undeniably sustained tremendous blows and had nevertheless performed major services for the United Nations cause. The United States and other United Nations had avidly desired Soviet entry into the war against Japan, and none can be sure of the "might-have-been" that could have resulted from the Soviet Union's taking another course. It is nevertheless to be remarked that, at a very small cost to itself, the USSR had recovered much of the privileged position tsarist Russia once had enjoyed in Manchuria. China's sovereignty there had been accorded due recognition. In terms of exploitative right to the Chinese Changchun Railway and appurtenances and usufruct of the ports of Port Arthur and Dairen, however, Stalin had got what he wanted. But the Chinese side expressed its satisfaction with the agreements; the Nationalists thought that they had made a good deal.[8] The agreements were ratified simultaneously in China and the Soviet Union on August 24, the day that hostilities were victoriously terminated in Manchuria, and ratifications were duly exchanged at Chungking on December 5, 1945.

Implementation of the agreements began soon after the end of the war. There was early action with regard to the status of Outer Mongolia. Chiang Kai-shek, in an address of August 24 before the Supreme National Defense Council, stated that Outer Mongolia had attained de facto independence a quarter century before and that in accord with "the basic principles of the national revolution" it was necessary to recognize that independence, to the end that there might be friendly relations between the two countries.[9] A plebiscite was in fact held on October 20, the Mongols voted unanimously in favor of independence, and on January 5, 1946, the National government formally recognized the Mongolian People's Republic.

With the future of Outer Mongolia thus assured, Manchuria became the focus of attention. Japan was now out of the picture, with the Kwantung Army formally dissolved on September 17. But the United States was in occupation of Japan and had poured over 100,000 troops into China to help the Nationalists accomplish their "takeover" task. By agreement of the American and Soviet general staffs, Soviet and American forces jointly occupied Korea, with the Soviets in the North and the Americans in the South. But Manchuria was solely under the occupation of some 300,000 Soviet troops, with Marshal Rodion Ya. Malinovski in supreme command.

Stalin had originally assured T. V. Soong that Soviet forces would be withdrawn from Manchuria within ninety days after the cessation of hostilities against Japan. With V-J Day, the National government promptly initiated action to assert its authority over the area it had never controlled other than nominally (1928–1931), and where it had lacked even that nominal control for fourteen years. Chungking on August 31, 1945, announced that there would be established at Changchun (Hsinking) a Northeast Headquarters of the Military Affairs Commission, under Hsiung Shih-hui as director. The headquarters was to be charged with overall direction and supervision of the provincial administrative organs in liaison, for the time being, with Marshal Malinovski's headquarters.

In a situation so important for Sino-Soviet relations, Chiang Ching-kuo was once more dispatched to the scene. He had served for six years under Hsiung Shih-hui in Kiangsi during the Sino-Japanese War, and now he was appointed special foreign affairs commissioner for the Northeast, to work with Hsiung in Manchuria. He accompanied Hsiung to Changchun in mid-October, with responsibility for diplomatic relations with the Soviet military command headed by Malinovski.

Ching-kuo had hard work cut out for him. Chiang Kai-shek early sought to exploit, once more, American influence against the Soviet position. On October 1, Foreign Minister Wang Shih-chieh informed the Soviet embassy at Chungking that thirteen divisions of Nationalist troops were being sent to Manchuria and would be disembarked at Dairen — from U.S. naval transport vessels. On October 6, the Soviet ambassador delivered Moscow's re-

MONGOLIAN
PEOPLE'S REPUBLIC
1924–1970

300 KM.

S.   LAKE   S.
                    BAIKAL
U.   Chita   R.
        Irkutsk   Ulan Ude

            UBSA   DALAI   Sukhe
            NOR   NOR   Bator   Kiakhta
BAYAN   KHUBSU   Altan Bulag
OLOGEI   UBSA   SELENGA   DORONOD   Nomonhan
                                                                      BUIR
Jirgalanta   DZABHAN   BULAGAN   TOB   Choibalsan   NOR
                            ARA   Ulan   KHENTEI
        Jibhalanta   KANGAI   Bator
KOBDO   SUKHE
                            UBUR   BATOR
        GOBI   BAYAN   KHANGAI
        ALTAI   KHONGOR   DUNDA GOBI
                                              DORONO
                                              GOBI
                OMONO GOBI   N

C   BOUNDARY
                   SETTLEMENT
                   OF 1962
    H   I

MONGOLIAN
PEOPLE'S REPUBLIC   MANCHOUKUO

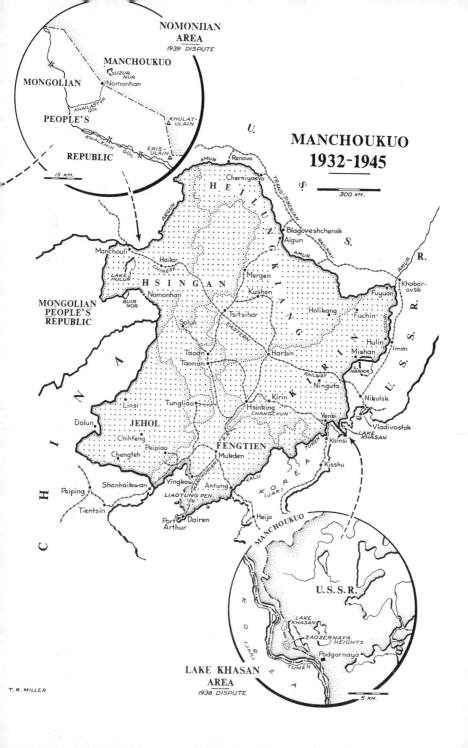

NOMONIIAN
AREA
1939 DISPUTE

MANCHOUKUO

MONGOLIAN

PEOPLE'S

REPUBLIC

SUZUR
NUR
Nomonhan

KHAILASTYN
GOL

KHULAT-
ULAIN

KHALKHIN
GOL
ERIS-
ULAIN

15 KM.

U.

S.

S.

MANCHOUKUO
1932-1945

300 KM.

AMUR
Renovo

Cherniyaevo

HEILUN

TRANS-SIBERIAN

Blagoveshchensk
Aigun

AMUR

RAILWAY

Khabar-
ovsk

AMUR
R.

Manchouli

Hailar

CHINESE

ARGUN

LAKE
HULUN

HSINGAN

Mergen

Kushan

Nomonhan

Tsitsihar

EASTERN

Holikang

Fuyuan

Fuchin

BUIR
NOR

MONGOLIAN
PEOPLE'S
REPUBLIC

Solun

Taoan

Taonan

Harbin

KIRIN

Ninguta

Hulin
Mishan

Iman

HANKA

U. S. S. R.

RAILWAY

Nikolsk

Linsi

Tungliao

Kirin

Hsinking

Vladivostok

CHANGCHUN

Yenki

LAKE
KHASAN

Dolun

JEHOL

Chihfeng

Peipiao

Chengteh

FENGTIEN

Mukden

Kainsi

Kisshu

TUMEN

Peiping

Shanhaikwan

Yingkow

Antung

NALU

KOREA
(JAP.)

Tientsin

LIAOTUNG PEN.

Port
Arthur

Dairen

Heijo

CHINA

MANCHOUKUO

MANCHURIAN

KOREA
(JAP.)

U.S.S.R.

LAKE
KHASAN

ZAOZERNAYA
HEIGHTS

Podgornaya

TUMEN

LAKE KHASAN
AREA
1938 DISPUTE

5 KM.

T. R. MILLER

fusal: Dairen, it was argued, had been designated in the Sino-Soviet treaty as a commercial port, not to be used by other military forces than those of China and the USSR. Admiral Daniel E. Barbey, commanding the U.S. Seventh Amphibian Force, tried to land his Nationalist charges at Hulutao and Yingkow seriatim, only to find those ports held by Chinese Communist forces. He finally put the Nationalist troops ashore at Chinwangtao, safely held by U.S. Marines.

The chief difficulties met by the Nationalists in effecting the takeover of Manchuria centered on, first, competition from the rapidly moving and fast-growing Communist forces and, second, Chungking's failure, in large measure almost certainly because of the enlistment of American support, to achieve agreement and a smooth working relationship with the Soviet Union. Stalin had suggested his terms in the earlier discussions with T. V. Soong and Chiang Ching-kuo; Chiang Kai-shek, looking at the character of the American collaboration, had decided that he could safely reject those terms.

The Nationalists showed an inclination to interpret the Sino-Soviet treaty as binding the USSR to support them against revolution as well as against the Japanese; in any event, they were confident that the United States would assist in any emergency.[10] But Chiang's confidence in his prowess — and in the significance of American support — was not fully shared in all quarters. General Albert C. Wedemeyer, still acting as Chiang Kai-shek's chief of staff as well as commanding general of the U.S. forces in the China Theater, on November 14 reported to Washington that "He [Chiang Kai-shek] will be unable to occupy Manchuria for many years unless satisfactory agreements are reached with Russia and the Chinese Communists."[11] He offered further, related, conclusions: "Russia is in effect creating conditions for the realization of Chinese Communist and possibly their own plans in north China and Manchuria." And, "It appears remote that a satisfactory understanding will be reached between Chinese Communists and the National Government." Those judgments were the background for Wedemeyer's final recommendation to Washington: he proposed that the United States, Britain, and the USSR jointly establish a trusteeship to be exercised over Manchuria until the National government might possess the strength and stability to assume responsibility for full control.

Chiang Kai-shek was determined, however, to seize and exercise full control of that highly important area for his own power ends. He began the advance of his troops from North China into Manchuria, by land, on November 15, the day after Wedemeyer made his pessimistic report to Washington. The situation in Manchuria was in fact distinctly unfavorable, as Wedemeyer had warned, for the easy imposition of Nationalist authority. Japanese and Manchoukuo military forces throughout the region had been disarmed by the Soviet Army, it was true, but local administrations were either in Soviet hands or had already been seized by "autonomous elements" whose political complexion was often uncertain, but which even at that early date sometimes seemed possibly Communist—and were often patently anti-Kuomintang.

It had already become obvious that the transfer of authority from the Soviet Army to the National government could not be accomplished within the ninety-day time limit. Discussions were held between the Chinese and Soviet sides at Changchun, and it was decided by agreement of November 30 between Chiang Ching-kuo and Malinovski to fix January 3, 1946, as a new date for withdrawal of the Soviet forces from Manchuria.

The power issue between the Nationalists and Chinese Communists, still unresolved as of V-J Day, became a major factor with respect to developments in Manchuria. On December 9, Hsiung Shih-hui flew to Nanking to report on the deteriorating situation. A Nationalist-Communist confrontation centered on Changchun brought new political maneuvers, new delays. The date for Soviet troop withdrawal was again extended, this time to February 1, "to facilitate the Nationalist troops' advancing to take over defense." [12] Molotov stated at the time of the Three Ministers Conference (of American, British, and Soviet foreign ministers) in December, and the evidence indicates, that the postponements in Soviet troop withdrawal to the date February 1, 1946, were at the request of the National government. [13] The Nationalist regime desired the Soviet forces to remain in place, as custodial troops, until its military units were in position to take over control directly from the Soviet Army.

Chiang Ching-kuo had remained in Changchun, in contact with Malinovski. About the time that General George C. Marshall arrived in China on his mediation mission, Stalin invited Ching-kuo to visit the Soviet Union. [14] On December 25, Ching-kuo left for Moscow as Chiang Kai-shek's personal representative. He remained in the Soviet capital from December 30 to January 5, 1946.

A Soviet-American conflict over jurisdiction in the Far East had begun to shape up some time before. Moscow had desired to have Soviet troops occupy Hokkaido as well as the Kuriles, and also to share in the occupation of the rest of Japan Proper, but had been balked by the Americans. The Three Ministers Conference, which met in Moscow from December 14 to 26, gave further evidence of conflict — over China. There, Secretary of State James F. Byrnes proposed that one subject for discussion should be the matter of Soviet transfer of Manchuria to Nationalist control. Molotov rejected the proposal, holding that the existence of a Sino-Soviet agreement on the subject, and the absence of disagreement between the two countries regarding the matter, made such discussion unnecessary. He instead pressed the Soviet desire to discuss the presence of American troops in China. Byrnes held that U.S. forces were present in China at the request of the National government and solely for the purpose of assisting the Chinese to disarm the Japanese troops, and he agreed to inclusion of that issue on the agenda only as limited to the function in point. American refusal to enter upon an agreement for a simultaneous withdrawal of U.S. and Soviet troops could only have aggravated Moscow's suspicions of American motives.

There was, in fact, little satisfaction received on either side. The communiqué issued at the close of the conference contained a section relative to China, as follows:

> The three Foreign Secretaries exchanged views with regard to the situation in China. They were in agreement as to the need for a unified and democratic China under the National Government, for broad participation by democratic elements in all branches of the National Government, and for a cessation of civil strife. They reaffirmed their adherence to the policy of noninterference in the internal affairs of China.[15]

The "agreement" was modest enough in all truth, given especially the failure to define "democracy." It was accompanied by an equally insignificant "accord" between the American and Soviet representatives:

The two Foreign Secretaries were in complete accord
as to the desirability of withdrawal of Soviet and
American forces from China at the earliest practicable
moment consistent with the discharge of their obligations
and responsibilities.

This communiqué made one thing entirely clear: the old power
struggle over China had been resumed, with a new cast of characters.

This was evidenced in the course of Chiang Ching-kuo's mission to the USSR. In Moscow, Ching-kuo met twice with Stalin.
He has written an account of those meetings in his book *Wo-ti fu-ch'in* (My Father), and his father has supplemented the account
with a later version of the event.[16] In essence, the Soviet dictator
proposed postwar collaboration between China and the Soviet
Union, offering Soviet assistance with respect to the postwar rehabilitation of China, and particularly of Manchuria and Sinkiang. But, according to Chiang Kai-shek, Stalin expressed himself as opposed to the introduction of the influence of any third
power (the United States) into Manchuria, and "He urged China
to adopt an independent policy, leaning neither to one side nor
to the other."[17] There was a corollary to this understanding fully
appreciated by the two sides, even if it was not made explicit:
Chiang Kai-shek should accept coexistence with the Chinese
Communists as well as with the Soviet Union. Stalin, through
Ching-kuo, who got back to China on January 14, invited Chiang
Kai-shek to meet with him either in Moscow or on the Sino-Soviet
border. Chiang Kai-shek refused the invitation. His policy had
been fixed, probably not without regard for the prospect of a
worsening of Soviet-American relations, along other lines than
Sino-Soviet and KMT-CCP collaboration.

The major Sino-Soviet issues remained very much in being.
There was the military question: when, and how, should the Soviet forces withdraw from Manchuria? And there was another,
related economic question of no small dimensions. The Soviet occupying forces had early begun the dismantlement and removal,
in a liberal interpretation of the term "war booty," of key elements of the rich industrial establishment built up by the Japanese through the decades. They stripped Manchuria of nearly
$900 million worth of the most valuable industrial components.
The dollar equivalent was not the sum total of the loss suffered.

The approximate measure of the economic significance of the loss was indicated by the (American) Pauley Mission's statement:

> The value of the [Manchurian] properties removed by the Soviets is probably one-tenth of the amount of damage and economic collapse resulting from these same removals. . . . The loss of continuing production in the disabled plants and the loss of livelihood of the workers will be felt for years to come.[18]

In their actions with respect to Japanese property the Soviets were doubtless motivated in part by a national recollection of the Russo-Japanese War of 1904–1905, and the Soviet policy in Manchuria with regard to "war booty" was in general line with the approach to that issue in Germany. It also appears not unlikely that a calculation of the effect that a weakening of the Manchurian economy would have for a hostile Chiang Kai-shek's power ambitions might well have been a factor in their policy.

The Soviets went further in their efforts to obtain the final measure of benefit from their military occupation. On the one hand, they confiscated the gold discovered in Manchoukuo banks, and on the other they emitted large quantities of "Red Army notes." With that fiat currency, the Soviets purchased large quantities of commodities and property; the notes were left behind for redemption by the successor government. In addition, the Soviet authorities proposed that certain concessions be made by the Chinese with respect to Manchurian heavy industry and other enterprises as a condition of the take-over. On November 24, Soviet economic adviser Slatkovsky, in a communication delivered to the head of the Northeast Economic Commission, Chang Kiangau, proposed that there should be joint Sino-Soviet operation of 154 industrial and mining enterprises, comprising 80 percent of the heavy industry of Manchuria.[19]

In the absence of agreements with respect to (1) the withdrawal of U.S. forces from China and (2) a joint control of Manchurian industry as proposed by Moscow, February 1 passed without completion of Soviet troop evacuation from Manchuria. The Soviet explanation was that winter weather conditions had hampered troop movement, and that evacuation consequently would not be finished until March 1. The delay, which was doubtless coupled in the Chinese mind with the negotiations aimed at obtaining a share for the Soviet Union in exploitation of the Manchurian industrial establishment, evoked a Chinese propaganda move: "student demonstrations" were staged, first in Chungking and then in other urban centers, to demand that Soviet forces depart Manchuria. A week later, on February 26, Malinovski's chief of staff announced that the troop evacuation had been duly resumed on January 15, that most occupation forces had already departed, and that complete withdrawal was now to be accomplished without further delay. The Soviet embassy and the Chinese Foreign Ministry entered upon a new agreement providing that the Soviet forces would entirely withdraw from Manchuria by the end of April. The Soviet garrison force at Mukden in fact evacuated its position from March 9 to 12, and the Nationalists triumphantly occupied the town, the Northeast's industrial and communications center, on March 15.

Moscow made a final attempt to get Chinese agreement respecting the joint management of Manchurian industries. On March 27, Soviet Ambassador Aleksandr S. Panyushkin shifted the Soviet position, proposing the establishment of a Sino-Soviet joint-stock company, with ownership divided equally between China and the USSR, administered by a Chinese chairman and a Soviet vice chairman, to operate Manchurian industry. Chungking refused to discuss the proposal, holding that negotiations were impossible until the Soviet Union had retired its troops from Manchuria.

In March and April, the Soviet forces moved rapidly out of Chinese territory and back to their homeland. On May 3, Moscow announced that the movement had been completed. But the "victory" of the Nationalists was less than total: as the Soviet troops moved out, Chinese Communist forces entered into control of all of North Manchuria. So undisputed was the Communist advance that, when the Soviet forces evacuated Harbin, the Chinese Nationalist officials stationed there chose to accompany the retiring troops and returned to Nationalist territory via the Soviet Union. The Communist control now reached from the Amur south to the Sungari, midway between Changchun and Harbin.

Stalin offered Chiang Kai-shek a last opportunity to change his mind — and his policy. In May, the month the National government officially resumed functioning at Nanking after eight and a half years' absence, Stalin transmitted through Military Attaché Roshchin and Chiang Ching-kuo a renewed invitation to Chiang Kai-shek for a meeting. Chiang again rejected the invitation. He subsequently explained why:

> I felt that if I should accept the invitation the only road
> before us in diplomacy would be to follow the Russian
> Communists' consistent strategy toward China, i.e.,
> cooperation between Kuomintang and the Chinese
> Communist Party, the joint establishment of a coalition
> government and complete dependence on Soviet Russia.[20]

This suggests the hard reality: as confirmed by decisions reached in March by the KMT Central Executive Committee, the Nationalists under Chiang's leadership had committed themselves against broadening the base of government to include the Communists, in favor of relying upon a continuation of American aid for maintenance of the one-party dictatorship and destruction of the Communist armed power by force of arms. General Marshall in mid-January had succeeded in arranging a truce between the Nationalists and Communists. But the issue of peace or war between the two factions had centered in large measure on the matter of control of Manchuria, and even as the Soviet forces completed their evacuation of the area, in March and April, heavy fighting developed between the opposing Chinese forces for the control of key points. With the expiry of the truce on June 30, 1946, the civil war resumed in full fury. The only alien troops remaining in China at that time were the American and Japanese forces, and, insofar as involved at all, both were on the Nationalist side.

Chiang Ching-kuo had come under heavy criticism at the March KMT Central Executive Committee session for his handling of the Manchurian problem, and at the beginning of September he resigned his post as special commissioner for foreign affairs in the Northeast. No reason for the resignation was given. None was needed: Ching-kuo had fulfilled his mission vis-à-vis the Soviets to the utmost, and now, with Nanking's policy committed to alignment with the United States in opposition to the Soviet Union, there was nothing left for him to do in the diplomatic field. The future of Sino-Soviet relations would be determined by the outcome of the "third revolutionary civil war" between the Nationalists supported by the United States, and the Communists—who commanded sympathy, but no material support, from the Soviet Union.

26 REVOLUTIONARY CHANGE

THE COMMUNIST OFFENSIVE of May–June, 1947, in Manchuria won a major strategic victory and marked a turning of the tide in the Chinese civil war. The indications were that the Chinese Communist leadership, after having earlier anticipated a protracted war against the materially stronger Nationalists, now saw the possibility of victory within the visible future. In a directive issued on September 1, 1947, Mao Tse-tung laid down the strategy for the year ahead in a mandate for a nationwide counteroffensive.[1] Within the framework of the thinking set forth in his earlier doctrine "On Protracted War,"[2] the decision would have been based upon an estimate that the Communist forces now enjoyed strategic superiority over their enemy. Three weeks after Mao's command came down, the People's Liberation Army (PLA) launched a new, massive offensive in Manchuria, and a manifesto issued in the army's name on October 1 was essentially a call for a national uprising for overthrow of the Chiang Kai-shek regime.

It is to be assumed that Moscow's estimate of developments in China paralleled, to a degree, those of the CCP leadership. The thinking of Communist theoreticians at about that time took on broader dimensions. There was of course early Bolshevik precedent for this approach. Zinoviev at the Baku Congress of Peoples of the East in 1920 had envisaged a utopian development of international socialist solidarity. He held that, from the moment when one country (Russia) tore itself away from capitalism, "we can say that China, India, Turkey, Persia and Armenia can and must begin the struggle for a soviet construction." The workers of Europe would help, and "such countries can and must now prepare themselves for a soviet revolution . . . in order to create a Labor State and to form a close alliance with the organized workers of the whole world." Zinoviev expressed the belief that a great force was developing in the East, and that in the not distant future there would issue forth a movement which, uniting in a powerful Eastern International, together with the Western proletariat would "strike to the very heart of world capitalism." [3]

A lot of water had gone over the dam since 1920, in both Soviet Russia and the Far East. Yet, it was perhaps notable that Mao Tse-tung, in an interview granted the journalist Edgar Snow in 1936, had set forth the prerequisites for Japan's defeat as including the creation of an international united front against Japan and the emergence of a revolutionary movement in Japan and its colonies.[4] With the signature of the August, 1945, treaty between Moscow and the National government at Chungking, the Communist press had enthusiastically foreseen the future development of close Sino-Soviet collaboration.[5] From that time onward, there was apparent in China a strong desire of left-wing and middle-of-the-road elements for new and closer relations with the country's Soviet neighbor. Such a development was in line with one segment of Mao's concept of a decade earlier. Japan, however, had now in fact been defeated; by the theory, a new "enemy" was required.

The thinking of the Communist leadership, as it approached victory in the civil war, was given a distinctly aggressive outward expression in a number of important policy statements indicative of the CCP's probable future stance regarding foreign affairs. One such statement was CCP Information Department Chief Lu Ting-yi's "Explanation of Several Basic Questions Concerning the Postwar International Situation," as published at the beginning of 1947.[6] Lu held that the existing situation had in it two imperatives: (1) the anti-democratic ("imperialist") forces would of necessity attack; and (2) the democratic (Communist-led) forces would be victorious. "The struggle between the forces of democracy and anti-democracy will cover a greater part of the world. . . . Thus the actual dominant political contradiction in the world between democratic and anti-democratic forces is within the capitalist world and not between the Soviet Union and the

United States." That is, domestic revolution was the task. Then, after describing the United States as being in the process of becoming "a fortress of the world reactionary forces," Lu Ting-yi asserted that the duty of all in the democratic camp was "to call the people in America, in all capitalist, colonial and semi-colonial countries to fight for their own existence and to resist the attacks and aggressions of the American imperialists, their real enemies."

Lu Ting-yi envisaged the creation of a worldwide united front, which would comprise "well over one billion people," to be deployed against "American imperialism and reactionaries in all countries." Said Lu, "This world-wide united front will undoubtedly have the sympathy and moral support of the socialist Soviet Union." And he concluded on a confident note: "It may be forecast categorically that the face of China and the world will be vastly different after three to five more years. All comrades of our party and all people of China must resolutely fight for a new China and a new world."

The Lu Ting-yi formulation of 1947, in holding at one and the same time for wars of national liberation (that is, Communist-led national revolutions) and for the presentation of a world united front against the United States, with the USSR expected to manifest "sympathy and moral support," reflected both the current position of the Chinese Communists, still far short of victory in China and unable to offer any lead, and their revolutionary aspirations for the future. For the time being, the CCP leadership had to stand for international solidarity.

The Asian concept voiced by Lu Ting-yi had to be viewed against the background of postwar developments in Europe. There, the Moscow leadership had reverted in some degree to the revolutionary thinking and tactics of the Bolshevik chieftains of 1917–1920, this time with a larger measure of success. It had evidently been assumed in Moscow, during wartime, that victory over the Germans, combined with the devastating and dislocating effects of six years of total war, would induce, or at least make possible, revolutionary change – to the benefit of the USSR. The struggle over the future of Poland that began during wartime between the conservative (Anglo-American) and radical (Soviet) factions of the United Nations had by February, 1947, ended with the effective consolidation of a Communist regime in Warsaw. With even greater dispatch, Communist regimes, with Soviet influence dominant, had been established in Rumania, Bulgaria, and Hungary. Moscow applied heavy pressure against Turkey and Iran (ex-Persia) with the aim of achieving transfers of "lost territory" to the Soviet Union and, in the case of Turkey, to obtain agreement to the proposition that the Soviet Union and Turkey should share responsibility for the defense of the Dardanelles. Turkey and Iran stood firm, and Soviet expansionism was temporarily contained in that sector. But Greek Communists, supported from the outside — and in particular by Albania and Yugoslavia — had in 1946 begun a civil war with the acknowledged aim of overthrowing the monarchical regime that had returned to power in March.

There had been certain fundamental differences between the points of view entertained by Roosevelt and Churchill on the one hand and Stalin on the other even during wartime. The Soviet leadership could not forget the interventions of 1918–1920 and the maneuvers at the time of Munich; the Atlantic powers, for their part, had entered upon an alliance with the Soviet Union as a simple marriage of convenience, to stop Hitler and Tojo. It was therefore hardly to be expected that either (1) Stalin would be content to see a restoration of the status quo ante bellum, with the Soviet Union encircled by rehabilitated "democracies" in the Western pattern and under the Atlantic powers' aegis; or (2) the Anglo-American combine would be content to see an expansion of Moscow's "Communist" control. And the destruction of German and Japanese military might on the western and eastern flanks of Soviet Russia, relieving Moscow of the two main threats to Soviet national existence, had automatically facilitated Soviet expansionism.

It was thus in line with the basic long-term course of events that President Harry S Truman, speaking to a joint session of Congress in March, 1947, with reference to the situation in Greece and Turkey, requested authorization for an aid program for the threatened countries, saying that "it must be the policy of the United States to support free peoples who are resisting attempted subjugation by armed minorities or by outside pressures." The "Truman Doctrine" had come into being. In June, Secretary of State George C. Marshall launched the concept for economic aid to European countries that would shortly become a working "Marshall Plan," providing massive economic assistance for the purpose of combating tendencies toward radicalization of the European situation. The Cold War, envisaged by American political leaders as a war of "containment" that had to be waged against an aggressive "International Communism," had begun.

In September, 1947, the representatives of nine European Communist parties met at Wiliza Gora, in Poland, and there heard a major address by Andrei A. Zhdanov, member of the CPSU Politburo who, as Lu Ting-yi, acted as his party's watchdog over the ideology of the faithful, especially in the realm of literature. And just as Lu acted as the mouthpiece of Mao Tse-tung, so it could be assumed that Zhdanov voiced the thoughts of Stalin. On this occasion, Zhdanov addressed himself to politics, in what was quite obviously a critical formulation of Communist strategy.[7]

Zhdanov found that World War II had sharply changed the relationship between the two world systems, the capitalist and socialist, to the benefit of the socialist. The USSR, he held, had been the guiding force and spirit in the military defeat of Germany and Japan, and "The progressive forces of the whole world have united around the Soviet Union."[8] There had come into being a powerful upsurge of national-liberation movements in colonial and dependent countries, thus creating a threat to the rear of the capitalist systems; "The ruling classes of the metropoles can no longer as before control the colonies."[9] He said that the United States, the only surviving capitalist nation that had come out of World War II in a strengthened position, had now embarked upon a frankly expansionist course, having as aim the achievement of American imperialism's world supremacy. Alarmed at the successes of socialism in the USSR, at the progress of the new democracies, and at the democratic movement in all countries, in the postwar period, the United States was bent on assuming the role of savior of the capitalist system from Communism. The imperialist camp, he asserted, was undertaking preparations for a new war.

One of the prerequisites for the construction of Communism was external peace, Zhdanov went on, and the Soviet foreign policy was predicated upon coexistence of capitalism and socialism over a protracted period. "The Soviet Union has demonstrated its will and desire for collaboration."[10] But the projected "collaboration" was not without qualification. Since most of the leadership of European socialist parties was coming forward to act as agents for U.S. imperialist circles, Zhdanov said, "upon Communists falls the historic role of leading the resistance to the American plan for the enslavement of Europe."[11]

On October 5, it was announced simultaneously in various Communist capitals that the Warsaw meeting of September had decided to create a Communist Information Bureau (Cominform) "to organize the exchange of experiences" and "where necessary to coordinate the activities of the Communist parties on the basis of mutual agreement." The conference manifesto, broadcast that same day, was heavily redolent of the Zhdanov speech (made public only on October 22). The CCP was not a member party of the Cominform. Zhdanov barely mentioned China in his speech, and then only with reference to American support of the "reactionary" Nationalist military force. The European Communist thinking nevertheless neatly fit the Chinese Communist needs: the United States was the prime enemy, and "wars of liberation" were a device for combating that enemy.

The Zhdanov doctrine was couched in defensive terms, but the Soviet offensive against "hostile" elements on the Russian western flank continued, and the Beneš government in Czechoslovakia was overthrown by a Communist coup of February, 1948. Shortly afterward, however, the USSR met a setback in Yugoslavia, where it had endeavored to arrogate to itself the key powers usually enjoyed by a suzerain over its vassal. In that same February, Stalin had demanded that Yugoslavia federate with Bulgaria. As Tito put it, "we came to the conclusion that its [the proposal's] aim was the subjection of Yugoslavia. We therefore rejected it on the ground that actual conditions for federation were not yet ripe." [12] Four months later, the Cominform expelled Yugoslavia from the Communist bloc. It was in view of the totality of the Soviet-Yugoslav relationship from 1945 to 1948 that Tito, speaking in September, 1949, would charge that "The Soviet Union in its action towards our country has violated all the rights of small nations." That complaint was lodged against Moscow in particular, but something else he said in the same speech might have been given wider circulation:

> We are a small country, but we intend jealously to defend the independence of our foreign policy. . . . We wish our policy to be a warning to all the great Powers, whether of the east or the west, that the fate of small nations cannot be gambled with nor decided upon without the consent of the nations concerned. [13]

The following January, Moscow moved to establish a counterweight, *within* the Communist bloc, to the Organization of

European Economic Cooperation (OEEC), which had been formed by a number of western and southern European countries in connection with implementation of the Marshall Plan. There was organized a bloc Council for Mutual Economic Assistance (CMEA), with the proclaimed aim of coordinating and assisting the economic development of the member states, comprising (in the beginning) the Soviet Union, Poland, Czechoslovakia, Hungary, Bulgaria, and Rumania. The basic purpose underlying the formation of CMEA appeared to be a closer economic integration of the Eastern European countries with the Soviet Union—with the ultimate aim of furthering political integration as well.

The Communist leadership driving to power in China was thus being offered a wealth of illuminating examples in the field of foreign affairs. It can be assumed that they were filed for possible future reference. The two-camp-world concept was evidently early accepted by the Chinese Communist leadership—just as, in 1935, they had been prompt to adopt the united-front tactic formulated at the Seventh Comintern Congress. In April, 1949, when the North Atlantic Treaty Organization (NATO) was born to serve what the United States viewed as being the needs of the "free world" in waging the Cold War against "International Communism," Mao Tse-tung on behalf of the CCP joined with the representatives of nine "democratic" parties to warn that China would side with the USSR in the event of war. In his major policy statement of June 30, 1949, "On the People's Democratic Dictatorship," Mao confirmed that China would thenceforth "lean to one side," the side of the Soviet Union, for "Neutrality is mere camouflage and a third road does not exist." But he spoke mainly of the aid that China could not logically expect to receive from "capitalist" countries and therefore planned to get from the Soviet Union.

This overall reassessment by Chinese and Soviet leaders of the changing world situation in the period 1947–1949 was accompanied by a major change in Sinkiang. There, the Altai Kazakh Usman Bator, a born fighter, had in the spring of 1943 established contacts with the Mongolian People's Republic that brought him arms and a measure of encouragement for resistance against Sheng Shih-ts'ai's government at Urumchi. In June of that year, Usman led his people into open rebellion.

The Urumchi government endeavored to move large numbers of the rebellious Kazakhs from their ancestral home in the Altai region into southern Sinkiang. Facing that prospect, many

Kazakhs fled across the Sinkiang border into the Mongolian People's Republic, where they were given refuge. In March, 1944, Usman inflicted a heavy defeat on the Chinese forces in the field. Sheng had already charged publicly that a foreign power was aiding Usman's movement and now protested to the Soviet consulate general. The Soviets rejected Sheng's charge of intervention as "provocation"; and Tass at Ulan Bator on April 2 issued a fuller exposition of the matter in which it asserted that Chinese forces in pursuit of fleeing Kazakhs had crossed the Mongolian frontier —and had been expelled by MPR troops.

By the time Sheng departed the provincial scene in October of that year, the Kazakh rebellion had won (Sinkiang) Mongol converts and grown stronger. The Kazakh-Mongol actions influenced the Sarts of the Ili region, where there had already been organized a "Sinkiang Turki National Liberation Committee." On November 7, under the leadership of the Uighur Akhmedjan Kasimov, the Turki rebels launched an attack on Kuldja.

The rebel force took the town on January 31, 1945, and there was proclaimed the establishment of an "Eastern Turkestan Republic" headed by the Uzbek Ali Khan Türe as president. Usman had already reached agreement with the Ili group, and other dissident elements promptly joined the revolutionary movement. In July, the rebels occupied Chuguchak. They now controlled the whole of the Ili, Altai, and Tarbagatai regions, and turned to menace Urumchi. The "Ili rebellion" had taken on dimensions that threatened the Chinese rule in Sinkiang.

There were those Chinese who assumed that the uprising naturally had Soviet sympathy and support.[14] But if Soviet influence were there, it would logically have been exercised with extreme care at that juncture: the Sino-Soviet treaty, designed to incorporate the winnings of Yalta, was under negotiation at Moscow, and the USSR was preparing to enter the war against Japan. Again, as at the time of Ma Chung-ying's rebellion, the major Soviet interest would have counseled against gambling recklessly in sideshows. There was too much at stake on the center stage.

The signature of the Sino-Soviet treaty and accompanying agreements, in one of which Moscow professed a policy of noninterference in the internal affairs of China, brought about a temporary relaxation of the tensions afflicting Sinkiang. But the issue of local autonomy had not yet been settled. The new chairman, Wu Chung-hsin, proved unable to bring peace back to the troubled province. During the 1945 summer, White Russian émigrés and others joined the Ili rebellion. In early September, the rebel forces administered a severe defeat to the Nationalist Second Army. The Chungking government dispatched General Chang Chih-chung, recently appointed director of the generalissimo's Northwest headquarters at Lanchow, to Urumchi to deal with the deteriorating situation. General Chang went to what presumably was thought by the Nationalists to be the source of the trouble: on September 13, he informed the Soviet consul general that, unless hostilities immediately ceased, China would make an international issue of the matter.[15] This was implicitly a threat to evoke the interest of the United States in the developments, to exacerbate relations between that country and the USSR in the Asian sphere. Two days later, Moscow transmitted to Chungking a rebel request that the dispute be mediated, accompanied by an expression of Soviet willingness to act in such mediatory capacity.

Negotiations began at Urumchi on October 10, with Chang Chih-chung as chief negotiator for the Nationalist Chinese and Akhmedjan Kasimov heading a three-man mission from Ili. Soviet consular officials duly mediated. The talks centered on two main issues: (1) the composition of a new government for Sinkiang in which the non-Chinese peoples should be duly represented and (2) the future form of military organization for the province. As an essential preliminary move, the Ili group dropped the appellation "Eastern Turkestan Republic" for their domain.

On January 2, 1946, after prolonged bargaining, there was finally signed an agreement of "eleven points" that nominally guaranteed to the minority peoples of Sinkiang a considerable measure of cultural independence and an important share in the provincial government. Chiang Kai-shek reported on that agreement to a March 12 meeting of the KMT Central Executive Committee. He explicitly acknowledged that the Soviet Union had mediated the dispute and said that the resultant agreement provided for a large degree of autonomy for Sinkiang, within the framework of the Chinese Republic. It appeared as if the minority peoples of Sinkiang were at long last to be granted a substantial share in the government of their homeland. Chang Chih-chung replaced Wu Chung-hsin as provincial chairman and on June 6 reached a supplementary agreement providing for the de facto autonomy of the dissident Ili, Altai, and Chuguchak districts, and also for a proportional representation of those districts in a reorganized provincial government.

The government envisaged by the January agreement was inaugurated on July 1, 1946, with Chang Chih-chung formally assuming his post as provincial chairman. The two vice chairmen, as chosen by the popular groups, were the Tatar Burhan Shahidi and the Uighur Akhmedjan Kasimov. Masud Sabri, a wealthy Uighur who had since 1935 been a member of the KMT Central Executive Committee and had long been associated with the reactionary C–C Clique,* was given the post of supervisory commissioner for Sinkiang. A Soviet source would later charge that Masud Sabri was a Pan-Turanian who had long served, seriatim, the intelligence services of Germany, Britain, Japan, and the United States.[16] Turki leaders, Kazakhs, Tatars, Mongols, Dungans, and Chinese received other appointments in the new government at Urumchi.

In May, 1947, Chang Chih-chung resigned the post of provincial chairman, and was succeeded by Masud Sabri the C–C man. Masud organized a new government at Urumchi at the end of the month, and C–C policies were given fuller rein. Outraged at the open flouting of their nationalistic aspirations in disregard of the commitments earlier assumed, Akhmedjan Kasimov and his followers first formally protested the changed orientation. This move being fruitless, the Ili group in July once more went into open revolt against the Chinese authority, and in August, 1947, the "coalition" government at Urumchi fell apart. Chang Chih-chung remained in Urumchi to assist Masud, for the time being, in the arduous task of government.

Early in June, a clash had occurred on Sinkiang's border with the Mongolian People's Republic. The *China News Agency* duly reported that, on June 5, a Mongolian force in regimental strength supported by four planes marked with the Soviet red star had begun an invasion of Sinkiang in the vicinity of Peitashan. The National government, through its ambassador at Moscow, protested to the Soviet Union against the invasion. The Moscow radio broadcast a Tass denial that Soviet planes had been in-

---

* A KMT faction so named for the powerful, conservative brothers who led and dominated it, KMT organization chief Ch'en Kuo-fu and Minister of Education Ch'en Li-fu.

volved in the military action, and this was followed by a denial by Ulan Bator that Mongolian troops had attacked Sinkiang; on the contrary, said Ulan Bator, Peitashan was in MPR territory and the Chinese had done the attacking, thus causing the border incident. Those initial broadcast responses were followed by a formal Soviet note delivered to the National government at Nanking suggesting that an aggravation of the conflict might call into operation the Soviet-Mongol mutual-defense treaty of 1936. Minister of Information Hollington Tong on June 18 announced that the situation had quieted down.

The Mongol version of developments appears to have been closer to the facts than was the Chinese. Usman Bator had broken away from the Ili insurgent group in April and lost most of his following. General Sung Hsi-lien, the Nanking commander in chief in Sinkiang, thereupon enlisted the rebel on the Nationalist side. Usman and his force of half a hundred men participated in the Nationalist strike against an MPR frontier post, and the attackers overran the Mongolian position, killing the officer in command. But the initial success was due to exploitation of the surprise factor against a weak military position. The Mongols threw cavalry and planes against the invaders, and the Nationalist-Usman force was thrust out of the border region. The Mongols were thus left in possession of the territory they claimed — and it was then that the Chinese side took their complaint to the world airwaves. Maps going back as far as 1920, including the official Chinese Postal Map, indicate that the boundary in the Peitashan area was far from being clearly defined. But the so-called "Peitashan Incident" rested, a clear victory for the Mongolian People's Republic.

The Peitashan Incident was only a temporary diversion from the main business at hand. After the Ili delegation departed Urumchi with the quite evident intent of never returning, Chang Chih-chung went through the motions of striving for reconciliation. In a letter of September 1, 1947, addressed to Akhmedjan Kasimov at Ili,[17] Chang remarked the circumstance that talk in the Ining (Kuldja) area was often of "running dogs of the Hans" and "reactionary elements." He presumed that such language must be based upon the premise that those supporting the Hans were reactionary while those in opposition were revolutionary, that those friendly to the Soviets and opposing the Hans were revolutionary also, whereas those friendly to the Hans and opposing the Soviets were "reactionary elements." Chang said that if this was in fact the significance of the usage, it was in grave error, because China was "your [the Turki] fatherland," while the Soviet Union was for China a "friendly country." Chang added that the Turki phraseology was not susceptible of logical explanation; but if the Turki idea was that Sinkiang was not China's, then there was nothing to be said.

Akhmedjan Kasimov and Rahim-jan Sabir-hadji, in behalf of the Ili group, replied (lengthily) to Chang's letter only in mid-October. Their letter revealed the vast chasm that yawned between the Chinese rulers and their Turki subjects, and it seems to have elicited no immediate response from the Chinese side. Chang Chih-chung at last left Urumchi to return to Nanking. Failing any resolution of the issue of government, the situation remained stalemated, with the Ili regime lacking military strength to challenge the provincial forces, and the Chinese, given particularly the deteriorating military situation in China Proper, in no position to embark on an all-out campaign to suppress the rebellion. On December 31, 1948, Burhan Shahidi succeeded Masud Sabri as Sinkiang provincial chairman. But by this time Nationalist power over China as a whole was in collapse.

In January, 1949, to the accompaniment of the staggering Nationalist defeats on the battlefield and the retirement of Chiang Kai-shek from his position as head of the Chinese state, Chang Chih-chung returned to Urumchi to participate in negotiations with the Soviet side for a new agreement to replace the ten-year treaty signed by Sheng Shih-ts'ai in 1939 governing Sino-Soviet economic collaboration in Sinkiang. The advantage to the Soviets of having a new agreement to replace the old was obvious: Moscow could confront any successor regime with a valid document that would at least have to be taken into consideration in the working out of any new Sino-Soviet relationship. But the Nationalists, standing at the very eve of the expiry of their Mandate of Heaven, clearly could derive no advantage whatsoever from entering now upon treaty negotiations with the power whose approaches Chiang Kai-shek had spurned a short three years before. After several sessions with the Soviet negotiators, Chang Chih-chung returned to Lanchow. In May, Nanking and Moscow agreed on a five-year extension of Soviet rights to operate the airline between Urumchi and Alma-Ata, but nothing more was achieved in the months when the Nationalist regime was crumbling.

By July, General P'eng Teh-huai's Communist army stood at the gates of Sinkiang. In August, an imposing delegation of Turki leaders, led by Akhmedjan Kasimov, left Ili to participate in the proceedings of the national conference engaged in organization of a new government and to make the voice of Sinkiang's minorities heard in Peking, China's new capital. The whole group on August 27 was killed in a reputed plane crash — which, oddly, went unreported for several weeks. With the leading spokesmen for Turki nationalism dead, the function of representing the Turki peoples of Chinese Turkestan passed to one Uighur leader who happened not to be on the plane, Saifudin Azizov, and, more or less automatically, to Burhan. As, effectively, the sole survivor of the Ili regime's leadership, Saifudin was isolated politically; power flowed naturally into the hands of Burhan. Saifudin attended the Chinese People's Political Consultative Conference as representative of the Ili group — and now spoke with the voice of *Chinese* nationalism. The Ili revolt, by the new (Communist) interpretation, had not been at all an effort of the Turki peoples to achieve independence of Chinese rule, but instead was a social antifeudal movement directed against the corrupt KMT regime. On September 29, the 80,000 Nationalist troops in Sinkiang turned over to the Communist side. Burhan had proved the instrumentality.

On October 1, the new Communist regime was inaugurated at Peking (Peiping); its political authority had already been confirmed in Sinkiang. PLA units entered the province on October 20. With their leaders dead or in the Chinese Communist camp, and Burhan working for the consolidation of Communist control over the province, the power of the Turki dissidents was broken. Chang Chih-chung in late November accompanied Communist military leader P'eng Teh'huai back to Urumchi and on that occasion made a speech asking rhetorically if the Kuomintang had not deserved defeat and sketching a glorious future in which, after having passed through the stages of (Mao Tse-tung's) New Democracy, socialism, and communism, humanity would be found in a state of world universalism (*shih-chieh ta-t'ung*).

The Ili rebellion was over. Sinkiang, given the new protestations of friendship between Peking and Moscow, had no friendly power to which it might turn for sympathy and aid, and had to be viewed as solidly in the Chinese political embrace. On December 18, 1949, Peking announced the establishment of a new political regime at Urumchi. Burhan Shahidi and Saifudin Azizov were respectively chairman and vice chairman of the civil administration, while P'eng Teh-huai and Chang Chih-chung were put in command of the Urumchi headquarters of the Sinkiang military establishment. Usman Bator, who had once more taken up the banner of revolt against the Hans, was hunted down, captured, and executed.

The Chinese Communist power in Sinkiang was now consolidated beyond possibility of effective challenge from the Turki nationalists. Once more, the factionalism and political infighting of the Turki, Kazakh, and Mongol peoples of Sinkiang had critically weakened their campaign for independence from China. All outward appearances suggested that the opportunity would probably never come again. Yet, Yang Tseng-hsin had warned that "The history of several thousands of years can repeat itself." Besides, across the frontier demarcated between the expanding Chinese and Russian empires only in the nineteenth century, there resided the blood brothers of the peoples of Sinkiang, and also another and different type of Communist rule — the Soviet Russian. To the new rulers of China, history and contemporary circumstances alike dictated the desirability of amalgamating Sinkiang more solidly than before with the body of China, as Manchuria had been welded to the Eighteen Provinces a half century earlier, through political, economic, and ethnic measures.

27 MID-CENTURY:
NEW DIRECTIONS

IN THE LAST DAYS of Nanking, the Nationalists undertook two final significant maneuvers with respect to the Soviet
Union. One move was made by Generalissimo Chiang Kai-shek.
Facing military defeat, Chiang in his New Year's message of January 1, 1949, asserted that, "Being a strong believer in the Three
People's Principles and abiding by Dr. Sun's bequeathed teaching, I did not have any intention to fight the Communists at the
end of the war." [1] And when the National government on January
8 appealed for foreign mediators in its dispute with the Communists, it sent its request to Moscow as well as to London, Paris,
and Washington. The Soviet government's reply of January 17,
not surprisingly, as the American and British replies of two days
earlier, offered no helping hand.

A second move originated in another Nationalist sector.
Chiang Kai-shek retired from the presidency of China on January
21, 1949. His successor to the post, Vice President Li Tsung-jen,
seemingly even before that date had established contact with the
Soviet embassy at Nanking, and on January 23 a representative
of General Li called on the American embassy to report that the
Chinese and Soviet sides had reached a tentative three-point
agreement, which the Soviet ambassador had taken with him on
departing for Moscow a few days earlier. The agreement provided
for: (1) China's strict neutrality in any future international conflict, (2) the elimination to the greatest extent possible of Ameri-

can influence from China, and (3) the establishment of a basis for effective cooperation between China and the USSR. General Li's representative requested a public statement of American support for his superior's position, saying that Li felt that such a statement would strengthen his hand in negotiations regarding the details of the agreement that had been reached in principle. The American ambassador duly transmitted the message to Washington, and an obviously shocked State Department promptly replied that it considered it "incredible that Li Tsung-jen should seek a United States statement indicating support for the purpose of strengthening his position while at the same time arranging a tentative agreement with Russia calling for the elimination of American influence from China." [2] The ambassador was instructed to convey the Department's views to General Li.

A new deal between Nanking and Moscow was not to be. Li's government, undercut by Chiang's political maneuvering and unbefriended, was forced to abandon the capital in April before the menace of a Communist advance across the Yangtze. It fled first to Canton, then to Chungking, and on to Chengtu. The National government finally abandoned the Szechwan capital for Formosa in December, and Kuomintang rule on the mainland came to an end. The Soviet proposition of the previous January, presumably predicated upon an assumption that Li might either reach a political compromise with the Communists (and contacts had already been established for negotiations) or that he might succeed in holding South China, therefore never bore fruit. When the Communists set up their government in Peking on October 1, 1949, Moscow promptly, the next day, extended formal recognition to the new regime. The rest of the Communist camp, including the Mongolian People's Republic, quickly followed suit. A new era in Sino-Russian relations began.

Russian Asia was at this time in a vastly stronger position than when the beleaguered Bolsheviki had sued for China's attention in the 1917–1924 period. In World War II, as contrasted with World War I, the Soviet Union was a victor nation. As a member of the winning coalition, it had recovered not only positions lost in the Russo-Japanese War of forty years before, but also got the return of the Kurile chain ceded to Japan in 1875. The Sea of Okhotsk was consequently transformed into a Soviet lake. The Soviet position vis-à-vis the United States in the North

Pacific thus was stronger, in terms of simple geography, than at any time since the sale of Alaska in 1867.

Soviet Asia is richly endowed with natural resources. Siberia is wealthy not only in the furs and gold sought by the first generations of Russian adventurers, but also in terms of huge deposits of coal and iron ore — the very bones of an industrial society.[3] Further, Siberia possesses a tremendous potential for hydroelectric power.

The Soviets had early undertaken the exploitation of their vast resources in the East. By 1941, when the USSR was thrown headlong into World War II, the Ural industrial bases were already contributing substantially to the Soviet heavy industrial output. With the German advance into the Donbas, the Soviets lost much of their European production. But they did not lose all of the physical plant itself: insofar as possible, elements of threatened industrial plants were removed to the Urals and reinstalled there.

In actuality, all Siberia was strengthened economically as a result of the blows dealt Soviet Russia on the western front. Where in prewar times Siberia had not been self-sufficient even with regard to grain, now the loss of much of European Russia's grain land made it necessary that Siberia feed itself, or starve. Since large quantities of American Lend-Lease goods were shipped to the USSR via the Pacific Ocean and Vladivostok, the double-tracking of the Trans-Siberian Railway was completed, to meet the inexorable demands on its carrying capacity. Airfields were built, and airlines developed, to supplement the long and tenuous rail line to Moscow. Increased pressure was put on the Pacific Coast fisheries to augment the supply of salmon and other fish, for benefit of the scanty Soviet food supply. Petroleum production was pushed on Sakhalin, towns like Komsomolsk were erected with backbreaking effort, and the Irkutsk area underwent considerable development as a protected base for any Far Eastern warfare. Through the Arctic Ocean, every summer, more and more convoys of ships made the difficult passage, to lighten the load on the railway and to strengthen the Soviet Arctic economy as well.

In sum, intent and events had by 1950 combined to introduce a new balance into the Soviet economy: the center of gravity was notably farther to the east than in tsarist times. The former concentration of heavy industry in the Donbas, and of light industry at various points in western European Russia, had given way. There had been a shift of plant and power to the iron of Magnitogorsk in the Urals, to the coal of the Kuzbas 1,300 miles to the east, to the enterprises of Omsk and Novosibirsk and Irkutsk, and much farther—right on to the Soviet Far East itself. In the heart of Asia, a powerful heavy industry was being constructed. There had been tremendous losses in both industrial power and manpower in European Russia, and the cost of course had to be counted on a national scale, but Asiatic Russia, overall, was now both relatively and absolutely stronger than before.[4] The Soviet Union thus ranked, in mid-century, as an Asiatic great power.

In 1947 Zhdanov had pointed up the circumstance that the world balance of power had radically changed as a result of World War II: of the six so-called great imperialist powers, he said, Germany, Italy, and Japan had suffered military defeat, and France had been so weakened that it had lost its position as a great power. That left only Britain and the United States in the field—and the position of Britain had been undermined. The United States, he said, now aimed at taking over the world markets not only of ex-enemies but also of wartime allies. And the "imperialist" world was threatened besides by the upsurge of national-liberation movements in the colonial and dependent countries.[5]

In the five years from the end of World War II to mid-century, there had indeed been tremendous changes in the power structure of the Far East. Japan had been destroyed as an empire and returned to the four islands it occupied a century before; its navy had been sunk, army disbanded, war-making capacity eliminated —and, at American insistence, by its new constitution it undertook a commitment never again to arm or to make war. In 1947, Britain abandoned its imperial sway over India and Burma, and they became independent. Similarly, the Dutch were forced out of the Netherlands East Indies. The United States had played an important role, during wartime and after, in committing the British and Dutch to such withdrawal of imperial power. And at this beginning of Asia's postimperial era, the United States, at long last, gave freedom to its own East Asian colony, the Philippines.

One development along the lines forecast by Zhdanov seemed already to be taking place: in the Philippines, Indonesia, Burma, and Malaya, Communist-led insurrections were in course, with the aim of overthrowing the "bourgeois nationalist" governments that had come into being upon the withdrawal of colonial power. In an even more aggravated form, a major war was being waged in Indo-China between the French and the Vietnamese nationalists led by the Communist Vietminh. The United States, earlier eager to have the French renounce their rights of empire in Indo-China, in 1950 began to lend aid in money and arms to the French colonialists, to help them to stay. American "anti-Communism" now took precedence over the earlier traditional American "anti-colonialism."

Zhdanov had pointed up the USSR's concern with the American anti-Communism; in a sense, Mao Tse-tung had done the same on China's behalf. Both countries were concerned, however, with major domestic problems as well as foreign-policy issues. Unlike the United States, both were faced with tremendous tasks of economic rehabilitation, for repair of the ravages of war. China's was the more difficult position: it had suffered less material war damage by far than the Soviet Union, but it was in any event an underdeveloped country and still confronted the fundamental task of economic construction sketched a generation earlier by Sun Yat-sen. The issue was how the two countries, jointly or severally, would fix their national priorities.

The men in Peking were indeed to be viewed as Communists — but first as Chinese. The Chinese Communist Party, a member of the Comintern until the demise of the international Communist organization in 1943, had in the past been consistently loyal to Moscow's foreign-policy line; not being in power, it could well afford orthodoxy — and could *not* afford to act counter to the wishes of the one country that might show sympathy and, upon occasion, offer material support. As Mao Tse-tung and his cohorts approached power in China, however, they were confronted by various hard issues of practical foreign policy. What should be the approach of the Chinese People's Republic to the world of the twentieth century? It was to be anticipated that, upon occasion, the "Chineseness" of the new rulers of the Middle Kingdom might well show through the veneer of Marxism-Leninism that was supposed to be their faith.

In November, 1949, the new Chinese regime's concepts of the world revolutionary struggle were given concrete formulation. Communist theorist Liu Shao-ch'i, speaking to the opening session of the Australasian Trade Unions Conference at Peking, asserted that "the people's fighters for liberation" in Indo-China, Burma, India, Malaya, and the Philippines were acting entirely correctly: it was only through victory in the struggle for liberation and by explusion of imperialism that those several countries could achieve a basic solution of the problem of living standards. Liu laid down four revolutionary procedures for use in such countries, and they amounted to a declaration of revolutionary warfare to be waged until the Communist order was established throughout Asia. For that was the underlying significance of Liu's including, in the year 1949, India, the Philippines, and Burma in the same category as Indo-China and Malaya.

Mao Tse-tung, as Lenin, gave first priority to political matters, and only second place to economic affairs. Liu's address was focused on the need, and desirability, for revolution, not on the tasks of national economic reconstruction. The emphasis in Zhdanov's talk of 1947, contrariwise, had been at least outwardly on the need for peace, and defensive measures; the wounds suffered by the USSR in the devastating war against Germany required close attention for healing. Zhdanov had been primarily concerned with the confrontation between his country and the United States, and it could in all logic be assumed that Stalin proposed no wars of adventure for the Soviet Union. Chinese theoretician Lu Ting-yi on the other hand had in 1947 considered that the chief "contradiction" was that between democratic and antidemocratic forces *within* the capitalist world. His doctrine proposed the export of revolution.

The CCP's world outlook at this juncture had to be viewed in the light of China's history. As had all Chinese nationalists of the Republican period, the CCP chieftains desired first and foremost to achieve the restoration of China to its traditional position of preeminence in Asia. They wanted to have China's frontiers include all territory won by the conquering *Manchus,* not simply that ruled by the regressive Ming Chinese. No Chinese leader in modern times has been prepared to accept as legal and final any past transfer of territory that has been to China's *detriment;* the reverse operation is entirely acceptable.

Chiang Kai-shek was one such Chinese who thought in terms of restoration of China's imperial boundaries; [6] Mao Tse-tung was another. The Communists in the beginning, as the Kuomintang in its salad days, had voiced liberal sentiments regarding the right of China's minority peoples to "self-determination." As the party came closer to power, however, it increasingly manifested an inner urge toward the "Great Han chauvinism" that assumed an inherent right of the Chinese to rule over all peoples who once had been brought into the empire by the Manchus. Even in 1936, Mao Tse-tung, in an interview with Edgar Snow, said that "When the people's revolution has been victorious in China the Outer Mongolian republic will automatically become a part of the Chinese federation, at their own will." [7] Mao, the author of the philosophic concept "On Contradiction," seemingly saw no contradiction in his thought that the Outer Mongols, "at their own will," would "automatically" become a part of the Chinese Communist federated republic.

Mao Tse-tung would thus contemplate liaison with the Eurasian land power against the dominant sea and air power with clear geopolitical purpose in mind and China's national interests in full view. Economic factors might temporarily occupy the foreground, but in the ultimate analysis political and military factors would consistently be given priority over the economic. Moreover, regardless of the verbiage, national aggrandizement would occupy a firm position in the minds of the new Chinese leadership.

Even before the establishment of formal diplomatic relations between Moscow and Peking, a solid beginning had been made in the development of economic ties between the Soviet Union and the Communist power in China. After the military victories of 1948 gave the Chinese Communists possession of important urban and industrial centers, particularly in Manchuria, Mao Tse-tung appealed to the Soviet Union for trained technicians and engineers. In response, "A big group of Soviet specialists went to China and helped Mao Tse-tung to sort out the economic chaos, and submitted necessary recommendations." [8] "Under the influence of Soviet specialists," the second plenum of the CCP central committee in March, 1949, proceeded to formulate a national economic policy based upon a conservative general line, namely: "During a more or less long period of time to implement gradually the socialist industrialization of the country and to carry out gradually the socialist remaking of agriculture, of cottage industry, of capitalist industry and commerce." [9]

In July, 1949, a Manchurian delegation headed by Kao Kang went to Moscow, and on July 31 the Soviet press announced the conclusion of a barter agreement to govern exchanges of goods between the USSR and Manchuria.[10] It was only on August 27 that there was organized, at Mukden, a Northeastern People's Government (NEPG) with Kao Kang at its head. The Soviet Union's economic collaboration with the new "people's authority" in China thus had already begun before the establishment of the Central People's Government at Peking on October 1 and the beginning of formal diplomatic relations with the arrival, in early October, of the new Soviet ambassador, sometime military attaché N. V. Roshchin.

It was therefore in line with the revolutionary concept envisaging the extension of massive aid by the more advanced socialist countries to backward revolutionary nations, and in accord with tendencies toward closer union that were viewed as entirely logical (if not quite foreordained), that Mao Tse-tung made his first journey abroad, to Moscow. Accompanied by aides and Ambassador Roshchin, he arrived in the Soviet capital on December 16. China's new premier, Chou En-lai, joined him there on January 20. Chou was accompanied by important personalities from the economic field, with the Manchurian interest well represented. Among those present were NEPG Vice Chairman Li Fu-ch'un, Vice Minister of Industry Lü Tung, and Vice Minister of Trade Chang Hua-tung. Peking Minister of Trade Yeh Chi-chuang and Eastern Europe section chief Wu Hsiu-ch'uan, both of whom had earlier occupied posts in Manchuria, were also in the party.

Mao Tse-tung in December, 1949, was already bound by certain commitments. He was openly pledged to a pro-Soviet policy, and from 1946 onward the Chinese Communists had burned various international bridges behind them. He was engaged further by Communist theory regarding the Asian revolution. Those ideological ties had led inevitably to full acceptance of the Sino-Soviet agreements of August, 1945, by the CCP, and if the Soviets would have blushed to ask their brother Communists for like concessions in the first instance, they could enter upon a conference with Mao in 1949 with equanimity, having the goods in hand as "treaty rights." Finally, Mao Tse-tung was committed by his canny nature to adherence to his own advice always to guide actions according to objective conditions: "ideas, if not based on and not in keeping with objective facts, are merely fancies, falsehood, and they will lead to failure if they are carried out." [11] If to Mao's intellectual position and political orientation there be added the hard objective facts of the situation then existing in

East Asia, it will be appreciated that Mao and his party did not make their pilgrimage in the capacity of fully free agents.

Few will ever know whether, as rumored in Peking at the time, Mao Tse-tung made the trip in question only reluctantly. It is conceivable that the Chinese Communist leaders, who for more than twenty years had borne a hard and dangerous existence, might have experienced some twinge of inner longing for some respite, a little breathing spell, before undertaking new responsibilities in the international field in addition to those confronting them at home. Still, it was clear enough that only by attacking certain foreign problems could some of China's domestic tasks be accomplished, and it seems probable that there was no important hesitation on the part of either Mao or any of his hard-fibered lieutenants: they went because they knew they must, in accordance with Communist compulsions.

After Mao Tse-tung had left, but before the departure of Chou En-lai from Peking, the Communists burned another bridge behind themselves — or, perhaps, it was burned behind Mao in particular. There had been some early speculation regarding possible American recognition of the new government that had come to power in China. Washington in the end had held back, in obedience to the axiomatic injunction "Let the dust settle," and on January 6 the Peking Military Control Commission in defiance of pertinent treaty provisions took the first steps toward "requisitioning" the former military barracks of the official American, British, French, and Dutch establishments in Peking. The American barracks had been converted into the consulate general, so the Chinese proposed in effect to confiscate the United States consular establishment — undoubtedly, with malice aforethought. They in fact consummated the act of confiscation on January 14, and the United States consequently withdrew all diplomatic and consular personnel from China.

It is permissible tentatively to put forward the hypothetical proposition that, just as some political strategist in the Li Tsung-jen camp a year earlier had been prepared to undertake to eliminate American influence in China in return for close Sino-Soviet collaboration, so there was quite possibly a faction in the CCP leadership that thought it politically astute further to alienate the United States while Mao Tse-tung was negotiating in Moscow in order thus (1) to give the Soviet leadership clear evidence of

Peking's bona fides and (2) to isolate Communist China so defini-
tively from the old American relationship that there would
remain no chance of its restitution in changed form. Mao Tse-
tung had said, six months before, that one was either in the camp
of the socialist countries or in the imperialist camp; he now was in
the socialist camp, willy-nilly.

The action taken against the American position in China was
in contravention of a basic tenet of Chinese international political tactics: "use barbarians to control barbarians." The estrangement of China from the United States at that juncture could have
had only one result for the position of Mao and his fellow negotiators in Moscow: their bargaining position was weakened, for
they clearly had nowhere else to turn for great-power support.
Given the extent of China's needs — and desires — this was a serious political handicap in negotiating the terms of the new Sino-
Soviet relationship.

Mao's aspirations with respect to Soviet aid, while perhaps
not on the exaggerated scale of Sun Yat-sen's proposal that the
victorious powers assembled in the Paris Peace Conference of
1919 supply $20 billion in credits to China for its economic mod-
ernization, in all probability were substantial. One source states
that Mao had figured China's needs as being in the order of U.S.-
$2 billion to $3 billion.[12] If his philosophy (voiced by his lieutenants as well as by himself) is any guide, Mao would also
have desired that, with regard to world affairs, China should be
a full partner in the revolutionary Communist enterprise — except
in terms of responsibilities, for there it could argue that it was the
weaker, whereas the Soviet Union was the stronger and thus
should assume the greater burden.

The negotiations were long and patently difficult, reflecting
the vast gap between Mao Tse-tung's demands and the degree of
Soviet willingness to act as both shield bearer and rich Communist uncle to indigent China. The attitude of Stalin, given his
long experience with China, can only have been reserved. Borodin
had warned, after his return to Moscow in 1927, "When the next
Chinese General comes to Moscow and shouts, 'Hail to the World
Revolution,' better send at once for the G.P.U. (state police). All
that any of them want is rifles."[13] Was there any real assurance
that Mao Tse-tung would prove, in the end, any less self-serving,
any less Chinese, than Chiang Kai-shek, Feng Yü-hsiang, and
Sheng Shih-ts'ai? And regardless of Mao Tse-tung's personal

bona fides, could nationalism be counted so outworn a force that Soviet Russia would assuredly suffer no strategic disadvantage from assisting in the development of a powerful China on its flank?

One could see the conflict of national interests reflected in the agreements signed on February 14, 1950, which: (1) confirmed the main concessions formulated at Yalta and incorporated into the accords signed by the Nationalists in 1945, (2) extended the scope of previous arrangements to bring about what was essentially a restoration of the close Sino-Soviet collaboration existing in Sinkiang from 1934 to 1942 under the regime of Sheng Shih-ts'ai, (3) created an effective Peking-Moscow axis possessing military, political, and economic aspects, with Manchuria as the fulcrum for Northeast Asia, and (4) concurrently and consequently increased the liaison of China with the USSR — and correspondingly removed China farther from the orbit of possible attraction to Occidental powers. An outstanding feature of the official American reaction to developments was the evident assumption that China, as the Eastern European states, had simply become a satellite of the Soviet Union, in a further extension of the domain of International Communism as controlled by Moscow.[14]

The main instrument agreed upon that day was a thirty-year Treaty of Friendship, Alliance, and Mutual Assistance between the People's Republic of China and the USSR, as signed by Chou En-lai for China and Andrei Ya. Vyshinsky for the Soviet Union.[15] The treaty was accompanied by an exchange of notes agreeing to the invalidation of the Sino-Soviet treaty of August 14, 1945. The new agreement, as the earlier one, provided for a joint defensive stance against Japan, but with significant change in wording: by Article I, the signatories undertook jointly "to adopt all necessary measures at their disposal for the purpose of preventing the resumption of aggression and violation of peace on the part of Japan *or any other state that may collaborate with Japan directly or indirectly in acts of aggression*" (emphasis added). Given the American occupation of Japan at the time of signature, the most obvious "any other state" was logically the United States. A further provision of the same article committed each signatory to render immediate military and other aid "by all means at its disposal" in the event of an attack by Japan "or any state allied with her." But it was notable that the wording of the treaty focused on Japan and any ally, and inferentially on actions within that alliance, and was therefore limited in geographical scope: it would not function automatically, that is, in the event of hostilities with the United States arising out of a situation in some other sector of the Asian periphery.

The treaty expressed the readiness of the two contracting parties to participate in sincere cooperation with "all international actions aimed at ensuring peace and security throughout the world," and opted for early conclusion of a peace treaty with Japan "jointly with the other powers which were allies in the Second World War." Each party committed itself not to conclude an alliance directed against the other signatory nation or to participate in any coalition or actions or measures aimed at the co-signatory. They agreed, by Article IV, to "consult with each other in regard to all important international problems affecting the common interests of China and the Soviet Union." And Article V provided that China and the Soviet Union, with due respect for the principles of equality, mutual benefit, mutual respect for each other's sovereignty and territorial integrity, and noninterference in the other's internal affairs, should render to each other "all possible economic assistance, and carry out necessary economic cooperation."

A second agreement of the same date provided for the transfer by the USSR to China, without compensation, of all Soviet rights in the joint administration of the Chinese Changchun Railway, together with all property belonging to the railway, immediately upon the conclusion of a peace treaty with Japan, "but not later than the end of 1952." Soviet armed forces were to withdraw from the jointly utilized naval base of Port Arthur within the same time schedule, but with the Chinese government this time charged with compensating the USSR for expenses incurred in restoration and construction of installations since 1945. There was a qualification here: should either state become involved in hostilities as a result of aggression committed against it by Japan "or any state that may collaborate with Japan," by the proposal of the Chinese government and agreement of the Soviet government the two states might again jointly use the naval base for the conduct of "joint military operations against the aggressor." A final article of the same agreement provided that the matter of the port of Dairen should be given further consideration upon conclusion of a peace treaty with Japan; in the meantime, however, all property in Dairen "now temporarily administered by or leased to the Soviet Union" should be transferred to the Chinese government.

A third agreement of February 14 demonstrated that Moscow's generosity, even to the Chinese who purported to be the most revolutionary of all Chinese "revolutionaries" who had gone to Moscow in search of material aid, had rather narrow limits: it provided for a Soviet credit of U.S.$300 million, expendable in equal portions of one fifth annually over a period of five years from January 1, 1950, and repayable with 1 percent interest in ten annual installments beginning "not later than" December 31, 1954, and ending December 31, 1963. The credits would be used for payment of Soviet deliveries of equipment and materials and repayments would be in the form of "raw materials, tea, gold, American dollars." [16]

On the eve of his departure for home, Mao Tse-tung forecast a bright and fruitful future for the alliance:

> All see that the solidarity of the great Chinese and
> Soviet peoples, consolidated by the Treaty, is durable,
> unbreakable, and steadfast. This solidarity will
> inevitably influence not only the well-being of the great
> powers China and the Soviet Union, but also the future
> of all humanity and will lead to the victory of justice
> and peace throughout the whole world.[17]

Mao the political figure thus left the Moscow scene, but economists and others remained behind, and representatives from Sinkiang now joined the negotiating party. The talks with the Soviets resulted in the signature of three new agreements on March 27. Two thirty-year accords provided for the resumption and further development of the Sinkiang-USSR arrangements that had been effective under Sheng Shih-ts'ai until 1942 for the exploitation by Sino-Soviet joint-stock companies of, first, petroleum, and, second, nonferrous and rare metals in Sinkiang.[18] The third agreement provided for the establishment of another such joint-stock company to operate civilian airlines, for ten years, over three routes between the two countries: Peking-Chita, Peking-Irkutsk, and Peking–Alma-Ata. This was again in the pattern of the service that had functioned, until the 1942 rupture, between Alma-Ata and points in Sinkiang. And finally, on April 19, 1950, three more accords were signed. One was a protocol to govern the delivery of Soviet goods to China in 1950–1952 in service of the credit agreement of February 14, a second comprised a regular Sino-Soviet trade agreement, and a protocol for the exchange of goods in 1950 made up the third.

By outward evidence, a Sino-Soviet axis had come into being. It was, however, to be remarked that, whereas East Germany and Albania became members of the Council for Mutual Economic Assistance in 1950, China remained outside that bloc economic organization. This circumstance probably reflected as much Moscow's estimate that China as an underdeveloped country would be difficult to incorporate into a system based upon economic reciprocity (to a degree), as any current Chinese desire to maintain its economic independence.

1. Cossack chieftain Yermak's conquest of Sibir began Russian expansion east of the Urals

2. Emperor K'ang-hsi, apprehensive of Mongol power in Central Asia, signed a treaty with Russia in 1689

3. Peter the Great, near the end of his reign, began an eastward thrust, warring against Persia

4. The Manchu siege of the Russian position at Albazin induced negotiations resulting in signature of the 1689 treaty

5. Although devoid of major accomplishments, the Izbrandt mission brought Russia better understanding of China

6. Captain Kruzenstern, in circling the globe, visited Canton. **7.** State Counselor Rezanov (print) sailed with him, and tried to open relations with Japan

8. Nikolai N. Muraviev helped win the region on the left bank of the Amur for Russia in 1858. **9.** General Tso Tsung-t'ang recovered Dzungaria and Eastern Turkestan for Manchu rule after their revolt

10. Before the building of the Trans-Siberian Railway, undertaken in 1891 but not completed until 1917, **11.** Russian transport and communications labored under great difficulties

12. Russian soldiers played a major role during the Boxer Rebellion of 1900

13. The Amur region, at the time of Russian penetration, was inhabited by petty indigenous tribes such as the Goldi (shown here), Daurs, and Olchei

14. The Russo-Japanese War began with naval engagements off Chemulpo and Port Arthur, leased from China as a naval base

15. The Battle of Mukden was the last and biggest land engagement of that war

16. Soviet Russia, beset by foreign intervention, used revolutionary activity in China as a flanking measure: Michael Borodin, adviser to Sun Yat-sen's Nationalist forces, and a Nationalist general

17. General Vasili K. Bluecher ("Galen") helped to create the National Revolutionary Army finally commanded by Chiang Kai-shek. **18.** Marshal Feng Yü-hsiang obtained Soviet aid through professions of revolutionary aims, but in 1927 joined Chiang Kai-shek to demand withdrawal of the Russians from the revolution

credits: **14** and **15.** Colliers, *The Russo-Japanese War* (New York, 1905); **16.** U.S.I.A., National Archives, 306-NT-167.576C; **17.** Wide World Photos; **18.** Eastfoto

19. After the collapse of military efforts of tsarist loyalists in Russia, many Russian émigrés continued to wage the "anti-Bolshevik" struggle from Manchuria. The pictured demonstration celebrates the German-Japanese Anti-Comintern Pact of 1936

credits: **19** and **21.** U.S.I.A., National Archives, 306-NT-998E-1 and 306-NT-124.752.C; **20** and **22.** Zhukov, *Marshal Sovetskogo Soyuza* (Moscow 1969)

20. Samurai swords, Soviet trophies from the Battle of Nomonhan, where General Georgi K. Zhukov won a smashing victory

21. After the 1936 pact with Nazi Germany, Japan tested Soviet will at Changkufeng on the Manchoukuo border. 22. Soviet troops face the big military test near Nomonhan

23. With headquarters at Yenan, Chinese Communists fought the common foe, Japan, 1937–45. 24. Rugged terrain in Northwest China, once a refuge, was the main Communist base when civil war began after V-J Day

25. At the Yalta Conference, Moscow formally agreed to enter the war against Japan.

26. Soviet forces went into action against the Japanese in Manchuria two days after Hiroshima

27. Soviet forces defeated Japanese armies in Manchuria, and also removed important components of Japanese industrial plants located there as "war booty"

credits: **27** and **28**. Library of Congress, 43816/2 and 43816/3; **29**. Eastfoto

29 (below right). Marshal Malinovsky, commander-in-chief of Soviet occupational forces in Manchuria, with Mongol leader Marshal Choibalsan at an anniversary celebration of Outer Mongolia's independence

28. In the fighting between Chinese Nationalists and Chinese Communists after V-J Day, Communist sabotage brought further damage to railways and industrial plants in Manchuria

credits: **30.** U.S.I.A., National Archives, 306-NT-995A-7; **31.** Eastfoto; **32 and 33.** Wide World Photos

30. U.S. tanks for China being loaded at Houston. The United States continued to give support to the Chinese Nationalist regime during the Chinese civil war

31. China's new leader, Mao Tse-tung, made his second trip to Moscow in 1957, but was disappointed in his political and economic expectations. With him are Mme. Sun Yat-sen and Soviet Premier Bulganin

32. In the midst of the Great Proletarian Cultural Revolution, a decade after Mao's second Moscow visit, the Red Guards of Mao's creation laid siege to the Soviet embassy in Peking

33. Soviet troops on guard in 1969 after a major border clash between Chinese and Soviet armed forces at Damanski Island in the Ussuri

34. A Soviet Arctic border patrol, Chukotsk Peninsula. Since 1941, the United States has been a major factor in Sino-Russian relations. Only the Bering Strait separates the peninsula from Alaska

28 REVOLUTIONARY WAR AND THE ECONOMIC FACTOR

IN MID-CENTURY, despite the collapse of Asian empires, there was little opportunity for China to advance its interests substantially in South and Southeast Asia. The only sectors that were seemingly open to direct Chinese action of military or revolutionary character were Formosa and Korea.

The United States had in 1945 by its unilateral decision handed Formosa and the Pescadores over to the Nationalist Chinese; now the remnant Nationalists, having fled the mainland, were in refuge there — with little left for their defense. In Korea, by decision of the American and Soviet general staffs, the Thirty-eighth Parallel had been adopted as the temporary boundary between the respective Soviet and American occupation zones in North and South. Given his urge for national aggrandizement, Mao Tse-tung would not willingly brook the continued presence of his domestic enemy, Chiang Kai-shek, on Formosa, or *either* the American or Soviet presence in Korea.

It is to be presumed that Mao Tse-tung and Stalin had talked long and in broad scope of the political situation in the Far East. It can further be assumed, given the logic of a situation in which Mao's combined nationalism and anti-imperialism would naturally mold his thinking, that in those conversations the Chinese leader took certain initiatives respecting "Communist" policy in the Far East. On the basis of the inquiring principle "cui bono?" and given the assumption by China of responsibility at the critical strategic juncture, it can tentatively be deduced that the Communist strategy for Korea was in good part formulated and probably even proposed by Mao Tse-tung, and accepted, with suitable qualifications, by Stalin. Other Western observers indeed credit the Soviet side with the initiative in this regard; however, it is to be noted that Peking, even in its bitterest polemical moments, has never put the blame on Moscow.

In general, it was as if Mao Tse-tung's arrival in Moscow signaled the critical entry of China into a new political stage. Hainan had not yet been captured, but at that early date the Communists publicly addressed themselves to the matter of "liberation" of Formosa, where Chiang Kai-shek had again resumed control of the remnants of the Nationalist regime. There was bellicose reaction from the Taipei sector to the Communist threat. Nationalist leaflets scattered by airplane over the mainland on February 19 bore Chiang Kai-shek's promise that a mainland offensive would soon be launched, Mao Tse-tung executed, and Stalin tried as a war criminal.

The Peking official organ had even before this charged that, during separate visits by Nationalist secret-police chief Cheng Kai-min and Yü Ta-wei (soon to become minister of defense) to the United States in November and December, arrangements had been made for further American assistance to the Nationalists.[1] Significantly, both *Pravda* and *Izvestiya* carried the *New China News Agency* (NCNA) report of that "secret agreement." Peking's press campaign was expanded to give coverage to other sectors of China's Pacific front, and the alleged American plans were put into geopolitical perspective in a treatment at the beginning of April of "Two Major Elements of the So-Called [American] Asia Policy."[2] Here it was stated that, after ex-Ambassador William C. Bullitt and two others had met in conference with General Douglas MacArthur in early February,[3] it had been planned to convert Japan into a permanent American base, with the construction of military bases and the reconstituting of the Japanese army in the guise of a 500,000-man police force. That strengthened Japan, always according to NCNA, was to be the central bastion of a Pacific offensive line reaching from the Aleutians via South Korea, Japan, and the Ryukyus to the Philippines. By virtue of the Korean-American $10 million arms aid agreement of

January 26, it was charged, Korea would be made a part of that MacArthur Line, with the United States permitted to maintain a "military advisory group" in South Korea on a long-term basis. And, the article went on, the dispatch of American military supplies to the French in Indo-China constituted a threat to the Vietminh.

The line of thought of the Peking leaders was clearly visible: in the South Korean, Japanese, Formosan, and Indo-Chinese sectors of contest, they saw the menace of American power. The Chinese Communists made new dispositions of their forces opposite Formosa and began to render aid to the Vietminh. Their role with respect to particular developments in Korea cannot be established, but logic demands that it be assumed that the Korean War that began in June, 1950, came as no surprise to Peking.

In August, by unconfirmed report, Soviet Foreign Minister Molotov visited Peking and, reached an agreement with Mao Tse-tung that, if United Nations (i.e., American) forces crossed the Thirty-eighth Parallel, China would send its own forces into Korea.[4] In a long speech of October 1 (the day MacArthur called upon the North Korean army to surrender), Premier Chou En-lai proclaimed that the Sino-Soviet alliance bound nearly 700 million people together in a close military, economic, and cultural combination. Ratifications of the Sino-Soviet agreements of the preceding February had been formally exchanged at Peking the day before.

In the UN debate of October 6, the American and British delegates promised that their countries would withdraw their forces from Korea as soon as possible and would menace neither the Soviet Union nor China. The United Nations General Assembly (UNGA) resolution as passed the following day provided that the United Nations should take "all appropriate steps" to "ensure conditions of stability throughout Korea" – and this was seized upon by MacArthur as sanction for UN military action north of the Thirty-eighth Parallel. By his command the U.S. First Cavalry Divison promptly went into action, in full disregard of a warning by Chou En-lai on October 3 that China would intervene if UN forces crossed the Thirty-eighth Parallel.

A generation before the Korean War broke out, the editor of a foreign English-language periodical published in Shanghai had remarked that some of China's enemies had depicted China as being the "international cry baby that yelled when it was hit, but did not strike back." [5] Washington's easy disregard of Peking's warning suggests that the top American strategists still held to the traditional estimate of the Chinese potential for retaliation. They were due to experience an unpleasant surprise. On October 16, the first Chinese troops entered Korea; on October 25, transparently camouflaged as "volunteers," they intervened in the fighting in North Korea. By the end of December, the position of the UN command had badly deteriorated, and MacArthur recommended that, unless there were blockade of the coast of China, destruction by naval and air bombardment of China's industrial capacity to wage war, and both the unleashing of the Nationalist forces for action against the mainland and the securing of other Nationalist troops for reinforcement in Korea, the UN forces should fall back on the Pusan beachhead for evacuation. [6]

The Chinese offensive launched on New Year's Day of 1951 thrust the UN forces from North Korea, and on January 3 and 4 the Chinese forces occupied respectively Seoul and Inchon. In February, however, in the vicinity of Wonju, the Chinese were repulsed. There was no evacuation. By June, 1951, the UN forces had restored the position roughly at the Thirty-eighth Parallel.

It had been made apparent by the statements of Peking's delegate, Wu Hsiu-ch'uan, before the UNGA in December, 1950, and from the Soviet position as set forth at that time of distress for the UN coalition, [7] that the basic Communist aim was to effect the expulsion of all foreign forces from the peninsula. They had nearly succeeded, but the course of events on the battlefield led also to a changed Communist assessment — and, incidentally, to the replacement of Lin Piao by P'eng Teh-huai as Chinese commander in chief in Korea. There were now three factors that operated against the Communists: (1) world opinion, as manifested in the UN, was ranged against the North Korean aggression, with which China had become formally associated by virtue of a UNGA resolution (sponsored by the United States) of January, 1951; (2) the Chinese and North Koreans alone lacked the military power, deployed as it was across the narrow waist of the peninsula, to eject the UN forces from Korea; and (3) if the matter were left in the military framework, an American military faction favoring MacArthur's strategy of extending the war to China (regardless of Anglo-American assurances voiced in the UN) might carry the day, and the "police action" might be transformed into a general war — which was not desired by the Soviet Union in particular. On June 23, over a radio program, Soviet UN delegate Malik dropped the suggestion that it was possible to settle the Korean question by political means. Formal negotiations for a Korean truce began at Kaesong on July 10, 1951. By December, now at Panmunjom, they had stalemated on the issue of what should be done with the prisoners of war (POWs) in UN hands.

During the hostilities, the demands of the People's Liberation Army for new and replacement matériel were met by the Soviet service of supply, with China charged for eventual payment. MIG fighters, supplied by the USSR, were employed by the Chinese "volunteers" from the beginning of November. Soviet tanks, artillery, and other equipment also made their appearance on the Korean battlefield.

At the same time, the Sino-Soviet relationship was also both fulfilling incidental functions and undergoing new developments in the economic field. China was doing more than simply fighting the war. When the Chinese military intervention began in 1950, Manchuria was entering upon its third year of economic rehabilitation and construction. The Northeast was not directly damaged in any major respect by the war; on the contrary, it was considerably strengthened in the course of being equipped to function as the strategic base for military operations in Korea. Wartime needs constituted an automatic stimulus to the mining of coal and the production of steel and electric power.

Soviet economic support of China was broader in character than spelled out in the terms for the $300 million credit. Machinery was an especially important item of Soviet goods imported. Several tens or "upwards of 100" Soviet plants had been installed in various machineshops at Mukden by 1950, but more important still, it was reported, were the services of Soviet specialists who helped with Manchuria's reconstruction.[8]

Since the exchange of ratifications of the February, 1950, agreements took place only in September of that year, implementation of the credit arrangement was delayed for months. On February 10, 1951, however, it was announced by Peking and Moscow jointly that the USSR had transferred to China, gratis, various property located in Peking, Dairen, and the Northeast generally. The gift was substantial, including as it did an impressive number of power plants, factories, warehouses, residences, cinemas, and the like,[9] and it probably contributed to the development of a spirit of good trade relations. A new protocol to govern trade exchanges during 1951 was signed by the two countries at Moscow on June 15. At the same time, there was signed an agreement for the current delivery to China of Soviet equipment and materials under the terms of the 1950 credit arrangement.[10]

The Soviet Union was not the only Communist country with which China traded at that early date. A Polish mission arrived in Peking in January, 1950, for discussions with the Ministry of Trade, and a commercial agreement between the two countries was signed in March. Other Eastern European countries likewise signed trade agreements. In a contemporary survey of China's foreign trade, it was reported that 1950 saw a big increase in foreign commerce (inferentially, over 1949), and that trade then doubled in 1951, with disappearance of the unfavorable balance that had been characteristic of the "imperialist period."[11] Trade with the USSR and Eastern Europe, which in 1950 was 25 percent of the total, rose to 61 percent in 1951 and in 1952 constituted about 70 percent. In those years, the UN embargo on trade with "aggressor" China exercised an important pressure toward the reorientation of China's trade—for which the Communist bloc was presumably grateful.

The restriction of the warfare to the Korean peninsula, taken in conjunction with the truce talks, permitted China to carry on with most of its normal economic activities. But the war naturally imposed certain limitations on the economic effort. On July 1, 1952, as the POW impasse continued—and shortly after American bombing raids against the Suiho Dam on the Yalu—Ambassador Roshchin left Peking for Moscow. In August, while both the Panmunjom negotiations and military action in the field remained stalemated, Chou En-lai headed a new mission to the Soviet capital. His entourage included both Deputy Chief of General Staff Su Yü and important representatives from economic organs. Vyshinsky and Stalin, for the Soviet side, took part in the discussions. MPR Premier Tsedenbal also met at Moscow with the Chinese and Soviet leaders. Peking's mission remained in the Soviet capital for a month, and it would seem certain that the joint discussions touched upon major questions of strategy in Asia, and also upon the more peaceful pursuits of economic development. The second was clearly related to the first: while engaged in a major war, China could not well embark upon a general program of economic development.

Not only was the Korean War a factor of threatening uncertainty, but in 1952 the Japan Peace Treaty, and the accompanying American-Japanese Security Pact, both signed in September, 1951, came into effect. Japan was again a free nation, with the sovereign right to rearm — if it chose. The Communist estimates of the changed international situation of 1952, of the new exigencies confronting the Moscow-Peking axis, and of the requirements of China itself, were presumably reflected in the Sino-Soviet agreements reached as a result of the conference in Moscow. It was announced on September 16 that, in accordance with a Chinese request, the Soviet right of joint occupation of the Port Arthur naval base was to be extended, but Soviet rights in the Chinese Changchun Railway would be returned to China, without compensation, by the end of 1952 as scheduled. Other agreements, in the economic realm, suggested a relaxed attitude on the part of the allies. Moscow also agreed to an increase in supply of war materials to China — but quite evidently advanced no further in its support of the Chinese position in Korea. Before leaving for home soon afterward, Chou En-lai expressed the belief that Sino-Soviet friendship would develop day by day — and generation by generation.

On the eve of the Nineteenth CPSU Congress (convened on October 5, 1952), there appeared Stalin's essay on "Economic Problems of Socialism in the U.S.S.R." [12] Of critical importance as formulating the orthodox line in Moscow's foreign policy was the concept there set forth that the world market, once universal, as a consequence of World War II and the subsequent division of various states into the two opposed camps had now disintegrated and been replaced by two parallel world markets, also opposed to each other. [13] Party Secretary G. M. Malenkov, taking off from that theme in his report to the congress, reflected more clearly the judgment, suggested in Stalin's treatment, that competition between the two world markets would result in victory for the socialists: "We are confident that in peaceful competition with capitalism the socialist economic system will prove its superiority over the capitalist economic system more and more strikingly with each passing year." [14] In his treatment of the international situation, Malenkov was finally found standing for political peace and competitive economic cooperation between nations — and between the two opposing political systems.

It is to be remarked that a concept envisaging the peaceful

coexistence of capitalism and socialism, regardless of the question of whether or not it was orthodox Marxism-Leninism, was entirely alien to the basic philosophical concepts of Mao Tse-tung. Speaking before the CCP Central Committee in November, 1938, Mao had been categorical:

> All things grow out of the barrel of a gun. According to the Marxist theory of the state, the army is the chief component of state power. Whoever wants to seize and retain state power must have a strong army. Some people ridicule us as advocates of "the omnipotence of war." Yes, we are advocates of the omnipotence of revolutionary war; that is good, not bad, it is Marxist.[15]

The strategy of peaceful coexistence and economic competition was not suited to the temperament of China's new leader.

Mao Tse-tung believed fundamentally in the merits of permanent revolution and aimed at the overthrow of imperialism — naturally, as he saw it, to the major benefit of China. If he accepted the Communist line of the CPSU congress for the time being, he doubtless did so as a tactical matter, not because he deemed it a basic change in strategy. For the present, China was operating within the Communist bloc in accordance with the tenets of the Communist "united front" concept; but Mao knew, and probably Stalin did too, that the united-front relationship, always employed only as a *pis aller* to confront a critical tactical situation, might also in the present case prove to be only a temporary expedient.[16] There was thus a potential for trouble in the Sino-Soviet relationship if Moscow were to persist in the course fixed by the Nineteenth CPSU Congress past the point where it might appear to Peking that militant action in furtherance of the world revolution was feasible, and therefore advisable.

In 1952, however, prime military considerations and the economic imperative governed with respect to China's foreign policy. Indications of the scope and direction of the Sino-Soviet discussions at Moscow continued to issue. On October 4, there was signed, at Peking, a Sino-Mongolian agreement, to run for ten years, for "economic and cultural cooperation." A few days later, an NCNA dispatch from Peking announced the beginning of construction of the railway line to run from Lanchow, in Kansu Province, into Sinkiang. This was the rail line that, by later design, was to meet at Khorgos, on the Sino-Soviet frontier in

Central Asia, with a spur from Aktogai on the Turk-Sib Railway. In November, another economic mission headed by Minister of Foreign Trade Yeh Chi-chuang arrived in Moscow. It would remain there until March, 1953.

In early October, in view of the stalemate over the POW issue, the UN delegation had withdrawn from the truce conference at Panmunjom pending receipt of more constructive proposals from the Communist side, and the year ended without resumption of the truce negotiations. But there were signs of a shift in the Communist position, in line with the attitudes adopted at the October CPSU congress. On December 24, Stalin in a letter of reply to James Reston of the *New York Times* reaffirmed his belief that war between the Soviet Union and the United States "cannot be considered inevitable, and that our countries can continue to live in peace," and expressed his readiness to cooperate in bringing an end to the Korean War.[17] On the same day, Premier Chou En-lai announced that the Peking government proposed in 1953 (1) to hold elections for an All-China People's Congress and (2) to inaugurate a five-year plan for industrial and agricultural development. Those were not warlike moves. A competent student of the Chinese economic scene later put the developments into perspective:

> During 1951, there were indications that some heavy industries were moved from the Northeast to the Northwest, but from the latter part of 1952, large-scale industrial projects were going full blast in Manchuria. . . . All these events seem to indicate that Peking had decided late in 1952 or early in 1953 to end the Korean fighting.[18]

The Chinese and Soviets had been maintaining a united front of opposition to an Indian plan put forward in the UN for resolution of the conflict; nevertheless, the UNGA vote of 54 to 5 (Nationalist China abstaining) in favor of the plan left the Communist bloc in a clear minority, and isolated with respect to "peace" in Korea — an awkward position in the light of the Communist bloc's contemporary support of the World Peace Council. It was then obviously too late in the American Democratic administration for radical changes, or decisive action, to be anticipated from the side of the makers of U.S. policy; nor would it have been easy for the Communist side to find an occasion within the next two months for embarking upon a new tack. But the newly elected president, General Dwight D. Eisenhower, had promised the American public to bring about peace in Korea. In his State of the Union message of February 2, 1953, he "unleashed" Chiang Kai-shek.

It could hardly have been for fear of Chiang's armies that Chou En-lai on February 4 called for a resumption of the recessed truce negotiations and for an immediate cease-fire. Chiang Kai-shek actually took no aggressive action, limiting himself to the statement that he would wait upon a general war against Communism. On February 25 he proclaimed the abrogation of the August, 1945, Sino-Soviet treaty (already ruled null and void by the February, 1950, agreement between Peking and Moscow), with Foreign Minister George Yeh stating in explanation that the Soviet Union had repeatedly violated the treaty "in carrying out its program of aggression in China."

Whether Stalin's death on March 5 was in fact a critical factor is impossible to say, but Chou En-lai in his next démarche notably softened his stand. On March 30, he again called for a resumption of truce negotiations, and besides made a set of counterproposals close to the terms of the Indian resolution. Molotov on April 1 expressed the Soviet Union's "full solidarity with this lofty act," and Churchill described the move as "a considerable event." On April 2, President Eisenhower said that the United States was ready to meet every honest advance from the other side, and then, on April 16, he called for an armistice leading to "free elections in a united Korea."

April 18, 1953, saw a rare example of unanimity in the UN General Assembly: by a vote of 60 to 0, there was passed a Brazilian resolution expressing the hope that further negotiations would bring about an early armistice in Korea. There is no evidence that there existed any fundamental difference of opinion among Moscow, Peking, and Pyongyang respecting the aspiration voiced in that resolution. Truce negotiations resumed a week later. On May 22, having concluded that the Chinese were again using obstructionist tactics, Dulles on behalf of the Eisenhower administration sent a private message to Peking through Indian channels threatening the use of atomic bombs against China unless it got down to business at Panmunjom.[19] Agreement for an armistice in the Korean War was actually achieved on July 27, 1953. It is entirely evident that the date would have been earlier, had it not been for Syngman Rhee's arbitrary release of some 27,000 enemy POWs whom Pyongyang and Peking had demanded should be forcibly repatriated. Had the Communist side desired to "escape" from an armistice, Rhee's action would have given them a last good occasion. The Communists did not seize upon that opportunity, for they clearly did not want it: the Korean affair had been squeezed dry of benefits for the Sino-Soviet allies, and was programed for liquidation.

The Korean War had cost China heavily and demonstrated the country's basic weakness: its economic base was inadequate to support a great-power role. China had been able to perform militarily as well as it had only because of (1) the self-imposed UN limitations restricting the scope of operations to Korea, and (2) Soviet material aid. In the distant past, China had regarded treaties as simply instruments of political convenience, which might be violated at such time as circumstances so dictated. Nor had the treaty arrangements of 1896 with Russia and 1918 with Japan operated or been viewed as effective alliances between equals: China was the inferior in the arrangements and had entered upon them with no other purpose than the national profit. By 1953, the Sino-Soviet treaty of 1950 had shown its major political worth for China as well as for the Soviet Union. Now the time had come to ascertain whether it would also work equally well for mutual benefit in the economic sphere, for which it was also designed.

The form that Soviet economic assistance would take in general would naturally be determined by the nature of Chinese economic planning. The period of rehabilitation was in truth effectively completed by the end of 1952, at which time Peking claimed that agricultural and industrial production had been restored to the highest pre-1937 levels. The net national production for that year was approximately 20 percent higher than in 1933 — although only 6 percent higher in per capita terms.[20] China was ready to undertake new construction, with the aim of becoming a major economic power.

In contemplation of that massive task, Peking in November, 1952, had established a National Planning Commission, headed by Kao Kang, who had played so important a role in postwar Manchuria. Jao Shu-shih was made Kao's deputy in the new organization. Jao was a man who seems to have spent some time in Moscow in the early 1930s. He had long been associated with

Liu Shao-ch'i and had attended the Nineteenth CPSU Congress at Moscow in 1952 with him. Jao Shu-shih was an able, seasoned — and evidently entirely reliable — Communist functionary.

When it was proclaimed to the Chinese nation that the first five-year economic plan would be undertaken in 1953, no details of the plan were disclosed. Basing his conclusions in part upon disclosures made in a *People's Daily* editorial of September 16, 1953, one observer analyzed the situation as follows:

> What appears to have happened is that the Russians
> were not satisfied with the draft plan as it stood and also
> thought that there were some things in which the
> Chinese were asking for help that they might accomplish
> on their own. . . . From this it would appear that the
> draft plan received a fairly drastic overhauling from the
> Russian experts who studied it and that the Chinese, in
> view of their need for help, had to consent to this.[21]

The death of Stalin could have been expected to make a difference in the long-term prospects. For one thing, Stalin was *sui generis;* so was Mao Tse-tung, who was now senior, in terms of years and revolutionary experience, to the leadership that had succeeded to power at Moscow. The Chinese Communists went to considerable length to express their official grief at the death of Stalin, whose harsh dictatorship they clearly regarded as a model for China. And Premier Chou En-lai made another trip to Moscow to convey the Central People's Government's condolences and attend the funeral. But Stalin had died in the heated atmosphere of the "doctors' plot," in which an alleged terrorist group of nine doctors was charged with having caused the deaths of Politburo member Aleksandr S. Shcherbakov in 1945, of Zhdanov in 1948, and of plotting against the lives of various military leaders, all in behalf of the American and British secret services. A new Stalinist purge, in sum, had been in the offing when Stalin died. It seemed less than certain that Georgi M. Malenkov would be able to retain the position of chairman of the council of ministers (premier) and that the new triumvirate of Malenkov, Molotov, and Lavrenti P. Beria (minister of internal affairs) would provide a steady successor rule to that of the dead dictator. Mao Tse-tung could only have viewed the developments in Russia as holding the potential for change in favor of himself and China, in both the political and economic fields.

29 SINO-SOVIET COLLABORATION, 1953–1955

THE RELATIVE "LIBERALISM" of Malenkov seemed to have an early reflection in Sino-Soviet relations. Soon after Stalin's death, there was a substantial advance in economic cooperation between the two countries. V. V. Kuznetsov, a metallurgical expert, in early March replaced Panyushkin as ambassador at Peking. Yeh Chi-chuang's mission reaped the fruits of its labors with announcement on March 26, 1953, of the signature "recently" of a trade protocol for 1953, a second protocol governing use of the 1950 Soviet credit for the same year, and an agreement providing for the extension of Soviet assistance for the expansion of existing power plants and the construction of new ones. It was in this context that Kao Kang proceeded to Peking to take up his posts as vice premier and chief of the State Planning Commission. His lieutenant, Jao Shu-shih, was made head of the CCP Central Committee's powerful Organization Bureau.

China still lacked the wherewithal for the formulation of a substantial five-year economic plan. The relatively meager Soviet credit of 1950 had not been designed to support a national five-year plan for a country the size of China. Finally, however, on September 15, after the termination of the Korean War, Li Fu-ch'un in his capacity of vice chairman of the Committee on Economic and Financial Affairs announced that negotiations had been completed for a new program of long-term Soviet economic assistance that included the construction of ninety-one new enterprises for China. It also provided for the renovation of fifty more, to make a total of 141 to be built or modernized.

Manchuria had been a heavy exporter of goods to the Soviet Union since 1949, and it was to be assumed that much of the new economic construction would be in that critical region.[1] The effort, nevertheless, would not be exclusively concentrated there: China now was going to undertake the development of new industrial centers, based upon two major considerations: (1) industrial plants would be established near important deposits of raw materials; and (2) a measured dispersal of the nation's industry would render China strategically less vulnerable. Existing hydraulic and thermal power plants in Manchuria were to be expanded, but new power plants would also be constructed elsewhere. Steel plants were to be built at Paotow and Tayeh, to increase China's capacity for steel output by approximately 4 million tons annually. Petroleum production in China's Northwest was to be expanded, and tin production in Yunnan Province would be increased.

In all of those projects, the Soviet Union was to lend a hand. But no new Soviet credit was extended: China was still limited by the yearly allocation from the original U.S.$300 million credit (now already half spent), and by its ability to export goods for current payment. In this equation, there was a critical factor: the Soviet Union already qualified as an industrialized nation; China, while proudly demanding to be treated as a political equal of the USSR, was in an inferior stage of economic development. With reference to the Soviet Union, it was in the relationship of countryside to town.

The new Sino-Soviet arrangement for economic "collaboration" was moreover not to be divorced from significant political developments flowing from the death of Stalin. The release in April of those arrested and charged by the Ministry of Internal Affairs (MVD) in connection with the "doctors' plot" was followed in due course by the removal of Beria from the post of MVD minister and his expulsion from the CPSU Central Committee, on the grounds that:

> This hireling of foreign imperialist forces was hatching plans to seize the leadership of the Party and the

country, with the real object of destroying our
Communist Party and substituting for the policy worked
out by the Party over many years, a policy of
capitulation which, in the final analysis, would have led
to the restoration of capitalism.[2]

Beria was indicted and tried on those general grounds, and on
December 24 it was announced that he had been executed.

It was of passing significance that, about this time, South
Korean President Syngman Rhee paid a state visit to Nationalist
President Chiang Kai-shek, who had once more come under the
American aegis as an incidental result of the Korean War, and
on November 28, at the conclusion of their discussions, they
issued a joint communiqué identifying Korea and China as "the
first victims of Russia's Communist aggression in Asia," and proclaimed their stand against compromise or coexistence with
Communism: "We are certain that victory over Communism in
Asia is the key to world peace and stability." They pledged their
governments and peoples to stand united in the determination to
mobilize their forces against "the aggressor in Asia," further:

Our two countries . . . jointly appeal to all Governments
and peoples of the free countries in Asia to organise a
united anti-Communist front and earnestly hope that our
desire to achieve solidarity in this part of the world will
have the moral and material support of other
freedom-loving nations, particularly those bordering on
the Pacific such as the United States of America.[3]

Chiang and Rhee were both subscribers to the containment
strategy.

The Korean War had provided exigent political reasons
for Sino-Soviet collaboration, but it had also introduced an important element of rivalry into the new relationship. In the 1945–1950
period, the Soviet Union had enjoyed dominant influence in North
Korea, thanks to the initial presence of Soviet troops and advisers.
With the entry of large Chinese forces into the country during the
Korean War, however, Chinese influence replaced the Soviet
brand. In September, 1953, North Korean Premier Kim Il Sung
headed a mission to Moscow that won a grant of one billion rubles
(U.S.$250 million) for aid in rehabilitation. Then, in November,
Kim made a visit to Peking, where he concluded a ten-year Agree-

ment for Economic and Cultural Cooperation—and received China's commitment to forgo Pyongyang's repayment of costs of all materials supplied North Korea during the course of the Korean War and a Chinese grant of U.S.$200 million in gratis aid to be extended over three years. Since China was currently going into debt to the Soviet Union in the process of striving for its own modernization, the political nature of the Sino-Korean deal was as clear to Moscow as it was to Pyongyang.

China was naturally not yet in a position to export any substantial quantities of machinery and capital goods; it had still to become self-sufficient in that regard. In January, 1954, China and the Soviet Union reached a new agreement for increasing their commerce and fixed upon the usual protocol to govern the year's deliveries of Soviet goods under the terms of the 1950 credit. The categories of goods involved in the exchanges reflected China's stage of economic development: it would import chiefly machinery, industrial and mining equipment, rolled steel, chemical products, and tractors; it would export agricultural products and nonferrous metals.

China's prime political and economic relations were with the USSR. The USSR, on the other hand, was engaged in the Cold War with the United States. Moscow consequently looked toward an expanding relationship with critical elements of the Third World, and in Eastern Europe had created a supporting system of states that in important respects balanced, both politically and economically, the continental mass that was China. The Council for Mutual Economic Assistance had been slow in developing, but in 1954, with the introduction of a new concept for the international socialist division of labor, it began a fresh advance. The Soviet Union's 1954–1955 "New Course" in economic affairs gave a considerable stimulus to CMEA. China was not Moscow's only care, or sole option.

Yet, in 1954, the Communist regime in China was to feel a degree of "maturity." It had been in power for five years and had consolidated political control over the country and steadied the tottering economy. China had played an important, independent role in the 1954 Geneva conference that ended the Indo-China War. In September, 1954, evidencing the regime's confidence, the first National People's Congress approved a new constitution for the Chinese People's Republic (CPR). An imposing Soviet delegation, headed by Nikolai A. Bulganin and Nikita S. Khrushchev and including Mikoyan and others, arrived in Peking to participate in the ceremonies in celebration of the CPR's fifth anniversary on October 1.

That the Soviet mission had more than a ceremonial purpose was made evident in joint declarations issued on October 12 respecting a number of matters, chiefly economic. Moscow promised to help China construct fifteen more industrial enterprises, and extended an additional long-term credit of U.S.$130 million for use in that connection. Another agreement provided for the exchange, over five years, of technical "documents" and scientific information, and of specialists, to further scientific and technical cooperation between the two countries. An accord was reached on the construction of the transcontinental rail line from Lanchow to Aktogai, with the Soviet Union to extend technical aid in connection with work on the Chinese section of the line. The accord took due note of work begun by China on the Lanchow-Yümen sector in 1953. Similarly, a Sino-Soviet-Mongolian tripartite agreement was reached regarding completion by 1955 of the rail line from Tsining, on the Peking-Suiyuan line in Inner Mongolia, to connect with the railway linking Ulan Bator with the USSR.

But the Peking leadership was still governed by an innate chauvinism that would no longer suffer anything in the nature of a special, "privileged" position for another power in China — even though it might be to China's benefit. That feeling would be buttressed by a sharp alertness to situations that might tend to keep China in a supporting role, such as the "town-country" relationship. Other agreements were reached that reflected Peking's concern that China fully enjoy its "sovereign economic rights." A joint communiqué, remarking the termination of war in both Korea and Indo-China and making note further of "the strengthening of the defense potential of the Chinese People's Republic," announced that Soviet military forces were to be withdrawn from the Port Arthur naval base area, with installations transferred without compensation to China, by May 31, 1955. (The Soviet withdrawal was effected six days before due date.) China thus caused the removal from its soil of the Soviet shield against attack from the direction of Japan.

And although Peking from the beginning had been strongly hostile to the "revisionist" regime in Yugoslavia, it seems to have taken due note of one of Prague's complaints against Soviet policy, namely that the operation of the two Soviet-Yugoslav joint-stock companies had made substantially more profits for the USSR than for Yugoslavia. China had entered upon similar arrangements for four joint-stock companies, with those for the exploitation of nonferrous and rare minerals and for the extraction and refining of petroleum, in Sinkiang, to run for thirty years. Now, four years later, those two Sinkiang combines, together with the joint-stock company charged with operation of civil airlines between the two countries, and a combine that had been formed for shipbuilding and repair in Dairen, were all to be liquidated, with the Soviet shares in the several enterprises to be transferred to China on January 1, 1955, payment therefor to be made in Chinese export products over a period of years.

The rationale set forth in the communiqué was simple enough: "Chinese economic organizations have accumulated the necessary experience and can themselves manage the activity of enterprises which are part of the mixed companies." [4] But the statement, which did logical violence to the original agreement that the joint enterprises should continue for three decades, did not carry full conviction. Whether China, which during the reign of Sheng Shih-ts'ai had engaged in exactly the same type of economic arrangements in Sinkiang, was actually getting the short end of the deal, is difficult to say. One source, a Polish Communist who defected to the West in 1956, has reported that Mikoyan argued in the July, 1955, plenum of the CPSU Central Committee for dissolution of the "mixed companies" that functioned in the "people's democracies" of Eastern Europe, since they resulted in economic exploitation of those countries and thus were a manifestation of Soviet imperialism. By this account, Mikoyan buttressed his position by reporting that, after Stalin's death, Moscow had proposed to Peking that there be organized joint-stock companies for the production and export of tropical fruits to the Soviet Union. Mao rejected the proposition, suggesting that China instead export the fruits on a regular commercial basis; "Mao gave a very eloquent appraisal of the mixed companies' activities from the point of view of Chinese interests." [5]

If Mikoyan was present at the time Mao gave his exposition, as is logically to be inferred, the occasion could only have been at the time of the Soviet mission's visit to Peking in September–October, 1954; but even if the exchange had not been face-to-face and had come earlier, it would appear that Mao Tse-tung in October, 1954, felt some deep dissatisfactions which led, presumably, to the decision to press for the dissolution of the four Sino-Soviet joint-stock companies. That the proud ruler of the "New China" could not bear to have a foreign power reap *any* substantial profit from a joint "partnership" seems probable on the record. Consequently the Soviet influence — but as manifested in scientific and technical terms, as well as in the form of an intangible political prestige — was caused to withdraw. The transfer of ownership took place on January 1, 1955, as agreed.

A new factor automatically flowed from the 1954 developments: China was rapidly increasing its debit balance vis-à-vis the Soviet Union. On top of the original credit of $300 million, there had been piled the cost of Soviet munitions supplied to China for use in the Korean War. The support of Soviet technicians in China and of the many Chinese technicians and military men and others studying in Soviet institutions, all increased the charges to be paid currently out of agricultural and mining production. Now, expulsion of the Soviets from the four partnerships substantially increased China's outstanding indebtedness. The move may have been a balm to the Peking leadership's self-esteem; it was clearly costly in the larger national sense. It can only be considered a propitiatory beau geste that the Soviet mission, on that October, 1954, occasion, made a gift to China of a number of Soviet machine tools and agricultural machines then on exhibit in Peking, and promised to equip and help organize, at Soviet expense, a 20,000-acre state farm in Heilungkiang Province. The farm was to be named, suitably enough, "Sino-Soviet Friendship State Farm."

There was in course at that time a development in the CCP's internal politics that, although not known in all its aspects, appears to have had a connection with Sino-Soviet relations. That was the case of the new State Planning Commission chiefs, Kao Kang and Jao Shu-shih. Kao Kang, known from Yenan days as a trusted lieutenant of Mao Tse-tung and viewed in 1952 as being one of the ten most powerful men in the Communist hierarchy, did not long enjoy the limelight after getting to Peking: his last known public appearance was in January, 1954. He failed to be named to a high post in the new "constitutional" government inaugurated at Peking in October of that year. In official statements, there appeared veiled references to those who had come to regard particular areas as "their individual inheritance or individual kingdom." Then Teng Hsiao-p'ing, speaking on behalf of the CCP central committee in April, 1955, announced that Kao Kang had been found guilty by the CCP congress that sat in late March of having endeavored to make of Manchuria "the independent kingdom of Kao Kang," of being "an agent of imperialism," and of having engaged in "antiparty conspiratorial activities" designed to seize leadership of the party and government.[6] He had consequently been expelled from the party central committee but, in a final act of betrayal of the party, had committed suicide. Jao Shu-shih was likewise expelled from the party, and by report was being subjected to "disciplinary action." He was not heard of again.

The major developments in this case, it would appear, had taken place not in 1955, but in *1954*. Jao Shu-shih may have been arrested as early as February, 1954. In that month, according to the Teng Hsiao-p'ing report, Kao Kang had been given a serious warning – which he proceeded to disregard. Kao was still listed as chairman of the Northeast Administrative Committee as late as September of that year.

Significant suggestions crept into the official explanation: Kao had tried to gain the posts of vice chairman of the party central committee and premier of the State Council – in which posts he would have succeeded Chou En-lai and stood in the line of succession to Mao Tse-tung. Kao Kang, thus, had ventured to compete for position with two of the three most powerful figures (Mao, Chou, and Liu Shao-ch'i) in the Peking Communist regime. Further, Kao's plotting was alleged to have dated back to 1949, the year in which he had headed a delegation to Moscow to negotiate a trade agreement between Manchuria and the USSR. An interesting suggestion was dropped in the debate between Khrushchev and P'eng Chen in their bitter confrontation at the Bucharest Communist meeting of June, 1960, when Khrushchev obliquely observed that Kao Kang's only crime had been to oppose his party's incorrect policy vis-à-vis the Soviet Union.[7]

It may be speculated that Kao possibly contended for closer economic collaboration with the Soviet Union, particularly in Manchuria. Speaking of the intramural struggles of the Chinese Communist Party, one writer has observed that "The one unpardonable offense seems to be to have, or seek to develop, unusually close Soviet connections and to try to use them in a power struggle or policy debate."[8] He thought that this was a factor in the purging of Kao Kang and P'eng Teh-huai. But there were also obvious similarities between Kao's case and that of Lavrenti Beria.

The fall of 1954 and early spring of 1955 were marked by the development of a critical situation in China's foreign relations. American Secretary of State Dulles, who had at the beginning of 1954 formulated the doctrine of "massive retaliation" for use against China, succeeded in creating the Southeast Asia Treaty Organization (SEATO) in September—although he was forced by the objections of European participants to omit Chiang Kai-shek's staunchly "anti-Communist" Nationalist regime from the alliance. In the face of this development, Peking launched a campaign for the reduction of Formosa, and as the "first Formosa Strait crisis" unfolded, the United States on December 2 signed a separate treaty of alliance with the Taipei government. The crisis built up until, by March, 1955, there was talk in Washington of war in April between the United States and China.[9]

But by then Peking had already shifted from the offensive to the defensive. With the new Soviet commitments of additional economic aid, a blueprint for the first five-year plan was completed (but not published) in February, 1955. Premier and concurrently Foreign Minister Chou En-lai in April, far from inviting war, attended the Bandung Afro-Asian Conference, and mirrored a bland and peaceful China standing strongly in support of Panch Shila—the Five Principles, envisaging peaceful coexistence and economic cooperation, as proclaimed by Chou and Indian Prime Minister Jawaharlal Nehru in June, 1954. The Formosa Strait crisis subsided, and in July a new head of the State Planning Commission, Kao Kang's old associate Li Fu-ch'un, made public the details of China's first five-year plan. In general, it was in the pattern of Soviet development, with the stress on heavy industry and relative neglect of light industry and agriculture, except that the capital investment devoted to heavy industry was to consume a greater proportion of China's available capital resources than Moscow had ever seen fit to allocate to that sector. It could thus safely be assumed that the plan was more a reflection of Mao's exuberant thinking than of the calculations of the cautious Armenian Mikoyan.

Given previous Sino-Soviet agreements, and especially those of 1954, it was no surprise that Soviet assistance, in the form of materials and technological knowledge and skills, was to provide the backbone for the planned industrial construction. The USSR was to build for China iron and steel enterprises, nonferrous metallurgical plants, petroleum-processing and machine-building plants, power plants, factories for the production of tractors and other motor vehicles, and to supply coal-mining, railway, and other heavy equipment. In June, 1955, Secretary of State Dulles testified in secret session before the House Appropriations Committee that the Soviet economic system was "on the point of collapsing." Evidence of this was not visible in the Sino-Soviet economic arrangements, and China swung fully into the rhythm of rapid industrial construction.

The promise of a further, and more substantial, advance in Sino-Soviet collaboration was discovered in Moscow's announcement on January 17, 1955, that it had made appropriate proposals to Poland, East Germany, Rumania, Czechoslovakia, and China that the Soviet Union extend them scientific and technological assistance in connection with the utilization of atomic energy for peaceful purposes. The proposals duly bore fruit: on May 1, Moscow reported that relevant agreements had been reached with those five bloc countries. A short time later, similar agreements were signed with Bulgaria and Hungary. The prospects for a fruitful realization of the projected economic and scientific cooperation of China and the Soviet Union appeared good.

And yet, new political factors having an important bearing on the future of that cooperative economic effort had been introduced into the equation at the very beginning. In early 1955, before Bandung, the Soviet leadership had been immersed in a power struggle that was resolved when Nikita S. Khrushchev won out against Premier Malenkov. With Malenkov's forced retirement, Nikolai A. Bulganin became premier, while Khrushchev wielded dominant power as the party first secretary. Victorious, Khrushchev effectively adopted Malenkov's concept of "peaceful competition" with capitalism.

It was the Bulganin-Khrushchev leadership that observed intently, from afar, the Bandung conference. Certain developments at that gathering were highly significant for the future of Sino-Soviet relations. From 1950 to 1955, it seemed as if Moscow was prepared, in something like a revolutionary division of labor, to allocate to China the task of furthering the national interests of the two partners, and the common cause of Communism, in

Asia. Such an appearance may, of course, only have reflected a Soviet preoccupation with domestic and European problems: there were quite enough, at the time, to distract the Soviet leadership. But it was in any event to be remarked that, to endure, such a policy of division of spheres of activity and influence would have depended upon the partners' substantial trust in each other's bona fides.

Regardless of the important position it occupied in Asia, the Soviet Union was not represented at that Afro-Asian conference of April, 1955; China was. And where Mao Tse-tung had affirmed in 1949 that there was no middle road between the socialist and imperialist camps, and Liu Shao-ch'i had proposed the violent overthrow of Asian bourgeois governments, the Peking regime through Chou En-lai at Bandung manifested a genial readiness to coexist with the bourgeois Asian and African states represented there, and at the same time seemingly assumed that China would naturally play the leading role in the world of emerging nations. Chou exercised so dominant an influence at Bandung, in fact, that India's Nehru, who had anticipated that the mantle of leadership would fall upon his own shoulders, was quite eclipsed by the Chinese. Insofar as Chou was acting as surrogate for the Communist bloc Moscow naturally would not find his performance objectionable. But that was just where a question came up: was Chou engaged in furthering bloc interests generally — or first and foremost the interests of China?

In both Russia and China, the sense of revolution joined with strong feelings of ethnic nationalism and with a historic impulse toward imperialism to offset the purported feeling of socialist brotherhood. Neither Soviet Russia nor Communist China was governed basically by the altrusitic desire to share socialist wealth, whether in terms of consumption goods, territories — or even power. Given the history of the long and troubled relation between them, many Chinese harbored the conviction (not originally Chinese) that "Scratch a Russian, and you'll find a Tatar." And one could easily perceive that the Soviet Union, with twice as much land area in Asia as China, was called upon to defend its position as an Asian power, even as in the days of empire, against the encroachments of a reviving Middle Kingdom. In the Third World, it similarly had to build up its position of influence in the face of competition from *both* the United States and China.

Beginning in 1955, in fact, Moscow substantially revised the entire grand strategy, and strategic concepts, inherited from Stalin. The Soviets of the new postrevolutionary generation had begun to see world forces, and military, political, and economic potentials, in a new light. In particular, there had probably been some at Moscow, including Stalin, who from the beginning in 1950 had seen reason to doubt that the Chinese at Peking, just because they were Communists, would be governed primarily by the spirit of socialist internationalism. For those who had assumed that the Chinese Communists would cooperate rather than strive for domination, the Bandung conference would have been an awakening. Concepts of national interest, and national survival, still had a role to play, even as in the time of Stalin, and new forces were engaged in an arena of action bigger than a generation before. The manner of meeting challenges was changing, becoming more subtle.

This circumstance was reflected in bloc relationships. From its European partners, the Soviet Union received something in the nature of a political return soon after negotiation of the agreements governing the extension of Soviet aid for atomic-energy projects. On May 14, 1955, after the accession of West Germany to NATO, there was signed at Warsaw a treaty (the "Warsaw Pact") providing for mutual defense and military aid among the bloc countries. The signatory powers comprised the same eight states (including Albania) which by now made up CMEA, and the new organization thus became in effect the military counterpart of the economic organization. Soviet Marshal Ivan S. Konev became supreme commander of the Warsaw Pact forces, with strategy, military systems, and arms of the Eastern European states thereafter to be patterned after those of the Soviet Union. Integration of the Occidental section of the socialist commonwealth had been advanced accordingly; but again China, and other Asian Communist states, remained outside the new system.

It was further to be taken as a sign of the new Soviet approach to world affairs when, after winning power, Khrushchev undertook to woo Yugoslavia. He and Bulganin did Soviet penitence in a trip to Belgrade. And where China had held off from normalization of Sino-Yugoslav relations ever since Belgrade's extension of recognition in 1949, Moscow in June, 1955, achieved at least a partial reconciliation, in a move toward bringing the wayward

Communist state fully back into the "socialist commonwealth." This done, Khrushchev and Bulganin in a sense followed in the footsteps of Tito and made a tour of Afghanistan, India, and Burma that, if not a complete substitute for participation in the Bandung conference, was at least an earnest of Moscow's intention to exploit energetically the full potential of its new world strategy. The place of China in that strategy would necessarily be different from what it had been before.

30 DEVELOPMENTS IN THE ALLIANCE, 1956–1957

THE YEAR 1956 was to prove of critical importance in relations between Moscow and Peking. In January, the Soviet Union and Yugoslavia reached a full reconciliation, with Moscow writing off Yugoslavia's debit of $90 million and granting new credits. Soviet foreign affairs generally were looking up. And in a press conference Secretary of State Dulles sounded a note of alarm contrasting strangely with his estimate of half a year earlier regarding the Soviet Union's economic future. He quoted a message from the American delegation to the United Nations which, he said, was viewed by the president and himself as so important that he now made it public: the USSR was using

> economic and social collaboration as a means for jumping, military as well as political barriers. . . . We are in a contest in the field of economic development of underdeveloped countries which is bitterly competitive. Defeat in this contest could be as disastrous as defeat in an armaments race. We could lose this economic contest unless the country as a whole wakes up to all its implications.[1]

Quite unconsciously, Dulles spoke for Peking as much as for Washington.

The new strategy was further publicized by the Soviets themselves at the Twentieth CPSU Congress in February. In an address to the gathering, Khrushchev proposed in effect that Communist parties endeavor to effect the peaceful capture of bourgeois parliaments, and that Communist countries undermine capitalist regimes by penetration of their overseas markets and the overseas sources of supply for their raw materials. War between the socialist and imperialist camps was not inevitable — peaceful coexistence was actually essential — and still capitalism might be brought down into the dust. His treatment was given further elaboration in a long contemporary article in the party's theoretical journal by the ideologue A. Sobolev.[2] The Soviet grand strategy had changed.

Although Khrushchev did not give credit, this ideological development was a natural projection of the Stalin thesis of 1952. There was a good reason why Khrushchev did not laud the original author: this was the occasion when, in his famous "secret speech," the Soviet leader sought to demolish the Stalin legend and all it stood for. The "de-Stalinization" of Soviet society had begun. It was simply in obedience to the inner logic of the changed situation that, on April 17, there was proclaimed the dissolution of the Cominform. It had lived less than a decade.

The developments were reflected in a redressing of dogma. In June, 1956, just one year after his first move toward reconciliation with Yugoslavia, Khrushchev joined Tito in a joint declaration at Moscow acknowledging that there might be "a multiplicity of forms of socialist development." A few days later, Italian Communist leader Palmiro Togliatti expounded the doctrine of a "polycentric system" of Communism in which individual parties enjoyed full autonomy and were bound by *bilateral* relations. Such a concept could not have been received with sympathetic appreciation by the Chinese, who had started upon their relationship with Yugoslavia by dutifully anathematizing it.

The introduction of increased flexibility into the Soviet Union's relations with the Third World, and the beginning of a "thaw" at home, were not unnaturally taken as marking a distinct mellowing of its attitude toward other Communist countries as well. In Poland the combined effect of the February de-Stalinization in Moscow and of economic distress at home was such that riots broke out in Poznan. The disorder spread until it threatened the very existence of the governing Stalinist leadership.

Mikoyan and the first secretary of the Polish United Workers party, Edward Ochab, in Peking to attend the Eighth Congress of the Chinese Communist Party in September, were brought together by Mao Tse-tung for a discussion of the future of Poland, and on that occasion Mao seemingly threw his support to Ochab against Mikoyan. The Polish delegation returned home with assurances of Chinese support in the event of conflict with the CPSU.[3]

It would appear probable that the Soviet leaders took judicious account of the Chinese support for Warsaw when they made their decision to stop short of using force to maintain in Poland the Stalinist pattern rejected for Soviet domestic affairs. But the major factor was doubtless the political skill of Wladislaw Gomulka, who consolidated his domestic support and at the same time convinced the Soviet leadership that he was determined to keep Poland in the Communist camp and on the Soviet foreign-policy line. Poland thus was able to buttress its autonomy.

Developments in Hungary followed a notably different course. That country, too, was afflicted by grave economic problems. The Hungarian people, taking their cue from developments in Poland, challenged the Communist authority itself at Budapest. It at first appeared as if the Polish pattern might prevail. But Imre Nagy was no Gomulka. The government lost control of the situation, and when Nagy on October 31 informed Mikoyan that Hungary proposed to withdraw from the Warsaw Pact, he sealed his fate—and that of Hungary. The Soviet army intervened in force the following day. Janos Kadar came to power. A principle had been established: a member state might not secede from the socialist commonwealth.

China had implicitly acceded to the de-Stalinization process, in one sense, when Mao Tse-tung at the beginning of May launched the "Hundred Flowers" movement, paralleling the liberalization and thaw in Eastern Europe. But it remained fairly evident that Khrushchev had not consulted the CCP in advance regarding his intent to downgrade Stalin, despite the significance of that revolutionary action for the world Communist movement. Peking at the time showed restraint; Mao Tse-tung nevertheless could hardly have felt other than barred from exercise of the full partnership that he assumed belonged to him—and to China—by right.

There was measured Chinese criticism of Stalin on ideological grounds, with an authoritative editorial carried by the *People's Daily* at the end of the year observing that the Soviet leader had made some serious mistakes regarding both the domestic and foreign policies of the Soviet Union. "His arbitrary method of work impaired to a certain extent the principle of democratic centralism both in the life of the Party and in the state system of the Soviet Union, and led to a partial disruption of socialist legality." [4] In many fields of work, the editorial continued, Stalin had estranged himself from the masses and made personal arbitrary decisions regarding important policies, and thus grave mistakes. "These mistakes stood out most conspicuously in the suppression of counter-revolution and in relations with certain foreign countries." He "wronged many loyal Communists and honest citizens," and in tackling certain questions in relations with brother countries and parties "showed a tendency toward great-nation chauvinism and himself lacked a spirit of equality. . . ."

The editorial found most of Stalin's errors to have occurred in the latter years of his life. Making a broad comparison between Lenin and Stalin, the editorial writer(s) reached a general judgment:

> The decisive factor is man's ideological condition. A series of victories and the eulogies which Stalin received in the latter part of his life turned his head. . . . He began to put blind faith in personal wisdom and authority. . . . As a result, some of the policies and measures he adopted were often at variance with objective reality. He often stubbornly persisted in carrying out these mistaken measures over long periods and was unable to correct his mistakes in time.

Peking's responses to the developments in Poland and Hungary indicated that the CCP's liberalism was tempered by a full measure of dogma. Peking supported Gomulka's drive for freedom from Moscow's close supervision and came out first in support of the Hungarian people and then against Nagy and in favor of the Soviet armed intervention when Budapest made crystal clear that it intended to take Hungary out of the Communist bloc altogether. By the interpretation of the *People's Daily*, the Soviet intervention had been for the purpose of restoring order at the request of the Hungarian government and in accordance with the "genuine desire" of the Hungarian people, and had been "entirely just."

In January, 1957, after visits to various countries of Southeast Asia and India and Pakistan, Chou En-lai traveled to Moscow, Warsaw, and Budapest, to play the role of the great conciliator. The joint communiqué issued January 16 at Warsaw by Chou and his hosts proclaimed that "Relations between socialist countries . . . must be based upon the principles of respect for their sovereignty, of non-interference in their internal affairs, of equality and of mutual benefit." But at the same time Chou demanded that Gomulka silence his revisionists and manifest flexibility respecting the Soviet Union.[5]

Two days later, with the Chinese delegation back again in the USSR, there was issued a joint Sino-Soviet communiqué in which the two sides agreed that, "By helping the Hungarian people to put down the counterrevolutionary rebellion, the Soviet Union has fulfilled its duty to the working people of Hungary and the other socialist states, which is completely in line with the interests of safeguarding world peace."[6] Nothing was said specifically about the case of Poland. But when Council of Ministers Chairman (Premier) Jozef Cyrankiewicz headed a Polish delegation to Peking in April, he and Chou En-lai joined in a communiqué asserting that the Chinese and Polish Communist parties "are determined to continue their best efforts to strengthen further the solidarity of the countries in the socialist camp based on the Marxist-Leninist principles of proletarian internationalism and equality among nations."[7] Further, "they should consistently combat all deviations, whether doctrinaire or revisionist." China's intervention in European affairs suggested to some observers that, although the Soviet Union might not have qualified in the eyes of all as an Asian power, China contrariwise stood in line to become a European power.

In China itself, the intellectuals, made wary by previous experience with Mao Tse-tung's wiles, long resisted the invitation to speak their minds freely. But in May and June of 1957, after much prodding, they finally gave vent, in the Hungarian pattern, to some of their innermost feelings with regard to the CCP and its monopolistic exercise of power. The Communist leadership thereupon first undertook a rectification campaign within the party apparatus and then launched an antirightist campaign.

Teng Hsiao-p'ing in September sounded the keynote: the bourgeoisie threatened the revolution and must be eliminated as a class.

One feature of the Hundred Flowers criticism shed a sidelight on Sino-Soviet relations. A number of the supposedly dissident intellectuals voiced cogent criticism of the operation of the alliance. Some of those critics developed the charge that the Peking authorities had required too unquestioning an acceptance of things Soviet, whether with reference to school curricula, Soviet ideology, or technical processes and standards. But the most political of the animadversions against the Soviet Union came from "democratic personage" (and sometime Nationalist warlord ruler of Yunnan) Lung Yun, whose "absurd views" as presented to "an important meeting" were broadcast to the world by NCNA, as follows:

1. It was unreasonable for China to bear all the expenses of the resist-America aid-Korea war.
2. During the Second World War, the United States granted loans and leases to her allies. Later, some of these allies refused to pay back the loans, and the United States excused some from repayment. It will take our country more than ten years to repay the loans from the Soviet Union, if we can ever repay them. Besides, we have to pay interest to the Soviet Union. China fought for socialism, but look at the result.
3. The Soviet Army dismantled and shipped away some of the machinery of our factories when it liberated northeast China. What was the price paid by the Soviet Union? Will the Soviet Union compensate us?
4. The foreign aid budget of our country is too big and should be curtailed.[8]

The fourth point seemed oddly out of line with the preceding three. But NCNA presumably proposed to show that Lung was unsparing in his revelations.

Those political developments were to be viewed against the background of China's economic development. Liu Shao-ch'i, in his political report to the Eighth CCP Congress of September,

1956, laid down the basic tasks of the second five-year economic plan, for the period 1958–1962. He placed the stress, as before, on the development of heavy industry. It was entirely evident that the Chinese leadership anticipated being able to proceed in a straight line of development through three five-year plans, as originally contemplated, for the construction of a broadly based, integrated socialist economy by the end of 1967 or before.

The fulfillment of this rosy expectation would have depended upon either a notably improved performance in agriculture, or massive new credits from the Soviet Union to bridge the gap between China's lagging agricultural production and the growing needs of both the nation's industry and a population now expanding at the net rate of 15 million annually. There were signs in 1956 that Moscow was in fact prepared to expand its existing commitment to further China's economic development. The year began with a good omen when, in January, the new trans-Mongolian rail line was formally opened to traffic, thus providing an additional transportation link between China and its economic benefactor. In April, Mikoyan made yet another trip to Peking, and as a result of his negotiations the USSR undertook to construct fifty-five more factories and industrial plants for China, supplying designer services, equipment, and technological skills, in the total value of U.S.$625 million. No new Soviet credit was involved: China was to pay by current deliveries of goods. A second agreement provided for completion by 1960 of the Lanchow-Aktogai rail line.

In August, Peking announced that China and the Soviet Union had agreed to undertake joint development of the hydraulic power potential of the Amur and Argun river basin by construction of a network of electric-power plants designed to generate seventy billion kilowatt-hours to meet the power demands of regional Chinese and Soviet urban and industrial centers. The network would also provide power to make possible the electrification of the Irkutsk-Vladivostok section of the Trans-Siberian Railway. Among the hydraulic-engineering projects contemplated was one for the construction of a new outlet for the Amur to facilitate the passage of deep-draft oceangoing vessels and reduce the long period when passage was infeasible because the shallow mouth was frozen shut.

There was also movement in Soviet-Japanese relations. In October, on the eve of the Hungarian affair, Moscow and Tokyo reached an agreement for termination of the technical state of war and for the resumption of diplomatic relations. China, on the other hand, remained without diplomatic relations with its Asian neighbor. And then, when the first Conference of Afro-Asian Solidarity convened at New Delhi in December, the USSR was represented by a delegation from its Asian republics. This was a marked change from the situation prevailing at the 1955 Bandung conference. Moscow was further building up influence in Asia.

In 1957, China and the Soviet Union stood in notable contrast to each other. This was the final, and critical, year for China's first five-year plan. Agriculture had made good showings in the early plan period, what with good climatic conditions, the reduction of waste, and domestic peace. But Mao's pushing through of full collectivization at a rapid pace beginning in 1955, the decline in crop area in 1957 as compared with 1956, and bad growing weather, combined to make 1957 a poor crop year. The claimed grain production was only 185 million metric tons, constituting a 1.3 percent increase over 1956 — less than the population increase.

China's accumulated debits to the Soviet Union, which had to be paid in the main by the export of agricultural products, were an important economic factor. China had served its national interest in intervening in the Korean War, had heeded its impatience in pressing forward with industrialization at headlong pace in the period 1954–1957, and indulged its nationalistic pride in forcing the liquidation of the Sino-Soviet joint-stock companies. It took 40 percent of all Soviet machinery exports in 1957.[9] Now the bills were up for payment. The outstanding debit to the USSR in 1957 was U.S.$2.4 billion, of which something over one half represented arms purchases during the Korean War, while the rest was for principal and interest still outstanding with respect to the 1950 and 1954 credits of $430 million, and reimbursement for the Soviet share in the joint-stock companies, and other Soviet property turned over to China.[10]

At a time when China confronted increasing difficulties, the Soviet Union was substantially improving its power position. In August, 1957, in advance of the United States, the Soviets unveiled an operational intercontinental ballistic missile (ICBM) system, and in early October they sent up "sputnik," the earth's first man-made satellite. Sputnik had a considerable impact on American public opinion; it also made a distinct impression on

Peking. On October 15, China obtained something in the nature of a Soviet commitment to supply it with models and the technological information required for the manufacture of atomic weapons. The Chinese were to share, to a degree, in the Soviet technological triumph. But China's deficiencies were building up new tensions in the relationship.

In November, 1957, as Peking's leaders viewed China's international debit position against the background of the year's poor harvest, Moscow celebrated the fortieth anniversary of the Bolshevik Revolution. The shockwaves of de-Stalinization had largely subsided on the Soviet Union's western periphery, and Eastern Europe was stabilized in a pattern that remained recognizably "socialist." The twelve states of the Communist bloc were all represented at the anniversary ceremonies in Moscow.

Suggesting the importance that Peking attached to the event, Mao Tse-tung himself headed the Chinese delegation. For Peking, however, the ceremonies constituted not only an occasion for rendering homage to the brother Communist nation that had gone so far in forty years, but also an opportunity for endeavoring to obtain massive aid for China in its difficulties. Mao would not, of course, picture China as nationalistic, and selfish. It was easy for him to argue, given the ideology he had long professed, that he believed in the higher strategic principle, which should govern either simple militarist or Communist, that those who gain the advantageous position should go over to the offensive and annihilate the enemy. That was the essence of the Maoist concepts voiced by Liu Shao-ch'i in 1949; now, less than a decade later, Mao at Moscow sought to gain wider acceptance for his doctrine.

On November 6, Mao addressed a joint session of the Soviet of the Union and the Soviet of the Nationalities. He praised the Soviet Union for its achievements over the forty years of its existence and thanked it warmly for assistance rendered to China in the task of socialist construction. He asserted that the Chinese revolution "has its own national characteristics and it is entirely necessary to take them into consideration," but in both revolution and socialist construction China had made full use of the rich experience of the CPSU and the Soviet people.[11]

Mao held that all nations should practice the Five Principles in their relations with each other. He charged, however, that the United States persisted in interfering in the internal affairs of other countries. That did not trouble him: capitalism had lost its superiority and socialism had become invincible. "If the imperialist warriors are determined to start a third world war, they will bring about no other result than the end of the world capitalist system." In concluding his speech, Mao stressed the importance of acceptance of the Soviet Union as leader: "We regard it as the sacred international obligation of all socialist countries to strengthen the solidarity of the socialist countries headed by the Soviet Union."

It was during this visit to Moscow that Mao Tse-tung made a figurative remark that attracted wide attention: "The East Wind is prevailing over the West Wind." This was generally interpreted at the time to mean that the socialist camp was prevailing over the imperialists. But there were undertones of a different theme to be discovered in the fuller version later made public by a Soviet source:

> Who is stronger, the under-developed or advanced countries? Who is stronger, India or Britain, Indonesia or Holland, Algeria or France? To my mind all the imperialist countries are in a position which is like the position of the sun at 6 P.M., but ours is like the position of the sun at 6 A.M. Thus the tide has turned. And this means that the Western countries have been left behind, that we have outdistanced them considerably. Undoubtedly, it is not the Western wind that prevails over the Eastern wind, for the wind from the West is so weak. Undoubtedly, the Eastern wind prevails over the Western wind, for we are strong.[12]

In sum, there was here a distinct suggestion (which Mao not unnaturally refrained from spelling out) that by "East" was meant the underdeveloped countries of the Third World of which China was a part, whereas the term "West" embraced the industrialized countries of North America and Europe — including the Soviet Union.

The representatives of the twelve Communist parties present in Moscow took the occasion to convene for a joint consideration of the world situation and the role of Communism with relation thereto. In an official declaration issued on November 16, they set forth their unanimous agreement.[13] They found that "The main content of our epoch is the transition from capitalism to socialism, which was begun by the Great October Socialist Revolution in

Russia." They held that "The question of war or peaceful co-existence is now the crucial question of world policy." The Moscow Declaration embodied a critical thesis:

> At the present time the forces of peace have grown to such an extent that there is a real possibility of averting wars. . . .

> The Communist and Workers' Parties taking part in the meeting declare that the Leninist principle of peaceful co-existence of the two systems "socialist" and "capitalist" . . . is the sound basis of the foreign policy of socialist countries and the dependable pillar of peace and friendship among the peoples.

The assembled parties effectively discarded an element of the Zhdanov doctrine and opted in favor of collaboration with socialist parties and "the freedom- and peace-loving forces of the world" (in line with the "united front" concept adopted by the Seventh Comintern Congress two decades earlier); also, they agreed that a resolute stand should be taken against revisionism and dogmatism alike. They eschewed a program of detailed Marxist-Leninist dogma, holding that the need was for "a creative application of the general principles of the socialist revolution and of building socialism, depending on the concrete conditions of each country. . . ."

The Declaration was on the general line of the Khrushchev-Sobolev theses of February, 1956. It did indeed incorporate some revision of Leninist doctrine in both its foreign and domestic application. China adhered to the Declaration, as did the other Communist parties, without qualification or condition. But in due time, it would become apparent that the Maoist delegation had opposed the European position, proposing a fundamentally different orientation and stance for the bloc in world affairs. There appear to have been four main Chinese propositions, which may be summed up as follows. First, the Communist bloc should accept direct confrontation with imperialism. Second, bloc economic aid to nationalist bourgeois governments, soon to be overthrown in any event by proletarian internationalism, should cease. Third, all available Communist aid should be channeled to the needier members of the bloc. And fourth, the Communist bloc should be more tightly organized to the indicated ends, with Moscow no longer determining strategy, which should be formulated by the whole membership.

The rationale for Mao's radical program was to be found both in his ideology and in Chinese pragmatism. His thinking characteristically incorporated a large measure of demonology: Maoism provided automatically for the continued existence of enemies at home until all classes were eliminated, and for enemies abroad until the last imperialist had been swept from the face of the earth. He needed enemies for the pursuit of his purposes in accordance with his theory of contradictions; and there in fact existed those who opposed the Chinese national purpose as determined by Mao Tse-tung, and thus were to be regarded as enemies and eliminated — by the facile manipulation of some other opposing force if possible.

Mao's aims, although left unspecified, were plain to see. He proposed that the Soviet Union, given its presumed technological advantage over the United States (an advantage presumed by the Chinese, but not by the Soviets), should engage in a Dullesian brinkmanship to advance the cause of Communism throughout the world even at the risk of nuclear war — which Mao disparaged. Six years later, Moscow would reveal that Mao on that November, 1957, occasion had contemplated the possible annihilation of one third to one half of the world's population in nuclear war — but with equanimity, since "imperialism would be destroyed entirely and there would be only socialism in all the world." [14] There was a consideration that Mao left unspoken: of the three powers, the United States, the Soviet Union, and China, underdeveloped poverty-stricken China in all probability had the least to lose from a nuclear war that would be fought, at least in its initial phases (and there might be no other), between the USSR and the United States.

The establishment of an abstract "socialism" was patently not Mao's prime concern: the defeat of the rich, industrialized nations of the world — Mao's "imperialists" — would bring an early division of the spoils and thus relieve Chinese poverty. The second and third demands were pointed to the same general end of getting a diversion of all available Communist economic aid to the "needy" Communist countries — and wasn't China, the biggest and most populous, the neediest of them all? Mao in effect demanded that the European members of the bloc stop their own economic progress until they had raised the economically backward Asian sector to the same economic level, so that all socialist countries might advance together into the state of communism.[15] Since the corollary to this proposition contemplated that the several populations of the respective Communist countries in the state of "equality" should enjoy the same per capita standard of living, and China had well over three times the population of the Soviet Union, implementation of that particular Chinese program would naturally bring China into a position where it was relatively over three times as strong as the country from which it was demanding aid.

And then, by the final proposition, Mao Tse-tung proposed to guarantee the ultimate service of Chinese ends: with strategy to be determined by the whole membership, the Soviet Union would be effectively prevented from serving "selfish" Soviet ends and could be pressured by "majority" opinion to serve the purposes of Peking, whereas Peking by its veto could always ultimately prevent a similar manipulation of itself. This all meant that China was to have an important voice in both the fomentation of war with the imperialist camp (and the distribution and employment of Soviet weaponry) and the distribution of the Soviet Union's economic wealth.

Mao's efforts were supported by an imposing Chinese military delegation that had arrived in the Soviet capital on November 6. The mission was headed by Marshal P'eng Teh-huai, minister of national defense and sometime commander of the Chinese "volunteers" in Korea, and included Chief of General Staff Su Yü and Marshal Yeh Chien-ying, who had played so important a role in both the 1927 Canton Commune and the Executive Headquarters at Peking twenty years later. The composition of the mission suggested that the Chinese had been desirous of obtaining larger supplies of modern weapons, for those three men were among the leading modernists of the People's Liberation Army: they stood for professionalism in military affairs. The Chinese argument must logically be presumed to have been that China required a modern military establishment in order to play its full role with respect to events impending in the international arena. If this was so, however, it is evident that the Soviets did not propose a rapid buildup of the PLA for the (assumed) task of overwhelming imperialism by force of arms.

Moscow had made its choice long before. The costs of World War I and the civil war and interventions that had followed in the wake of the 1917 Revolution, the 7.5 million military dead and missing and the economic destruction incidental to World War II, had qualified even Zhdanov's advocacy of the revolutionary approach to the solution of international problems. The 1952 and 1956 formulation of a strategy primarily economic in its approach, while unsuited to the purposes of economically backward China, quite obviously was serving the Soviet Union well in competition with the United States. A military confrontation, on the other hand, would lead at the least to so vast a destruction that the USSR, even if not the United States as well, would be reduced to the level of – China. There was no profit apparent in such an adventure. Moscow chose to maintain the existing "Bandung strategy" of peaceful coexistence and, as Malenkov had put it in 1952, competitive economic collaboration.

Mao Tse-tung returned to Peking empty-handed, except for the Soviet promise to provide China with prototypes of atomic weapons. In the period from 1953, when Stalin died, the Korean War ended, and the Chinese launched their first five-year plan, to 1957, the Soviet Union had refined its world strategy and developed a new set of international relations that gave it openings to both the West and the Third World. The evidence of subsequent events suggests that Mao failed to make an adequate appreciation of the new Soviet policy and power position.

31 GATHERING STORM, 1958-1959

AT THE END OF 1957, China stood confronted by hard, unyielding alternatives. Moscow was not prepared to support a strategy envisaging nuclear confrontation, nor was it prepared to bend its wealth and energies primarily to the task of transforming China into a major military and economic power for that alleged purpose. Without Soviet aid, China was not in an economic condition to equip the People's Liberation Army with an arsenal of modern weapons. Nor could it anticipate, by the usual pragmatic calculations, being able to create a modern industrial base in short order without outside assistance. In late 1957 Moscow announced a new economic plan for the seven years 1959–1965, and undertook appropriate adjustments of its economic relations with the Eastern European members of the bloc, within the framework of CMEA. But China was not a member of CMEA, so there was no special help available to it in that area.

China therefore either had to retrench and consolidate the acquired gains through the diversion of the limited available capital funds to the needs of agriculture, or it would have to invent new methods, in some fresh sinicization of Marxism-Leninism, which would solve the seemingly insoluble problem of bridging the widening gap between agricultural productivity and the growing needs of the nation for industrial raw materials, food supplies, and agricultural export products. Mao's China was over-committed politically and economically; it had either to cut down on its commitments, or perform a miracle.

In February, 1958, the National People's Congress called for a Great Leap Forward in economic developments over the next three years. The second session of the Eighth CCP Congress, held in May, gave its approval to the proposition (which it had undoubtedly fathered), and the campaign was launched with all the vigor of the party behind it. The governing slogan was "politics in command," the approved procedure "uncontrolled spontaneity." For CCP Chairman Mao Tse-tung, the subjective would form and create the objective; the revolutionary will of the "Red," not the restrained pragmatism of the "expert," was to dominate.

In May, 1958, also, at a CMEA meeting at Moscow, agreement was reached on an arrangement whereby Asian Communist states, including China, the Mongolian People's Republic, North Korea, and North Vietnam, might join the USSR and the Eastern European states in overall economic planning. But this would have required specialization along lines determined to some degree by alien will, and coordination with the activities of others. Peking was chauvinistically opposed to "foreign interference"; furthermore, the temper of May, 1958, was such that a tie-up with the Occidental section of the bloc would have been viewed as threatening a retardation of China's economic development. China did not avail itself of the opportunity offered. Instead it chose to follow the path laid down by the Thought of Mao Tse-tung.

In a literal interpretation of the Marx-Engels proposition that "production armies" should be formed for the performance of agricultural tasks, the peasant masses were mobilized into labor brigades. In August, the agricultural-commune system was formally launched. Then, too, in line with Lenin's sometime proposal that there should be created a people's militia comprising the great majority of males and females between the ages of eighteen and sixty-five, the Chinese masses were recruited in huge numbers into militia formations. Marx, Engels, and Lenin? The social organization undertaken in the countryside was strikingly reminiscent of the pattern proposed at the end of the nineteenth century by the liberal constitutional-monarchist K'ang Yu-wei, and the drive toward regimentation of the state smacked of the Legalist doctrine of two thousand years earlier. The program was in categorical violation of the "basic laws" voiced in the 1957 Moscow Declaration that the socialist reconstruction of agriculture should be *gradual,* and that national economic development should be *planned.*

With the advent of summer, Peking's attacks on revisionism generally, and Yugoslav revisionism in particular, took on new violence. Here it is well to remember the old Chinese proverb, "pointing at the mulberry to curse the locust," expressive of a timeworn Chinese trait of criticizing by indirection. The main target of Peking's antirevisionism had already become Khrushchev's "unrevolutionary" policy of peaceful coexistence. But Tito fought back on his own account and, speaking in June, charged that the Peking leadership, which calculated that if one half of China's 600 million people were killed there would still remain 300 million Chinese, counted on war as a means of consolidating its rule over Asia.[1]

The issue of peace or war had taken on more than philosophical importance, given particular developments in the field of China's foreign relations. For one thing, it was reported that it had been by Mao Tse-tung's insistence that there had been introduced into the Moscow conference's draft declaration the changes that had made it unacceptable to Yugoslavia. For another, Peking seemed now bent on giving an example to the timid by itself pursuing a "revolutionary foreign policy" distinctly reminiscent of that employed by the Nationalist government at Wuhan in 1927. The party's Military Affairs Committee (MAC) in late July completed a two-month-long session that appears to have been devoted to considerations of military organization and theory, and grand strategy. The evidence of China's foreign relations in 1958 suggests that the decision was to follow a radical foreign-policy line generally and, in particular, to take action against the Nationalist position on Quemoy.[2]

This intent probably was made known to Moscow, which, in view of the Middle East crisis then in course, would presumably not have been averse to China's undertaking a diversionary action in the Far East at that particular juncture — with strict limitations of risk and of Soviet responsibility. At the end of July, Peking received another visit from Khrushchev, this time accompanied by Defense Minister Malinovski, who was known to the Chinese from his administration of Manchuria as commander of the occupying Soviet forces in 1945–1946. The communiqué issued at the end of the three-day conference disclosed nothing of real substance respecting the agenda of this top-level meeting, but it was to be noted that Marshal P'eng Teh-huai participated, as the counterpart of Malinovski, and in the light of political developments in both the Middle East and the Formosa Strait, it can safely be assumed that the conference dealt with matters of major political and military significance.

It was probably at this highly important strategy meeting between the Soviet and Chinese leaders at time of crisis that the Soviets proposed that a joint Sino-Soviet naval command should be constituted for the West Pacific.[3] Since the Soviet Union was being called upon to assume not inconsiderable responsibilities with respect to the defense of China vis-à-vis the United States, Moscow's purpose in such a partnership would naturally have been to exert a degree of control and guidance over China's West Pacific strategy. That particular sort of "equality" would have been insufferable to Peking, and the Chinese later charged that "In 1958 the leadership of the CPSU put forward unreasonable demands designed to bring China under military control. These unreasonable demands were rightly and firmly rejected by the Chinese Government."[4] As evidenced by subsequent events, the Soviets consequently refused to shoulder the military undertakings urged upon them by the Chinese.[5]

When the Formosa Strait crisis sprung by the Communist bombardment of Quemoy reached its height in early September, Moscow limited its support to a vaguely worded warning statement by *Pravda* on September 5; Chou En-lai offered to negotiate on September 6; *then,* the following day, Khrushchev by letter to President Eisenhower stated that an attack on China would be regarded as an attack on the Soviet Union itself. And it was not until September 19, *after the crisis had effectively quite passed the danger point,* that Khrushchev in a second letter announced that, in the event of a nuclear attack on China, "then the aggressor will receive a fitting rebuff by the same means."[6]

Peking on October 6 announced that it had suspended the bombardment of Quemoy, and the crisis had effectively run its course — without victory for Mao Tse-tung. Mao's essay "Imperialists and All Reactionaries Are Paper Tigers" was published that same month. If he could not overwhelm his enemies in fact, Mao was always able to do so in theory. There was however no sign that his essay changed the thinking of Nikita S. Khrushchev on the desirability of avoiding World War III.

The Chinese were not without a modest consolation prize: on July 4, Peking and Moscow had signed a protocol to govern their scientific and technical collaboration, and on August 8, after Khrushchev and Malinovski had departed Peking, the two countries entered upon an agreement providing for Soviet aid in the design and installation of forty-seven more industrial plants.

But in October, with the second Formosa Strait crisis past, China claimed much greater results from its own efforts. Five months after undertaking the Great Leap in industry and two months after embarking upon the revolutionary reorganization of agriculture, Peking proudly proclaimed tremendous successes in all areas of political and economic endeavor during 1958. It would soon claim specifically to have doubled steel production, to reach a total of 11 million tons, and also to have doubled food-grain production, put at 375 million tons as compared with 185 million tons the year before. There had never been anything like this before in the history of mankind. And those putative accomplishments could of course be taken as substantiating the claim that Mao Tse-tung had not only discovered a universal pattern for revolution in the agrarian, backward, emerging nations of Asia, Africa, and Latin America, but that he had also evolved procedures for achieving socialist construction in a Great Leap, instead of slowly and laboriously.

Moscow was concerned in more ways than one with the revolutionary Chinese experiment: success would overturn orthodox Communist thinking on economic processes and justify Peking's claim, made in October, that it was entering the stage of communism (ahead of the Soviet Union); failure, on the other hand, would increase the economic burdens the Soviet Union would be called upon to bear—if it chose to redeem the mistakes of the Peking leadership. With its many technicians on the ground in China, Moscow occupied an advantageous position from which to observe the course of the Great Leap. It evidently listened to the paeans of victory with disbelief and judged the vast adventure (in which the sober advice of Soviet specialists had been ignored, where not scorned) a failure.[7]

Sobering doubts had evidently penetrated the Chinese party hierarchy as well. In a communiqué of December 17, the CCP Central Committee still lauded the agricultural communes and proclaimed a Great Leap Forward plan for 1959, but it also announced substantial changes in policy and practice, in the direction of moderation, gradualism, and the use of economic incentives. The central committee further reported its decision of December 10 to grant the "wish" of Mao Tse-tung to be relieved of the post of chairman of the Chinese People's Republic. His successor to that position, elected by the National People's Congress the following April, was the pragmatic organization man, Liu Shao-ch'i.

The achievements of 1958, then, had patently not been so decisive that China was prepared voluntarily to forgo any further economic assistance from abroad, and the logical prospective source was still its Soviet ally. The USSR had remitted the debts of "revisionist" Yugoslavia and was extending credits and other forms of economic assistance to "bourgeois nationalist" countries of the Third World; it had already given much economic aid, of various kinds, to China, and manifestly was in a position to continue with the program. Chou En-lai had in October given a measure of Communist-bloc aid by his report that, in the first decade of the Chinese People's Republic's existence, the Soviet Union had supplied China with the services of over 10,000 experts, and Eastern European countries had sent an additional 1,800. Given the ambitious program for the years ahead, and China's oppressive shortage of trained engineers and industrial administrators, Peking had good reason to desire even greater aid in the future. There was at this juncture no indication that China proposed to forgo the utilization of foreign experts, in favor of reliance upon its own "Reds."

It was only good politics, therefore, for Chou En-lai, accompanied by K'ang Sheng (who had spent several years in the Soviet Union in the 1930s), to attend the Twenty-first CPSU Congress held in Moscow in January, 1959. The doctrines developed by Khrushchev at the congress offered no concession to Mao's revolutionary romanticism. The Soviet leader stood by the previous CPSU positions respecting the requirements of the international situation. He quoted Lenin: "If Russia becomes covered with a dense network of electric stations and powerful technical equipment, our communist economic construction will become a model for the future socialist Europe and Asia." [8] This seemed to be a fairly obvious retort to the Maoist claim that China would supply the revolutionary patterns to, at least, the emerging Third World.

The Soviet Union had produced 55 million tons of steel in 1958, and if its grain output was only 140 million tons, it had a population less than one third the size of China's to feed. Its two-way trade in 1958 had totaled 34.6 billion rubles (U.S.$8.65 billion), as compared with China's U.S.$3.4 billion, and in 1957, according to Khrushchev's report, Soviet trade with underdeveloped countries was five times what it had been in 1953. Moscow bade fair to make its influence felt in concrete terms. If Khrushchev did not follow the Chinese pattern and claim a doubling of Soviet grain production in one year, he still reported that his country's 1958 grain output was 91 percent higher than in 1953 — and his statistics turned out to be closer to the reality than had been Peking's. Details of the 1959–1965 economic plan as presented to the congress displayed the flesh and bones of Moscow's theories. There was more of substance there than in the Chinese project for a continuation of the Great Leap Forward in 1959.

When Chou En-lai addressed the congress on January 28, he transmitted a message from Mao Tse-tung lauding "the correct leadership of the Central Committee of the Communist Party headed by Comrade Khrushchev," and the seven-year plan. Mao had not been able to forbear remarking that imperialism was currently suffering from economic crisis and social conflicts, and that the colonial system was disintegrating; "The deathbed struggles of the imperialists and all other reactionaries will never save them from final extinction." [9] As in 1957, he acknowledged a debt: "The Chinese people have received consistent brotherly assistance and support from the Soviet Union in their struggle to reconstruct and safeguard their country. In the name of the Chinese people, we express our heartfelt thanks to the people, the Government and the Communist Party of the Soviet Union." There were obvious differences in emphasis between the Soviet and Chinese formulations in the realm of foreign affairs, but Peking seemed to be at least outwardly in general agreement with the Moscow line.

The Chinese approach bore rich fruits. On February 7, Chou En-lai and Khrushchev signed an agreement providing that the Soviet Union would supply China with equipment, materials, technical assistance, and training for Chinese personnel, in the total value of 5 billion rubles (U.S.$1.25 billion) over the nine years 1959–1967. The agreement envisaged the construction of 78 large plants (in addition to the 47 plants for which commitment had been made in August) in the critical fields of metallurgy, machine building, chemistry, coal mining, electric power, and building materials. This made a grand total of 336 Chinese plants programed for construction or reconstruction with Soviet aid since 1950. Again there was a limiting factor: Moscow offered no new credits for use in purchasing this material and the related engineering services, Peking instead being required to pay for its purchases out of current production. Given the extravagant official claims that the output of such basic products as food grains and steel had doubled in 1958, China presumably felt that it faced no especial difficulty in contracting for the new purchases.

In hard fact, the success of the new program of economic construction depended chiefly upon (1) China's own economic capabilities and (2) the political and economic directions chosen by the Peking regime. The second factor in large measure governed the first. The CCP leadership kept its intramural dissensions mostly secret, but Mao Tse-tung's resignation of the chairmanship of the Chinese People's Republic had obviously been a move of great significance — for both nation and party. Now there came another development, reflecting a depth of division that became known only later.

P'eng Teh-huai, as Kao Kang, had gone on missions to the USSR and (if with different motives) favored the Soviet liaison. In May, 1959, while on a goodwill tour to the Eastern European bloc, he met Khrushchev in Albania. P'eng, a practical military man, had been opposed to the Great Leap in general and to the agricultural communes in particular. It is evident that he belonged to the group of Chinese militarists who felt the need of creating a modern army for China's use in self-defense and implementation of its national policy. It is logical to assume that he would have been opposed to the adventurousness of the 1958 operation in the Formosa Strait and the wasteful extravagances of the coincident organization of tens of millions of militia in service of the idea that they could act as a counterforce to American nuclear power. He had prepared a memorandum expounding his point of view and, although he had not yet submitted it to his own party, he presented a copy to Khrushchev.[10]

There was doubtless more to the exchange between Khrushchev and P'eng than we shall ever know, but it can be guessed that the Soviet leader at least obtained a fuller appreciation of both the reasons for Mao's retirement from state leadership and the bent of Chinese grand strategy. Subsequent developments bore heavily on the Sino-Soviet relationship. In accordance with an agreement of April, 1956, Moscow had in 1958 completed the installation of a nuclear reactor for China. There was also the Soviet undertaking of 1957 to assist their Chinese allies in developing a nuclear arsenal. But much water had flowed over the dam in 1958 in particular, and Peking was now to discover that Khrushchev's grand strategy operated to limit Soviet support for China's adventures. On June 20, in an action that became known only much later, the Soviet Union canceled the 1957 agreement to provide China with the technological knowledge requisite for the manufacture of atomic bombs.

Just a little over a month later, Moscow agreed to extend India a fresh credit of U.S.$378 million for economic development. Peking was then on the eve of acknowledging that it had sadly overestimated the country's economic accomplishments of 1958. Given the exasperations that attended the Chinese leadership in that hard year of 1959, it would have been only natural for the radicals of Mao's clique to conclude that the Soviet Union had embarked upon a policy in direct conflict with Chinese national aspirations. It required but one step more to reach the conclusion that Moscow's policy had become openly anti-Chinese.

P'eng Teh-huai's exchange with Khrushchev was presumably unknown to Mao Tse-tung at the time. At an August plenum of the CCP Central Committee at Lushan, however, with his determination probably strengthened by the Soviet cancellation of the program for aiding China to become a nuclear power,[11] P'eng presented his memorandum attacking Party policy. A major confrontation resulted. Mao seemingly fought desperately to destroy his major opponent,[12] and had his way. In September, there came the dismissal of P'eng Teh-huai as minister of national defense and of Huang K'e-ch'eng as his chief of general staff. They were replaced by Lin Piao and Lo Jui-ch'ing, respectively.

Nearly coincident with the Lushan meeting, a new crisis occurred in China's foreign relations. A movement of rebellion in Tibet had led, in March, to the intervention of Chinese troops and the flight of the theocratic ruler, the Dalai Lama, to India. This in turn resulted in a Sino-Indian conflict over the common frontier, with Chinese military units in late August breaching the border to occupy an Indian outpost. Prime Minister Nehru in a report of August 31 to the Upper House informed the Indian people, for the first time, that in 1957 the Chinese had built a highway across eastern Ladakh, claimed as Indian territory, and that subsequent negotiations with Peking regarding the matter had been fruitless. The Chinese action seemed in clear violation of the Five Principles proclaimed jointly in 1954 by Chou En-lai and

Nehru, and, following so closely in the wake of the new Soviet credit to India, it also had the earmarks of a challenge to Soviet policy.

Tass on September 9 issued a statement pointing the finger of blame at "certain political circles and the press in the western countries" for "a noisy campaign" with respect to the Sino-Indian border incident.[13] Tass went on to adopt, for Moscow, a basically neutral position:

> The incident on the Chinese-Indian frontier is certainly deplorable. The Soviet Union maintains friendly relations with the Chinese People's Republic and the Republic of India. The Chinese and Soviet peoples are linked by unbreakable bonds of fraternal friendship, based on the great principles of socialist internationalism. Friendly co-operation between the U.S.S.R. and India is developing successfully in keeping with the idea of peaceful co-existence.

> Soviet leading circles . . . express their confidence that the two governments will settle the misunderstandings that have arisen, taking into consideration their mutual interests and in the spirit of the traditional friendship between the peoples of China and India.

The Soviet "confidence" was misplaced: the Sino-Indian honeymoon was over.

It was against the background of both the Indian development and another spectacular Soviet technological achievement, the sending of a rocket to the moon, that Khrushchev visited the United States from September 15 to 28, 1959, with the avowed aim of improving Soviet-American relations. His mission was opposed by Peking, which under Mao's leadership favored conflict, not détente, between the two nuclear powers. The meetings between Khrushchev and President Eisenhower at Camp David could be called a brave try, but they produced no immediate results: the differences in points of view between the American and Soviet leaders were too great. It was an interesting coincidence that P'eng Teh-huai's dismissal occurred about the same time as the Camp David talks were being held. The talks over, Khrushchev reoriented himself and proceeded to Peking for participation in the celebration of the tenth anniversary of the founding of the Chinese People's Republic.

Khrushchev at Peking made no concessions to the Maoist view that socialism had become invincible and that, therefore, "the socialist countries headed by the Soviet Union" should take the offensive in world affairs in easy disregard of probable American reaction. Speaking upon his arrival September 30, he held that his talks in the United States had been "useful" and would lead to a relaxation of international tensions. Everything had to be done to clear the atmosphere and create conditions for friendship among peoples; "we must achieve such conditions in order to ensure peace throughout the world." [14] Then, speaking at a dinner held that evening in celebration of the Chinese People's Republic's tenth anniversary, he expounded more fully on the same theme of peace, saying that "We must and we shall defeat the capitalist countries in peaceful competition. . . . Socialism brings peace, that greatest of blessings, to men. . . . This is how the matter stands: either peaceful coexistence or war with its catastrophic consequences." The socialist countries were strong, but, "Of course, this does not in any way mean that . . . we should test the stability of the capitalist system by force. This would be wrong." [15]

Departing on October 4, Khrushchev spoke briefly to reiterate his belief that it was possible to "rule out war for all time as a means of solving international disputes." [16] The Chinese had doubtless heard him the first time, and they patently didn't like what they heard.

At the end of October, the Soviet press carried new attacks on Trotsky. Trotsky was long dead, but Moscow too knew the tactic of "pointing at the mulberry to curse the locust." Trotsky was serving as surrogate for Mao Tse-tung. Khrushchev did not limit himself to indirection: at the Seventh Hungarian Party Congress in early December, he attacked China's Great Leap and voiced condemnation of "arrogant leaders" in the Communist camp. The Soviet campaign against the Yugoslav leadership further moderated from about this time onward, with Soviet criticism of Yugoslav policies being limited to the realm of foreign affairs: Tito's brand of domestic "socialism," radically different though it might be from the Soviet brand, was inferentially once more acceptable to Moscow—but not to Peking. This made it all the more evident that fundamental differences had developed between Khrushchev and Mao Tse-tung respecting the world strategy to be followed—by the Soviet Union in particular.

This political development took place under conditions where the Chinese boasts that 1959 promised even more striking advances than 1958 had already been belied. Li Fu-ch'un had claimed that, "despite serious natural calamities," the summer harvest of 1959 had exceeded that of the year before by 2.5 billion catties (roughly, 1 million metric tons). In fact, the output of *food grains* in particular dropped from an estimated 194 million tons [17] (as distinct from the *adjusted* official Chinese figure of 250 million tons) in 1958 to an estimated 168 million tons in 1959. The trend in industrial production was still upward, for the time being, but before the next year was out industry too would go into a decline by reason of the shock of the Great Leap—and of additional blows that would soon be rained down upon it. In terms of foreign trade, 1959 was China's best year to date, with the total value of the two-way exchange reaching $4.4 billion. That year, China occupied first place in the Soviet Union's foreign trade. But with a declining agricultural output China was now living beyond its means, and in 1960 its foreign trade would plunge into a sharp decline. The attempted Great Leap Forward had been a massive failure.

The Soviet Union, on the other hand, had in 1959 driven ahead to implement its program for winning political sympathies and support by a broad program of trade and aid directed at the Third World. Moscow selected correspondent nations carefully, for, unlike the United States, the Soviet Union was not possessed of the resources that would have permitted it to be profligate with grants—even had this been deemed a desirable approach. International developments facilitated the strategy, and Soviet influence was perceptibly advanced in countries like Cuba, the United Arab Republic, Iraq, and Guinea. Fidel Castro came to power in Cuba on New Year's Day of 1959, and just a little over a year later would enter upon a barter agreement with the Soviet Union —and then, under the added urge of American hostility, would draw closer still to Moscow. The Soviet political presence was also made manifest in Afghanistan and Burma, on China's frontiers, and in Indonesia. In India, thanks to the Soviet aid program, the Bhilai steelworks went into production at the end of the year. China, as a "fraternal" socialist state, can only have thought that Soviet aid should be going more liberally to the more deserving country—itself.

32 1960: OPEN CONFLICT

THE YEAR 1960 began with a promise, born of the Camp David meeting, that there would be a summit conference of the four Occidental great powers (China thus excluded) for an attempted relaxation of the tensions between them — and particularly between the USSR and the United States. The status of Berlin was the prime item on the agenda. Khrushchev had begun in late 1958 to pressure the United States, Britain, and France to withdraw troops from West Berlin, and although he had refrained from attempting to effect the sanctions threatened in the event of failure to reach a settlement along the lines laid down, the situation was still ominous.

Khrushchev still voiced peaceful sentiments. In addressing the Supreme Soviet in mid-January, he spoke in favor of universal and total disarmament and announced a reduction of the Soviet armed forces from 3,623,000 to 2,423,000 men. He made only a few passing references to China.

In February, the Warsaw Pact powers met in Moscow. Again, there was a Chinese observer present — this time K'ang Sheng. Khrushchev continued his onslaught against Chinese policy and declared that the Soviet Union would not provide nuclear arms to China.[1] According to the information made public in August, 1963, the Soviet promise to provide an A-bomb model had at that date already been given — and rescinded. But this was not generally known at the time of the Warsaw Pact meeting at Moscow.

In a speech on that occasion, K'ang said that the Chinese people rejoiced at the projected convening of the summit conference, but he also took the occasion to state that China would not be bound by any international agreement reached without its formal participation and signature. The position was technically sound – but also obvious, not needing the saying. In the context, his statement appeared directed at the United States. But it naturally had an equal relevance to Soviet policy.

Soviet attention seemed at this time to be directed quite as much in other directions as toward China. Voroshilov had visited India and Nepal in January. In February, after the Warsaw Pact meeting was over, Khrushchev made a longer trip that took him to India, Burma, Indonesia, and Afghanistan. February 14, 1960, was the tenth anniversary of the signature of the Sino-Soviet treaty of alliance. On that date, Khrushchev was in India, where on February 12 there was signed a Soviet-Indian agreement, with Khrushchev and Nehru present at the signing ceremony, by which Moscow extended a credit of 1.5 billion new rubles (U.S.$1.65 billion) to India for use in connection with the joint construction or expansion of industrial and other enterprises during its third five-year plan, scheduled to begin in 1961. This was in addition to 3.13 billion (old) rubles (U.S.$782.5 million) in Soviet credits granted through 1959.

Soviet aid to India was beginning to bear fruits. Given the shattered state of China's *second* five-year plan, which had begun with the disastrous Great Leap of 1958, Khrushchev's presence in India on that significant date February 14, and his accomplishments there, could only have been viewed sourly by Peking. The remainder of Khrushchev's itinerary was designed to arouse China's nationalistic suspicions. Burma and Indonesia were "anti-imperialist," but not pro-Chinese, in their foreign policies, and Indonesia in particular promised to become a critical element in the future South Pacific balance of power. Afghanistan, even as in the nineteenth century, occupied a strategic position between Russia and India and on the flank of China, and Moscow and Washington were currently both striving to expand their influence there.

Peking was truly not in a position to complain that it had no share in the Soviet economic program. In March, China and the Soviet Union had signed a new trade protocol to govern exchanges during 1960, and the projected total contemplated an increase of

10 percent over that fixed by the 1959 protocol (but actual trade in 1959, at 8.2 billion [old] rubles [U.S.$2.05 billion] had been greater than contemplated by the protocol, reflecting in part sharply increased shipments of Soviet machinery and equipment to China). On the face of it, Sino-Soviet commercial exchanges seemed destined to bring increased profit to both parties.

It was at this time that the Chinese, who had undoubtedly been following developments in Moscow's foreign economic and political affairs with close attention, chose to go over to the attack. The occasion was the anniversary of Lenin's birth, and the means was a long article entitled "Long Live Leninism!" published in the April 16 issue of the *Red Flag*, the organ of the CCP Central Committee. The Soviets were later to ascribe authorship of the article to Mao Tse-tung himself.

The article was a polemic against those who, in the light of changed world conditions, would revise "the truths revealed by Lenin." It leaned upon the Moscow Declaration of 1957 to condemn the "modern revisionism" that would (allegedly) contend that Marxism-Leninism was outmoded. It cited the Sino-Japanese War in (spurious) support of a favorite Maoist theory that man, not technique, determines the fate of mankind. The introduction of nuclear arms into national arsenals had not altered the basic characteristics of the epoch in which, according to Lenin, proletarian revolution confronted imperialism. "Until the imperialist system and the exploiting classes come to an end, wars of one kind or another will always appear. . . . Revolution means the use of revolutionary violence by the oppressed class, it means revolutionary war." [2] And if there were nuclear war, "the result will certainly not be annihilation of mankind."

The article pro forma proclaimed China's devotion to peace, but emphasized the addiction of imperialists to war. It pointed the accusing finger directly at the "Yugoslav revisionists," who "deny the danger of the imperialists launching another big war, deny that it will be possible to do away with war only after doing away with the exploiting classes." [3] The article ended with what might have been taken as a war cry: "Long live great Leninism!" By this time it was crystal clear that, if Tito had been selected as official whipping boy, the real object of Mao Tse-tung's aroused "Leninist" scorn was Nikita S. Khrushchev.

If Mao was not actually the author, he would obviously have

been the inspirer of the article and have sanctioned its publication. His condemnation of any further rapprochement between the USSR and the United States, his adamant opposition to a Soviet policy of trade and aid with the Third World that promised benefits to the Soviet Union in which China could not hope to share, were logical from his viewpoint. What is not immediately apparent, however, is why Mao Tse-tung chose to launch so obvious a challenge to Moscow's contemporary foreign-policy line at that particular juncture.

Mao could have reasoned that (1) the Soviet Union could not in the ultimate analysis contemplate a break with China, (2) Moscow on previous occasion, even with respect to the 1957 Declaration, had made concessions to the Chinese point of view, and (3) faced with a serious challenge, Moscow would perhaps make the important concession of granting, publicly, that the United States was as much of an enemy for the Soviet Union as for China — or at least would offer substantial grants in aid to China, as a conciliatory gesture. Such a line of reasoning would have fit neatly the Maoist law of contradictions, or, be it said, traditional Chinese bargaining tactics in foreign affairs. But there would have been a flaw in that line of thought: Peking had not built up plausible alternatives to the Sino-Soviet alliance.

If Mao Tse-tung would employ the *Red Flag* as a channel for leveling a challenge at Khrushchev, the Soviet leader also had proxies at hand. The reply to the Chinese blast was given by Otto V. Kuusinen, member of the Soviet party's presidium, who was chief editor of a new comprehensive work, *Fundamentals of Marxism-Leninism*, published in 1960, setting forth authoritative Communist doctrine. That work presented in detail, inter alia, the new Soviet doctrine that "wars are not fatally inevitable," and stated categorically that "The official doctrine of Soviet foreign policy is the *Leninist principle of peaceful coexistence* of states regardless of the differences in their social and political systems." [4]

Kuusinen borrowed the occasion offered by the celebration at Moscow, on April 22, of the Lenin anniversary. In his analysis of the ideological problem, he stoutly supported the Khrushchevian policy and decried the Chinese dogma that major war was inevitable. From the standpoint of the Marxist-Leninist purists, he made a telling point when he related that Nadezhda Krupskaya, Lenin's widow, had reported that Lenin foresaw that "the time will come when war will be so destructive as to be impossible." [5]

Khrushchev's argument in favor of peaceful coexistence received a rude and unexpected setback when, on May 1, an American U-2 spy-plane penetrated the Soviet Union and was shot down 1,200 miles inside Soviet territory. Evasive tactics adopted by the U.S. government compounded the offense. The summit conference, so dependent for its success upon bona fides, had shown waning prospects because of the American attitude toward the German question; now, no promise was left, and Khrushchev's months' old public defense of Eisenhower had been blasted before the eyes of the world. The summit meeting convened on May 16, true, but it foundered the following day. Mao Tse-tung had on this occasion been proved right.

The Chinese did not forgo the opportunity to press their forensic advantage while the Soviets were off balance. When the council of the World Federation of Trade Unions sat in Peking from June 5 to 9, Soviet policy generally and Khrushchev in particular were brought under strong Chinese attack, and the Chinese now addressed themselves seriously to the task of creating anti-Soviet fractions in other Communist parties. The Chinese party's challenge to the dominance of the CPSU in the world Communist movement had taken overt form.

Moscow was seemingly not yet prepared to make a full, organized response to the Chinese campaign, which was probably in large measure unexpected — at least on the scale in which it appeared. But in June, 1920, Lenin had published a short work entitled *"Left-Wing" Communism: An Infantile Disorder*, in which he had condemned certain excesses of the German Communist left wing in particular. He held that anarchism and "petty-bourgeois revolutionism" were two "monstrosities" that had acted to complement each other in the working-class movement. Petty-bourgeois revolutionism, in particular, was to be viewed as barren and unstable and apt to be transformed into "a mad infatuation with one or another bourgeois 'fad.'" [6] He held that the German Left's rejection of all compromise "in principle" was simply left-wing Communism; the history of Bolshevism "is full of instances of manoeuvring, temporising, and compromising with other parties, bourgeois parties included!" [7]

It was evident from this document that Lenin would have

condoned no great leaps in social development, no putschism in the struggle to replace bourgeois-nationalist governments with Communist regimes. On the fortieth anniversary of the publication of that work, N. Matovsky in *Pravda* read a lesson on ideological rectitude to unnamed Communist parties that might in their radical fervor wish to skip historical stages of development (by Marxist-Leninist theory), or might quest for "separate paths" to socialism, saying "There is in life only one Leninist path, verified by historical experience, for building socialism and communism, the path of the Great October Socialist Revolution." [8]

The combination of adverse circumstances and Chinese argument led to no admission by Khrushchev that he had been wrong all along. Instead, it was as if the summit-conference episode had hardened Khrushchev's attitude toward the Chinese argument. Evidence of this came at the next confrontation, which took place at a conference of the twelve Communist parties, the first since 1957, held at Bucharest when the Rumanian party congress sat in June. Khrushchev was present, accompanied by Foreign Minister Gromyko and CPSU International Section Chief Boris N. Ponomarev, and so was CCP Politburo member P'eng Chen, to offer the Maoist point of view. The Soviets began their campaign early, circulating on the eve of the meeting a long memorandum by Ponomarev expounding the Soviet position and condemning the Chinese arguments. At the conference proper, Khrushchev spoke first, on June 21, and stood firmly on his previous position in support of the policy of coexistence. He spoke bluntly against an opposite policy: "Only lunatics and maniacs can now come out with appeals for a new world war." [9] Khrushchev went on to voice support of the principle of closer integration of the socialist commonwealth. P'eng Chen, speaking the next day, took as his theme Mao's obiter dicta regarding the predominance of the East Wind; said P'eng, "the days of imperialism are numbered." [10] He also reiterated the well-worn Chinese arguments for the support of revolutionary movements and for a strong stand against imperialism.

Those speeches, civil enough in outward aspects, were presented in the open sessions of the conference. On June 26, however, the Chinese circulated among the delegations a statement charging Khrushchev with having adopted in the encounter a "patriarchal, arbitrary and despotic" attitude and with having "completely violated the principle of regulation of common prob-

lems by way of discussion among fraternal parties." [11] In a confidential meeting at the end of the conference Khrushchev loosed
an angry assault on Chinese Communist policies with respect to
the Hundred Flowers campaign, agricultural communes, India,
and Algeria, and he attacked in particular Mao Tse-tung as an
ultradogmatist and left revisionist who, like Stalin, fostered a
personality cult.[12] P'eng is reported to have replied that Khrushchev had evidently organized the conference for the sole purpose of attacking the Chinese Communist party.

After the Bucharest meeting, there were new discussions between the Soviet and Chinese parties with the presumed aim of
easing tensions and working out a settlement. The USSR was depending heavily upon economic exchanges with countries in the
Communist bloc for implementation of its program of constructing
a socialist commonwealth. In 1959, a full three quarters of its
total trade turnover was with countries within the bloc, including
China. But for Moscow this was designed to be a two-way proposition. The work of supporting China's program of rapid industrialization, taken in conjunction with other demands on the Soviet
heavy industry, constituted an important drain on Soviet economic and technological resources. The question inevitably arose:
if the Soviet Union were to channel industrial goods to China that
it might be sending instead to more malleable sectors of the Third
World, and far from receiving gratitude would be cursed for nig-
gardliness, and be forced to contemplate the possibility that it
would at some time in the future be confronted by a Frankenstein
monster of its own creation, could the strategy be judged in its
national interest — or even in the interest of the rest of the Communist bloc?

A survey of Moscow's China policy from 1957 onward would
give support for the tentative judgment that, after the experiment
of making a measured contribution to China's power buildup
during the eight years 1950–1957, the Soviet leadership had
reached a strategic decision to take advantage of such political
opportunity as might offer to reduce aid to China under "justifi-
able" conditions and to establish new power relations with other
major elements on the periphery of China — such as Japan, India,
and Indonesia (while not neglecting countries like Afghanistan
and Burma). The hypothetical occasion offered itself when Peking
in 1960 chose to challenge Moscow's ideological *and political*

leadership in the Communist bloc and went over into open competition with the Soviet Union for influence in the Third World. Moscow thereupon stepped up its own activities in sectors where the Chinese threat took shape.

The rise of Sino-Soviet competition for influence in the Mongolian People's Republic presented an illustrative example. As would in due course become known, when Khrushchev visited Peking in 1954 the Chinese presented him with a demand, made in bland disregard of their earlier recognition of MPR independence, to the general effect that Moscow hand Outer Mongolia over to China. That gambit would naturally have alerted Moscow to China's imperial ambitions with respect to former "Chinese" territory. Now, six years later, the competition between the two countries for Mongol favor became more open after Peking and Ulan Bator on May 31, 1960, signed a Treaty of Friendship and Mutual Aid providing for consultation on all problems of common interest and a long-term Chinese loan of 200 million rubles to the MPR.

Moscow was in a position easily to match this move, and on September 9 reached an agreement with Ulan Bator for Soviet aid in connection with the Mongolian five-year economic plan for 1961–1965. The Soviet-Mongol agreement provided for Soviet help in the construction of fifteen industrial enterprises and other installations, the delivery of tractors and agricultural machinery for use in connection with the raising of Mongolian agricultural productivity and improvement of animal husbandry, the dispatch of Soviet specialists to the MPR, and training of Mongol workers and specialists in Soviet enterprises; besides, Moscow extended credits of 615 million rubles and granted a postponement of payment by the MPR of 245 million rubles due in 1961–1965. The two transactions showed in glaring light the unequal character of Sino-Soviet economic competition.

With the confrontation at Bucharest, seemingly, the Soviet dossier was replete with grievances, and the time had come for a major counteroffensive. In mid-July, the Soviet government sent the Peking regime a note charging misuse and mistreatment of Soviet experts employed in China's service. It was not only that the advice of those specialists was frequently disregarded, the note said, but Soviet personnel were caused to work under intolerable conditions, in which they were spied upon, had their mail opened and belongings searched, and upon occasion were even molested or attacked. As a consequence, the Soviet government had decided to recall, during July and August, all its specialists from China – engineers, technicians, scientists, others.[13]

Peking's reply of about a week later made an apparent effort to rebut the charges and to find them inadequate justification for the Soviet move, but to no avail. In July, the Soviet specialists began to depart, and by the end of August the withdrawal of 1,390 personnel (with families, nearly 4,000 persons) had been accomplished. They took with them not only their skills, but their blueprints as well. The action was highly reminiscent of the Soviet withdrawal of 1943 from Sinkiang and the recall of Soviet specialists from Yugoslavia in 1948, but it was on a much bigger scale and had major significance for China's program of modernization.

The matter of treatment of the Soviet specialists was clearly not by itself enough to have brought about the Soviet decision. In fact, Ambassdor Stepan Chervonenko, explaining the development to an audience of Soviet specialists gathered in the embassy at Peking, did not pretend that it was. He was reported [14] to have added to the charge of harassment the further complaint that the Chinese endeavored to proselytize their Soviet advisers with "subversive propaganda" (including the article "Long Live Leninism!").[15] But he reserved his main animadversions for China's foreign policy. Chervonenko condemned it particularly as applied to the United States, India, and Indonesia; he condemned also the unnecessary exacerbation of relations with Yugoslavia and the excessive Chinese friendship for Albania in opposition to Soviet policy. Besides, he noted, there was the obvious effort of the Chinese to establish a policy line in competition with Soviet policy – and to supplant Soviet leadership over the socialist bloc. The decision to withdraw the Soviet specialists, according to this source, had been taken by the CPSU Central Committee in plenary session in July.

S. Titarenko, writing on "Lenin's Teaching on the Victory of Socialism and the Present Day" in *Pravda Vostoka* of August 23, asked a pointed question that highlighted the Soviet action of withdrawal: "Can one imagine socialism being successfully built in present-day circumstances even in such a great country as, say, China if that country were in an isolated position and not supported by the cooperation and mutual assistance of all the other socialist countries?" [16] He answered his own question: that country would be subjected simultaneously to economic blockade and military blows, and even if it were able to withstand the enemy onslaught, "it would experience the most formidable difficulties."

Given the presumed flexibility in the Chinese policy-making establishment, one could have logically expected Peking to make a tactical retreat in order to redress its position and save the profitable relationship. A quarter of a century before, Mao Tse-tung had laid down discreet rules of military tactics that would have ordinarily counseled caution. One principle prescribed: "Oppose the strategy of striking with two 'fists' in two directions at the same time." Another proposed: "Oppose the policy of isolation, and affirm the policy of winning over all possible allies." [17] It would not make good political sense for China to be in hostile relationship to the United States and the Soviet Union simultaneously and thus isolated from both of the two major world power centers.

But Mao Tse-tung had committed an egregious blunder in launching the Great Leap of 1958, had come into bitter conflict with some of his Old Comrades in 1959, and now, in 1960, was seeking a way to stage a return to full power. The quarrel with Khrushchev was patently Mao's quarrel. He doubtless felt that he could not, upon the departure of the Soviet specialists, promptly admit a major error in the field of foreign affairs to top his blunder at home. He would gamble and play a few more cards.

For there was then impending a major conference of Communist parties, and Mao probably hoped to win something back at that meeting. The CPSU had on June 2 sent a letter to the Chinese party proposing a conference of Communist parties to resolve the differences between the two. Agreement had been reached at the Bucharest meeting for such a parley to be held in Moscow on the occasion of the celebration of the Bolshevik Revolution in November. As proposed by the Chinese, *all* Communist parties would be invited to attend. Peking's gambit was clear: the Chinese hoped to mobilize majority support against the CPSU.

On November 11, after the Soviet anniversary celebration was over, the international Communist conference met. Delegations from eighty-one of the world's eighty-seven parties were in attendance, to make this the most broadly representative gathering in the Communist world since the Seventh Comintern Congress of 1935. Its tasks were however perhaps more difficult of solution, even if less critical, than when German Nazism and Japanese imperialism threatened the Soviet Union and capitalist states alike.

There were major issues of Communist theory, deriving from the Sino-Soviet ideological contention, on the agenda. There was the question of Marxist-Leninist characterization of the contemporary historical stage: was the prime contradiction of the epoch between national liberation movements and imperialism as argued by the Chinese, or between socialism and capitalism as contended by the Soviets? Implicit in the whole was the critical practical issue of the Sino-Soviet dispute: were Soviet or Chinese patterns better fitted for not only revolution, but also for the development of the emerging nations of the Third World? In sum, should Soviet or Chinese policy guide the world Communist movement?

Mao Tse-tung did not brave the risk of being contradicted personally. The Chinese delegation was led, however, by Liu Shao-ch'i, Mao's longtime associate, Politburo member and CPR chairman, and he was supported by P'eng Chen, veteran of the political battle of Bucharest and of the planning sessions, and Teng Hsiao-p'ing, secretary general of the CCP Central Committee. Khrushchev headed the Soviet delegation. Togliatti, the Italian Communist chieftain, like Mao, did not attend, but Maurice Thorez, the veteran and powerful head of the French Communist Party, was among the elite who participated—and he personally attacked the Chinese for their factious activities.

The same well-trodden ideological ground was marched over again. The conference lasted two full weeks, this fact reflecting its importance—and difficulties. The eighty-one delegations actually reached an agreed position that was set forth in a Statement of December 5. That lengthy document incorporated important elements of compromise with the Chinese point of view. It obviously did not represent full conviction by the two chief contending parties that the words before them constituted the gospel truth as they saw it respectively. But any ambiguity that had crept into the phrasing to carpet over differences inevitably left the door open for individual interpretations as occasion might arise. In the circumstances, probably no other arrangement was possible: it had to be that way, for "agreement."

The Statement began with reaffirmation of the allegiance of the various parties to the Moscow Declaration of 1957.[18] This was an initial victory for the Soviets, who had in 1957 dominated, while not effectively monopolizing, the drafting of the twelve-party Declaration. The Statement declared that a new stage had begun in the development of the world socialist system, which was defined as "a social, economic, and political community of free and sovereign peoples united by the close bonds of international socialist solidarity; by common interests and objectives, and following the path of socialism and communism." The use of the term "community" was significant, as reflecting an urge, more Soviet than Chinese, toward closer association.[19]

The position taken on the moot issue of peace or war was clearly in favor of the Khrushchevian thesis. So was that on the matter of intervention by Communist states to foster revolution: the Statement opposed the export of revolution. If the concerned parties also voiced a determination to *"fight resolutely against the imperialist export of counterrevolution,"* the first factor was the more important issue between Peking and Moscow. There was condemnation of revisionism in general and of Yugoslav revisionism in particular. Strong words were also spoken against dogmatism and sectarianism, but the strictures were somewhat farther removed from specific targets. It was agreed that Marxist-Leninist parties were independent and possessed of equal rights: although the CPSU was put forward as a shining example, it was not designated high priest. "All Communist and Workers' Parties contribute to the development of the great theory of Marxism-Leninism." Khrushchev *or* Mao might equally define the Truth.

The Statement addressed itself to the matter of Marxist definitions and held that the main content of the epoch was "the transition from capitalism to socialism begun by the Great October Socialist Revolution. . . . *The main content, the main trend and the main features of the historical development of human society in the present epoch are determined by the world socialist system and the forces fighting against imperialism for a socialist reorganization of society."* [20] But there was still further qualification, for this was said to be an epoch also of "socialist revolutions and national-liberation movements, an epoch of the downfall of imperialism and abolition of the colonial system. . . ."

The Statement evidenced, particularly in some issues patently compromised and others left untreated, that existing differences had not all been resolved. It was later to be reported, without confirmation, that Peking's agreement was won only by Khrushchev's promising increased economic aid to China.[21] And Chinese self-seeking was not a good guarantee for a smooth future collaboration. Moscow was under no illusions in this regard, and even before the congress adjourned both Moscow and other Eastern European capitals began once more to make conciliatory gestures in the direction of Belgrade.

The Communist political exchanges did not bring unalloyed victory to Moscow. The year 1960 actually saw a major failure for Khrushchev's effort, begun earlier, to erect an institutional framework for a single socialist commonwealth centered on the Soviet Union. References to the need for solidarity could not hide the fact that the monolithic concept had been abandoned, for the time being, in favor of polycentrism, so that political entities as diverse as Yugoslavia and China, manifestly following very different "roads to socialism," might be accommodated within the same loose system.

It remained to be seen, even so, how useful the Statement would prove to be in practice as a renovated foundation for the Sino-Soviet relationship. The Soviets, from long habit, remained firm and categorical in the positions they had assumed — evidently more for pragmatic reasons having to do with Russian national interests than for considerations of dogma. The Chinese, for their part, ceded nothing to the Russians in terms of egocentrism and under Mao's direction they had evolved a doctrine, termed true Marxism-Leninism, designed to serve the *Chinese* national interest — regardless of what might happen to the rest of the world. Accommodation of the two Romes, each purporting to be the seat of doctrinal orthodoxy, was evidently a near impossibility.

It appeared clear that, if China could not be Middle Kingdom for the whole of the Communist world, it intended at least to become the political center for the Asian sector of it. China would nevertheless not make much substantial progress toward realization of its power aspirations in the period of hardship it was now enduring. Grave economic weaknesses were assailing the Chinese state.

33 BLOC POLEMICS, 1961-1963

OF THE 336 MAJOR industrial enterprises programed from 1954 to 1959 for construction in China with Soviet aid, only 154 had been completed by the end of 1960. Now the Soviet engineers had departed. Had the Chinese been prepared to make the most of the limited but truly substantial aid they were receiving from the Soviet Union, they could probably have achieved their ambition of building up a self-sufficient economy in the course of three five-year plans, that is, by 1967.[1] After that, if it chose, Peking could have challenged Moscow from a position of strength. But this strategy would have required a Machiavellian dissimulation, and restraint. And the aging Mao Tse-tung was not a patient man — no more than Wang Mang, Wang An-shih, or the emperor Kuang-hsu before him. Lacking outside aid, China now chose "self-reliance."

And indeed, after having hit near rock bottom in 1960, in 1961 China began once more the agonizingly arduous climb upward. In the beginning, the USSR still held out a helping hand. Minister of Foreign Trade Yeh Chi-chuang headed a Chinese delegation to Moscow that on April 7 signed the customary annual protocol for bilateral trade exchanges. No totals were announced, but that China was able to buy less than before was indicated by the circumstance that the pertinent communiqué issued at Moscow reported incidentally that, in the light of the "temporary difficulties" experienced by China, *the Soviet Union* had proposed the postponement for five years of payment of China's outstanding debit balance (amounting to U.S.\$320 million) for 1960, and that the Soviet Union would moreover supply China with 500,000 tons of sugar on interest-free credit before the end of August. The evidence was clear: China had become unable fully to meet its obligations under the terms of the August, 1958, and February, 1959, agreements for goods exchanges.

While the two countries still collaborated, the arena for competition between them expanded. On July 6, 1961, at Moscow, the Soviet Union and the Democratic People's Republic of Korea signed a Treaty of Friendship, Cooperation and Mutual Assistance; on July 11, at Peking, Premier Kim Il Sung signed another treaty, this time with Chou En-lai, acting on behalf of China. The texts of the two treaties were remarkably similar, but the Sino-Korean document made broader provision for mutual aid between the signatories with respect to socialist construction, this circumstance presumably reflecting the Chinese desire to play the major foreign role in the development of North Korea's economy.

Not long after this indirect political exchange over Korea, there occurred a fresh Sino-Soviet clash with more ominous overtones, and more important immediate results. The occasion was the Twenty-second CPSU Congress, held in October, 1961. Khrushchev, in his opening speech to the party conclave, took the occasion to treat the Albanian question. He charged the Albanian Party of Labor with having sharply changed course and diverged from the agreed Communist world line, "something which became particularly manifest from the middle of last year" (that is, from the time of the Bucharest conference).[2] He asserted that it was evident that the Albanian party disagreed with the conclusions of the 1957 and 1960 Moscow conferences that had approved the decisions of the Twentieth CPSU Congress and that the Albanian leaders were themselves now adhering to the methods followed in the Soviet Union during the period of the personality cult. He also said that the Soviet leadership was following the Leninist course laid down by the twentieth congress "and we cannot concede on this fundamental question to either the Albanian leaders or anyone else." Khrushchev did not need to say whom else he might have had in mind: it was clear that his description of Albanian attitudes was equally applicable to the policy positions of Peking. Khrushchev called upon the Albanians (and Chinese) to return to "the path of unity with the whole international Communist movement."

Chou En-lai, taking the rostrum on October 19, addressed himself to the issue. He made specific reference to Albania as one of the twelve fraternal countries making up the socialist camp; then, without naming either Albania or Khrushchev, he voiced opposition to the public airing of disputes between fraternal parties and, speaking for the CCP, hoped that fraternal parties between which there were disagreements would "reunite on the basis of Marxism-Leninism and . . . mutual respect for independence and equality." [3]

The Soviet leadership did not heed the Chinese admonition. Anastas Mikoyan and Mikhail Suslov, seriatim, leveled new blasts at the Albanian leadership. This was, if Mao chose to take it as such, the retort discourteous to the "fraternal" advice offered by Peking's representative. On October 21, Chou En-lai ceremoniously laid a wreath inscribed "To the Great Marxist-Leninist, J. Stalin" on the tomb of the dead dictator and then, while the Twenty-second CPSU Congress was still in session, left Moscow for home. His actions could not conceivably have been other than by the personal direction of Mao Tse-tung.

By taking up the cudgels for the Albanians (who had argued the Maoist case for the inevitability of war), Mao was thus seen as continuing the attack he had launched against Khrushchev in April, 1960. And Khrushchev, in disregarding the Chinese advice to use sweet reason with the Albanians, had in the end displayed a readiness to leave the Chinese together with the Albanians in the Communist purgatory.

The matter was swiftly brought to a logical denouement. Moscow withdrew its engineers and technicians, suspended economic credits, and abruptly stopped other economic aid to debilitated Albania, acting as it had with respect to China. The Soviet embassy at Tirana was closed, commercial representation was withdrawn, and, despite the protests of Tirana, the Albanian mission at Moscow was also forced to depart. Tirana laid the blame specifically on Khrushchev.

Albania, while still technically a member, was now ostracized by CMEA; when the Warsaw Pact powers met again at Prague at the end of the following January, no representative from Tirana was present. Albania had not been invited, and its later note of protest was rejected. Albania's was a deficit economy; now it would have to rely either upon "the imperialists" for help, as Khrushchev suggested was probable, or upon its fellow antirevisionist, China. China was then going through the throes of recovery from the disastrous attempted Great Leap. The herculean effort at economic recovery had begun to pay off: food-grain production climbed to an estimated 167 million tons in 1961. But this was still 18 million tons below the 1957 figure. And yet, for politics' sake, Peking in February, 1961, granted a loan of U.S.$125 million to its newfound ally, Albania.

China's woes were not coming singly. In 1961 also, there was built up the potential for a new confrontation with the United States. The year saw the beginning of American military intervention in Vietnam in service, once more, of the Dullesian doctrine of containment. Given the debility of Ngo Dinh Diem's Saigon regime, it could safely be assumed that the United States would shortly assume the main burden of the war and greatly increase its military strength in that strategic area bordering on China.[4] In circumstances where its alliance with the Soviet Union had been severely damaged, China faced the new danger of a growing American threat in Southeast Asia. For it was ultimately China, not just North Vietnam, that was to be "contained." Premier Chou En-lai's report to the third session of the second National People's Congress meeting in April, 1962, was a sober document. It spelled out, in sum total, a massive slowdown in China's industrialization and the rebirth of capitalism under what was the equivalent of a Chinese New Economic Policy (the NEP of the 1920s in the Soviet Union). It meant revisionism. Added to this was the thwarting of China's messianic international mission.

Moscow now was offering neither philosophical sympathy to Peking in its distress nor political aid to assist China in buttressing its international position. Peking, in April, proposed a cessation of polemics between the Soviet and Chinese parties, but linked this proposal with another, namely that there should be a restoration of normal relations between Moscow and Tirana. Moscow chose to go in quite the other direction. The progressive reconciliation between Moscow and Belgrade in the period April–October, 1962, naturally acted to crystallize Mao's antipathy toward Moscow. Adding insult to injury, a member of Czechoslovakia's State Planning Commission reported that China's economy had been found too backward to qualify it for membership in CMEA [5] – of which the Mongolian People's Republic was now a member.

There were fresh political developments. Since late March, the Albanians had manifested restraint in their anti-Soviet propaganda, but now the official organ *Zeri i Popullit* exhorted all true Marxist-Leninists to face up to an open schism in world Communism and achieve the overthrow of Khrushchev. Resuming its propaganda campaign against Tito at the same time, Tirana launched strong attacks against the CPSU and on Khrushchev personally. Almost automatically, it involved Peking in the new political drive. Mao Tse-tung had been trapped and was now being used by Party Secretary Enver Hoxha and Premier Mehmet Shehu in Albania's political warfare against both Yugoslavia and the Soviet Union.

It was in the fall of 1962 that major crises occurred in the foreign affairs of both China and the USSR. China became embroiled once more with India, and the USSR was found in dangerous confrontation with the United States over revolutionary Cuba. On October 12, Prime Minister Nehru informed the press that the Chinese had intruded into the Northeast Frontier Agency (NEFA) and posed a "real menace" to India, and that the Indian Army had been instructed to eject the intruders beyond the McMahon Line. The Chinese counterattacked massively against the Indian positions in both NEFA and Ladakh (infiltrated by the Indians during the previous months), inflicted heavy defeats on the Indians in both sectors, and then declared a unilateral cease-fire and withdrew to positions proposed in their negotiations earlier that year with New Delhi – namely what they had originally occupied in the Ladakh region, and the McMahon Line in NEFA. Having achieved their territorial objectives, the Chinese chose to avoid a larger military conflict. Politically, however, they came out of the affair with major loss: not only was India brought into closer military relationship with the British Commonwealth and the United States, with new sources of arms supply thus made available to it, but even the Soviet Union continued ready to implement a previous agreement to supply MIG-21s to the Indian Army.

Only a few days after the Chinese military assault of October 20, the Cuban missile crisis brought the United States and the USSR to the verge of thermonuclear war. At the end of a tense week, the crisis was resolved by the Soviet decision to remove the offending Soviet missiles from Cuba. Moscow claimed credit for saving the peace, and Khrushchev in his report of December 12 to the Supreme Soviet held also that he had obtained assurances from President John F. Kennedy that neither the United States nor other countries of the Western hemisphere would invade Cuba. Khrushchev purported that the Soviet Union had achieved what it had set out to do. And he criticized "the Albanian leaders," who had wanted to bring on a clash between the USSR and the United States.

The Peking leadership saw the matter very differently. It blamed Moscow for having emplaced missiles in Cuba in the first instance, condemning the action as foolish adventurism. But the Peking publicity organs equally condemned the Soviet Union's bowing to the threat of American military action: in *that* move, Moscow had been guilty of capitulationism. The *People's Daily* held that the assurances that there would be no invasion of Cuba, which Moscow comforted itself with having received from the United States, were simply "a hoax," and charged the Soviet Union with "cowardice." The Chinese organ promised that the 650 million Chinese, as distinct from the Soviets, would stand by the Cuban people to the end.

The stage was thus set for a new battle in the political war between Peking and Moscow, and it is evident that the Chinese were the ones who chose to force the issue. From November, 1962, to January, 1963, the Bulgarian, Hungarian, Czechoslovakian, Italian, and East German Communist parties held their respective congresses, and both Soviet and Chinese delegations attended all of the gatherings. Wu Hsiu-ch'uan, the tough-minded CCP central committee member who had argued China's case before the United Nations in late 1950, headed the Chinese delegation to the several bloc meetings. The Soviet delegations had equally powerful complements. Neither side can have expected other than a real confrontation. Both sides used the international platforms to try to mobilize support for their respective positions. Peking demanded the convocation of a new world Communist congress; Moscow rejected the idea.

The Chinese persisted in covering the same old doctrinal ground, and the Italian Communist Party leader, Palmiro Togliatti, was led at the Italian party congress to remark "a certain dissonance" introduced by CCP representative Chao Yi-ming, recalling that the questions Chao raised had been discussed and decided upon at the 1957 and 1960 congresses. At the East German congress, party chief Walter Ulbricht found the Chinese Communists at fault for failing to consult with, or even inform in advance, other Communist countries respecting Chinese moves in the border conflict with India. Togliatti, in an article published in *Pravda* on the opening day of the German congress, criticized Peking's polemical manners: "It seems that the Chinese comrades wish to open a unilateral discussion in which they alone can speak and the others must remain silent. There can be no discussion in which the Chinese comrades pronounce the anathema and excommunicate all those who do not think as they do." [6]

But the Chinese, after having spent a full month making violent attacks on the policies of the Soviet party, still protested against the making of open attacks on the Albanian party. In the end, they did not bring about a cessation of those attacks but instead drew the lightning down on their own heads. They attacked revisionism, but now heard the charge of dogmatism and sectarianism voiced in louder tones than before. And finally, by supporting Albania, Peking fostered the Soviet-Yugoslav reconciliation. Tito paid a formal visit to Moscow in December, 1962, and was warmly received. The Soviet Union and Yugoslavia had drawn closer together; the Soviet Union and China were moving farther apart.

Khrushchev in his report of December 12 to the Supreme Soviet dealt specifically with the China question. After taking note of the understandable exercise of Chinese restraint with respect to such colonial vestiges as Macao and Hong Kong, he referred to the Chinese action in proclaiming a unilateral ceasefire on the Sino-Indian front and in withdrawing its armed forces. He granted that China had probably been moved in part in its decision by the circumstance that the United States and Britain had come to the support of India, but approved the Chinese actions, which he said would be properly appraised "by peace-loving peoples." He made it easy to infer that the Chinese restraint at the Indian border had its similarities to Soviet restraint over Cuba.

The reference to Macao and Hong Kong was bound, whether by intent or not, to enrage the nationalistic Chinese. Peking rose to the bait. In an editorial entitled "Workers of All Countries, Unite to Oppose Our Common Enemy!" the *People's Daily* defended the CCP position with respect to all points at issue. Was it argued that the Chinese side in the debate stood in the minority, and was wrong? That made no difference to the *People's Daily:* "such questions as who is right and who is wrong, and who has the truth on his side, cannot be determined by who is in the majority or minority at a given moment." [7] The Chinese argumentation was repeated, time and again, in further polemics at the end of 1962 and beginning of 1963, with Peking heavily belaboring the issues. The *People's Daily* on New Year's Day of 1963 charged that China was being encircled by enemies who designed to isolate it. Now the "modern revisionists" were put in the same enemy company as the "imperialists."

Pravda in an editorial of January 7, 1963, denouncing "splitters" attacked the Chinese position directly: "The pretensions of a certain Communist Party in seeking to proclaim its right to infallibility and furthermore to ignore the opinion of other Communist Parties are altogether wrong and harmful to the interests of the Communist movement." [8] Khrushchev, speaking January 16 at the sixth congress of the German Unity Party proposed that polemics between the Communist parties be halted, that passions be permitted to subside, after which they might "be in a better position to talk things over." [9]

In January, Peking began to attack Khrushchev by name, in what developed into a clear campaign to unseat him – in the obvious hope that the succession Soviet leadership would prove more receptive to Chinese ideological tutoring. On February 21, the CPSU central committee nevertheless sent to the central committee of the CCP an even-tempered letter in which it proposed formally that the polemics cease, and that bilateral talks be held between representatives of the two parties for a joint consideration of "all important questions in which both parties are interested." [10] Such talks, it was argued, would be an important preliminary for the desired new conference of Marxist-Leninist parties. The focus of concern of that larger conference, from the Soviet point of view, should be "the common tasks of struggle against imperialism," advance of the people's liberation movement, solidarity of the socialist world, and "consolidation of the unity of the Communist movement."

Peking could not well quarrel with the objectives thus set forth. But it chose first to level another broadside at Moscow. Going far afield indeed in the quest for rationale, the CCP leadership seized upon a repetition on January 9 by the American Communist Party of Khrushchev's observations regarding Hong Kong, Macao, and Formosa. In an editorial of March 8, the *People's Daily* focused on the matter of nineteenth-century imperialism and mentioned various "unequal" treaties, including treaties with Russia, by virtue of which China lost territory during that century of decline. The editorial remarked that, at the time of inauguration of the Central People's Government, it had been announced that the new regime would examine old treaties and recognize, abrogate, or renegotiate them on their merits. Peking's policy regarding socialist countries, the editorial remarked, would be different from that for imperialist countries. "With regard to outstanding issues, which are a legacy from the past, we have always held that *when conditions are ripe,* they should be settled peacefully through negotiations, and that pending a settlement, the status quo should be maintained" (emphasis supplied).

The logic with which the editors approached the issue threw a glaring light on China's attitude toward international law, including treaties between states. First, it was taken for granted that an "unequal" treaty, being unjust, was without validity. Second, the Chinese government itself would unilaterally determine which of the treaties it had inherited should be maintained, discarded, or renegotiated. And third, it might be expected to take up such an old issue at any date, however distant in the future, "when conditions are ripe." There was thus a menace in the question posed by the *People's Daily* at the conclusion of its survey: "You are not unaware that such questions as those of Hong Kong and Macao are a series of questions left over from history, questions related to the unequal treaties forced upon China by imperialism. By raising questions of this category, may we ask, do you aim at reopening all the unequal treaty questions in order to have a general settlement?"

The reference to Russia in its tsarist character was plain. Peking's attitude demonstrated the perceptiveness of an American scholar's characterization of its foreign policy shortly after the regime's establishment:

Communist China typifies a new *kind* of state, organized and motivated by a new ethic thoroughly incompatible with the existing structure of international law and relations. It struggles to attain unbridled freedom of action for the implementation of doctrines which can no longer be exposed to objective scrutiny and evaluation. If it accepts restraint, it does so from political and tactical considerations alone and not from any sense of legal obligation under international law.[11]

Communist China was truly a direct lineal descendent of imperial China.

Having thus assuaged its amour propre, Peking on March 9 accepted the Soviet invitation for bilateral talks – in a self-justifying reply that argued the Chinese case further. In that response, the Chinese agreed to suspend, "temporarily," public replies via the press "to the public attacks which were directed by name against the Chinese Communist Party by comrades of the CPSU and other fraternal parties." [12] But the Chinese reserved their right to make public replies to public attacks.

The communication noted that Mao Tse-tung, in his conversation (of February 28) with Ambassador Chervonenko, had expressed the hope that Khrushchev would stop over in Peking for an exchange of views in the course of his visit to Cambodia. Khrushchev was not making a visit to Cambodia, and the CPSU central committee conveyed this information to the Chinese in a reply of March 30. It did more: making initial reference to the Chinese statement respecting the range of questions that should be discussed, it took the occasion to set forth its views on "some questions of principle," in the hope that this would help "to define the range of questions requiring an exchange of opinions at a bilateral meeting." But the Soviet letter set forth another purpose: "We are doing this so as to stress once again our determination to uphold firmly and consistently the ideological standpoint of the entire world communist movement, its general line as expressed in the 1957 Declaration and the 1960 Statement." [13] The Soviet position as outlined in the CPSU letter offered little promise of compromise to the Chinese.

The usual annual Sino-Soviet trade protocol was nevertheless signed at Moscow in April. Overall two-way trade between the two countries had dropped from 1,498,700,000 rubles (U.S.-$1.65 billion) in 1960 to 742,280,000 rubles (U.S.$816.5 million) in 1962. In early May, the two parties finally agreed that the bilateral conference should convene July 5 in the Soviet capital. The parties named their respective delegations. With all the necessary preliminaries completed, including an understanding of sorts regarding the agenda, it appeared that everything was in order. Nothing remained but the conference proper.

Despite the agreement in hand, and in full disregard of the tactical desirability at that juncture of adhering to the commitment to cease public polemics, on June 14 the Chinese side issued a long letter to the Soviet party, nominally in response to the CPSU's letter of March 30, once more giving the Chinese interpretation of the meaning of the 1957 and 1960 documents, and making twenty-five numbered propositions, with frequent citations from Lenin, respecting not only the general line of the international Communist movement, but also the Soviet Union's own domestic program for building communism.

The Chinese voiced the hope "that this expression of views will be conducive to mutual understanding by our two Parties and to a detailed, point-by-point discussion in the talks." [14] But the hard-line positions assumed by the Chinese ideologues with respect to the moot issues made compromise agreement at the upcoming conference highly improbable.[15] The pontifical, condescending tone of Peking's communication, the arrogance with which the Chinese leadership defined the true Marxist-Leninist line, and the reversion to pure polemics at the end of the message, practically guaranteed the failure of the meeting. Peking in effect still insisted, as it had all along, that Moscow accept Maoism as the true Marxism-Leninism, with validity for world Communism. If Moscow refused, it was by definition revisionist.

As might have been anticipated, Moscow reacted violently, charging breach of the agreement for termination of open polemics. The Communist-sponsored World Women's Congress, sitting at the time in Moscow, had earlier been the scene of disruptive actions staged by the Chinese delegation; on June 29, it adjourned to the accompaniment of stormy anti-Chinese and anti-Albanian demonstrations. And on July 4, on the eve of the talks proper, the Kremlin in an official statement asserted that the Chinese leaders had no desire to resolve existing differences between the two Communist parties and charged that "Chinese organizations are interfering in the internal affairs of our party and transferring the differences of opinion from the sphere of relations of parties to relations of states." [16]

It was ironic that the exchanges respecting matters of Communist doctrine and strategy took place simultaneously with Soviet negotiations with the United States for a limited nuclear-test ban. Moscow had a choice: should it undertake a partial agreement with the United States, in favor of a lessening of the dangers of war, or should it accept the Maoist proposals for waging relentless and adventurous war against the United States buoyed up by the belief that, even if thermonuclear war were to result, out of it would come a more beautiful civilization? The answer was foreordained. If besides the Peking delegation had proposed, as reported,[17] that a new world conference indeed be convened to settle the Sino-Soviet dispute, but that the voting procedure be changed from one-party-one-vote to one in which a delegation's voting power would be weighted according to both the size of the party (and the Chinese Communist Party possessed the biggest membership) and the population of the country represented (with China counting some 700 million to the Soviet Union's 200 million), Moscow would have realized that it was faced with a Chinese urge to power with which no compromise was possible — at least, for so long as Mao Tse-tung lived and ruled.

On July 14 — a good revolutionary anniversary — the CPSU central committee made extended public reply to Peking's open letter of June 14.[18] It offered neither surrender nor conciliation. The bilateral discussions broke up on July 20 without agreement, and on July 25 the Soviet government initialed, together with the United States and Britain, the limited test-ban treaty. Peking had almost certainly helped the three Occidental powers reach agreement.

The Sino-Soviet talks had nominally only "recessed," but none expected them to resume within the visible future. The Sino-Soviet relationship was in worse condition than before. And in fact the tripartite agreement on the limited test-ban treaty was taken by the Chinese as occasion for offensive action. Just six days later, the Peking government issued an official statement condemning the treaty — and now putting into a state document the essence of some of the previous party polemics, accusing the Soviet government of betraying the interests of the *Soviet* people, of the Chinese people, of the people of the socialist camp, and the interests of all the peace-loving people of the whole world. This, said Peking, constituted "capitulation to U.S. imperialism." [19]

The Soviet *government* took up the audacious challenge, and on August 3 made a long reply that was notably harsher in tone than the previous polemics of the CPSU proper. It was clear that Peking's proposition that it was only Mao Tse-tung (inferentially) who knew what was good for not only the Chinese people but the Soviet nation and the rest of the world had enraged the Moscow leadership. Peking nevertheless persisted in its course, and on August 15 the Chinese regime issued yet another partisan polemic. It was in this statement that the Chinese, by reporting that the Soviet Union had on October 15, 1957, concluded an agreement with China "on new technology for national defence," but had on June 20, 1959, "unilaterally" torn up that agreement "and refused to provide China with a sample of an atomic bomb and technical data concerning its manufacture,"[20] began the series of Chinese and Soviet disclosures regarding their confidential relations that was to win the rapt attention of non-Communist observers.

In the concluding section of its statement, Peking asserted that "it is our proletarian internationalist duty to point out that they [the Soviet leaders] have now betrayed the interests of the Soviet people and the entire socialist camp." The CCP had relegated the Soviet leadership to the category of "enemy." Between Peking and Moscow, therefore, there now existed, by the Maoist theory, an "antagonistic" contradiction that could be resolved only by the application of superior force. Peking had evidently chosen to carry the "struggle" against the existing Soviet leadership, particularly Khrushchev, through to the end. The occasion and procedure selected for implementation of this policy decision were not favorable to China in either the socialist camp or the world generally: Peking had first chosen to challenge majority opinion in the socialist community with respect to outstanding questions of political dogma and then had taken a position that was opposed to world sentiment for peace.

There was a heated exchange of charge and countercharge regarding *governmental* security breaches. Then, on September 6, Mao Tse-tung and his cohorts, once more clad in their party uniforms, took the polemics back into the arena of Communist party relationships. On that date, the editorial department of the CCP Central Committee organ *Red Banner* published the first of a series of nine essays purporting to treat of the subject "The Origin and Development of the Differences Between the Leadership of the CPSU and Ourselves," addressing their treatment to –the CPSU communication of July 14. The article dated the beginning of those differences back to the Twentieth Congress of the CPSU, that is, to Khrushchev's de-Stalinization and to the voicing of his proposition that there might be peaceful transition from capitalism to socialism. Further, Khrushchev had "tampered" with Lenin's doctrine on imperialism and war.[21]

The new Chinese polemical series continued up to a final article of July 14, 1964 – the anniversary of the Soviet communication that had been selected as Peking's target in the first instance. There was occasional spice introduced with the revelation of some happenings in interparty affairs that had previously been obscure, but Peking abandoned the practice of revealing state secrets: it presumably had some of its own that it did not want disclosed. In the main, the tiresome ratiocinations and fustian were the same as before.

But there was a new interest in the situation: it had by now become evident that there existed a Chinese will to broad hegemony. In early September, 1963, in fact, the pro-Chinese Italian Communist newssheet *Ritorniamo a Lenin* (Let Us Return to Lenin) of Rome, reporting widespread support in world Communism for the Chinese position, stated that "The Chinese comrades, preparing to set up a new trade-union center, a new Cominform, and new Communist parties in all the world, have put themselves decisively on the road to founding in a short time a new Communist international on revolutionary Marxist positions."[22] Mao Tse-tung had adopted Zinoviev's thought, voiced four decades before, that there should be organized an Asian International – but had added to it.

However, the sinews of power were still lacking: in 1963, China's food-grain production was only increased to an estimated 179 million tons – up a mere one million tons from the hard year before. And imports of foreign grain continued, for the purpose of feeding the Chinese people. These things were plain to the view. So too was the basic illogic in the Chinese position. After the middle of 1963, the first tendency of leftist elements in various Communist parties to swing into support of the "idealistic" Chinese "Marxist-Leninist" position on the question of war and revolution had been in large measure checked.

At a meeting in early December at Warsaw of the Communist-backed World Peace Council, which counted representatives from eighty countries, the Chinese delegation suffered two major defeats. The gathering voted overwhelmingly to defeat a Chinese resolution proposing the adoption of a militant anti-Western policy line. In addition, China's attempt to wrest leadership of the organization from the USSR through mobilization of Asian, African, and Latin American support failed utterly. Mao Tse-tung, seventy years of age that month, would continue impatient to bring his apocalyptic vision to fruition. But the tide had been reversed in favor of Moscow.

34 SINO-SOVIET
COLD WAR, 1964–1965

UNDER THE MAOIST LEADERSHIP, China now stood effectively isolated not only from the "imperialist camp," but also from the Communist "revisionists," who made up the great majority of the world Communist movement. It counted Albania as an (outwardly) loyal supporter, true, but, as the La Fontaine fable concluded, "A mouse is not an elephant." The CCP had in 1963 won the support as well of the Trotskyite Fourth International, but this was obviously more of an embarrassment than cause for self-congratulation for the Chinese party.

Peking needed a new world strategy. No longer an integral part of the socialist camp, China would have to seek allies elsewhere. This exigency presented the leadership with a philosophical problem. By Mao's doctrine of 1949, the world was divided into two camps, imperialist and socialist, and it was imperative to belong to one or the other. Now, unable to associate itself closely with either, China was left with the sole alternative of wooing "neutralist" bourgeois governments it would have scorned in 1949.

Rationalization did not come hard for Peking. In his interview of 1946 with Anna Louise Strong, Mao Tse-tung had seen the United States as preparing to wage a war against the Soviet Union. He suggested that the American project would be attended by difficulties. First, the "U.S. reactionaries" would have to attack the American people. And then: "The United States and the Soviet Union are separated by a vast zone which includes many capitalist, colonial and semi-colonial countries in Europe, Asia and Africa. Before the U.S. reactionaries have subjugated these countries, an attack on the Soviet Union is out of the question." [1] Mao predicted that "The day will come when the U.S. reactionaries find themselves opposed by the people of the whole world."

The concept of 1946 had been temporarily engulfed by Mao's thought of 1949. Now, in changed circumstances, the earlier theory was brought forward once more. Almost coincident with the reaching of an agreement with Paris for the establishment of regular diplomatic relations between China and France, Peking in January, 1964, enunciated its doctrine of the "intermediate zone," seen as located between the socialist camp and the "imperialist" United States.

The first sector of the intermediate zone — that where the *ultimate* victory would inferentially be won — was made up of those countries of Asia, Africa, and Latin America that, as colonies of the now moribund imperialist powers, had according to Maoism been despoiled of their natural wealth and had been enslaved. They contained the decisive potential for the final revolutionary overthrow of capitalism and imperialism throughout the world. The second sector of the zone comprised all industrialized capitalistic states excepting the United States. Having been divested of any substantive standing as "imperialists," they were viewed by Peking as being, even as the underdeveloped countries, the objects of American imperialist power and capitalist greed, and thus were considered potential allies of the socialist camp against "the common enemy of mankind," the United States. Mao had reverted to a variation of the "united front" doctrine of 1935.

There was a major difference — for the time being left unexpressed. In the situation of January, 1964, Peking was viewing Communist "revisionists" as apostates, and it was prima facie evident that China proposed that the "socialist camp" should be composed of itself and those elements of the Communist world who accepted Maoism as the True Doctrine, and that the heretics from this version of Marxism-Leninism would in due course be classified with the "imperialists." In more concrete terms, the Maoist leadership proposed to capture sole direction and control of the "revolution of rising expectations" of the emerging nations, buttress its power in the interim by permitting industrialized states to trade and have modest political relations with China; and in the ultimate stage, having become politically and economically strong while its enemies had (in theory) become enfeebled, would crush the two main enemies, the United States and the Soviet Union. The vision was bold enough; the question was whether China's leaders matched boldness with equal wisdom, and whether the country's power resources were adequate for implementation of the design.

A test was being made of the strategy even as it was enunciated. From mid-December, 1963, to mid-February, 1964, Premier Chou En-lai and Foreign Minister Ch'en Yi, accompanied by an entourage of some fifty officials, made an extended tour of Africa, visiting such critical countries as the United Arab Republic, Tunisia, Algeria, Morocco, Ghana, and Guinea. In a statement issued to newsmen upon his arrival in Cairo on December 14, Chou made clear that the main theme of his tour would be Afro-Asian solidarity. "I am convinced," he said, "that the Asian and African peoples, united, will certainly continue to win new victories in their common cause." In the course of his tour, the Chinese premier made it amply clear that when he spoke of "Asian peoples," and when he supported the idea of an Afro-Asian conference, he had no thought of including the Soviets.

Chou En-lai's ardent revolutionism crept through when, speaking at Mogadishu in Somalia on February 4, on the eve of his return to China, he remarked: "There is an excellent revolutionary situation on the African continent." Since most of the bourgeois nationalist governments that had entertained Chou's party viewed with a common distaste the possibility of Communist-led revolutions that might oust them from power, a pall was cast over the accomplishments of the Chinese mission. The mission was indeed to be credited with some accomplishments. Tunisia and several other countries extended recognition to Peking at this time. Yet, it was evident at the end of Chou's safari that Africa was not as ripe for the penetration of Chinese influence as Peking appeared to believe.

New developments loomed in the Communist camp. On February 12, 1964, immediately before a new plenary meeting of the CPSU central committee, the Soviet party sent a letter to other Communist parties, but not to the CCP, stating that the Chinese matter was to be discussed at the coming plenary and raising once more the question of holding a new world Communist congress. On February 20, the CCP demanded that it be provided with a copy of the letter. Moscow took the occasion to remark that the Chinese had not yet replied to the Soviet letter of November 29. Thus spurred, Peking on February 29 sent along its reply to the earlier Soviet communication. With regard to the proposal to hold another worldwide Communist conference, the Chinese expressed agreement in principle, but ruled that a resumption of Sino-Soviet party talks were a necessary prerequisite and proposed that such talks take place in Peking October 10-25, 1964, to be followed by the convening of a preparatory committee made up of representations from seventeen parties.

The matter of timing was a critical factor: Peking obviously desired to delay the negotiations as long as possible, hoping in the interim to be able to rally majority sentiment against the Soviet party. It was only natural that Moscow came up with the counterproposal that Chinese and Soviet delegations meet in Peking the coming May for a resumption of the talks broken off the preceding July, that a preparatory conference of *twenty-six* parties meet in June and July, and that, with agreement there, the projected world conference be held in the fall of 1964. A Rumanian delegation headed by Premier Ion G. Maurer, in Peking March 3-10 for the purpose of mediating the Sino-Soviet differences, bore back to the USSR Peking's categorical rejection of the proposed measures for a compromise. Maurer presumably carried the Chinese "conditions" for a settlement, but Mao Tse-tung had girded his loins to settle accounts with "revisionism" both at home and abroad, and any price that he might have asked to halt his ideological campaign and accept "peaceful coexistence" with Moscow could only have been too high.[2]

Evidence of this was discovered at the Afro-Asian Solidarity Conference, held at Algiers March 22-26. There the Chinese delegation led by Liu Ning-yi accused the Soviet government of a wide variety of counterrevolutionary crimes, including inter alia "imperialism," "racism," "betraying the Algerian revolution," "refusing to help the Arabs liberate Palestine," and even moral responsibility for the murder of Patrice Lumumba.[3] Back in Peking, the *Red Flag,* in its issue of March 31, held that capitalist forces in the Soviet Union had been transformed into a deluge sweeping over all Soviet life. "Now is the time – now it is high time – to repudiate and liquidate Khrushchev's revisionism!"[4]

In fact, Peking continued its attack against the Soviet position on all fronts. Paralleling the Chinese drive for trade and political sympathy in different areas of the "intermediate zone," CCP agents followed up the endeavor to build up pro-Maoist fractions in other Communist parties, in both the Third World and Europe. The Chinese efforts achieved some initial successes. But various Communist leaders had appreciated the danger and were already taking steps to meet it. The Australian party purged pro-CCP elements from its ranks early in the year. Like purges would follow in other parties.

Addressing a Soviet-Polish friendship rally at Moscow in mid-April, Khrushchev made a biting attack on Mao Tse-tung, by · name. Shortly thereafter, he received from Mao Tse-tung, Liu Shao-ch'i, Chu Teh, and Chou En-lai birthday greetings that in passing expressed the belief that the Sino-Soviet differences over Marxism-Leninism were only "temporary" and repeated the familiar Chinese refrain: "In the event of a major world crisis, the two parties, our two countries and our two peoples will undoubtedly stand together against our common enemy. Let imperialists and reactionaries tremble before our unity!" [5]

Again Lenin's birthday anniversary (April 22) provided an occasion for Marxist-Leninist philosophizing. The Soviet theoretician Yuri V. Andropov, speaking on that date, referred to the subject of Chinese "Left opportunism" and nationalism, which had created "a real danger of scission." [6] He said that the Chinese terms for reconciliation were unconditional surrender; as for the birthday message, he stigmatized it as hypocrisy.

Nor were political leaders in the Third World so obtuse that they could not see through the self-serving character of the Chinese doctrine. And when Moscow in late April made known its demand for participation in any new Afro-Asian conference on the grounds that two-thirds of its territory lay in Asia, that démarche evoked a favorable African response. Again Peking's myopic policies had militated against achievement of its aims.

It was on May 7 – and the Soviets had proposed that the Sino-Soviet talks be resumed that month – that the Chinese replied to the Soviet letter of exactly two months earlier. Peking found the May date unacceptable and moreover expressed the opinion that their own suggested date of October would be too early; perhaps May, *1965*, would be possible. The Chinese also roughly rejected the Soviet proposals for a world conference, and proposed indefinite postponement: it might take four or five years, they held, to complete preparations. Refusing a Moscow offer to return Soviet technicians to China and undertake an expansion of Sino-Soviet trade, Peking charged Moscow with using trade as a political lever and trying to retard the industrialization of certain Communist countries for the purpose of keeping them permanently in agricultural status, to be outlets for Soviet goods. The Chinese leadership pointed up one of their grievances by taking the occasion to demand that all CMEA members (and the reference was obviously to Albania) be treated as equals — and that all Communist countries (and here the reference was to China) enjoy the right of membership.

On May 10, the CPSU began a detailed attack, in installments, on the Chinese ideological position. Against the background of the evidence that Moscow intended to proceed along its chosen course, the CCP on July 28 sent along another letter in which it was contended that any decision on the holding of an international Communist conference on the moot subject of ideological differences should be unanimous, including the agreement of pro-Chinese fractions, and that if the CPSU convened the projected conference, there would result an "open split." [7] The CPSU nevertheless on July 30 invited the twenty-five other parties of *its* proposal to send delegations to Moscow on December 15 to prepare for a conference to be held in 1965. Various Communist parties were at the time dubious about the advisability of convening a world conference under existing conditions. On August 30, the CCP rejected the invitation.

In October, 1964, Peking celebrated two victories. China, which had obtained its first nuclear reactor (located at Peking) from the Soviet Union in 1958,[8] exploded its first atomic device, and thus entered the exclusive club of the nuclear powers. And then, Nikita Sergei Khrushchev, the prime and specific target of Peking's ideological attacks from January, 1963, onward, was expelled from his position of leadership in Moscow. Mao Tse-tung must have assumed that the CPSU Central Committee had done this as a sacrifice to better Sino-Soviet relations, which would now be based on the foreign-policy line dictated by Maoism. Mao, Liu Shao-ch'i, Chou En-lai, and Chu Teh joined in a message of greetings to the new Soviet leaders, CPSU First Secretary Leonid I.

Brezhnev, Chairman of the Council of Ministers (premier) Alexei N. Kosygin, and President Mikoyan. And Chou En-lai expressed China's hopes for improved relations with the Soviet Union.[9]

It was only natural that Chou En-lai should lead an imposing seven-man delegation to Moscow for the nominal purpose of attending the celebration of the Bolshevik Revolution. Almost certainly, the Chinese intended to ascertain what gifts the Soviet succession was prepared to make to mollify the Peking leadership. The delegation arrived in the Soviet capital on November 5. The following day, Brezhnev made a public speech in which he stated plainly that Moscow would continue with the foreign policy laid down by Khrushchev. He ritualistically called for unity in the world Communist movement but at the same time purported to see an "urgent necessity" for the convening of a new world conference of Communist parties — something the Chinese leadership had come to oppose.

Brezhnev and Kosygin demonstrated quite clearly that, with respect to outstanding Sino-Soviet issues, they were every bit as "revisionist" as Khrushchev. Chou and his party left Moscow on November 13, and a week later Peking's authoritative *Red Flag* made a violent denunciation of Khrushchev and warned Moscow against any attempt to revive "Khrushchevism without Khrushchev." *Pravda* announced on December 13 that the conference's preparatory commission, which by Khrushchev's proposal would have convened on December 15, would meet on March 1, 1965. Soviet Deputy Premier Aleksandr N. Shelepin, speaking at Cairo at the end of December, soothingly said that the Soviet Union was doing its best to effect a rapprochement with China and that the Peking-Moscow dispute "will certainly be settled." But the Chinese knew that they had their answer: Moscow was adhering to its chosen course.

At the end of 1964, China gave the appearance of being at its strongest for several years. When it became one of the nuclear powers, at least potentially, its world position had been automatically enhanced. Mao's personal "enemy," Khrushchev, had been eliminated. And, addressing the National People's Congress in Peking, Premier Chou En-lai reported that the country's economic recovery had been such that the third five-year economic plan would be launched in 1966.

These were the accents of strength and confidence. There were however flies in the ointment. For one thing, the Soviet

Union, which had suffered a disastrous crop failure in 1963 and had been forced to purchase twelve million tons of wheat abroad, was again showing signs of an economic upsurge: the country's national income was reported to have risen 7 percent in 1964, as compared with 5 percent in 1963 (and 8 percent in 1960).[10] This was an achievement the Chinese were unable to match.

Moscow was also demonstrating increased strength in the political field. The Havana conference of Latin American countries had roundly condemned party factionalism (to which the Chinese had devoted so much energy) and demanded an immediate end to public polemics. At the end of the year, the Mongolian party expelled three pro-Chinese members of its central committee for "fractional antiparty activities," and Premier Yumjagiin Tsedenbal about the same time leveled pointed charges against "demagogues" and those "stirring up nationalistic passions" and taking up "nihilistic" positions.[11] And the pro-Chinese faction of the Indian Communist Party was effectively crippled when the Indian government arrested more than five hundred members of the group, charging them with carrying on subversive activities in a manner threatening the security of the country, in collusion with, and with the financial support of, China.

These were warning signs – if Mao Tse-tung chose to give them heed. Peking actually tried a new gambit, but it was still along a radical line. Premier Chou En-lai, with reference to Indonesia's withdrawal from the United Nations, called on January 24, 1965, for formation of a new "revolutionary" United Nations of Afro-Asian nations. Visiting Indonesian Foreign Minister Roden Subandrio went partway along the road with this idea by joining Chou in a communiqué announcing that "the United Nations cannot reflect the anti-imperialist and anti-colonial desire of the people of the world, nor can it organizationally reflect the reality in which the new emerging and revolutionary forces have far outstripped the decadent forces."[12] But the organization of an Afro-Asian United Nations under Peking's leadership – and domination – was by the evidence not within the realm of present possibility.

Against the background of the accomplishments and planning of 1964, it can be deduced that the Peking leadership anticipated that the new year would be marked by substantial progress. Two major factors would operate in 1965, however, to the detriment of Peking's aspirations. In the first place, there was the matter of making concrete preparations for the new five-year plan. How was China to achieve major economic advance with weak capital accumulation, backward technology, and a damaged primitive agriculture? That this problem was foreseen can be taken for granted, but that it had yet to be resolved, given Mao Tse-tung's urge to accomplish miracles by harnessing the presumed limitless powers of the Chinese masses, and the resistance to that line posed by the pragmatists of the party, is also probable.

The second major problem could not have been anticipated other than in a general way. The United States in February, 1965, without even token concern for Chou En-lai's warning against any widening of the war, began the systematic strategic bombing of North Vietnam, explaining that this was in response to aggression from the North against South Vietnam. But long before this the argument had been put forward that the American involvement in Vietnam was for the purpose of containing Chinese Communism, which Washington held to be the source of revolution in Asia. The new move was within that strategic concept. The issue of China's national security had thus been raised in acute form.

In the circumstances, it would naturally have occurred to certain members of the CCP Politburo to seek a resolution of their problems of economic development and national defense through a reconciliation with the Soviet Union. This would, however, have required a recognition by Mao Tse-tung that his USSR policy was in error. Mao had not even yet confessed to having erred with regard to the 1958 Great Leap, and he had gone so far in his war against the Soviet Union that to back down would have brought great loss of prestige, with corresponding reduction of his chances for recovering the power position he had lost in 1958. Apart from that, Mao's campaign proposing the creation of a new Communist International centered on China had not yet been played out. And then, there was the hoary hope that China might benefit from some international calamity.

Speaking at the Soviet embassy in Peking on February 14, the occasion of the fifteenth anniversary of signature of the Sino-Soviet treaty of alliance, Foreign Minister Ch'en Yi in effect gave the Soviet Union yet another "last chance" to live up to Mao's revolutionary standard. Holding that peaceful coexistence with American imperialism was "out of the question," he said: "Only in concrete action against United States imperialism and its followers can the Chinese-Soviet alliance be tested and tempered and Chinese-Soviet unity be consolidated and developed." [13] This was a forceful restatement of the Chinese demand, first voiced in 1957, that Moscow throw down the ultimate challenge to American power.

But Peking was making its demands from a weakening political position. The Chinese mission had the month before been ejected from the tiny East African country of Burundi for having engaged in local political activities. In Nigeria, a small number of revolutionaries trained in China and Algeria had undertaken to overthrow the existing pro-Western regime through the waging of guerrilla warfare in the Maoist manner and had suffered a debacle. About the same time, Peking found it the better part of valor to give up its support of a guerrilla movement of rebellion in the Cameroon Republic. It also got into trouble with Kenya over the latter's well-substantiated charge that among the countries that had increased their trade with South Africa (boycotted by African nations) in 1962 and 1963 was – China.

On March 1, as scheduled, an international Communist gathering convened in Moscow. But there were only nineteen, not twenty-six, parties represented. China sent no delegation, and the North Korean, North Vietnamese, Japanese, and Indonesian parties were also without representation. The Mongolian People's Revolutionary Party and the Pro-Soviet fraction of the Indian Communist Party had sent delegations, but with the weak Asian representation, and in view of the reservations that some accepting parties had attached to their acceptances, the purpose of the meeting was changed from that of preparing for a world Communist conference to simple "consultation." The meeting terminated on March 5, and the final communiqué, while supporting in principle the idea of holding a new world conference, proposed that there first be held a preliminary meeting of representatives from the eighty-one Communist parties that had participated in the 1960 gathering. This pointed up the desirability of winning the dissidents, including the CCP, back into the fold. There had been less than a Soviet victory, with the setback hardly mitigated appreciably by the call for a cessation of polemics.

Peking would appear to have viewed the results as a *Chinese* victory; after March, 1965, it again demanded what amounted to full Soviet capitulation to the Chinese viewpoint. [14] The Chinese were at this time working hard to bar the Soviet Union from participation in the Afro-Asian "second Bandung conference" scheduled to be held in Algiers on June 29, 1965. Obviously with the purpose of furthering that aim, Premier Chou En-lai in late March and the beginning of April visited Algiers and Cairo. Playing to Arab emotions, Peking had regularly spoken more stridently than Moscow of its "firm support" for the Arab desire to obliterate Israel. But Chou spoke from a position of practical disadvantage: Soviet aid to Egypt had already been ten times that recently *promised* by Peking, and where China had committed itself prior to Chou's 1963 visit to extend $50 million in aid to Algeria, the Soviet aid credits of $250 million and supply of military equipment bulked far larger.[15] "Self-reliance"? The Arab countries would quite naturally ask "Why?" And they were manifestly not interested, any more than Cuba, in becoming simple pawns in the Sino-Soviet dispute.

Thus Chou won no converts. He made a four-day visit at the beginning of June to Tanzania, a country in which for the moment the Chinese influence was seemingly greater than that of the Soviet Union — not to mention the United States. He had planned to go on from there to Kenya, Uganda, Zambia, and Ethiopia, and then to crown his second African tour by participating in the Afro-Asian conference at Algiers at the end of the month. But China's trade with South Africa, and Chou's reiteration in Tanzania of his 1963 suggestion that Africa was ripe for revolution, alienated his prospective hosts in the East African countries, which refused to receive him. Kenyan Minister of Finance James Gichuru, speaking before the parliament, blasted China for subversive activities, including hidden arms shipments through the country, and threatened withdrawal of the Kenyan diplomatic mission from Peking. From Dar-es-Salaam, where he had proclaimed that "an exceedingly favorable situation for revolution prevails today not only in Africa but also in Asia and Latin America,"[16] Chou En-lai left for home.[17]

Even plain luck acted against the Chinese plan. On the very eve of the scheduled Afro-Asian conference, Colonel Houari Boumedienne staged a coup that overturned the Algerian government headed by Ahmed Ben Bella. A majority of French and British African states had already decided not to attend the conference. Peking, striving to save something from the burning, hurried to extend recognition to the new Algerian government.

But there was no salvation, for Afro-Asian countries found Peking's intent of causing them to take a stand simultaneously against the United States and the Soviet Union too radical for their own purposes. The aims of the first Bandung conference had been outdated; the concerned Afro-Asian countries had failed to find a satisfactory new common purpose for the second conference. So, for the time being, it was postponed. In July, in the wake of the Algiers debacle, Prime Minister Jomo Kenyatta ousted the NCNA contingent from Kenya. It had served as cover for the subversive activities that had aroused the Kenyan ire.

Peking still undertook to develop the theme of world revolution. The program adopted by the Sixth Comintern Congress at Moscow on September 1, 1928, had depicted a revolutionary opposition of underdeveloped states to developed states in the concept that "Colonies and semi-colonies . . . represent the world agricultural district in relation to the industrial countries, which represent the world city." [18] Now, in an article entitled "Long Live the Victory of the People's War!" published September 3 to commemorate the victory over Japan, Lin Piao built upon that theme to conclude that the world countryside, comprising the poor of the earth, would surround and overwhelm the world town, made up of the rich, industrialized states.

This was in a sense a portrayal of Mao's dream. The timing was perhaps significant. Lin and his chief may have expected to get an initial boost for their program, in circumstances where they had experienced setbacks farther afield, by reason of developments in Indonesia, thought "ripe for revolution." The Indonesian Communist Party (PKI), with three million members, was the largest party in the world after the Chinese and Soviet organizations, and it was headed by the pro-Chinese D. N. Aidit.

But the "September 30th Movement" that struck in Jakarta on October 1, with the PKI early involved even if it had not planned and triggered the coup, failed to achieve the seizure of power, and as one consequence the PKI was effectively destroyed (with party secretary Aidit killed). An estimated 300,000 Communists were massacred, some 170,000 were thrown into detention camps, and a national purge began. Further, there were widespread anti-Chinese riots, the burning of the Chinese-owned Republika University, and forceful entry of the Chinese commercial counselor's office in Jakarta. The October development effectively nailed the coffin lid down on Peking's hopes for an early massive assault by the dispossessed of the earth, under Peking's leadership, against the citadels of world power and wealth. The "ultimate victory" of the proletarian revolution over imperialism was still only a will-o'-the-wisp.

African and Asian states were not slow to read current developments as marking a decline of China's world importance. When the preparatory committee met at Algiers later in October in a renewed effort to make preparations for the holding of the second Afro-Asian conference, the Chinese delegation found it impossible to block a decision to invite the Soviet Union to the conference of Afro-Asian heads of states scheduled for November 5. The Chinese, who had earlier, with Jakarta at their side, been so eager to have the conference held, now gave formal notice that they would not attend; moreover, such a meeting would be illegal, they said, because decisions should be reached unanimously — and China had not agreed.

Nor did even the Sino-Cuban relationship, which had seemed after the Cuban missile crisis to promise much to Peking, contribute any longer to the credit side of China's foreign-affairs ledger. Peking had persisted in endeavoring to get Havana openly to take its side in the Sino-Soviet dispute, and was prepared to apply economic leverage in an effort to attain that end. China's actions at Algiers, and its objections to Soviet participation in the Tri-Continental Conference scheduled to convene in Havana in January, 1966, further alienated the Cubans. Peking had misjudged Havana. Castro's position in 1965 was less in favor of Peking than firmly oriented toward ideological independence of *both* Communist Romes — with this attitude accompanied by a willingness to accept needed aid from either. Castro was not wedded to Maoism, and Moscow, in the end, was able to offer the more substantial aid.

Peking reached the last quarter of 1965 with its "revolutionary foreign policy" in barren disarray. In a press conference on September 29, Foreign Minister Ch'en Yi voiced defiance:

> If the American imperialists have decided to launch a war of aggression against us, we hope that they will come, and the sooner the better. Let them then come tomorrow! Let the Indian reactionaries, the British imperialists and the Japanese militarists come with

them! Let the modern revisionists support them in the North! We will finish nevertheless by triumphing.[19]

Ch'en went on to express a doubt that "the great Soviet people and the great Communist Party of the Soviet Union" would permit so "criminal" a decision to be taken by their leaders. But he sounded uncertain.

The balance was tipped against Peking. In sum, Mao Tsetung's anti-Soviet campaign had indeed induced a certain erosion of Moscow's authority within the Eastern European sector of the bloc through its contribution to the feelings of polycentrism; however, far from strengthening the Chinese position correspondingly, the campaign had weakened Peking's attraction and influence: Communist countries and parties were evincing a demand for a polycentrism effective with respect to the Chinese as much as with regard to the Soviets. And the emerging nations of the world were found to be more interested in the substance of political power and economic progress than in Peking's preachments.

35 THE GREAT PROLETARIAN CULTURAL REVOLUTION AND SINO-SOVIET RELATIONS

IN SEPTEMBER, 1965, after the appearance of Lin Piao's article but before the attempted coup in Indonesia, the CCP Central Committee met in secret extraordinary session for a consideration of the grave issues facing China. Again there seem to have been those pragmatists who proposed that, for a resolution of the country's domestic and foreign difficulties, there should be a measure of reconciliation with the Soviet Union. Mao Tse-tung pushed the proposition that there should be an intensification of the struggle against "reactionary ideology," but was defeated. He retired to Shanghai, only to launch, two months later, a campaign designed to eliminate his "revisionist" opposition. Mao now seemed driven by an overpowering messianic urge to mold not only China's but the world's destiny, and in 1966 his drive against "enemies" would assume the form of the Great Proletarian Cultural Revolution (GPCR).

China's foreign affairs for the next three years reflected Mao's reckless revolutionism, with a notable step-up of the anti-Soviet drive. Peking sharpened the themes on which its attacks were based, charging notably that the Soviet Union had betrayed the cause of Communist world revolution, entered upon a "secret pact" with the United States and, with regard to Vietnam, was actually aiding the United States instead of helping the Vietnamese Communists to achieve victory. Peking did not deny that Moscow was providing aid to North Vietnam, but from 1965 onward it was argued that aid to the Vietnamese (and other) revolutionaries should be "commensurate with the strength of the Soviet Union." It was not. Peking ostentatiously concluded that this circumstance evidenced collusion with the imperialist enemy and proceeded to build up the theme of "imperialist-revisionist encirclement of China" as the chief bogey in China's foreign relations for the period of the GPCR.

The year 1966 began unpropitiously for Peking in the realm of foreign affairs. The Chinese leadership was patently desirous that the conflict between India and Pakistan, which had erupted into full-scale hostilities, should continue, and spread. But Moscow took steps to mediate the dispute and restore peace. Thanks to Kosygin's intervention, on January 5 discussions began at Tashkent (the Soviet Union's "Asian" capital) between Pakistani President Mohammed Ayub Khan and Indian Premier Lal Bahadur Shastri. The presence on the Soviet side of such top-ranking officials as Kosygin, Foreign Minister Gromyko, and Defense Minister Malinovski manifested the Soviet Union's concern — and its important role. The meeting ended in full success five days later with the signature of an agreement providing, inter alia, for the mutual withdrawal of troops, return of the ambassadors of the two countries to their posts, and the restoration of trade relations. Soviet influence was consequently enhanced in both countries.

A few days later, on January 15, the Soviet Union and the Mongolian People's Republic signed a new twenty-year Treaty of Friendship and Mutual Assistance to replace the expiring 1936 agreement. Gromyko and Malinovski, fresh from Tashkent, and CPSU chieftain Brezhnev, were all present at the signing ceremony in Ulan Bator. Marshal Tsedenbal was the chief Mongol representative. The treaty of ten articles provided for cooperation in all fields of national effort. Article 5 comprised provisions for mutual aid in ensuring development of the two countries' defense potential, for mutual consultation respecting important international problems of common interest, and for the joint undertaking of "all necessary measures, including military ones, with the aim of ensuring the security, independence, and territorial integrity of both countries." [1] Given especially the Chinese territorial pretensions that had been brought to light in the course of the Sino-Soviet polemics, the provision regarding "territorial integrity" would now have had a special meaning for Ulan Bator — and that meaning would not have been lost on Peking.

The two important conferences at Tashkent and Ulan Bator had a counterpart in another meeting half a world away. Sponsored by the Afro-Asian People's Solidarity Organization (AAPSO), a Tri-Continental Conference of Asian, African, and Latin American Solidarity was held at Havana from January 3 to 15, with its main purpose being "to oppose the world-wide enterprises of imperialism with a global revolutionary strategy." [2] The 500 delegates represented not only Communist countries and parties, but revolutionary groups and "national liberation" movements as well, and even a few governments of "nonaligned" African countries.

China and the USSR were both represented, evidencing the defeat of Peking's efforts to debar the Soviet Union from "Asian" gatherings. The Soviet delegation was headed by Sharif R. Rashidov, first secretary of the Uzbek Communist Party, who emphasized the need for unity of the anti-imperialist forces. Chinese delegate Wu Hsueh-chien chose to argue that there had been "revisionist treacheries" committed with respect to the Congo, the Dominican Republic, and Vietnam. But the various delegations had not come to Havana for the purpose of hearing once more the endless diatribes of the Chinese against their opposition. *Le Monde* reported that the great majority of the delegates, including those from Latin America, were shocked by "the extremeness of the Chinese, their exaggerations, and their bad faith in their attacks against the Soviet Union, and especially their divisive role at a 'unity conference.'" [3]

In the end, the conference decided to set up an Asian, African, and Latin American People's Solidarity Organization, with its headquarters at Havana. It was tentatively agreed that a second Tri-Continental Solidarity Conference should be held at Cairo in 1968 to determine the final structure of the new organization; in the meantime, the Afro-Asian People's Solidarity Organization would remain in being and would hold its 1967 meeting in Peking.

In the net, however, the Chinese had lost much at Havana through their intransigence.

Against the background of those international developments, Peking stepped up its anti-Soviet campaign. Was it alleged that China was charging transit fees, in dollars, for the transshipment of Soviet supplies to Vietnam? Moscow spread the report, said a Chinese spokesman, "to vilify China, sow discord in the relations between China and Vietnam and serve U.S. imperialism." [4] Had Premier Kosygin proposed that Japan collaborate in a vast project for the exploitation of Siberia's resources? This was at the request, Peking suggested, of the United States.

In a letter of February 14 to the parties of Eastern Europe, the CPSU Central Committee made charges of its own, in particular that the Chinese government was refusing to resume the border negotiations suspended in May, 1964, and was indoctrinating its people with the idea that it was necessary to prepare for a possible eventual military conflict with the Soviet Union.[5] Also, "One has every reason to affirm that one of the objectives of the policy of the Chinese leaders in the Vietnam affair is to provoke a military conflict between the USSR and the United States so as to be able, as they themselves say, 'to sit on the mountain and observe the fight of the tigers.' " [6]

Peking indeed professed to think war coming, but purported to see China in the midst of it. In an interview with a delegation of Japanese Communists on March 28, Mao Tse-tung let himself appear in an apocalyptic role. War between China and the United States, he said, was "inevitable," and the event would come perhaps in 1966 "or within two years at the latest." And as the United States attacked across the Vietnamese and Korean frontiers and from Okinawa and Formosa, the Soviet Union, with the "Sino-Russian pact as its pretext," would advance from Siberia and through Outer Mongolia to occupy Manchuria and Inner Mongolia — and there would be a confrontation between the Soviet forces and the People's Liberation Army across the Yangtze River. Mao gave one of his famous oversimplified analyses of the world political situation: "It is a mistake to say that in the world today there are war powers and peace powers confronting one another; there only exist revolutionary war powers and anti-revolutionary war powers. World revolution cannot come about by the evasion of war." [7]

Ch'en Yi on May 20 finally answered the Soviet allegations respecting frontier problems, asserting that it was Moscow that had refused a settlement on the basis of the old Sino-Russian treaties, as had been proposed by Peking, and had "insisted on going beyond these unjust treaties." [8] Ch'en built further on the foundation laid by Mao. The Soviet Union, he said, had concentrated troops on the common frontier and held military maneuvers targeted at China as the theoretical enemy.

It was noteworthy that, at a moment when Mao and his ministers were avowedly contemplating the nation's soon being plunged into war – somewhere – and Mao besides was harboring plans for a domestic upheaval of vast proportions, Peking stubbornly persisted on a bankrupt course in international Communist affairs. The Japanese Communist Party (CPJ) sent a mission to Peking under the leadership of its secretary general, Miyamoto Kenji, for the evident purpose of effecting a Communist reconciliation, but the mission failed of its purpose. The Japanese party moved away from the CCP and toward the CPSU. In July, it recalled its two representatives from their station in Peking, and a purge of pro-Peking elements in the CPJ began. The Rumanians had wanted to make one more try at mediation between the Chinese and Soviet parties, and in June, probably at least in part with reference to this plan, Chou En-lai headed a mission to Bucharest. His visit ended on June 24 with signs of strain between Chou and his hosts,[9] and it was entirely evident that the exchange was fruitless as far as Sino-Soviet relations were concerned. The following day, Chou left for Albania.

Nothing other than dogmatic inflexibility could have been expected in China's foreign policy at that juncture: Mao's attempt to purge his enemies in the party was now going into high gear, and his ingrained tactical concepts required, in the circumstances, that he maintain a radical position abroad as well as at home. In August, 1966, at the eleventh plenum of the CCP Central Committee, the Great Proletarian Cultural Revolution was formally inaugurated. There was the massing first of millions of youthful Red Guards and then of "revolutionary rebels," and finally the introduction of the PLA into the fray, in service of Mao's dual purpose of purging the CCP of "revisionism" and recovering dominant control of the political destiny of the nation.

The central committee's communiqué of August 13 indicated the relevancy of the GPCR for Peking's foreign policy. At last revealing that the June 14, 1963, "Proposal Concerning the General Line of the International Communist Movement" (which it now termed a programmatic document) had been drawn up under the direction of Mao Tse-tung himself, it asserted that "to oppose imperialism it is imperative to oppose modern revisionism." [10] So, although the CCP plenary called for the formation of "the broadest possible international united front" against American imperialism, it qualified that prescription by adding that the Soviet revisionists "cannot of course be included in this united front."

Thus Peking, caught up in the feverish Red Guard movement, maintained its attitude of unrelenting hostility toward the USSR. Almost coincident with the issuance of the central committee's communiqué, the Soviet vessel *Zagorsk* was detained at Dairen by the port authorities. On August 29, "popular" demonstrations began against the Soviet embassy in Peking. The following day, the *People's Daily* charged that Moscow was actively assisting the United States to shift the emphasis in American strategy from Europe to Asia; "Together they are working for the encirclement of China." However, the paper foresaw a favorable outcome: when the main American forces had been destroyed, there would be world revolution. [11]

Tass was soon to report that the Red Guard headquarters at Peking had organized an international relations department for the enlistment of foreigners into a "Red Guards Internationale," among the requirements for membership being recognition of Mao as head of the world revolution and acceptance of the Thought of Mao Tse-tung as "the summit of Marxism-Leninism." [12] It seemed a Maoist "contradiction": at a time when blind xenophobia was being given full rein, and the nation as a whole was retreating into an ideological isolationism reminiscent of the reign of the emperor Ch'ien-lung, the leadership went through the motions of aspiring to universalism.

On September 20, the Peking government informed foreign missions that all foreign students should leave China by October 10. On October 7, Moscow informed Peking in return that, since the educational arrangements were based upon reciprocity, all Chinese students should depart the Soviet Union by October 31. Peking protested, and fresh demonstrations were mounted against the Soviet embassy. In the USSR, a flood of news reports, articles, and commentaries poured forth in criticism of the GPCR and Chinese domestic and foreign policy. And the CPSU Central Committee plenum, sitting in mid-December, passed a resolution condemning "the great-Power nationalist course of the present Chinese leaders," and, to make matters crystal clear, the policy of "Mao Tse-tung and his group." [13]

On January 25, 1967, Chinese students passing through Moscow en route from France and Finland back to China provoked a clash with the Soviet police in Red Square. The following day, new disturbances surged up in front of the Soviet embassy in Peking, which was brought under a siege that lasted for two full weeks. Early in February, Soviet embassy dependents were evacuated— with Chinese crowds interposing humiliating difficulties. On February 9, Moscow delivered a stiff note to China, demanding that harassment of the embassy cease immediately and that the embassy staff enjoy freedom of movement for the performance of their functions. "Unless this is done within the shortest period of time, the Soviet side reserves the right to take necessary measures in reply." [14] Three days later, demonstrations against the Soviet embassy ceased as suddenly as they had begun.

Peking's verbal attacks nevertheless continued in full force. The meeting of Premier Kosygin with President Lyndon B. Johnson at Glassboro was characterized in an NCNA broadcast of June 23 as marking "a new phase of closer, wider, and more brazen counterrevolutionary collaboration between Washington and Moscow." The Glassboro confrontation was nearly coincident with the Arab-Israeli "six-days' war." In a political reflex that had become almost automatic, Peking charged Moscow with betrayal of the Arabs. [15]

The Prague radio on December 11, 1966, had proffered the information that Peking had been critical of the Soviet Union for not creating new areas of tension, particularly on the frontier between East and West Germany, in order to aid North Vietnam. [16] In an interview granted the NBC television network in July, 1967, Khrushchev made an even more grisly revelation.

In 1959, Mao Tse-tung said to me: "You must provoke a war with the United States, and then I will send you as many divisions as you need: a hundred, two hundred, a thousand." I explained to Mao that, in the present era, two missiles would suffice to transform those divisions into radio-active offal. He told me that there was nothing to this. Apparently, he took me for a coward.[17]

The Chinese could not match this revelation. But in August, the Dairen authorities again detained a Soviet merchant ship, the *Svirsk*, jailed the captain, badgered the crew, and plastered the ship itself with insulting inscriptions. The cause alleged for this violence was that the ship's second officer had not only refused to wear a badge bearing Mao Tse-tung's picture, but had thrown it overboard. The captain was released, and the ship was permitted to sail, after Premier Kosygin sent Chou En-lai a telegram remarking that those "arbitrary and lawless acts" were "placing in doubt the fulfillment of existing trade relations between the Soviet Union and China." [18]

On August 14, the day after the *Svirsk* sailed, however, new Red Guard demonstrations were directed against the Soviet embassy in Peking, and three days later its consular section was invaded and files burned. Moscow the following day sent Peking a formal note charging that the attack was "premeditated, organized and carried out by the Mao Tse-tung group," and was "incompatible with normal relations between states." [19] Mao Tse-tung's "revolutionary diplomacy" had patently been carried too far. In the face of a stiff British protest against the burning (August 21–22) of the British chancery at Peking, and a minatory tone assumed by the Soviet press, Chou En-lai was reported soon after to have ordered that "Red Guards must not intrude into foreign embassies or missions or indulge in acts of violence and destruction." [20]

China's relations with the Third World were at this time going from bad to worse. The Council of the Afro-Asian People's Solidarity Organization (AAPSO), meeting at Nicosia in February, expelled the pro-Chinese delegations and then decided that the 1967 AAPSO conference should not be held at Peking as originally planned, but at Algiers. Peking's relations with Asian countries were worst of all.[21] It had become evident that Mao's revolutionism was sometimes no more popular with the poor than with the rich of the earth. The irrationality of Chinese behavior operated to the benefit of Soviet foreign policy, with Soviet sobriety and support of the principle of peaceful coexistence appearing the more attractive by contrast. Moscow presumably felt on safe ground in announcing, in late November, that a meeting of Communist parties would convene at Budapest the following February, to prepare for the holding of the mooted world Communist conference.

The preparatory meeting actually convened at Budapest on February 29, 1968. Fourteen parties refused to attend (Peking did not even reply to the Soviet invitation)—this circumstance probably reducing the possibilities for discord. It was decided that the projected world conference should be held at Moscow in late 1968, and an organizing committee, meeting subsequently, fixed on November 25 as the exact date.

Developments in Eastern Europe conspired against that schedule and incidentally gave China a new occasion for attacking Moscow. On the night of August 20, the USSR and four other Warsaw Pact powers intervened militarily in Czechoslovakia. This was the end-result of a Czechoslovak process of liberalization that had begun in January and gathered momentum over the months. The five powers, after meeting at Warsaw July 14–15, had given Prague forewarning in a letter addressed to the Czechoslovak party. That letter set forth a policy stand: "We shall never agree to imperialism, using peaceful or non-peaceful methods, making a breach, from inside or from outside, in the socialist system and changing the correlation of forces in Europe, in favor of imperialism." [22] The doctrine of "limited sovereignty" had been evoked. With Hungary as a historical precedent, the military action would thus have come as no surprise to Communist capitals.

The intervention was nevertheless a major development for the relations between Peking and Moscow. The Maoist drive for hegemony in 1965–1966 had substantially reduced Peking's influence in the Communist world. Now, the strong condemnation of the Soviet action by not only the Yugoslav but also the French, Italian, and other parties in the Occident had opened up the possibility that Communists *outside* the bloc would become alienated from Moscow and organize themselves as a separate force with their own "liberal" Marxism-Leninism, perhaps reoriented toward a new power center. Had there existed a liberal-minded leadership in Peking at this juncture, it would have been the CCP's opportunity, but liberalism had always been anathema to Mao Tsetung, being one of the evil "bourgeois" elements that he saw in revisionism. In the GPCR, he was engaged in pushing antiliberalism to the extreme.

There thus existed no doubt regarding Peking's disapproval of the Czechoslovak liberalization. Yet, the CCP leadership patently viewed the development in Eastern Europe as something that by extension might constitute a longer-term threat to Albania or China, or both. In any event, Peking was offered a neat opportunity to reap propaganda gains in the quarrel with Moscow. On August 21, at a reception in the Rumanian embassy, Chou En-lai departed from the 1956 pattern with respect to Hungary and condemned the Soviet occupation as "an abominable crime against the Czechoslovak people" that derived, he suggested, from a Soviet policy of collaboration with the United States "with a view to the domination of the world." [23] But he also castigated in severe terms "the revisionist Czechoslovak governing clique."

Albania supported China down the line, and Peking returned the favor. On September 13, the People's Assembly at Tirana approved the formal withdrawal of Albania from the Warsaw Pact (in which it had been inactive for years). Prime Minister Shehu had already indicated that Albania counted on China for its protection. Peking obliged by again assuming an unflinching posture. On September 17, Mao Tse-tung, Lin Piao, and Chou En-lai made their position public: "The seven hundred million Chinese always and in all circumstances will be found firmly at the side of their brother people of Albania." [24]

On the same day NCNA announced that the foreign ministry had delivered a note to the Soviet chargé d'affaires, Yuri Razdukov, protesting Soviet violations of Chinese airspace in the vicinity of Tunghua, in Heilungkiang Province. Remarking 119 violations of Chinese airspace by Soviet military aircraft in the course of the year 1967, and 29 during August alone, the note said that those intrusions "have been thoroughly organized and planned by the Soviet government in order to support the kind of atrocious aggression perpetrated against Czechoslovakia." [25] And where Moscow had been accusing Peking of "social chauvinism" and Peking had thought of nothing better than to call the nonproliferation treaty "nuclear colonialism," now Peking began to characterize the Moscow regime as "social imperialist."

At the end of September, Chou En-lai further elaborated upon the Chinese charge that Moscow was planning military aggression. He accused the USSR of deploying military forces to menace Albania and China, of acting to encircle China in particular by massing troops along the Sino-Soviet and Sino-Mongol frontiers; he warned that such action would have no effect on the Chinese and Albanian peoples, "who are armed with Marxism-Leninism." [26]

In July and August, however, the moderate forces, and in particular the PLA, appeared once more to gain the upper hand in China's GPCR. The events in Czechoslovakia were perhaps a contributory factor in the final defeat of Mao's campaign for permanent revolution, in the form of revolutionary anarchism, at home and abroad: the strategy had demonstrably become too dangerous and too undependable. Caution and moderation were once more manifested in the field of China's foreign affairs. Demonstrations against foreign missions in Peking had ceased long before. Now China undertook to patch up its damaged relations with other countries, excepting the Soviet Union.

The eighth central committee of the CCP sat in plenary session October 13–31, 1968. It was marked by sobriety, whereas the nineteenth central committee plenum of two years earlier had been ebullient. Significantly, the emphasis was primarily on the home front, where the 1966 plenum had given considerable attention to the significance of the GPCR for the world of the latter part of the twentieth century. The outside world was indeed not quite forgotten: the communiqué took the occasion to contend that China was not isolated inasmuch as the people who desired revolution, who made up 90 percent of the globe's population (logically excepting China), "are our friends." It had, however, become evident to all by this time that the GPCR was not in fact accepted by humanity as the wave of the future.

The Soviet Union, though it had been subjected to a setback with regard to its policy line of "peaceful coexistence," had lost neither military nor economic power. Moscow had the direct support of the four Eastern European countries that had participated in the invasion, and other Communist parties, if feeling distress, could not see clearly where else to go if they were to renounce their allegiance to Moscow as leader. It was obvious that none would find more than qualified and calculating hospitality at the hands of either China or the United States.

The fate of the projected world Communist meeting, originally scheduled for November 25, thus held especial interest, given particularly the common assumption that the Soviet position had been so damaged that the other Communist parties would reject the project out of hand. This did not happen. The preparatory commission, made up of sixty-seven party delegations, met in Budapest on November 18 and decided, with only three delegations opposing, that the world conference should only be postponed, not canceled; it would be held in May, 1969, with all Communist parties, including those refusing to attend the preparatory meeting (as the Chinese), to be invited.

It was notable that Rumania supported the Soviet proposal for a conference, that it also participated in a meeting of the Warsaw Pact powers at Bucharest November 26–30, and that Yugoslavia did not diverge further from the bloc. As of that date, none of the Western European parties that had been critical of the action against Czechoslovakia had declared independence of Moscow. They had found no other haven, in East or West.[27]

So the test of relative influence was to be made. The Chinese turn at conferences came first. The GPCR had reached its term, after weakening the country in the process, and it was essential for Mao Tse-tung and his cohorts to dress developments up as an overall success. After eight years' delay beyond schedule, the Ninth CCP Congress was held at Peking April 1–24, 1969. It was characterized as "a congress of unity and a congress of victory," but it was patently neither. Mao Tse-tung indeed celebrated a "victory" over his chief domestic enemy, Chairman of the Chinese People's Republic Liu Shao-ch'i, but this was a Pyrrhic accomplishment: in his drive to recover power, Mao had effectively wrecked the CCP power apparatus. Further, with the elevation of his Thought into the status of immutable Law, the Peking government was left without direct exit from the political and economic impasse into which Maoism had led the country. It was not accidental that Lin Piao's report (the main document of the congress) offered no program for the economic field and no more than Maoist generalities for the domestic political realm.

Lin Piao devoted much attention to foreign affairs. He asserted that China's foreign policy would be governed by the five Bandung principles, including that of peaceful coexistence. But here he indulged in a Maoist contradiction, saying that "China has drawn a clear line between herself on the one hand and U.S. imperialism and Soviet revisionism on the other."[28] As foreshadowed by the CCP Central Committee pronunciamento of August, 1966, American "imperialism" and Soviet "revisionism" were now equally China's "enemies," and beyond the pale. The essence of this principle was written into the new party constitution; Mao proposed that that element of foreign policy should be frozen in the mold of his design.

Lin voiced the familiar principle that China would support and aid foreign revolutionary movements, and, reverting once more to the intermediate-zone theme, he sounded a militant note: "All countries subjected to aggression, control, intervention or bullying by U.S. imperialism and Soviet revisionism, unite and form the broadest possible united front and overthrow our common enemies!" He quoted the omniscient Mao: "An unprecedently gigantic revolutionary mass movement has broken out in Japan, Western Europe and North America, the 'heartlands' of capitalism." The clichés were old and uninspired, and they told the inner truth of the CCP ninth congress: Mao and his supporters, winning to power against the opposition within the party, had been entrapped in an institutionalized dogma.

Exigent economic and political problems made the situation the more difficult for the Chinese leadership at that hour. Lin Piao's report made no reference to the country's third five-year plan. The reason was obvious: that plan had been wrecked. Following the damping down of the GPCR in mid-1968, there had been a modest upturn in some sectors of the economy. But a return to rapid progress in economic development was not now to be expected. A study of the Chinese economy made by the Japanese Foreign Ministry reached the conclusion that, as a result of the ravages of the GPCR, China for the foreseeable future could be expected to have an economic growth rate of no more than 4 percent annually — as compared with the average of 8.9 percent achieved during the first five-year plan.[29] The substitution of revolutionism for technology had stunted China's growth rate. And Mao's war against both "imperialists" and "modern revisionists" had left him no place to turn for gratis aid.

The Soviet Union occupied a much more favorable power position. Moscow thus was naturally attended by greater fortune in the world conference of Communist parties that assembled in Moscow, at long last, on June 5, 1969. Representations were mustered from a full seventy-five parties, despite the Czechoslovak affair — and the Sino-Soviet dispute. China, although refusing to participate, had been unable to prevent most of the rest of the Communist world from attending the gathering held in the "enemy" capital under "revisionist" auspices. The Chinese defeat was the greater in that several of the Asian parties that stayed away—such as the North Korean, North Vietnamese, and Japanese—obviously did so for other reasons than pure loyalty to CCP Chairman Mao Tse-tung.

One major purpose of that Moscow-sponsored meeting was the restoration of a measure of international unity. More diversity of views was expressed there than at either of the two preceding postwar Communist congresses, but the gathering benefited by the acknowledgment of the complex reality of intrabloc relations, and the admission of diversity was discovered not necessarily to mean that the socialist camp would be torn apart by the clash of nationalistic forces: centripetal forces were also at work. As the Hungarian and Polish crises of 1956, the Czechoslovakian affair of 1968 was lamented, but ultimately accepted.

It had been agreed at the preliminary meetings that the conference's principal document would make no reference to China. But the agreement to shelve Sino-Soviet polemics in written form did not deter the Soviet and other delegations from treating the matter in the conference sessions. Brezhnev in particular condemned the Maoists for their "political adventurism" and charged that "China's foreign policy has to all intents and purposes broken with proletarian internationalism and lost its socialist class content." [30] He nevertheless indulged in no sweeping condemnation of the Chinese nation, instead outwardly holding out hope for a change:

> We are profoundly convinced that the genuine national rebirth of China can be achieved and its socialist development ensured not on the path of struggle against the U.S.S.R. and other socialist countries and against the entire Communist movement but on the path of alliance and fraternal cooperation with them.

Moscow's quarrel was depicted as being with the Maoist faction alone.

That position was moderate and restrained, as compared with Peking's fulminations, and led to various parallel statements—but no walkouts. On June 17, at the end of the conference, the great majority of the participants agreed upon a text setting forth the results of their deliberations. The document was anti-imperialist in content—with the "imperialists" including other capitalist countries than the United States. There was no subscription, that is, to the Maoist intermediate-zone theory, and the Soviet Union was thus left in a more comfortable position than one of polarized confrontation with the United States. The strategy still leaned heavily upon "all-embracing cooperation" between the socialist countries for the ensuring of fresh successes in "the decisive areas of economic competition" between the socialist and capitalist systems — a field of competition where China could make only a weak showing. The document also eschewed the thought that there was a "leading center" to the international Communist movement, holding instead that all parties possessed equal rights and that the objective was the development of a fraternal alliance of the socialist countries through "strict adherence to the principles of proletarian internationalism, mutual assistance and support, equality, sovereignty and noninterference in each other's internal affairs." [31] The menace of "limited sovereignty" had retired into the wings — at least for the time being.

Those several parties that either refused to sign the document or signed only with qualifications appear in no instance, so far as the available evidence shows, to have been motivated by sympathy with Peking's pronouncement of anathema on the gathering. As agreed, the formal document made no mention of Mao Tse-tung, his Thought, or even China. In some respects, thus to be ignored was perhaps a greater blow to the CCP's position than if the Sino-Soviet question had been made the subject of extended treatment: as it was, Mao's camp had literally nothing to say. Although Peking had on various occasions warned ominously that the sky would fall if such an international Communist conference were held without China's participation, it did not. The Sino-Soviet dispute was no longer viewed as a major factor disturbing Moscow's relations with other world Communist parties.

36 CONFRONTATION IN THE BORDERLANDS

THE MAJOR CONFRONTATION between Soviet Russia and Communist China had for some time been not in the Communist councils of the world, but in the Sino-Soviet borderlands. Two great nation-states, one Asian and the other Eurasian, faced each other in belligerent mood, as they had often done in the past, along 4,500 miles of frontier. Both were aroused by the irredentism which Mao had evolved in the years of his campaigning against Moscow.

Back in 1962, the eight hundredth anniversary of the birth of Genghis Khan, Peking had caused indignation in Soviet Russia by exalting the Mongol conqueror and theorizing that his westward drive to empire had been a civilizing, "cultural" force. Here it has to be remembered that the modern Chinese political theorists have adopted the Mongols (together with Manchus, Tibetans, and Central Asian Turkis) as a part of the "Chinese" people of which the Hans too are only a part — if by far and away the greater, and "leading" part. Genghis Khan, thus, had been a civilizing "Chinese" influence. From the Pax Mongolica concept to Pax Sinica was an easy step.

That this particular manifestation of Chinese chauvinism might possess contemporary political significance was suggested by tensions that developed along the Sino-Soviet frontier — also beginning in 1962. The Sinkiang-Uighur Autonomous Region (SUAR), which had been deeply stirred by the 1956–1957 urge toward autonomy, had remained restless within the oppressive Chinese pattern. Finally, driven to desperation, some 62,000 Kazakhs and Uighurs fled from Sinkiang into neighboring areas of the Soviet Union between April, 1962, and mid-1963.

For reasons unstated, other than by reference to "deteriorating relations" between the parties concerned, Peking was reported to have closed down the Soviet consular offices in Urumchi and Kuldja about September, 1962.[1] The "Friendship Railway" that was to have linked China Proper with Soviet Kazakhstan via Sinkiang remained uncompleted. The USSR had finished construction of the spur from Aktogai to the Dzungarian Pass by January, 1961, and had founded a border settlement named "Druzhba" (Friendship), but although the Chinese and Soviet sections were to have been connected in that same year, the Chinese for the time being had stopped construction at Urumchi.

Against the background of reports of heavy Chinese troop movements into Sinkiang, the *People's Daily* on September 3, 1963, brought the border troubles to the attention of the outside world, putting all the blame on Moscow. Soviet agencies and personnel, it alleged, had in April and May of 1962 carried out "large-scale subversive activities in the Ili region of Sinkiang and incited and coerced several tens of thousands of Chinese citizens [the Kazakhs and Uighurs] into going to the Soviet Union."[2] In a related radio broadcast, Peking charged that Moscow had refused to repatriate the refugees "on the pretext of a sense of Soviet legality and humanitarianism." It was entirely evident that the Chinese were not content with the Russian explanation.

Moscow replied, obliquely, in an official statement of September 21 alleging that the Chinese had "systematically violated" the Soviet border, with over 5,000 Chinese violations occurring in 1962 alone, and charging further that "Attempts are also being made to 'develop' some parts of Soviet territory without permission."[3] The Moscow statement further disclosed that the Soviet government had on a number of occasions invited Peking to enter upon talks to determine separate sections of the border, but that the Chinese side had avoided such talks. Moscow offered a pointed estimate: "The artificial creation of any territorial problems in our times, especially between Socialist countries, would be tantamount to embarking on a very dangerous path." And there was a warning: a continuation of hostile Chinese acts against the Soviet Union would meet "a most decisive rebuff."

In an interview in January, 1964, with the American writer Edgar Snow, Chou En-lai revealed that an agreement had been reached with Moscow for negotiations on Sino-Soviet border problems. Those talks began at Peking on February 25. On February 29, as remarked above, the Chinese made reply to a Soviet letter of November 29. They took up the boundary question, which they characterized as a legacy of the past. It could be settled, the Chinese letter said, through negotiations, and, pending settlement, there should be maintenance of the status quo. They took the occasion, however, to charge Moscow with frequent violations of that status quo and with subverting minority peoples residing in China's borderlands. Shortly afterward, it was reported that China had dispatched additional troops to Sinkiang and had cleared and fortified a security zone twenty miles in depth along hundreds of miles of the border with the Soviet Union.[4]

The prospects for the negotiations at Peking thus appeared unpromising. They in fact made no headway, for the simple reason that the two capitals approached the talks from fundamentally different angles. Moscow was understood to desire a limitation of negotiations to specific local issues, such as that pertaining to the ownership of certain islands in the Amur River, whereas Peking was reported to have demanded a comprehensive border review. The Chinese approach would naturally have required a reassessment of historical developments. The Chinese delegation, according to a *Pravda* report months afterward, actually put forward a claim to over 1.5 million square kilometers (580,000 square miles) of Soviet territory — while modestly stating that Peking would refrain for the moment from demanding satisfaction of that claim. In May, 1964, the talks were suspended.

Mao Tse-tung, in an interview of July 10 with a group of visiting Japanese Socialists, gave some confirmation of the scope of Chinese territorial desires, and at the same time added fuel to Japanese (and other) irredentism. He said that, after World War II, the Soviet Union occupied "too many places," in Eastern Europe and in Northeast Asia as well. Moscow had brought Outer Mongolia under its rule, and Peking had raised this question with Khrushchev and Bulganin when they visited China in 1954, "but they refused to discuss it." "Some people," he said, had suggested that Sinkiang should be included in the Soviet Union. "China has not yet asked the Soviet Union for an accounting about Vladivostok, Khabarovsk, Kamchatka, and other towns and regions east of Lake Baikal which became Russian territory about 100 years ago." [5] He offered a sop to his visitors by voicing support for the return to Japan of "the northern islands" (the Kuriles).

Pravda, in an editorial comment of September 2, stated the obvious when it said that the USSR was faced with "an openly expansionist programme with far-reaching pretensions." [6] Khrushchev, as was his habit, put the matter into rather more picturesque language: he found little merit in the claims of those who persisted in referring to "the frontiers of the Old Testament." And in a meeting with visiting members of the Japanese Diet on September 15, he expressed himself at some length on Mao Tse-tung's irredentist views, which he found "offensive." He observed that Chinese emperors, even as Russian tsars, had engaged in wars of conquest, and voiced a warning: "The borders of the Soviet Union are sacred, and he who dares to violate them will meet with a most decisive rebuff on the part of the peoples of the Soviet Union." [7]

The Soviet warning had teeth in it. The (British) Institute of Strategic Studies in late 1964 estimated the Soviet armed forces to number 3.3 million men, as compared to 2.476 million men for China. Moreover, the Soviet forces were fully equipped with powerful offensive weapons, including nearly 200 intercontinental ballistic missiles, whereas the Chinese army was "gravely short of heavy and self-propelled artillery as well as transport," and "had little strategic mobility, due to its primitive logistics." [8] China's recent explosion of a nuclear device, by the institute's estimate, did not promote China "even to the status of a medium military power." The history of the Sino-Soviet conflict of 1929 would have warned Peking not to venture a military confrontation with its Soviet neighbor.

Of major strategic significance in the borderlands confrontation between the two Communist giants was the buffer state of Mongolia. Its relations with China could now be taken as a barometer of Moscow's relations with Peking. Ulan Bator was assured that the agreements binding it to the Soviet Union had practical value in terms of national defense. The Mongolian legal position had moreover been strengthened by the signature, in December, 1963, of an accord with Peking by virtue of which the Sino-Mongol frontiers were defined — with no major concessions by the Mongol side.

Its position thus buttressed, Ulan Bator reacted in April,

1964, to the proselytizing and subversive activities of Chinese construction workers and others, sent from 1955 onward to implement the aid program that had been set up in the Mongolian People's Republic, by requesting the Chinese, numbering over 20,000, to depart. By late June, 5,200 Chinese workers had been brought home from the MPR and another 900 were preparing to leave.[9]

In June also, the Mongolian People's Revolutionary Party made public charges of the previous December that China had been using various kinds of pressure to force the MPR to enter the Chinese sphere of influence. In August, with Chinese influence reduced rather than increased, Moscow stepped up its program of economic aid to the Mongols. Earlier, it had been ostentatiously announced at Ulan Bator by the MPR minister of defense that there would be special anniversary observance, that summer, of the 1939 Nomonhan campaign, which, he said, had forged an unbreakable friendship between the Mongol and Soviet peoples and demonstrated their ability to crush any forces that might be sent against them.[10] The Chinese at Peking were thus reminded again of the significance of the Soviet-Mongol mutual defense pact.

Finally, in September, Ulan Bator took official notice of the irredentism expressed in Mao Tse-tung's talk with the visiting Japanese Socialists, and in a statement published in *Pravda* said that "The Chinese nationalists' shady schemes to do away with the state independence of the Mongolian People's Republic are absurd and unrealizable."[11] Ulan Bator laid down the rationale for its expression of confidence:

> Every working person in the Mongolian People's Republic is fully aware that if our country had not linked its destiny with the Soviet Union, Mongolia would not be independent and would not have had the successes that have now been achieved. It is clear that if the Chinese leaders' schemes had been carried out, our people would have shared the fate of the Inner Mongolians and other national minorities of China toward whom the policy of great-Han chauvinism is being pursued.

There was no logical countervailing argument that Peking might have offered. Peking's policies, far from prying the Mongolian People's Republic away from the Soviet Union, had driven it closer into the Soviet embrace, as the sole refuge.

In the course of the GPCR, there were new maneuvers in the border regions. In May, 1966, as the Cultural Revolution entered its primary stage, foreign minister Ch'en Yi reiterated the Maoist theme in an interview with a group of visiting Scandinavian journalists: the Russians, he said, were thieves who had annexed one and a half million kilometers of Chinese territory in the nineteenth century and even afterward. In October, as the Revolution swirled around the gates of the Soviet embassy in Peking, the Moscow press charged that Chinese troops had begun to fire indiscriminately at Russian ships plying the Amur, and Occidental correspondents in Moscow reported that, according to a Soviet source, organized Chinese "people's" movements in the Amur region and Sinkiang were calling for the return of "lost territories." [12]

Soviet troop strength in the Soviet Far East was at that time put at twelve divisions on war footing and five divisions in reserve. The Chinese strength in Manchuria was estimated at twenty-four divisions. But it was notable that, as the GPCR took on full fury, Moscow built up the Soviet defense position in both the Soviet Far East and the Mongolian People's Republic. China for its part, with the PLA heavily engaged with the complex responsibilities of the GPCR, was not able to make much change in its own military dispositions.

Peking's war against the USSR was waged mostly in words during the period 1966–1968. With the de facto end of the GPCR in October, 1968, however, Mao Tse-tung and his lieutenants needed an issue that might promise to strengthen their position in the upcoming party congress. On March 2, 1969, Chinese and Soviet forces clashed on obscure Damanski (Chen Pao) Island in the Ussuri River, and the Soviets suffered thirty-four killed. Given the heavy Soviet casualties, and the circumstance that only a Soviet border patrol was involved, logic leads to the conclusion that, as charged by Moscow, China initiated the attack.

It is interesting to view the subsequent developments in the light of the history of the 1939 clash at Changkufeng. The Chinese claimed victory, but the evidence indicates that the Soviets brought up reinforcements and reoccupied the island. Then, in a note delivered to the Soviet embassy and published in Peking on March 13, the Chinese charged new Soviet aggressions in the disputed sector – as if building up a case. According to a Soviet source,[13] Defense Minister Lin Piao made a tour of inspection to the Damanski sector. On March 15, there was a new, and much bigger, armed clash on that battleground.

A diplomatic exchange followed promptly. On the very day of the clash, the Chinese Ministry for Foreign Affairs delivered a note to the Soviet embassy at Peking charging that a large number of Soviet forces accompanied by armored cars and tanks had penetrated Damanski Island "and the region west of that island," and then had sent in reinforcements, with more armor, which had leveled artillery fire deep into the Chinese interior. "The incident was thus extended."[14] The Chinese note said further that "The Soviet government must bear the entire responsibility for all the grave consequences which could result from this."

The Soviet government on the same day addressed to the Chinese government a note which, referring to the clash, stated that "This new and impudent provocation by the Chinese authorities is heavy with consequences."[15] The message contained a plain warning: "the Soviet government declares that if the legitimate rights of the U.S.S.R. are mocked, that if new attempts are made to violate the integrity of Soviet territory, the Soviet Union and all of its peoples will defend it resolutely and will oppose a crushing riposte to such violations." The Chinese chargé d'affaires at Moscow refused to accept the note, but he undoubtedly gave heed to its contents and reported appropriately to his government.

Significantly, no detailed report was made by either side. But what appears to have happened was that the Chinese had again attacked the Soviet position on Damanski Island, in regimental force, employing both mortars and artillery. The Soviets effected a withdrawal, thus leading the Chinese to mass in the Damanski sector, whereupon the Soviets, who had anticipated the attack, opened up on the Chinese along a front several kilometers in length with artillery, missiles, tanks, and air power. According to travelers from the Soviet Far East, the Chinese lost 800 men as compared with about 60 Soviet dead, and the island of Damanski was "practically erased from the map."[16] Soviet circles seemed assured that the "lesson" had gotten across to the Chinese; "This time," it was said, "they have understood."[17]

There seems little doubt that Mao Tse-tung and his cohorts now were finally brought to a realization that they had exceeded the limits of China's prowess – and of Soviet forbearance. Mao would have won no personal political gain from the action, but would instead have once more proved himself wrong in the eyes of his soberer colleagues. Where the *People's Daily* of Peking had earlier declared vaingloriously that "The anti-Chinese scum will end badly," [18] it must have been a chastened Chinese leadership that read a communication delivered by the Soviet government to the Chinese embassy in Moscow on March 29 regarding Sino-Soviet relations, and then promptly made public, right on the eve of the opening of the Ninth CCP Congress. [19]

The declaration began with a consideration of recent events on the Ussuri. Significantly, it gave fewer details regarding the second clash than about the first, recounting simply that "Units of the regular Chinese army, supported by artillery fire, attacked the Soviet frontier armed forces defending Damanski island. The attack was firmly repulsed. It claimed new victims." But even more significantly it stated with respect to the question of the Ussuri boundary that: "In 1861, the two sides signed a map on which the frontier line in the Ussuri region was traced. Near Damanski island, that line passes directly along the Chinese shore of the river. The originals of those documents are held by the Chinese government as well as by that of the U.S.S.R."

The declaration then reviewed the Sino-Soviet relationship as it had developed since 1917. Moscow did not omit to mention the outcome of the clashes with the Japanese at Lake Khasan and Khalkhin Gol in 1938 and 1939. The historical account would have been of interest to others than historians: it would have jogged the memories of the political pragmatists as well. When Moscow at the end of the declaration invited the government of the Chinese People's Republic to abstain from all action along the frontier that "would risk bringing about complications," and called upon Peking to resolve any differences "in calm and by means of negotiations," through the prompt resumption of the border negotiations undertaken at Peking in 1964, it was assured of an audience at the ninth congress. Symbolically, low-lying Damanski Island would about this time have been submerged by the spring floods on the Ussuri.

Lin Piao in his April report to the congress acknowledged receipt of the Soviet offer and said cryptically but revealingly that "Our Government is considering its reply to this." It was notable in this connection that the Bulgarian minister for foreign affairs in an interview granted Austrian journalists on April 4 observed that it was conceivable that Warsaw Pact forces might intervene in a case where incidents on the Sino-Soviet frontier "would menace the security of the socialist camp."[20] Here was thinly veiled threat of action in the pattern of the intervention in Czechoslovakia. When the conservative West German *Frankfurter Allgemeine Zeitung* about a week later, referring to "informed circles in the Austrian capital," reported that symbolic contingents of Warsaw Pact forces "faithful to the Moscow line" were en route to the Sino-Soviet frontier,[21] again Peking would have "understood."

On May 12, Peking announced that it had sent a message to the Soviet Union accepting in principle the Soviet proposal for resumption of the work of the mixed commission for the regulation of traffic on the border rivers and proposing that the date be fixed for mid-June. Moscow agreed, naming June 18 as the exact date. A few days after that exchange, on May 18, the Peking *People's Daily,* as if to demonstrate that there had been no Chinese surrender, denounced the "new Soviet tsars'" policy of naval expansion in the Mediterranean, the Red Sea, the Indian Ocean, and the Pacific. It appears probable that the *People's Daily* hoped that the advertisement also would make an impression on the American high naval command.

About this time, Soviet President Nikolai V. Podgorny visited North Korea and the Mongolian People's Republic on a tour that was obviously designed to strengthen Moscow's political fences. Delicately considerate of the desire of his Korean hosts to maintain the semblance of neutrality, he refrained from attacking Peking while in the North Korean capital. In Ulan Bator, however, where Premier Tsedenbal on May 19 in a personàl interview with an American newsman condemned Mao Tse-tung as a "great-power chauvinist" and expressed concern about, inter alia, the Sino-Soviet conflict,[22] Podgorny on the following day joined with Tsedenbal in a denunciation of the Mao regime. The two men spoke against the background of a sharp increase in Sino-Mongolian border incidents over recent months.[23] It was undoubtedly with due deliberation that Tsedenbal referred confidently to the Soviet-Mongolian association that, as he remarked, had then endured for fifty years. At this time, the USSR was entering the fourth year of an intensive buildup of its military establishment in the region east of Lake Baikal especially. Air facilities had been considerably expanded, and estimates of the Soviet troop strength located east of Irkutsk ranged as high as 1.5 million men; further, some 100,000 to 200,000 Soviet troops, including missile-launching units, had by report been deployed in the MPR —within easy reach of Paotow and Lanchow, two of China's nuclear centers.[24]

The Sino-Soviet frontier issue was still pending. In a statement published by the NCNA on May 24, the Chinese government complained that Soviet gunfire on the Ussuri had continued as an evident attempt to force negotiations, but in the end it agreed in principle to the Soviet proposal, suggesting that the date and place of the projected negotiations regarding the Sino-Soviet frontier "be discussed and decided by the two parties through the diplomatic channel."[25] The statement contained in the Chinese note asserting that "all of the treaties relative to the present Sino-Soviet frontier are unequal treaties, and all should be annulled,"[26] could be viewed as in main ritualistic.

There were at the same time, in May, reports of recent clashes on the Sinkiang-Kazakhstan frontier. The information offered was uncertain and inconclusive, but suggestive of new friction. One initial report had it that a thousand Chinese troops, advancing behind shepherds moving their flocks in annual migration to pastures in the higher plateaus, had penetrated eastern Kazakhstan in the vicinity of Bakhty and were in occupation of several square kilometers of Soviet territory. A later version gave a roughly similar tale, but had Soviet forces ejecting the intruders, with a woman sheepherder losing her life.

Then there came a Chinese protest against the alleged intrusion of a large Soviet armored force into SUAR territory in the vicinity of Yumin in early June. A new clash occurred in the same general region in mid-August, with each side accusing the other of frontier violation, but the casualty figures again suggested a Chinese defeat. In the light of historical precedents, one might with reasonable assurance speculate with respect to at least the earlier phase that the Chinese had engaged in probes across the Soviet frontier and had been summarily thrust back.[27] It appears probable in any event that no Chinese troops were long in occupation of Soviet territory after March 2, 1969—no matter how far removed from Moscow.

In the meantime, the Sino-Soviet joint river-navigation commission had resumed its functioning at Khabarovsk on June 18, as scheduled. Peking seemed constrained to indicate that it had no hope for amicable agreement. At the beginning of July, a functionary speaking at a meeting of senior officials in Canton reputedly declared that war with the Soviet Union was "definitely imminent" and, asserting that he spoke on behalf of higher authority, stated that World War III would begin in October.[28] Such apocalyptic pronouncements had of course been made before — with direct attribution to Mao Tse-tung. There was no solid evidence, however, that the Peking leadership had such faith in its own words that it had begun to deploy its armed forces in anticipation of the event.

There was, nevertheless, evidence to show that Peking considered its relations with Moscow so deteriorated that it had to proceed with exceptional care. On July 8, shortly after the prognostication of war, the Chinese charged that the Soviets had violated Chinese territory by intruding into Goldinski (Pacha) Island in the Amur near Khabarovsk. Moscow described the incident as a *Chinese* violation of the existing frontier and charged that the Chinese had staged a "malicious provocation" with the aim of sabotaging the Khabarovsk talks. In an address of July 10, Foreign Minister Gromyko, while speaking in favor of good relations with the United States, voiced a categorical warning to China: "We rebuffed and we shall rebuff all the attempts to speak with the Soviet Union in terms of threats or, moreover, weapons. What happened in March of this year near Damansky Island on the Ussuri River must make certain people consider more soberly the consequences of their actions."[29] Gromyko did not have to spell out, for the Chinese, what had happened in March.

The next development seemed to bear out the Moscow charge that the Goldinski Island clash was a "provocation" designed to abort the river-navigation negotiations. The Chinese delegation at Khabarovsk on July 12 broke off the talks. But on the following day, according to a Tass account, the delegation reversed itself and informed the Soviet side that, "contrary to its statement of July 12, it has decided to remain in Khabarovsk and agreed to the continuation of the commission's work."[30] Presumably, the Chinese delegation had in the first instance acted in accordance with its instructions — only to have those instructions suddenly reversed. Peking was now beginning to give heed to the hard facts of power. Interestingly enough, nothing more was heard of the Goldinski incident.

The Chinese spoke out defiantly on August 1, Army Day. In a common editorial, the *People's Daily, Red Flag,* and the *Liberation Army Daily* condemned the "military expansionism" of the United States and the Soviet Union and the reputed collusion of the two Western powers in anti-Chinese maneuvers, and asserted in conclusion: "If the United States and the Soviet Union desire to impose war upon us, we will give suitable return to them to the end, whether in a little or a big war, a conventional war or a nuclear war." [31]

Despite Peking's brave words, the Soviet Union was the readier for war, and the CCP leadership knew it. The Chinese economy had been weakened by Mao Tse-tung's Great Purge, and the PLA remained a second-rate army. Mao's voluntarism had not sufficed to overcome China's concrete difficulties. A week after the celebration of Army Day, an agreement was signed at the Khabarovsk conference to govern navigation of the border rivers in the current year, and provision was made for holding further talks regarding the matter in 1970. Then, on September 11, Premier Kosygin, after reaching Dushanbe in Tadjikstan en route home after attending Ho Chi Minh's funeral, proceeded to Peking and met there with Premier Chou En-lai. This was the first meeting of the two in four and a half years – that is, since Chou's trip to Moscow in January, 1965.

According to a report brought back by American Communist Party leader Gus Hall after a meeting with Brezhnev at Moscow,[32] the meeting was at the Soviet initiative, and Kosygin presented specific proposals that (1) critical border issues be taken up promptly at the deputy ministerial level, (2) the Soviet and Chinese ambassadors immediately return to their respective posts at Peking and Moscow, and (3) negotiations be undertaken regarding trade and economic relations. Different from earlier press accounts, which put the meeting at one hour, this version stated that the talk between the two premiers lasted for four hours. The American Communist leader expressed the qualified view that external and internal pressures were pushing the Chinese toward a resolution of the Sino-Soviet conflict.

At the Chinese National Day celebrations on October 1, 1969, after twenty years of power, Peking appeared in a quiet mood. The day was not the gala occasion staged by the CCP leaders a short decade earlier. The nation's domestic accomplishments in those ten last years had been scantier by far than anticipated when China embarked upon its second five-year economic plan in 1958, and honored foreign guests were few, evidencing the battered state of China's foreign relations. Mao Tse-tung "appeared," and thus performed his function. Lin Piao spoke, damning "U.S. imperialism" specifically, but leaving the identifying adjective off his condemnation of "social imperialists." At the same time, he asserted that Peking in its foreign policy had "always" upheld the Five Principles of peaceful coexistence. This time, in striking contrast to the position he had assumed at the Ninth CCP Congress six months before, he excepted neither the Soviet Union nor the United States from the benefits of that doctrine. His final appeal to the people of the world to "unite and oppose the war of aggression launched by any imperialism or social-imperialism" [33] seemed but a feeble echo of his earlier call to *overthrow* "our common enemies" — identified specifically as "U.S. imperialism and Soviet revisionism." China's "enemies" had become faceless. Peking had bowed to the inevitable.

One week later, on October 7, 1969, it was officially announced by Peking that differences on questions of (Communist) principle "should not prevent China and the Soviet Union from maintaining normal *state* relations on the basis of the five principles of peaceful coexistence" (emphasis supplied), and that "There is no reason whatsoever for China and the Soviet Union to fight a war over the boundary question." [34] The Chinese government, the statement said, had "never" demanded the return of territory annexed by tsarist Russia "by means of the unequal treaties," and had "always" stood for the settlement of existing boundary questions in "earnest all-round negotiations." Then, "The Chinese Government and the Soviet Government have now decided through discussion that negotiations are to be held in Peking between the Chinese and Soviet sides on the Sino-Soviet boundary question at the level of Vice Minister of Foreign Affairs." The Kosygin proposals had been accepted. To all indications, the provisions of the "unequal treaties" of the nineteenth century would not be the prime issue at the forthcoming negotiations.

This was the logical denouement of the deliberations of the twelfth CCP Central Committee plenary of just one year before. China would not be at war in October. The shattered Chinese leadership was undertaking the long, arduous road toward adjusting to the world, instead of remaking it immediately in Maoist design. In accordance with the principle of peaceful coexistence, it had at last manifested a readiness to accept a measure of reconciliation with Moscow. Perhaps, eventually, it would even become less strident in its campaign against "U.S. imperialism."

EPILOGUE CHINESE, RUSSIANS, AND AMERICANS

THE LIFE OF EMPIRES is uncertain, as amply demonstrated by the Mongol, Spanish, and Manchu experiences—to select some striking early examples. Nazi Germany, according to its founders, was to last a thousand years; it hardly lived a decade. In combating imperial and Nazi Germany in two world wars, however, the British and French empires were broken, and little remains of them today. The very principle of "empire," insofar as it signifies the right of powerful states to dominate other peoples, has been discredited.

The urge to power nevertheless is inherent in expansive polities. Thus, in an era when empires are viewed as anachronistic, three remain—China, the Soviet Union, and the United States. In a world too small for modern warfare, they are in contact in many sectors; true to the nature of imperial states, they compete, and are currently in conflict. The future of each will be influenced in large measure, inevitably, by domestic developments. The "Han cycle" is found in more than Chinese affairs. But the future of all mankind may be decided by the outcome of the contest of the three in the world arena.

The Sino-Russian relation in the latter part of the twentieth century must therefore properly be considered with due reference to other forces operative in today's world, and especially to Amer-

THE CHINESE PEOPLE'S REPUBLIC AND
THE UNION OF SOVIET SOCIALIST REPUBLICS

| | DISPUTED AREAS | RUSSIA 1598 | MING CHINA 1580 |

1000 KM

T.R. MILLER

ican power and strategy. Peking's policy vis-à-vis the Soviet Union has from the beginning been molded in good part by the urge to *li yung* (profitably utilize) Soviet strength to achieve the expulsion of American power from the Asian peripheral sectors where it is posed to "contain" China. And Soviet policy toward China has been dictated to an important degree by considerations of American strategic objectives. There is more than direct reciprocity in the Sino-Soviet relationship.

The main sectors of the triangular military confrontation are Northeast Asia, where the three powers meet in a zone of hostility centered on the divided Korean Peninsula; Southeast Asia, where the United States purports to fight for the purpose of stemming the advance of Chinese influence; and Southwest Asia and the Balkans, where all three maneuver in the field of conflicting Arab-Israeli, Greco-Turk, and Albanian-Yugoslav rivalries.

In order to achieve hypothetical expansionist objectives of (1) gaining access to new spaces for its surplus tens of millions of people and (2) winning a redistribution of the world's wealth in order to relieve its poverty, China would either have to succeed in maneuvering the United States and the USSR into a suicidal nuclear collision or else, in a slower and more laborious process, achieve such control of the rising anger of the poor nations against the rich as would enable it to overwhelm the "imperialist" and "revisionist" enemies through the instrumentality of that "world revolution."

That the first strategy is not entirely out of the realm of possibility must be admitted: American and Soviet security interests clash in many critical world sectors. The military element is increasingly dominant in both the American economy and American foreign policy, and the Soviet Union competes strenuously in armaments and in other fields. But the Peking leadership has been less discreet than either the Soviet or the American government with respect to the veiling of some of its darker thoughts, and it would appear that both Washington and Moscow are at least alerted to Mao Tse-tung's concept that the civilization which had its beginning in the Mediterranean shall come to its end in the NATO-Warsaw Pact arena.

Barring such a violent denouement, the Third World would constitute a critical unknown in any peaceful equation. That inchoate political entity, the object of Mao's philosophical concern, by definition is viewed as embracing all of the poor and under-developed but emerging nations of Asia, Africa, and Latin America, excepting, effectively, China itself (set apart more by its politics than by its economics). That massive sector of the world is hag-ridden by the problems of political integration and economic development, in circumstances where, because of the shortage of domestic capital and technological and administrative skills, the exploitation of resources is often in the hands of foreign entrepreneurs. There has been UN assistance, unilateral aid, and bilateral trade, but the hard fact is that many of those poor countries are now finding it difficult to service outstanding debt charges from existing foreign-exchange resources and thus find their international purchasing power further reduced instead of expanded. It is now almost trite to remark the obvious fact: the rich countries are getting richer, while the poor get poorer.

The attitudes finally adopted by that great turbulent mass of the economically disadvantaged nations with respect to the various great-power drives will substantially influence the outcome of the struggle. The Peking leadership is correct in its assessment of the importance of the underlying "antagonistic contradiction" between poor nations and rich. Many of the peoples of Asia, Africa, and Latin America were fascinated by the Chinese political and economic achievements in the 1950–1957 period (from China's intervention in the Korean War to the end of the first five-year plan); then disenchantment set in. China's accomplishments fell off, and it came to be realized that Peking's words and deeds were of two different categories. Professions of disinterested altruism have not carried conviction to China's Asian neighbors. The several striking manifestations of the imperial spirit, such as the voicing of claims to vast "lost" territories, Peking's reiterated demand that the Mongols return to the Chinese fold, and fitful attempts to make China's diktat run for not only Burma and Korea but also Japan and Indonesia, have alerted China's Asian neighbors to the circumstance that the present Chinese leaders, though endowed with the adjective "Communist," are Great Hans still. The Maoist intellectual arrogance, and Chinese great-power chauvinism, were not designed to win the emerging nations to a common cause of Asians against Occident, or of Africans and Latin Americans against either the United States or the Soviet Union.

The psychological advantage thus fell automatically to the Russians, charged by the Chinese with collaborating with the United States to halt the course of world revolution. That allegation hardly touched the emerging nations to the quick, concerned as they are with nationalistic aspirations and economic betterment. Peking's philosophical excesses and tactical political errors have helped, more than they hurt, the Soviet Union. Insofar as there was profit to be had from the Chinese posturing and troublemaking, it was mostly reaped by Moscow, not Peking.

If the chief concern of any "imperial" power can be assumed in general to be national aggrandizement, the particular imperial objectives naturally often differ. So it is with the Soviet Union and China. The chief Soviet concern in Europe has evidently been to maintain a solid buffer zone of "socialist" allies against the West. In Asia, Moscow proposes similarly to keep China functioning as a barrier between the Soviet Union and American sea and air power in the West Pacific, and to have the Mongolian People's Republic perform a valuable buffer role against China itself. It would further block any advance of China against Soviet dominions, and besides flank the renascent Chinese empire, by building up, through a combination of economic and political efforts, positions of influence in such critical countries as Japan, India, and Indonesia. At the same time, it would wage secondary campaigns against American and Chinese influences in Africa and Latin America. If successful, according to the Stalin thesis of 1952, the "socialist" world would continue to expand and the "capitalist" world contract, until capitalism had been quite swallowed up by socialism. And in that new socialist world the Soviet Union, not China, would stand out as the dominant force and figure.

It can be deduced that for Chinese of the "revolutionary" Maoist stamp the paramount strategic objectives would be Siberia to the north with its natural wealth, Russian Turkestan to the west, Africa in the distant southwest, and Australia far to the southeast, all three areas offering rich prizes for the resource-poor and power-hungry Chinese nation. China's needs in that respect evoke no altruism in Moscow. As Khrushchev indicated plainly, the USSR would repulse with rude military force any Chinese attempt to "liberate" Tungusi, Mongol, and Turki lands now under the Soviet imperium. Peking has consequently found it expedient to limit its actions in the Inner Asian borderlands to minor military harassments, political maneuvers, and simple holding operations.

To the south lies India, another Asian country that has a major role in the Great Game being played in Asia in the last half of the twentieth century. It occupies a geographic position of high strategic importance with respect to China's expansive goals. As an avowedly "socialist" state, India competes with China for world political prestige. It faces some of the same economic problems that burden China, and the relative success or failure of the two countries will show up in the development of their national powers. China, having by its actions divorced itself from major sources of gratis outside aid, or of liberal credits, perforce glories in its "self-reliance." But by adopting an openly anti-Indian policy Peking has left New Delhi with no other option than the not entirely unpleasant one of accepting both military and economic aid from the British Commonwealth, the United States, and the Soviet Union. India has been receiving in the neighborhood of U.S.$1 billion annually in grants and credits from interested industrialized nations. It can evidently expect to continue to receive massive outside help during the course of the next critical decade of its economic modernization.

The weakening of India would require its flanking on east or west (or both). That particular Chinese cause has not been advanced on India's eastern flank, in Southeast Asia, despite the presence there of some 12 million Overseas Chinese, or by developments that have swirled around Vietnam as an Asian storm center. The influence of China in that region actually declined from 1965 to 1968 as a consequence of developments in Thailand, Malaysia, and Indonesia, the three main areas of Chinese ethnic concentration, and in Vietnam itself. The gateway to the south has not been pried ajar. And yet, the escalation of the Vietnam War into Laos and Cambodia automatically demanded an augmented Chinese commitment to the "anti-imperialist" side. The final accounting of the Second Indo-China War is yet to be made.

India's western flank, comprising the triangular region made up of Afghanistan, Pakistan, and Iran, opening onto the Arab lands, is the traditional land route to Africa. Afghanistan, grown wise from having long been the object of covetous imperialists, maintains an independence which, with American and Soviet "aid" neatly balancing each other, is largely invulnerable to Chinese initiatives. Iran similarly presents China with the problem of overcoming both American and Soviet competition. Pakistan, a member of the Central Treaty Organization (CENTO) and Southeast Asia Treaty Organization (SEATO), both "free world" combines, has demonstrated that it does not intend to sacrifice its national interests for either. And, having obtained Chinese aid and a good boundary settlement in return for an anti-Indian attitude that it would at the time have entertained in any event, Karachi turned to mend its fences with the USSR. China has achieved no solid foothold in Pakistan, Afghanistan, or Iran. The Soviet Union has more prestige and influence by far in that critical triangle.

Nor has Peking been able to discover greater hospitality for its aspirations farther still to the southwest. The Maoists of today are prepared to call the Arabs and blacks of the Middle East and Africa "brothers" in the service of their grand strategy, which contemplates the exploitation of racism against the Occident. With respect to the Arab world, however, China suffers from the same disabilities it experiences elsewhere: it can hardly win influence over military regimes and Arab sheikhs by proposing their overthrow, and it has no lever with which to push the Arab masses into a rebellion designed to advance *Chinese* interests in the Middle East. Here Moscow, which is inclined to frown upon the enthusiasms of radical Iraqi revolutionaries and Egyptian Communists as threatening to complicate Soviet relations with the established governments of countries of prime importance such as Turkey, Egypt, and Algeria, would appear to be following a course that promises richer results. China has indeed established a presence in the Middle East, but its influence there remains minute, whereas the Soviet influence there is of such dimensions as to challenge the American position. And Africa is even farther away in strategic terms, and out of the effective political and economic reach of poverty-stricken China. Consequently, the CCP leadership is caused to concentrate most of the nation's slender resources for empire-building in the nearest and most dangerous of the three arenas, and the main Chinese thrust remains today, as in times past, to the southeast.

This circumstance requires reference again to the overall strategic situation. At the beginning of the twentieth century, the focus of imperial struggle was in East Asia, where the beleaguered Chinese empire was under siege by land and sea powers. The new confrontations of China, Russia, and the United States on the world scene replace those of seventy years ago. Excepting in the military aspect, China and the Soviet Union no longer confront each other primarily in their borderlands, but in those countries on the periphery of Asia that are destined to play prime roles in the power politics of Asia's future. Unless China can make political progress in its immediate geopolitical environment, it will patently stand little chance of making headway in Africa and Latin America, which are far away from the Celestial Kingdom in history, culture, and feeling.

The question whether the Chinese or the Soviet strategy promises the greater success in the Third World reduces itself to this: which country presents the more attractive political image, and which has the more effective economic approach? Mao Tse-tung's regime from 1958 to 1968 persisted in calling upon the masses to revolt against their "bourgeois" rulers under the leadership of the "proletariat" (Communists); Moscow has endeavored since Bandung days to woo bourgeois nationalist governments with trade and aid.

The comparative merits of the two strategies must be deemed reasonably clearly established. At the beginning of 1953 (the year China embarked upon its first five-year plan), the Soviet Union had trade and payments agreements with three Third World countries—but a decade later with thirty-five. It seemed in 1953–1957 that the underdeveloped world was to be China's oyster, but the diversion of Chinese effort from the Bandung policy to jousting with the phantasmagoria of "imperialism" and "revisionism," with employment of that variety of expedients that betrays the inadequacy of a philosophy or strategic plan, favored instead Soviet success in the field of the emerging nations. By 1968, the revolutionary foreign-policy line adopted in the year of the Great Leap had met disaster in the Third World.

A major reason for China's failure in the arena of trade-and-aid competition was Peking's decision, manifested in the launching upon a public quarrel with Moscow in 1960, to exploit its Soviet ally to the Soviet disadvantage and its own prime benefit. Communist China in the end proved itself as incapable as Imperial China of conceding that *both* parties to an alliance should derive the measured national benefit that is the usual expectation in such arrangements between equally sovereign states. If China had been content to see the Soviet Union's power grow at the same time as its own, even though this was to China's disadvantage with respect to any theoretical ultimate conflict with the Soviet Union, it would today have been a much more powerful political, military, and economic entity. But this would have meant political and economic gradualism, and Mao Tse-tung's impatient millennialism would not bear with the prospect.

The policies of Mao Tse-tung thus resulted in the nearly complete isolation of China. And yet, insofar as China responds to the urge to press into Southeast Asia, it confronts the United States as its chief antagonist. For so long as the American ring of steel is maintained in the West and South Pacific (that "Nan Yang" — South Seas — long regarded by Chinese as the natural outlet for surplus millions of people and for expansive commercial endeavor), there exists no logical basis for the working out of a sympathetic relationship between the United States and China. The American treaty of alliance with the Nationalist faction on Formosa is only an added guarantee that the postures of reciprocal hostility will be broken down only laboriously, and over a long term.

If China's ultimate task is to overcome the American strategy, its first problem is then to protect its flank and rear, and if possible to enlist some international support. For the reasons set forth by Mao Tse-tung in July, 1949, China needs a strong ally. There are in the Asian environment other wills to power than those of the three major empires. The Japanese are well known to the Chinese, Russians, and Americans alike for their military qualities, and the leadership at Peking, in line with Sun Yat-sen's recurrent thought, would like to enlist the hard-fighting samurai in their "Asian" crusade. But the Japanese would in that case be compelled to accept a subordinate position, and serve the national interests of others. By their economic effort alone, they are already making much more substantial headway in non-Communist Asia, Australia, and Africa (to limit the consideration to the three areas) than Mao Tse-tung has been able to do with all of his revolutionary philosophy. A generation ago, they lost an empire as the result of undertaking to destroy Occidental power in Asia. Having now attained the position of Asia's greatest industrial power (and third in the world), they are hardly likely to accept the shield-bearer's role proffered by Peking. The greater probability is that Japan and the Soviet Union, discovering common political and economic interests, will draw closer to each other.

A measured reconciliation with Moscow thus must seem to conservative elements in the CCP to constitute the most feasible alternative in a complex of difficult and sometimes distasteful choices. The Sino-Soviet rift was basically of Mao Tse-tung's personal choice and making, instead of representing a Moscow decision—or even the consensus of opinion in the eighth CCP Central Committee before Mao's purge. The quarrel was between two party leaderships that happened to be in charge of their respective states. This was the interpretation of Aleksei Adzhubei, chief editor of *Izvestiya* (and incidentally Khrushchev's son-in-law), as set forth in an interview published in *Der Spiegel* on August 2, 1964. Responding to a question regarding the effect of the Sino-Soviet conflict on Moscow's German policy, Adzhubei said that "we do not have a conflict with the Chinese People's Republic but with the leaders of the Communist Party of China."

From the time when Moscow directed its attack specifically against Mao Tse-tung, it has been apparent that if Mao were to be removed from power and his hostile policy vis-à-vis the USSR were abandoned by his successors, the Sino-Soviet alliance (with a decade still to run) could once more be made into a working political and economic arrangement. The Sino-Soviet relationship can hardly be restored to the condition it was in during the 1950–1956 honeymoon period. Yet, Mao Tse-tung will pass, and the Chinese revolutionary development will then be directed by a new leadership—probably a more pragmatic one. And with the advent of pragmatists to power in Peking, the Sino-Soviet alliance could, without any great difficulty, be made to operate in a fashion that would service some of China's basic needs—and would, in corresponding satisfaction of a Soviet desideratum, preserve China as a buffer zone between Soviet Siberia and the American naval and air power in the West Pacific.

This estimate points up the circumstance that the imperial struggle has changed vastly since the time, three centuries ago, when the three land powers of China, Russia, and Mongolia contended for power in Inner Asia. For one thing, Russia is no longer simply a land power. Peter the Great fathered the Russian navy. After making a respectable beginning at becoming a sea power, Russia was returned to the status of land power by the Russo-Japanese War, but subsequent developments have reversed that setback. The Soviet navy has now reached maturity as a world strategic force of first rank: in 1960, it had in active service twice the tonnage of the British Royal Navy. And the Soviet merchant fleet, comprising 3 million tons in 1953, at the end of another decade had nearly doubled. Soviet Russia has been transformed into a combined land and sea power. It is consequently able readily either to deter Maoist military adventures or to underwrite a grand strategy of undercutting China politically and economically, either in the South Seas or elsewhere in the Third World, as the need might arise.

Soviet power also confronts the United States in the North, West, and South Pacific (omitting consideration of the Mediterranean). Excluded from the Washington conference that in 1921–1922 deliberated upon Pacific and East Asian issues, Soviet Russia is now a major influence in both areas. And China, for all its travail, is almost certainly destined to grow in power and play an increasingly important role in world affairs. To mount a cordon of containment against both the Soviet Union and China, the United States has deployed a massive nuclear establishment. But it has not yet designed a grand strategy fitted to cope with the Asian nationalism that brought an end to other empires; it has failed to align American strategy, molded so rigorously to suit its impassioned China policy, with the course of political, economic, and social change taken by Asia's thousand million people. Given its present strategic aims, the United States is predestined to fight counterrevolutionary wars on China's periphery – if not against China itself.

Both the players and the rules of the Great Game of Asia are changed substantially from what they were in the nineteenth century. The old-style imperialists who ruled in China, Russia, and Mongolia in the seventeenth century, despite important differences in viewpoint, were probably better able to understand each other than are the governments of the three empires that stand in hostile confrontation in the world arena today. But, as in the Sino-Russian-Mongol triangle, two of the concerned powers will be inclined, for reasons of self-preservation, to align with each other against the third. *As things stand today,* it must be anticipated that China and the USSR will probably find compelling reasons to sustain a measure of collaboration in Asia – even after three centuries of massive contest.

The future inevitably remains clouded and uncertain. The present Chinese, Russian, and American leaderships, that of Mao Tse-tung among them, will all pass, without any one of them having achieved a millenarian solution to the problem of world power. Hopeful logic suggests that the instinct for self-preservation coupled with a humanistic wisdom may eventually prevail against the struggle for domination. But willful men, self-right-eous and prone to resort to physical force to uphold their assumed right to prevail, are apt to rise to power at the head of imperial states. Contemporary nationalistic passions could easily flare into a global conflagration. Or messianic world outlooks could lead imperialistically motivated governments, as has happened in the not-distant past, to strike out in an endeavor to impose their will and political patterns — either revolutionary or counter-revolutionary — on Third World peoples caught up in the process of change. Here too, the conflict would tend naturally to become global. Therein lies the danger that the triangle of Sino-Russian-American confrontation in Asia will give birth, at some point, to a world holocaust.

NOTES

INTRODUCTION. CHINESE, RUSSIANS, AND MONGOLS

1. George Vernadsky, *The Mongols and Russia* (2d ed., New Haven, 1959), p. 54.

2. See in this connection J. Dyer Ball, "Early Russian Intercourse with China," *Anglo-Russian Literary Society Proceedings* (Oct.-Nov.-Dec., 1912), pp. 34–57.

3. See René Grousset, *The Rise and Splendour of the Chinese Empire* (London, 1952), pp. 256–57, for an interesting descriptive passage respecting this phenomenon; also Wang Gungwu, "Early Ming Relations with Southeast Asia: A Background Essay," in John K. Fairbank, ed., *The Chinese World Order* (Cambridge, Mass., 1968), pp. 34–62.

4. Mahmetkul is sometimes identified as Kuchum's son; I here follow Vincent Chen, *Sino-Russian Relations in the Seventeenth Century* (The Hague, 1968), p. 14.

5. The year is also given as 1584. I follow the *Sovetskaya Istoricheskaya Entsiklopediya* [Soviet historical encyclopedia] (hereinafter cited as *SIE*) (Moscow, 1961–), s.v. "Ermak Timofeevich," Vol. 5, cols. 508–9.

6. I. F. Demidova and V. S. Myasnikov, *Pervye russkie diplomaty v Kitae* ("*Rospis*" *I. Petlina i stateinyi spisok F. I. Baikova*) [The first Russian diplomats in China (The "Catalog" of I. Petlin and essay list of F. I. Baikov)] (Moscow, 1966), pp. 15, 17. For Godunov's promise to the English, and the later requests of others for travel facilities to China, see Ball, "Early Russian Intercourse with China," *Anglo-Russian Literary Society Proceedings*, pp. 46–47.

7. Andrei Grigorevich Bannikov, *Pervyi russkie puteshestviya v Mongoliyu i Severnyi Kitai Vasilii Tyumenets, Ivan Petlin, Fedor Baikov* [The first Russian journeys by Vasilii Tyumenets, Ivan Petlin, and Fedor Baikov to Mongolia and North China] (Moscow, 1949), pp. 11–13.

8. Quoted in Demidova and Myasnikov, *Pervye russkie diplomaty v Kitae*, p. 19, from TsGADA, f. *Snosheniya Rossii c Angliei* [Relations of Russia with England] (1604), Book 4, p. 230.

9. Following the usual form of this name. But Demidova and Myasnikov, *Pervye russkie diplomaty v Kitae*, pp. 22–23, make it "Madov."

10. The present account follows Demidova and Myasnikov, *Pervye russkie diplomaty v Kitae*, pp. 23–26.

11. Following Demidova and Myasnikov, *Pervye russkie diplomaty v Kitae*, p. 26. Vincent Chen and Bannikov both make it June.

12. So for instance *SIE*, s.v. "Petlin, Ivan," Vol. 11, cols. 91–92. Another Russian source, A. Artemev, *Prebyvanie kitaiskogo posolstva v Kazan* (Otd. ott. iz Pribavlenii k Kazanskim gubernskim vedomostyam 1845 No. 1, 2, 3 i 5) [Sojourn of a Chinese mission in Kazan (Extracted from the Supplement to the Kazan provincial gazette 1845, Nos. 1, 2, 3, and 5)], (n.p., n.d.), pp. 1–2, reports that Ivan IV in 1567 dispatched two Russian Cossacks, Ivan Petrov and Burnash Yalychev, to explore the lands east of Russia, and that the two men actually reached Peking but, not having brought presents with them, were not received by the emperor and after a lengthy stay in Peking returned to their homeland. This account, which appears elsewhere, is seemingly deemed apocryphal by Russian historians. See in this connection Vincent Chen, *Sino-Russian Relations*, pp. 34–35.

CHAPTER 1. THE MEETING OF EMPIRES

1. Sh. B. Chimitdorzhiev, "Pervye svyazi mezhdu Rossiei i Khalkha-Mongoliei (XVII vek)" [The first ties between Russia and the Khalkha-Mongols (XVII century)] (pamphlet, Ulan Ude, 1959), pp. 8–9.

2. See F. A. Golder, *Russian Expansion on the Pacific, 1641–1850; An Account of the Earliest and Later Expeditions Made by the Russians along the Coast of Asia and North America; Including Some Related Expeditions to the Arctic Regions.* (Glendale, Calif., 1914), p. 46.

3. "Le Koteou en Russie," *T'oung Pao ou Archives de l'Asie Orientale*, IV (1893), 114, citing the memoirs of the historian Tallemant des Reaux. See also Ball, in "Early Russian Intercourse with China," *Anglo-Russian Literary Society Proceedings,* who states that the custom persisted until abolished by Peter I.

4. Gantimur is also identified as a Solon, that is, a Tungusi; see Arthur W. Hummel, ed., *Eminent Chinese of the Ch'ing Period (1644–1912)* (2 vols.; Washington, 1943), s.v. "Ghantimur," I, 269. I here follow, arbitrarily, the accepted Russian interpretation.

5. L. A. Derbov, "Nachalo diplomaticheskikh i torgovykh otnoshenii Rossii s Kitaem," *Uchënye zapiski vypusk istoricheskii, posvyashchennyi 50-letiyu Universiteta 1909–1959* ["The beginning of diplomatic and trade relations of Russia with China," *Scholarly notes: historical publication in commemoration of the 50th year of the University 1909–1959*] (Sarat) 68 (1960), 98, 98n.

6. For text, see Vincent Chen, *Sino-Russian Relations*, p. 72; see also, in this connection, Derbov, "Nachalo diplomaticheskikh . . . ," *Uchënye zapiski . . .* , 68 (1960), 105–6. It is of interest to remark that the official Ch'ing Dynasty history, noting that Russian traders (presumably referring to the Seitkul Ablin missions) on coming to Peking submitted communications, further recorded that K'ang-hsi in 1676 received the "merchant Nikolai" (presumably Spathar-Milescu) in audience to demand that the Russians stop harassing the frontiers. *Ch'ing-shih kao* [Draft history of the Ch'ing Dynasty] (Peking, 1927), pang chiao [International relations], p. 1.

7. The Tatars and Kirgizi called those fugitive Mongols "Kalmyk," or remnant, and the term came to be applied generally by the Russians to the Oirat group.

8. Ilya Yakovlevich Zlatkin, *Istoriya Dzhungarskogo Khanstva (1635–1758)* [History of the Dzungar khanate (1635–1758)] (Moscow, 1964), p. 246.

9. *Ibid.*, p. 257.

10. Quoted by "An Indian Officer" (Captain H. Mullaby), *Russia's March Towards India* (2 vols.; London, 1894), I, 37.

CHAPTER 2. THE "NORMALIZATION" OF RUSSO-MANCHU RELATIONS

1. From French-language text in Godfrey E. P. Hertslet, with the assistance of Edward Parkes, *Treaties, &c., between Great Britain and China; and between China and Foreign Powers; and Orders in Council, Rules, Regulations, Acts of Parliament, Decrees, &c., Affecting British Interests in China, in Force on the 1st January, 1908* (hereinafter cited as Hertslet's *Treaties*) (3d ed., 2 vols.; London, 1908), I, 437–38.

2. Gaston Cahen, *Histoire des relations de la Russie avec la Chine sous Pierre le Grand* (Paris, 1911), p. 70; Nikolai Nikolaevich Bantysh-Kamenskii, *Diplomaticheskoe sobranie del mezhdu Rossiiskim i Kitaiskim gosudarstvami s 1619 po 1792-i god* [Diplomatic collection of affairs between the Russian and Chinese governments from 1619 to 1792] (Kazan, 1882), pp. 5–6. (L. A. Derbov, whose article "Nachalo diplomaticheskikh . . ." is cited above, made considerable use of this second work.)

3. This account of origins follows "Missions of the Russian Orthodox Church in Asia and America," *The East and the West* (April, 1904), pp. 143–63. See also Vincent Chen, *Sino-Russian Relations*, pp. 112–14.

CHAPTER 3. THE KIAKHTA AGREEMENT AND MONGOL DISASTER

1. Quotations from text in John M. Maki, *Selected Documents: Far Eastern International Relations (1659–1951)* (mimeographed, Seattle, 1957), pp. 2–6.

2. For a detailed account of the audience, see Bantysh-Kamenskii, *Diplomaticheskoe sobranie*, pp. 175–76.

3. For this first mission from China to Russia, and the following mission, see also Gaston Cahen, "Deux ambassades chinois en Russie au commencement du XVIIIᵉ siecle," *Revue Historique*, 133 (1920), 82–89.

4. Some sources indicate that Amursana's body was in fact handed over. I here follow Zlatkin, *Istoriya*, pp. 460–61. See also Bantysh-Kamenskii, *Diplomaticheskoe sobranie*, pp. 274–75, 279–98.

5. Zlatkin, *Istoriya*, p. 374.

6. For some details of this typical example of the workings of the Russo-Manchu commercial relationship as reflected in Chinese documents, see *A Documentary Chronicle of Sino-Western Relations (1644–1820)*, Compiled, Translated, and Annotated by Lo-shu Fu (2 vols.; Tucson, 1966), I, 281–91.

CHAPTER 4. TRIANGLE IN EAST ASIA

1. For text of Macartney's instructions, see Hosea Ballou Morse, *The Chronicles of the East India Company trading to China, 1635–1834* (4 vols.; Oxford, 1926), II, 232–42; for similar instructions given Lieutenant Colonel Charles Cathcart, designated ambassador to China in 1787, who died en route in June 1788, see *ibid.*, pp. 160–67.

2. For Kruzenstern's account, see Ivan Fedorovich Kruzenshtern, *Puteshestvie vokrug sveta v 1803, 4, 5 i 1806 po poveleniyu ego imperatorskogo velichestva ALEKSANDRA PERVAGO, po korablyakh Nadezhde i Neve . . .* [Voyage around the world in 1803, 4, 5 and 1806 by command of his imperial highness ALEX-

ANDER THE FIRST, by the ships *Nadezhda* and *Neva* . . .] (Parts I, II, St. Petersburg, 1810, 1812).

3. *"Voyage round the World*, in the years 1803, 4, 5, and 6, by order of his imperial majesty Alexander the First, on board the ships Nadeshda and Neva, under the command of Captain A. Y. Von Krusenstern. Translated from the original German by Richard Belgrave Hopper, Esq."; and, *"Voyages and Travels in various parts of the world, during the* years 1803, 4, 5, 6, and 7. By G. H. Von Langsdorf, Aulic Counsellor to his majesty the Emperor of Russia, &c." (essay review from *The Electic Review) Analectic Magazine* (June, 1815), pp. 441–82.

4. *Ibid.*, p. 475.

5. Quoted in "A Prophecy about Japan" (from *La Revue Russe*, March 24, 1904) *Anglo-Russian Literary Society Proceedings* (Feb.-Mar.-Apr., 1904), pp. 105–7.

6. Wu Hsiang-hsiang, *O-ti ch'in-lueh Chung-kuo shih* [The history of Russian imperialism's aggression against China] (Taipei, 1954), p. 26. Morse in his account (*Chronicles*, III, 3) makes no reference to British ownership of the cargo.

7. Kruzenshtern, *Puteshestvie*, II, 334n. See also Langsdorf, *Voyages and Travels*, per review in *Analectic Magazine* (June, 1815), p. 482.

8. E. V. Bunakov, "Iz istorii russko-kitaiskikh otnoshenii v pervoi polovine XIX v." [From the history of Russo-Chinese relations in the first half of the nineteenth century], *Sovetskoe vostokovedenie* (1956), No. 2, pp. 96–104.

9. *Ibid.*

10. A. L. Galperin, "Russko-Kitaiskaya torgovlya v XVIII-pervoi polovene XIX veka (opyt sravneniya Kyakhtinskogo torga s torgovlei cherez Guanchzhou)" [Russo-Chinese trade in the eighteenth and first half of the nineteenth century (test comparison of Kiakhta trade with trade through Kwangchow [Canton])], *Problemy Vostokovedeniya* (1959), No. 5, pp. 215–27. One authority estimates the two-way trade through Kiakhta (inferentially, in both the public and private sectors) in mid-eighteenth century at approximately 4 million rubles (US$100 million at present currency values). Hector Chevigny, *Russian America, the Great Alaskan Venture 1741–1867* (New York, 1965), pp. 43–46.

11. For a description of the Sino-Russian trade at Kiakhta, see Bunakov, "Iz istorii . . . ," *Sovetskoe Vostokovedenie* (1956), No. 2, pp. 98–99; for an earlier assessment of prospects for Sino-Russian commerce, see Kruzenshtern, *Puteshestvie*, II, 376–77.

CHAPTER 5. CONFRONTATION IN THE WEST PACIFIC,
MID-NINETEENTH CENTURY

1. Kuo T'ing-yi, *Chin-tai Chung-kuo shih-shih jih-chih* [Diary of historical matters of recent Chinese history] (2 vols.; Taipei, 1964), I, 144.

2. For text, see Hertslet's *Treaties*, I, 449–53.

3. This account follows Chevigny, *Russian America*, pp. 213–16.

4. *Ch'ing-shih kao*, "pang-chiao" 1, 2.

5. Prince A. Lobanov-Rostovsky, *Russia and Asia* (New York, 1933), pp. 137–38.

6. Thomas Taylor Meadows, *The Chinese and Their Rebellions* (Stanford, 1953 [originally published 1856]), pp. 473–74.

7. See in this connection R. K. I. Quested, *The Expansion of Russia in East Asia 1857–1860* (Singapore, 1968), pp. 106 ff.

8. Kuo T'ing-yi, *Chin-tai Chung-kuo*, I, 280–81.

9. From text in P. E. Skachkov and V. S. Myasnikov (compilers), *Russko-Kitaiskie otnosheniya 1689-1916 — ofitsialnye dokumenty* [Russo-Chinese relations 1689-1916 — official documents] (Moscow, 1958), pp. 30-34.

10. See Quested, *Expansion*, pp. 240 ff.

11. Chevigny, *Russian America*, p. 223.

12. *Ibid.*, p. 245.

CHAPTER 6. THE "GREAT GAME" IN CENTRAL ASIA

1. The Russian usage is to term the three groups the Younger, Middle, and Elder Hordes. I here follow Geoffrey Wheeler, *The Modern History of Soviet Central Asia* (New York, 1964).

2. Following *SIE*, s.v. "Kokandskoe khanstvo" [Kokand khanate], Vol. 7, col. 471. Other dates for the reign of both Alim Khan and his successors are found.

3. Quoted by Mullaby, *Russia's March*, I, 118. Mullaby mistakenly indicates that Muraviev's voyage was in 1822, whereas that was only the date of the book containing his report, *Puteshestvie v Turkmeniyu i Khivu v 1819 i 1820 gg.* [Journey to Turkmenia and Khiva in 1819 and 1820] (Moscow, 1822). The names are identical, but this is not the Muraviev of Amur fame.

4. Nikolai Modestov, "K istorii osvobozhdeniya russkikh plennikh iz Khivy" [Regarding the history of the freeing of Russian prisoners from Khiva], *Russkii arkhiv, 1915*, pp. 31-48.

5. From text in Mullaby, *Russia's March*, Vol. II, App. II, pp. 302-8.

6. Wheeler, *Modern History*, p. 58.

7. Lord John Laird Mair Lawrence, the new viceroy of India, was of the opinion that "Russia might prove a safer ally, a better neighbour, than the Mohammedan races of Central Asia and Kabul." Great Britain, Foreign Office, *Papers Relating to Central Asia and Quetta*, 1879, p. 41.

8. Great Britain, Foreign Office, *British and Foreign State Papers 1872-1873* (London, 1879), Vol. 63, p. 672.

9. See in this connection *ibid.*, pp. 660-61, 668-71.

10. *British and Foreign State Papers, 1873-1874*, Vol. 65, pp. 92-93.

11. *Ibid.*, p. 93.

12. Cited by Wheeler, *Modern History*, p. 56.

CHAPTER 7. CONFRONTATION IN CENTRAL ASIA,
MID-NINETEENTH CENTURY

1. One writer holds that 130,000 Manchus were killed at Urumchi, but he credited that small Asian town with a population of two million, "probably with the suburbs." A. K. Geina, "O vosstanii musulmanskogo naseleniya ili Dungenei v zapadnom Kitai" [Of the uprising of the Muslim population or Dungans in western China], *Geografîcheskaya Izvestiya*, Vol. II, No. 3 (1866), p. 87.

2. Arminius Vambery, *Central Asia and the Anglo-Russian Frontier Question, A Series of Political Papers*, trans. by F. E. Bunnett (London, 1874), pp. 252-53.

3. *British and Foreign State Papers 1872-1873*, Vol. 63, p. 681.

4. *Ibid.*, p. 676. For Shaw's favorable estimate of Yakub Beg's regime reached as the result of his visit to Sinkiang and set forth in a letter of July, 1869, to Forsyth, see *ibid.*, p. 681.

5. Demetrius Charles Boulger, *The Life of Yakoob Beg* (London, 1878), pp. 175-77.

6. V. M. Alekseev, L. I. Duman, and A. A. Petrov, *Kitai* [China] (Moscow, 1940), pp. 168–69.

7. M. Nemchenko, "Kolonialnyi rezhim i agrarnye otnosheniya v Sintsyane" [The colonial regime and agrarian relations in Sinkiang], *Problemy Kitaya*, Nos. 8–9 (3–4) (1931), pp. 181–90.

8. See in this connection N. Przhevalskii, "Sovremennoe polozhenie tsentralnoi Azii" [Contemporary position of Central Asia], *Russkii vestnik*, 186 (1886), 473–524.

9. Quoted by J. O. P. Bland, *Li Hung-chang* (London, 1917), pp. 195–96.

10. G. E. Grum-Grzhmailo, *Opisanie puteshestviya v zapadny Kitai* [Notes on a journey to Western China] (3 vols.; St. Petersburg, 1899), II, 4. For a further account of the flight of Dungans and others before Tso Tsung-t'ang's armies, see E. M. Zhukov, ed., *Mezhdunarodnye otnosheniya na Dalnem Vostoke 1840–1949* [International relations in the Far East 1840–1949] (2d ed.; Moscow, 1956), pp. 91–92; also G. B. Nikolskaya, "Nekotorye dannye ob otkhodnichestve iz Severozapadnogo Kitaya v Turkestan (v kontse XIX – nachale XX veka)" [Various data on the exodus from Northwestern China into Turkestan (at the end of the nineteenth and beginning of the twentieth century)], *Trudy Tashkentskogo Universiteta im. V. I. Lenina* [Works of the Tashkent Lenin University] (Tashkent, 1962), pp. 43–60.

11. Note, *Geograficheskaya Izvestiya*, Oct. 3, 1866.

12. Zhukov, *Mezhdunarodnye otnosheniya*, pp. 91–92.

13. This account follows Ann Sheehy, "Russia and China in the Pamirs: 18th and 19th Centuries," *Central Asian Review*, Vol. XVI, No. 1 (1968), pp. 4–14.

14. Francis Henry Skrine and Edward Dennison Ross, *The Heart of Asia* (London, 1899), pp. 408–9.

CHAPTER 8. FIN DE SIÈCLE IN EAST ASIA

1. G. Efimov, *Vneshnaya politika Kitaya 1894–1899 gg.* [The foreign policy of China 1894–1899] (Moscow, 1958), p. 71.

2. Sergei I. Witte, *The Memoirs of Count Witte*, trans. by Abraham Yarmolinsky (Garden City, 1921), p. 83.

3. Hugh Borton, *Japan's Modern Century* (New York, 1955), p. 209.

4. Following Efimov, *Vneshnaya politika*, p. 122.

5. *Ibid.*, p. 177.

6. See in this general connection "The Various Stages of Russian Influence and Activities in Manchuria," *Contemporary Manchuria* (Nov., 1937), pp. 10–11.

7. Efimov, *Vneshnaya politika*, p. 221.

8. Tien-fong Cheng, *A History of Sino-Russian Relations* (Washington, 1957), p. 60.

9. Witte, *Memoirs*, p. 101.

10. A. N. Kuropatkin, *The Russian Army and the Japanese War*, trans. by Captain A. B. Lindsay (2 vols.; London, 1909), I, 71–72.

11. Efimov, *Vneshnaya politika*, p. 256.

12. Witte, *Memoirs*, pp. 106–7.

13. June 21 is often given for the date of declaration of war; however, Prince Tuan issued the appropriate war orders to the governors general on June 20; see dispatch No. 272, July 8, 1900, from the U.S. consul general at Shanghai to the secretary of state, Department of State, *U.S. Foreign Relations* (hereinafter cited

as *USFR) 1900*, I, 252–54. For text of the imperial decree as *published* in the *Peking Gazette* on June 21, 1900, see *ibid.*, pp. 168–69. For use of the date June 20, see also Zhukov, *Mezhdunarodnye otnosheniya*, p. 167, and J. O. P. Bland and E. Backhouse, *China Under the Empress Dowager* (Philadelphia, 1910), p. 265.

14. Witte, *Memoirs*, pp. 107–8.

15. For this account of military actions in Manchuria, I follow mainly George Alexander Lensen, *The Russo-Chinese War* (Tallahassee, 1967). For a somewhat different version, see Chester C. Tan, *The Boxer Catastrophe* (New York, 1955), particularly chap. 8, "Russia Acts in Manchuria."

16. Witte, *Memoirs*, p. 110.

17. The dates November 10, November 11, and November 30 also alternately appear. I here follow Kuo T'ing-yi, *Chin-tai Chung-kuo*, II, 1110.

CHAPTER 9. WAR, REVOLUTION, AND IMPERIALISM

1. 1. Vl. B., "The Yellow Peril," *Novoe Vremya* [New Times], in *Anglo-Russian Literary Society Proceedings* (Oct.-Nov.-Dec., 1903), pp. 120–21. Re the position occupied by Chinese in Eastern Siberian trade, see *ibid.* (Feb.-Mar.-Apr., 1896), pp. 39–61. See also E. H. Parker, "The Yellow Peril," *ibid.* (Feb.-Mar.-Apr., 1904), pp. 62–80, for an argument that fears that the Chinese would engulf other peoples were groundless.

2. Cited by Chester C. Tan, *The Boxer Catastrophe*, p. 207.

3. Yoshi S. Kuno, *Japanese Expansion on the Asiatic Continent* (Berkeley, 1940), pp. 355–58.

4. Quoted by Lensen, *The Russo-Chinese War*, p. 254.

5. From text in (*Collier's Magazine*), *The Russo-Japanese War, A Photographic and Descriptive Review of the Great Conflict in the Far East, gathered from the reports, records, cable dispatches, photographs, etc., etc., of Collier's war correspondents* (New York, 1905), p. 16. See this work for a useful collection of the related Japanese correspondence of 1903-1904.

6. *The Outlook* (Jan. 9, 1904), 97–98.

7. For a summary discussion of the matters at issue at that juncture, including the reputed control by Russia of the strategic port of Masampho (between Mokpho and Fusan), see *ibid.* (Jan. 16, 1904), pp. 164–65.

8. *The Russo-Japanese War*, p. 23.

9. Other figures for the size of the squadron sometimes appear. I here follow *Sovetskaya Bolshaya Entsiklopedia* [Soviet great encyclopedia], "Russko-Yaponskaya Voina 1904–1905," [Russo-Japanese War 1904–1905] Vol. 37, pp. 473–76.

10. *USFR 1904*, pp. 121–22.

11. See *ibid.*, pp. 125, 139–40.

12. *The Outlook* (March 5, 1904), 528.

13. J. C. O'Laughlin, "The War and the Powers," *ibid.* (March 26, 1904), 735–39.

14. Kuo T'ing-yi, *Chin-tai Chung-kuo*, II, 1199.

15. A. H. Ford, "Some Notes on 'Influence of America on Siberia and Russia,'" *Anglo-Russian Literary Society Proceedings* (Feb.-Mar.-Apr., 1901), pp. 49–67.

16. See text provided by Victor A. Yakhontoff, *Russia and the Soviet Union in the Far East* (New York, 1931), Appendix, pp. 375–76.

17. Lobanov-Rostovsky, *Russia and Asia*, p. 248.

18. George Kennan, *E. H. Harriman, A Biography* (2 vols.; Boston and New

York, 1922), II, 28. The name is spelled by this source "Kokovtsev," identified as minister for foreign affairs. But the then minister for foreign affairs was Izvolski, and there can be no real doubt that the personality in question was Minister of Finance Kokovtsov. See in this general connection also Harold M. Vinacke, *A History of the Far East in Modern Times* (6th ed.; New York, 1959), p. 197.

CHAPTER 10. REVOLUTION AND THE MANCHU BORDERLANDS

1. *USFR 1912*, p. 50.

2. *Ibid.*, p. 75.

3. Ivan Barsukov, *Graf Nikolai Nikolaevich Muravev-Amurskii po ego pismam, offitsialnym dokumentam, razskazam sovremennikov i pechatnym istochnikam (materialy dlya biografii)* [Count Nikolai Nikolaevich Muravev-Amurskii according to his letters, official documents, narratives of contemporary and printed sources (materials for a biography)] (2 vols.; Moscow, 1891), II, 110–13.

4. See, for a detailed account of this mission, Gerard M. Friters, *Outer Mongolia and Its International Position* (London, 1951), pp. 56–60.

5. See *ibid.*, p. 66, for the April 13, 1912, estimate of Foreign Minister Sazonov to that general effect. See also Louis M. Kervyn, *Ourga (1912–1930) – La politique chinoise en Mongolie* (Peking, 1932), pp. 108–10, 120–22, for a description of the Mongolian political environment in which the Russians had to work – consequently their judicious restraint.

6. J. Levine, *La Mongolie historique, geographique, politique* (Paris, 1937), p. 85. See Peter S. H. Tang, *Russian and Soviet Policy in Manchuria and Outer Mongolia 1911–1931* (Durham, N.C., 1959), p. 305, for a somewhat different version.

7. See Robert A. Rupen, *Mongols of the Twentieth Century* (2 parts, The Hague, 1964), Part I, pp. 61–64, for an exchange of correspondence between Yuan Shih-k'ai and the Khutukhtu.

8. For text, see Yakhontoff, *Russia*, Appendix, pp. 380–81.

9. Westel W. Willoughby, *Foreign Rights and Interests in China* (2 vols.; Baltimore, 1927), I, 383–84n.

CHAPTER 11. THE RUSSIAN REVOLUTION AND CHINA

1. John Van Antwerp MacMurray, *Treaties and Agreements with and concerning China, 1919–1929* (2 vols.; Washington, 1929), II, 1407–9.

2. Hishida Seiji, *Japan Among the Great Powers, A Survey of Her International Relations* (London, 1940), p. 227.

3. MacMurray, *Treaties*, II, 1411–12.

4. Quoted by James W. Morley, *The Japanese Thrust into Siberia, 1918* (New York, 1957), pp. 32–33.

5. MacMurray, *Treaties*, II, 1413–14.

6. For a description of the development of Kolchak's regime, see the item *SIE*, s.v. "Kolchakovshchina" [Kolchakism], Vol. 7, cols. 547–49.

7. Text in Ministry of Foreign Affairs of the USSR, *Dokumenty vneshnei politiki SSSR* [Documents of the foreign policy of the USSR] (Moscow, 1958), II, 221–23, citing *Izvestiya*, August 26, 1919, for original publication. Interestingly enough, there was forwarded from Irkutsk and Vladivostok, by telegram and radio, a text containing an additional paragraph promising the outright return of the CER to China. For discussion based upon the assumption that the offer was in fact made, see Allen S. Whiting, *Soviet Policies in China 1917–1924* (New York,

1953), pp. 30–33, and Peter S. H. Tang, *Russian and Soviet Policy*, pp. 137–39; for a Soviet explanation of what had happened, see A. N. Kheifets, *Sovetskaya Rossiya i sopredelnye strany Vostoka 1918–1920* [Soviet Russia and contiguous countries of the East 1918–1920] (Moscow, 1964), p. 392n.

8. Vl. Vilenskii (Sibiryakov), *Yaponiya* [Japan] (Moscow, 1923), p. 97.

9. See *USFR 1920*, I, 760 for the U.S. Secretary of State's negative response of March 20, 1920 – three months later.

10. The date for Kolchak's transfer of power is also given as January 4, 1920. I here follow Kheifets, *Sovetskaya Rossiya*, p. 376; and P. S. Parfenov (Altaiskii), *Borba za Dalnii Vostok 1920–1922* [Struggle for the Far East 1920–1922] (2d ed., rev., Moscow, 1931), p. 41, which carries the text of Kolchak's order.

11. See B. Shereshevskii, *Zabaikale v period Dalnevostostochnoi Respubliki 1920–1922* [Trans-Baikal in the period of the Far Eastern Republic 1920–1922] (Chita, 1960), pp. 10–11.

CHAPTER 12. CHINA, OUTER MONGOLIA, AND THE FAR EASTERN REPUBLIC

1. This datum is usually challenged by Chinese sources. I here follow M. S. Kapitsa, *Sovetsko-Kitaiskie otnosheniya* [Soviet-Chinese relations] (Moscow, 1958), p. 65.

2. Rupen, *Mongols*, I, 141. See Ken Shen Weigh, *Russo-Chinese Diplomacy* (Shanghai, 1928), pp. 201–5, for more on the relationship of Chang Tso-lin to the Ungern-Sternberg affair.

3. Rupen, *Mongols*, I, 144.

4. The date July 11 also appears. I here follow *SIE*, s.v. "Mongolskaya narodnaya revolyutsia 1921" [The Mongolian people's revolution 1921], Vol. 9, col. 612.

5. A. T. Yakimov, "Mongolskaya narodno-revolyutsionnaya partiya – organizator i vdokhnovitel pobed Mongolskogo naroda" [The Mongolian People's Party – organizer and inspirer of the victories of the Mongolian people] in Akademiya Nauk SSSR, Institut Vostokovedeniya, *Mongolskaya Narodnaya Respublika – sbornik statei* [The Mongolian People's Republic – a collection of articles] (Moscow, 1952), p. 72.

6. Kheifets, *Sovetskaya Rossiya*, p. 395.

7. *Ibid.*, p. 389.

8. Memorandum of Interview between (U.S.) Minister Charles R. Crane and Chang Tso-lin [sic. Chang Shih-lin], Jan. 8, 1921, in the possession of John O. Crane.

9. For details, see Kheifets, *Sovetskaya Rossiya*, p. 411. For the Narkomindel proposals regarding content of a new treaty of friendship between the two countries, see Kapitsa, *Sovetsko-Kitaiskie otnosheniya*, pp. 56–57. An English-language version of those proposals which has various shades of difference is available in Tien-fong Cheng, *History*, pp. 110–11.

10. Crane memorandum of Jan. 8, 1921.

11. Secretary of State Colby to Minister Crane, telegram Sept. 21, 1920, *USFR 1920*, I, 763–64.

12. Paraphrased copy of telegram of Oct. 7 from Chinese Foreign Office to Chinese legation in Washington as left by the Chinese minister at the Department of State, Oct. 8, 1920, *ibid.*, pp. 770–71.

13. Whiting, *Soviet Policies*, p. 118, quoting V. Vilenskii, "Kitaiskaya Kom-

munisticheskaia Partiia" [The Chinese Communist party], *Novyi Vostok* [New East], No. 2 (1922).

14. Tien-fong Cheng, *History*, p. 111. It is Kheifets, *Sovetskaya Rossiya*, p. 406, who dates the Chinese proposals as following upon Yurin's presentation of November 30.

15. Whiting, *Soviet Policies*, pp. 162, 312n.

CHAPTER 13. TURMOIL IN CENTRAL ASIA

1. For Yang's official correspondence, I have depended upon his *Pu-kuo Chai jih-chi* [Diary of the Redeeming Studio), 20 t'ao (cases) (n.p., 1921).

2. For details, see Aitchen K. Wu, *China and the Soviet Union, A Study of Sino-Soviet Relations* (New York, 1950), pp. 252–54.

3. *Boevoi put voisk Turkistanskogo voennogo okruga* [The fighting path of the troops of the Turkestan military region] (Moscow, 1959), p. 186.

4. Whether Togan's advice in this connection arrived before Enver's rejection of the offer is not entirely clear, but it is evident from Enver's character that he would not have acted otherwise than he did, with or without the advice to negotiate. Togan had in the first instance advised Enver Pasha not to become engaged in Turkestan, but rather to proceed to Afghanistan, where his efforts might produce richer fruits.

5. See "The Basmachis – The Central Asian Resistance Movement, 1918–24," *Central Asian Review*, Vol. VII, No. 3 (1959), pp. 236–50, for a fuller account of this complicated phenomenon.

6. The dates September and November also appear. I here follow Kapitsa, *Sovetsko-Kitaiskie otnosheniya*, p. 382.

CHAPTER 14. REESTABLISHMENT OF STATE RELATIONS

1. Quoted by Peter S. H. Tang, *Russian and Soviet Policy*, p. 112.

2. Harish Kapur, *Soviet Russia and Asia 1917-27, A Study of Soviet Policy towards Turkey, Iran and Afghanistan* (Geneva, 1966), p. 61.

3. *China Year Book 1924* (Tientsin, 1924), p. 866.

4. Kapitsa, *Sovetsko-Kitaiskie otnosheniya*, pp. 102–3.

5. Lawrence Impey, "An Interview with Mr. Karakhan," *China Weekly Review*, (Jan. 12, 1924), pp. 233–34.

6. See Whiting, *Soviet Policies*, pp. 221–24, and Tien-fong Cheng, *History*, pp. 114–15, for additional details. The full text is given in *China Year Book 1924*, pp. 880–83.

7. In this paragraph, I follow Kapitsa, *Sovetsko-Kitaiskie otnosheniya*, pp. 108–9, and *China Year Book 1924*, pp. 883–85.

8. Whiting, *Soviet Policies*, p. 224. See also Ch'en Po-wen (comp.), Wu Ching-heng, Ts'ai Yuan-p'ei, Wang Yun-wu (eds.), and Wang Cheng-t'ing (collator), *Chung-O wai-chiao shih* [History of Sino-Russian foreign relations] (Shanghai, 1928), p. 118, for a report that Wang and Koo had privately quarreled over Wang's full powers to sign. But Koo's position was almost certainly not unrelated to the foreign pressure that had been brought to bear on him.

9. Tien-fong Cheng, *History*, p. 115.

10. This survey of the treaty follows the version of the text given in Aitchen K. Wu, *China and the Soviet Union*, Appendix A, pp. 347–50.

11. Xenia Joukoff Eudin and Robert C. North, *Soviet Russia and the East* (Stanford, 1957), pp. 316–18.

12. Kapitsa, *Sovetsko-Kitaiskie otnosheniya*, p. 125.

13. Henry Kittredge Norton, "Trouble Behind the Trouble in China," *China Weekly Review* (Jan. 30, 1926), pp. 237–44.

14. Rupen, *Mongols*, I, 192.

15. For pertinent extract from Sh. Nachudorji, *Life of Sukhebatur*, in translation, see Owen Lattimore, *Nationalism and Revolution in Mongolia* (New York, 1955), pp. 174–75.

16. See Yakimov, *Mongolskaya Narodnaya Respublika*, pp. 75–76; and Rupen, *Mongols*, I, 193.

17. For text, see *China Year Book 1926-7* (Tientsin, 1926), pp. 795–800.

18. Whiting, *Soviet Policies*, p. 234.

CHAPTER 15. PEKING-MOSCOW RELATIONS IN CRISIS

1. Quoted by Harriet L. Moore, *Soviet Far East Policy 1931-1945* (Princeton, 1945), p. 20.

2. Kapitsa, *Sovetsko-Kitaiskie otnosheniya*, p. 157.

3. *China Weekly Review* (May 1, 1926), pp. 239–40.

4. *Ibid.* (May 8, 1926), p. 276.

5. J. B. P. [John B. Powell, editor], "Michael Borodin, 'Cleverest Revolutionist in the World Today!'" *China Weekly Review* (July 16, 1927), pp. 159–61.

6. A limited and noncommittal American version of the background of the raid is given in the April 7, 1927, account of Minister MacMurray to the secretary of state, *USFR 1927*, II, 316–17. For an extract from Oudendijk's own version, see Aitchen K. Wu, *China and the Soviet Union*, pp. 192–93. The journalist Lawrence Impey offered an eyewitness account in "Chang Tso-lin Raids the Soviet in Peking," *China Weekly Review* (April 23, 1927), pp. 198–99.

7. See in this connection Charles Dailey, "Was the Soviet Plotting to Make All China Red?" *China Weekly Review* (May 14, 1927), pp. 280–85.

8. Impey, "Chang Tso-lin . . . ," *China Weekly Review* (April 23, 1927), pp. 198–99.

9. Editorial, "Raiding of Embassies, A Dangerous Business," *China Weekly Review* (May 28, 1927), pp. 341–42. See also for corroborative testimony Aitchen K. Wu, *China and the Soviet Union*, pp. 189–91.

10. Editorial, "Raiding . . . ," *China Weekly Review* (May 28, 1927), pp. 341–42, quoting Dr. Fox.

11. *China Weekly Review* (April 16, 1927), p. 190; *China Year Book 1928*, p. 792.

12. For extensive presentation and consideration of the seized documents, see *Documents on Communism, Nationalism, and Soviet Advisers in China 1918-1927: Papers Seized in the 1927 Peking Raid*, Edited, with Introductory Essays, by C. Martin Wilbur and Julie Lien-ying How (New York, 1956). (Hereinafter, cited as Wilbur and How, *Documents*.) Moscow cited various circumstances to support its charge that there had been forgery, as see Kapitsa, *Sovetsko-Kitaiskie otnosheniya*, pp. 175–76. Wilbur and How themselves found reason to suspect some of the items made public, but most of the published documents were evidently authentic.

13. Quoted by Aitchen K. Wu, *China and the Soviet Union*, p. 195.

CHAPTER 16. MOSCOW AND CHINESE REVOLUTIONARIES, 1923–1926

1. *China Weekly Review* (Dec. 16, 1922), pp. 88–89.

2. *Ibid.*

3. Text from *China Year Book 1924*, p. 863, as quoted by Aitchen K. Wu, *China and the Soviet Union*, pp. 312–13.

4. A. I. Cherepanov, *Zapiski voennogo sovetnika v Kitae, iz istorii pervoi grazhdanskoi voiny (1924–1927)* [Notes of a military adviser in China, from the history of the first civil war (1924–1927)] (Moscow, 1964), p. 11. Cherepanov was a member of the first group, served in China 1924–1927 (with an interval in early 1926) and (as chief Soviet military adviser) during the war against Japan 1937–1945, and revisited the country in 1956.

5. *SIE*, s.v. "Mikhail Markovich Borodin," Vol. 2, col. 623.

6. See in this general connection Howard L. Boorman, ed., *Biographical Dictionary of Republican China* (New York, 1967–), s.v. "Chiang Kai-shek," I, 319–38, esp. 322.

7. A. S. Perevertailo (chief ed.), V. I. Glunin, K. V. Kukushkin, V. N. Nikiforov, *Ocherki istorii Kitaya v noveishee vremya* [Outlines of the history of China in the contemporary period] (Moscow, 1959), p. 101.

8. Cherepanov, *Zapiski*, p. 64.

9. Eudin and North, *Soviet Russia and the East*, p. 272.

10. Other sources have Bluecher variously arriving at Canton in the company of Borodin in October, 1923, and assisting in the organization of the Whampoa Military Academy in May, 1924. I here follow Cherepanov, *Zapiski*, p. 119.

11. Quoted in Wilbur and How, *Documents*, pp. 158–59.

12. George E. Sokolsky, "The Kuomintang," *China Yearbook 1928* (Tientsin, 1928), esp. p. 1325.

13. Kuibyshev's pseudonym is sometimes given as "Kisanko." I here follow A. I. Cherepanov, *Severnyi pokhod Natsionalnorevolyutsionnoi armii Kitaya* [The Northern Expedition of the National-revolutionary army of China] (Moscow, 1968), p. 15.

14. It has been estimated as "likely" that Feng reached "some kind of arrangements" with the Russians as early as February, 1925. James E. Sheridan, *Chinese Warlord – The Career of Feng Yü-hsiang* (Stanford, 1966), p. 164. But see also in this connection "Jen Te-chiang's Letter to Frunze on Alliance with Feng Yü-hsiang," Wilbur and How, *Documents*, pp. 336–40. From an authoritative Soviet account, it would appear that the general decision leading to the approach was made only on February 22. Cherepanov, *Severnyi pokhod*, p. 40. The date April appears, but logic suggests that the critical meeting occurred in late February or early March. That an earlier arrangement had been made to supply munitions to the *Second* Kuominchün, commanded by Hu Ching-yi, is established. After the death of General Hu on April 10, 1925, the advisers and munitions intended for the Second were diverted to Feng's First Kuominchün.

15. Quoted by Wilbur and How, *Documents*, p. 342.

16. See *ibid.*, p. 221. For a specific and somewhat lurid account, see Tien-fong Cheng, *History*, p. 133, presumably following Chiang Kai-shek, *Soviet Russia in China* (New York, 1957), p. 39. Chiang's account was thirty years after the event, and circumstances had radically changed.

17. As see Cherepanov, *Severnyi pokhod*, pp. 83–86.

18. See Wilbur and How, *Documents*, pp. 228, 230–31. The chief opposition at

this time to the Northern Expedition evidently came from the Chinese Communists, who feared (as proved by the event, not without grounds) that one result would be an increase of the power of Chiang Kai-shek and the KMT Right. There was indeed some Soviet reluctance, but it would appear to be related more closely to a fear that an expedition against the outwardly much more powerful forces of Wu P'ei-fu, Sun Ch'uan-fang, and Chang Tso-lin was then premature.

CHAPTER 17. END OF THE REVOLUTIONARY ALLIANCE

1. Wilbur and How, *Documents,* p. 251. For a fuller estimate of Chiang in the context of the Chung Shan Incident, see *ibid.,* pp. 251–52, and for Chiang's relations with his Soviet advisers, *ibid.,* pp. 215–17. For a Soviet account of that relationship, see Cherepanov, *Zapiski,* pp. 160, 165–71, 190, 204, 231–32.

2. Wilbur and How, *Documents,* p. 264.

3. For text of theses, see Eudin and North, *Soviet Russia and the East,* pp. 356–64.

4. Quoted, *ibid.,* pp. 364–65.

5. From text as given, *ibid.,* pp. 303–4.

6. Conrad Brandt, *Stalin's Failure in China, 1924–27* (Cambridge, Mass., 1958), p. 139.

7. Quoted by Charles Dailey, "Manchurian Tiger's New Role," *China Weekly Review* (July 2, 1927), pp. 107–8.

8. J. B. P., "Michael Borodin . . . ," *China Weekly Review* (July 16, 1927), pp. 159–61.

9. A. Stetzki (Moscow), "China – As a Communist Sees the Situation," *China Weekly Review* (July 23, 1927), p. 190.

10. Tien-fong Cheng, *History,* pp. 144–45.

11. For a contemporary Soviet analysis of the deteriorating situation in China, see "Resolution on the International Situation," as approved by a joint plenum of the central committee and central control commission of the Communist Party of the Soviet Union against the background of a report made on August 9 by Bukharin, in *Inprecor* [International Press Correspondence] (Aug. 18, 1927), pp. 1072–76, esp. pp. 1075–76.

12. Perevertailo, *Ocherki,* p. 198; Nikiforov, in *ibid.,* p. 34. Perevertailo includes the French.

13. Quoted by Tien-fong Cheng, *History,* p. 148.

14. J. B. P., "Michael Borodin . . . ," *China Weekly Review* (July 16, 1927), pp. 159–61.

CHAPTER 18. CONFLICT IN MANCHURIA

1. Dispatch from U.S. consul at Harbin to U.S. minister at Peking, Dec. 31, 1928, *USFR 1929,* II, 186–88.

2. Harbin dispatch to the U.S. minister at Peking, Jan. 9, 1929, *ibid.,* pp. 188–89.

3. Mukden dispatch to U.S. minister at Peking, Feb. 7, 1929, *ibid.,* p. 189.

4. Quoted by Peter S. H. Tang, *Russian and Soviet Policy,* p. 195.

5. From text in *China Year Book 1929–30* (Tientsin, 1929), pp. 1217–20.

6. Telegram from U.S. legation at Peking to secretary of state, July 21, 1929, *USFR 1929,* II, 221: report of U.S. military attaché at Peking, July 26, 1929, *ibid.,* pp. 251–52. See also the legation's telegram of July 20, 1929, *ibid.,* p. 220,

for a pertinent report by the naval attaché regarding Chinese intentions. See also in this general connection John Erickson, *The Soviet High Command* (London, 1962), pp. 240–41.

7. *China Year Book 1929–30*, p. 1221.

8. Telegrams from secretary of state to U.S. minister at Peking, July 18, 1929, *USFR 1929*, II, 210; July 19, 1920, *ibid.*, pp. 215–17.

9. Telegram from legation at Peking to secretary of state, *ibid.*, p. 211.

10. From text given in translation in *China Year Book 1929–30*, pp. 1223–24.

11. Text in *USFR 1929*, II, 231–32.

12. *Ibid.*, p. 267.

13. Telegram from U.S. embassy at Berlin to secretary of state, Aug. 13, 1929, *ibid.*, p. 275.

14. Following Kapitsa, *Sovetsko-Kitaiskie otnosheniya*, pp. 208–9, instead of Tien-fong Cheng, *History*, pp. 154–55. Cheng states that "On August 27 the German Government offered its good offices for mediation," and, implicitly on the same date, proposed (by inference, at its own instead of Nanking's initiative) that the joint manifesto be issued.

15. Kapitsa, *Sovetsko-Kitaiskie otnosheniya*, p. 208.

16. For a fuller description of the military engagements of the Sino-Soviet conflict of 1929, see O. Edmund Clubb, "Armed Conflict in the Chinese Borderlands," in Raymond L. Garthoff, ed., *Sino-Soviet Military Relations* (New York, Washington, and London, 1966), esp. pp. 20–25.

17. *China Year Book 1929–30*, pp. 1227–29.

18. For further details on the extent of the Chinese debacle, see *China Year Book 1931*, "The Sino-Russian Conflict," p. 432.

19. *USFR 1929*, III, 350.

20. *China Year Book 1931*, p. 496.

21. Peter S. H. Tang, *Russian and Soviet Policy*, p. 255.

22. For text of Khabarovsk Protocol, see *China Year Book 1931*, p. 497.

23. Chiang Kai-shek, *Soviet Russia in China*, p. 58.

CHAPTER 19. CHINA, JAPAN, AND THE USSR, 1931–1935

1. *The First Congress of the Toilers of the Far East* (Petrograd, 1922), p. 33.

2. *Ibid.*, p. 35.

3. Following Zhukov, *Mezhdunarodnye otnosheniya*, p. 455. See also Tien-fong Cheng, *History*, p. 184. Aitchen K. Wu, *China and the Soviet Union*, p. 214, has *Japan* making the proposal for a nonaggression pact, and the Soviet Union refusing.

4. (Japanese Foreign Office), Document B, *Relations of Japan with Manchuria and Mongolia* (revised ed., Tokyo, 1932), pp. 26–27.

5. Texts of the Yen and Litvinov statements, Aitchen K. Wu, *China and the Soviet Union*, pp. 218–19. For Wu's full account of negotiations for the resumption of diplomatic ties, see pp. 213–21.

6. So Kapitsa, *Sovetsko-Kitaiskie otnosheniya*, p. 258. Aitchen K. Wu, himself a Chinese diplomat, says merely that, "For some reason, . . . this non-aggression pact did not materialize after the resumption of relations." *China and the Soviet Union*, p. 221. Tien-fong Cheng, another Chinese diplomat, observes as tersely that "somehow the proposed non-aggression pact did not materialize until four years later." *History*, p. 183.

7. Quoted in Aitchen K. Wu, *China and the Soviet Union,* p. 238.

8. For text of the agreement, see *ibid.,* Appendix B, pp. 380–91.

9. *China Year Book 1934,* pp. 723–25.

10. *Ibid.,* pp. 725–26.

11. No official version of the three principles was made public, and there consequently exists no accepted true version. The present version is based in the main on that set forth in *China Year Book 1936,* p. 176, modified as seems suggested logically by reference to Zhukov, *Mezhdunarodnye otnosheniya,* p. 464, and Dorothy Borg, *The United States and the Far Eastern Crisis of 1933–1938* (Cambridge, Mass., 1964), p. 158. Dr. Borg herself offers an alternate version, as given by Hirota to American Ambassador Grew, in Chap. V, p. 588n.65. That latter version would quite possibly have been somewhat watered down for American consumption.

12. Tien-fong Cheng, *History,* p. 190. Cheng traveled to Europe on the same ship with Ch'en Li-fu.

CHAPTER 20. SINO-SOVIET RELATIONS IN SINKIANG, 1934–1937

1. Aitchen K. Wu, who was then Nanking's foreign affairs representative in Sinkiang and participated in the negotiations, presents an interesting account of Sinkiang developments in the book *Turkestan Tumult* (London, 1940).

2. On the full extent of Ma Chung-ying's naïve ambitions, see Sven Hedin, *The Flight of Big Horse,* trans. by F. H. Lyon (New York, 1936), p. 16: "In conversation with his advisers he [Ma Chung-ying] calmly worked out a plan for the conquest of the whole world in alliance with Germany, Russia and Turkey. In that dance, of course, the Great Powers were to follow his piping." (For "Russia," Hedin might have better written "Japan.")

3. This treatment of P'eng Chao-hsien's role in the critical developments of January, 1934, in Sinkiang relies upon P'eng Chao-hsien, as told to Ling Yun (pseud.), "Sheng Shih-ts'ai shih tsen-yang chueh-ch'i Sinkiang-ti?" [How did Sheng Shih-ts'ai rise to eminence in Sinkiang?], *Ch'un Ch'iu* [Hong Kong], No. 148 (Sept. 1, 1963), pp. 7–8 ff. Internal evidence suggests that the Ling Yun account is not entirely reliable; however, it can probably safely be assumed correct in general substance. See in this connection Chang Ta-chün, *Szu-shih-nien tung-luan Sinkiang* [Forty-years turbulent Sinkiang] (Hong Kong, 1956), p. 46, for quotation from a letter from Sheng Shih-ts'ai to Chiang Kai-shek acknowledging, at an unspecified later date, that he had proposed to Moscow that Sinkiang be communized in exchange for Soviet military aid—which, he explained, was essential to save Sinkiang from the designs of Ma Chung-ying and Sabit Mullah. Sheng Shih-ts'ai in an English-language retrospection suggests, implausibly enough, that the initiative for military intervention came from Moscow. See Allen S. Whiting and Sheng Shih-ts'ai, *Sinkiang: Pawn or Pivot?* (East Lansing, 1958), p. 164. This latter Sheng version runs contrary to all other evidence.

4. Aitchen K. Wu, *China and the Soviet Union,* pp. 257–58. See, however, Alexander Barmine, *One Who Survived* (New York, 1945), pp. 231–32, on the Soviet intervention. Barmine, who was personally involved in the matter, records that the Soviet estimate was that the British were behind Ma Chung-ying's move.

5. Sir Eric Teichman, "Chinese Turkestan," *Journal of the Royal Central Asian Society* (Oct., 1936), p. 568.

6. It is, however, the contention of a Chinese writer that one of the conditions

under which the Soviets intervened on Sheng's behalf in 1934 was that although the White Russian forces generally might be retained by Sheng, the former imperial officer Papingut had to go. Chang Ta-chün, *Sinkiang chin-szu-shih-nien pien-luan chi-lueh* [A Record of the recent forty years of disorder in Sinkiang] (Taipei, 1954), p. 34. (The characters for the given name "Ta-chün" of this author differ from those in the name "Chang Ta-chün" as author of *Szu-shih-nien tung-luan Sinkiang*, but the two names are reliably reported to identify one and the same man.)

7. For a description of Sinkiang prison conditions under Sheng's rule by a Turkish traveler who wrote from personal experience, see Ahmad Kamal, *Land Without Laughter* (New York, 1940).

8. Whiting and Sheng Shih-ts'ai, *Sinkiang: Pawn or Pivot?* p. 35.

9. Quoted from Kitada's correspondence with Foreign Minister Hirota, *ibid.*, p. 36.

10. *Ibid.*, p. 37.

11. Chang Ta-chün, *Szu-shih-nien tung-luan Sinkiang*, pp. 63–64. See Tien-fong Cheng, *History*, p. 174, for a briefer, somewhat different account.

12. For a fuller account of this 1937 struggle, see Chang Ta-chün, *Szu-shih-nien tung-luan Sinkiang*, pp. 56–60, and Chang Ta-chün, *Sinkiang chin-szu-shih-nien pien-luan chi-lueh*, pp. 41–42.

13. Whiting and Sheng Shih-ts'ai, *Sinkiang: Pawn or Pivot?* p. 178. In Sheng's report to Stalin after the event, he included the British among the imperialist plotters behind the reputed Trotskyites. See Chang Ta-chün, *Szu-shih-nien tung-luan Sinkiang*, pp. 96–97, for a direct quotation of Sheng's report.

14. See, however, Sheng, in Whiting and Sheng Shih-ts'ai, *Sinkiang: Pawn or Pivot?* p. 179, for the statement that "only 33 were sentenced to death." There is obviously the possibility of equivocation here. Many were killed *without the formality of judicial action,* or simply "died in prison."

CHAPTER 21. YEAR OF DECISION: 1936

1. Borg, *The United States and the Far Eastern Crisis,* p. 177.

2. For text, see Wang Chien-min, *Chung-kuo kung-ch'an-tang shih-kao* [Draft history of the Chinese Communist party] (3 vols.; Taipei, 1965), III, 42–45.

3. Zhukov, *Mezhdunarodnye otnosheniya,* p. 467.

4. Quoted by Tien-fong Cheng, *History,* p. 165, from *Tikhii Okean* [Pacific Ocean] (1936), No. 3, p. 77.

5. From translated text in Aitchen K. Wu, *China and the Soviet Union,* pp. 392–93.

6. Mongol personalities, with names transliterated from the Chinese. For a series of contemporary reports on this case, see *China Weekly Review,* April 18, April 25, May 2, and May 9, 1936.

7. C. Y. W. Meng, "Japan Now Meeting Its 'Waterloo' in Suiyuan," *China Weekly Review* (Dec. 19, 1936), pp. 85–86.

8. International Military Tribunal for the Far East (hereinafter, IMTFE), *Record,* pp. 22, 481 (May 19, 1947).

9. Wang Chien-min, *Chung-kuo kung-ch'an-tang shih-kao,* pp. 65–66.

10. Perevertailo, *Ocherki,* p. 291. See also in this general connection Wang Chien-min, *Chung-kuo kung-ch'an-tang shih-kao,* pp. 98–99.

11. Cited by Charles B. McLane, *Soviet Policy and the Chinese Communists, 1931–1946* (New York, 1958), p. 82.

12. Perevertailo, *Ocherki*, p. 292. For an interesting anticipation by the Shanghai *Nichi Nichi* of this and certain other elements of the agreement, over a month before, see *China Weekly Review* (Nov. 7, 1936), p. 350.

13. For fuller accounts of the Sian Incident, see McLane, *Soviet Policy*, pp. 79–91; Edgar Snow, *Red Star over China* (London, 1938); Agnes Smedley, *Battle Hymn of China* (New York, 1943); Earl Albert Selle, *Donald of China* (New York, 1948); and James M. Bertram, *First Act in China: The Story of the Sian Mutiny* (New York, 1938).

CHAPTER 22. THE USSR AND THE SINO-JAPANESE WAR, 1937–1941

1. For pertinent extract of the military court's verdict, see "Tukhachevsky, Mikhail Nikolaevich," *The New International Year Book, 1937* (New York and London, 1938), pp. 726–27. For a version purporting that Tukhachevski's group had plotted to stage a coup against Stalin and the G.P.U., see Isaac Deutscher, *Stalin, A Political Biography* (New York and London, 1949), pp. 379–80.

2. Following Kapitsa, *Sovetsko-Kitaiskie otnosheniya*, p. 266. This version differs from that offered by Aitchen K. Wu, *China and the Soviet Union*, p. 264.

3. Harold Denny, *New York Times,* Feb. 12, 1936.

4. Chiang Ching-kuo, *My Days in Soviet Russia* (dated May 27, 1937, Wenchangkeh, Hsi-K'ou, Chekiang Province, Republic of China; preface dated Taipei 1963; n.p., n.d.), pp. 33–34.

5. *New York Times,* April 29, 1937. There are varying accounts of Chiang Ching-kuo's activities in the Soviet Union. For a general biographical sketch offering a treatment of that phase of the subject person's life, see Boorman, *Biographical Dictionary,* I, 306–12.

6. Borg, *The United States and the Far Eastern Crisis,* pp. 277–78, collated with the account in Ho Kan-chih, *A History of the Modern Chinese Revolution* (Peking, 1960), p. 324.

7. Tien-fong Cheng, *History,* p. 212. In a German Foreign Office report of the latter part of July sent to the German embassy at Tokyo, it was stated that Germany did not view with favor the Japanese action against China, since the Anti-Comintern Pact did not envisage warring on Bolshevism on the territory of a third state; and it complained against Tokyo's seeking at least a moral German commitment of support for a war portrayed by Japan as a fight against Communism. IMTFE, *Record,* pp. 5975–79 (Sept. 20, 1946).

8. For text in translation, see Aitchen K. Wu, *China and the Soviet Union,* pp. 394–95.

9. Borg, *The United States and the Far Eastern Crisis,* p. 474.

10. *Ibid.,* p. 475. For a stiffer version of what was inferentially the same set of terms, see *China Weekly Review* (Jan. 8, 1938), p. 161.

11. Aitchen K. Wu, *China and the Soviet Union,* p. 268.

12. See, in this connection, *ibid.,* pp. 268–70; Kapitsa, *Sovetsko-Kitaiskie otnosheniya,* pp. 284–85; F. F. Liu, *A Military History of Modern China, 1924–1949* (Princeton, 1956), pp. 166–70.

13. *USFR 1938,* III (Far East), 457.

14. Chargé Kirk, Moscow, to Department of State, Sept. 14, 1938, *USFR 1938,* III (Far East), 484–85.

15. Erickson, *The Soviet High Command*, p. 517n.

16. Winston Churchill, *The Second World War* (6 vols.; Boston, 1948–1953), I, *The Gathering Storm*, 362–63.

17. Rupen, *Mongols*, I, 235. See *ibid.*, 250n.47, for detailed charges against Gendun and his alleged fellow conspirators.

18. Yassuo Misshima and Tomio Goto, *A Japanese View of Outer Mongolia* (condensed translation of *The Outer Mongolian People's Republic* [Tokyo, 1939]), trans. and summarized from the Japanese by Andrew J. Grajdanzev (Institute of Pacific Relations mimeograph, New York, 1942), p. 1.

19. Zhukov, *Mezhdunarodnye otnosheniya*, p. 507.

20. Quoted by Rupen, *Mongols*, I, 226.

21. Louis Aragon, *A History of the USSR from Lenin to Khrushchev*, trans. from the French by Patrick O'Brian (London, 1964), p. 343. For a fuller account of the Nomonhan battle, see O. Edmund Clubb in Garthoff, *Sino-Soviet Military Relations*, pp. 36–39.

22. *USFR 1939*, III (Far East), 53.

23. Max Beloff, *Foreign Policy of Soviet Russia 1929–1941* (2 vols.; London, 1949), II (1936–1941), 248n.2.

CHAPTER 23. THE USSR AND SINKIANG, 1937–1943.

1. For Sheng's version of this unusual international episode, see Whiting and Sheng Shih-ts'ai, *Sinkiang: Pawn or Pivot?* pp. 200–6.

2. See, in this connection, Chang Ta-chün, *Sinkiang chin-szu-shih-nien pien-luan chi-lueh*, p. 33. There had been speculation through the years regarding the fate of the doughty Dungan Ma Chung-ying, with one report contending that he had died upon arrival in Moscow. "Rebellion in Chinese Turkestan," *Journal of the Royal Central Asian Society*, Vol. XII, Part 1 (Jan., 1935), pp. 100–5. For Sheng Shih-ts'ai's own unconvincing account of the manner in which Ma met his death, see Whiting and Sheng Shih-ts'ai, *Sinkiang: Pawn or Pivot?* pp. 192–96.

3. For text in translation, *ibid.*, Appendix B, pp. 280–86.

4. For Ch'en Hsiu-ying's alleged confession, see *ibid.*, Appendix E, pp. 293–301. For an informed, if necessarily speculative, account of this bizarre episode, see Chang Ta-chün, *Szu-shih-nien tung-luan Sinkiang*, pp. 118–21.

5. Whiting, in Whiting and Sheng Shih-ts'ai, *Sinkiang: Pawn or Pivot?* pp. 85–86, offers as one alternative explanation of Sheng Shih-ch'i's death that "Sheng Shih-ch'i protested acceptance of Chungking's terms, or perhaps resisted the anti-Communist purge. Given his position of military power, swift execution may have been his punishment."

6. From text in English-language translation, *ibid.*, Appendix C, pp. 287–90; for text in translation of Tu Chung-yuan's reputed confession, see *ibid.*, Appendix D, pp. 291–92.

7. Chang Ta-chün, *Szu-shih-nien tung-luan Sinkiang*, pp. 138–39. Another source reports that Sheng requested Stalin to incorporate Sinkiang into the Soviet Union. Owen Lattimore et al., *Pivot of Asia* (Boston, 1950), p. 81, quoting dispatch by Christopher Rand, dated Urumchi, Sept. 22, 1947, in *New York Herald Tribune*, Sept. 23, 1947.

8. Chang Ta-chün, *Szu-shih-nien tung-luan Sinkiang*, pp. 140–41.

CHAPTER 24. TWILIGHT IN THE SINO-JAPANESE WAR

1. Charles F. Romanus and Riley Sunderland, *United States Army in World War II: China-Burma-India Theater* (3 vols.; Washington, 1953), I, *Stilwell's Mission to China*, pp. 168, 326.

2. Churchill, *The Second World War*, V, *Closing the Ring*, 328.

3. Romanus and Sunderland, *United States Army*, II, 70. See also Churchill, *The Second World War*, V, 328.

4. *Ibid.*

5. U.S. Department of State, *United States Relations with China with Special Reference to the Period 1944-1949* (hereinafter cited as *China White Paper*) (Washington, 1949), p. 72. At the beginning of June, 1944, Soviet military attaché N. V. Roshchin in conversation with an officer of the U.S. embassy at Chungking expressed bewilderment at the Chinese policy of noncooperation with the Americans and British at a time when relations with the USSR were being deliberately ruined, and spoke "bitterly" of Chungking's failure to utilize the services of Soviet military advisers. Ambassador Gauss to secretary of state, *USFR 1944*, VI (China), 96–97.

6. *China White Paper*, p. 73.

7. See Borg, *The United States and the Far Eastern Crisis,* Chap. VII, "Views of American Officials on the Chinese Communists and the Sian Incident," pp. 196–234.

8. McLane, *Soviet Policy*, p. 175.

9. Version from George A. Lensen, "Yalta and the Far East," in John L. Snell, ed., *The Meaning of Yalta* (Baton Rouge, 1956), pp. 150, 152.

10. Robert J. C. Butow, *Japan's Decision to Surrender* (Stanford, 1954), p. 84.

11. Quoted, *ibid.,* p. 122.

12. *Ibid.,* p. 123n.

13. *China White Paper,* p. 57.

14. *Ibid.,* p. 92.

15. *Ibid.,* p. 86. There is to be remarked the close similarity between this characterization and that of Molotov in the August 31 meeting (as quoted "roughly" by Hurley): "The so-called Chinese Communists are not in fact Communists at all." *Ibid.,* p. 93. It would appear possible that Hurley may have adopted the estimate offered by Molotov. But Hurley presumably expressed his real belief (if adopted), whereas Molotov could reasonably be suspected of having indulged in some dissimulation.

16. *Ibid.,* p. 93.

CHAPTER 25. THE CRITICAL YEAR

1. For a catalog of the meetings, see Aitchen K. Wu, *China and the Soviet Union,* pp. 287–88.

2. In this treatment, I follow Tun Chai (pseud.), "Chiang Ching-kuo ho Shih-ta-lin tang-nien yi-hsi-t'an" [Chiang Ching-kuo's conversation with Stalin that year], *Ch'un Ch'iu,* No. 143 (June 16, 1963), pp. 2–4, "Li Chin k'ou-shu Ch'in Ling-yun pi-lu" [Statements of Li Chin recorded by Ch'in Ling-yun].

3. Aitchen K. Wu, *China and the Soviet Union,* p. 288.

4. See Ts'ao Chü-jen, *Chiang Ching-kuo Lun* [Discussion of Chiang Ching-kuo] (Singapore and Hong Kong, 1954), p. 61.

5. For military details of the campaign, see chap. 4, Raymond L. Garthoff,

"Soviet Intervention in Manchuria," in Garthoff, ed., *Sino-Soviet Military Relations*, pp. 57–69.

6. F. C. Jones, Hugh Borton, and B. R. Pearn, *The Far East, 1942–1946* (London and New York, 1955), p. 178; Stuart Schram, *Mao Tse-tung* (New York, 1966), p. 218.

7. This quotation and other citations from the August 14 agreements are taken from Aitchen K. Wu, *China and the Soviet Union*, Appendix C.

8. See, in this connection, *China White Paper*, pp. 120–21; but also Aitchen K. Wu, *China and the Soviet Union*, pp. 291–94.

9. For Chinese text, see pamphlet *Statements and Speeches by Generalissimo Chiang Kai-shek* (Shanghai, 1945), I (Aug.–Oct., 1945), 5–6. The accompanying English-language translation is unreliable.

10. See Herbert Feis, *The China Tangle* (Princeton, 1953), p. 416. By the Yalta Pact, of course, Moscow had committed itself to entering upon a pact with the Nationalist regime solely "in order to render assistance to China with its armed forces for the purpose of liberating China from the Japanese yoke."

11. *China White Paper*, p. 132.

12. T'ang Yun (comp.), *Tung-pei wen-t'i chih chen-hsiang* [The true nature of the Northeastern Question] (Nanking, 1946), p. 69.

13. *China White Paper*, p. 125.

14. Chiang Kai-shek, *Soviet Russia in China*, p. 147. Other evidence, not without its inner logic, suggests that the visit was by Chiang Kai-shek's initiative. See in this connection, McLane, *Soviet Policy*, p. 212.

15. *China White Paper*, p. 125.

16. Chiang Kai-shek, *Soviet Russia in China*, pp. 147–49.

17. *Ibid.*, p. 147.

18. Edwin W. Pauley, *Report on Japanese Assets in Manchuria to the President of the United States, July 1946* (Washington, 1946), p. 36. See Jones, Borton, and Pearn, *The Far East*, pp. 225–31, for a summary account of the economic consequences of the Soviet occupation.

19. See, in this connection, Kao Hsi-ping, *Yuan-tung hung-huo-ti ch'ien-yin hou-kuo* [The causes and fruits of the Red calamity in the Far East] (Taipei, 1950), p. 65; Carsun Chang, *The Third Force in China* (New York, 1952), p. 167; and *China White Paper*, pp. 123–24. (Kao Hsi-ping was chairman-designate for Antung Province, and was present in Changchun at the time under consideration.)

20. Chiang Kai-shek, *Soviet Russia in China*, p. 148.

CHAPTER 26. REVOLUTIONARY CHANGE

1. Mao Tse-tung, "Strategy for the Second Year of the War of Liberation," in *Selected Military Writings of Mao Tse-tung* (Peking, 1963), pp. 327–32.

2. For text, see *ibid.*, pp. 187–266.

3. *Pervii Sezd Narodov Vostoka* [The First Congress of the Peoples of the East] (stenographic record, Petrograd, 1920), pp. 40, 169.

4. *Selected Military Writings of Mao Tse-tung*, p. 191.

5. See, for instance, editorials in the (Communist) *Hsin-hua jih-pao*, Aug. 17 and Aug. 27, 1945.

6. *Chieh-fang jih-pao*, Jan. 4–5, 1947, in translation in *China White Paper*, pp. 710–19.

7. A. Zhdanov, *O mezhdunarodnom polozhenii, Doklad, cdelannyi na Informatsionnom soveshchanii predstavitelei nekotorykh kompartii v Polshe v kontse sentyabrya 1947 g.* [On the international situation, A report made to the information conference of representatives of several Communist parties in Poland at the end of September, 1947] (Moscow, 1947).

8. *Ibid.,* p. 8.

9. *Ibid.,* p. 9.

10. *Ibid.,* p. 22.

11. *Ibid.,* pp. 44–45.

12. Royal Institute of International Affairs (hereinafter cited as RIIA), *Documents on International Affairs 1949-1950* (hereinafter cited as *Documents,* for various years) (London, New York, and Toronto, 1953), p. 499.

13. *Ibid.,* pp. 472–73.

14. So, for example, Chang Ta-chün, *Szu-shih-nien tung-luan Sinkiang,* p. 175. Neither Aitchen K. Wu, Tien-fong Cheng, nor Henry Wei, however, makes a similar accusation.

15. Whiting and Sheng Shih-ts'ai, *Sinkiang: Pawn or Pivot?* p. 107.

16. N. G. Mingulov, "The National Liberation Movement in Sinkiang as Part of the Chinese Revolution (1944-1949)," *Central Asian Review,* Vol. XI (1963) No. 2, pp. 181-95, translated from *Voprosy Istorii Kazakhstana i Vostochnogo Turkestana* [Problems of the history of Kazakhstan and Eastern Turkestan] (Alma-Ata, 1962).

17. According to a later newspaper article, "Chang Chih-chung's Sinkiang Sickness," *Shih-chieh-jih-pao,* Jan. 30, 1948.

CHAPTER 27. MID-CENTURY: NEW DIRECTIONS

1. *Vital Speeches* (Jan. 15, 1949), p. 203.

2. *China White Paper,* p. 293.

3. See S. Besborodov, *The Bolsheviks Discover Siberia* (Moscow, 1933), p. 44, and George B. Cressey, *How Strong Is Russia? A Geographic Appraisal* (Syracuse, 1954), p. 33, for estimates putting the Kuznetsk coal reserves at variously 400 and 450 billion tons; and Harry Schwartz, *Russia's Soviet Economy* (New York, 1950), p. 20, for a calculation of better-grade iron ore in the Urals at 1,143 million tons – and 382 million tons for the rest of Siberia.

4. See André Pierre, "La Sibérie Nouvelle," *Révue de Défense Nationale* (Jan., 1960), Part II, pp. 79-95, for a revealing treatment of the Siberian economy.

5. Zhdanov, *O mezhdunarodnom polozhenii,* pp. 8-13 passim.

6. See, for example, Chiang's statement that, "in the territory of China a hundred years ago, comprising more than ten million square kilometers, there was not a single district that was not essential to the survival of the Chinese nation, and none that was not permeated by our culture." Chiang Kai-shek, *China's Destiny & Chinese Economic Theory,* with notes and commentary by Philip Jaffe (New York, 1947), p. 34. Those measurements of course included Mongolia, Tibet, and Sinkiang, all conquered by the Manchus, and other peripheral elements left outside Chiang's China.

7. Snow, *Red Star Over China,* p. 96n.

8. Fyodor Dmitriev, pamphlet "Whither China? (Comments on the Economic Policy of Mao Tse-tung)" (Moscow, n.d.), p. 9.

9. *Ibid.,* pp. 9-10.

10. See, in this connection, Kapitsa, *Sovetsko-Kitaiskie otnosheniya*, pp. 343–44, and Max Beloff, *Soviet Policy in the Far East 1949–1951* (London, 1953), pp. 69–70.

11. Compare this with Mao's general rules for guidance in warfare: "Those who direct the war shall not strive for victory beyond the limits permitted by objective conditions. They must, however, within the limits of those objective conditions, actively strive for victory of the war." Mao Tse-tung upon occasion quoted the old Chinese adage that prompts against a thoughtless dissipation of resources: "As long as we preserve the green forest, we don't have to worry about firewood."

12. François Fejtö, *Chine-URSS, La fin d'une hégémonie* (2 vols.; Paris, 1964), I, *Les origines du grand schisme communiste, 1950–1957*, 73.

13. Anna Louise Strong, *China's Millions* (New York, 1928), p. 242.

14. For a good summary account of the December, 1949, to March, 1950, negotiations and a perceptive comparison between the agreements of 1950 and those of 1945, and especially for an account of official American reaction to the developments in Sino-Soviet relations, see Beloff, *Soviet Policy*, pp. 70–78.

15. For text see Garthoff, *Sino-Soviet Military Relations*, Appendix B, pp. 214–15.

16. For this agreement, following the text as given in translation in Aitchen K. Wu, *China and the Soviet Union*, pp. 420–21.

17. *Izvestiya*, Feb. 18, 1950, quoted in Pyn Min (P'eng Ming), *Istoriya Kitaiskogo-Sovetskoi druzhby* [The history of Sino-Soviet friendship] (Moscow, 1959), p. 273.

18. See *Jen-min jih-pao* [People's Daily] (hereinafter cited as *JMJP*), March 27, 1950, for a description of the joint administration provided.

CHAPTER 28. REVOLUTIONARY WAR AND THE ECONOMIC FACTOR

1. "U.S. Imperialist Continues to Aid Bandits and Plots Aggression against Taiwan," *JMJP*, Jan. 4, 1950.

2. *Ibid.*, April 2, 1950.

3. The participants in this conference were presumably as identified in a news item, *ibid.*, Feb. 14, 1950: Ambassador Philip C. Jessup, Assistant Secretary of State W. Walton Butterworth, ex-Ambassador William C. Bullitt, and General MacArthur.

4. *New York Times*, Aug. 17, 1950.

5. Editorial, *China Weekly Review* (June 26, 1920), p. 207.

6. "Military Situation in the Far East," *Hearings before the Committee on Armed Services and the Committee on Foreign Relations* (hereinafter cited as MacArthur Hearings), U.S. Senate, 82d Congress, 1st Session (Washington, 1951), p. 331.

7. See Ya. Victoroff, "The American Aggressor's Lost Gamble," *Pravda*, Jan. 7, 1951, as summarized in *Current Digest of the Soviet Press* (hereinafter cited as *CDSP*), Vol. III, No. 1, p. 16.

8. Ai Fang, "New China Strains Forward toward Industrialization," *JMJP*, April 10, 1950.

9. See U.S. Consulate General, Hong Kong, *Current Background* (hereinafter cited as *CB*), No. 62 (March 5, 1951), for list.

10. U.S. Consulate General, Hong Kong, *Survey of the China Mainland Press* (hereinafter cited as *SCMP*), No. 122 (June 22–23, 1951).

11. Yeh Chi-chuang, "The Chinese People's Republic's Foreign Trade during the Past Three Years," *Jen-min chou-pao* (Oct. 10, 1952), pp. 33–34, from *JMJP*, Sept. 30, 1952.

12. Officially published in the September 15 *Bolshevik*, which however did not issue until early October; also published in *Pravda*, Oct. 3–4, 1952.

13. It is of interest to compare this concept with Liu Shao-ch'i's theory, set forth in his November, 1948, treatment of the theme *Internationalism and Nationalism* (p. 21), that after World War I and the October Revolution, "the world was divided into two different economic systems."

14. Leo Gruliow, ed., *Current Soviet Policies, The Documentary Record of the 19th Communist Party Congress and the Reorganization after Stalin's Death* (New York, 1953), p. 106.

15. "Problems of War and Strategy," *Selected Military Writings of Mao Tse-tung*, p. 273.

16. For a penetrating contemporary analysis of Peking's foreign-affairs concepts as revealed in 1950, see H. Arthur Steiner, "Mainsprings of Chinese Communist Foreign Policy," *American Journal of International Law*, 44 (1950), 69–99.

17. *New York Times*, Dec. 26, 1952.

18. Chao Kuo-chün, "The Government and Economy of Manchuria," *Far Eastern Survey*, Part II (Jan., 1954), pp. 9–14.

19. Walter LaFeber, *America, Russia, and the Cold War, 1945–1966* (New York, 1967), p. 152; *Encyclopaedia Britannica* (1968 ed.), VI, 44C (essay by Walter Millis, "Cold War," 43–44F).

20. Joint Economic Committee, Congress of the United States, *An Economic Profile of Mainland China* (hereinafter cited as *Economic Profile*) (2 vols.; Washington, 1967), I, ix.

21. RIIA, *Survey of International Affairs 1953* (hereinafter cited as *Survey*, for various years), pp. 236–37.

CHAPTER 29. SINO-SOVIET COLLABORATION, 1953–1955

1. See, in this connection, Chao Kuo-chün, "The Government and Economy of Manchuria," *Far Eastern Survey*, Part II (Jan., 1954), pp. 173–74.

2. RIIA, *Documents 1953*, pp. 19–20.

3. *Ibid.*, pp. 458–59.

4. RIIA, *Documents 1954*, p. 325.

5. Seweryn Bialer, "I Chose Truth," *News from Behind the Iron Curtain* (Oct., 1956), pp. 3–16.

6. Howard L. Boorman, ed., *Biographical Dictionary*, s.v. "Kao Kang," II, 233–35.

7. Fejtö, *Chine-URSS*, p. 96.

8. Harold C. Hinton, *Communist China in World Politics* (Boston, 1966), p. 54.

9. For a consideration of the first Formosa Strait crisis, see O. Edmund Clubb, "Formosa and the Offshore Islands in American Policy, 1950–1955," *Political Science Quarterly* (Dec., 1959), pp. 517–31.

CHAPTER 30. DEVELOPMENTS IN THE ALLIANCE 1956–1957

1. *New York Times*, Jan. 12, 1956. See also, for a French scholar's assessment of the character and significance for China of the change in Soviet strategy, H. Car-

rère d'Encausse, "La pénétration chinoise en Asie," *Révue de Défense Nationale* (Jan., 1958), pp. 100–19.

2. A. Sobolev, "Vsemirno-istoricheskoe znachenie sotsialisticheskogo lagerya" [The world-wide historical significance of the socialist camp], *Kommunist,* No. 3 (Feb., 1956), pp. 15–32.

3. Fejtö, *Chine-URSS,* p. 163; RIIA, *Survey 1956–1958,* p. 78; and Donald S. Zagoria, *The Sino-Soviet Conflict 1956–1961* (Princeton, 1962), pp. 55–56.

4. Editorial, "More on the Historical Experience of the Dictatorship of the Proletariat," *JMJP,* Dec. 29, 1956, in Center for International Affairs and the East Asian Research Center, Harvard University, *Communist China 1955–1959 — Policy Documents with Analysis* (hereinafter cited as *Communist China Policy Documents*) (Cambridge, Mass., 1962), pp. 257–72.

5. Fejtö, *Chine-URSS,* p. 178.

6. RIIA, *Documents 1957,* pp. 467–73.

7. *Ibid.,* pp. 497–502.

8. Roderick MacFarquhar, ed., *The Hundred Flowers Campaign and the Chinese Intellectuals* (London, 1960), p. 50.

9. RIIA, *Survey 1956–1958,* p. 527.

10. The figure U.S.$2 billion is sometimes taken as representing solely costs of armaments purchased during the Korean War. But for support of the present calculation, see B. Apremont, "Les relations économiques sino-soviétiques," *Politique Étrangère,* 8 (1958), 509–31.

11. All quotations from text in *Communist China Policy Documents,* pp. 389–93.

12. As quoted by B. Zanegin, *Nationalist Background of China's Foreign Policy* (pamphlet; Moscow, n.d.), p. 57. For the somewhat different and notably milder Chinese "fuller version," see the Chinese statement of Sept. 1, 1963, replying to an earlier Moscow statement, William E. Griffith, *The Sino-Soviet Rift* (Cambridge, Mass., 1964), pp. 371–87.

13. Following English-language text in RIIA, *Documents 1957,* pp. 527–39.

14. Soviet government statement, Sept. 21, 1963, in Griffith, *Sino-Soviet Rift,* pp. 427–61.

15. For another aspect of the matter, see Zanegin, *Nationalist Background,* p. 55.

CHAPTER 31. GATHERING STORM, 1958–1959

1. *New York Times,* June 16, 1958.

2. For treatment of the developments of 1958 in the Formosa Strait, see John R. Thomas, "The Limits of Alliance: The Quemoy Crisis of 1958," in Garthoff, *Sino-Soviet Military Relations,* pp. 114–49.

3. See *ibid.,* p. 88; Hinton, *Communist China,* p. 134; and *Le Monde,* March 11, 1967.

4. "The Origin and Development of the Differences between the Leadership of the CPSU and Ourselves," *JMJP,* Sept. 9, 1963, as quoted by Hinton, *Communist China,* p. 134.

5. The breakdown of the plan for a joint naval command for the Pacific has been cited as a major issue contributing to development of the Sino-Soviet dispute. See Edward Crankshaw, "The Moscow-Peking Clash Exposed," *The Observer,* Feb. 12, 1961.

6. See Thomas, in Garthoff, *Sino-Soviet Military Relations*, pp. 119–23, for a speculative consideration of factors making for Soviet caution during this second Formosa Strait crisis.

7. For a subsequent Soviet treatment of developments in the Chinese economy in this critical period, see Dmitriev, *Whither China?* pp. 21–54.

8. *CDSP*, Vol. X, No. 49 (Jan. 14, 1959), p. 10.

9. From text in RIIA, *Documents 1959*, pp. 572–73.

10. I here follow Jean Baby, *La grande controverse sino-soviétique (1956–1966)* (Paris, 1966), p. 67; but see David A. Charles (pseud.), "The Dismissal of Marshal P'eng Teh-huai," *The China Quarterly* (Oct.–Dec., 1961), pp. 63–76, for a version purporting that P'eng sent a letter to the Soviet party – in the same sense.

11. For speculative support of this assumption, see Ellis Joffe, "Moscow and the Chinese Army," *Far Eastern Economic Review* (April 2, 1964), pp. 13–15.

12. See especially Charles, "The Dismissal . . . ," *The China Quarterly* (1961), p. 68.

13. From text in RIIA, *Documents 1959*, pp. 573–74.

14. *CDSP*, Vol. XI, No. 39 (Oct. 28, 1959), p. 19.

15. *Ibid.*, p. 21.

16. *Keesings Contemporary Archives* (hereinafter cited as *KCA*), 17142.

17. Following the estimate of the agricultural officer, U.S. Consulate General, Hong Kong, as recorded in Ta-chung Liu, "The Tempo of Economic Development of the Chinese Mainland, 1949–65," *Economic Profile*, I, 70. Other estimates frequently use the round figure of 200 million tons – "or less."

CHAPTER 32. 1960: OPEN CONFLICT

1. Baby, *La grande controverse*, p. 71.

2. *CB*, No. 617 (April 26, 1960).

3. From extracts in RIIA, *Documents 1960*, pp. 198–209.

4. O. Kuusinen, *Fundamentals of Marxism-Leninism* (2d impression; London, 1961), p. 581.

5. From extracts of Kuusinen's speech, RIIA, *Documents 1960*, pp. 209–13.

6. V. I. Lenin, *"Left-Wing" Communism: An Infantile Disorder* (New York, 1934), p. 17.

7. *Ibid.*, pp. 51–52.

8. *CDSP*, Vol. XII, No. 24 (July 13, 1960), p. 4. The Soviet theoretical journal *Kommunist* on June 23 gave added specificity to the condemnation of "left-wing Communism"; see *KCA,* 17559.

9. Extracts in RIIA, *Documents 1960*, pp. 213–14; text in *CDSP*, Vol. XII, No. 25 (July 20, 1960), pp. 3–9.

10. Extracts in RIIA, *Documents 1960*, pp. 214–16; text in *CDSP*, Vol. XII, No. 26 (July 27, 1960), pp. 11–12.

11. André Fontaine, *Histoire de la Guerre Froide* (2 vols.; Paris, 1965), II, 388.

12. Here see Baby, *La grande controverse*, p. 80; but also Fontaine, *Histoire*, II, 387–88, and Edward Crankshaw, "The Moscow-Peking Clash Exposed," *The Observer*, Feb. 12, 1961, for a somewhat different picture.

13. Mikhail A. Klochko, *Soviet Scientists in Red China* (New York, 1963), pp. 177–78; see also with respect to the treatment of Soviet personnel the Feb. 14, 1964, report of Mikhail A. Suslov to the CPSU Central Committee, *New York Times*, April 4, 1964.

14. Klochko, *Soviet Scientists*, pp. 181–87.

15. See in this connection Robert Guillain, "Chine nouvelle, an XV," Installment VII, "La 'derussification' et le retour à la Chine," *Le Monde,* Sept. 25, 1964.

16. *CDSP*, Vol. XII, No. 35 (Sept. 28, 1960), pp. 8–10.

17. "Strategy in China's Revolutionary War," *Selected Military Writings of Mao Tse-tung*, pp. 95–96.

18. For extracts from the statement, see RIIA, *Documents 1960*, pp. 222–38.

19. See in this general connection Todor Zhivkov, "Unity of the Socialist Countries Is Decisive in Building Socialism," *World Marxist Review* (Jan., 1963), pp. 3–11.

20. *CDSP*, Vol. XII, No. 48 (Dec. 28, 1960), p. 3.

21. Harry Schwartz, *New York Times*, Feb. 19, 1961.

CHAPTER 33. BLOC POLEMICS, 1961–1963

1. See in this connection Arthur G. Ashbrook, Jr., "Main Lines of Chinese Communist Economic Policy," in *Economic Profile*, I, 26.

2. From extracted text in Alexander Dallin, ed., *Diversity in International Communism: A Documentary Record, 1961–1963* (New York and London, 1963), pp. 4–32.

3. From text, in *ibid.,* pp. 45–54.

4. See in this connection O. Edmund Clubb, "Trap in Vietnam," *The Progressive* (April, 1962), pp. 16–20.

5. *New York Times*, Aug. 12, 1962.

6. Paul Wohl, *Christian Science Monitor*, Jan. 21, 1963.

7. From text in Dallin, *Diversity,* pp. 695–706. Cf. Mao Tse-tung in an address to the party central committee in 1938 on "The Role of the Chinese Communist Party in the National War": one of the four fundamental tenets of party discipline was that "the minority is subordinate to the majority." *Selected Works of Mao Tse-tung*, II, 204.

8. *CDSP*, Vol. XV, No. 1 (Jan. 30, 1963), pp. 3–10.

9. From text in Dallin, *Diversity,* pp. 746–62.

10. From text in *ibid.*, pp. 814–19.

11. H. Arthur Steiner, "Mainsprings of Chinese Communist Foreign Policy," *American Journal of International Law* (Jan., 1950), pp. 69–99, esp. p. 99; for a fuller treatment of *imperial* China's attitude toward the international law and order constructed by the Occident, with some striking parallels, see Arthur Desjardins, "La Chine et le droit des gens," *Révue des Deux Mondes,* 162 (1900), 522–49, 815–44.

12. From text in Dallin, *Diversity,* pp. 820–26.

13. From text in Griffith, *Sino-Soviet Rift,* pp. 241–58.

14. From text in *ibid.,* pp. 259–88.

15. For more detailed analyses of the issues outstanding between the two parties and their respective positions, see Geoffrey Goodsell, "Rendezvous on July 5," *Christian Science Monitor*, Parts I and II, June 28 and June 29, 1963; *National Observer,* July 8, 1963; and "Summary of Major Points in Soviet-Chinese Dispute," *New York Times*, July 15, 1963.

16. Seymour Topping, *New York Times*, July 4, 1963.

17. *New York Times*, July 10, 1963.

18. For text, see *New York Times*, July 15, 1963.

19. From text in Griffith, *Sino-Soviet Rift*, pp. 326–29.

20. From text, *ibid.*, pp. 340–53; see also *New York Times*, Aug. 15, 1963.

21. For text, see *New York Times*, Sept. 14, 1963.

22. *Christian Science Monitor*, Sept. 5, 1963.

CHAPTER 34. SINO-SOVIET COLD WAR, 1964–1965

1. *Selected Works of Mao Tse-tung*, IV, 99.

2. For some details of the Rumanian mission, see Paul Underwood, *New York Times*, April 9, 1964, and *ibid.*, April 27, 1964.

3. *KCA*, 20364; see also *New York Times*, March 28 and March 29, 1964, and Takashi Oka, *Christian Science Monitor*, March 30, 1964.

4. *New York Times*, March 31, 1964.

5. *Ibid.*, April 17, 1964.

6. Michel Tatu, *Le Monde*, April 24, 1964. See also Henry Tanner, *New York Times*, April 23, 1964.

7. *New York Times*, July 31, 1964.

8. China had subsequently, in the main through its own efforts, built three more – at Hanyang, Chungking, and Sian.

9. *New York Times*, Oct. 29, 1964.

10. Soviet government's annual economic report, cited in *New York Times*, Jan. 31, 1965.

11. *New York Times*, Jan. 4, 1965.

12. Quoted in Guy J. Pauker, "The Rise and Fall of Afro-Asian Solidarity," *Asian Survey* (Sept., 1965), pp. 425–32.

13. *New York Times*, Feb. 15, 1965.

14. Kevin Devlin, "Which Side Are You On?" *Problems of Communism* (Jan./Feb., 1967), pp. 52–59.

15. John K. Cooley, *Christian Science Monitor*, April 3, 1965.

16. Lawrence Fellows, *New York Times*, June 13, 1965.

17. See also in this connection Editorial, "China Too Far Too Fast?" *Christian Science Monitor*, June 12, 1965.

18. *Blueprint for World Conquest As Outlined by the Communist International* (Washington and Chicago, 1946), p. 213.

19. Baby, *La grande controverse*, p. 232; see also *Peking Informers* (Oct. 16, 1965), pp. 5–6.

CHAPTER 35. THE GREAT PROLETARIAN CULTURAL REVOLUTION AND SINO-SOVIET RELATIONS

1. *KCA*, 21209.

2. *Ibid.*, 21219.

3. Quoted, *ibid.*, 21220.

4. David Oancia, *The Globe and Mail* (Toronto), in *New York Times,* Jan. 18, 1966.

5. *KCA*, 21633.

6. Baby, *La grande controverse*, p. 240.

7. Kikuzo Ito and Minoru Shibata, "The Dilemma of Mao Tse-tung," *China Quarterly* (July–Sept., 1968), pp. 58–77, esp. 67n.

8. *KCA*, 21633.

9. Henry Kamm, *New York Times*, June 24, 1966.

10. From extracts in *New York Times*, Aug. 14, 1966.

11. *Asian Recorder* (Sept. 24–30, 1966), pp. 7329–30.

12. *Ibid.* (Oct. 29–Nov. 4, 1966), p. 7360.

13. *KCA*, 22045.

14. *Ibid.*, 22047.

15. See in this connection Tillman Durdin, *New York Times*, June 26, 1967.

16. *KCA*, 22045.

17. *Le Monde*, July 9–10, 1967.

18. *KCA*, 22279.

19. *Le Monde*, Aug. 20–21, 1967.

20. *KCA*, 22280; see also *Le Monde*, Sept. 9, 1967.

21. For a survey of China's deteriorated relations with its immediate neighbors to the south, see François Joyaux, "La revolution culturelle en Chine et ses repercussions en Asie du sud-est," *Le Monde Diplomatique*, Nov., 1967.

22. *KCA*, 22887.

23. *Le Monde*, Aug. 25–26, 1968.

24. Alain Bouc, *Le Monde*, Oct. 6–7, 1968.

25. *Le Monde*, Sept. 18, 1968. See also *ibid.*, Sept. 24, 1968, and Alain Bouc, *ibid.*, Sept. 19, 1968.

26. *Le Monde*, Oct. 1, 1968.

27. See in this general connection Paul Wohl, *Christian Science Monitor*, Dec. 13, 1968.

28. From text of Lin Piao "Report to the Ninth National Congress of the Communist Party of China," *Peking Review* (April 30, 1969), pp. 16–35.

29. Peter Grose, *New York Times*, May 19, 1969.

30. From text in *CDSP*, Vol. XXI, No. 23 (July 2, 1969), pp. 3–17.

31. From excerpts in *New York Times*, June 19, 1969.

CHAPTER 36. CONFRONTATION IN THE BORDERLANDS

1. *New York Times*, Nov. 30, 1962.

2. *KCA*, 20361; see also *New York Times* and *Christian Science Monitor*, both Sept. 7, 1963.

3. *KCA*, 20362; *Christian Science Monitor*, Oct. 2, 1963.

4. *New York Times*, April 16, 1964.

5. *KCA*, 20368.

6. *KCA*, 20368.

7. *CDSP*, Vol. XVI, No. 38 (Oct. 14, 1964), pp. 3–6.

8. James Feron, *New York Times*, Nov. 13, 1964; for more on the deleterious effects of the Sino-Soviet dispute on the Chinese military establishment see Takashi Oka, *Christian Science Monitor*, Feb. 21, 1964, and *New York Times*, May 16, 1965.

9. *Christian Science Monitor*, June 25, 1964.

10. Harrison E. Salisbury, *New York Times*, May 24, 1964.

11. *CDSP*, Vol. XVI, No. 37 (Oct. 7, 1964), pp. 15–16.

12. Robert Guillain, *Le Monde*, March 5, 1969.

13. *Ibid.*, March 18, 1969.

14. *Ibid.*

15. *Ibid.*

16. For this paragraph, I follow *Le Monde*, March 15–18 and May 13, 1969;

see also Harrison E. Salisbury, *New York Times*, May 11, 1969, for a report, written from Irkutsk, putting Chinese casualties in the March 15 attack at 300 to 400.

17. *Le Monde,* May 13, 1969.

18. *Ibid.,* March 16-17, 1969.

19. For complete text, see *ibid.,* April 1, 1969.

20. *Ibid.,* April 11, 1969.

21. *Ibid.,* April 13-14, 1969.

22. Harrison E. Salisbury, *New York Times*, May 21, 1969.

23. *Ibid.,* May 26, 1969.

24. *Ibid.,* May 24, 1969.

25. *Le Monde,* May 25-26, 1969; *New York Times*, May 25, 1969. Radio Peking about ten days later announced that the Soviets since March 15 had fired 8,000 shells into Chinese territory, inferentially at various points along the frontier; at Moscow, the chief of the press service of the Foreign Affairs Ministry declared that, according to their information, "the most complete calm" reigned on the frontier. *Le Monde,* June 7, 1969.

26. *Le Monde,* May 27, 1969.

27. For reports on this affair, see *Le Monde,* May 13, 1969; Alain Jacob, *ibid.,* May 15; and *ibid.,* June 12 and 13, 1969.

28. Ian Stewart, *New York Times*, July 6, 1969. For speculation on a presumed debate between Soviet "hawks" and "doves" on the desirability of waging a preventive war against China, see Sidney I. Ploss, *Los Angeles Times*, in *Ithaca Journal,* July 23, 1969.

29. *New York Times*, July 11, 1969.

30. *Ibid.,* July 14, 1969.

31. *Le Monde,* Aug. 2, 1969.

32. Harrison E. Salisbury, *New York Times*, Sept. 25, 1969.

33. *New York Times*, Oct. 2, 1969.

34. From text in *New York Times*, Oct. 8, 1969.

GLOSSARY

ahung	(Muslim) religious teacher
aimak	(Mongol) tribe; now, administrative subdivision
altyn-khan	golden khan
Alty-shar	The Six Cities – Eastern Turkestan
amban	high commissioner
Ankuochün	National Pacification Army
ataman	hetman, chieftain
baturbashi	commander in chief
bek (beg, bey)	prince
Bogdo Gegen	"Living Buddha of Urga" (bogdo – heavenly; gegen – holy man)
boyar	member of the (Russian) aristocracy
cohong	official trading combine (at Canton)
Cominform	Communist Information Bureau
Comintern	Communist (Third) International
gobi	arid steppe
gol	river
hoppo	superintendent of trade (Canton)
hoshun	(Mongol) clan
khoja	member of a religio-political clan
khural	council
khutukhtu	living Buddha
kontaisha	prince (also, "Khontaiji")
kul	lake
Kuominchün	People's Army
kush-begi	"lord of the family" – commander
Li-fan Yuan	Court for Administration of Borderlands
mir	chief
Narkomindel	Commissariat for Foreign Affairs
nur, nor	lake
oblast	district
orda	tribal grouping of nomads (or, as known in the West, "horde")
ostrog	fortified strong point
Profintern	Trade Unions International
revvoensovet	revolutionary military council
sotnik	commander of a hundred

| soviet | council |
| Sovsintorg | Soviet-Sinkiang Trading Company |

taoyin	circuit intendant
tsar	Caesar
Tsungli Yamen	Office in General Charge of Affairs of All (foreign) Nations
tuchün	military governor
T'ung-meng Hui	Alliance Society
tutuh	military governor

| ukaz | decree |
| ulus | (petty) tribe |

| voevoda | military commander |

yamen	(Chinese) administrative office
yasak	tribute in furs
yuan	hall, court (1 of 5 branches of KMT central govt.)
yurt	tent (equivalent to family)

| zemski sobor | territorial assembly |

ABBREVIATIONS

AAPSO	Afro-Asian People's Solidarity Conference
ASSR	Autonomous Soviet Socialist Republic
CCP	Chinese Communist Party.
CER	Chinese Eastern Railway
CMEA	Council for Mutual Economic Assistance
CPR	Chinese People's Republic
CPSU	Communist Party of the Soviet Union
ECCI	Executive Committee of the Communist International
FER	Far Eastern Republic
GPCR	(Chinese) Great Proletarian Cultural Revolution
GPU	(Soviet) state police
KMT	Kuomintang
MAC	(CCP) military affairs committee
MPR	Mongolian People's Republic
MPRA	Mongolian People's Revolutionary Army
MVD	(Soviet) Ministry for Internal Affairs
NEP	(Soviet) New Economic Policy
PKI	Communist Party of Indonesia
PLA	People's Liberation Army
POW	prisoner of war
RSFSR	Russian Soviet Federal Socialist Republic
SMR	South Manchurian Railway
SSR	Soviet Socialist Republic
SUAR	Sinkiang-Uighur Autonomous Region

SELECTED BIBLIOGRAPHY

Ahmad Kamal. *Land Without Laughter.* New York, 1940.

Akademiya Nauk SSSR, Institut Vostokovedeniya. *Mongolskaya Narodnaya Respublika—Sbornik Statei.* Moscow, 1952.

Alekseev, V. M., L. I. Duman, and A. A. Petrov. *Kitai.* Moscow, 1940.

Allworth, Edward, ed. *Central Asia.* New York, 1966.

Aragon, Louis. *A History of the USSR from Lenin to Khrushchev.* London, 1964.

Baby, Jean. *La Grande Controverse Sino-Soviétique (1956–1966).* Paris, 1966.

Baddeley, John F. *Russia, Mongolia, China.* 2 vols. London, 1919.

Badmaev, P. A. *Rossiya i Kitai.* St. Petersburg, 1905.

Bannikov, Andrei Grigorevich. *Pervye Russkie Puteshevstviya v Mongoliyu i Severnyi Kitai. Vasilii Tyumenets, Ivan Petlin, Fedor Baikov.* Moscow, 1949.

Bantysh-Kamenskii, Nikolai N. *Diplomaticheskoe Sobranie del mezhdu Rossiiskim i Kitaiskim Gosudarstvami s 1619 po 1792-i god.* Kazan, 1882.

Barmine, Alexander. *One Who Survived.* New York, 1945.

Barsukov, Ivan. *Graf Nikolai Nikolaevich Muravev-Amurskii po ego pisman, offitsialnym dokumentam, razskazam sovremennikov i pechatnym istochnikam (materialy dlya biografi).* 2 vols. Moscow, 1891.

Beloff, Max. *Foreign Policy of Soviet Russia 1929–1941.* 2 vols. London, 1949.

Bertram, James M. *First Act in China: The Story of the Sian Mutiny.* New York, 1938.

Besborodov, S. *The Bolsheviks Discover Siberia.* Moscow, 1933.

Bland, J. O. P. *Li Hung-chang.* London, 1917.

Blueprint for World Conquest as Outlined by the Communist International. Introduction by William Henry Chamberlain. Washington, D.C./Chicago, 1946.

Boevoi Put Voisk Turkestanskogo Voennogo Okruga. Moscow, 1959.

Boorman, Howard L., ed. *Biographical Dictionary of Republican China.* 4 vols. New York, 1967–

Borg, Dorothy. *The United States and the Far Eastern Crisis of 1933–1938.* Cambridge, Mass., 1964.

Borton, Hugh. *Japan's Modern Century.* New York, 1955.

Boulger, Demetrius. *Central Asian Questions: Essays on Afghanistan, China, and Central Asia.* London, 1885.

Brandt, Conrad. *Stalin's Failure in China, 1924-1927.* Cambridge, Mass., 1958.

Brandt, Conrad, Benjamin Schwartz, and John K. Fairbank. *Documentary History of Chinese Communism.* New York, 1966.

Butakov, Alexander Ivanovich, and Aleksandr Evgenevich Tizengauzen. *Voiny Evropeitsev s Kitaem 1840-42, 1856-58, 1859, i 1860 g.g. po Frantsuskim Nemetskim i Angliiskim Istochnikam. Sost. Gen. Shtaba Podpolk. Butakovym i kap. bar. Tizengauzenom.* St. Petersburg, 1884.

Butow, Robert J. C. *Japan's Decision to Surrender.* Stanford, 1954.

Cahen, Gaston. *Histoire des Relations de la Russie avec la Chine sous Pierre le Grand (1689-1730).* Paris, 1911.

Cambridge History of British Foreign Policy, 1783-1919. 3 vols. Cambridge, 1922-23.

Caroe, Olaf. *Soviet Empire.* London, 1953.

Center for International Affairs and the East Asian Research Center, Harvard University. *Communist China, 1955-1959: Policy Documents with Analysis.* Cambridge, Mass., 1962.

Chang Ta-chün. *Szu-shih-nien tung-luan Sinkiang* (Forty-years Turbulent Sinkiang). Hong Kong, 1956.

—— *Sinkiang chin-szu-shih-nien pien-luan chi-lueh* (A Record of the recent forty years of disorder in Sinkiang). Taipei, 1954.

Ch'en Po-wen, comp., Wu Ching-heng, Ts'ai Yuan-p'ei, Wang Yun-wu, eds., and Wang Cheng-t'ing, collator. *Chung-O wai-chiao shih* (History of Sino-Russian foreign relations. Shanghai, 1928.

Chen, Vincent. *Sino-Russian Relations in the Seventeenth Century.* The Hague, 1968.

Cheng, Tien-fong. *A History of Sino-Russian Relations.* Washington, D.C., 1957.

Cherepanov, A. I. *Zapiski Voennogo Sovetnika v Kitae, iz Istorii Pervoi Grazhdanskoi Voiny (1924-1927).* Moscow, 1964.

—— *Severnyi pokhod Natsionalnorevolyutsionnoi Armii Kitaya.* Moscow, 1968.

Chevigny, Hector. *Russian America: The Great Alaskan Venture 1741-1867.* New York, 1965.

Chiang Ching-kuo. *My Days in Soviet Russia.* (Dated May 27, 1937, Wenchangkeh, Hsi-k'ou, Chekiang Province, Republic of China; preface dated Taipei, 1963.)

Chiang Chung-cheng (Kai-shek). *Soviet Russia in China: A Summing Up at Seventy.* New York, 1957.

Chiang T'ing-fu (T. F. Tsiang). *Chung-kuo chin-tai shih* (Recent history of China). Hong Kong, 1954.

Chimitdorzhiev, Sh. B. *Pervie Szyazi mezhdu Rossiei i Khalkha-Mongoliei (XVII vek).* Ulan-Ude, 1959.

China Year Book. Tientsin/Shanghai, various years.

Clemens Jr., Walter C. *The Arms Race and Sino-Soviet Relations.* Stanford, 1968.

Cobden, Richard. *Russia and the Eastern Question.* Boston, 1854.

Colliers Magazine. *The Russo-Japanese War (by Colliers war correspondents).* New York, 1905.

Cressey, George B. *How Strong Is Russia? A Geographic Appraisal.* Syracuse, 1954.

Curzon, Hon. George N. *Russia in Central Asia in 1889 and the Anglo-Russian Question.* London, 1889.

Czaplicka, M. A. *The Turks of Central Asia in History and at the Present Day: An*

Ethnological Inquiry into the Pan-Turanian Problem, and Bibliographical Material Relating to the Early Turks and the Present Turks of Central Asia. Oxford, 1918.

Dallin, Alexander, ed. *Diversity in International Communism: A Documentary Record, 1961-1963.* New York/London, 1963.

Davidson-Houston, J. V. *Russia and China from the Huns to Mao Tse-tung.* London, 1960.

Editorial Collegium: L. P. Delyusin, M. A. Persits, A. B. Rezhikov, Prof. R. A. Ulyanovskii, chief ed. *Komintern i Vostok, Borba za Leninskuyu Strategiyu i Taktiku v Natsionalno-osvoboditelnom Dvizhenii.* Moscow, 1969.

Demidova, N. F., and V. S. Myasnikov. *Pervye Russkie Diplomaty v Kitae ("Rospis" I. Petlina i Stateinyi Spisok F. I. Baikova).* Moscow, 1966.

Efimov, G. *Vneshnaya Politika Kitaya 1894-1899 g.g.* Moscow, 1958.

Erickson, John. *The Soviet High Command.* London, 1962.

Eudin, Xenia Joukoff, and Robert C. North. *Soviet Russia and the East, 1920-1927: Documentary Survey.* Stanford, 1957.

Fairbank, John K., ed. *The Chinese World Order.* Cambridge, Mass., 1968.

Far Eastern and Russian Institute, University of Washington. *A General Handbook of China.* 2 vols. Seattle, 1956.

Fejtö, François. *Chine-URSS: La Fin d'une Hégémonie.* 2 vols. Paris, 1967.

The First Congress of the Toilers of the Far East. Petrograd, 1922.

Fontaine, André. *Histoire de la Guerre Froide.* 2 vols. London, 1951.

Friters, Gerard M. *Outer Mongolia and Its International Position.* London, 1967.

Fu Lo-shu, comp., tr., and annotater. *A Documentary Chronicle of Sino-Western Relations (1644-1820).* 2 vols. Tucson, 1966.

Furmanov, Dmitrii A. *Myatezh.* Kiev, 1956.

Garthoff, Raymond L., ed. *Sino-Soviet Military Relations.* New York/Washington/London, 1966.

Gataulina, L. M., chief ed. *Materialy po Istorii Russko-Mongolskikh Otnoshennii (1607-1636).* Moscow, 1959.

Gibert, Lucien. *Dictionnare Historique et Géographique de la Mandchourie.* Hong Kong, 1934.

Gittings, John. *Sino-Soviet Dispute, 1956-63.* London, 1964.

Golder, F. A. *Russian Expansion on the Pacific, 1641-1850: An Account of the Earliest and Later Expeditions Made by the Russians Along the Pacific Coast of Asia and North America, Including Some Related Expeditions to the Arctic Regions.* Glendale, Calif., 1914.

Great Britain: Foreign Office. *British and Foreign State Papers.* London, various years.

—— *Papers Relating to Central Asia and Quetta.* London, 1879.

Griffith, William E. *The Sino-Soviet Rift.* Cambridge, Mass., 1964.

Gruliow, Leo, ed. *Current Soviet Policies: The Documentary Record of the 19th Communist Party Congress and the Reorganization After Stalin's Death.* New York, 1953.

Grum-Grzhmailo, G. E. *Opisanie Puteshestviya v Zapadny Kitai.* 3 vols. St. Petersburg, 1899.

Gubelman, M. I. *Borba za Sovetskii Dalnii Vostok, 1918-1922.* Moscow, 1958.

Hedin, Sven. *The Flight of Big Horse.* Trans. by F. H. Lyon. New York, 1936.

Hertslet, Godfrey E. P., with the assistance of Edward Parkes. *Treaties, &c., Between Great Britain and China; and Between China and Foreign Powers; &*

Orders in Council, Rules, Regulations, Acts of Parliament, Decrees, &c., Affecting British Interests in China, in Force on the 1st January, 1908. 3d ed. 2 vols. London, 1908.

Hinton, Harold. *Communist China in World Politics.* Boston, 1966.

Hishida, Seiji. *Japan Among the Great Powers: A Survey of Her International Relations.* London/New York/Toronto, 1940.

Holdsworth, Mary. *Turkestan in the 19th Century: A Brief History of the Khanates of Bukhara, Kokand & Khiva.* Issued by The Central Asia Research Centre in Association with St. Anthony's College. Oxford, 1959.

Hsu, Immanuel. *The Ili Crisis (1871-81): A Study of Sino-Russian Diplomacy, 1878-1881.* Oxford, 1965.

Hummel, Arthur W., ed. *Eminent Chinese of the Ch'ing Period (1644-1912).* 2 vols. Washington, D.C., 1943.

The International Military Tribunal for the Far East, Record (Tokyo, 1946-48).

Institut National de la Statistique et des Études Économiques, Direction de la Conjoncture et des Études Économiques, Études et Documents. *L'Asie Soviétique, Études et Documents Serie D 3.* Paris, 1949.

Japanese Foreign Office Document B. *Relations of Japan with Manchuria and Mongolia.* Rev. ed. Tokyo, 1932.

Jelavich, Charles and Barbara, eds. *Russia in the East, 1876-1880: The Russo-Turkish War and the Kuldja Crisis as Seen Through the Letters of A. G. Jomini to N. K. Giers.* Leiden, 1959.

Jones, F. C. *Japan's New Order in East Asia: Its Rise and Fall, 1937-45.* London, 1954.

—— *Manchuria Since 1931.* London, 1949.

Jones, F. C., Hugh Borton, and B. R. Pearn. *Survey of International Affairs, 1939-1946; The Far East, 1942-46.* London, 1955.

Kao Hsi-ping. *Yuan-tung hung-huo-ti ch'ien-yin hou-kuo* (The causes and fruits of the Red Calamity in the Far East). Taipei, 1950.

Kao Yin-tsu. *Chung-hua Min-kuo ta-shih chi* (Record of major events of the Chinese Republic). Taipei, 1957.

Kapitsa, M. S. *Sovetsko-Kitaiskie Otnosheniya.* Moscow, 1958.

Kapur, Harish. *Soviet Russia and Asia, 1917-1927: A Study of Soviet Policy Towards Turkey, Iran, and Afghanistan.* Geneva, 1966.

Kardelj, Edvard. *Socialism and War: A Survey of Chinese Criticism of the Policy of Coexistence,* translated from the Serbo-Croatian by Alec Brown. London, 1961.

Kennan, George. *E. H. Harriman, A Biography.* 2 vols. Boston/New York, 1922.

Kervyn, Louis M. *Ourga (1912-1930) La Politique Chinoise en Mongolie.* Peking, 1932.

Kheifets, A. N. *Sovetskaya Rossiya i Sopredelnyi Strany Vostoka, 1918-1920.* Moscow, 1964.

Klochko, Mikhail A. *Soviet Scientists in Red China.* New York, 1963.

Kruzenshtern, Ivan Fedorovich. *Puteshestvie Vokrug Sveta v 1803, 4, 5, i 1806 godakh po Poveleniyu Ego Imperatorskogo Velichestva Aleksandra Pervago, na Korablakh Nadezhda i Neva.* 3 parts. St. Petersburg, 1809-1812.

Kuno, Yoshi S. *Japanese Expansion on the Asiatic Continent.* Berkeley, 1940.

Kuo T'ing-yi. *Chin-tai Chung-kuo shih-shih jih-chih* (Diary of historical matters of recent Chinese history). 2 vols. Taipei, 1964.

Kuropatkin, A. N. *The Russian Army and the Japanese War,* trans. by Captain A. B. Lindsay. 2 vols. London, 1909.

Lantzeff, George V. *Siberia in the Seventeenth Century.* University of California Publication in History, Vol. 30. Berkeley, 1943.

Lattimore, Owen. *Manchuria, Cradle of Conflict.* New York, 1932.

―― *Nationalism and Revolution in Mongolia.* New York, 1955.

Lattimore, Owen, and others. *Pivot of Asia: Sinkiang and the Inner Asian Frontiers of China and Russia.* Boston, 1950.

Lensen, George Alexander. *The Russian Push Toward Japan: Russo-Japanese Relations, 1697-1875.* Princeton, 1959.

―― *The Russo-Chinese War.* Tallahassee, 1967.

Lensen, George Alexander, ed. *Russia's Eastward Expansion.* Englewood Cliffs, N.J., 1964.

Levin, M. G., and L. P. Potapov, eds. *The Peoples of Siberia.* Originally published by Russian Academy of Science, Moscow, 1956, under title *Narody Sibiri.* Trans. from the Russian by Scripta Technica, Inc., English translation edited by Stephen Dunn, Institute of Russian Studies, Fordham University. Chicago, 1964.

Levine, J. *La Mongolie Historique, Géographique, Politique.* Paris, 1937.

Liddell Hart, B. H., ed. *The Red Army.* New York, 1956.

Lobanov-Rostovsky, Prince A. *Russia and Asia.* New York, 1933.

Lupach, V. S. *I. F. Kruzenshtern i Yu. F. Lisyanskii,* under the editorship of M. S. Bodnarsk. Moscow, 1953.

Macintosh, J. M. *Strategy and Tactics of Soviet Foreign Policy.* London/New York/Toronto, 1962.

McLane, Charles B. *Soviet Policy and the Chinese Communists, 1931-1946.* New York, 1958.

MacMurray, John V. A. *Treaties & Agreements with and Concerning China, 1894-1919.* 2 vols. Oxford, 1921.

Maki, John M. *Selected Documents: Far Eastern Relations (1689-1951).* Seattle, 1957.

Manning, Clarence. *The Siberian Fiasco.* New York, 1952.

Meadows, Thomas Taylor. *The Chinese and Their Rebellions* (originally published 1856). Stanford, 1953.

Michael, Franz. *The Origin of Manchu Rule in China: Frontier and Bureaucracy as Interacting Forces in the Chinese Empire.* Baltimore, 1942.

Moore, Harriet L. *Soviet Far East Policy, 1931-1942.* Princeton, 1945.

Morley, James W. *The Japanese Thrust into Siberia, 1918.* New York, 1957.

Morse, Hosea Ballou. *The International Relations of the Chinese Empire.* 3 vols. London, 1910.

Morse, Hosea Ballou, and Harley Farnsworth MacNair. *Far Eastern International Relations.* Boston, 1931.

(Mullaby, Captain H.) "An Indian Officer." *Russia's March Towards India.* 2 vols. London, 1894.

Nikiforov, V., G. Erenburg, and M. Yurev. *Narodnaya Revolyutsiya v Kitae.* Moscow, 1950.

North, Robert C. *Kuomintang and the Chinese Communist Elites.* Stanford, 1952.

Norton, Henry Kittredge. *The Far Eastern Republic of Siberia.* London, 1923.

Orlov, B. P. *Pervoe Russkoe Krugosvetnoe Plavanie (1803-1806 g.g.).* Moscow, 1954.

Parfenov, P. S. (Altaiskii). *Borba za Dalnii Vostok 1920–1922.* 2d ed., rev. Moscow, 1931.

Park, Alexander G. *Bolshevism in Turkestan, 1917–1927.* New York, 1957.

Pasvolsky, Leo. *Russia in the Far East.* New York, 1922.

Pauley, Edwin W. *Report on Japanese Assets in Manchuria to the President of the United States, July 1946.* Washington, D.C., 1946.

Perevertailo, A. S., chief ed., V. I. Glunin, K. V. Kukushkin, and V. N. Nikiforov. *Ocherki Istorii Kitaya v Noveishee Vremya.* Moscow, 1959.

Pervii Sezd Narodov Vostoka (Stenographic record). Petrograd, 1920.

Pierce, Richard A. *Russian Central Asia, 1867–1917: A Study in Colonial Rule.* Berkeley, 1960.

Pyn Min (P'eng Ming). *Istoriya Kitaisko-Sovetskoi Druzhby.* Moscow, 1959.

Quested, R. K. I. *The Expansion of Russia in East Asia, 1857–1860.* Singapore, 1968.

Roy, M. N. *Revolution and Counter-Revolution in China.* Calcutta, 1946.

Royal Institute of International Affairs. *Survey of International Affairs.* London, various years.

—— *Documents on International Affairs.* London, various years.

Rupen, Robert A. *Mongols of the Twentieth Century.* 2 parts. Bloomington, Ind., 1964.

Salisbury, Harrison E. *War Between Russia and China.* New York, 1969.

Savvin, V. P. *Vzaimootnosheniya Tsarskoi Rossii i SSSR s Kitaem.* Moscow/ Leningrad, 1930.

Schram, Stuart. *Mao Tse-tung.* New York, 1966.

Schram, Stuart, and Hélène Carrère d'Encausse. *Le Marxisme et l'Asia 1853–1964.* Paris, 1965.

Schwartz, Harry. *Tsars, Mandarins, and Commissars.* New York, 1964.

Sebes, Joseph. *The Jesuits and the Sino-Russian Treaty of Nerchinsk, 1689.* Rome, 1961.

Sevrikov, K., ed. *Kak My Bili Yaponskikh Samuraev.* Moscow, 1938.

Shastina, N. P. *Russko-Mongolskie Posolskie Otnosheniya XVII veka.* Moscow, 1958.

Shereshevskii, B. *Zabaikale v Period Dalnevostochnoi Respubliki.* Chita, 1960.

Sheridan, James E. *Chinese Warlord: The Career of Feng Yü-hsiang.* Stanford, 1966.

Shursunov, Kh. *Vosstanie 1916 Goda v Srednei Azii i Kazakhstani.* Moscow, 1966.

The Sino-Soviet Dispute Documented and Analysed by G. F. Hudson, Richard Lowenthal and Roderick MacFarquhar. London, 1961.

Skrine, F. H. *The Expansion of Russia.* Cambridge, 1915.

Skrine, Francis Henry, and Edward Dennison Ross. *The Heart of Asia.* London, 1899.

Snell, John N., ed. *The Meaning of Yalta.* Baton Rouge, 1956.

Stalin, Joseph. *Marxism and the National Colonial Question.* New York, 1935.

Tan, Chester C. *The Boxer Catastrophe.* New York, 1955.

Tang, Peter S. H. *Russian and Soviet Policy in Manchuria and Outer Mongolia, 1911–1931.* Durham, 1959.

T'ang Yun, comp. *Tung-pei wen-t'i chih chen-hsiang* (The true nature of the Northeastern Question). Nanking, 1946.

Tchao Tchun Tcheou. *Évolution des Relations Diplomatiques de la Chine avec les Puissances (1587–1929).* Paris, 1931.

Thornton, Richard C. *The Comintern and the Chinese Communists, 1928–1931.* Seattle/London, 1969.

Ts'ao Chü-jen. *Chiang Ching-kuo Lun* (Discussion of Chiang Ching-kuo). Singapore/Hong Kong, 1954.

USSR: Ministry of Foreign Affairs. *Dokumenty Vneshnei Politiki SSSR.* Moscow, 1958.

U.S. Congress: Joint Economic Committee. *An Economic Profile of Mainland China.* 2 vols. Washington, D.C., 1967.

U.S. Department of State. *Foreign Relations of the United States.* Washington, D.C., various years.

—— *Chinese Correspondence, 1857–59.* Washington, D.C., 1860.

—— *United States Relations with China, with Special Reference to the period 1944–1949.* Washington, D.C., 1949.

Vámbéry, Árminius. *Central Asia and the Anglo-Russian Frontier Question: A Series of Political Papers,* trans. by F. E. Bunnett. London, 1874.

Vernadsky, George. *Kievan Russia.* 2d ed. New Haven, 1951.

Vernadsky, George, and Michael Karpovich. *A History of Russia.* 2d ed. Vol. IV: *The Mongols and Russia.* New Haven, 1959.

Vilenskii, Vl. (Sibiryakov). *Yaponiya.* Moscow, 1923.

Wang Chien-min. *Chung-kuo Kung-ch'an-tang shih-kao* (Draft history of the Chinese Communist Party). 3 vols. Taipei, 1965.

Weigh, Ken Shen. *Russo-Chinese Diplomacy.* Shanghai, 1928.

Wheeler, Geoffrey. *The Modern History of Soviet Central Asia.* New York, 1964.

White, John Albert. *The Siberian Intervention.* Princeton, 1950.

Whiting, Allen S. *Soviet Policies in China, 1917–1924.* New York, 1954.

Whiting, Allen S., and Sheng Shih-ts'ai. *Sinkiang: Pawn or Pivot?* East Lansing, 1958.

Wilbur, C. Martin, and Julie Lien-ying How, eds. *Documents on Communism, Nationalism and Soviet Advisers in China, 1918–1927; Papers Seized in the 1927 Peking Raid.* New York, 1956.

Witte, Sergei I. *The Memoirs of Count Witte,* trans. by Abraham Yarmolinsky. Garden City, 1921.

Wu, Aitchen K. *China and the Soviet Union, A Study of Sino-Soviet Relations.* New York, 1950.

—— *Turkestan Tumult.* London, 1940.

Wu Hsiang-hsiang. *O-ti ch'in-lueh Chung-kuo shih* (The history of Russian imperialism's aggression against China). Taipei, 1954.

Yakhontoff, Victor A. *Russia and the Soviet Union in the Far East.* New York, 1931.

Yakovleva, P. T. *Pervyi Russko-Kitaiskii Dogovor 1689 Goda.* Moscow, 1958.

Yang Tseng-hsin. *Pu-kuo Chai jih-chi* (Diary of the Redeeming Studio). 1921.

Zagoria, Donald S. *The Sino-Soviet Conflict, 1956–1961.* Princeton, 1962.

Zhukov, E. M., chief ed. *Mezhdunarodnye Otnosheniya na Dalnem Vostoke 1840–1949.* Moscow, 1956.

Zlatkin, I. Ya. *Istoriya Dzhungarskogo Khanstva (1635–1758).* Moscow, 1964.

—— *Ocherki Novoi i Noveishei Istorii Mongolii.* Moscow, 1957.

PUBLICATIONS OF THE EAST ASIAN INSTITUTE

STUDIES

The Ladder of Success in Imperial China, by Ping-ti Ho. New York: Columbia University Press, 1962.

The Chinese Inflation, 1937–1949, by Shun-hsin Chou. New York: Columbia University Press, 1963.

Reformer in Modern China: Chang Chien, 1853–1926, by Samuel Chu. New York: Columbia University Press, 1965.

Research in Japanese Sources: A Guide, by Herschel Webb with the assistance of Marleigh Ryan. New York: Columbia University Press, 1965.

Society and Education in Japan, by Herbert Passin. New York: Bureau of Publications, Teachers College, Columbia University, 1965.

Agricultural Production and Economic Development in Japan, 1873–1922, by James I. Nakamura. Princeton: Princeton University Press, 1966.

Japan's First Modern Novel: Ukigumo of Futabatei Shimei, by Marleigh Ryan. New York: Columbia University Press, 1967.

The Korean Communist Movement, 1918–1948, by Dae-Sook Suh. Princeton: Princeton University Press, 1967.

The First Vietnam Crisis, by Melvin Gurtov. New York: Columbia University Press, 1967. Paperback edition, 1968.

Cadres, Bureaucracy and Political Power in Communist China, by A. Doak Barnett. New York: Columbia University Press, 1967.

The Japanese Imperial Institution in the Tokugawa Period, by Herschel Webb. New York: Columbia University Press, 1968.

Higher Education and Business Recruitment in Japan, by Koya Azumi. New York: Teachers College Press, Columbia University, 1969.

The Communists and Chinese Peasant Rebellion: A Study in the Rewriting of Chinese History, by James P. Harrison, Jr. New York: Atheneum Publishers, 1969.

How the Conservatives Rule Japan, by Nathaniel B. Thayer. Princeton: Princeton University Press, 1969.

Aspects of Chinese Education, edited by C. T. Hu. New York: Teachers College Press, Columbia University, 1969.

Economic Development and the Labor Market in Japan, by Koji Taira. New York: Columbia University Press, 1970.

The Japanese Oligarchy and the Russo-Japanese War, by Shumpei Okamoto. New York: Columbia University Press, 1970.

Japanese Education: A Bibliography of Materials in the English Language, by Herbert Passin. New York: Teachers College Press, Columbia University, 1970.

Documents of Korean Communism, 1918–1948, by Dae-Sook Suh. Princeton: Princeton University Press, 1970.

Japan's Postwar Defense Policy, 1947–1968, by Martin E. Weinstein. New York: Columbia University Press, 1971.

Election Campaigning: Japanese Style, by Gerald L. Curtis. New York: Columbia University Press, 1971.

China and Russia: The "Great Game," by O. Edmund Clubb. New York: Columbia University Press, 1971.

Imperial Restoration in Medieval Japan, by H. Paul Varley. New York: Columbia University Press, 1971.

Li Tsung-jen: A Memoir, edited by T. K. Tong. Berkeley: University of California Press, forthcoming.

Money and Monetary Policy in Communist China During the First Five Year Plan, by Katharine H. Hsiao. New York: Columbia University Press, forthcoming.

Law and Policy in China's Foreign Relations, by James C. Hsiung. New York: Columbia University Press, forthcoming.

OCCASIONAL PAPERS PUBLISHED BY COLUMBIA UNIVERSITY PRESS

Taiwan: Studies in Chinese Local History, edited by Leonard H. D. Gordon. New York: Columbia University Press, 1970.

The Introduction of Socialism into China, by Li Yu-ning. New York: Columbia University Press, 1971.

The Early Chiang Kai-shek: A Study of His Personality and Politics, 1887–1924, by Pichon P. Y. Loh. New York: Columbia University Press, forthcoming.

INDEX

UNION OF
SOVIET SOCIALIST REPUBLICS

.... S.S.R. BOUNDARY
·················· A.S.S.R. BOUNDARY
················ OBLAST, OKRUG, AND KRAI BOUNDARY

1000 KM.

GREENLAND
(DEN.)

UNITED
KINGDOM

NORTH
SEA

SPITZBERGEN
(NOR.)

FRANZ
J.L.A.

NORWAY
Oslo

DENMARK

SWEDEN

ARCTIC CIRCLE

Murmansk

ARCTIS

NOVAYA
ZEMLAYA

WEST
GERMANY
EAST
Berlin

Stockholm

BALTIC SEA

FINLAND

Helsinki

ESTONIAN
S.S.R.

LATVIAN
S.S.R.

Riga

KARELIAN
A.S.S.R.

Leningrad

Archangel

KOMI
A.S.S.R.

Vorkuta

POLAND
Warsaw

LITHUANIAN
S.S.R.

Sale-
chard

SOVIET

CZECHO.

Minsk

BELORUSSIAN
S.S.R.

Smolensk

Vologda

RUSSIAN

RUMANIA

Kiev

MOSCOW

Kirov

Serov

MOLDAVIAN
S.S.R.

UKRAINIAN
S.S.R.

Tula

Gorki

Perm

Sverdlovsk

Kursk

MARI
A.S.S.R.

Kazan

Tyumen

Odessa

Dnieperpetrovsk

MORDV.
A.S.S.R.

TATAR
A.S.S.R.

BASHKIR
A.S.S.R.

IRTYSH

Sevastopol

Zaporozhe

Saratov

Kuibyshev
A.S.S.R.

Ufa

Omsk

BLACK
SEA

Rostov

Volgo-
grad

VOLGA

Magnito-
gorsk

Novo-
sibirsk

ABKHAZ
A.S.S.R.

KALMYK
A.S.S.R.

Astrakhan

URAL

Petro-
pavlovsk

TURKEY

Batum

GEORGIAN
S.S.R.

DAGESTAN
A.S.S.R.

K A Z A K H

Tselinograd

Karaganda

ARMENIAN
S.S.R.

NAKHI-
CHEVAN
A.S.S.R.

Tbilisi

CASPIAN
SEA

S.S.R.

Semi-
palatinsk

AZERBAIJANIAN
S.S.R.

Baku

ARAL
SEA

KARAKALPAK
A.S.S.R.

LAKE
BALKHASH

Aktogai

IRAQ

IRAN

Krasno-
vodsk

Khiva

UZBEK
S.S.R.

Chimkent

Dzhambul

Kuldja

TURKOMEN
S.S.R.

Ashkhabad

Bukhara

Tashkent

Alma-Ata

Arak

Tehran

Merv

Kokand

KIRGIZ
S.S.R.

Frunze

Kuch

TADJIK
S.S.R.

Kashgar

Yezd

AFGHANISTAN

Yarkand